The Disintegration of the World Economy Between the World Wars
Volume II

The Growth of the World Economy

Series Editor: Nick F.R. Crafts
  Professor of Economic History
  The London School of Economics

1. Trade in the Pre-Modern Era, 1400–1700 (Volumes I and II)
   Douglas A. Irwin

2. Trade and the Industrial Revolution, 1700–1850 (Volumes I and II)
   Stanley L. Engerman

3. The Integration of the World Economy, 1850–1914 (Volumes I and II)
   C. Knick Harley

4. The Disintegration of the World Economy Between the World Wars (Volumes I and II)
   Mark Thomas

5. The Reconstruction of the International Economy, 1945–1960
   Barry Eichengreen

The Disintegration of the World Economy Between the World Wars
Volume II

Edited by

Mark Thomas

Associate Professor of History
University of Virginia, US

THE GROWTH OF THE WORLD ECONOMY

An Elgar Reference Collection
Cheltenham, UK • Brookfield, US

© Mark Thomas 1996. For copyright of individual articles please refer to the Acknowledgements.

All rights reserved. No part of this publication may be reproduced, stored in a retrieval system, or transmitted in any form or by any means, electronic, mechanical, photocopying, recording, or otherwise without the prior permission of the publisher.

Published by
Edward Elgar Publishing Limited
8 Lansdown Place
Cheltenham
Glos GL50 2HU
UK

Edward Elgar Publishing Company
Old Post Road
Brookfield
Vermont 05036
US

British Library Cataloguing in Publication Data
Disintegration of the World Economy
Between the World Wars. – (Growth of the
World Economy Series; No. 4)
I. Thomas, Mark II. Series
330.9

Library of Congress Cataloguing in Publication Data
The disintegration of the world economy between the world wars / edited by Mark Thomas.
    p. cm. — (The growth of the world economy ; 4) (An Elgar reference collection)
   Includes bibliographical references and index.
   1. International trade—History—20th century. 2. Commercial policy—History—20th century. 3. International economic relations—History—20th century. 4. Economic history—1918-1945.
   I. Thomas, Mark. II. Series. III. Series: An Elgar reference collection.
HF1379.D57 1996
337'.09'04—dc20
95-37715
CIP

ISBN 1 85278 986 7 (2 volume set)

Printed in Great Britain by Galliard (Printers) Ltd, Great Yarmouth

Contents

Acknowledgements ix
An introduction to both volumes appears in Volume I.

PART I   THE EMERGING CRISIS, 1929–1931

1. Irving Fisher (1933), 'The Debt-deflation Theory of Great Depressions', *Econometrica*, **1**, 337–57   3
2. Barry Eichengreen (1992), 'The Origins and Nature of the Great Slump Revisited', *Economic History Review*, **XLV** (2), May, 213–39   24
3. Andrew Newell and J.S.V. Symons (1988), 'The Macroeconomics of the Interwar Years: International Comparisons', in Barry Eichengreen and T.J. Hatton (eds), *Interwar Unemployment in International Perspective*, Chapter 2, Dordrecht: Kluwer Academic Publishers, 61–96   51
4. David Williams (1963), 'The 1931 Financial Crisis', *Yorkshire Bulletin of Economic and Social Research*, **15** (2), November, 92–110   87
5. D.E. Moggridge (1970), 'The 1931 Financial Crisis – A New View', *The Banker*, **120** (8), August, 832–3, 835–7 and 839   106
6. Ehsan U. Choudhri and Levis A. Kochin (1980), 'The Exchange Rate and the International Transmission of Business Cycle Disturbances', *Journal of Money, Credit, and Banking*, **12** (4), November, 565–74   112
7. Ben Bernanke and Harold James (1991), 'The Gold Standard, Deflation, and Financial Crisis in the Great Depression: An International Comparison', in R. Glenn Hubbard (ed.), *Financial Markets and Financial Crises*, Chicago: National Bureau of Economic Research, Chapter 2, 33–68   122
8. Harold James (1992), 'Financial Flows Across Frontiers During the Interwar Depression', *Economic History Review*, **XLV** (3), August, 594–613   158
9. James Foreman-Peck, Andrew Hughes Hallet and Yue Ma (1992), 'The Transmission of the Great Depression in the United States, Britain, France and Germany', *European Economic Review*, **36** (3), 685–94   179

PART II	THE RESPONSE TO CRISIS	
	10. H.V. Hodson (1933), 'Tariffs and Exchange Control: The Struggle to Escape', in Arnold J. Toynbee (ed.), *Survey of International Affairs, 1932*, Oxford: Oxford University Press, 3–40	191
	11. Svenska Handelsbanken (1933), 'The Great Trade War', *Index*, **VIII** (86), January, 2–13	229
	12. Peter Alexis Gourevitch (1984), 'Breaking with Orthodoxy: The Politics of Economic Policy Responses to the Depression of the 1930s', *International Organization*, **38** (1), Winter, 95–129	241
	13. Clemens A. Wurm (1989), 'International Industrial Cartels, the State and Politics: Great Britain Between the Wars', in Alice Teichova, Maurice Lévy-Leboyer and Helga Nussbaum (eds), *Historical Studies in International Corporate Business*, Chapter 10, Cambridge: Cambridge University Press, 111–22	276
	14. Donald MacDougall and Rosemary Hutt (1954), 'Imperial Preference: A Quantitative Analysis', *Economic Journal*, **LXIV** (2), June, 233–57	289
	15. Patricia Clavin (1991), 'The World Economic Conference 1933: The Failure of British Internationalism', *Journal of European Economic History*, **20** (3), Winter, 489–527	314
	16. T.J.T. Rooth (1986), 'Tariffs and Trade Bargaining: Anglo-Scandinavian Economic Relations in the 1930s', *Scandinavian Economic History Review*, **XXXIV** (1), 54–71	353
	17. Alan S. Milward (1981), 'The Reichsmark Bloc and the International Economy', in Gerhard Hirschfeld and Lothar Kettenacker (eds), *Der 'Führerstaat': Mythos and Realität*, Stuttgart: Klett-Cotta, 377–411	371
	18. Larry Neal (1979), 'The Economics and Finance of Bilateral Clearing Agreements: Germany, 1934–8', *Economic History Review*, **XXXII** (3), August, 391–404	406
	19. Volker Hentschel (1990), 'Indicators of Real Effective Exchange Rates of Major Trading Nations from 1922 to 1937', *German Yearbook on Business History 1988*, Berlin: Springer-Verlag, 47–72	420
	20. Barry Eichengreen and Jeffrey Sachs (1985), 'Exchange Rates and Economic Recovery in the 1930s', *Journal of Economic History*, **XLV** (4), December, 925–46	446
PART III	TRADE POLICY, GLOBAL DEPRESSION AND THE DEVELOPING WORLD	
	21. C.H. Lee (1969), 'The Effects of the Depression on Primary Producing Countries', *Journal of Contemporary History*, **4** (4), October, 139–55	471

22.	Vladimir P. Timoshenko (1933), 'The Collapse of 1929-30' and 'The Spread of Depression', in V.P. Timoshenko, 'World Agriculture and the Depression', *Michigan Business Studies*, **V** (5), 66–100	488
23.	Barry Eichengreen and Richard Portes (1986), 'Debt and Default in the 1930s: Causes and Consequences', *European Economic Review*, **30** (3), 599–640	523
24.	Ippei Yamazawa (1975), 'Industrial Growth and Trade Policy in Prewar Japan', *Developing Economies*, **XIII** (1), March, 38–65	565
25.	Carlos F. Diaz Alejandro (1984), 'Latin America in the 1930s', in Rosemary Thorp (ed.), *Latin America in the 1930s: The Role of the Periphery in World Crisis*, London: Macmillan, 17–49	593
26.	José Manuel Campa (1990), 'Exchange Rates and Economic Recovery in the 1930s: An Extension to Latin America', *Journal of Economic History*, **L** (3), September, 677–82	626

PART IV CONTEMPORARIES LOOK FORWARD

27.	D.H. Robertson (1938), 'The Future of International Trade', *Economic Journal*, **XLVIII** (1), March, 1–14	635
28.	Robert B. Bryce (1942), 'Basic Issues in Postwar International Economic Relations', *American Economic Review*, **XXXII**, 165–81	649

Name Index 667

Acknowledgements

The editor and publishers wish to thank the following who have kindly given their permission for the use of copyright material.

Alan S. Milward for his own article: (1981), 'The Reichsmark Bloc and the International Economy', in Gerhard Hirschfeld and Lothar Kettenacker (eds), *Der 'Führerstaat': Mythos and Realität*, 377–411.

American Economic Association for article: Robert B. Bryce (1942), 'Basic Issues in Postwar International Economic Relations', *American Economic Review*, **XXXII**, 165–81.

Banca di Roma for article: Patricia Clavin (1991), 'The World Economic Conference 1933: The Failure of British Internationalism', *Journal of European Economic History*, **20** (3), Winter, 489–527.

Basil Blackwell Ltd for articles: D.H. Robertson (1938), 'The Future of International Trade', *Economic Journal*, **XLVIII** (1), March, 1–14; Sir Donald MacDougall and Rosemary Hutt (1954), 'Imperial Preference: A Quantitative Analysis', *Economic Journal*, **LXIV** (2), June, 233–57; Barry Eichengreen (1992), 'The Origins and Nature of the Great Slump Revisited', *Economic History Review*, **XLV** (2), May 213–39; Harold James (1992), 'Financial Flows Across Frontiers During the Interwar Depression', *Economic History Review*, **XLV** (3), August, 594–613; David Williams (1963), 'The 1931 Financial Crisis', *Yorkshire Bulletin of Economics and Social Research*, **15** (2), November, 92–110.

Cambridge University Press for articles and excerpt: Barry Eichengreen and Jeffrey Sachs (1985), 'Exchange Rates and Economic Recovery in the 1930s', *Journal of Economic History*, **XLV** (4), December, 925–46; José Manuel Campa (1990), 'Exchange Rates and Economic Recovery in the 1930s: An Extension to Latin America', *Journal of Economic History*, **L** (3), September, 677–82; Clemens A. Wurm (1989), 'International Industrial Cartels, the State and Politics: Great Britain Between the Wars', in Alice Teichova, Maurice Lévy-Leboyer and Helga Nussbaum (eds), *Historical Studies in International Corporate Business*, Chapter 10, 111–22.

Econometric Society for article: Irving Fisher (1933), 'The Debt-deflation Theory of Great Depressions', *Econometrica*, **1**, 337–57.

Elsevier Science Publishers BV for articles: Barry Eichengreen and Richard Portes (1986), 'Debt and Default in the 1930s: Causes and Consequences', *European Economic Review*, **30** (3), 599–640; James Foreman-Peck, Andrew Hughes Hallet and Yue Ma (1992), 'The Transmission of the Great Depression in the United States, Britain, France and Germany', *European Economic Review*, **36** (3), 685–94.

Financial Times Magazines for article: D.E. Moggridge (1970), 'The 1931 Financial Crisis – A New View', *The Banker*, **120** (8), August, 832–3, 835–7 and 839.

Svenska Handelsbanken for its own article: (1933), 'The Great Trade War', *Index*, **VIII** (86), January, 2–13.

Institute of Developing Economies for excerpt: Ippei Yamazawa (1975), 'Industrial Growth and Trade Policy in Prewar Japan', *Developing Economies*, **XIII** (1), March, 38–65.

Kluwer Academic Publishers for article: Andrew Newell and J.S.V. Symons (1988), 'The Macroeconomics of the Interwar Years: International Comparisons', in Barry Eichengreen and T.J. Hatton (eds), *Interwar Unemployment in International Perspective*, Chapter 2, 61–96.

Larry Neal for his own article: (1979), 'The Economics and Finance of Bilateral Clearing Agreements: Germany, 1934–8', *Economic History Review*, **XXXII** (3), August, 391–404.

Macmillan Press Ltd and St Martin's Press for excerpt: Carlos F. Diaz Alejandro (1984), 'Latin America in the 1930s', in Rosemary Thorp (ed.), *Latin America in the 1930s: The Role of the Periphery in World Crisis*, 17–49.

MIT Press Journals for article: Peter Alexis Gourevitch (1984), 'Breaking with Orthodoxy: The Politics of Economic Policy Responses to the Depression of the 1930s', *International Organization*, **38** (1), Winter, 95–129.

Royal Institute of International Affairs for excerpt: H.V. Hodson (1933), 'Tariffs and Exchange Control: The Struggle to Escape', in Arnold J. Toynbee (ed.), *Survey of International Affairs, 1932*, (published by Oxford University Press for the Royal Institute of International Affairs), 3–40.

Sage Publications Ltd for article: C.H. Lee (1969), 'The Effects of the Depression on Primary Producing Countries', *Journal of Contemporary History*, **4** (4), October, 139–55.

Scandinavian Economic History Review for article: T.J.T. Rooth (1986), 'Tariffs and Trade Bargaining: Anglo-Scandinavian Economic Relations in the 1930s', *Scandinavian Economic History Review*, **XXXIV** (1), 54–71.

University of Chicago Press for excerpt: Ben Bernanke and Harold James (1991), 'The Gold Standard, Deflation, and Financial Crisis in the Great Depression', in R. Glen Hubbard (ed.), *Financial Markets and Financial Crises*, Chapter 2, 33–68.

University of Michigan for article: Vladimir P. Timoshenko (1933), 'The Collapse of 1929-30' and 'The Spread of Depression', *Michigan Business Studies*, 'World Agriculture and the Depression', V (5), 66–100.

Volker Hentschel for his own article: (1990), 'Indicators of Real Effective Exchange Rates of Major Trading Nations from 1922 to 1937', *German Yearbook on Business History 1988*, 47–72.

Every effort has been made to trace all the copyright holders but if any have been inadvertently overlooked the publishers will be pleased to make the necessary arrangement at the first opportunity.

In addition the publishers wish to thank the library of the London School of Economics and Political Science, the Alfred Marshall Library, Cambridge University and the Photographic Unit of the University of London Library for their assistance in obtaining these articles.

Part I
The Emerging Crisis, 1929–1931

[1]

THE DEBT-DEFLATION THEORY OF GREAT DEPRESSIONS

By Irving Fisher

INTRODUCTORY

In *Booms and Depressions*, I have developed, theoretically and statistically, what may be called a debt-deflation theory of great depressions. In the preface, I stated that the results "seem largely new," I spoke thus cautiously because of my unfamiliarity with the vast literature on the subject. Since the book was published its special conclusions have been widely accepted and, so far as I know, no one has yet found them anticipated by previous writers, though several, including myself, have zealously sought to find such anticipations. Two of the best-read authorities in this field assure me that those conclusions are, in the words of one of them, "both new and important."

Partly to specify what some of these special conclusions are which are believed to be new and partly to fit them into the conclusions of other students in this field, I am offering this paper as embodying, in brief, my present "creed" on the whole subject of so-called "cycle theory." My "creed" consists of 49 "articles" some of which are old and some new. I say "creed" because, for brevity, it is purposely expressed dogmatically and without proof. But it is not a creed in the sense that my faith in it does not rest on evidence and that I am not ready to modify it on presentation of new evidence. On the contrary, it is quite tentative. It may serve as a challenge to others and as raw material to help them work out a better product.

Meanwhile the following is a list of my 49 tentative conclusions.

"CYCLE THEORY" IN GENERAL

1. The economic system contains innumerable variables—quantities of "goods" (physical wealth, property rights, and services), the prices of these goods, and their values (the quantities multiplied by the prices). Changes in any or all of this vast array of variables may be due to many causes. Only in imagination can all of these variables remain constant and be kept in equilibrium by the balanced forces of human desires, as manifested through "supply and demand."

2. Economic theory includes a study both of (a) such imaginary, ideal equilibrium—which may be stable or unstable—and (b) dis-equilibrium. The former is economic statics; the latter, economic dynamics. So-called cycle theory is merely one part of the study of economic dis-equilibrium.

3. The study of dis-equilibrium may proceed in either of two ways.

We may take as our unit for study an actual historical case of great dis-equilibrium, such as, say, the panic of 1873; or we may take as our unit for study any constituent tendency, such as, say, deflation, and discover its general laws, relations to, and combinations with, other tendencies. The former study revolves around events, or *facts;* the latter, around *tendencies.* The former is primarily economic history; the latter is primarily economic science. Both sorts of studies are proper and important. Each helps the other. The panic of 1873 can only be understood in the light of the various tendencies involved—deflation and other; and deflation can only be understood in the light of the various historical manifestations—1873 and other.

4. The old and apparently still persistent notion of "the" business cycle, as a single, simple, self-generating cycle (analogous to that of a pendulum swinging under influence of the single force of gravity) and as actually realized historically in regularly recurring crises, is a myth. Instead of one force there are many forces. Specifically, instead of one cycle, there are many co-existing cycles, constantly aggravating or neutralizing each other, as well as co-existing with many non-cyclical forces. In other words, while a cycle, conceived as a *fact*, or historical event, is non-existent, there are always innumerable cycles, long and short, big and little, conceived as *tendencies* (as well as numerous non-cyclical tendencies), any historical event being the resultant of all the tendencies then at work. Any one cycle, however perfect and like a sine curve it may tend to be, is sure to be interfered with by other tendencies.

5. The innumerable tendencies making mostly for economic dis-equilibrium may roughly be classified under three groups: (a) growth or trend tendencies, which are steady; (b) haphazard disturbances, which are unsteady; (c) cyclical tendencies, which are unsteady but steadily repeated.

6. There are two sorts of cyclical tendencies. One is "forced" or imposed on the economic mechanism from outside. Such is the yearly rhythm; also the daily rhythm. Both the yearly and the daily rhythm are imposed on us by astronomical forces from outside the economic organization; and there may be others such as from sun spots or transits of Venus. Other examples of "forced" cycles are the monthly and weekly rhythms imposed on us by custom and religion.

The second sort of cyclical tendency is the "free" cycle, not forced from outside, but self-generating, operating analogously to a pendulum or wave motion.

7. It is the "free" type of cycle which is apparently uppermost in the minds of most people when they talk of "the" business cycle. The yearly cycle, though it more nearly approaches a perfect cycle than

any other, is seldom thought of as a cycle at all but referred to as "seasonal variation."

8. There may be equilibrium which, though stable, is so delicately poised that, after departure from it beyond certain limits, instability ensues, just as, at first, a stick may bend under strain, ready all the time to bend back, until a certain point is reached, when it breaks. This simile probably applies when a debtor gets "broke," or when the breaking of many debtors constitutes a "crash," after which there is no coming back to the original equilibrium. To take another simile, such a disaster is somewhat like the "capsizing" of a ship which, under ordinary conditions, is always near stable equilibrium but which, after being tipped beyond a certain angle, has no longer this tendency to return to equilibrium, but, instead, a tendency to depart further from it.

9. We may tentatively assume that, ordinarily and within wide limits, all, or almost all, economic variables tend, in a general way, toward a stable equilibrium. In our classroom expositions of supply and demand curves, we very properly assume that if the price, say, of sugar is above the point at which supply and demand are equal, it tends to fall; and if below, to rise.

10. Under such assumptions, and taking account of "economic friction," which is always present, it follows that, unless some outside force intervenes, any "free" oscillations about equilibrium must tend progressively to grow smaller and smaller, just as a rocking chair set in motion tends to stop. That is, while "forced" cycles, such as seasonal, tend to continue unabated in amplitude, ordinary "free" cycles tend to cease, giving way to equilibrium.

11. But the exact equilibrium thus sought is seldom reached and never long maintained. New disturbances are, humanly speaking, sure to occur, so that, in actual fact, any variable is almost always above or below the ideal equilibrium.

For example, coffee in Brazil may be over-produced, that is, may be more than it would have been if the producers had known in advance that it could not have been sold at a profit. Or there may be a shortage in the cotton crop. Or factory, or commercial inventories may be under or over the equilibrium point.

Theoretically there may be—in fact, at most times there must be—over- or under-production, over- or under-consumption, over- or under-spending, over- or under-saving, over- or under-investment, and over or under everything else. It is as absurd to assume that, for any long period of time, the variables in the economic organization, or any part of them, will "stay put," in perfect equilibrium, as to assume that the Atlantic Ocean can ever be without a wave.

12. The important variables which may, and ordinarily do, stand

above or below equilibrium are: (a) capital items, such as homes, factories, ships, productive capacity generally, inventories, gold, money, credits, and debts; (b) income items, such as real income, volume of trade, shares traded; (c) price items, such as prices of securities, commodities, interest.

13. There may even be a *general* over-production and in either of two senses: (a) there may be, in general, at a particular point of time, over-large inventories or stocks on hand, or (b) there may be, in general, during a particular period of time, an over-rapid flow of production. The classical notion that over-production can only be relative as between different products is erroneous. Aside from the abundance or scarcity of particular products, relative to each other, production as a whole is relative to human desires and aversions, and can as a whole overshoot or undershoot the equilibrium mark.

In fact, except for brief moments, there must always be some degree of general over-production or general under-production and in both senses—stock and flow.

14. But, in practice, general over-production, as popularly imagined, has never, so far as I can discover, been a chief cause of great dis-equilibrium. The reason, or a reason, for the common notion of over-production is mistaking too little money for too much goods.

15. While any deviation from equilibrium of any economic variable theoretically may, and doubtless in practice does, set up some sort of oscillations, the important question is: Which of them have been sufficiently great disturbers to afford any substantial explanation of the great booms and depressions of history?

16. I am not sufficiently familiar with the long detailed history of these disturbances, nor with the colossal literature concerning their alleged explanations, to have reached any definitive conclusions as to the relative importance of all the influences at work. I am eager to learn from others.

17. According to my present opinion, which is purely tentative, there is some grain of truth in most of the alleged explanations commonly offered, but this grain is often small. Any of them may suffice to explain *small* disturbances, but all of them put together have probably been inadequate to explain *big* disturbances.

18. In particular, as explanations of the so-called business cycle, or cycles, when these are really serious, I doubt the adequacy of over-production, under-consumption, over-capacity, price-dislocation, maladjustment between agricultural and industrial prices, over-confidence, over-investment, over-saving, over-spending, and the discrepancy between saving and investment.

19. I venture the opinion, subject to correction on submission of

future evidence, that, in the great booms and depressions, each of the above-named factors has played a subordinate rôle as compared with two dominant factors, namely *over-indebtedness* to start with and *deflation* following soon after; also that where any of the other factors do become conspicuous, they are often merely effects or symptoms of these two. In short, the big bad actors are debt disturbances and price-level disturbances.

While quite ready to change my opinion, I have, at present, a strong conviction that these two economic maladies, the debt disease and the price-level disease (or dollar disease), are, in the great booms and depressions, more important causes than all others put together.

20. Some of the other and usually minor factors often derive some importance when combined with one or both of the two dominant factors.

Thus over-investment and over-speculation are often important; but they would have far less serious results were they not conducted with borrowed money. That is, over-indebtedness may lend importance to over-investment or to over-speculation.

The same is true as to over-confidence. I fancy that over-confidence seldom does any great harm except when, as, and if, it beguiles its victims into debt.

Another example is the mal-adjustment between agricultural and industrial prices, which can be shown to be a result of a change in the general price level.

21. Disturbances in these two factors—debt and the purchasing power of the monetary unit—will set up serious disturbances in all, or nearly all, other economic variables. On the other hand, if debt and deflation are absent, other disturbances are powerless to bring on crises comparable in severity to those of 1837, 1873, or 1929-33.

THE ROLES OF DEBT AND DEFLATION

22. No exhaustive list can be given of the secondary variables affected by the two primary ones, debt and deflation; but they include especially seven, making in all at least nine variables, as follows: debts, circulating media, their velocity of circulation, price levels, net worths, profits, trade, business confidence, interest rates.

23. *The chief interrelations between the nine chief factors may be derived deductively*, assuming, to start with, that general economic equilibrium is disturbed by only the one factor of over-indebtedness, and, in particular, assuming that there is no other influence, whether accidental or designed, tending to affect the price level.

24. Assuming, accordingly, that, at some point of time, a state of over-indebtedness exists, this will tend to lead to liquidation, through

the alarm either of debtors or creditors or both. Then we may deduce the following chain of consequences in nine links: (1) *Debt liquidation* leads to *distress selling* and to (2) *Contraction of deposit currency*, as bank loans are paid off, and to a slowing down of velocity of circulation. This contraction of deposits and of their velocity, precipitated by distress selling, causes (3) *A fall in the level of prices*, in other words, a swelling of the dollar. Assuming, as above stated, that this fall of prices is not interfered with by reflation or otherwise, there must be (4) *A still greater fall in the net worths of business*, precipitating bankruptcies and (5) *A like fall in profits*, which in a "capitalistic," that is, a private-profit society, leads the concerns which are running at a loss to make (6) *A reduction in output, in trade and in employment* of labor. These losses, bankruptcies, and unemployment, lead to (7) *Pessimism and loss of confidence*, which in turn lead to (8) *Hoarding and slowing down still more the velocity of circulation*.

The above eight changes cause (9) *Complicated disturbances in the rates of interest*, in particular, a fall in the nominal, or money, rates and a rise in the real, or commodity, rates of interest.

Evidently debt and deflation go far toward explaining a great mass of phenomena in a very simple logical way.

25. The above chain of causes, consisting of nine links, includes only a few of the interrelations between the nine factors. There are other demonstrable interrelations, both rational and empirical, and doubtless still others which cannot, yet, at least, be formulated at all.[1] There must also be many indirect relations involving variables not included among the nine groups.

26. One of the most important of such interrelations (and probably too little stressed in my *Booms and Depressions*) is the direct effect of lessened money, deposits, and their velocity, in curtailing trade, as evidenced by the fact that trade has been revived locally by emergency money without any raising of the price level.

27. In actual chronology, the order of the nine events is somewhat different from the above "logical" order, and there are reactions and repeated effects. As stated in Appendix I of *Booms and Depressions:*

The following table of our nine factors, occurring and recurring (together with distress selling), gives a fairly typical, though still inadequate, picture of the

---

[1] Many of these interrelations have been shown statistically, and by many writers. Some, which I have so shown and which fit in with the debt-deflation theory, are: that price-change, after a distributed lag, causes, or is followed by, corresponding fluctuations in the volume of trade, employment, bankruptcies, and rate of interest. The results as to price-change and unemployment are contained in Charts II and III, pp. 352–3. See references at the end of this article; also footnote 2, page 345, regarding the charts.

cross-currents of a depression in the approximate order in which it is believed they usually occur. (The first occurrence of each factor and its sub-divisions is indicated by italics. The figures in parenthesis show the sequence in the original exposition.)

    I. (7) Mild *Gloom* and Shock to *Confidence*
       (8) Slightly *Reduced Velocity* of Circulation
       (1) Debt *Liquidation*

   II. (9) *Money Interest* on Safe Loans Falls
      (9) But Money Interest on Unsafe Loans Rises

  III. (2) *Distress Selling*
      (7) More Gloom
      (3) *Fall in Security Prices*
      (1) More Liquidation
      (3) *Fall in Commodity Prices*

  IV. (9) *Real Interest Rises;* REAL DEBTS INCREASE
      (7) More Pessimism and Distrust
      (1) More Liquidation
      (2) More Distress Selling
      (8) More Reduction in Velocity

   V. (2) More Distress Selling
      (2) *Contraction of Deposit Currency*
      (3) Further Dollar Enlargement

  VI. (4) *Reduction in Net Worth*
      (4) Increase in *Bankruptcies*
      (7) More Pessimism and Distrust
      (8) More Slowing in Velocity
      (1) More Liquidation

 VII. (5) *Decrease in Profits*
      (5) *Increase in Losses*
      (7) Increase in Pessimism
      (8) Slower Velocity
      (1) More Liquidation
      (6) *Reduction in Volume of Stock Trading*

VIII. (6) *Decrease in Construction*
      (6) *Reduction in Output*
      (6) *Reduction in Trade*
      (6) *Unemployment*
      (7) More Pessimism

  IX. (8) *Hoarding*

   X. (8) *Runs on Banks*
      (8) *Banks Curtailing Loans* for Self-Protection
      (8) *Banks Selling Investments*
      (8) *Bank Failures*
      (7) Distrust Grows
      (8) More Hoarding
      (1) More Liquidation
      (2) More Distress Selling
      (3) Further Dollar Enlargement

As has been stated, this order (or any order, for that matter) can be only approximate and subject to variations at different times and places. It represents my present guess as to how, if not too much interfered with, the nine factors selected for explicit study in this book are likely in most cases to fall in line.

But, as has also been stated, the idea of a single-line succession is itself inadequate, for while Factor (1) acts on (2), for instance, it also acts *directly* on (7), so that we really need a picture of subdividing streams or, better, an interacting network in which each factor may be pictured as influencing and being influenced by many or all of the others.

Paragraph 24 above gives a logical, and paragraph 27 a chronological, order of the chief variables put out of joint in a depression when once started by over-indebtedness.

28. But it should be noted that, except for the first and last in the "logical" list, namely debt and interest on debts, *all the fluctuations listed come about through a fall of prices*.

29. When over-indebtedness stands alone, that is, does *not* lead to a fall of prices, in other words, when its tendency to do so is counteracted by inflationary forces (whether by accident or design), the resulting "cycle" will be far milder and far more regular.

30. Likewise, when a deflation occurs from other than debt causes and without any great volume of debt, the resulting evils are much less. It is the combination of both—the debt disease coming first, then precipitating the dollar disease—which works the greatest havoc.

31. The two diseases act and react on each other. Pathologists are now discovering that a pair of diseases are sometimes worse than either or than the mere sum of both, so to speak. And we all know that a minor disease may lead to a major one. Just as a bad cold leads to pneumonia, so over-indebtedness leads to deflation.

32. And, vice versa, deflation caused by the debt reacts on the debt. Each dollar of debt still unpaid becomes a bigger dollar, and if the over-indebtedness with which we started was great enough, the liquidation of debts cannot keep up with the fall of prices which it causes. In that case, the liquidation defeats itself. While it diminishes the number of dollars owed, it may not do so as fast as it increases the value of each dollar owed. Then, *the very effort of individuals to lessen their burden of debts increases it, because of the mass effect of the stampede to liquidate in swelling each dollar owed*. Then we have the great paradox which, I submit, is the chief secret of most, if not all, great depressions: *The more the debtors pay, the more they owe*. The more the economic boat tips, the more it tends to tip. It is not tending to right itself, but is capsizing.

33. But if the over-indebtedness is not sufficiently great to make liquidation thus defeat itself, the situation is different and simpler. It is then more analogous to stable equilibrium; the more the boat

rocks the more it will tend to right itself. In that case, we have a truer example of a cycle.

34. In the "capsizing" type in particular, the worst of it is that real incomes are so rapidly and progressively reduced. Idle men and idle machines spell lessened production and lessened real income, the central factor in all economic science. Incidentally this under-production occurs at the very time that there is the illusion of over-production.

35. In this rapid survey, I have not discussed what constitutes over-indebtedness. Suffice it here to note that (a) over-indebtedness is always relative to other items, including national wealth and income and the gold supply, which last is specially important, as evidenced by the recent researches of Warren and Pearson; and (b) it is not a mere one-dimensional magnitude to be measured simply by the number of dollars owed. It must also take account of the distribution in time of the sums coming due. Debts due at once are more embarrassing than debts due years hence; and those payable at the option of the creditor, than those payable at the convenience of the debtor. Thus debt embarrassment is great for call loans and for early maturities.

For practical purposes, we may roughly measure the total national debt embarrassment by taking the total sum currently due, say within the current year, including rent, taxes, interest, installments, sinking fund requirements, maturities and any other definite or rigid commitments for payment on principal.

ILLUSTRATED BY THE DEPRESSION OF 1929–33[2]

36. The depression out of which we are now (I trust) emerging is an example of a debt-deflation depression of the most serious sort. The

[2] Note the charts, pp. 352–7:

Chart I shows: (1) the price level (P) and (2) its percentage rate of rise or fall (P'). When the last named is lagged with the lag distributed according to a probability curve so that the various P''s overlap and cumulate we get $\bar{P}'$, as in Charts II and III. This $\bar{P}'$ is virtually a lagged average of the P''s.

Charts II and *III* show: $\bar{P}'$ contrasted with employment (E). $\bar{P}'$ may be considered as what employment would be if controlled *entirely* by price-change.

Chart IV shows the Swedish official (retail) weekly index number contrasted with the American weekly wholesale and monthly retail indexes.

Chart V shows the estimated internal debt in the United States contrasted with the estimated total money value of wealth. The unshaded extensions of the bars upward show what the 1933 figures would be if enlarged 75 per cent to translate them into 1929 dollars (according to the index number of wholesale commodity prices).

Chart VI shows estimated "fixed" annual charges (actually collected) contrasted with estimated national income. The unshaded extensions of the bars upward show what the 1932 figures would be if enlarged 56 per cent to translate them into 1929 dollars.

Charts VII and *VIII* show the chief available statistics before and after March 4, 1933, grouped in the order indicated in Article 27 above.

debts of 1929 were the greatest known, both nominally and really, up to that time.

They were great enough not only to "rock the boat" but to start it capsizing. By March, 1933, liquidation had reduced the debts about 20 per cent, but had increased the dollar about 75 per cent, so that the *real* debt, that is the debt as measured in terms of commodities, was increased about 40 per cent $[(100\% - 20\%) \times (100\% + 75\%) = 140\%]$. Note Chart V.

37. Unless some counteracting cause comes along to prevent the fall in the price level, such a depression as that of 1929-33 (namely when the more the debtors pay the more they owe) tends to continue, going deeper, in a vicious spiral, for many years. There is then no tendency of the boat to stop tipping until it has capsized. Ultimately, of course, but only after almost universal bankruptcy, the indebtedness must cease to grow greater and begin to grow less. Then comes recovery and a tendency for a new boom-depression sequence. This is the so-called "natural" way out of a depression, via needless and cruel bankruptcy, unemployment, and starvation.

38. On the other hand, if the foregoing analysis is correct, it is always economically possible to stop or prevent such a depression simply by reflating the price level up to the average level at which outstanding debts were contracted by existing debtors and assumed by existing creditors, and then maintaining that level unchanged.

That the price level is controllable is not only claimed by monetary theorists but has recently been evidenced by two great events: (1) Sweden has now for nearly two years maintained a stable price level, practically always within 2 per cent of the chosen par and usually within 1 per cent. Note Chart IV. (2) The fact that immediate reversal of deflation is easily achieved by the use, or even the prospect of use, of appropriate instrumentalities has just been demonstrated by President Roosevelt. Note Charts VII and VIII.

39. Those who imagine that Roosevelt's avowed reflation is not the cause of our recovery but that we had "reached the bottom anyway" are very much mistaken. At any rate, they have given no evidence, so far as I have seen, that we had reached the bottom. And if they are right, my analysis must be woefully wrong. According to all the evidence, under that analysis, debt and deflation, which had wrought havoc up to March 4, 1933, were then stronger than ever and, if let alone, would have wreaked greater wreckage than ever, after March 4. Had no "artificial respiration" been applied, we would soon have seen general bankruptcies of the mortgage guarantee companies, savings banks, life insurance companies, railways, municipalities, and states. By that time the Federal Government would probably have be-

come unable to pay its bills without resort to the printing press, which would itself have been a very belated and unfortunate case of artificial respiration. If even then our rulers should still have insisted on "leaving recovery to nature" and should still have refused to inflate in any way, should vainly have tried to balance the budget and discharge more government employees, to raise taxes, to float, or try to float, more loans, they would soon have ceased to be our rulers. For we would have insolvency of our national government itself, and probably some form of political revolution without waiting for the next legal election. The mid-west farmers had already begun to defy the law.

40. If all this is true, it would be as silly and immoral to "let nature take her course" as for a physician to neglect a case of pneumonia. It would also be a libel on economic science, which has its therapeutics as truly as medical science.

41. If reflation can now so easily and quickly reverse the deadly down-swing of deflation after nearly four years, when it was gathering increased momentum, it would have been still easier, and at any time, to have stopped it earlier. In fact, under President Hoover, recovery was apparently well started by the Federal Reserve open-market purchases, which revived prices and business from May to September 1932. The efforts were not kept up and recovery was stopped by various circumstances; including the political "campaign of fear."

It would have been still easier to have prevented the depression almost altogether. In fact, in my opinion, this would have been done had Governor Strong of the Federal Reserve Bank of New York lived, or had his policies been embraced by other banks and the Federal Reserve Board and pursued consistently after his death.[3] In that case, there would have been nothing worse than the first crash. We would have had the debt disease, but not the dollar disease—the bad cold but not the pneumonia.

42. If the debt-deflation theory of great depressions is essentially correct, the question of controlling the price level assumes a new importance; and those in the drivers' seats—the Federal Reserve Board and the Secretary of the Treasury, or, let us hope, a special stabilization commission—will in future be held to a new accountability.

43. Price level control, or dollar control, would not be a panacea. Even with an ideally stable dollar, we would still be exposed to the

---

[3] Eventually, however, in order to have avoided depression, the gold standard would have had to be abandoned or modified (by devaluation); for, with the gold standard as of 1929, the price levels at that time could not have been maintained indefinitely in the face of: (1) the "scramble for gold" due to the continued extension of the gold standard to include nation after nation; (2) the increasing volume of trade; and (3) the prospective insufficiency of the world gold supply.

debt disease, to the technological-unemployment disease, to over-production, price-dislocation, over-confidence, and many other minor diseases. To find the proper therapy for these diseases will keep economists busy long after we have exterminated the dollar disease.

DEBT STARTERS

44. The over-indebtedness hitherto presupposed must have had its starters. It may be started by many causes, of which the most common appears to be *new opportunities to invest at a big prospective profit*, as compared with ordinary profits and interest, such as through new inventions, new industries, development of new resources, opening of new lands or new markets. Easy money is the great cause of over-borrowing. When an investor thinks he can make over 100 per cent per annum by borrowing at 6 per cent, he will be tempted to borrow, and to invest or speculate with borrowed money. This was a prime cause leading to the over-indebtedness of 1929. Inventions and technological improvements created wonderful investment opportunities, and so caused big debts. Other causes were the left-over war debts, domestic and foreign, public and private, the reconstruction loans to foreigners, and the low interest policy adopted to help England get back on the gold standard in 1925.

Each case of over-indebtedness has its own starter or set of starters. The chief starters of the over-indebtedness leading up to the crisis of 1837 were connected with lucrative investment opportunities from developing the West and Southwest in real estate, cotton, canal building (led by the Erie Canal), steamboats, and turnpikes, opening up each side of the Appalachian Mountains to the other. For the over-indebtedness leading up to the crisis of 1873, the chief starters were the exploitation of railways and of western farms following the Homestead Act. The over-indebtedness leading up to the panic of 1893 was chiefly relative to the gold base which had become too small, because of the injection of too much silver. But the panic of 1893 seems to have had less of the debt ingredient than in most cases, though deflation played a leading rôle.

The starter may, of course, be wholly or in part the pendulum-like back-swing or reaction in recovery from a preceding depression as commonly assumed by cycle theorists. This, of itself, would tend to leave the next depression smaller than the last.

45. When the starter consists of new opportunities to make unusually profitable investments, the bubble of debt tends to be blown bigger and faster than when the starter is great misfortune causing merely non-productive debts. The only notable exception is a great war and even then chiefly because it leads *after it is over* to productive debts for reconstruction purposes.

46. This is quite different from the common naïve opinions of how war results in depression. If the present interpretation is correct, the World War need never have led to a great depression. It is very true that much or most of the inflations could not have been helped because of the exigencies of governmental finance, but the subsequent undue deflations could probably have been avoided entirely.

47. The public psychology of going into debt for gain passes through several more or less distinct phases: (a) the lure of big prospective dividends or gains in *income* in the remote future; (b) the hope of selling at a profit, and realizing a *capital* gain in the immediate future; (c) the vogue of reckless promotions, taking advantage of the habituation of the public to great expectations; (d) the development of downright fraud, imposing on a public which had grown credulous and gullible.

When it is too late the dupes discover scandals like the Hatry, Krueger, and Insull scandals. At least one book has been written to prove that crises are due to frauds of clever promoters. But probably these frauds could never have become so great without the original starters of real opportunities to invest lucratively. There is probably always a very real basis for the "new era" psychology before it runs away with its victims. This was certainly the case before 1929.

48. In summary, we find that: (1) economic changes include steady trends and unsteady occasional disturbances which act as starters for cyclical oscillations of innumerable kinds; (2) among the many occasional disturbances, are new opportunities to invest, especially because of new inventions; (3) these, with other causes, sometimes conspire to lead to a great volume of over-indebtedness; (4) this, in turn, leads to attempts to liquidate; (5) these, in turn, lead (*unless counteracted by reflation*) to falling prices or a swelling dollar; (6) the dollar may swell faster than the number of dollars owed shrinks; (7) in that case, liquidation does not really liquidate but actually aggravates the debts, and the depression grows worse instead of better, as indicated by all nine factors; (8) the ways out are either *via laissez faire* (bankruptcy) or scientific medication (reflation), and reflation might just as well have been applied in the first place.

49. The general correctness of the above "debt-deflation theory of great depressions" is, I believe, evidenced by experience in the present and previous great depressions. Future studies by others will doubtless check up on this opinion. One way is to compare different countries simultaneously. If the "debt-deflation theory" is correct, the infectiousness of depressions internationally is chiefly due to a common gold (or other) monetary standard and there should be found little tendency for a depression to pass from a deflating to an inflating, or stabilizing, country.

SOME NEW FEATURES

As stated at the outset, several features of the above analysis are, as far as I know, new. Some of these are too unimportant or self-evident to stress. The one (No. 32 above; also 36) which I do venture to stress most is the theory that when over-indebtedness is so great as to depress prices faster than liquidation, the mass effort to get out of debt sinks us more deeply into debt.[4] I would also like to emphasize the whole logical articulation of the nine factors, of which debt and deflation are the two chief (Nos. 23, 24, and 28, above). I would call attention to *new investment opportunities* as the important "starter" of over-indebtedness (Nos. 44, 45). Finally, I would emphasize the important corollary, of the debt-deflation theory, that great depressions are curable and preventable through reflation and stabilization (Nos. 38–42).

Yale University

[4] This interaction between liquidation and deflation did not occur to me until 1931, although, with others, I had since 1909 been stressing the fact that deflation tended toward depression and inflation toward a boom.

This debt-deflation theory was first stated in my lectures at Yale in 1931, and first stated publicly before the American Association for the Advancement of Science, on January 1, 1932. It is fully set forth in my *Booms and Depressions*, 1932, and some special features of my general views on cycle theory in "Business Cycles as Facts or Tendencies" in *Economische Opstellen Aangeboden aan Prof. C. A. Verrijn Stuart*, Haarlem, 1931. Certain sorts of disequilibrium are discussed in other writings. The rôle of the lag between real and nominal interest is discussed in *The Purchasing Power of Money*, Macmillan, New York, 1911; and more fully in *The Theory of Interest*, Macmillan, New York, 1930, as well as the effects of inequality of foresight. Some statistical verification will be found in "Our Unstable Dollar and the So-called Business Cycle," *Journal of the American Statistical Association*, June, 1925, pp. 179–202, and "The Relation of Employment to the Price Level" (address given before a section of the American Association for the Advancement of Science, Atlantic City, N. J., December 28, 1932, and later published in *Stabilization of Employment*, edited by Charles F. Roos, The Principia Press, Inc., Bloomingdale, Ind., 1933, pp. 152–159). See Charts I, II, III. Some statistical verification will be found in *The Stock Market Crash and After*, Macmillan, New York, 1930.

A selected bibliography of the writings of others is given in Appendix III of *Booms and Depressions*, Adelphi Company, New York, 1932. This bibliography omitted Veblen's *Theory of Business Enterprise*, Charles Scribner's Sons, New York, 1904, Chapter VII of which, Professor Wesley C. Mitchell points out, probably comes nearest to the debt-deflation theory. Hawtrey's writings seem the next nearest. Professor Alvin H. Hansen informs me that Professor Paxson, of the American History Department of the University of Wisconsin, in a course on the History of the West some twenty years ago, stressed the debt factor and its relation to deflation. But, so far as I know, no one hitherto has pointed out how debt liquidation defeats itself via deflation nor several other features of the present "creed." If any clear-cut anticipation exists, it can never have been prominently set forth, for even the word "debt" is missing in the indexes of the treatises on the subject.

CHARTS

The following eight charts are all on the "ratio scale" excepting Charts II, III, V, VI, and curve P' of Chart I. The particular ratio scale used is indicated in each case.

It will be noted that in Charts VII and VIII all curves have a common ratio scale, as indicated by the inset at the right in both charts, except "Brokers' Loans" in Chart VII and "Failures Numbers," "Failures Liabilities," and "Shares Traded" in Chart VIII, which four curves have another, "reduced" i.e., smaller, common scale, as indicated by the inset at the left of Chart VIII.

It will be further noted that "Money in Circulation," "Failures Numbers," and "Failures Liabilities" are inverted.

The full details of how $\overline{P'}$ in Charts II and III is derived from P' in Chart I and also how P' in Chart I is derived from P are given in "Our Unstable Dollar and the So-Called Business Cycle," *Journal of the American Statistical Association*, June, 1925.

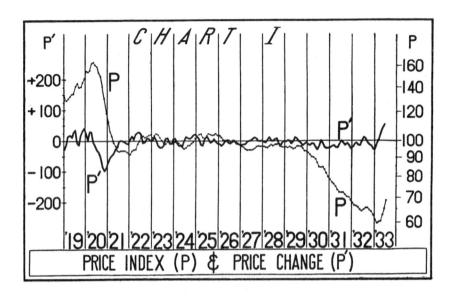

CHART I
PRICE INDEX (P) & PRICE CHANGE (P')

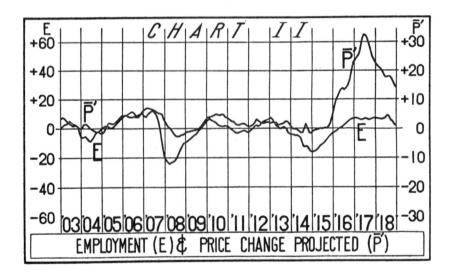

CHART II
EMPLOYMENT (E) & PRICE CHANGE PROJECTED (P̄')

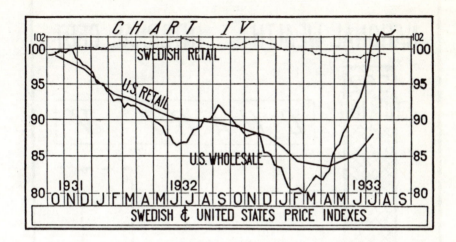

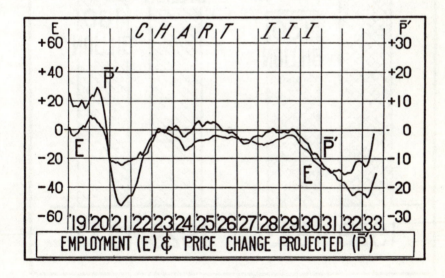

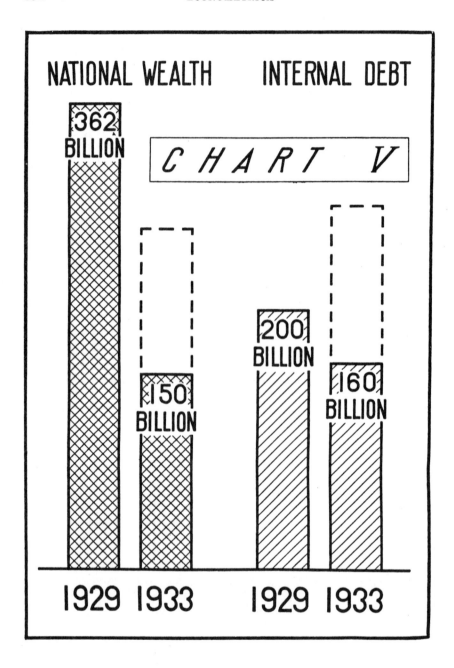

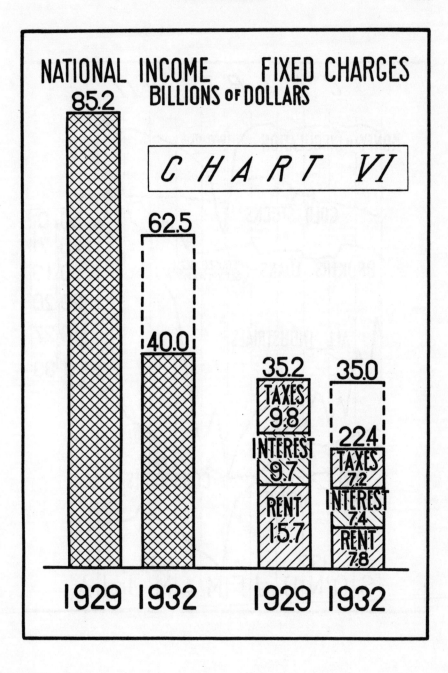

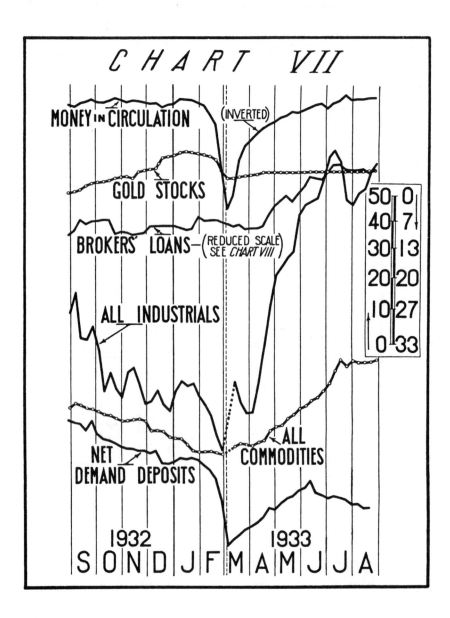

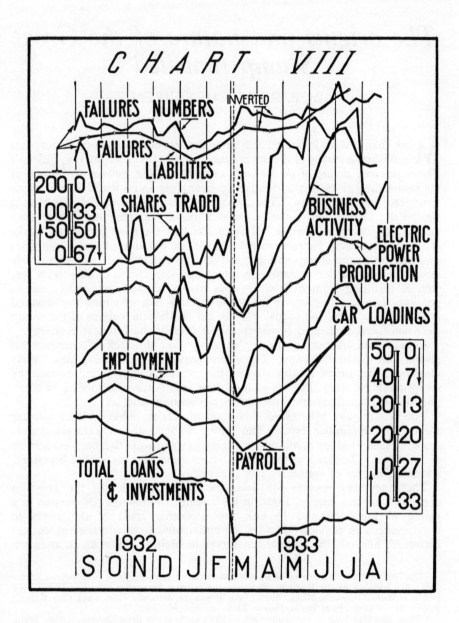

The origins and nature of the Great Slump revisited

By BARRY EICHENGREEN[1]

More than a decade has passed since the Economic History Society last published a survey of the depression of the 1930s. That survey, Fearon's *The origins and nature of the Great Slump, 1929-1932*, proved to be one of the best-selling titles in the 'Studies in Economic and Social History' series sponsored by the Society.[2] The appeal of Fearon's pamphlet was that it treated the Depression of the 1930s as a global phenomenon. Rather than focusing on events in the United States, as had the most influential works of preceding years, Fearon treated the US as but one of many countries succumbing to the slump and emphasized the linkages between them.[3] He resurrected an earlier literature in which the depression of the 1930s was seen as resulting from instabilities that had developed over the course of previous decades. Implicit in his account, fully half of which was devoted to World War I and the 1920s, was the notion that the origins of the slump were somehow connected to structural features of the interwar economy.

A disturbing feature of Fearon's survey was the lack of consensus it revealed on the central issues. The events requiring explanation were clearly identified: the onset of the slump, the persistent downward spiral, the inception of recovery. But for each of these events there seemed to be many potential explanations and little agreement among scholars.

The reader may ask, given this state of affairs, what justifies another survey of such familiar terrain. The answer, I contend, is that the last decade has witnessed a hidden revolution in our understanding of the macroeconomics of the 1930s. On many of the central issues raised by the earlier literature, a striking degree of consensus has emerged.

There are two reasons for using Fearon's pamphlet as the point of departure for this survey. First, in his attempt to view the Depression as a global phenomenon and to link the economic crisis of the 1930s to developments in previous decades, he anticipated trends in the subsequent literature. Second, the comparison serves to highlight how much attention

---

[1] This is a greatly revised version of a paper first presented to a meeting of the European Science Foundation Network on the Economic History of the Interwar Years. For helpful comments I am grateful to Michael Bernstein, Michael Bordo, Steve Broadberry, Alexander Field, Adam Klug, Kenneth Mouré, Martha Olney, Peter Temin, Eugene White, and especially Mark Thomas.

[2] Where American scholars universally refer to this episode as the Great Depression, their British counterparts reserve the term for the period 1873-93: Fearon calls the depression of the 1930s the Great Slump. In this article I use Great Depression and Great Slump interchangeably to refer to the decline in economic activity that began in 1929.

[3] Two of the most influential and certainly most widely cited studies of the Depression published in the 1960s and 1970s were Friedman and Schwartz, *Monetary history*, and Temin, *Did monetary forces cause the Great Depression?* Both focused almost exclusively on the US.

has been devoted subsequently to the macroeconomics of the interwar years. Only six items are common to the bibliographies of his survey and mine.[4]

I

One of the most enduring themes in research on the Depression is that changes in economic structure during World War I and the 1920s were responsible for the crisis of the 1930s.[5] Four variants of the hypothesis recur frequently in the literature. Not all of them have emerged unscathed from recent scholarship.

The first is *changes in the composition of production*. In the literature on Britain this transformation is couched in terms of the decline of the staple trades (iron and steel, coal, textiles, shipbuilding) and the rise of the 'new industries' (chemicals, electrical engineering, motor vehicles). Analogous shifts are evident in other countries where dependence on the staple trades never reached comparable levels. The rapid pace of structural change in industry is portrayed as heightening vulnerability to cyclical instability.

Not only is the mechanism unclear, however, but recent research calls into question the notion that structural change was exceptionally rapid between the wars. For Britain, where changes in the composition of industrial production have received close attention, Matthews, Feinstein, and Odling-Smee find that structural change, measured as the dispersion of growth rates across industries, was slower between the wars than after World War II, when no comparable episode of cyclical instability occurred.[6]

Alternatively, it could be that the direction rather than the pace of structural change heightened the economy's vulnerability to cyclical disturbances. The growing importance of consumer durables was one such change. The motor car epitomized the shift: production in the United States rose from fewer than two million units in 1919 to more than five million in 1929. The importance of the sector was evident in the decline in US industrial production in 1927, which coincided with Henry Ford's decision to shut down his assembly line for six months to retool for the Model A.

The question is whether this had important implications for the cycle. Did it constitute a 'consumer durables revolution'? Data for the US show a rise in the share of durables in consumption from less than 9 per cent in the first two decades of the century to 11 per cent in the 1920s. Motor vehicles, furniture, household appliances, radios, and gramophones, to which

---

[4] In this survey I have consciously sought to emphasize new directions in research on the macroeconomics of the 1930s. This is why important earlier studies are omitted. Moreover, owing to space limitations it is impossible to provide a comprehensive listing of recent contributions to the literature. Specialists in British economic history may consult Broadberry, *British economy between the wars*. A comprehensive survey of the recent literature on the US is Fearon, *War, prosperity and depression*. Temin's Robbins Lectures, *Lessons from the Great Depression*, also summarize and synthesize the recent literature from an international perspective.

[5] Two influential statements of the view are Svennilson, *Growth and stagnation*, and Steindl, *Maturity and stagnation*. More recently, Temin, *Lessons from the Great Depression*, linked the depression of the 1930s to World War I, and Bernstein, *The Great Depression*, related it to changes in economic structure in the 1920s.

[6] See Matthews, Feinstein, and Odling-Smee, *British economic growth*, and von Tunzelmann, 'Structural change and leading sectors'.

4.3 per cent of US consumption spending had been devoted in 1900-19, accounted for 7.3 per cent in 1920-9.[7] These are modest but noticeable changes. But the US was clearly in the vanguard of this movement. In the UK the consumer durables revolution was delayed by at least a decade.[8] That there is little literature on the consumer durables revolution in other countries is probably indicative of the fact that the sector was of still less importance there.

Insofar as the depression was unusually severe in the US, it is worth exploring the possibility that the growth of this sector contributed to the cyclical instability of the American economy. Consumer durables being costly, their demand is notoriously sensitive to cyclical conditions (figure 1). In periods of uncertainty, households hesitate to tie up their savings—or, if they purchase on the instalment plan, their future incomes—in durable goods of limited resale value.[9] Thus, the shift in production and consumption towards consumer durables may have heightened the sensitivity of American industry to cyclical fluctuations.

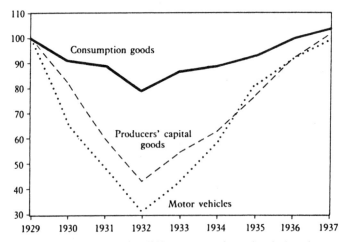

Figure 1. *Indices of production by different manufacturing industries, 1929-1937* (1929 = 100)
Source: League of Nations, *World production and prices, 1937/8*, p. 44

The instalment contracts under which consumer durables were purchased in the US reinforced the economy's responsiveness to the cycle. Durables were so expensive that many households could purchase them only on

---

[7] These are Olney's estimates, from 'Consumer durables'. For the period 1900-19, I have taken unweighted averages of her figures for the first two decades of the century.

[8] See Bowden, 'Consumer durables revolution'. For interesting French comparisons, see Marseille, 'Les origines'.

[9] This mechanism is emphasized by Mishkin, 'Household balance sheet'. Inability to ensure that they were properly maintained made durables difficult to rent, while informational asymmetries worked to limit resale value. The main informational asymmetry—that sellers had more information about reliability than did buyers—is developed by Akerlof, 'Market for lemons'. Romer, 'The Great Crash', emphasizes that the early phases of the depression were characterized by unusual levels of uncertainty.

credit.[10] This provided an additional channel through which disruptions to financial markets, typical of economic downturns, could magnify cyclical instabilities. Moreover, in contrast to present day instalment contracts, households that missed instalments and had their durables repossessed received no credit for previous payments.[11] When income turned down, as in 1929, a small increase in the risk of job loss, raising the danger that an instalment payment would be missed, thus acted as a deterrent to households that otherwise might have been willing to enter into new instalment contracts. Households already in possession of such contracts had an exceptional incentive to compress other forms of spending so as not to miss a payment and risk repossession. Thus, there is some reason to think that the growth of consumer durables spending heightened cyclical sensitivity, but mainly in the US.

Accompanying these changes in the composition of industrial activity were changes in primary production. East European and Russian grain exports had been disrupted by the war, prompting producers elsewhere to step into the breach. US farmers boosted acreage and exports. Canadian acreage under wheat was expanded by 80 per cent between 1913 and 1918. Argentine producers raised their exports of meat, those in New Zealand their production of meat and dairy products. An abundance of cheap credit, together with limited supplies of manufactured goods, fuelled a boom in farm land prices during and after the war. When interest rates rose in 1920 and east European grain supplies came back on stream, commodity prices turned down and land prices collapsed. Having shifted resources into the production of grain, meat, and dairy products, farmers now hesitated to withdraw that capacity from production.[12] They found themselves saddled with low output prices and a heavy burden of mortgage debts.[13] The danger that they would default on those debts if crop prices again declined posed an obvious threat to the financial system, while the pressure farmers applied for cheap credit and tariff protection continued to shape policy throughout the decade.[14]

The second potential change in economic structure highlighted by the recent literature concerns *the operation of labour markets*. High unemployment throughout the industrial world characterized the 1920s. The official unemployment rate in Britain, calculated on an average annual basis, fell below double digits only once during the decade. Trade union returns for Germany show unemployment never falling below 6.8 per cent after 1922. The available statistics for most other industrial countries paint the same

---

[10] See Olney, 'Credit as production smoothing device'.

[11] See *idem*, *Buy now, pay later*, from where the points in the remainder of this paragraph are drawn.

[12] The plausibility of this mechanism, in which temporary relative price movements have permanent effects, is supported by recent theoretical work in economics analysing permanent effects of the US dollar's temporary appreciation in the 1980s. See Dixit, 'Hysteresis'; his model, in which there are fixed costs entering and exiting a market, seems particularly suitable to analysing agricultural supply decisions in the 1920s.

[13] Farm foreclosure rates in the US averaged more than 10 per 1,000 farms between 1921 and 1925 and rose significantly in the second half of the decade. The comparable figure for 1913-20 was 3 per 1,000; see Alston, 'Farm foreclosures', tab. 1.

[14] The concentration of US bank failures in regions heavily exposed to agricultural risk is emphasized by Temin, *Monetary forces*. The role of the agricultural lobby in the passage of the US Smoot-Hawley tariff in 1930 is reviewed by Eichengreen, 'Political economy of Smoot-Hawley'.

dismal picture.[15] Only in the US, for which Lebergott's estimates show unemployment reaching a low of 2.9 per cent in 1925, was the record reasonably satisfactory.[16]

The pervasiveness of high unemployment before the advent of the depression points to the possibility of a deterioration in the flexibility and adaptability of labour markets during or after World War I. Collective bargaining is said to have restricted the downward flexibility of wages. Rates of unionization reached unprecedented levels in this period. Between one-third and one-half of the interwar British labour force was covered by collective agreements.[17] Powerful German unions are said to have placed upward pressure on wages in the second half of the 1920s.[18] Unionism in the US scaled new heights, leading employers to raise wages in order to ward off the threat of organization.[19] Yet it is also true that levels of union density in many countries declined after World War I. The vast majority of workers were still not covered by collective bargaining agreements. There is little evidence outside the US of a change in the wage determination process. Hatton's prewar and interwar comparisons for Britain do not indicate a decline in labour market flexibility. Nor does Thomas's analysis of labour market flows.[20]

The difference in the US was the rise of personnel departments and internal labour markets in key sectors dominated by large enterprises. Under their guidance workers and firms increasingly agreed to implicit contracts covering an entire sequence of wage bargains, which reduced the cyclical sensitivity of wages.[21] This appears to have been a distinctively American phenomenon. As yet, there is no evidence for other countries of a significant spread in the importance of internal labour markets.[22] Gordon's time-series analysis reveals a decline after World War I in the responsiveness of wages to fluctuations in GNP for the US but not for Britain and Japan.[23]

Any analysis of interwar labour markets is incomplete without a discussion of unemployment benefits and other policy-induced labour market distortions. The bad name acquired by the hypothesis of benefit-induced unemployment in the UK is attributable to the strong terms in which the argument has

---

[15] These unemployment rates are tabulated and their construction is discussed in Eichengreen and Hatton, 'Interwar unemployment', pp. 6-7.
[16] Lebergott, *Manpower*, p. 512.
[17] Thomas, 'Institutional rigidity'.
[18] The notion that high real wages were the source of German unemployment in the second half of the 1920s has come to be known as the 'Borchardt thesis'; see Borchardt, *Perspectives on modern German history*. A recent analysis that is generally supportive of the Borchardt thesis is Corbett, 'Unemployment'.
[19] This is, for example, the explanation for Henry Ford's famous decision to double daily wages to $5, in Raff, 'Five dollar day at Ford'.
[20] Hatton, 'Institutional change'; Thomas, 'Institutional rigidity'.
[21] The leading study of personnel departments is Jacoby, *Employing bureaucracy*. It builds on the literature on implicit contracts in economics, viz. Azariadis, 'Implicit contracts'.
[22] See Thomas, 'Institutional rigidity'; *idem*, 'How flexible were wages?'.
[23] Gordon, 'Why U.S. wage and employment behavior differs'. Gordon's conclusions are consistent with the findings of Cagan and Sachs of a decline in US wage and price flexibility over the course of the twentieth century; Cagan, 'Changes in recession behavior'; Sachs, 'Changing cyclical behavior'. Note that the argument is not that American labour markets were perfectly flexible before the war. (For evidence that they were not, see Carter and Sutch, 'The labor market in the 1890s'.) It is that the extent of wage flexibility declined further between the prewar and interwar periods.

been couched. Benjamin and Kochin's assertion that the bulk of British unemployment between the wars was caused by excessively generous insurance benefits does not withstand scrutiny.[24] But subsequent studies for Britain using both microeconomic and macroeconomic data continue to show that benefits had a small impact on unemployment.[25] Corbett's study of Germany yields a picture similar to that which has emerged for Britain, one which features 'at most a very modest role for relief benefits in inducing search unemployment'.[26] In any case, the main effect of overly generous unemployment benefits would have been to raise the 'natural' or equilibrium rate of unemployment. Except insofar as the replacement rate (the ratio of benefits to wages) rose with the deflation that accompanied recessions, it is not clear that insurance schemes should have reduced the cyclical sensitivity of wages.

The third change in economic structure receiving attention in recent years is *the operation of the international monetary system*. Britain's return to gold in 1925 and France's *de facto* stabilization in 1926 marked the re-establishment of a truly international gold standard. A number of factors limited that system's capacity to accommodate balance of payments disturbances and heightened its vulnerability to destabilizing shocks. The share of foreign exchange in international reserves rose by more than 50 per cent between the end of 1913 and the end of 1928.[27] A loss of confidence in sterling or the dollar which led to the liquidation of foreign exchange reserves was sure to apply intense balance of payments pressure to Britain and the US, the principal reserve currency countries, and unleash a deflationary scramble for gold, threatening the stability of the entire international system.

Further contributing to the fragility of the interwar gold standard was the prevalence of policies insulating domestic output and employment from external disturbances. Violations of the 'rules of the game', in which policymakers prevented domestic credit from rising and falling with international reserves, became increasingly frequent as the period progressed.[28] The markets therefore subjected the stated commitment to gold to early and repeated tests.[29]

Moreover, central bankers and governments failed to appreciate that international monetary stability should be regarded as a collective good. International support operations like those undertaken in response to the crises of 1890 and 1907 proved difficult to arrange.[30] To defend the

---

[24] Benjamin and Kochin, 'Searching for an explanation'. A good review of the subsequent literature critical of the hypothesis is Hatton, 'The British labour market in the 1920s'. An authoritative recent study, if not the final word, is Dimsdale, Nickell, and Horsewood, 'Real wages and unemployment'.

[25] This was my conclusion based on the analysis of a survey of London households, as reported in Eichengreen, 'Unemployment in interwar Britain'. It is also the conclusion of Dimsdale, Nickell, and Horsewood, 'Real wages and unemployment' on the basis of their analysis of aggregate quarterly data.

[26] Corbett, 'Unemployment insurance and induced search'.

[27] Lindert, *Key currencies and gold*, pp. 12-5. The implications of this fact for the stability of the system are emphasized by Hamilton, 'Role of the gold standard'.

[28] Eichengreen, 'International monetary instability', pp. 94-6.

[29] Hamilton, 'Role of the gold standard'.

[30] The importance of international support operations under the prewar gold standard is argued by Eichengreen, 'Credibility and cooperation'. The contrast with the interwar period is a theme of Eichengreen, *Golden fetters*.

convertibility of currency into gold, countries had to rely on their domestic resources, despite the extent to which one country's crisis threatened to undermine confidence in other currencies. More generally, the cross-border repercussions of domestic monetary policies were inadequately taken into account. The surplus countries, the US and France, raised interest rates and restricted domestic credit in a non-cooperative struggle to obtain gold reserves, forcing other countries to do likewise.[31]

Three factors limited the extent of international cooperation: domestic political constraints, international political disputes, and incompatible conceptual frameworks.[32] Domestic interest groups with the most to lose were able to stave off adjustments in economic policy that would have facilitated international cooperation. The dispute over war debts and reparations disrupted international negotiations, contaminating efforts to redesign the gold standard system and to manage it cooperatively. The competing conceptual frameworks employed in different countries prevented policy-makers from reaching a common understanding of their economic problems, much less from agreeing on a solution.

The fourth and final change in structure emphasized in the recent literature concerns *the pattern of international settlements*. These changes went back to World War I. As soon as European merchandise exports to Latin America were curtailed in 1914, US producers leapt in to fill the void. Having set up marketing and distribution networks, they proved difficult to dislodge. In Asia, the new competitor, Japan, was different, but the consequences were the same. Japanese exporters, like their US counterparts, once they had incurred the fixed costs of establishing a marketing infrastructure, proved difficult to dislodge following the armistice.[33] The consequence was a deterioration in the competitive position of European exports, aggravated in some cases (notably that of Britain) by the decision to return to the gold standard at an overvalued exchange rate.[34]

Moreover, World War I had transformed the US from a net foreign debtor to a net foreign creditor. Net interest transfers, traditionally a debit item in the balance of payments accounts, turned positive overnight. Superimposed upon this current account imbalance were war debts and reparations. The victorious powers received nearly $2 billion of transfers from Germany between 1924 and 1929. A substantial portion of this was passed on from western Europe to the US as principal and interest on war debts, amounting to about $1 billion between mid 1926 and mid 1931.

In the 1920s New York surpassed London as the leading international financial centre. The surge of US lending was a response to these shifts in the pattern of balance of payments settlements. US lending to central and eastern Europe served to recycle European balance of payments deficits.[35]

---

[31] Two treatments of monetary policy in the 1920s as a non-cooperative game are Eichengreen, 'Central bank cooperation', and Broadberry, 'Monetary interdependence and deflation'.
[32] See Eichengreen and Uzan, 'The 1933 world economic conference', for further development of these points.
[33] Again, see Dixit, 'Hysteresis'.
[34] See Redmond, 'The sterling overvaluation in 1925'.
[35] The recycling analogy is explicit in Schuker, 'American "reparations" to Germany'.

Debate centres on the rationality of the process. In principle, a country running a current account deficit has two options: financing it or adjusting to eliminate it. A temporary deterioration in the external position should be financed: the deficit country should borrow to smooth the time profile of spending. The impact of a permanent deterioration in international competitiveness should be eliminated through adjustment (a competitiveness-enhancing decline in real wages and a permanent cut in domestic spending).[36] Those critical of US lending to Germany in the 1920s suggest that the underlying disturbance to the balance of payments, namely reparations, was long lived, and that too much financing and too little adjustment took place.[37] US lenders and German borrowers should have recognized that Germany would be unable to sustain its rising burden of external debts.

Recent research lends mixed support to this view. Whether Germany's debt would have grown unsustainably hinges on the rate of growth of consumption relative to the rate of growth of domestic production.[38] Klug's review of the evidence for 1925-9 suggests an annual growth rate of real net national product of 2.4 per cent and of real consumption of 3.1 per cent.[39] Only if Germany had been consuming significantly less than it produced at the start of the period could consumption have grown more quickly than production without violating the national budget constraint. But, as is evident in the fact that Germany was already borrowing in 1924, consumption was too high to remove the discrepancy.

Before concluding that US lenders were reckless or irrational, it is important to note that contemporary experts systematically overestimated the growth rate of German output in the 1920s, in some cases sufficiently to suggest that the country was solvent.[40] Their judgements concerning the advisability of international lending therefore hinged on the realism of the assumption that Germany's rapid growth would continue indefinitely. In fact, the 1920s were widely viewed, especially in the US, the leading creditor of the period, as a new era of continuous growth. Cyclical downturns were regarded as a thing of the past. Assuming growth and lending continued uninterrupted, there seemed no reason to doubt that the process could be sustained.[41]

---

[36] See for example Sachs, 'The current account and macroeconomic adjustment'.

[37] Schuker, 'American "reparations" to Germany'.

[38] If the growth rate exceeded the interest rate, the debt/GNP ratio would decline in the absence of additional borrowing. Insofar as domestic spending fell short of domestic production, the excess could be used to repay foreign debt, thereby reducing it as a share of GNP. See Cohen, 'How to evaluate solvency'.

[39] Klug, 'American loans to Germany'.

[40] Klug argues (ibid.) that contemporary observers had exaggerated the destructiveness of the war and the fall in output in the latter stages of the hyperinflation. Thus, they overstated the rate of growth of output from an artificially low base in 1924-5 to the end of the 1920s.

[41] In theory, there was no reason why Germany ultimately had to repay the principal or even to stop borrowing. It could continue to borrow as its economy grew, devoting a constant fraction of GNP to debt service. Conditions under which this result obtains are spelled out in Eichengreen, 'Trends and cycles in foreign lending'. See also Klug, 'American loans to Germany'. The belief that recessions were a thing of the past can also be invoked to rationalize the rise of the New York stock market on the grounds that high stock prices were rational assuming that economic growth (and hence dividends) would now proceed without interruption. This explanation for the stock market boom is advanced by Sirkin, 'The stock market of 1929', and has been criticized recently by White, 'When the ticker ran late'.

All four changes in economic structure could have helped set the stage for the post-1929 depression. The first two—the rising importance of consumer durables and the declining flexibility of labour markets—were limited mainly to the US. Together they go some way towards explaining why the post-1929 decline of activity in the US was exceptionally severe. The other two—the growing fragility of the gold standard and shifts in the pattern of international settlements—were global phenomena. The fragility of the gold standard heightened the danger of capital flight and intensified the pressure for national central banks to choose between policies to restore internal and external balance. Shifts in the pattern of international settlements increased the dependence of the global commercial and financial system on continued lending by the US. Any interruption of lending was sure to force severe dislocations on the borrowers. From 1928 the consequences became readily apparent.

II

For many years the least conclusive strand of literature on the Great Depression was that concerned with its onset. A consensus now seems to have emerged that increasingly stringent US monetary policy contributed significantly to the onset of the slump. Field and Hamilton presented evidence showing that, in response to growing Federal Reserve concern over stock market speculation, US monetary policy turned in a restrictive direction in 1928.[42] The rate of growth of US monetary aggregates decelerated, as shown in figure 2. American interest rates rose. The Federal Reserve Board sterilized gold inflows.

In terms of its impact on economic activity worldwide, US monetary policy might seem to have been a small tail wagging a large dog. Restrictive monetary policy in the US had such powerful effects because it induced restrictive monetary policy in other countries. Monetary restriction by the Fed brought US foreign lending to a halt. Unpropitiously this coincided with the movement of gold towards France, where capital inflows were required to rebuild money balances following the franc's stabilization.[43] As the US and France siphoned off gold and financial capital from the rest of the world, foreign central banks were forced to raise their discount rates and to restrict the provision of domestic credit in order to defend their gold parities. Superimposed upon already weak foreign balances of payments, these shifts in US and French policy provoked a greatly magnified shift in monetary policy in other countries. Table 1, based on official statistics compiled by the League of Nations, shows that between 1927 and 1928 the rate of growth of monetary aggregates, while falling by 2 per cent in the US and Canada, fell by 5 per cent in both Europe and Latin America. Between

[42] Field, 'A new interpretation of the Great Depression'; *idem*, 'Asset exchanges'; Hamilton, 'Monetary factors in the Great Depression'.
[43] Eichengreen, 'The Bank of France and the sterilization of gold'. See also Mouré, 'The Bank of France and the gold standard'. Dornbusch, Sturzenegger, and Wolf, 'Extreme inflation', citing a number of historical and contemporary episodes, show that this increase in the demand for real money balances is a standard response to credible stabilizations.

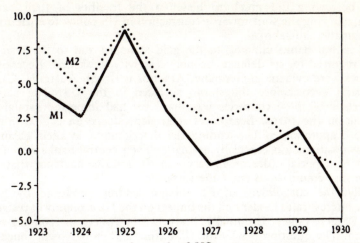

Figure 2. *Annualized rates of growth of US monetary aggregates, 1923-1930*
Source: Hamilton, *Monetary factors*, p. 151.

1928 and 1929, monetary growth rates fell by an additional 4 per cent in North America but by an additional 5 per cent in the rest of the world. This shift in policy worldwide, and not merely in the US, was the source of the contractionary impulse that set the stage for the 1929 downturn.

Table 1. *Percentage change in M1 between ends of successive years (per cent)*

	1926-1927	1927-1928	1928-1929
North America	5.20	3.04	−0.91
Central and South America	12.14	7.53	2.66
Europe	11.54	7.82	2.45
Far East	1.38	5.37	0.20

Note: All figures are unweighted averages of data for constituent countries. North America includes Canada and the United States. Central and South America includes Argentina, Brazil, Chile, Colombia, Uruguay, Venezuela, El Salvador, and Mexico. Europe includes Belgium, France, Netherlands, Poland, Switzerland, Austria, Germany, Bulgaria, Czechoslovakia, Hungary, Italy, Yugoslavia, Denmark, Finland, Norway, Sweden, the UK, and Ireland. Far East includes Australia, New Zealand, and Japan.
Source: Eichengreen, *Golden fetters*, p. 223.

This view of the importance of US policy might be interpreted to mean that the US initiated the slump. Some, such as Temin, argue instead for shared causation.[44] In fact, there is no incompatibility between the two views. The shift in policy in the US may have provided the initial impulse, but it produced a crisis rather than merely a deceleration in growth because it was superimposed upon the already critical position in which other countries found themselves. French policies, as described above, were partly to blame. In addition, the failure of other countries to adjust to changing international competitive conditions and their consequent dependence on

[44] Temin, *Lessons from the Great Depression*.

foreign borrowing did much to heighten the fragility of their external position, allowing the shift towards contraction in US policy to elicit an even more dramatic shift abroad.

With central banks clinging to the gold standard and to the restrictive policies required for its defence, economic activity weakened. Recessionary tendencies were evident in Germany, Argentina, Brazil, Australia, Canada, and Poland even before the slump surfaced in the US. The common characteristic of these countries was that they had imported capital on a large scale in the 1920s. Because of their dependence on capital imports, with the evaporation of US lending the deterioration in their balance of payments positions was especially dramatic. Their central banks were forced to adopt an especially draconian response. It is no coincidence that these were the first countries to enter the slump.[45]

Initially, the curtailment of US foreign lending produced by higher domestic interest rates moderated the impact on the US economy of restrictive Federal Reserve policy. Eventually, however, the American economy began to weaken. The question is why the US output and employment, once they began to decline, spiralled downwards so precipitously. One contributing factor was the deterioration of US export markets. Since a number of other countries entered the recession before the United States, US exports peaked before US industrial production.[46] The growing importance of consumer durables, for reasons described above, could have lent an additional fillip to the early stages of the slump. So could the 1929 stock market crash. Economic historians long ago dismissed the crash as a factor in the decline of output and employment, on the grounds that equities were only a fraction of total household wealth and that the marginal propensity to spend out of wealth was small. Recently Romer has suggested additional channels through which the Great Crash could have contributed to the onset of the depression.[47] The rise in stock market volatility, Romer argues, inaugurated a new era of uncertainty. Not knowing whether the crash signalled a decline in incomes and employment prospects, households deferred their purchases of expensive items. Thus, Romer's analysis neatly ties the consumer durables revolution of the 1920s to the economic instability of the 1930s.[48]

The Federal Reserve Board did not loosen its policy significantly in response to the deepening slump. Admittedly, the New York Federal Reserve Bank purchased more than $100 million of government securities in the

---

[45] Other factors such as the weakness of primary commodity prices may also have contributed to the difficulties of many of these countries. But some, notably Germany, were primary-commodity importers to whom the argument does not apply. The debate over whether the onset of the slump in Germany was due to the curtailment of capital inflows or to independent sources of weakness in Germany, as argued by Temin, seems to have been resolved in favour of an eclectic view. See Temin, 'Beginning of the Great Depression in Germany', and, for a recent assessment of the debate, Balderston, 'Beginning of the depression in Germany'. Alternatives like Temin's have not been suggested, in any case, for the other countries to experience an early onset of the depression.

[46] Fleisig, *Long-term capital*; Eichengreen, *Golden fetters*, ch. 8.

[47] Romer, 'The Great Crash'. Much other work on the 1929 crash was stimulated by its 1987 counterpart. See for example Santoni and Dwyer, 'Bubbles or fundamentals'; Rappoport and White, 'Was there a bubble?'

[48] Romer's argument is buttressed by time-series evidence linking output in industries producing consumer durables to the volatility of equity prices.

wake of the crash. But these purchases were initiated to bail out New York banks that had extended brokers' loans. Once those loans were discharged, expansionary open market operations were halted. In addition, the New York Federal Reserve Bank's intervention had not been authorized by the Federal Reserve Board but was undertaken independently. George Harrison, Governor of the New York Reserve Bank, was put on the carpet; the conflict helped to shift authority over monetary policy to Washington, D.C., where there was less agreement on the need for policy activism.

The question is whether US monetary policy again became tight after the New York Federal Reserve Bank's post-crash operations were unwound, from about the middle of 1930. Temin's conclusion for the US—that money was not tight since interest rates were low—has been challenged on the grounds that low nominal rates in 1930 could have reflected anticipated deflation rather than accommodating monetary policy.[49] Low nominal interest rates could have concealed high real rates that served to depress investment and consumption. Evidence from commodity futures markets suggests, in fact, that prices were not expected to decline.[50] But futures prices for agricultural commodities, which depend on the weather and other factors unlikely to affect the industrial and service sectors, may be imperfect indicators of overall price expectations.[51] This observation led Hamilton to analyse the correlation between commodity futures and the aggregate price level.[52] He concluded that the 5 per cent decline in the US price level in the first year of the slump (September 1929 to September 1930) was not anticipated. In contrast, about half the decline in consumer prices in the second and third years of the depression could have been forecast by market participants. These conclusions are consistent with Nelson's survey of the financial press.[53] They imply that *ex ante* real interest rates were higher than nominal interest rates after September 1930, signalling a role for tight money in the intermediate stages of the slump. This conclusion does not apply to the first year of the depression, however.

Thus, while there does not appear to be a satisfactory single factor explanation for the exceptionally rapid contraction of the American economy, a more eclectic approach has considerable explanatory power. The stage was set for the US recession by the turn to contraction in monetary policy. Interacting with existing imbalances in the pattern of international settlements, the shift in Federal Reserve Board policy provoked an even more contractionary shift in policy abroad. Hence US exports weakened. Next the Wall Street crash led consumers to defer spending on expensive items, magnifying the cyclical sensitivity of the durables sector to the downturn. In the second half of 1930, another move towards contraction in monetary policy reinforced deflationary tendencies. And the decline in the flexibility of American labour markets limited the economy's ability to adjust.

---

[49] Temin, *Monetary forces*; Schwartz, 'Understanding 1929-1931'.
[50] Hamilton, 'Monetary factors'.
[51] This point is emphasized by Cecchetti, 'Prices during the Great Depression'.
[52] Hamilton, 'Was the deflation during the Great Depression anticipated?'
[53] See Nelson, 'Was the deflation of 1929-30 anticipated?'

III

The decline in US economic activity was transmitted to other countries through several mutually reinforcing channels. These channels operated powerfully because national economies were linked together by the fixed exchange rates of the gold standard.[54] Price deflation in the US produced price deflation abroad, since the US accounted for more than one-third of the global demand for primary products. Federal Reserve monetary policy, which was less than accommodating, reinforced by the shift from bank deposits into currency induced by financial instability, attracted a steady stream of gold towards the US and drained reserves from foreign central banks, forcing them to restrict domestic credit in order to defend gold convertibility. The decline of US merchandise imports, initiated by the contraction but reinforced by the Smoot-Hawley Tariff, created difficulties for foreign manufacturers.

So long as they remained committed to the fixed exchange rates of the gold standard, other countries could do little to insulate themselves from the destabilizing impulse emanating from the US. A reduction in the central bank discount rate, open market purchases, or an increase in public spending stimulated net commodity imports, encouraged capital outflows, and caused a loss of international reserves. Unless the expansionary initiative was reversed quickly, a convertibility crisis ensued. Before departing from gold, countries importing the destabilizing impulse from abroad thus had virtually no capacity to offset it.[55]

Britain and Germany are two prominent examples of countries bound by the gold standard in 1931.[56] But even the US and France, the two countries with the largest shares of international reserves, faced essentially the same constraints. The US and France each possessed roughly 30 per cent of the world's monetary gold reserves. If any countries had the capacity to relax global credit conditions by loosening credit at home, it was one of these two. Yet both repeatedly ran up against the external constraint.

Friedman and Schwartz have criticized the Fed for failing to prevent the decline in US money supply following Britain's devaluation in September 1931. It is hard to see what else could have been done, however, by a central bank committed to defending the fixed dollar price of gold. Prior to the passage of the Glass-Steagall Act in 1932, the Fed had to worry about the problem of free gold. Government securities did not qualify as collateral for Federal Reserve notes in circulation; the Fed consequently could engage in expansionary open market operations only to the extent that it possessed free gold. With the reserve losses it experienced following the devaluation

---

[54] Choudri and Kochin, 'The exchange rate', provides evidence on the operation of these linkages for countries that went off the gold standard at different times. The point has been re-emphasized by Eichengreen, *Golden fetters*, and Temin, *Lessons from the Great Depression*.

[55] This is a theme of Eichengreen, 'Relaxing the external constraint'; Temin, *Lessons from the Great Depression*; Bernanke and James, 'The gold standard, deflation and financial crisis'.

[56] Cairncross and Eichengreen, *Sterling in decline*, ch. 3; Borchardt, 'Could and should Germany have followed Great Britain?'

of sterling, the Fed's free gold fell to less than half a billion dollars. Hence the scope for expansionary open market operations was limited.[57]

In 1934-5 it was the turn of France. The Flandin government's policies were less deflationary than previous programmes. Flandin's initiatives, based on government budget deficits financed by the issue of short-term debt, much of which was discounted by the Bank of France, led within months to the loss of 15 per cent of the central bank's international reserves. The government fell, and its successor reverted to a policy of concerted deflation. Once the crisis passed, the new Laval government resumed its predecessor's policy of deficit spending financed by central bank discounts of Treasury bills—though, in contrast to Flandin, Laval denied that his government engaged in the practice. The result, in any case, was renewed reserve losses and another crisis of the franc.[58]

There is little question that countries on the gold standard were unable to insulate themselves from the fall in international prices so long as they remained on gold. Figure 3 illustrates the coherence of price level trends until 1931. More controversial is the mechanism through which falling prices led to a persistent fall in output. The traditional explanation is that money wages failed to keep pace with falling prices. Figure 4 confirms the tendency in several countries for real wages in manufacturing to rise in the early stages of the slump. This rise in real wages increased production costs, depressing output and discouraging employment. In a closed economy the effect of real wages on output is theoretically ambiguous, but the effect is unambiguously negative in an open economy whose export sales depend on relative costs.[59] Evidence for a variety of countries suggests that this negative effect dominated in the early stages of the slump.

It is not easy to understand why nominal wages persistently lagged behind falling prices even while unemployment scaled unprecedented heights. In part, policy was to blame. In the US, President Herbert Hoover pressed employers to forswear wage cuts, hoping that stable labour incomes would sustain demand.[60] But firms responded by laying off costly workers and limiting hours of work.[61] Similarly, the National Industrial Recovery Act is blamed for the anomalous rise in US real wages in 1933-4, when unemployment was still hovering around 20 per cent.[62] In Britain, unemployment benefits were not reduced at the same pace as prices and wages,

---

[57] It might seem perplexing that free gold was so scarce in light of the fact that the US had been importing gold for much of the period. The explanation is that the supply of eligible paper which qualified as backing for as much as 60 per cent of Federal Reserve notes in circulation declined along with business activity in the early stages of the slump. As eligible paper became scarce, the Fed was forced to substitute gold, locking up its reserves. Eichengreen, *Golden fetters*, ch. 10.

[58] Jackson, *The politics of depression*; Eichengreen, *Golden fetters*.

[59] In a closed economy, the real wage-employment relationship is theoretically ambiguous because higher real wages, while increasing production costs, also stimulate demand; Dimsdale, Nickell, and Horsewood, 'Real wages and unemployment'. In an open economy, demand is given by global conditions so only the first effect operates; Eichengreen and Sachs, 'Exchange rates and economic recovery'; Temin, *Lessons from the Great Depression*. Newell and Symons, 'Macroeconomics of the interwar years', uses the closed economy model to analyse the world as a whole, and finds that the negative relationship between real wages and output dominates.

[60] Barber, *New era to New Deal*.

[61] Bernanke, 'Employment, hours and earnings'.

[62] See Weinstein, *Recovery and redistribution*. Additional econometric analysis of the impact on wages of the NIRA codes is provided by Eichengreen, *Golden fetters*, ch. 11.

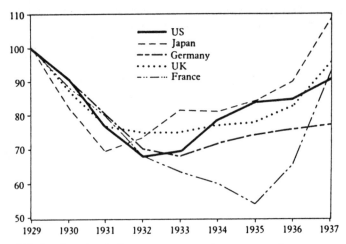

Figure 3. *Wholesale price indices, 1929-1937* (1929 = 100)
Source: League of Nations, *World production and prices*, 1937/8, p. 54.

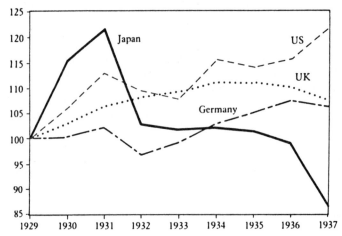

Figure 4. *Product wages (nominal wages/manufacturing prices), 1929-1937* (1929 = 100)
Source: Eichengreen and Hatton, 'Interwar unemployment', p. 15.

allowing the replacement rate to scale new heights. As the demand for labour fell, workers were encouraged to share the available employment, alternating three days of work with three days on the dole, rather than offering to work full time at lower hourly rates.[63] Since pay was negotiated through collective bargaining, union leaders pushed for the highest wages consistent with the employment of their currently active members; they saw little reason to

---

[63] The prevalence of this alternating pattern, known as the OXO system, should not be exaggerated. Thomas, 'Labour market structure', suggests that in 1934 fewer than one in four British workers on short-time participated in formal OXO schemes.

moderate their demands in order to improve the employment prospects of idle workers who had dropped off their membership rolls.[64]

A final factor contributing to the failure of wages to adjust lies in what economists refer to as coordination failure.[65] Employees in both the public and private sectors would have been willing to accept lower wages had they been confident of the readiness of others to do likewise. Workers would have been prepared to accept lower wages had they been confident of the willingness of rentiers to accept lower nominal rents and interest on bonds. Similarly, rentiers would have agreed to accept lower money incomes if they had been convinced that workers would accept lower wages and that the cost of commodities would decline accordingly. Only government intervention could break this log-jam. This is what the Laval government in France attempted in 1935. The resistance of public sector unions to nominal wage cuts doomed its efforts to failure.

Scholars sceptical on *a priori* grounds that nominal inertia in labour markets could have persisted for years have emphasized alternative channels through which deflation depressed output and employment. One of these was disruptions to the operation of the banking system. The fall in prices made it difficult for debtors to repay their loans, weakening bank balance sheets and undermining confidence in national banking systems. Banking crises and financial panics resulted, especially in countries whose universal or mixed banking systems were vulnerable to the decline of industry profits.

Banking panics disrupted the provision of financial services and the financial system's ability to allocate capital efficiently across competing uses. Small firms in need of working capital found themselves unable to obtain it at any price, and were forced to curtail operations. Enterprises with profitable but risky investment opportunities found themselves unable to obtain the external finance required to exploit them. It is not obvious how the operation of market forces could have brought to an end the self-reinforcing spiral of bank failures and declining output. In the absence of intervention by a lender of last resort, declining output which led to bank failures and disintermediation simply reinforced the decline in output, worsening the financial crisis and further depressing economic activity.

The damage caused by financial instability has been most persuasively documented for the US.[66] But bank failures and financial crises were a pervasive feature of the 1930s in other countries as well.[67] Only countries like Britain and Canada, whose banking systems were highly concentrated, widely branched, and less than intimately connected to industry, were immune from banking panics and their effects.[68]

---

[64] See Crafts, 'Long-term unemployment', which draws on the 'insider-outsider' models of unemployment developed by Lindbeck and Snower in *The insider-outsider theory*.

[65] A clear statement of the approach can be found in Cooper and John, 'Coordinating coordination failures'. This is essentially a formalization of Keynes's theory of wage relativities and wage rigidity: Keynes, *General theory*.

[66] Bernanke, 'Nonmonetary effects of the financial crisis'.

[67] Bernanke and James, 'The gold standard', presents evidence of the importance of bank failures for output trends in more than 20 countries.

[68] On Canada see Haubrich, 'Non-monetary effects of financial crises'. The contrast between the performance of the US and Canadian banking systems is also a theme of White, 'Banking crisis of 1930'.

The monetary and non-monetary effects of financial crises were containable only through lender-of-last-resort intervention. Here the gold standard again figured as a constraint. Where gold and foreign exchange reserves had already fallen to the legal minimum, the extension of additional domestic credit violated a basic provision of the gold standard. Countries had the option of suspending or modifying gold cover restrictions, but either action threatened to undermine confidence in convertibility. To defend the gold standard, central banks were forced to restrain the impulse to intervene, sacrificing the stability of the domestic banking system. It is no coincidence, then, that banking panics were most prevalent in countries which held fast to the gold standard.[69]

Indeed, where the gold standard prevailed, lender-of-last-resort intervention could be not only difficult but counterproductive. The provision of additional liquidity when the ratio of gold reserves to monetary liabilities approached its statutory minimum signalled that the authorities attached a higher priority to the condition of the banking system than to the maintenance of gold convertibility. Fears of devaluation induced depositors to withdraw their bank balances and to shift into gold or foreign currency. The faster liquidity was injected into the banking system, the faster it leaked out again. Lender-of-last-resort intervention only encouraged the liquidation of deposits and provoked capital flight. Suspending gold convertibility was therefore a precondition for effective intervention to stabilize the banking system.[70]

Circumventing this dilemma required internationally coordinated lender-of-last-resort intervention. If the free reserves of the entire group of gold standard nations had been made available to the country experiencing the speculative crisis, it no longer followed that the provision of liquidity courted devaluation. Similarly, if reflationary monetary and fiscal initiatives had been coordinated internationally, the pursuit of such policies would no longer have been inhibited by the gold standard constraints. Expansion at home would still have weakened the balance of payments, but expansion abroad would have strengthened it. Had domestic and foreign intervention been coordinated, their impact on the balance of payments could have been eliminated.[71]

Why then was coordinated reflation so difficult to arrange? One problem was that statutory restrictions inspired by the memory of postwar inflation limited central banks' freedom of action. The Bank of France and the German Reichsbank were essentially prohibited from engaging in expansionary open market operations. The Federal Reserve System effectively found itself in the same position before collateral requirements on Federal Reserve notes were modified in 1932.[72] But these restrictions were themselves symptomatic of deeper disagreements among countries over the appropriate response to the depression. In Britain, the slump was attributed to inadequate provision of money and credit under the prevailing depressed business conditions.

---

[69] The linkage between the gold standard and financial panics is emphasized by Eichengreen, 'International monetary instability'; Bernanke and James, 'The gold standard'; Temin, *Lessons from the Great Depression*.
[70] Two examples of the destabilizing effect of lender-of-last-resort intervention under the gold standard were the Austrian and German banking crises in the summer of 1931; Eichengreen, *Golden fetters*, ch. 9.
[71] Eichengreen, 'Central bank cooperation'; Broadberry, 'Monetary interdependence and deflation'.
[72] Eichengreen, 'The Bank of France'; James, *The German slump*.

There existed a well-articulated model of the benefits of monetary reflation, courtesy of Keynes's Macmillan Committee evidence, and a powerful counter-example in the form of the depressing effects of Bank of England policy in the 1920s.[73] In France, by contrast, monetary expansion was regarded as the problem rather than the solution. In light of France's pre-1927 experience with inflation, monetary expansion was associated not with prosperity but with financial and political chaos. The depression itself was viewed as a consequence of excessive credit creation undertaken in the 1920s by central banks that failed to abide by the rules of the gold standard game. Cheap credit had fuelled unhealthy speculation, setting the stage for the crash of 1929. For central banks again to intervene when prices finally had begun to fall to more realistic levels threatened to provoke another round of speculative excesses and, ultimately, an even more catastrophic depression. It would be healthier in the long run, in the prevailing French view, to purge speculative excesses from the system by liquidating enterprises that had over-extended themselves prior to the crash. A similar liquidationist view conditioned US monetary policy until Roosevelt took office in 1933. Given the prevalence of these incompatible conceptual frameworks, it is not hard to see why policymakers in different countries found collaboration so difficult.[74]

IV

The alternative to coordinated reflation was for countries to disengage themselves from the international system in order to reflate unilaterally. Two means of doing so were currency depreciation and trade restrictions, both of which helped to insulate the balance of payments from the effects of expansionary initiatives. Several of the primary producing nations that had been battered first by the collapse of US lending and then by the decline of commodity prices began surreptitiously to abridge gold convertibility as early as 1929. Britain led some two dozen countries, mainly its Scandinavian trading partners and members of its commonwealth and empire, off the gold standard in September 1931. A bloc of countries, led by France and including the US until April 1933, clung to the gold standard but adopted increasingly comprehensive tariffs and quotas to neutralize the effects on the balance of payments of currency depreciation abroad. Germany and much of eastern Europe used tariffs, quotas, and clearing arrangements to the same end.

The older literature on the depression indicts these tariffs and quotas for greatly exacerbating the slump. The Smoot-Hawley tariff imposed by the US in 1930 is blamed for having unleashed a global wave of retaliatory trade restrictions. Simple income-expenditure models have been used to argue that, by obstructing exports, trade warfare destroyed one of the few remaining sources of autonomous demand.[75] Curiously, these analyses essentially ignore the expenditure-switching effects of tariffs. As a tax on imports, a tariff

---

[73] An excellent recent analysis of monetary thought in official circles in the early 1930s is Clarke, *Keynesian revolution*.

[74] On French policy, see Mouré, 'La perception de la crise'. On US policy in the Hoover years, see Barber, *New era to New Deal*.

[75] An example of this modelling approach is Friedman, *Impact of trade destruction*.

switches demand from imports towards domestic goods; taken in isolation, a tariff like Smoot-Hawley is likely to redistribute the depression internationally (moderating it in the country imposing the tariff, whose industries benefit from the tariff-induced shift in expenditure towards it, but intensifying it in other countries, whose industries experience a decline in demand), without significantly altering the severity of the depression worldwide.[76]

Retaliation changes the story. Insofar as foreign tariffs neutralized the expenditure switching effects of Smoot-Hawley, leaving the international allocation of spending roughly unchanged, the *macroeconomic* effects would have been minimal. Insofar as import tariffs placed modest upward pressure on prices, they tended to moderate the impact of debt deflation on national financial systems. But insofar as the monetary authorities failed to respond, upward pressure on prices exacerbated the scarcity of real money balances, tending to raise interest rates at the worst possible time. Since the two effects worked in opposite directions, on balance the aggregate effects of trade restrictions in the 1930s were probably small.[77]

This is not to deny that tariffs and quotas had implications for the composition of spending within countries. They aggravated the difficulties of some industries and moderated those of others.[78] The point is not that tariffs should be ignored by scholars conducting studies of industry in the 1930s; rather, it is that those concerned to understand the sources of the *macroeconomic* crisis have probably paid undue attention to protectionism. Only to the extent that tariffs switched demand towards sectors exhibiting increasingly returns to scale were they likely to have had a significant effect on aggregate levels of output and productivity.[79]

Perhaps the most important effect of trade warfare in the 1930s was in aggravating the balance of payments problems of debtor nations. The US was the single largest importer of primary commodities; the Smoot-Hawley tariff surely increased the difficulties faced by commodity exporters seeking to service their debts. The first wave of Latin American defaults came less than a year after the imposition of Smoot-Hawley. Default in Latin America and eastern Europe intensified the balance of payments pressure on the creditors. Interest and dividends earned abroad were the component of the British balance of payments that deteriorated most markedly in the year leading up to the 1931 sterling crisis.[80] Protectionism can therefore be allotted some responsibility for the collapse of the gold standard system.

The more important means of loosening the link to the international system was currency depreciation. By suspending gold convertibility and

---

[76] This still-controversial conclusion was emphasized by Kindleberger, *World in depression*, and Fearon, *Origins and nature*. It is also the conclusion of Eichengreen, 'Political economy of Smoot-Hawley', and Temin, *Lessons from the Great Depression*, among others. My own estimates suggest that, in the absence of retaliation, Smoot-Hawley would have raised US output by perhaps 5 per cent.

[77] Estimates in Eichengreen, 'Political economy of Smoot-Hawley', suggest that the favourable price-level effect probably dominated the damaging interest-rate effect in the 1930s.

[78] Capie, *Depression and protectionism*, calculated effective rates of protection for Britain as a way of estimating the sectoral impact of the 1932 General Tariff.

[79] Kitson and Solomou, *Protectionism and revival*, provides some evidence for Britain that the 1932 General Tariff shifted activity in this direction.

[80] Moggridge, 'The 1931 financial crisis'.

allowing the currency to depreciate, countries could enhance the competitiveness of their exports. The exports of countries that abandoned the gold standard recovered more quickly than those of countries that clung to it.[81] As with tariffs, however, this effect only redistributed the impact of the depression internationally and could be neutralized by competitive depreciation abroad. More significant was that currency depreciation provided additional scope for the unilateral pursuit of expansionary policies. Countries that allowed their currencies to depreciate could expand their money supplies without having to worry about the consequences for the balance of payments. Depreciation removed the pressure to cut government expenditure and raise taxes in order to defend the exchange rate. The adoption of more expansionary policies enabled countries with depreciated currencies to edge their way towards recovery. Moreover, countries continued to benefit from the more expansionary policies facilitated by currency depreciation even if other countries depreciated their currencies as well.

The timing and extent of depreciation can explain much of the variation in the timing and extent of economic recovery.[82] Britain's early devaluation, for example, helps to explain the early date of its recovery so evident in figure 5. Japan's early and extensive depreciation helps to account for its unusually rapid growth in the 1930s. US recovery coincided with the dollar's devaluation.[83] France's delayed recovery was clearly associated with its unwillingness to devalue until 1936. Table 2, which expands the sample of countries to all those for which comparable data on industrial production are available for the 1930s, confirms the generality of the point. There is a strong contrast between relatively rapid recovery in countries which abandoned the gold standard and the persistence of the slump in countries which maintained it.

Countries that devalued did not all pursue reflationary initiatives to the same extent. In a few cases, policymakers expanded domestic credit aggressively following the abandonment of gold. Prices and domestic demand rose in its wake. Interest-sensitive sectors like construction were special beneficiaries of cheap money (figure 6). Since the expansion of domestic credit stimulated domestic demand and placed upward pressure on prices, there was little growth of exports. Instead, recovery was led by the home market. More commonly, policymakers hesitated to capitalize upon their new found freedom. The association of currency depreciation with inflation, inherited from the 1920s, remained strong. Policymakers waited for evidence that depreciation did not automatically auger inflation before turning to reflationary policies. Limited expansion of domestic credit meant limited stimulus to domestic demand and little upward pressure on prices (figure 3). Exports were not crowded out. The improvement in the trade balance, along with the reflux of financial capital, strengthened the balance of payments. Eventually capital inflows helped to relax domestic credit conditions and put upward pressure on money supplies (figures 7 and 8).

---

[81] Eichengreen and Sachs, 'Exchange rates and economic recovery'.
[82] Ibid.; Campa, 'An extension to Latin America'; Temin, *Lessons from the Great Depression*.
[83] This point is emphasized by Temin and Wigmore, 'The end of one big deflation'.

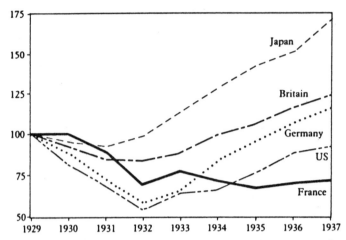

Figure 5. *Indices of industrial production, 1929-1937* (1929 = 100)
Source: League of Nations, *World production and prices, 1937/8*, p. 44.

Table 2. *Percentage growth of industrial production, 1929-1936*

	1929-1932	1929-1933	1929-1934	1929-1935	1929-1936
Gold bloc countries	−28.17	−22.60	−21.84	−20.60	−13.94
Exchange control countries	−35.70	−31.70	−21.24	−10.28	−2.30
Sterling area countries	−8.75	−2.53	8.88	18.05	27.77
Other countries with depreciated currencies	−17.48	−1.63	3.26	14.13	27.06

Note: figures are calculated as unweighted averages of data for constituent countries.
Gold bloc: Belgium, France, Netherlands, Poland, and Switzerland
Exchange control: Austria, Czechoslovakia, Germany, Hungary, and Italy
Sterling area: Denmark, Finland, New Zealand, Norway, Sweden, and the UK
Other depreciators: Brazil, Colombia, Chile, Mexico, Costa Rica, Guatemala, Nicaragua, El Salvador, and the US
Source: Eichengreen, *Golden fetters*, p. 351.

One reason why complete recovery was so long in coming, however, was that central bank and treasury officials, curiously fearful of inflation when deflation was the real and present danger, remained hesitant to act. In only a few countries was expansionary monetary policy used systematically.

Because monetary expansion remained tentative, currency depreciation in the 1930s was beggar thy neighbour. Countries depreciating their currencies and shifting demand towards the products of domestic industry satisfied their growing demands for money and credit by importing gold and capital from abroad. Their reserve gains were reserve losses for countries still on gold. The central banks of countries still on the gold standard were forced to retrench. Precisely when exporting to countries with newly depreciated currencies became more difficult, domestic demand was compressed. But the real problem in the 1930s was not that competitive depreciation took

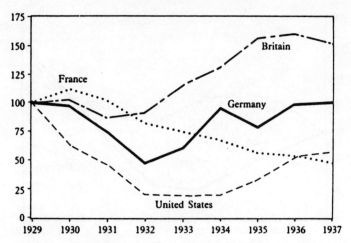

Figure 6. *Indices of building activity, 1929-1937* (1929 = 100)
Source: League of Nations, *World production and prices, 1937/8*, p. 27.

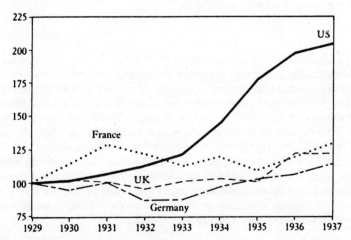

Figure 7. *Monetary base (notes, coins, and central bank sight liabilities), 1929-1937* (1929 = 100)
Source: League of Nations, *Monetary review, 1937/8*, tab. 3.

place; on the contrary, it was that depreciation was not more widespread and that it did not occasion more expansionary domestic policies.

Thus, the recent literature, by emphasizing the contribution of domestic and international monetary initiatives to economic recovery in the 1930s, has inverted the previous tendency to dismiss monetary policy as ineffectual and to regard fiscal policy as the critical policy variable. Upon reflection, this is not surprising. In the US, the most important fiscal change of the period, in 1932, was a tax increase, not a reduction. Observed budget deficits were small. Cyclically

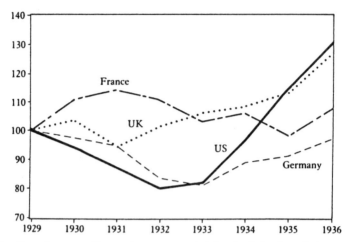

Figure 8. *Broad money (base plus commercial bank sight deposits), 1929-1936* (1929 = 100)
Source: League of Nations, *Monetary review, 1937/8*, tab. 3.

corrected budget deficits were smaller still.[84] Even in the presence of large fiscal multipliers, the increment to aggregate demand attributable to fiscal policy remained modest until rearmament spending got under way in the second half of the 1930s.[85] In contrast, in countries like the US (and to a lesser extent the UK), the expansion of currency and bank deposits was enormous. The one significant interruption to monetary expansion in the US, in 1937, revealingly coincided with the one significant interruption to economic recovery.[86] Nor is there evidence for Britain of a liquidity trap that would have rendered monetary policy ineffectual.[87] Even in Sweden, renowned for having developed Keynesian fiscal policy before Keynes, monetary policy did most of the work.[88] Clearly, the tendency to dismiss monetary policy in the 1930s on the grounds that one 'cannot push on a string' has been pushed too far.

[84] This is the conclusion of Brown, 'Fiscal policy in the thirties', for the US; Middleton, *Towards the managed economy*, for Britain; and Jonung, 'The depression in Sweden', for Sweden.
[85] The only case for which the effects of rearmament on recovery have been systematically assessed is Britain; Thomas, 'Rearmament and economic recovery'.
[86] This episode is analysed by Romer, 'The great expansion', who arrives at essentially the same conclusions.
[87] Mills and Wood, 'Money substitutes'. Other analyses of British experience consistent with this view are Worswick, 'The sources of recovery'; Wright, 'Britain's inter-war experience'; Cairncross and Eichengreen, *Sterling in decline*. The only recent study to attempt directly to estimate the impact of monetary policy on a component of aggregate demand is Broadberry, 'Cheap money', whose conclusion is that monetary policy was responsible for part but not all of the housing boom of the 1930s.
[88] Jonung, 'The depression in Sweden'.

V

From the most recent generation of studies, a coherent picture of the Great Depression has emerged. It links the slump of the 1930s to changes in economic structure that took place during World War I and in the 1920s: to the expanding production of consumer durables and the declining flexibility of labour markets in the US, to the growing fragility of the international monetary system, and to the dependence of the pattern of international settlements on US lending. Each of these changes served to magnify the impact of the principal shift in economic conditions at the end of the 1920s: increasingly restrictive US monetary policy and the reinforcing policy shift it elicited from foreign countries.

With the disintegration of the financial system, the economy's self-correcting mechanisms were rendered weak and ineffectual. Policy initiatives were required to lay the foundations of recovery. Abandoning the gold standard was a necessary precondition for their adoption. By stabilizing money supplies and banking systems, governments succeeded in bringing the downward spiral to a halt. As they abandoned the gold standard and allowed domestic credit conditions to relax, economic recovery gradually got under way. In most cases, the expansion of domestic credit remained tentative, however, and domestic financial stringency was eliminated mainly through capital inflows. Capital inflows for countries with depreciated currencies meant capital outflows for countries still on gold. Hence currency depreciation had beggar-thy-neighbour effects. But more widespread depreciation still would have been helpful for recovery, especially insofar as it occasioned more rapid expansion of domestic credit.

The traditional distinction between two views of the depression of the 1930s, which attribute it to structural instabilities in the world economy and to misguided policies, loses much of its force in the light of recent scholarship. Policy may have provided the initial destabilizing impulse, but changes in economic structure strengthened the propagation mechanism. A better understanding both of the policy choices and of the structures shaping their effects is the obvious agenda for research.

University of California at Berkeley

Footnote references

Official publications
League of Nations, *World production and prices, 1937/38* (Geneva, 1938).
League of Nations, *Monetary review, 1937-8* (Geneva, 1938).

Secondary sources
Akerlof, G., 'The market for lemons: quality uncertainty and the market mechanism', *Qu. J. Econ.*, LXXIV (1970), pp. 488-500.
Alston, L. J., 'Farm foreclosures in the United States during the interwar period', *J. Econ. Hist.*, XLIII (1983), pp. 885-903.
Azariadis, C., 'Implicit contracts and underemployment equilibria', *J. Pol. Econ.*, 83 (1975), pp. 1183-1202.
Balderston, T., 'The beginning of the depression in Germany, 1927-30: investment and the capital market', *Econ. Hist. Rev.*, 2nd ser., XXXV (1983), pp. 395-415.
Barber, W. J., *From new era to New Deal* (Cambridge, 1985).

Benjamin, D. and Kochin, L., 'Searching for an explanation for unemployment in interwar Britain', *J. Pol. Econ.*, 87 (1979), pp. 441-78.
Bernanke, B., 'Nonmonetary effects of the financial crisis in the propagation of the Great Depression', *Amer. Econ. Rev.*, 73 (1983), pp. 257-76.
Bernanke, B., 'Employment, hours and earnings in the depression', *Amer. Econ. Rev.*, 76 (1986), pp. 82-111.
Bernanke, B. and James, H., 'The gold standard, deflation and financial crisis in the Great Depression: an international comparison', in R. Glenn Hubbard, ed., *Financial markets and financial crises* (Chicago, 1991), pp. 33-68.
Bernstein, M., *The Great Depression: delayed recovery and economic change in America, 1929-1939* (New York, 1987).
Borchardt, K., 'Could and should Germany have followed Great Britain in leaving the gold standard?', *J. Eur. Econ. Hist.*, 13 (1984), pp. 471-98.
Borchardt, K., *Perspectives on modern German economic history and policy* (Cambridge, 1991).
Bowden, S. M., 'The consumer durables revolution in England, 1932-1938: a regional analysis', *Exp. Econ. Hist.*, 25 (1988), pp. 42-59.
Broadberry, S. N., *The British economy between the wars: a macroeconomic survey* (Oxford, 1986).
Broadberry, S. N., 'Cheap money and the housing boom in interwar Britain: an econometric appraisal', *Man. School*, 55 (1987), pp. 378-91.
Broadberry, S. N., 'Monetary interdependence and deflation in Britain and the United States between the wars', in M. Miller, B. Eichengreen, and R. Portes, eds., *Blueprints for exchange rate management* (New York, 1989), pp. 47-69.
Brown, E. C., 'Fiscal policies in the 1930s: a reappraisal', *Amer. Econ. Rev.*, 46 (1956), pp. 857-79.
Cagan, P., 'Changes in the recession behavior of wholesale prices in the 1920s and post-World War II', *Exp. Econ. Res.*, 2 (1975), pp. 54-104.
Cairncross, A. and Eichengreen, B., *Sterling in decline* (Oxford, 1983).
Campa, J. M., 'Exchange rates and economic recovery in the 1930s: an extension to Latin America', *J. Econ. Hist.*, L (1990), pp. 677-82.
Capie, F., *Depression and protectionism* (1983).
Carter, S. and Sutch, R., 'The labor market in the 1890s: evidence from Connecticut manufacturing', in E. Aerts and B. Eichengreen, eds., *Unemployment and underemployment in historical perspective* (Leuven, 1990), pp. 15-24.
Cecchetti, S. G., 'Prices during the Great Depression: was the deflation of 1930-32 really unanticipated?', *Amer. Econ. Rev.* (forthcoming, 1992).
Choudri, E. and Kochin, L., 'The exchange rate and the international transmission of business cycle disturbances', *J. Money, Credit & Banking*, 12 (1981), pp. 565-74.
Clarke, P., *The Keynesian revolution in the making* (Oxford, 1988).
Cohen, D., 'How to evaluate the solvency of an indebted nation', *Econ. Policy*, 1 (1985), pp. 139-57.
Cooper, R. and John, A., 'Coordinating coordination failures in Keynesian models', *Qu. J. Econ.*, CIII (1988), pp. 441-60.
Corbett, D., 'Unemployment insurance and induced search in interwar Germany', in E. Aerts and B. Eichengreen, eds., *Unemployment and underemployment in historical perspective* (Leuven, 1990), pp. 76-87.
Crafts, N. F. R., 'Long-term unemployment and the wage equation in Britain, 1925-39', *Economica*, 56 (1989), pp. 247-54.
Dimsdale, N. H., Nickell, S. J., and Horsewood, N., 'Real wages and unemployment in Britain during the 1930s', *Econ. J.*, 99 (1989), pp. 271-92.
Dixit, A., 'Hysteresis, import penetration and exchange rate passthrough', *Qu. J. Econ.*, CIV (1989), pp. 205-28.
Dornbusch, R., Sturzenegger, F., and Wolf, H., 'Extreme inflation: dynamics and stabilization', mimeo, Massachusetts Institute of Technology, 1990.
Eichengreen, B., 'Central bank cooperation under the interwar gold standard', *Exp. Econ. Hist.*, 21 (1984), pp. 64-87.
Eichengreen, B., 'The Bank of France and the sterilization of gold, 1926-32', *Exp. Econ. Hist.*, 23 (1986), pp. 53-84.
Eichengreen, B., 'Unemployment in interwar Britain: dole or doldrums?', *Oxf. Econ. Pap.*, 39 (1987), pp. 597-623.
Eichengreen, B., 'The political economy of the Smoot-Hawley tariff', *Res. Econ. Hist.*, 12 (1989), pp. 1-44.
Eichengreen, B., 'International monetary instability between the wars: structural flaws or misguided policies?', in Y. Suzuki, J. Miyake, and M. Okabe, eds., *The evolution of the international monetary system* (Tokyo, 1990), pp. 71-116.
Eichengreen, B., 'Credibility and cooperation under the gold standard', *Kinyu J.*, 3 (1990), pp. 40-6.
Eichengreen, B., 'Relaxing the external constraint: Europe in the 1930s', in G. Alogoskofis, L. Papademos,

and R. Portes, eds., *External constraints on macroeconomic policy: the European experience* (Cambridge, 1991), pp. 75-117.
Eichengreen, B., *Golden fetters: the gold standard and the Great Depression, 1919-1939* (New York, 1992).
Eichengreen, B., 'Trends and cycles in foreign lending', in H. Seibert, ed., *Capital flows in the world economy* (Kiel, 1992), pp. 3-28.
Eichengreen, B. and Hatton, T. J., 'Interwar unemployment in international perspective: an overview', in B. Eichengreen and T. J. Hatton, eds., *Interwar unemployment in international perspective* (Dordrecht, 1988), pp. 1-50.
Eichengreen, B. and Sachs, J., 'Exchange rates and economic recovery in the 1930s', *J. Econ. Hist.*, XLV (1985), pp. 925-46.
Eichengreen, B. and Uzan, M., 'The 1933 World Economic Conference as an instance of failed international cooperation', in R. Putnam *et al.*, *Diplomacy and domestic politics* (forthcoming).
Eichengreen, B., Watson, M., and Grossman, R., 'Bank rate policy under the interwar gold standard: a dynamic probit model', *Econ. J.*, 95 (1985), pp. 725-45.
Fearon, P., *The origins and nature of the Great Slump, 1929-1932* (1979).
Fearon, P., *War, prosperity and depression: the U.S. economy, 1917-45* (1987).
Field, A., 'Asset exchanges and the transactions demand for money, 1919-29', *Amer. Econ. Rev.*, 74 (1984), pp. 43-59.
Field, A., 'A new interpretation of the onset of the Great Depression', *J. Econ. Hist.*, 44 (1984), pp. 489-98.
Fleisig, H., *Long-term capital flows and the Great Depression* (New York, 1975).
Friedman, M. and Schwartz, A. J., *A monetary history of the United States, 1867-1960* (Princeton, 1963).
Friedman, P., *The impact of trade destruction on national incomes: a study of Europe, 1924-1938* (Gainesville, Fla., 1974).
Gordon, R. J., 'Why U.S. wage and employment behaviour differs from that in Britain and Japan', *Econ. J.*, 92 (1982), pp. 13-44.
Hamilton, J., 'Monetary factors in the Great Depression', *J. Monetary Econ.*, 13 (1987), pp. 1-25.
Hamilton, J., 'Role of the international gold standard in propagating the Great Depression', *Contemp. Policy Issues*, 6 (1988), pp. 67-87.
Hamilton, J., 'Was the deflation during the Great Depression anticipated? Evidence from the commodity futures market', *Amer. Econ. Rev.* (forthcoming, 1992).
Hatton, T. J., 'The British labor market in the 1920s: a test of the search-turnover approach', *Exp. Econ. Hist.*, 22 (1985), pp. 257-70.
Hatton, T. J., 'Institutional change and wage rigidity in the U.K., 1880-1985', *Oxf. Rev. Econ. Policy*, 4 (1988), pp. 74-86.
Haubrich, J. G., 'Nonmonetary effects of financial crises: lessons from the Great Depression in Canada', *J. Monetary Econ.*, 25 (1990), pp. 223-52.
Jackson, J., *The politics of depression in France, 1932-1936* (Cambridge, 1985).
Jacoby, S., *Employing bureaucracy* (New York, 1985).
James, H., *The German Slump* (Oxford, 1986).
Jonung, L., 'The Depression in Sweden and the United States: a comparison', in K. Brunner, ed., *The Great Depression revisited* (Boston, 1981), pp. 286-315.
Keynes, J. M., *The general theory of employment, interest and money* (1936).
Kindleberger, C. P., *The world in depression, 1929-1939* (Berkeley, 1973).
Kitson, M. and Solomou, S., *Protectionism and revival: the British inter-war economy* (Cambridge, 1990).
Klug, A., 'The theory and practice of reparations and American loans to Germany, 1925-29', Working Paper in International Economics no. G-90-03, International Finance Section, Department of Economics, Princeton University, 1990.
Lebergott, S., *Manpower in economic growth* (New York, 1964).
Lindbeck, A. and Snower, D., *The insider-outsider theory of employment and unemployment* (Cambridge, Mass., 1988).
Lindert, P., *Key currencies and gold, 1900-1913* (Princeton Studies in International Finance no. 24, 1969).
Marseille, J., 'Les origines "inopportunes" de la crise de 1929 en France', *Revue Économique*, 31 (1980), pp. 648-84.
Matthews, R. C. O., Feinstein, C., and Odling-Smee, J., *British economic growth, 1865-1973* (Stanford, 1982).
Middleton, R., *Towards the managed economy* (1985).
Mills, T. C. and Wood, G. E., 'Money substitutes and monetary policy in the U.K., 1922-1974', *Eur. Econ. Rev.*, 10 (1977), pp. 19-36.
Mishkin, F. S., 'The household balance sheet and the Great Depression', *J. Econ. Hist.*, 38 (1978), pp. 918-37.
Moggridge, D., 'The 1931 financial crisis—a new view', *The Banker* (1971), pp. 832-9.
Mouré, K., 'The Bank of France and the gold standard, 1928-1936', *Proc. Annual Meeting Western Soc. for French Hist.*, 17 (1990), pp. 459-68.

Mouré, K., 'La perception de la crise par les pouvoirs politiques', *Le Mouvement Social*, 154 (1991), pp. 131-56.
Nelson, D. B., 'Was the deflation of 1929-30 anticipated? The monetary regime as viewed by the business press', unpublished manuscript, University of Chicago (1990).
Newell, A. and Symons, J., 'The macroeconomics of the interwar years: international comparisons', in B. Eichengreen and T. J. Hatton, eds., *Interwar unemployment in international perspective* (Dordrecht, 1988), pp. 61-96.
Olney, M., 'Credit as a production-smoothing device: the case of automobiles, 1913-1938', *J. Econ. Hist.*, XLIX (1989), pp. 377-92.
Olney, M., 'Consumer durables in the interwar years: new estimates, new patterns', *Res. Econ. Hist.*, 12 (1989), pp. 119-50.
Olney, M., 'Demand for consumer durable goods in 20th century America', *Exp. Econ. Hist.*, 27 (1990), pp. 322-49.
Olney, M., *Buy now, pay later: advertising, credit and consumer durables in the 1920s* (Chapel Hill, N.C., 1991).
Raff, D., 'Wage determination theory and the five dollar day at Ford', *J. Econ. Hist.*, XLVIII (1988), pp. 387-400.
Rappoport, P. and White, E., 'Was there a bubble in the 1929 stock market?' unpublished manuscript, Rutgers University (1991).
Redmond, J., 'The Sterling overvaluation in 1925: a multilateral approach', *Econ. Hist. Rev.*, 2nd ser., XXXVII (1984), pp. 520-32.
Romer, C., 'The Great Crash and the onset of the Great Depression', *Qu. J. Econ.*, CV (1990), pp. 597-624.
Romer, C., 'The great expansion', unpublished manuscript, University of California at Berkeley.
Sachs, J., 'The changing cyclical behavior of wages and prices, 1890-1976', *Amer. Econ. Rev.*, 70 (1980), pp. 78-90.
Sachs, J., 'The current account and macroeconomic adjustment in the 1970s', *Brookings Papers on Econ. Activity*, 1 (1981), pp. 201-68.
Santoni, G. J. and Dwyer, G. P., 'Bubbles or fundamentals: new evidence from the great bull markets', in E. White, ed., *Panics and crashes: the lessons from history* (New York, 1990), pp. 188-210.
Schuker, S. A., 'American "reparations" to Germany, 1919-33: implications for the Third World debt crisis' (Princeton Studies in International Finance no. 61, 1988).
Schwartz, A. J., 'Understanding 1929-1931', in K. Brunner, ed., *The Great Depression revisited* (Boston, 1981), pp. 5-48.
Sirkin, G., 'The stock market of 1929 revisited: a note', *Bus. Hist. Rev.*, LXIX (1975), pp. 223-31.
Steindl, J., *Maturity and stagnation in American capitalism* (New York, 1979).
Svennilson, I., *Growth and stagnation in the European economy* (Geneva, 1954).
Temin, P., 'The beginning of the Great Depression in Germany', *Econ. Hist. Rev.*, 2nd ser., XXIV (1971), pp. 240-8.
Temin, P., *Did monetary forces cause the Great Depression?* (New York, 1976).
Temin, P., *Lessons from the Great Depression* (Cambridge, Mass., 1989).
Temin, P. and Wigmore, B., 'The end of one big deflation', *Exp. Econ. Hist.*, 27 (1990), pp. 483-502.
Thomas, M., 'Rearmament and economic recovery in the late 1930s', *Econ. Hist. Rev.*, 2nd ser., XXXVI (1983), pp. 552-79.
Thomas, M., 'Labour market structure and the nature of unemployment in inter-war Britain', in B. Eichengreen and T. J. Hatton, eds., *Interwar unemployment in international perspective* (Dordrecht, 1988), pp. 97-148.
Thomas, M., 'How flexible were wages in interwar Britain?', in G. Grantham and M. MacKinnon, eds., *The evolution of labor markets* (Montreal, forthcoming 1992).
Thomas, M., 'Institutional rigidity in the British labour market, 1870-1939: a comparative perspective', in S. N. Broadberry and N. F. R. Crafts, eds., *Britain in the world economy, 1870-1939: essays in honour of Alec Ford* (Cambridge, forthcoming 1992).
Von Tunzelmann, G. N., 'Structural change and leading sectors in British manufacturing, 1907-68', in C. Kindleberger and G. De Tella, eds., *Economics in the long view*, III (1982), pp. 1-49.
Weinstein, M., *Recovery and redistribution under the NIRA* (Amsterdam, 1980).
White, E. N., 'A reinterpretation of the banking crisis of 1930', *J. Econ. Hist.*, XLIV (1984), pp. 119-38.
White, E. N., 'When the ticker ran late: the stock market boom and crash of 1929', in idem, ed., *Crashes and panics: the lessons from history* (New York, 1990), pp. 143-87.
Worswick, G. D. N., 'The sources of recovery in the UK in the 1930s', *Nat. Inst. Econ. Rev.*, 110 (1984), pp. 85-93.
Wright, J. F., 'Britain's interwar experience', in W. A. Eltis and P. J. N. Sinclair, eds., *The money supply and the exchange rate* (Oxford, 1981), pp. 282-305.

[3]

The Macroeconomics of the Interwar Years: International Comparisons

Andrew Newell and J S V Symons

1 Introduction

This paper is a study of the interwar years for fourteen countries, which we shall collectively describe as the world. Our major aim is to give an account of the Great Depression. Neither of us is an economic historian, as may become apparent, and our primary motivation in undertaking this work is to see if models we have developed to explain the last thirty years or so can explain the interwar years.

Many of the historical accounts of the Great Depression locate its epicentre in economic events in the United States. Close to sixty years on it is still difficult to draw out the critical events from such a history (see, *inter alia,* Kindleberger, 1973). Capital flights, stock market crashes, waves of protectionism, banking collapses and devaluations followed one another in a bewildering succession. The time-series evidence does allow some stylised facts to be established. Business activity peaked in the United States in early 1929, and the beginnings of a recession were perceptible from, say, the middle of that year. The New York stock market crash in October sent share prices falling worldwide and seemed to impart a further downward step in US industrial activity. Most historians note a period of brief respite in the early months of 1930, after which the "slide into the abyss" (Kindleberger, 1973, p.128) set in.

The story is different in other countries. Germany and Australia, for instance, were experiencing a steadily deepening depression from at least 1929 onwards, whereas in France the decline in activity started almost a year later.

That period of respite in the US has led some authors (notably Hicks, 1974, p.210) to characterise the US experience as a "double dip" - a severe depression superimposed on an already extant normal downturn. If that was the case the natural focus of attention would be the causes of the depression in the United States from mid-1930 onwards. The emphasis to date has largely been on the forces which caused that downturn in aggregate demand. The debate over this is perhaps familiar territory (the conference volume edited by Brunner (1981) provides an excellent introduction). We should state at the outset that we do not doubt that such a fall in aggregate demand happened, or that it was the major cause of the Depression, not only in the US, but worldwide - indeed the latter part of this paper discusses its origins.

Our aim here is to present a coherent supply-side story which we believe to be an essential supplement to the fall in aggregate demand in explaining the path of unemployment over the period. We have surely learned over the last twenty years that we ignore the supply side at our peril.

To focus our argument, consider Table 2.1. This traces the movement of wholesale prices for several countries from mid-1929 to October 1930. Note that from October 1929 onwards all the indices show an abrupt downwards change in trend. From October 1929 to June 1930 all the indices fell around 10 per cent. Generally, prices continued to fall until around 1933. Our major contention is that these price falls, in conjunction with the lack of a similar movement in wages, put a massive squeeze on profitability, in particular the profitability of employing labour.

Output is both demanded and supplied, and if the Great Depression was a fall in demand, it must equally have been a fall in supply. If the labour market clears, so that, in price-output space, the aggregate supply curve is vertical, then any leftwards shift of the aggregate demand curve will produce a fall in prices, but no fall in output or employment: the Great Depression could not have happened without an upwards-sloping supply curve. The primary task of this chapter is to document this supply curve, though we will say something about demand as well.

The model we shall use is more or less that of Newell and Symons (1985). Here labour demand depends on the real wage and the real interest rate. The real wage depends on the unemployment rate and the tax and import wedge. Our analysis is conditioned on the path of the labour force, and hence on the participation decision of individual workers. If some significant part of unemployment in the 1930s was due to increased participation then our analysis will not explain this. For our sample of countries we shall see that the labour demand equation works very well indeed, giving a pleasing consistency between interwar and postwar results, and, indeed, between these results and British and US data prior to the First

Table 2.1 Wholesale Price Indices, June 1929 - October 1930
(October 1929 = 100)

	US	UK	France	Germany
June 1929	97.7	99.6	103.6	98.5
August 1929	101.5	99.8	101.2	100.7
October 1929	100.0	100.0	100.0	100.0
December 1929	97.8	97.4	97.7	97.9
February 1930	95.6	93.9	95.7	94.2
April 1930	94.2	90.9	93.0	92.3
June 1930	90.1	88.7	90.3	90.7
August 1930	87.2	86.6	90.2	90.9
October 1930	85.8	83.0	86.2	87.6

Source: League of Nations *Monthly Bulletin of Statistics.*

World War. The wage equations, however, show an intriguing difference. We find nominal rigidity for the interwar years, i.e. an increase in inflation reduces (would have reduced) the real wage: thus we have our upwards-sloping supply curve. This contrasts with post-Hitler's war wage equations (Newell and Symons, 1986a) which show little or no nominal wage rigidity. In our analysis "nominal wage rigidity" means just that the inflation rate enters the real-wage equation with a negative sign. What is the economic behaviour corresponding to this? It might be that inflation proxies expectational errors; but the different results for pre- and post-Hitler's war then present a problem. Our feeling is that Occam's razor supports Keynes and suggests the explanation that workers will resist, by and large, a fall in the nominal wage. Prewar the price level was falling and equilibrium required wage cuts; postwar the price level was rising and such wage cuts were seldom required.

We do not find nominal rigidity for the US. The transmission mechanism from deflation to the real economy in the US was not the real wage. We find that monetary and demand conditions acted directly on employment in the United States via, effectively, a Lucas supply curve. But in most other countries nominal wage rigidity was crucial.

Since we have inflation in the wage equation, we need to explain the price level, i.e. we need a demand side. This contrasts with the postwar years where we find no nominal rigidity and the only role for demand-side variables is through transient shocks. Our demand-side models are the usual IS-LM-BP apparatus. These enable us to trace the impact of world prices and world trade on open economies, and we find very powerful linkages from them to domestic prices.

Thus it is possible to give an account of the Great Depression in individual open economies if one can explain the behaviour of world prices and world output. To explain these in turn we thus require a world model. The world is an appealing object of study as it is a closed economy. We develop a world IS curve, a world LM curve, and a rudimentary world aggregate supply schedule. The IS curve gives output as a function of world wealth - a weighted sum of labour income, equity prices, and money balances. It is via wealth that the stock market crash of 1929 and the subsequent decline in profitability enter our model. The LM curve is conventional. We find however a large leftwards shift over the 1930s corresponding to a huge increase in liquidity preference. This increase is most naturally associated with the continuing poor performance of equities over this period.

What of the Great Depression? Figure 2.1 plots the world average of the important time series. As we see it, what seems to have happened is this. For open economies, the price and volume of traded goods fell around 1930. This, and diminished wealth due to falling equity prices, led to a fall in domestic prices. In consequence the real interest rate and real wage rose, the latter due to nominal wage rigidity. Thus employment fell through adverse shifts in factor prices as these economies moved down their supply curves.

Why did world prices and world trade fall? For similar reasons. The fall in world stock prices led to a fall in world wealth and to an increase in liquidity preference: both the world IS and the world LM curves shifted left, the latter exacerbated in a minor way by monetary contraction. It seems likely, as Kindleberger (1973, p.125) emphasises, that the first wave of price deflation to hit the world economy was directly attributable to liquidation of stocks of commodities following the crash. With an upwards-sloping world supply curve (nominal rigidity again), world prices and world demand fell in consequence.

This chapter is organised as follows. Section 2 compares unemployment performance in the Depression across countries. We show that the extent of the fall in prices in each country is a good explanation of inter-country differences; that it Granger caused unemployment; and that the inflationary consequence of abandoning fixed exchange rates led to recovery. We argue that the fall in prices flowed through to the real economy by causing changes in relative prices. Section 3 describes our model in detail and uses some comparative statics to elucidate its workings. In Section 4 we give estimation results. We find nominal rigidity in the wage equation, and strong real wage and real interest rate effects in the employment equation. (For previous work on real wage effects on employment between the wars, see the survey by Hatton (1986) for Britain, and Bernanke (1985) for the United States.) We find swift and powerful effects of world

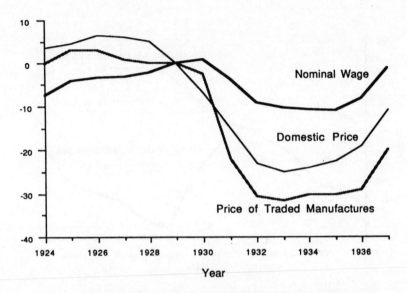

Figure 2.1a Nominal Wages, Domestic Prices and Price of Traded Manufactures (unweighted averages of fourteen countries)

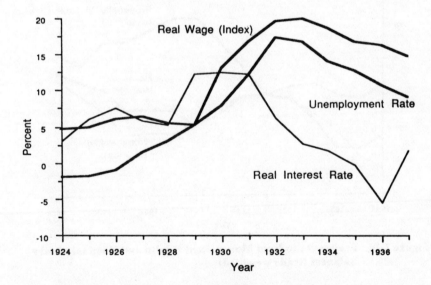

Figure 2.1b Real Wages, Real Interest Rate and Unemployment (unweighted averages of fourteen countries)

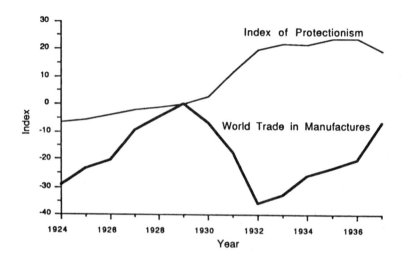

Figure 2.1c World Trade in Manufactures and Index of Protection (log scale, 1929=0)

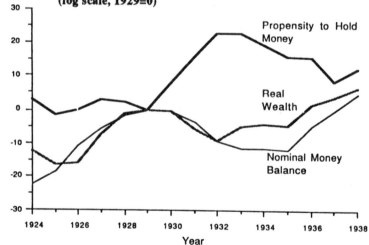

Figure 2.1d Propensity to Hold Money, Real Wealth and Nominal Money Balances (trade weighted)

Note: The propensity to hold money is the inverse of velocity. Real wealth is a weighted sum of labour income, equity prices (as a proxy for the valuation of the capital stock), and money balances. See Appendix 2.1 for details.

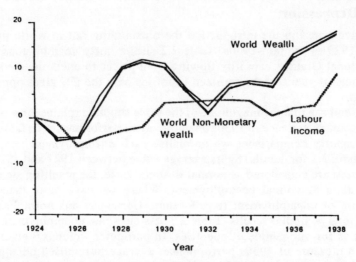

Figure 2.1e The Components of World Wealth (log scale, 1924=0)

Note: The components of wealth may be recovered from this diagram: labour income plus equity prices equals non-monetary wealth; and non-monetary wealth plus real money balances equals wealth.

prices on domestic prices. Section 5 develops and estimates a world model. Our intention here is to endogenise world prices and output. Section 6 gives a brief concluding discussion.

It seems to us that the proximate cause of the Great Depression was the fall in world stock prices, acting directly on the world IS curve, and indirectly on the LM curve by increasing liquidity preference. Blaming stock prices entails the implicit assumption that they must have had a large exogenous component. We do not attempt to decompose stock prices into an endogenous component influenced by economic activity and an exogenous component corresponding to something like animal spirits.

Where do we stand on the spending versus money debate as set out, for example, in Brunner's volume? We take bits and pieces from both. What got the Depression rolling was price deflation directly due to the Wall Street crash. The crash, and subsequent bearish profit expectations, led to an important deflationary wealth effect; but still more important in propagating the Depression was the shift in liquidity preference due almost certainly to poor performance of equities. This could have been eliminated at any time by a monetary expansion.

2 Relative International Performance in the Great Depression

We have noted in the introduction the outstanding fall in world prices from 1929 to the mid-1930s. Table 2.2 shows fairly unambiguous unidirectional Granger causality flowing from prices to unemployment for the interwar years: of the fourteen countries only the UK gives opposite results.

We shall see that the magnitude of the price shocks explains most of the inter-country variance in 1930s unemployment performance. To facilitate inter-country comparisons we normalise each unemployment rate (see Appendix 2.1 for details) by its average value between 1921 and 1929. If the 1920s are considered as normal in some sense, the resulting measure is in units of normal unemployment. Where we have more than one measure of unemployment (e.g. Sweden, Germany) this normalisation tends to give similar results. Table 2.3 sets out some unemployment rate statistics for our sample of countries. In particular, column 6 gives our chosen measure of 1930s performance: average normalised unemployment between 1930 and 1938. Note that continental Europe does badly, while Scandinavia and the UK do well. The US is about average.

The model in the first row of Table 2.4 shows that the 1929-32 price shock explains 65 per cent of the variance of inter-country unemployment performance. This is about the same in row 2 if we replace the 1929-32 price change with the total price change from 1929 to each country's price trough. The variance explained rises to 78 per cent if we include the positive price shock from trough to 1938. On the face of it these results show that the balance of inter-country differences can be explained by a negative price shock in the early 1930s - and a subsequent positive price shock. We shall argue below that these shocks caused important changes in relative prices, in particular the real wage and the real interest rate, which acted as the transmission to the real economy. There is some evidence that nominal wage cuts, moderating real wage growth during the first price shock, led to superior performance: see row 4.

The real wage acts over this period to distort simple Okun-type relationships between unemployment and the output gap. Table 2.5 estimates such a relationship including the lagged real product wage as an additional variable. These results show that even if one adopted an extreme Keynesian position where output is exogenous, still one finds that a given increase in aggregate demand drew forth a smaller increase in employment if the real wage rose. Note that the US and UK differ from the other results: we shall say more on this later.

We argue below that the first price shock is derived from a fall in the price of goods in world trade - which itself we shall seek to explain later.

Table 2.2 Granger Causality Between Unemployment and Inflation, 1923-38

(A) Unemployment on lagged inflation

	u_{t-1}	$\dot{p}_{t-1}$	trend	DW
Europe	0.61	-4.51	0.09	1.6
	(3.2)	(-1.7)	(1.0)	
Scandinavia	0.53	-2.69	0.02	1.3
	(2.2)	(-1.2)	(0.6)	
United Kingdom	0.95	4.46	-0.02	1.2
	(4.0)	(1.2)	(-0.9)	
United States	0.51	-9.88	0.08	1.6
	(2.4)	(-2.1)	(1.3)	
World average	0.60	-4.09	0.05	1.5
	(2.9)	(-1.4)	(0.8)	

(B) Inflation on lagged unemployment

	$\dot{p}_{t-1}$	u_{t-1}	trend	DW
Europe	0.37	0.03	0.00	1.8
	(1.5)	(0.4)	(-1.2)	
Scandinavia	0.09	0.00	0.00	1.6
	(0.3)	(-0.1)	(0.8)	
United Kingdom	-0.19	-0.04	0.00	1.5
	(-1.1)	(-4.1)	(4.3)	
United States	0.61	0.02	0.00	1.9
	(2.0)	(1.1)	(-0.6)	
World average	0.25	0.01	0.00	1.8
	(0.9)	(0.4)	(0.02)	

Note: Starting dates vary between countries: see Appendix 2.1.
The country groupings are: Europe - Belgium, Czechoslovakia, France, Germany, Italy and the Netherlands; Scandinavia - Denmark, Finland, Norway and Sweden; World - Europe, Scandinavia, Australia, Canada, UK and US.
t statistics in brackets. For the grouped countries averages of parameters and statistics are reported. If parameter estimates were independent, significance levels for country groupings would be Europe - 0.8, Scandinavia - 1.0, World - 0.5. Since independence is unlikely, some rounding up of these levels is desirable. With complete dependence, the appropriate level would be t=2. Experience with intercountry data has led us to believe that an increase of, say, 50 per cent is required for robust inference. Thus in part (A) of the table we would count the European, US, and World average results as significant with Scandinavia marginal.

Table 2.3   Selected Unemployment and Inflation Data

	Average unemp't rate 1921-29 (1)	Average unemp't rate 1930-38 (2)	Peak unemp't rate (3)	Year of peak (4)	Peak $\bar{U}$ (5)	Average $\bar{U}$ 1930-38 (6)	% change in price level 1929-32 (7)
Belgium	2.4	14.1	19.0	1932	7.9	5.9	-48
Czechoslovakia	2.6	11.9	17.4	1934	6.7	4.6	-28
France	3.8	10.2	15.4	1932	4.1	2.7	-42
Germany	6.5	15.2	30.1	1932	4.6	2.3	-24
Italy	3.3	9.6	11.8	1933	3.6	2.9	-28
Netherlands	2.4	8.7	11.9	1936	5.0	3.6	-20
Denmark	17.1	21.9	31.7	1932	1.9	1.3	-15
Finland	1.6	4.1	6.2	1933	3.9	2.6	-15
Norway	5.8	8.1	10.2	1931	1.8	1.4	-10
Sweden	14.2	15.8	23.3	1933	1.6	1.1	-20
Australia	5.8	13.5	19.1	1932	3.3	2.3	-17
Canada	3.5	13.3	19.3	1933	5.5	3.8	-20
UK	8.3	11.7	15.6	1932	1.9	1.4	-7
US	5.1	14.5	22.9	1932	4.5	2.8	-23
World average				1932	4.0	2.8	-23

Note: $\bar{U}$ is our normalised measure of unemployment, i.e. U / Col.(1). Col.(6) is Col.(2) / Col.(1). Col.(6) we argue is appropriate for inter-country comparison.

Which countries experienced severe price shocks? Half the variance is explained by whether the countries were still on fixed exchange rates by 1932: see Table 2.4, row 5. One might expect that trading countries would fare worse if the price shock was trade-derived. There is some evidence for this in row 6. The relatively low proportion of variance explained in rows 5 and 6 is due to Australia which experienced a large fall in prices due to extremely low prices for her raw material exports. Without Australia, the model in row 6 explains 76 per cent of the inter-country price shocks.

We have seen that countries which had abandoned the gold standard by 1932 experienced less of a price shock. We now investigate in more detail the role of monetary factors in inter-country performance. Table 2.6(A) gives unemployment U_t as a function of a lagged dependent variable, world average U_t, and a version of the real interest rate $(r-\dot{p})_{t-1}$. We think of the real interest rate here as an index of general monetary stance which is, of course, constrained under fixed exchange rates. We have controlled for average U_t to see if an expansionary monetary policy leads to better unemployment performance relative to the world. The results show

Table 2.4 Inter-Country Unemployment Performance, 1930s

Dependent variable: average normalised 1930s unemployment rates

% price change 1929-32	% price change 1929 to price trough	% price change price trough to 1938	% real wage change 1929-32	R^2
-0.13 (4.3)	-	-	-	0.65
-	-0.11 (4.3)	-	-	0.65
-	-0.11 (5.1)	-0.06 (2.3)	-	0.78
-	-0.08 (3.3)	-0.07 (3.1)	0.01 (1.9)	0.85

Dependent variable: percentage price change 1929-32

Dummy if on gold, 1932	Share of exports in GDP, 1929	R^2
-12.0 (4.0)	-	0.47
-11.6 (2.9)	-20.4 (1.1)	0.53

Note: In these regressions each of twelve countries is the unit of observation. Here and elsewhere in this chapter "prices" means the national GDP deflator. As discussed in Appendix 2.1 we do not have GDP deflators for Belgium, Finland and France and in other sections of this chapter we use rough proxies. Since intercountry comparability is paramount here we have discarded Finland and France from our set of countries. Data in Mitchell (1980) give national account statistics for Belgium at enough dates to enable GDP deflators to be reasonably interpolated using WPI data.

Table 2.5 Okun Regressions, 1923-38 (dependent variable unemployment rate)

	$(y-\bar{y})_t$	$(w-p_v)_{t-1}$	trend	DW	SE
Europe	-0.43 (-4.5)	0.15 (2.3)	0.001 (3.1)	1.6	0.022
Scandinavia	-0.49 (-4.3)	0.25 (3.1)	-0.002 (-0.6)	1.5	0.019
UK	-0.64 (-7.4)	0.04 (0.2)	0.001 (0.6)	1.7	0.013
US	-0.43 (-7.9)	0.04 (0.2)	0.005 (1.3)	0.6	0.019
World average	-0.45 (-4.7)	0.18 (2.1)	0.001 (1.6)	1.4	0.020

Note: t statistics in brackets. Starting dates vary between countries; see Appendix 2.1. For a listing of the country groupings and a brief discussion of the interpretation of average t statistics, see notes to Table 2.1. $(y-\bar{y})_t$ is the deviation of real GDP from a linear trend.

Table 2.6 Unemployment and Exchange Rate Policy, 1923-38

(A) *Dependent variable: unemployment rate*, U_t

	U_{t-1}	World average U_t	$(r-\dot{p})_{t-1}$	DW
Europe	0.41	1.17	0.20	1.9
	(4.6)	(6.2)	(1.3)	
Scandinavia	0.29	0.37	0.14	1.3
	(1.2)	(4.0)	(3.0)	
UK	-0.03	0.36	0.14	1.7
	(-0.1)	(3.5)	(3.1)	
US	-0.31	1.60	0.21	1.5
	(-2.2)	(9.4)	(2.5)	
World average	0.26	0.91	0.19	1.6
	(2.2)	(5.4)	(2.1)	

(B) *Dependent variable: central bank discount rate*, r_t

	r_{t-1}	Gold standard dummy	DW
Europe	0.63	-0.50	1.6
	(3.4)	(-0.7)	
Scandinavia	0.49	-1.10	1.8
	(2.7)	(-2.2)	
UK	0.10	-2.12	1.9
	(0.4)	(-3.7)	
US	0.53	-1.08	1.7
	(2.5)	(-2.3)	
World average	0.52	-0.86	1.7
	(4.3)	(-3.0)	

Note: t statistics in brackets. Starting dates vary between countries: see Appendix 2.1. For a listing of country groupings and a brief discussion of the interpretation of average t statistics, see note to Table 2.2.

quite clearly this was the case. In Table 2.6(*B*) we complete the chain of causation by showing that abandoning the gold standard did indeed release the nominal interest rate. The European countries do not show up well here: by and large they maintained parity until the late 1930s, suffering, in consequence we argue, higher nominal and real interest rates and worse unemployment.

The above analysis has brought out the following points:

(i) The proximate cause of unemployment in the Great Depression as a world phenomenon was a fall in prices.

(ii) This fall in prices was associated with fixed exchange rates.
(iii) Recovery was via a rise in prices associated with leaving the gold standard.
(iv) The fall in prices caused changes in relative prices, in particular the real wage and the real interest rate, which had important effects on the real economy.

The notion that abandoning fixed exchange rates was the source of recovery for many countries has been persuasively argued by Eichengreen and Sachs (1985). Our findings here thus support their conclusions.

3 A Model of the Open Economy, World Prices Given

In this section we shall develop and estimate small structural models to show in more detail the linkages suggested in section 1. First the labour market. We assume a labour demand schedule (here and elsewhere in logs) of the form

$$n^d = n^d (k, w-p_v, \rho) \qquad (1)$$

where k is capital, $w-p_v$ is the value-added product wage and $\rho = r - \dot{p}_v^e$ is the real interest rate. Sometimes we shall drop the subscript $_v$ from p_v. Technical progress should also be included but is omitted in this exposition. Given diminishing returns, we expect a negative sign on the wage, independently of market structure provided only that firms profit maximise and the price elasticity of output demand they face is not violently procyclical. With fixed capital the presence of the real interest rate is nonstandard. This variable, which we have found to be important empirically in virtually all employment time series we have studied (e.g. Newell and Symons, 1987), should be interpreted as measuring the price of capital not included in fixed capital (stocks, firm-specific human capital). There may be other explanations, and for the purposes of our analysis we need only think of it as the direct effect of monetary policy on the hiring decision of firms. It is sometimes convenient to interpret (1) as an output supply equation:

$$y^s = y^s (k, w-p_v, \rho) \qquad (1')$$

The real wage is assumed to be the outcome of a bargain between workers and firms (Nickell and Andrews, 1983; Newell and Symons, 1987).

$$w-p_v = h (k-l, p_c-p_v, u, \rho) \qquad (2)$$

Here l is the labour force, p_c is the consumption deflator, p_c-p_v is the tax-import wedge, and ρ is the real interest rate. This model is the appropriate generalisation of the competitive wage outcome to a bargaining setting. The capital-labour ratio gives the path of the equilibrium wage; the wedge p_c-p_v is present because firms and workers employ different price deflators; u is specific to the bargaining interpretation and reflects workers' concern for the prospects of displaced workers; and ρ is present because it shifts the labour demand curve. Given w-p_v, employment is determined from (1).

This equation works well for the post-Hitler's war period (Newell and Symons, 1986a). A crucial distinction between the interwar and postwar years is that the latter presumably seldom required a fall in money wages to achieve equilibrium, however defined. Keynes argued about his own period (*General Theory*, chapter 19) that workers would resist a fall in the money wage. In terms of a bargaining approach to wage formation, workers might rationally resist a fall in the nominal wage to maintain employment if this was likely to be misinterpreted as a sign of bargaining weakness bound to cause problems in subsequent negotiations. If, at the micro level, wages move to clear markets with the single restriction that they may not fall in some markets, the economy-wide wage equation will exhibit a form of nominal rigidity:

$$w\text{-}p_v = h\ (k\text{-}l,\ p_c\text{-}p_v,\ u,\ \rho,\ \Delta p_c) \tag{2'}$$

Note that an identical equation could be derived without assuming nominal rigidity from a wage equation containing unanticipated inflation if Δp_c were an appropriate proxy for it. We should also note that the parameter on Δp_c is expected to shift between periods of different average rates of inflation. In fact in previous work we have found no nominal rigidity post-Hitler's war, whereas we shall see below that nominal rigidity is definitely present between the wars. These issues are discussed in more detail in Newell and Symons (1986a).

Conditional on the nominal interest rate, the model could be closed by a reduced form price equation from the demand side of the economy, but we shall develop this in a little more detail as it is useful for descriptive purposes and will be of importance below. Here the model is standard. We assume demand for domestic value-added takes the form:

$$y^d = y^d\ (\rho,\ \theta,\ W^*,\ W^*\text{-}W) \tag{3}$$

where θ is competitiveness, $\theta = p^*+e-p$, W^* is world wealth, defined as current plus expected future income, and W is domestic wealth, defined as expected future income. The relative wealth term is required if domestic income is spent in greater proportion on domestic output. If foreigners have different propensities to consume our output out of current and future income we require also current world income in (3). The LM curve takes the form:

$$m = m^d (y, p, r) \qquad (4)$$

We have transactions balances in mind here but we leave open the prospect of wealth effects.

Finally, balance of payments equilibrium is given by

$$0 = b (y, \theta, r^* + e^e - r, W^*, W^* - W) \qquad (5)$$

Equations (1'), (2'), (3), (4) and (5) give five equations in five unknowns, y, r, p, w, and e or m, depending on the exchange rate regime. We find it helpful to consider the subsystem consisting of (1'), (3), (4) and (5). These equations can be solved to yield quasi-reduced forms for y, m, r and p in terms of the remaining variables. For prices, in particular,

$$p = p (e+p^*, w, \dot{p}^e, r^* + \dot{e}^e, W^*, W^* - W, k) \qquad (6)$$

The variable $r^* + \dot{e}^e$ is only present if financial capital is internationally mobile, and for most countries at the time this was much less important than currently. Discarding this, and employing an adaptive scheme for $\dot{p}^e$ so that it becomes embodied in the dynamics of the equation, we have

$$p = p (e+p^*, w, W^*, W^* - W, k) \qquad (6')$$

which is what we shall estimate. Equation (6) is a well-defined relationship irrespective of the exchange rate regime, with the proviso that e will become endogenous for most countries towards the end of the period. One might also consider the possibility that, after floating exchange rates, there might be a shift in (6') due to altered expectation formation. In general this is at the end of the sample for a handful of observations and econometrically is conveniently handled by allowing an intercept shift.

The comparative statics of the open economy on fixed exchange rates are given in Figure 2.2. We assume no relative wealth effects; no real interest rate in y^s; $\dot{p}^e = 0$; no capital mobility; and a severe form of nominal rigidity so that the nominal wage is predetermined. We draw the balance of payments curve (5) and an aggregate demand curve derived from (3) and (4) in p - y space, and also in θ - y space. If we begin at equilibrium at A, a simultaneous fall in the price of goods in trade p* and world wealth W* shifts down both b and AD in p - y space. Equilibrium

76 - Newell and Symons

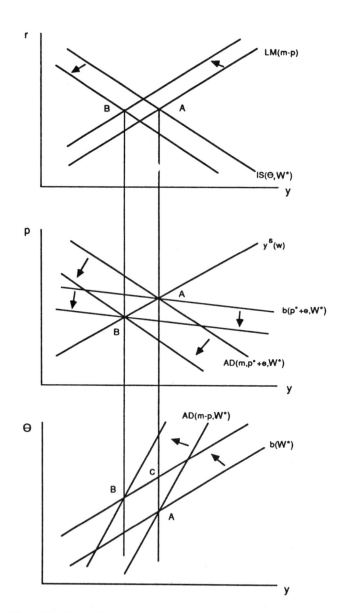

Figure 2.2   The Open Economy

Note: See text for discussion.

is established at B where b meets y^s. If temporarily the economy rests at a y^s = AD equilibrium not at B, monetary changes associated with the balance of payments shift the AD curve until it cuts b at B. On gold, with the world stock of money given, some countries will find themselves temporarily in trade surplus, some in deficit. In θ - y space both schedules shift back with no necessary change in competitiveness. Changes in real money balances, wealth and competitiveness shift both IS and LM curves to a consistent equilibrium at B. For the typical economy there is no change in competitiveness and demand falls because of a fall in world demand for domestically produced goods. Supply falls because prices have fallen and the real wage has risen.

If the economy depicted in Figure 2.2 abandons fixed exchange rates it is able to increase real money balances, so shifting out the AD curve to cut the b curve at C in θ - y space and y^s at A in p - y space. Both competitiveness and prices rise. Aggregate demand rises because of the increased competitiveness. Interest rates may or may not fall because both IS and LM curves shift out. Aggregate supply increases because the real wage falls. If *all* countries pursue this policy, average competitiveness will not change but interest rates will fall because of the increase in real balances. Thus domestic demand will rise and increase further via the current account because of the revival in world activity. With the addition of a few wrinkles this is the story of most countries' experience of the Great Depression.

4 Estimation Results

We discuss first the labour demand equation (1). See Table 2.7. Capital is represented by a trend. We allow for dynamic adjustment by including a lagged dependent variable. We employ the lagged wage and real interest rate to minimise instrumentation. On average (row 5) the results are most pleasing. The average wage elasticity is about -0.7. The wage is wrong-signed in three countries (though insignificantly): Italy and, notably, the US and the UK (rows 3 and 4). We shall study the latter two countries in more detail below. The real interest rate performs even better than the wage: it is wrong-signed only in Belgium (t = 0.1). We wondered whether there was any separate effect from the nominal interest rate. Adding this we found it insignificant in all countries, $\bar{t}$ = 0.005, a comprehensive rejection. Thus tying the nominal interest rate and inflation together in this way is most consistent with the data. We should note that the significance of the wage in this analysis is in no way an artefact of the inclusion of the real interest rate. Without it we find an average t of -2.0, establishing the existence of a raw correlation between employment and the wage over the period, as is obvious anyway from study of

78 - Newell and Symons

Table 2.7 Labour Demand Equations, 1923-38 (dependent variable employment, n_t)

	n_{t-1}	$(w-p)_{t-1}$	$(r-\bar{p}^e)_{t-1}$	trend	DW	SE
Europe	0.74	-0.19	-0.54	0.001	1.9	0.03
	(5.3)	(-2.0)	(-2.7)	(0.8)		
Scandinavia	0.44	-0.39	-0.61	0.008	1.5	0.04
	(2.2)	(-2.1)	(-2.2)	(1.8)		
UK	0.74	0.12	-0.08	0.001	1.3	0.02
	(3.0)	(0.3)	(-0.5)	(0.4)		
US	0.61	0.29	-0.53	-0.008	1.8	0.04
	(3.6)	(0.9)	(-2.5)	(-1.4)		
World average	0.59	-0.27	-0.53	0.003	1.7	0.03
	(3.9)	(-2.0)	(-2.7)	(1.4)		

Note: t statistics in brackets. Starting dates vary between countries; see Appendix 2.1. For conventions, see notes to Tables 2.2 and 2.3.

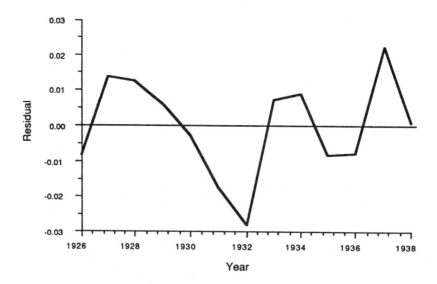

Figure 2.3 Average Residuals from the Labour Demand Equation, 1926-38

the plots in Figure 2.1. All in all, these results are strikingly consistent with what we have found postwar (e.g. Newell and Symons, 1987).

In Figure 2.3 we plot the average residuals from this model for our sample of fourteen countries. Note that only 1931 and 1932 show up with large negative unexplained components: about 2 and 3 per cent respectively. These are small relative to the large falls in employment over the period; and the implication is that the path of relative prices can more or less explain the Great Depression.

For the US and UK it is natural to ask whether the insignificant results for the wage are due simply to chance over a turbulent period or whether they point away from our theoretical framework. For both these countries we have long time series stretching back into the last century and we can estimate the model over longer time periods. See Table 2.8. For both these countries we have measures of capital and technical progress and these have been included. Constant returns to scale have been imposed. We exclude war and war-influenced years from our data, and also the early 1920s from Britain which were characterised by violent but transient changes in relative prices. It will be seen (rows 1 and 4) that the model fits well over the longer period and is consistent with the character of the international interwar results. For the interwar period the wage is wrong-signed in both but, most importantly, it is imprecisely estimated and the Chow test of parameter stability between the two periods is easily accepted. Thus the dependence of employment on relative prices over the interwar years is perfectly consistent with our model.

A generalisation of our model would allow transient demand shocks to influence employment, given relative prices (e.g. as in Newell and Symons, 1986b). If we include shocks (see the notes to Table 2.8 for construction) in the equation over the interwar period (rows 3 and 7) we obtain very similar results to those obtained over the longer period. Plots of these shock variables are given in Figure 2.4. Note the marked negative shocks in the US in 1932 and 1933. We conclude from this analysis that the difficulty of identifying real wage effects on employment for these two countries over this period is wholly due to the amount of noise over a turbulent period.

In summary, we find strong but slow-acting effects of the real wage on employment as well as powerful real interest rate effects. The burden of explanation for the level of employment throughout the Great Depression is thus passed back to explaining these variables.

We turn now to the real wage equations (2'). The real interest rate ρ was very weak in all experiments and typically wrong-signed. Given this, the fact that the real interest rate depresses employment according to the employment equation (1) means that a rise in the real interest rate will increase unemployment because the real wage does not fall to offset the fall

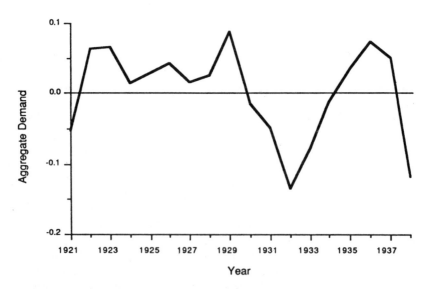

Figure 2.4a   Aggregate Demand Shocks in the United States, 1921-38

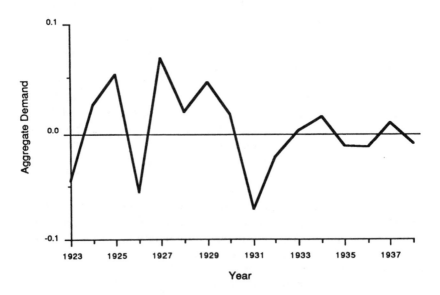

Figure 2.4b   Aggregate Demand Shocks in the United Kingdom, 1923-38

Table 2.8   UK and US Labour Demand Equations (dependent variable log employment - capital ratio $(n - k)_t$)

	$n_{t-1}-k_t$	$(w-p_v)_{t-1}$	$(r-\dot{p}^e)_{t-1}$	λ_t	$(y-y^e)_t$	DW	SE
UK 1872-1913	0.84	-0.11	-0.61	-0.01		1.9	0.02
and 1923-38	(13.9)	(-2.0)	(-4.5)	(-2.5)			
UK	1.00	0.32	-0.75	-0.002		2.4	0.01
1923-38	(6.3)	(0.9)	(-3.0)	(-1.9)			
UK	0.81	-0.14	-0.65	-0.01	0.28	2.2	0.01
1923-38	(2.6)	(-0.2)	(-2.5)	(-0.6)	(1.8)		
US 1892-1916	0.92	-0.22	-0.53	0.14		1.6	0.04
and 1921-38	(9.3)	(-2.3)	(-2.5)	(1.5)			
US	1.15	0.01	-0.79	-0.31		1.8	0.05
1921-38	(6.1)	(0.0)	(-1.4)	(-0.7)			
US	0.81	-0.46	-0.61	0.35	0.69	1.6	0.02
1921-38	(7.1)	(-1.9)	(-2.1)	(1.4)	(5.3)		

Note: t statistics in brackets. The model estimated is (in logs)

$$(n-k)_t = \alpha_0 (n_{t-1} - k_t) - \alpha_2 (w - p_v)_{t-1} - \alpha_3 (r - \dot{p}^e)_{t-1} + \alpha_4 \lambda_t + \alpha_5 (y - y^e)_t$$

where λ_t is the log of an index of labour augmenting technical progress, calculated by the Solow residual method (see Newell and Symons (1985) for details), and y-y^e is unexpected demand, which is represented by the residuals from a regression of y on lagged values of real wages, real interest rates, and real money balances. The real interest rate is its fitted value from a regression on lagged variables. Where appropriate, we take account of the endogenity of y- y^e by using current changes in nominal money balances as an instrument. The equations without unexpected demand pass a Chow test for parameter stability over the two subsamples, the relevant F statistics being 1.65 for the US and 0.9 for the UK, where the 5 per cent significance level is around 4.5 in both cases.

in the demand for labour. It would be paradoxical if a perfectly forecast increase in the real interest rate created unemployment rather than merely reducing the wage. What this seems to mean is that, when the wage bargain is struck, it is assumed that the real interest rate will turn out to be at some normal level. It will be seen, for example, in Figure 2.1 that the real interest rate had returned to normal levels by 1932.

Without the real interest rate, a version of our real wage equation is given in Table 2.9. The capital-labour ratio is represented by a trend. The wedge $p_c - p_v$ is entered in Δ (first difference) form, rather than in levels. This transformation was suggested by our previous work on post-Hitler's war data (Newell and Symons, 1985) and implies that changes in the tax and import wedge are incident only transiently on the product wage and

Table 2.9   Real wage equations 1923-38 (dependent variable real product wage $(w-p_v)_t$)

	$(w-p_v)_{t-1}$	$(\dot{p}_c-\dot{p}_v)$	$\dot{p}_c$	$\dot{p}_v$	U_{t-1}	trend	DW	SE
Europe (i)	0.82	0.85	-0.49		-0.004	0.007	2.2	0.03
	(4.8)	(2.2)	(-2.2)		(-1.0)	(2.6)		
(ii)	0.70			-0.64	-0.009	0.009	2.2	0.03
	(7.1)			(-4.0)	(-1.1)	(3.7)		
Scandinavia (i)	0.71	0.76	-0.81		-0.035	0.008	2.0	0.04
	(3.0)	(1.1)	(-1.0)		(-0.9)	(0.9)		
(ii)	0.66			-0.76	-0.037	0.009	1.7	0.04
	(4.0)			(-2.7)	(-1.2)	(2.2)		
UK (i)	0.16	-0.14	0.21		0.007	0.006	2.6	0.01
	(0.5)	(-0.6)	(1.2)		(0.4)	(1.6)		
(ii)	0.13			0.21	0.006	0.006	2.5	0.01
	(0.4)			(1.3)	(0.4)	(1.8)		
US (i)	0.50	-0.66	0.60		-0.004	0.010	1.8	0.03
	(1.3)	(-0.9)	(3.1)		(-0.4)	(1.1)		
(ii)	0.48			0.60	-0.004	0.010	1.8	0.03
	(1.9)			(3.7)	(-0.5)	(1.7)		
World average (i)	0.68	0.65	-0.43		-0.011	0.007	2.2	0.03
	(3.4)	(1.6)	(-1.2)		(-0.7)	(1.8)		
(ii)	0.58			-0.51	-0.013	0.009	2.0	0.03
	(4.6)			(-2.6)	(-0.8)	(2.8)		

Note: For general notes and conventions, see notes to Table 2.2. Method of estimation: instrumental variables. Current prices or inflation rates were treated as endogenous: instruments were lagged values and lagged world prices and world trade. Here unemployment rates are normalised on their average value 1921-29, so as to make the coefficients internationally comparable.

hence influence employment only transiently. On average (row 9) the model is well supported. The wedge term is fairly strong, indicating that, for our sample of countries, the fall in commodity prices in the late 1920s was benign for employment. Nominal rigidity is significant on average but fairly sporadic. Unemployment is quite weak, indicating that the feedback from unemployment to the wage was weak: this is presumably part of the problem. Inspection of the parameters on $\dot{p}_c - \dot{p}_v$ and $\dot{p}_c$ suggests that these terms could be approximately replaced by $\dot{p}_v$ and this is done in row 10. The estimate is considerably sharpened. Much the same story holds for the European and Scandinavian groups of countries (rows 1 to 4). The results for the UK and the US are contrary. If we estimate this equation for the UK up to 1913 we obtain similar results to the average reported in row 9, though much more sharply estimated. Between the wars our experiments indicate that the UK real wage behaved more or less as a random walk with drift. There is no sign of nominal rigidity, and no indication of unemployment feedback. It should be noted that the UK received only a very minor price shock in 1929. Similarly, for the US we find no nominal rigidity and no unemployment feedback. It would be hard to maintain that nominal wage rigidity was a feature of the US over this period. The nominal wage fell quite sharply in 1931; and Mitchell (1986) shows that wage cuts were common in the US in the 1920s. Our preferred real wage equation for the US is simply:

$$w-p_v = 0.79 \ (w-p_v)_{-1} + 0.21 \ (w-p_v)^*$$
$$\quad\quad\quad (5.5) \quad\quad\quad\quad (imposed)$$

$$DW = 1.9 \quad\quad SE = 0.037 \quad\quad 1921\text{-}38,$$

where $(w-p_v)^*$ is the equilibrium wage defined as that wage which equates the labour force and employment in the long-run version of the model in Table 2.7, row 4. This means that nominal rigidity cannot be part of our account of the US Great Depression: the logic of our analysis suggests that this must be due to slow recovery from massive demand and/or monetary shocks in the early 1930s. This slowness is due to natural inertia in employment evident in all the employment equations in Tables 2.7 and 2.8. Thus the reduced form supply equation in this model is effectively a dynamic Lucas supply curve of the sort discussed by Sargent, (1973, equation 23). The fact that there is little feedback from unemployment to real wages is characteristic also of US data since the last war. We have discussed this elsewhere (Newell and Symons, 1987): the theoretical meaning of this long-standing phenomenon is still unclear.

In accordance with the comparative statics analysis in section 2, nominal wage rigidity correlates fairly well with unemployment performance over the Depression. See Figure 2.5. Denmark is an outlier, but Denmark experienced a very high level of average unemployment during the 1920s suggesting that our performance measure, which normalises on this average, may give a misleading picture in this case.

We estimate a version of our price equation (6') in Table 2.10. We include results for the US for consistency though the open-economy perspective is in this case clearly misleading. Appendix 2.1 gives details of our construction of the wealth terms W and W*. We found relative wealth W - W* to be weak and we shall not discuss it here. World wealth W* is correctly signed on average, though more diffusely estimated across countries than one would wish. Of course W* is the appropriate variable to represent foreigners' demand for domestic output only in a world of perfect capital markets. If this is not the case current and future foreign income will appear with different weights. In the models labelled (ii) we replace W* with the current and lagged levels of world trade. The improvement in fit is marked, and we prefer these models.

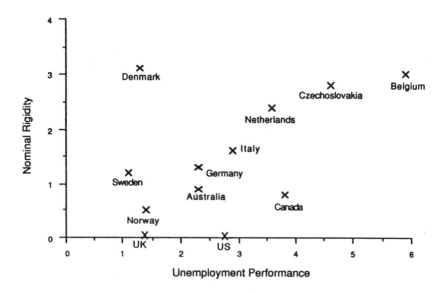

Figure 2.5   Unemployment Performance and Nominal Rigidity

Note: The long-run inflation parameters from the wage equations in Table 2.8 are on the vertical axis (absolute value). On the horizontal axis is the ratio of average 1930s unemployment to average 1920s unemployment.

The effect of world prices on domestic prices is powerful and quite quick-acting: the mean lag is about a third of a year on average. We have sought to include the effect of tariffs on prices by developing an index of the world rate of effective protection τ. This variable is strongly correlated with p* and world trade, and if entered separately in (6') tends to be very imprecisely estimated. The impact effect of tariffs should be one for one with world prices but decline as domestic resources are moved to the production of the protected good. A simple approximation to this is to enter tariffs as a first difference with the same parameter as p*. This is done in Table 2.10: the implied restriction was always easy to accept. Note that in terms of our model tariffs work by allowing an increase in prices without a deterioration in the balance of trade.

The remaining part of the model is just as one might expect: wages are correctly signed and significant everywhere; and the level of world trade exerts a powerful impact effect on domestic prices. We experimented with dummy variables for the exchange rate regime, but these were always insignificant. This was true also for government expenditure.

Table 2.10 Price Equations, 1923-38 (dependent variable inflation, $p_t - p_{t-1}$)

	$(p^*_t + \dot{\tau} - p_{t-1})$	(w_t-p_{t-1})	(world wealth)$_t$	(world trade)$_t$	(world trade)$_{t-1}$	DW	SE
Europe (i)	0.35	0.13	0.32			1.4	0.05
	(3.5)	(2.1)	(0.9)				
(ii)	0.30	0.38		0.56	-0.49	2.2	0.03
	(3.5)	(3.2)		(3.1)	(-3.3)		
Scandinavia (i)	0.46	0.36	0.67			1.9	0.03
	(4.6)	(2.9)	(2.8)				
(ii)	0.46	0.58		0.43	-0.15	1.6	0.03
	(3.4)	(4.6)		(2.7)	(-1.0)		
UK (i)	0.11	0.46	0.04			2.6	0.01
	(3.8)	(5.9)	(0.6)				
(ii)	0.09	0.44		0.05	-0.02	2.3	0.01
	(2.7)	(5.9)		(1.4)	(-0.6)		
US (i)	0.22	0.22	-0.02			1.5	0.02
	(4.7)	(3.7)	(-0.2)				
(ii)	0.15	0.19		0.14	-0.16	1.7	0.02
	(2.4)	(4.0)		(1.2)	(-1.5)		
World average (i)	0.33	0.29	0.32			1.7	0.04
	(3.6)	(2.7)	(1.2)				
(ii)	0.32	0.42		0.45	-0.31	2.0	0.03
	(3.1)	(3.6)		(2.6)	(-2.3)		

Note: For general notes and conventions, see notes to Table 2.2. Method of estimation: instrumental variables. All current variables were treated as endogenous: instruments were lagged values of these variables plus lagged values of the world trade and real money balances variables, as well as a dummy variable for the exchange rate regime. τ_t is a world index of protection. See text for discussion.

We have thus developed a three-equation model for each of our sample of countries: an unemployment equation, a real wage equation, and a price equation. Figure 2.6 gives a flow chart of the implied causation. The models employed are the average version of each of the three preferred specifications. Thus the model used refers to no particular country but is rather an unweighted average of all models. We take as exogenous the price of traded goods, world trade, tariffs and the nominal interest rate. Each cell gives the change in the variable over the indicated period. On each arrow we have written the contribution made by each variable to the change in the variable it influences. These contributions were calculated as follows. We simulated the average model from 1925 to 1937 allowing all independent variables their observed (averaged across all countries) values. The model was then simulated holding each

86 - *Newell and Symons*

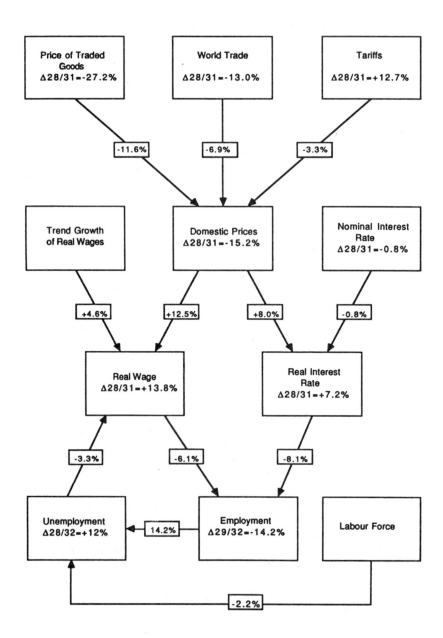

Figure 2.6 Linkages in the Great Depression

independent variable at its 1928 value, once for each independent variable. The change in the simulated dependent variable between each simulation was then attributed to the behaviour of the variable being held constant. For convenience the inflows to each cell, where their total was discrepant with the observed change in the cell, were factored to achieve equality.

Let us now trace the course of the Great Depression. The price of traded goods fell between 1928 and 1931 by 27 per cent, and the level of world trade fell by 13 per cent. In direct consequence domestic prices would have fallen by 18.5 per cent if protectionism had not raised prices by 3.3 per cent. Thus domestic prices fell by 15.2 per cent leading to potential rises of 12.5 per cent and 8.0 per cent in the real wage and real interest rate respectively. Trend growth contributed 4.6 per cent to the wage; but increased unemployment reduced it by 3.3 per cent: the sum of the three effects gives a rise of 13.8 per cent. The nominal interest rate fell by 0.8 per cent so the real interest rate rose by 7.2 per cent. The real interest rate and the real wage contributed 8.1 per cent and 6.1 per cent respectively to the fall in employment. Since the labour force fell by 2.2 per cent, the unemployment rate rose by twelve points, on average. (One feedback is missing in our model: from wages to prices. This was tiny and is omitted.) These numbers should not be taken too seriously: they merely suggest orders of magnitude to the various causalities in our model.

5 The World

So far we have taken world prices and output as given. In this section we apply our model to the world, considered as a single economic entity. The world IS curve takes the form

$$y^* = y^* (\rho^*, W^*)$$

We shall take W^* as a trade-weighted average of industrial country wealth; and ρ^* is a similar average of real interest rates. An estimate of a version of this model is given in Table 2.11. We have imposed the restriction that output is unit-elastic with respect to wealth in the long run, which was almost exactly true in the unrestricted model. Note that a permanent 1 percentage point increase in the real interest rate would produce about a 1 percentage fall in demand, wealth held constant, with a mean lag of about two years. Since W^* fell by about 9 per cent between 1929 and 1932, mainly due to the fall in real stock prices, and ρ^*_{t-1} rose by a similar amount, both are strong variables in accounting for the fall in output.

Table 2.11　The World Model, 1924-38

IS curve:　$y^*_t - W^*_t = 0.71\,(y^*_{t-1} - W^*_t) - 0.39\,\rho^*_{t-1}$ 　　　　　　　(4.7)　　　　　　　　(-3.3)	SE = 0.02,　DW = 2.3
LM curve:　$(m - p - y)^*_t = -3.06\,r^*_t + S$ 　　　　　　　(-3.4)	SE = 0.03,　DW = 2.7
$S = 0.04\,D30 + 0.15\,D31 + 0.23\,D32 + 0.20\,D33 + 0.17\,D34 + 0.09\,D35$ 　(1.1)　　　　(4.3)　　　　(6.7)　　　　(5.6)　　　　(4.6)　　　　(2.3)	
Output supply:　$y^*_t = 0.94\,y^*_t + 0.42\,p_t$ 　　　　　　　　(14.1)　　　(4.0)	SE = 0.02,　DW = 2.3

Note: Both independent variables in the IS curve are endogenous with instruments: lagged nominal interest rates, labour income, wealth and the change in world trade. In the LM curve, r^*_t is instrumented by its own lagged value and the lagged change in world trade. In the output supply equation $\dot{p}_t$ is instrumented with lags of wealth, money balances, and nominal interest rates. For simulations p^e in the expression for the real interest rate was replaced by the fitted value from a regression of $\dot{p}$ on its own lagged value and two lags of output.

This analysis implies that the fall in world wealth from 1929 to 1932 was a major deflationary force causing the Great Depression, as was the rise in the real interest rate. We turn now to money.

Money is held for transactions and as an asset. A fall in world wealth will produce a negative income effect on the demand for money as an asset, but a fall in the expected return on equities, as must surely have happened, will produce an opposite substitution effect. A further complication arises from the role of bank collapses which will reduce the demand for deposits and increase the demand for currency. Rather than attempt to unpick these complex interactions we shall simply allow the demand for money function to shift over the 1930s. Thus we estimate:

$$m - p - y = \lambda\,(m-p-y)_{-1} - \alpha\,r + S$$

where S is a set of year dummies for the first half of the 1930s. The results across all countries are summarised in Table 2.12. We especially include Canada as it provides an interesting contrast with the United States.

The dummies reveal a Λ-shaped increase in the demand for money, centred on 1932, which is strikingly consistent across countries. We have cumulated these dummy variables via the lagged dependent variable to give the total shift in the demand for money in Table 2.13. On average there was a fairly modest shift, but in North America the shift was much

Table 2.12 Demand for Money Equations, 1923-38 (dependent variable, m-p-y)

	$(m-p-y)_{t-1}$	(interest rate)$_t$	D30	D31	D32	D33	D34	D35	DW	SE
Europe	0.29	-0.08	0.04	0.03	0.14	0.05	0.04	0.05	2.5	0.09
	(1.6)	(-1.6)	(0.4)	(0.2)	(1.3)	(0.3)	(0.2)	(0.0)		
Scandinavia	0.32	0.00	0.11	0.14	0.10	0.14	0.04	0.00	1.8	0.08
	(1.0)	(0.1)	(1.3)	(1.5)	(1.1)	(1.3)	(0.2)	(0.2)		
UK	-0.54	-0.06	-0.08	0.02	0.07	0.09	0.06	0.01	2.0	0.04
	(0.7)	(-1.6)	(-1.1)	(0.5)	(1.6)	(2.0)	(0.9)	(0.3)		
US	0.51	-0.05	0.06	0.08	0.17	0.08	-0.02	0.05	2.4	0.03
	(2.7)	(-1.8)	(1.3)	(2.1)	(4.2)	(1.3)	(-0.3)	(1.5)		
Canada	0.56	-0.04	-0.03	0.11	0.17	0.17	0.02	0.05	1.9	0.04
	(2.3)	(0.6)	(-0.3)	(0.8)	(2.3)	(1.7)	(0.2)	(0.6)		
World average	0.27	-0.04	0.04	0.07	0.12	0.09	0.04	0.03	2.3	0.08
	(1.2)	(-1.1)	(0.4)	(0.8)	(1.6)	(0.9)	(0.3)	(0.4)		

Note: r_t is instrumented by r_{t-1}, r^*_{t-1}.

Table 2.13 Cumulated Effect of Shift in Demand for Money Functions

	1930	1931	1932	1933	1934	1935
World average	0.04	0.08	0.14	0.13	0.07	0.05
UK	-0.08	0.06	0.04	0.07	0.02	0.00
US	0.06	0.11	0.23	0.20	0.07	0.09
Canada	-0.03	0.09	0.22	0.29	0.18	0.15

stronger: in particular the increase in Canadian demand for money was much greater than in the US. Equities fell much less in Europe and in consequence one would expect a lesser increase in the demand for money. The relative behaviour of Canada and the US, which experienced similar equity behaviour, has been explained by Friedman and Schwartz as due to the absence in Canada of bank failures:

> The bank failures made deposits a much less satisfactory form in which to hold assets than they had been before in the United States or than they remained in Canada ... the demand for the sum of deposits and currency was reduced by the diminished attractiveness of deposits. Of course that effect was not strong enough to offset completely the increased demand for money relative to income as a result of ... the great increase in uncertainty, the decline in

Table 2.14   Simulations, 1930-33

	Change (%) in World GDP	Change (%) in World GDP deflator
Due to decline in wealth	-3.4	-13.8
Due to shift in the demand for money	-4.2	-16.3
Due to monetary contraction	-1.5	-5.7
Simulated	-9.1	-35.9
Actual	-7.0	-22.0

attractiveness of equities and real goods, and so on. (Friedman and Schwartz, 1965, p. 57)

The trade-weighted world version of the LM curve is given in Table 2.11. The Λ-shaped shift is again apparent. It is possible to obtain a similar equation replacing the dummy shifts with changes in world equity prices; but we think our approach is superior in that it allows for changes in wealth, and also for changes in banking risk.

We complete the world model with an aggregate supply equation, giving output as a function of the inflation rate. As discussed above, we think of this as due to nominal wage rigidity, but others may prefer to think of it simply as a Lucas supply equation with $\dot{p}^e = 0$. Alternatively we could replace this supply equation with one giving output as a function of the real wage and the real interest rate lagged: in fact this leads to similar results.

The reduced form of this system gives each of the endogenous variables p^*, y^* and r^* as functions of W^*, S and m. In order to see which of these is the most potent in explaining the Great Depression, we adopted the procedure described at the end of section 4. We simulated the model from 1929 allowing the exogenous variables to take their observed paths, and then held each endogenous variable constant in turn at its 1929 value. The difference between the simulations was, as before, attributed to the behaviour of the variable held constant.

Simulating our model from 1929 we obtain a trough in 1933 rather than 1932. Table 2.14 compares the simulated model at 1933 with observed values and also apportions changes in the endogenous variables to the behaviour of each exogenous variable. We find that the shift in the LM curve is the main culprit: it explains 46 per cent of the simulated fall in output, versus 37 per cent for the fall in wealth. Direct monetary contraction exerted only a minor influence.

6 Concluding Remarks

Let us summarise our argument. We have shown that the world economy was characterised between the wars by significant nominal rigidities on the supply side. These, as a consequence of a collapse in demand in the 1930s, led to increases in the real wage and real interest rates, and hence to the Great Depression. With regard to the fall in demand, we have compared three proximate sources: an observable shift in monetary behaviour, a decline in the money stock, and a fall in world wealth associated principally with a fall in equity prices (see Figure 2.1e). In the preceding section we have shown that the change in monetary behaviour - an increase in liquidity preference - caused a larger fall in demand than the fall in wealth and that the direct contribution of the fall in the money stock was quite slight.

But in a deeper sense this increase in liquidity preference was surely caused in large part by the continued poor performance of the equity market. Can one base an account of the Great Depression on "animal spirits"?

The argument would run like this. The bursting of the Wall Street bubble in 1929, coinciding with a natural downturn, sets in train a rapid deflation derived essentially from a wealth effect on aggregate demand. Pessimistic expectations are transmitted to the rest of the world. Nominal rigidities translate the fall in demand into a fall in real income so that pessimism becomes in part self-fulfilling. A complex of vicious circles is set up, as illustrated in Figure 2.7. The process continues until any lower valuation of the capital stock is implausible. This seems to us a convincing story. What are the problems?

The main problem is that financial panics do not always lead to Great Depressions. In particular Brunner (1981) asks why, if the 1929 crash was the key event in causing the Great Depression, did not the stock market fall in 1974 have catastrophic effects? According to our analysis a num-

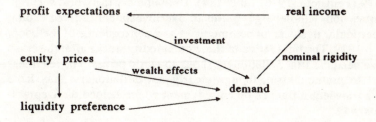

Figure 2.7 **Transmission Mechanisms in the Depression**

ber of preconditions are required before a collapse in demand can lead to a major depression.

(i) Nominal rigidities. An inwards shift of the aggregate demand schedule can produce enduring effects only if nominal rigidities ensure the aggregate supply schedule is upwards-sloping. We have argued that nominal rigidities become important only at low levels of core inflation. Inflation was very low worldwide in 1929, very high in 1974.

(ii) Governments must be unwilling or unable to take offsetting expansionary monetary action. We have seen how important was the increase in liquidity preference in propagating the Depression. If this increase in the demand for money had been met by an increase in the supply of money, we estimate the unemployment effects of the Depression would have been at least halved. We have shown in the first section that the sooner countries abandoned fixed exchange rates and hence gained control over their stock of money, the better they fared. Presumably only the United States could have acted unilaterally in this regard. We thus accept the central hypothesis of Friedman and Schwartz (1965) that US monetary policy must get the lion's share of the blame.

(iii) International linkages. When the bourses of the world are just a telephone call away, bearishness can rapidly spread from country to country. Kindleberger (1978) quotes Meyer von Rothschild saying in 1875, "The whole world has become a city." A related point is that the development of interest-sensitive international capital flows places greater constraints on short-run domestic monetary policy than those imposed merely by the current account.

Our contention is thus that a low level of core inflation, interlinked capital markets and a regime of fixed exchange rates mean that the world is particularly prone to depressions of the sort experienced after 1929. The most obvious precursor is the depression that followed the financial crash of 1873 ("the first significant international crisis", Kindleberger, 1978, p.132) when for example the British unemployment rate rose steadily until 1879 (Feinstein, 1976, Table 124). Undoubtedly the world was ripe for a depression. Kindleberger points to overinvestment in fixed capital and in particular in stocks of commodities as a consequence of the boom ending in 1929. The liquidation of these commodity stocks after the crash may have been the first deflationary shock to world prices. The readiness to resort to protectionism, though clearly not deflationary, may have exerted a transient influence on employment which helped the Depression on its way.

APPENDIX 2.1   Data

The data for the United States and United Kingdom regressions in Table 2.8 were all taken from *Long-Term Economic Growth in the US* (Department of Commerce, 1964) and Feinstein (1976) respectively.

In all the interwar regressions the starting dates were: 1922 for Australia, Finland, Italy, Norway, the United Kingdom and the United States; 1923 for Belgium, Canada, Denmark, France and the Netherlands; 1924 for Sweden; 1925 for Czechoslovakia; 1926 for Germany.

N   Employment. The employment data used here are discussed in detail in Newell (1986). The intention was to find time series of total civilian employment for every country. This proved impossible in a number of cases, and as a result the series employed vary in quality from official estimates or elaborately reconstructed series (i.e., Australia, Canada, Denmark, Netherlands, Norway, United Kingdom, and United States) to indices calculated employing the few materials available (Finland, France, Sweden).

U   The unemployment rate. There is a detailed discussion of the unemployment rate series in Newell (1985b). The series used here were chosen on two criteria: reliability of source and closeness of definition to the employment series. Series derived from trade union records are used for Australia, Belgium, Czechoslovakia, Denmark and Sweden. For the other countries series are derived in the main from the operation of unemployment insurance schemes.

w   The nominal wage rate. The construction of these data is described in detail in Newell (1986). Our intention was to find series reflecting annual averages of hourly earnings in the widest possible industry grouping. In fact wage rate series are used for Australia, Belgium, Canada, Czechoslovakia, France, Germany, Italy, Netherlands and Norway. Earnings series are used for Denmark, Finland, Sweden, the United Kingdom and the United States.

p_v The GDP deflator. Taken from national historical data sources and from Mitchell (1980, 1983). No series were available for Belgium, Finland and France. The series used for these countries were wholesale price indices adjusted according to the formula:

$$p_v = (1+s) p_o - s\, p_m$$

where p_o is the wholesale price index, p_m is an import price index and s is the ratio of imports to GDP.

p_c Consumer price index. Taken from national historical data sources and from Mitchell (1980, 1983).

M   A broad monetary aggregate. Taken from national historical data sources and from Mitchell (1980, 1983). The definition used generally is notes and coins in circulation plus all deposits in commercial banks, thus perhaps corresponding to a contemporary definition somewhere between M2 and M3. Sources were the League of Nations *Review of World Trade and Monthly Bulletin of Statistics*.

r   The nominal interest rate. The data are central bank discount rates from League of Nations *Monthly Bulletin of Statistics*.

τ   Tariffs. The average tariff rate. This variable is the average across the fourteen countries of $\bar{p}-p^*$, where $\bar{p}$ is the log of the wholesale price index and p^* is defined below.

y   Real GDP. Taken from national historical data sources and from Mitchell (1980, 1983).

p^* The world price of manufacturing value-added in US dollars. This was constructed using two series, p_m the world price of traded manufactures, and p_o the world price of other goods, according to the formula: $p^* = 1.25\, p_m - 0.25\, p_o$. Both raw series were taken from the UN *Statistical Yearbook 1969*.

    World Trade. A quantum index of world trade in manufactures from UN *Statistical Yearbook 1969*.

e   Annual average exchange rate as a percentage of gold parity. Sources were: League of Nations *Review of World Trade* and *Monthly Bulletin of Statistics*.

W   Wealth. A geometric average of real labour income, real stock prices, and real money balances, with weights 0.7, 0.28, 0.02, respectively. The stock price data were taken from League of Nations, *Monthly Bulletin of Statistics*.

The world variables W^*, y^*, etc. are trade-weighted averages of the data from the fourteen countries. Trade weights at 1929 from UN *Statistical Yearbook 1969*.

REFERENCES

Bean, C., Layard, P.R.G. and Nickell, S.J. (1986), "The Rise in Unemployment: A Multi-country Study", *Economica*, May.

Bernanke, B.S. (1985), "Employment, Hours, and Earnings in the Depression: An Analysis of Eight Manufacturing Industries", National Bureau of Economic Research, Working Paper no. 1642, June.

Brunner, K. (ed.) (1981), *The Great Depression Revisited*, The Hague: Martinus Nijhoff.

Eichengreen, B. and Sachs, J. (1985), "Exchange Rates and Economic Recovery in the 1930s", *Journal of Economic History* 45, no.4, pp.925-46.

Feinstein, C.H. (1976), *Statistical Tables of National Income, Expenditure and Output of the UK, 1855-1965*, Cambridge: Cambridge University Press.

Friedman, M. and Schwartz, A.J. (1965), *The Great Contraction*, Princeton, New Jersey: Princeton University Press.

Hatton, T.J. (1986), "The Analysis of Unemployment in Interwar Britain: A Survey of Research", in *Economic Perspectives*, London: Harwood.

Hicks, J.R. (1974), "Real and Monetary Factors in Economic Fluctuations", *Scottish Journal of Political Economy*, pp.205-214.

Kindleberger, C.P. (1973), *The World in Depression 1929-1939*, Berkeley: University of California Press.

Kindleberger, C.P. (1978), *Manias, Panics and Crashes*, New York: Basic Books.

Mitchell, B.R. (1962), *Abstract of British Historical Statistics*, Cambridge: Cambridge University Press.

Mitchell, B.R. (1980), *European Historical Statistics*, London: Macmillan, 2nd edn.

Mitchell, B.R. (1983), *Historical Statistics of the Americas, Asia and Australasia*, London: Macmillan.

Mitchell, D.J.B. (1986), "Explanations of Wage Inflexibility: Institutions and Incentives", in W. Beckerman (ed.), *Wage Rigidity and Unemployment*, London: Duckworth.

Newell, A.T. (1985a), "The Revised OECD Data Set", London School of Economics, Centre for Labour Economics, Working Paper no. 781.

Newell, A.T. (1985b), "Historical Unemployment Rate Data", London School of Economics, Centre for Labour Economics, Working Paper no. 804.

Newell, A.T. (1986), "Annual Data for Interwar Employment and Wages", London School of Economics, Centre for Labour Economics, Working Paper no. 841.

Newell, A.T. and Symons, J.S.V. (1985), "Wages and Unemployment in the OECD Countries", London School of Economics, Centre for Labour Economics, Discussion Paper no. 219.

Newell, A.T. and Symons, J.S.V. (1986a), "The Phillips Curve as a Real Wage Equation", London School of Economics, Centre for Labour Economics, Discussion Paper no. 246.

Newell, A.T. and Symons, J.S.V. (1986b), "Showdown for the Labour Demand Curve", London School of Economics, Centre for Labour Economics, Working Paper no. 885.

Newell, A.T. and Symons, J.S.V. (1987), "Corporatism, the Laissez-faire, and the Rise in Unemployment", *European Economic Review* 31, pp. 567-602.

Nickell, S.J. and Andrews, M. (1983), "Unions, Real Wages, and Employment in Britain 1951-1979", *Oxford Economics Papers*, November.

Okun, A.M. (1981), *Prices and Quantities: A Macroeconomic Analysis*, Oxford: Blackwell.

Sargent, T.J. (1973), "Rational Expectations, the Real Rate of Interest, and the National Rate of Unemployment", Brookings Institution, Washington, DC, Brookings Papers on Economic Activity, no. 2.

Symons, J.S.V. (1985), "Relative Prices and the Demand for Labour in British Manufacturing", *Economica* 52, pp. 37-51.

[4]

THE 1931 FINANCIAL CRISIS

This article reviews some of the main causes that led to the most severe financial crisis in monetary history. Those causes were many and complex and involved both economic and political factors. The crisis itself, like the circumstances out of which it arose, is unique. It began in the second half of 1928 with the liquidation of the gold exchange standard by one of the leading financial powers at a time of incipient economic depression in the agricultural debtor countries of the southern hemisphere. It ended in the Autumn of 1931 with the devaluation of sterling and, within, three months, of thirty-five other currencies. The structure of international payments collapsed and the fixed exchange rate system of the late 1920's was converted into the system of chaotically fluctuating exchange rates of the later 'thirties.[1]

The development of the crisis can be divided broadly into four periods. First, there occurred a steady liquidation of the gold exchange standard between mid-1928 and late 1929 with a consequent drain of liquid resources from the main international money markets of Europe, particularly London and Berlin. Second, one of the main effects of the decline in economic activity in the underdeveloped areas was to cause a rise in demand for funds, especially from London, between 1928 and early 1930. When the supply of funds proved to be insufficient, the first wave of devaluations occurred and the fixed exchange rate system of the later 'twenties began to show signs of breaking up. The rise in demand for liquidity increased further as depression spread to the rest of the world in the latter half of 1929 and throughout 1930. The various national monetary institutions, however, became less able to accommodate the rising demand for liquidity because of the heavy depreciation of, particularly, commercial bank assets. This creeping insolvency during 1930 and early 1931 was particularly important in the great international short-term creditor nations like France and the United States, both of which experienced acute internal bank failures.

The general rise in demand for liquidity, moreover, had international repercussions because of the widespread foreign ownership of short-term assets (outstandingly in the form of commercial bank deposits). Banks were subject to an internal drain of cash which was dependent on internal economic conditions; but they were also liable to an external drain of funds which depended on economic (and political) conditions in foreign countries, as well as foreign reaction to economic and political developments within a bank's own country. Indeed, the heart of the crisis is to be found in the fact that countries were forced—or induced—to draw on foreign money markets to satisfy their internal needs

---

[1] It has been estimated that the gross amount of short-term international indebtedness (foreign liabilities of European countries and the U.S.A. only) declined from 70,000 million Swiss francs at the end of 1930 to 32,000 million at the end of 1933. The Bank for International Settlements, *Fourth Annual Report* (Basle, 1934), p. 27.

for liquidity. And these internal needs for liquidity were a direct result of the more general economic depression with which most of the world was inflicted. The international money markets—in the last resort, London—were, however, unable to accommodate the demands for liquidity, particularly in face of the panic demand for funds which arose after the collapse of the Austrian banking system in May 1931.

The final, or panic, stage of the crisis (May–September 1931) was a consequence of the realisation that banking systems were becoming illiquid and, in many cases, insolvent as a result of the effects of the fall in economic activity on the asset structure of financial institutions. Funds were converted increasingly into foreign exchange as doubts arose first about the possibility of continued convertibility at fixed exchange rates and, second (after the Standstill Agreements of July 1931), on whether funds would be transferable at any exchange rate.

The Gold Exchange Standard

The international monetary system of the 1920's was a gold exchange standard and central banks regarded foreign exchange as the equivalent of gold. There is nothing inevitably or inherently unstable about this system, nor is there strong evidence that the 1931 crisis was a result of the adoption of the gold exchange standard in the early 'twenties. But the possibility exists that any exchange standard might be unable to withstand shocks arising from changes in the structure of demand for international financial assets. Towards the end of the 'twenties important changes occurred in the structure of demand for international assets.

In the first place, some countries, especially France, were intent on a self-liquidation of the gold exchange standard, and of substituting the holding of gold for foreign exchange. Second, the collapse in economic activity—with its consequent effects on the viability of financial institutions and general level of confidence— induced a rise in the demand for liquidity which involved a general conversion of short-term assets held abroad into national liquid assets or gold. The gold exchange system failed, in brief, to provide sufficient security, convenience or prestige to prevent a policy of self-liquidation by some of the leading creditor countries.

The instability of the gold exchange standard was due, in part, to the peculiar development of international financial practices during the 'twenties. Post-war reconstruction—especially in Central Europe—was financed to a large extent by private funds made available to debtor nations on a short-term basis. These funds were easily and quickly shifted, when interest rate differentials changed or confidence declined in any one centre.[1] This large stock of international cash was a new phenomenon.[2] Its instability was due, however,

---

[1] The pattern of interest rate differentials was relatively fixed throughout the later 'twenties. Germany usually maintained a differential of about 1½–2 per cent over the main financial centres. English rates were usually about 1–1½ per cent above New York which in turn maintained higher rates than France, the most important creditor on short-term account by the end of the decade.

[2] It is impossible to estimate accurately the size of the international short-loan fund during the later 1920's. New York held over £600,000,000 of foreign balances in 1930, *Committee on Finance and Industry*, Min. of Evid. Vol. II, Q. 7795. I have estimated that London held about £760,000,000 in June 1930. "London and the 1931 Financial Crisis", *Economic History Review*, Vol. XV (No. 3, 1963). Over 40 per cent of total bank deposits in Germany in 1930 were

not only to its highly liquid character and to the fact that funds moved in response to changes in confidence (an element largely absent before 1914) as well as to interest differentials, but also to the manner in which a large proportion of these funds was employed in the receiving countries.

The banks, perhaps improperly, regarded these internationally-owned deposits as part of their ordinary deposits and used them accordingly. Very broadly, funds borrowed on short-term from abroad were used within various countries as working capital (of which a large number of European countries had been drained after the inflations of 1920-24). In some cases—outstandingly Central Europe—bank funds or funds lent directly to industry on a short-term basis were used for other purposes, mainly for investment in essentially longterm projects.

The inflow of foreign-owned bank deposits did, of course, increase the exchange holdings of the central banks of countries experiencing a short-term capital influx. The newly acquired reserves were used, however, to support the rapid rise in economic activity—with a consequent rise in imports—which most countries experienced in the early and mid-'twenties. Some countries—especially Germany—financed reparation payments out of the short-term capital inflow. New York and, more particularly, London were able to finance large-scale long-term capital exports without causing undue pressure in their local capital markets and on their balances of payments. The increased foreign exchange 'backing' needed to finance the rise in local banknote issues was another 'drain' on the newly acquired reserves. Finally, from 1928/29 onwards central bank reserves were used increasingly to support exchange rates, which, in the light of the sharp fall in prices and trade which occurred after 1928, were palpably overvalued for many debtor countries. The main effect of the large scale inflow of funds which many debtor countries experienced was to stimulate economic activity. It also obviated the necessity of some countries to balance international earnings with current international financial commitments.

The manner in which the foreign-owned funds were used internally, and the use to which their foreign exchange equivalent was put by central banks, did not ensure their self-liquidation in terms of foreign exchange. The funds were not automatically self-liquidating in a manner which would have generated their foreign exchange equivalent. Foreign-owned funds used, for instance, in South America to finance the holding of agricultural stocks did little to earn foreign exchange, so that the borrowing country could not automatically amortise the debt. Similarly, the use made of such funds in Europe did relatively little to increase the foreign exchange earnings of the borrower or even assure lenders of constant liquidity of their funds. The consequence of heavy foreign short-term borrowing was to transfer abroad effective ownership of some countries' international monetary reserves.[1]

---

foreign owned. *Economist*, Banking Supplement, 9 May 1931, p. 8 also H. Clay, *Lord Norman* (London, 1957) p. 377. The commercial banks of most countries in East and Central Europe owed between 20-40 per cent of their total deposits to foreigners, F. Rona, *Currency and Banking in Central Europe, 1919-39* unpublished M. Sc. (Econ.) thesis (London, 1947) p. 258. It would seem that the international short-loan fund was of the order of £2,700 million—£3,000 million in mid-1930.

[1] The phenomenon of borrowed reserves can be briefly defined as one when a country's short-term liabilities exceed her short-term foreign assets plus internally held gold and foreign exchange reserves. Dr. Per Jacobsson has commented that "the exchange reserves of many of the European countries had been acquired by large-scale short-term borrowing, and they melted away when the short-term loans were not renewed .." *Proceedings*, Annual Meeting of I.M.F. (Vienna, 1961), p. 24.

Some countries not only effectively mortgaged their short-term international reserves, but they also endangered the liquidity of their internal banking systems; and, by so doing, threatened the collapse of the international financial structure. Under such conditions, international compensatory finance was urgently needed by the debtor countries, not only to cover the possible withdrawal of short-term capital, but also to bolster their internal banking systems and thus avoid the need for a deliberate policy of monetary restriction and deflation. Such finance was not forthcoming on an adequate scale when it was needed. The reasons are many and complex: partly, the chief creditor countries themselves suffered internal banking problems or felt too weak to extend credit; partly, international aid was essentially a matter of private enterprise where matters of confidence and economic risk outweighed political interests; and partly the onset of the financial crisis was used by governments as a means of achieving their political aims.[1]

The manner in which foreign-owned funds were used locally was particularly important because the gold exchange standard of the 'twenties was accepted as a matter of expediency. Once the chief results of the gold exchange standard had been achieved—stabilisation of exchange rates and the strengthening of monetary reserves—there was increasing pressure by some important countries to revert to a gold bullion standard. The gold exchange standard was never accepted as anything but a temporary palliative by France; Germany and the smaller countries of West and Central Europe had a strong desire to hold as much gold as was possible. The gold exchange standard in the 'twenties was regarded not only as an expedient, but as a temporary expedient. Under these conditions it was impotrant that the international financial system should have been highly liquid. In practice, it meant that international short-term debtor countries should have held sufficient reserves to meet an outflow of capital without the necessity of having to impose strict policies of deflation to reduce the demand for foreign exchange on the current account of the balance of payments. It was not so much a shortage of international reserves that caused difficulty in the later 'twenties as the consequences of misuse of funds.

It was France, however, who was not only the most insistent in desiring to liquidate the gold exchange standard but also in the strongest position to carry out her desires. From 1928 onwards French policy and financial practice led to a liquidation of her gold exchange commitments. This proved to be an important source of disequilibrium and deflation for the international monetary system.[2] France tended to drain the system of liquidity.

The French franc was informally stabilised in December 1926 [3] and *de jure* stabilisation was achieved in June 1928. The rate chosen in 1926 and legalised in 1928 tended to undervalue the franc *vis-à-vis* other currencies.[4] The consequence was an enormous surplus on the overall balance of payments

---

[1] Cf. E. W. Bennett, *Germany and the Diplomacy of the Financial Crisis, 1931* (Harvard, 1962).

[2] Liquidation of the gold exchange standard had a deflationary effect on the whole international monetary system because the gold losing centres reacted to the loss of gold by higher interest rates and restrictions on foreign lending; the gold receiving centre, however, simply exchanged one class of assets (foreign exchange) for another (gold) and was not induced to change its internal monetary policy.

[3] "... the franc would be restrained from fluctuating on the exchange, although no legal par value would be set against gold or foreign currencies". M. Wolfe, *The French Franc Between the Wars* (New York, 1951), p. 47.

[4] *Ibid.*, pp. 58–59.

THE 1931 FINANCIAL CRISIS

which resulted in a sharp increase in French gold and foreign exchange reserves. From the beginning of 1927 France began to build up a position which, by 1930, made her the biggest international short-term creditor nation in the world.[1] It was not, however, a stable creditor position.

After June 1928, all notes issued by the Bank of France and all sight deposits held at the Bank had to be covered by a minimum of 35 per cent gold. The Bank could no longer acquire foreign exchange as part of its reserves, any increase in Bank liabilities would therefore mean an increased demand for gold. Secondly, the amount of foreign exchange held by the Treasury was closely related to the fiscal needs of the Government; a budget deficit could be, and was, financed by first disposing of foreign exchange. Thirdly, the extent to which the commercial banks could maintain large foreign balances abroad depended not only, or even mainly, on considerations of interest rate differentials, but on the demand for financial accommodation within France and the cash needs of the banks themselves. To this extent, therefore, a rise in economic activity in France—with a consequent rise in the demand for notes and bank finance—would attract gold to France. The institutional structure of French finance after the passing of the 1928 stabilisation law led, irrevocably, to a liquidation of the gold exchange standard.

The international financial structure as it developed in the 'twenties was subject, then, to two important sources of disequilibrium. Firstly, the structure was built up by an extensive system of private international deposit banking, the liquidity of which depended on the manner in which these funds were utilised in local, but temporary, repositories. Secondly, the gold exchange standard had been adopted as a means of quickly stabilising foreign exchanges which had become disorganised due to the war and immediate post-war economic dislocation. The widespread extension of international deposit banking after 1925 further involved central banks in holding foreign exchange rather than gold. Most European central banks—outstandingly the Bank of France—however, regarded the gold exchange standard as a temporary expedient. The desire—and ability—to return to a gold bullion standard was strong.

Economic Depression

It was on this relatively unstable international monetary structure that the Great Depression impinged. The beginning of the Great Depression is usually dated from the third quarter of 1929. In most countries outside Europe, however, the agricultural industries had suffered a relatively severe depression

---

[1] It is not possible to calculate exactly the extent of French short-term claims on foreigners as no official balance of payments statistics were published before 1945. However, Wolfe (*ibid.*, p. 60) has noted that the 'sundry assets' of the Bank of France increased from 4 milliards francs in 1926 to 31 milliards in June 1928, and its foreign portfolio amounted to 43 milliards of francs. In addition, the French Treasury held Fr. 7·8 milliards of foreign currencies in December 1928, 9·9 milliards in 1929, 5·1 milliards in 1930 and Fr. 1·7 milliards in 1931—see M. G. Myers, *Paris as a Financial Centre* (London, 1936), p. 85. Further, the French commercial banks are believed to have held very large balances in New York and London up to 1929: "From June 1929 to January 1931, the banks drew on their foreign exchange portfolios to meet the public's demand for currency, as is evidenced by the fact that, against the 19 billion francs of gold added to the Bank's stock, 13·5 billion of notes were issued" W. H. Wynne, *Journal of Political Economy*, 1937, p. 490. There was, also, a very large capital outflow on private account before 1926, which was not fully repatriated after 1928. In total, French claims on foreign centres might have amounted to about 130 milliards of francs in 1929.

for at least two years before the more general economic downturn.[1] The agricultural depression was substantially one of overproduction at a time of falling demand for some agricultural products—notably cereals.[2] Agricultural prices, however, tended to decline only slightly in some countries, e.g., the U.S.A. and Continental Europe, with the result that large stocks of some commodities began to accumulate after the bumper harvest of 1928/29.[3] A further important feature of the developing agricultural crisis was the relative shift in importance of the main centres of production. Europe was becoming more self-sufficient in foodstuffs at the expense mainly of the traditional exporters like Argentina and Australia.[4]

The financial consequences of this agricultural depression were significant. First, the holding of stocks was largely financed by money borrowed on short-term from the main international financial centres.[5] Secondly, all the agricultural exporting countries, with the exception of the U.S.A., were debtor countries on a relatively large scale.[6] Borrowing merely to finance stocks and maintain prices meant increased indebtedness and less likelihood that earnings from exports would recover sufficiently to absorb the increased indebtedness as well as cover amortisation and interest charges on previous borrowings.

The outer Sterling Area, for instance, was in overall balance of payments deficit amounting to over £80 million in 1928, nearly £100 million in 1929 and £120 million in 1931. Japan, Argentina and Brazil all lost gold heavily in 1929 and 1930. Total gold stocks for South America declined from $927 million at the end of 1929 to $558 million at the end of 1930. Over the same period Asia's gold stock fell from $738 million to $601 million; the gold stocks of Oceania (mainly Australia and New Zealand) fell $150 million from $255 million during 1929 and 1930. On the other hand, European gold stocks increased from $4,425 million to $5,192 million and those of North America increased from $4,332 million to $4,787 million from the end of 1928 to the end of 1930.[7]

The most important reactions to the continued fall in gold reserves were devaluation and deflation. Argentina and Uruguay suspended gold payments in December 1929. Canada, in effect, suspended payments in January 1929. In 1930, four more Latin American countries abandoned the gold standard and these were joined by Australia and New Zealand.[8] The break-up of the pattern of fixed exchange rates had the result of significantly reducing the flow of capital funds from the developed to the underdeveloped world.

The main direct effect of the depression in the underdeveloped areas on Europe was, however, in the decline of international trade. European exports

---

[1] League of Nations, *The Agricultural Crisis* (Geneva, 1931), p. 7.
[2] League of Nations, "*Memorandum on Production and Trade 1925 to 1929/30*" (Geneva, 1931), p. 8: ibid. *The Course and Phases of the World Economic Depression* (Geneva, 1931), pp. 44–5 and 323.
[3] *Ibid. The Agricultural Crisis*, pp. 9–11. *The Statist* index of average wholesale prices (100–1913) fell from 165 in 1924 to 142 in 1928. See also Royal Institute of International Affairs, *World Agriculture* (London, 1937), pp. 89, 91–100 and League of Nations, *World Production and Prices, 1925–32* (Geneva, 1932), App. I table 6. p. 130.
[4] *Ibid.*, p. 21.
[5] J. B. Condliffe, *The Commerce of Nations* (London, 1951), pp. 478, 488.
[6] Cf. *The Course and Phases of the World Depression*, p. 36.
[7] League of Nations, *Final Report of the Gold Delegation of the Financial Committee* (Geneva, 1932). pp. 78–81.
[8] Final Report of the Gold Delegation, *op. cit.*, p. 9; also W. A. Brown, *The International Gold Standard Reinterpreted 1914–34* (New York, 1940), esp. Chap. 24.

THE 1931 FINANCIAL CRISIS

to the underdeveloped world slumped sharply from the beginning of 1929.[1] In addition, prices of manufactured exports fell more rapidly than did their costs of production. European exports became relatively less profitable after 1929 with the consequence that the incentive to push sales of exports abroad was gravely weakened.[2] The European export trades were faced with increasing excess capacity, rising costs and increasing unemployment. Depression which spread throughout Europe was, in part, due to the decline in activity in the export trades; to this extent Europe imported the 'Great Depression.'

Meanwhile, the Amercan economy had begun its long downward swing which was to last from mid-1929 to the Spring of 1933. This further reduced the volume of international trade and greatly increased the deflationary pressure on Europe and the rest of the world. The forces of deflation were, however, also gathering strength independently in Europe. The cessation of the flow of international investment to Europe in 1928/29, previously on a large scale, slowed down economic activity on the Continent. The decline in economic activity in Germany after 1928 "was related to a diminution in the inflow of funds".[3] The collapse of world agricultural prices and the emergence of vast surpluses of agricultural commodities greatly affected the economies of Eastern and Central Europe, as did the cessation of capital exports to that area. Economic activity fell sharply, and large and continuous deficits on the balance of payments occurred after 1928.[4]

The surplus countries—outstandingly France, some of the smaller countries of Western Europe and the United States—did not, however, make funds available to the debtor countries either on a short- or long-term basis. This, in part, reflected internal monetary difficulties, with a consequently increased demand for liquidity, which the creditor countries experienced between late 1929 and 1931. It also reflected the decline in confidence of the creditor nations in the creditworthiness of many of the borrowing countries.[5] France experienced a net import of capital in both 1929 and 1930.[6] The United States maintained foreign lending in 1929 and 1930, but at a much reduced rate.[7] The United Kingdom maintained its capital outflow at a surprisingly high rate, especially in view of a reduction in the surplus of the balance of payments.[8] But the

---

[1] "From 1929 to 1931, the quantum of European exports fell three to four times as much as that of European imports", League of Nations, *Review of World Trade 1931 and 1932* (Geneva, 1932) p. 19. The volume of British exports was 38 per cent lower in 1931 than 1929. U.S. exports fell 35 per cent over the same period and most European industrial countries experienced declines in exports of between 20–26 per cent. German exports, however, were higher in 1931 than 1927 a considerable proportion of which was accounted for by exports to Russia financed by German (and, indirectly, British and American) credit, *ibid.*, pp. 19 and 35. On the other hand, "the quantum of trade in agricultural products ... (was) ... maintained roughly at the same level as before the depression", *ibid.*, p. 16. The price of agricultural goods, however, fell enormously, so that "the excess in value of European imports over exports was reduced, as a result of the unequal fall in import and export prices", *ibid.*, p. 19.

[2] Germany was an exception: "Ever since 1927 when the import of foreign capital began to decline the domestic demand for goods has contracted, and the share of exports in industrial production is estimated to have increased considerably". *Ibid.*, p. 23.

[3] C. T. Schmidt, *German Business Cycles, 1924–33* (New York, 1940) p. 268.

[4] Cf. League of Nations, *Balance of Payments* (Geneva, 1933) pp. 38–39.

[5] Cf. Clay, *op. cit.*, p. 369.

[6] League of Nations, *Balances of Payments, 1930*; Wolfe. *op. cit.*, pp. 96–99.

[7] Private net investment declined from $1,541 million in 1928 to $555 million in 1930; the U.S. gained $450 million of gold in 1929–30. *Survey of Current Business*, July 1954.

[8] As Clay pointed out: "It was not in the tradition of London to cut off sharp, at the first signs of difficulty, the accommodation it gave to its debtors..." *Lord Norman*, p. 361. Long-term capital

total sums made available were pathetically inadequate to meet the needs of the main debtor countries. The international loan-fund, i.e., the quantity of funds available for international investment, was shrinking at a time when it was most in need of being expanded. From the middle of 1930, as international trade deficits increased, there was a sharp fall in the level of liquidity available to finance them; the alternatives were income deflation or repudiation of debt.

Owing to the fact that government expenditure is generally more inflexible than government revenues, budgets become unbalanced as incomes fall. The twin phenomenon of budget and balance of payments deficits—associated in the minds of many as causes of inflation—was sufficient to induce many governments to introduce strict deflationary policies in 1930–1931 in an attempt to eradicate these deficits. The severe depression in trade was thus turned into a catastrophe.

In conditions of depression, reductions in expenditure, as an attempt to eradicate budget deficits and remedy balance of payments disequilibrium, often cause a further contraction in incomes without necessarily remedying the balance of payments and budget deficits. Incomes fall faster than deficits can be closed, especially when deficits are in part determined by obligations of debt repayment. Some accommodating finance must be found—even if it is involuntary—to cover the deficits. In many respects the 1931 financial crisis was the result of the general failure by certain creditor countries to provide accommodating finance as a means of overcoming the international effects of depression and the ensuing collapse of confidence which made itself felt in a virtual cessation of international lending and a move by many creditors to demand repayment of earlier loans. The only feasible alternative to a policy of continuous deflation was repudiation of international obligations contracted on a gold price level, which in the light of 1930–31 seemed vastly inflated. The 1931 crisis was, in this sense, a crisis of repudiation of international debts.

The Liquidity Crisis

The liquidity crisis is often regarded as a panic demand for cash and gold, which raged between May and September 1931. The scramble for cash was, however, a culmination of a prolonged increase in the demand for liquidity—i.e., easy and assured realisability of assets into cash—which had been apparent since the middle of 1928. It was only when it was thought that short-term assets might no longer be easily or even automatically realisable or transferable that panic broke out. The liquidity crisis itself is, to a large extent, an account of the progressive deterioration in the quality and increasing difficulty in the realisability of short- and long-term assets as well as a decrease in the demand for short-term foreign assets. The decline in the liquidity of, and the fall in demand for, paper assets was, in the last resort, a consequence of the decline in economic activity and the effect which this had on the viability of financial institutions.[1] The onset of the crisis can be traced to the cessation of

---

outflow was £46 million in 1929 and £35 milion in 1930, though the balance of payments surplus on current account fell from £103 million in 1929 to £27·5 million in 1930, see, T. C. Chang, *Cyclical Movements in the Balance of Payments* (Cambridge, 1951) table facing p. 144.

[1] This is not to deny that overinvestment might have occurred in some industries in the late 'twenties, or, indeed, that malinvestment also occurred, with the inevitable consequence of bad debts which, sooner or later, would have appeared. It is maintained, however, that it was the onset of economic depression which fundamentally weakened the international monetary system of the 'tewnties.

THE 1931 FINANCIAL CRISIS

capital outflow from the creditor countries to the debtor countries in the second half of 1928.[1] The exceptionally strong boom in the industrial countries—especially the United States—absorbed savings which might otherwise have been exported. In addition to the boom in economic activity, New York and, to a lesser extent, London, experienced a sensational rise in stock market values which attracted funds both from local and foreign sources.[2] Further, the legal stabilisation of the French franc in June 1928 ended a long period of speculation against that currency. Henceforward there was an increasing tendency to remit to France the proceeds of the large export surplus which was being earned at that time. International investment in the underdeveloped parts of the world declined after 1928, partly because of the decrease in the profitability of investments there at a time when the creditworthiness of these countries was suspect—vide the decline in bond prices which occurred after 1928.[3]

As Clay pointed out: "The check to the (outward) flow of funds .. had the same effect as a contraction of credit".[4] Adequate financial help to the debtor countries was not forthcoming during the period of active industrial and financial activity between 1927 and late 1929. By the beginning of 1930 the economic situation had deteriorated alarmingly and there was, as a consequence, little desire to increase financial commitments in the debtor and agricultural producing areas.[5] From about June 1930 to March 1931, the crisis was one of a steady contraction of credits and was stimulated largely by a general decline in confidence consequent upon the deepening of the depression.

The fall in economic activity, output and prices, the consequent relative rise in costs, sharp increase in bankruptcies, the exchange depreciations in, and consequent capital flight from, the underdeveloped countries [6] all contributed to the tendency to liquidate previous international investments. This exercised a futher pressure on the world's foreign exchanges—in addition to the continued gold flow to the chief creditor countries due to their large surpluses on current trading account. During the course of 1930, however, a series of banking crises in many countries broke out and these increased enormously the demands for liquidity.

Unfortunately, the first banking crises were experienced in the great creditor countries of France and the U.S.A. In the early Autumn of 1930 a series of frauds involving the *Banque Oustric* "gave a serious check to depositors'

---

[1] League of Nations, *Balances of Payments, 1930* (Geneva, 1932), p. 30.

[2] "New capital issues for foreign account in the United States fell off heavily and the surplus of capital in other lending countries that would normally have been available for investment in underdeveloped countries was attracted by New York or by local domestic booms". *Ibid.*, p. 15.

[3] *Ibid.*, p. 35. The decline in creditworthiness was, in part, a consequence of the large amount of debts which these countries had incurred between 1923–27.

[4] *Op. cit.*, p. 373.

[5] There was a brief revival of long-term lending in the first half of 1930, but it was clearly of an exceptional and temporary nature. It included the Young Loan which ended inter-Governmental Reparations, British loans to the Government of India and refunding issues in New York. The net increase in outstanding long-term debt was small. For instance, the U.S. exported $555 million of capital in 1930 (a sixth of which was the U.S. subscription to the Young Loan) but this was converted into an inflow of $756 million in 1931. *Survey of Current Business, loc. cit.* Even in the U.K. earlier portfolio investment in foreign securities was liquidated and some short-term assets realised. U.K. balances held in New York fell from $328 million in May 1930 to $214 million in December of the same year. *Federal Reserve Bulletin*; also Chang, *op. cit.* p. 144.

[6] Cf. League of Nations, *Balances of Payments, 1930*, pp. 27–31.

confidence, and was followed by several failures in the (French) provinces".[1] The banking crisis spread, involving about a dozen provincial banks and one of the biggest of the Paris banks—*Banque Nationale de Crédit*. The consequences of the banking crisis were twofold. First, the demand for bank notes rose sharply.[2] Secondly, the commercial banks were induced to increase their liquidity ratios.[3] The main result of these events was to increase French demand for gold (with the increase in the note issue and the rise in deposits of the Bank of France) and also cause a repatriation of commercial bank funds held abroad. In addition, the foreign exchange reserves held by the French Treasury were run down as the budget moved into deficit. The strain on the foreign exchanges —especially on sterling—was thus greatly increased from the early Autumn of 1930 onwards in order to meet the demands for liquidity within France.[4]

The French, however, also began to withdraw their funds from abroad for other reasons. Funds were steadily withdrawn from Germany from the late summer of 1930 mainly because of the possibility that Germany would declare a moratorium on repatriation payments.[5] After the large electoral gains made by the Nazi party in September 1930, confidence in the political stability of Germany decreased greatly; there was, in consequence, a large and continous outflow of funds.[6] It also seems probable that France withdrew funds held on short-term accounts with banks in Eastern Europe and Austria.[7] The reasons for withdrawals are complex. Firstly, there was an obvious deterioration in the economies of Eastern Europe owing primarily to the slump in agricultural prices. Secondly, the financial structure looked none too sound, especially in the light of the substantial involvement by the banks in local industry, and the continued decline in bank liquidity.[8] Thirdly, French foreign lending in the late 'twenties was strongly motivated by political considerations, and it is possible that, especially where Austria was concerned, funds were withdrawn, in part, for political reasons.[9] In short, the increased needs for

---

[1] Myers, *op. cit.*, p. 116.

[2] Fr. 2·7 milliards, B.I.S. *Capital Flows* (Basle, 1932).

[3] The cash ratios of the four leading Paris commercial banks increased from 7·5 per cent in mid-1929 to 32·5 per cent in November 1931. Wynne, *loc. cit.*, p. 72.

[4] Gold reserves at the Bank of France increased from 36·6 milliards of francs in mid-1929 to 58·6 milliards in August 1931. At the end of 1931 France held nearly 25 per cent of the world's total gold stock, as compared with a holding of only 8 per cent at the end of 1926.

[5] Cf. Bennett, *op. cit.*, p. 15.

[6] *Ibid.*, p. 15. After the September elections "nearly 1 milliard Reichsmarks (£50 million) left the country". *Documents on British Foreign Policy* (London, 1947), 2nd Series, Vol. II., p. 174. The *Reichsbank* estimated an outflow of RM 1·3 milliards and H. S. Ellis estimated RM 1·6 milliards, cf. *Quarterly Journal of Economics*, 1940 (supp.). "After the withdrawals following the September 1930 elections, little in the way of French funds was left in Germany, so that there was no such concern over German credit in Paris as there was in New York or London". Bennett, *op. cit.*, p. 171, see also Documents, *op. cit.*, p. 195.

[7] There had, for instance, been a withdrawal of funds from Poland from the end of 1929 onwards; foreign-owned short-term debt in Poland was reduced from 673 million Zloty in 1929 to 640 million at the end of 1930. Foreign credits of the Austrian *Credit Anstalt* were reduced by nearly 30 per cent between December 1929 and April 1931; cf. League of Nations, *Commercial Banks 1932* (Geneva, 1933), pp. 56 and 173.

[8] Cash and other items of a cash nature as percentage of total deposits of banks in Austria fell from 3·6 in 1929 to 2·8 in 1930; in Hungary from 10·7 to 9·3; in Poland from 12·3 to 10·6; *ibid.*, pp. 53–54.

[9] Bennett has commented, with regard to the collapse of the *Credit Anstalt* in May 1931, that "... if France did not cause the collapse, it is quite possible that she precipitated the announcement" (of the true state of affairs of the bank), *op. cit.*, p. 101. If this is true, it is likely that French funds would have been withdrawn well in advance of the impending collapse of the bank.

liquidity within France, the timidity of her investors who had made advances abroad, and an early reading of the European financial/economic position caused a wholesale repatriation of capital to France throughout 1930 and early 1931. The withdrawals caused irreparable damage to the international payments system.[1]

America also began to reduce her international financial commitments during 1930. Germany and Eastern Europe suffered a steady loss of funds between December 1930 and June 1931,[2] a large proportion of which flowed to the United States. The withdrawal of short-term capital from abroad was, in part, associated with the large number of commercial bank failures, and the substantial rise in demand for liquidity, which occurred in the United States after the collapse of the stock market in October 1929. 1,345 banks collapsed in 1930 and 687 disappeared in the first six months of 1931.[3] The demand for notes rose almost continuously throughout 1931 mainly for hoarding purposes. In addition, by the third quarter of 1930, foreign-owned deposits were being withdrawn from New York banks on an increasing scale due in part to the fear of further commercial bank closures.[4] American investors in turn, sharply reduced their direct investments abroad and realised some of their previous foreign investments with the fall in profits and dividends of those investments. America absorbed a considerable amount of long-term capital in 1930 and by the first half of 1931 "the outward movement of long-term capital was converted into a net inward movement".[5]

The deterioration in the liquidity of financial institutions in the leading creditor countries was matched if, perhaps, in a less obvious manner, in the debtor countries of, particularly, Europe. The wave of bank failures was, surprisingly, later in the debtor countries than in the important creditor countries. This was partly due to various central banks heavily rediscounting bills for the commercial banks (with a consequent strain on foreign exchange reserves), partly due to a rapid decline in bank liquidity (which was, to some extent, masked by the misleading way of publishing bank balance sheets and even delaying the publication of balance sheets) and, finally, to a sharp rise in industrial bankruptcies which, though imposing capital losses on banks, realised some immediate cash assets. Further, many bank failures occurred throughout Continental Europe from late 1929 onwards, but, in most cases, such banks were absorbed by their stronger brethren.

These techniques simply delayed matters. A large section of Continental commercial banking was being dragged down by the weight of insolvent and depressed industry. The banking system of Europe was disintegrating under pressure of falling economic activity, continued declines in the marketable value of the banks' realisable assets, the consequence of some ill-judged in-

---

[1] The French government attempted to mitigate the effects of the withdrawal of funds from abroad by offering long-term loans to some governments—e.g., to Germany in late 1930, to England in early 1931 and, later, to Austria, "but it was always apparent that political conditions would accompany such loans" and they were, therefore, refused. Bennett, *op. cit.*, p. 93.

[2] For instance, RM 2·9 milliards of foreign-owned funds were withdrawn from Germany between December 1930 and the beginning of May 1931—even though the bulk of French funds had been withdrawn in the last quarter of 1930.

[3] Nearly $1,400 million deposits were, as a consequence, lost; League of Nations, *Memorandum on Commercial Banks 1929-33*, p. 245.

[4] U.S. short-term liabilities amounted to $2,640 million in September 1930; by May 1931 they had fallen to $1,109 million. *Federal Reserve Bulletin*.

[5] W. A. Brown, *op. cit.*, p. 982, also *Survey of Current Business*, 1954 *loc. cit.*

vestments. Unless there occurred a sharp rise in economic activity or a resumption of investment by foreign depositors a credit crisis was inevitable; the financial system had overstretched its liquid resources, at a time when the demand for liquidity, particularly by foreign creditors, was rising sharply throughout the latter half of 1930 and 1931. To meet these demands for liquidity meant deflation and a forced realisation of assets. This policy further weakened the structure of financial institutions and helped destroy foreigners' confidence in those institutions.

Though there was only a small decline in the total of bank deposits in most European countries during 1930, the amount of credit extended to industry increased quite sharply. But one might have expected that with the fall in prices and economic activity the volume of bank credit outstanding would also have fallen. Loans and advances by European banks to industry and bank participations in industry increased on average by between 18 and 20 per cent in 1930.[1] Bank credit was, in fact, becoming frozen. "To sustain ... firms in the difficult period and protect loans already granted, the commercial banks had frequently to grant fresh credits, especially when their relationship with industry was of an intimate character".[2]

Bank funds, which were becoming available through the liquidation of commercial bills and discounts throughout 1930 were, in fact, used to buttress industry. Bank cash ratios on the whole fell and the effective liquidity of Continental banks decreased. This tendency was exacerbated in some countries —outstandingly Germany—which experienced a contraction of credit during the first eighteen months of depression. "From the end of 1929 to May 1931 the contraction in credit was almost exclusively confined to the most liquid part of the banks' portfolio ... security holdings, participations and current account loans to 'affiliated' industries remained substantially unchanged".[3] Similarly in Eastern Europe, the close connection between the banks and agriculture severely limited the possibilities of quick realisation of commercial bank assets. The banks were finding it increasingly difficult even to attempt realisation of their assets: "Owing to their (the banks') close association with industry, they were caught in a vicious circle, every attempt to increase their liquidity by calling in credit involving the freezing of part of their remaining industrial assets and a further fall in the value of their security holdings".[4]

As bank liquidity declined, the possibility of a withdrawal of bank deposits, especially foreign-owned bank deposits, increased with the rise in demand for liquidity abroad. For many European countries, about 25 per cent or over of their banks' liabilities seemed to have been foreign-owned.[5] This was in part a consequence of the closely meshed financial structure of European banking [6]

---

[1] League of Nations, *Commercial Banks 1928–33* (Geneva, 1934) Appendix III, pp. 50–51. For example: "... the big Berlin banks increased their current account advances to customers other than banks by over RM 100 million; an analysis of the cover behind these advances shows that advances covered by securities not quoted on the stock exchange increased by over RM 200 million". *Ibid.*, p. 16. Similar increases were recorded for other European countries.
[2] *Ibid.*, p. 16.
[3] *Ibid.*, p. 114.
[4] *Ibid.*, p. 56.
[5] This would seem to be true, for instance, in Germany, Austria, Hungary, Italy, Poland and Roumania.
[6] For instance, Germany had important bank affiliations in Austria, Holland, Poland and elsewhere in Eastern Europe: cf., P. B. Whale, *Joint Stock Banking in Germany* (London, 1930), pp. 298–301. Most of the largest banks in Poland and Yugoslavia, Latvia, etc. were, in effect,

but also due to the fact that the U.S.A. and Britain had lent heavily to European banks either by granting acceptance credits or by placing deposits in Continental banks.[1] In addition, the great borrowing centres—Berlin and Vienna— re-lent a large percentage of these foreign-owned deposits to the other countries of Central and Eastern Europe.[2] The international liquidity of one banking centre—say, for example, London—depended almost entirely on liquidity in the secondary banking centres, such as Berlin and Vienna. It was in these secondary banking centres, however, that it became most difficult to maintain liquidity owing to the rapid fall in economic activity (which, in effect, determined the liquidity of the banks) and the sudden cessation of the continuous inflow of funds.

The fact that so many important countries experienced internal bank crises during 1930 and 1931 was instrumental in causing the final collapse of the international monetary system. Moreover, the internal bank crises had common causes—the collapse in trade, the fall in stock exchange security values and a rise in liquidity preference. The fortunes of the banks—and so the confidence of the investors—depended increasingly on the fortunes of industry, and there was little in the condition of much European, or even world, industry to allay the general deterioration in confidence. But the magnitude of the crisis and the fact that it turned out to be an international financial crisis was due to the widespread foreign ownership of national bank deposits.

The withdrawal of cash from abroad by the creditor countries, which proceeded over much of 1930 [3] and accelerated sharply in the first half of 1931, had the same effect as a leakage of cash (notes and coin) from an internal banking system which did not include a central bank. There was a multiple destruction of credit.

The various elements of crisis—the sharp fall in agricultural prices; the intractable balance of payments deficits of many debtor countries; the rise in demand for liquidity (and hoarding) in the main creditor countries which was, in part, a consequence of internal banking failures; the rapid decline in the effective liquidity of the debtor countries; the growing weaknesses in the structure of financial institutions under the impact of prolonged economic depression—all had been of increasing importance since the end of 1929.[4]

---

affiliates of important west European banks, cf. *Commercial Banks*, op. cit., pp. 133, 147, 173, 224.

[1] Germany was, of course, by far the biggest borrower, and by 1929/30 about 45 per cent of the total deposits of the big Berlin banks were foreign-owned, and, in addition "more than half the short-term debts of industry and commerce are also due to foreign banks and financial establishments, either in the form of direct debts or acceptance credits", *ibid.*, p. 110.

[2] As did London in relending heavily to Germany and Austria. Austria seems to have held foreign assets equal to nearly 80 per cent of her foreign liabilities—and Germany up to about 40 per cent of her liabilities, *ibid.*, pp. 57 and 111.

[3] London lost £125 million of foreign funds between June 1930 and June 1931, my estimate; German reserves declined from RM 3,000 million to RM 1,400 million over the same period though withdrawals of credits amounted to over RM 3,500 million. W. A. Brown has calculated that "26 Debtor and Periphery Countries" lost gold and foreign exchange reserves of S.F. 1,637 million in 1929; S.F. 2,276 million in 1930 and S.F. 2,568 million in the first half of 1931. Brown, *op. cit.*, table 67.

[4] Periods of deflation are usually characterised by 'excess' supplies of money and relatively increasing liquidity when account is taken of the fall in prices and incomes. The demand to hold money normally falls, at least in nominal terms. The uniqueness of the 1929–31 period lies in the fact that owing to increasingly adverse expectations and weakening of the fabric of financial institutions the demand for liquidity greatly increased, but effective supply fell. During late 1930 and 1931 the loss of confidence in financial institutions induced a further shift from bank

The European crisis of 1931 had already been foreshadowed and was, in part, caused by the 1929–30 crisis in the countries of the southern hemisphere. The basic cause of the 1930 and 1931 crises was the same—the increasing inability of debtor countries to finance their overall deficits (by borrowing or by expanding exports) at current exchange rates and the impossibility of attempting to overcome progressive financial illiquidity by continued income deflation.

The Final Phase

The crisis reached its final phase—the scramble for cash and for gold—between May and September 1931. It came suddenly and unexpectedly.[1] Vienna was the first important international banking centre—but one which was not a great net international short-term debtor—to show the effects of the impact of the decline in economic activity on the viability of financial institutions. Already, by November 1929, the second most important commercial bank in Austria, the *Boden Credit-Anstalt*, had become illiquid and was absorbed by the *Creditanstalt für Handel und Gewerbe*. As a consequence of this merger the *Credit Anstalt* accounted for over two-thirds of the total deposits of Austrian banking. Its assets reflected the decline in trade and security values which occurred between the summer of 1929 and early 1931. When its balance sheet for the year 1930 was published on 11 May 1931 the bank showed losses—which were later shown to have been underestimated—almost equal to its capital.

The publication of the 1930 balance sheet was followed immediately by withdrawals of funds by foreign and domestic depositors even though new capital was subscribed by the Government, the National Bank and Rothschilds. The Government guaranteed, in the first instance, the safety of certain categories of deposits; subsequently it guaranteed all foreign deposits "in return for a two years' Standstill Agreement from foreign creditors". It later guaranteed all deposits. Government guarantee of deposits was not, however, sufficient to stop the run. Indeed, the proposal to negotiate Standstill Agreements on Austria's foreign debt weakened confidence in the currency—confidence in the banking system was already weak—and precipitated the withdrawal of capital from Austria. Withdrawals of deposits and capital continued for the remainder of 1931.[2]

For the first time, considerations regarding both the safety (liquidity) and automatic convertibility (transferability) of funds had to be taken into account when deciding to withdraw capital from foreign centres. The possibility—either through Standstill Agreements, exchange control or currency depreciation—that automatic transferability of currencies might be endangered turned the run into a panic which affected both domestic and foreign depositors. The panic spread from Austria to Germany and hence to the rest of Eastern Europe and, finally, England, not only because the serious losses incurred by the *Credit*

---

deposits and near-money into bank notes. These bank notes in turn (in contrast to bank deposit money) needed to be fully covered with central bank holdings of gold and/or foreign exchange.

[1] Montagu Norman felt as late as the third week of April that "there was as yet no urgent sense of crisis" Clay, *op. cit.*, p. 375.

[2] The League of Nations, *Commercial Banks, 1925–33*, (Geneva, 1934) estimated that between 700–900 million schillings were withdrawn between May and December 1931, of which nearly 50 per cent was Austrian capital. p. 18. Bennett's estimate of an outflow of $56 million in May 1931 is almost certainly too high. *op. cit.*, p. 117.

Anstalt had endangered the liquidity of other European banks but also because of the fear that, in order to safeguard domestic financial institutions various national monetary authorities would restrict the withdrawal of deposits in terms of foreign currencies. This fear quickly hardened into a belief that because many European countries had overborrowed, these countries were, in fact, in no position to repay lenders.

The shock to confidence resulting from the illiquid state of the *Credit Anstalt* weakened confidence in all the European banks. Germany was especially vulnerable to a withdrawal of short-term credits. Germany had, in fact, experienced a major outflow of foreign funds following the elections of September 1930. Though the outflow of funds had virtually ceased by the early months of 1931, the international political crisis which arose following the announcement (21 March 1931) that Germany and Austria intended to form a customs union (to which France was violently opposed) in addition to the acute problem of a budget deficit (mid-April) and the prevalent rumour that Germany was soon going to suspend Reparation payments, further weakened confidence in Germany. She experienced a steady outflow of funds—some of which reflected a flight of domestic capital—from the end of March onwards.

The *Credit Anstalt* crisis made matters worse in the sense that it directly increased the demand for liquidity in Germany and also led to a withdrawal of Austrian balances held in Germany, as well as inducing an outflow of German funds.[1] It worsened, but did not directly cause, the German financial crisis. As Benett has pointed out "The Germans seemed to be making the worst of their situation, and their groans did not go unheard: the foreign creditors began to wonder about the security of their loans".[2] From the last week of May, a wholesale flight of funds occurred as the internal political and economic (especially budgetary) situations worsened, and also as it became clear that the amount of help Germany was likely to receive from outside was limited. Up to the end of June, however, the crisis could be regarded as another crisis of confidence which Germany had periodically experienced throughout the 'twenties and which she had, in part, caused by her own actions.[3]

The opening days of July, however, mark the turning point of the crisis. The impact of the depression—in the form of the collapse of the *Norddeutsche Wollkämmerei* endangered the solvency of two of the big Berlin banks. "The flight of capital was accentuated and the *Reichsbank* steadily lost gold".[4] The *Darmstädter und Nationalbank (Danat)* collapsed on 13 July 1931 and all banks were closed the following day. The internal banking system succumbed to the double weight of economic depression, which had caused a heavy depreciation of bank assets, and of having to meet demands for liquidity which were, in part, a consequence of that economic collapse. The *Reichsbank* immediately (14 July 1931) decided that all foreign exchange dealings must be centralised

---

[1] Bennett argues that the withdrawal of balances by foreign creditors "were prefaced by the flight of Austrian and German capital". *op. cit.*, p. 117. See also League of Nations, *Commercial Banks, 1925–33*, esp. p. 112.
[2] *Ibid.*
[3] As Bennett remarks: "foreign policy itself had precipitated a financial upheaval". *Ibid.*, p. 237. Mr. Norman commented on 13 June 1931 "The immediate thing was to get through the present Austrian crisis ... the difficulties of the German Government ... was a less urgent problem. Germany had already gone through two or three financial crises which would have been fatal to any other country ... and she might well get through again". *Documents on British Foreign Policy, op. cit.*, p. 74.
[4] *Commercial Banks*, op. cit. p. 112.

with it, and that foreign exchange would have to be rationed "to ensure that they *(devisen)* were used for 'economically justified purposes'".[1] Standstill Agreements on the repayment of creditors were arranged in late July, agreed in August and became effective for six months after 1 September 1931.

The collapse of the German banking system—with bank liabilities of foreign origin of at least RM 6 milliard immobilised—had grave repercussions throughout Europe.[2] Banks in Central and Eastern Europe experienced runs and the monetary authorities there were forced to impose exchange controls and to negotiate Standstill Agreements with foreign creditors.[3] There was no longer the assurance of automatic transferability of funds from many European countries. The main effect of the German collapse was felt in London, which was, at that time, the world's most important short-term money market.

Very broadly, the London crisis can be regarded as a crisis of confidence, firstly in the liquidity and solvency of important British financial institutions; and secondly, in the convertibility of assets into gold at a fixed rate of exchange. The fact that doubts arose about both institutional liquidity and convertibility explains the severity of the crisis. London had experienced a rising foreign demand for liquidity ever since the Autumn of 1930 in connection with the growing European monetary difficulties. Such pressure was enormously increased after the beginning of June 1931. French demands for funds from London increased rapidly after 8 June 1931, which followed the hesitant French acceptance of the terms of the Hoover one-year Moratorium on payments of war debts and reparations. Further, the sterling exchanges suddenly broke on 15/16 July—two days after the publication of the Report of the Macmillan Committee on Finance and Industry and also immediately after the collapse of the German banking system. The chief significance to foreigners of the Macmillan Report was that it showed, for the first time, London's international short-term debtor position. This had the same effect as a bank, when under pressure, publicising the extent of its weaknesses, not as it ought to announce its position of strength. In addition, the closure of the German banks on 13/14 July 1931 immobilised German bank liabilities and British banks were widely believed to have been heavily involved in granting acceptances to German banks. These acceptances [4] and the bulk of other British short-term assets in Europe had become frozen, and had in some cases been converted into liabilities. This seriously impaired the liquidity of some British banking institutions—particularly those banks which, like the merchant banks, depended heavily on foreign deposits. Substantial withdrawals of funds from London followed the locking up of British assets in Europe.[5] Withdrawals increased as it became apparent that France would not participate in an international credit to Germany, except on political conditions. There was, as a result, little possibility of quickly realising British short-term investments in Germany.[6] Pressure was increased further as various countries—the

---

[1] *Ibid.*

[2] The short-term foreign liabilities of industrialists, local authorities, etc., were also estimated at RM 6 milliard. *Commercial Banks, op. cit.*, p. 113.

[3] Cf. *ibid.*, pp. 111, 133, 147, 172-3, 224.

[4] Of which about £70 million was outstanding in Germany, though total British short-term assets in Germany and central Europe were probably in excess of £120 million.

[5] Cf. Clay, *op. cit.*, p. 383, P. Einzig, *The Tragedy of the Pound* (London, 1932), esp. pp. 66-67, League of Nations *Commercial Banks, op. cit.*, p. 208.

[6] *The Times*, 16 July 1931, pointed out "the refusal of France to participate in an international credit to Germany, except on political conditions which Dr. Bruning is unable to accept,

THE 1931 FINANCIAL CRISIS

U.S.A. and, especially, the smaller countries of Europe—withdrew funds from various debtor countries in sterling and then sold the sterling in London for gold, dollars or francs, and also sold sterling securities in London.

The immediate break of the sterling exchanges can, then, be directly attributed to the Continental financial crisis. The extent and severity of the crisis can, however, be explained only with reference to the growing awareness of the long-run weaknesses of London as an international banking centre, taken in conjunction with a rapid decline in confidence in London's ability or willingness to maintain the existing parity of sterling.

Ever since the end of 1928 London had become increasingly involved in the growing international monetary difficulties of the underdeveloped areas, as well as those of Europe. London had financed the trading deficits of the Sterling Area, extended short-term aid to South America and, at the same time, financed the foreign liquidation of its own very substantial short-term liabilities. This continuous outflow of funds from late 1928 onwards imposed a considerable strain on London's liquid resources. The prolonged and intensified depression in the outer Sterling Area was leading to a severe financial crisis. By April 1930 both Australia and New Zealand had effectively devalued their currency *vis-à-vis* sterling, and a break-up of the post-1925 sterling exchange system was not inconceivable. This could have had disastrous effects in the outer Sterling Area on the liquidity—and transferability—of London assets.

There was, in addition, the further problem that the economic recovery in Britain after 1921 had been distressingly incomplete and this seriously weakened foreigners' confidence in the viability of the British economy. Of all the major powers, her economic progress had been the least impressive. It was becoming increasingly accepted that one reason—if not the most important reason—was an overvaluation of sterling. There was, in addition, widespread belief that the gold standard and 'dear money' caused unemployment in the 1920's.[1] It was also becoming obvious that as world costs and prices were falling, the degree of overvaluation of sterling, and consequent pressure on the British economy, was tending to increase. The long-run decline in confidence in the British economy was never taken fully into account in determining economic policy and it accounts partially for the relative ineffectiveness of long-run policy at that time.

All this was becoming apparent in a most significant manner—namely that the resources of the London money and capital market were becoming strained, and were, in fact, inadequate to meet world demands for liquidity.[2] This could be interpreted in the sense that London had overcommitted its current resources and that the liquidity of the 'bank' was low.

From mid-1930 onwards there was, then, for a variety of reasons, increasing nervousness about the international position of London and the strength of sterling. However, from the beginning of 1931, this nervousness was increased by a series of internal events which served to emphasise London's long-run weaknesses. Firstly, the position of the Government was not strong and its continuance in power appeared to be in some doubt. Political instability was

---

has brought about a situation which threatens the financial stability of almost every country in Europe".

[1] R. S. Sayers, *Central Banking After Bagehot* (London, 1957), pp. 78-9.
[2] Clay, *op. cit.*, p. 371.

an unusual phenomenon in England.¹ A consequence of the relatively weak and split-minded Government was the inconsequential budget of the Spring of 1931 which affected foreign opinion adversely. A budget deficit was virtually a certainty and this gave substance to the charge that Government policy was 'irresponsible'. This budget led to further political instability— and to a change of government—at the height of the crisis in August 1931. Further, Bank of England policy was generally weak and passive throughout the crisis and this again tended to exaggerate the loss of confidence (interest rates were falling, and Bank Rate was reduced to 2½ per cent as late as May 1931).²

The British position was further weakened by the publication of the Macmillan Report (on Finance and Industry) at the time of the collapse of the German banking system and the May Report (on National Expenditure) at the height of the crisis. Both Reports—but especially the May Report, which produced grossly distorted figures regarding the effective budget deficit— tended to make the British economic situation seem rather worse than was the case, and, to that extent, further weakened confidence in London.³

The final blow came with the locking up of British assets in Europe. With London no longer impregnably sound—and becoming less sound with the development of the political crisis, the need to borrow heavily from the U.S.A. and France, and the consequences of the September budget—the whole European financial system seemed to be in imminent collapse. Liquidation, virtually regardless of cost, was the order of the day. The financial crisis—the roots of which are to be found in the economic collapse of the primary producing countries of the world, the intensification of world deflationary forces after the Autumn of 1929, and the progressive deterioraton in the liquidity of national banking systems which had disastrous effects both internationally and internally— reached its climax on 21 September 1931 when the Bank of England was relieved of its obligation to sell gold at a fixed statutory price.

The age of the gold standard was over. Many Continental Governments imposed moratoria on debt repayments and on international capital movements

---

¹ Cf. R. Bassett, *1931 Political Crisis* (London, 1958), esp. p. 44.

² It is, perhaps, impossible to come to any definite conclusions regarding British interest rate policy in the 1931 crisis. The case for a policy of raising interest rates from early 1931 rests on the belief that higher rates might well have avoided later trouble. Funds had been draining out of London from the middle of 1930, and it was contrary to Bank of England tradition to acquiesce in such a drain without increasing rates of interest. The effects of an early rise in rates might have been twofold. Firstly, it might have checked the foreign demand for finance in London, or even diverted borrowing to other centres. Secondly, higher—or rising—interest rates might have had important confidence and incentive effects which might have attracted foreign funds to, and retained existing funds in, London. In any case, an attempt might have been made to try and mobilise world liquidity relatively early in the European crisis. An increase in rates after the crisis had gained momentum had little effect in restoring confidence or mobilising extra liquidity. See my article: *Economic History Review, loc. cit.* esp. pp. 522–5.

³ In this respect, the publication of these Reports played much the same role as the publication of the Berlin Manifesto of June 1931 which, as Bennett has concluded"... whatever the manifesto was intended to do, its effect on German credit abroad was likely to be disastrous", *op. cit.*, p. 128. Whilst admitting that the 1931 crisis was partly due to our own ineptness at international public relations, Sir Roy Harrod seems to go much too far when he argues that: "The collapse of the gold standard in 1931 was not ... the inevitable, or even the avoidable, consequence of the chain of events since 1925 or of those *specifically related to the world slump*. It was simply that we British talked the world into it". (My italics) *Policy Against Inflation*. (London, 1958) p. 47, also pp. 43–47 and 49.

but maintained their exchange rates. Internal liquidation was attempted by draconian budgetary policies, the political consequences of which were later seen to have been disastrous. In Britain, on the other hand, an attempt was made to achieve the substance of recovery rather than chase the shadow of economic stability in the form of rigid exchange rates.

The University, Hull.   DAVID WILLIAMS

Britain's financial difficulties in recent years lend new interest to the 1931 financial crisis, which had such a traumatic effect on British economic history between the wars. The following article by Mr Moggridge, Fellow of Clare College, Cambridge, takes a fresh look at the 1931 crisis in the light of Britain's international experience in the 1960s. Mr Moggridge is the author of The Return to Gold 1925 *and is currently engaged on an historical study of British financial policy.*

D. E. MOGGRIDGE

THE 1931 FINANCIAL CRISIS—A NEW VIEW

Thirty-nine years ago this month, Britain was in the midst of one of the most severe balance-of-payments crises in her history. During the crisis, which eventually ended in the suspension of gold convertibility on September 21, 1931, the authorities sold over £200 millions of owned or borrowed gold and foreign exchange in their attempt to defend the parity of $4·86. If one converts this sum to current prices and foreign exchange equivalents, it compares well with the size of modern support operations as it exceeds £1,000 millions. Thus even by recent standards, it was a massive crisis.

Most historical treatments of the 1931 crisis have concentrated on its political repercussions—on the fall of the Second Labour Government, the formation of the National Government and the charges that it was a 'bankers' ramp' which brought the latter to power—or on the economic events of the summer months surrounding the final stages of the crisis. They have generally ignored the underlying causes of the crisis and official 'attempts' to deal with it, in its early stages, as a balance-of-payments problem. Many contemporary observers, such as Mr Samuel Brittan in his excellent book *Steering the Economy*, have made a point of saying that the years 1966–67 were not comparable to 1931, as in these years Britain suffered from a balance-of-payments problem rather than a financial crisis. This article attempts to look at the events of the summer of 1931 in the broader context of Britain's international economic position at the time. This re-examination suggests that the international turmoil of the summer of 1931 only brought matters to a head and that even if it had not occurred, the underlying balance-of-payments trends of the time would probably have forced Britain from gold at some stage during 1931–32, given the policy decisions of the authorities. In short, I will suggest that examining 1931 in a broader context is as rewarding as looking at the events of November 1967 in the light of Britain's international position in the years after 1960.

Let us look first at the evolution of Britain's international position in the years before 1931. In 1925, in an heroic but fundamentally misguided attempt

TABLE
UNITED KINGDOM BALANCE OF PAYMENTS ON CURRENT ACCOUNT (1924–31)

(£m)	1924	1925	1929	1930	1931 (estimate)	1931 (actual)
Visible Trade						
Exports of UK goods	+801	+773	+729	+571	—	+391
Retained Imports	−1,137	−1,167	−1,111	−958	—	−797
Balance of Trade	−336	−394	−382	−387	−387	−406
Invisible Trade						
Shipping (net)	+140	+124	+130	+105	+ 85–90	+ 80
Investment Income (net)	+220	+250	+250	+220	+150–180	+170
Short interest and commissions (net)	+ 60	+ 60	+ 65	+ 55	+ 35–45	+ 30
Other Private Invisibles (net)	+ 15	+ 15	+ 15	+ 15	+ 10	+ 10
Government Transactions (net)	− 25	− 11	+ 24	+ 19	+ 19	+ 14
Balance of Invisibles	+410	+438	+484	+414	+299–344	+304
Current Account Balance	+ 74	+ 44	+102	+ 27	− 88–43	−102

Sources: *Board of Trade Journal*
1931 estimates from Public Record Office, Cab. 58/18, Economic Advisory Council, Committee on Economic Information, Provisional Board of Trade Estimates of Changes in the Balance of Trade, 3 September, 1931; Balance of Trade, Memorandum by the Board of Trade, 21 September, 1931.

to ignore the results of World War I on her international position, Britain returned to gold at the pre-war parity of $4·86. In the circumstances, given official policy goals, this parity overvalued sterling by a minimum of 10 per cent. During the years after 1925, particularly after the General Strike of 1926, official policy did nothing fundamental to remove this overvaluation, although by a variety of palliative measures it limited its domestic impact on occasion. At the same time price, productivity and exchange rate developments in Britain and abroad, if anything increased the overvaluation. However, an expanding volume of world trade enabled British exports to grow roughly in line with the imports drawn in by rising British incomes and increased invisible earnings, as did reparations receipts on the Government account. Meanwhile foreigners, spurred on by high returns and occasional official pressure, increased their sterling balances. As a result, the Bank of England saw its gold and hidden foreign exchange reserves rise in 14 of the 19 quarters between March 1925 and December 1929. Nevertheless, the situation was precarious even during this period, and on more than one occasion Montagu Norman, Governor of the Bank of England, believed the parity of $4·86 to be sufficiently threatened by current developments to warn *foreign* central bankers that Britain might be forced from gold.

Effect of the slump on invisibles

However, with the collapse of international prices and production after 1928–29, this already precarious position became more dangerous. The slump did not greatly affect the balance of trade, as falling import prices offset the combined effects of declining British competitiveness and income and tariff-induced falls in overseas demand for British goods. But the decline in the volume of international trade, coupled with the effects of the slump on the earnings of overseas companies wreaked havoc with the invisibles position, as outlined in the Table. Thus even before the financial crisis, Britain's 1929 current account surplus was falling away into serious deficit and official observers expected further deterioration, on unchanged policies, as long as the slump continued.

Pressures from abroad

By itself, a developing current account deficit might not have alarmed the authorities in some circumstances. In 1926, Britain had run up a current account deficit of £14 millions and allowed £85 millions in new long-term foreign lending, and yet gained £23 millions in gold and foreign exchange reserves. However, in 1926 the countries making up what was to become the overseas sterling area had been in balance-of-payments surplus and had placed their increased balances in London, as had those withdrawing capital from France and others attracted by the high yields and liquidity offered by London investments. By contrast, in 1930-31 the proto-overseas sterling area countries were themselves in severe balance-of-payments difficulties and were reducing their sterling balances, which when transferred to foreigners were often taken from London in gold. In addition the French government was drawing on its large London funds to meet a budget deficit, French banks were drawing down their sterling secondary reserves to increase their cash reserves and allow for deposit and currency expansion, and as interest rates fell to low levels, foreigners, often anticipating liquidity problems at home, found it prudent to either reduce their sterling balances or, at best, not to increase them. Thus, even without any abnormal international events, Britain faced a substantial balance-of-payments problem in 1931 in very unfavourable circumstances—a problem that would grow progressively worse as the slump continued.

To meet this potential deficit, in so far as Britain was unable to attract funds from abroad by raising interest rates, the Bank had gold reserves of roughly £150 millions, plus exchange reserves, largely hidden from the Treasury, of roughly £30 millions. However, not all of this £180 millions was available for exchange defence, as over £100 millions was needed to cover the domestic note issue and as only a small part of this, say one third, might be released from this rôle by agreement with the Treasury. In addition, the Bank might borrow from foreign central banks, as she had done in 1927, 1929 and 1930, but these banks were becoming less willing to lend and the Bank of England less willing to borrow. At the roots of this reduced willingness lay the belief, expressed by one of the Bank's advisers in 1930, that such loans 'merely postpon[ed] the setting in motion of the forces which will correct the underlying situation ... [and] foster[ed] the willingness of England to take her difficulties sitting down, instead of standing against them'. Finally, as in 1925, the Government of the day could arrange to borrow abroad.

Now, given these underlying conditions, did the authorities recognize that, at the least, the potential for a crisis existed? The answer must be a qualified yes. During a series of discussions with French Treasury representatives early in 1931, the British officials involved came to admit that at the roots of British gold losses to France in 1930 lay a British payments problem rather than technical defects in French financial institutions, the original British position. However, there was a tendency in Treasury circles to argue that the onus for adjustment lay on France and that Britain should do nothing.* Governor

---

* At this time the Treasury rejected, on political grounds, the offer of a French loan to fund French sterling balances and increase Britain's reserves. Governor Norman, while admitting that he would have welcomed the assistance, accepted this decision.

Norman took a somewhat different line and suggested that

> the main troubles of this country were due to the defects of our financial policy during the past few years and the consequent lack of confidence in British Government securities and in sterling. Our exchange was depreciated not only with France but with all foreign centres and he [Norman] felt the French were right in the emphasis which they threw on the lack of confidence... The mistrust of sterling had got to such a point that some foreigners were now [February 1931] taking out credits in sterling with a view to repaying them ultimately on a cheaper basis.

Such a tone did not suggest inaction was the best policy, particularly when it was echoed by members of the Prime Minister's Economic Advisory Council.

Such warnings, plus business and political unease over the size of the Budget deficit, seem to have affected the Treasury, for when Sir Richard Hopkins presented the Treasury's evidence to the Royal Commission on Unemployment Insurance, he stressed in his oral evidence the impact of an unbalanced budget on foreign confidence during 'a period of economic stress and strain' in Britain, given her international connections. Moreover, during the early spring of 1931, Hopkins went so far as to ask R. G. Hawtrey, the Treasury's Director of Financial Enquiries, to make a case for defending the existing parity. Hawtrey refused. Finally, when the Government, under Opposition pressure, set up a Committee under Sir George May to recommend means of reducing public expenditure, the Chancellor specifically mentioned the impact of the current situation on Britain's international position.

Decision to deflate

However, recognizing the existence of a problem does not solve it. In the spring of 1931 there were four possible solutions to the payments problem available to the authorities: co-ordinated international reflation, devaluation, protection and domestic deflation. International reflationary collaboration, politically the most difficult to achieve quickly in any case, was blocked by France and America, as the fate of Governor Norman's proposals to stimulate international investment through an institution similar to the present World Bank indicated. Devaluation, despite Hawtrey and Ernest Bevin, was ruled completely out of court in official discussions*. As a deliberate act of policy to solve a balance-of-payments problem, it had never found use before and it had no public support from bankers, civil servants or economists. In fact, except by Bevin, devaluation was never seriously discussed in the press or recommended to a Minister until after the crisis broke in July, when Keynes privately advised the Prime Minister that a departure from $4·86 was inevitable and that the Government should immediately devalue by 25 per cent and invite the Empire and other iterested countries to join Britain in a currency bloc at this rate. Protection, although favoured by the Conservatives, was anathema to the Chancellor, whose wife returned Keynes' public tariff/subsidy proposals unread and who, at the height of the crisis, when outvoted on the issue in a Cabinet committee, stopped action by a threat of resignation. Thus, by elimination, the authorities were left with the option of deflation, at a time when unemployment exceeded 20 per cent, and when to achieve a reduction of, say, £60 millions in imports national income would have to fall by at least £200 millions (employment by 1 million or another 10 per cent).

This often implicit acceptance of the need for deflation accorded well with contemporary preoccupations with an unbalanced budget. However, it created severe strains within the Government and the Labour party, largely because

---

* In this connection it is interesting to note that when presented with the alternatives of protection or devaluation during the private discussions of the Macmillan Committee, Lord Bradbury, formerly of the Treasury, and Cecil Lubbock, formerly Deputy Governor of the Bank, stated that they would prefer devaluation, if the situation required such a choice.

the Government's parliamentary position and the public's current preoccupations made deflation synonymous with cuts in social expenditure rather than increases in taxation. Throughout the spring of 1931 the Government temporized, telling of future disasters while merely attempting to hold the existing position until the autumn, when armed with the relevant committee reports it might do later what it couldn't do then. Thus Governor Norman was perfectly correct when he cabled Governor Harrison of the Federal Reserve Bank of New York in February 'The future here depends more on politics than on finance . . . '. That was still the position when Britain's difficulties were compounded by an international liquidity crisis.

Demands on the reserves

The crisis began with the announcement of the difficulties of the Credit Anstalt of Vienna on May 11, which partially resulted from politically inspired French withdrawals. In such a situation, particularly in a slump which had already produced some banking problems in France and America, banks and individuals in other countries, finding some of their supposedly liquid assets frozen, moved to improve their positions by calling funds from other banks or financial centres, starting with those most likely to be in future difficulties. Of course, this simply transferred pressures to other banks or countries where further failures or payments moratoria increased desires for liquidity. In these conditions, it was almost inevitable, as financial crises swept Germany and Central Europe, that London, the premier money market of Europe, where Dutch, Belgian, French and Swiss banks kept much of their liquid reserves would be subject to demands for funds eventually. This at a time when Britain's overall international position called for fresh *inflows* of funds to finance a balance-of-payments deficit and when sterling had been under a cloud for over six months.

This explains the violence of the first demands on Britain's official reserves in mid-July. In the two weeks ending July 29 she lost one quarter of her official reserves. At this point, firm in the belief that any action could wait until Parliament reassembled in October, the Government, in a masterpiece of mistiming, released the *Report* of the May Committee. This *Report*, which Sir Richard Hopkins admitted showed 'no mercy', painted the budgetary picture in the blackest possible terms and recommended large, politically impossible cuts in unemployment expenditure. At the same time, the Government refused to take any steps to secure medium term credits to support sterling. Thus the Bank was forced to continue its exchange defence with very short-term central bank credits of $250 millions while it pressed the Government to pursue a severe retrenchment programme. In its efforts to persuade the Government of the gravity of the situation, the Bank went so far as to withdraw its support from the franc exchange for one day, August 4, when the rate broke badly and there were rumours that the Bank of France would not support sterling until Governor Norman resigned, hardly the best thing for confidence. It also pressed its views on the Government by letters and by word of mouth as its loans dribbled away in exchange support. Moreover, as a result of an unexplained change in its operating policies in exchange markets, the extent of the Bank's support, the very existence of which was unknown during its extensive previous operations in 1928–29, was known by the market each day to the extent that *The Times* of August 24 could announce within $1 million how much of the credits had found use. Meanwhile the Cabinet, finally recalled in haste to consider the May *Report*, struggled over a retrenchment policy suitable for backing additional open market loans in New York and Paris and eventually disintegrated. The decisions of the new National Government on economies came just in time as the Bank had exhausted its credits before the new loans of $400 millions were announced. However, despite the economies, these loans proved difficult to raise as operations normally taking weeks were compressed into two or three days, with over 100 banks and finance houses involved in New York alone. As J. P. Morgan and Company reported to the Treasury, conditions were so difficult that 'the amount of declinations from possible participants whom we invited was measurably greater than any other similar operation that we have ever conducted'. This did not bode well for the future.

With the new credits in hand and with all of the London clearing banks brought in to its operations to mask the extent of official support, the Bank continued to defend sterling. It even went so far as to drive the rate up in an attempt to increase confidence. Finally a 'mutiny' in the Atlantic fleet, election rumours and fresh financial crises and bank failures on the Continent brought new demands on London and exhausted the credits on Saturday, September 19. On Monday, September 21, the Gold Standard (Amendment) Act suspended gold convertibility, and, within days, officials, with apparent relief, began arguing as to what would be the best future rate for sterling. Discussions centred on the range $3·40–$4·10. Within three months, the market had settled on $3·40, 30 per cent below $4·86.

Underlying weakness

Now, what conclusions can one draw from this story. First one must accept that at the bottom of Britain's 1931 difficulties lay a weakened international financial position and a large payments deficit, both of which stemmed from previous policy decisions and current economic conditions. Second, the events of August and September 1931 were, to a considerable extent, dependent on the decisions of the authorities as to the means of dealing with the underlying problems at hand and the official refusal to carry out these decisions. This unwillingness to carry out the decisions of the early part of the year is all the more remarkable, when one realizes that the authorities had known of the probability of a German collapse for over a year and had recognized even earlier that such a collapse would result in heavy demands for funds from London which might, *in themselves*, drive Britain from gold. In this, as in other areas, Snowden's comment of November 1930 was, '[We] can do nothing now but wait'. This fatalistic policy of drift left the authorities in the position where a crisis and the need to borrow reserves, on the open market, would force them to impose a hasty deflation and to appear to be submitting to the demands of 'bankers', a difficult situation for a Labour Government at the best of times, without any prospect of achieving their goal, staying on gold. Finally, even if the authorities had acted earlier to cure the deficit or if the Conservatives had been in power and had deflated and introduced protection, it is very much an open question whether Britain would have remained on gold, even without a liquidity crisis, for the continuing slump would have probably required another series of measures to deal with the further deterioration occurring the next year. In fact, perhaps one of the saddest aspects of the episode was that a major political party was condemned to the political wilderness for attempting the impossible: removing the legacy of 1925 and countering the effects of depression on the balance-of-payments by deflation.

[6]

EHSAN U. CHOUDHRI
LEVIS A. KOCHIN*

The Exchange Rate and the International Transmission of Business Cycle Disturbances

Some Evidence from the Great Depression

1. INTRODUCTION

ADVOCATES OF THE FLEXIBLE EXCHANGE RATE SYSTEM have often claimed that this financial system insulates an economy from foreign business cycle disturbances. This claim has been viewed lately with considerable skepticism. Many leading economists have argued that while flexible exchange rates enable a country to independently determine (the rate of growth of) its money supply, they will not prevent foreign disturbances from affecting the demand for real cash balances through channels such as capital flows, currency substitution, or the wage-price setting process. Domestic output and prices, thus, will not be much more independent of foreign output and prices under flexible exchange rates.[1]

The theoretical arguments purporting that the insulation powers of the flexible exchange rate are limited have found empirical support in the recent experience in which output and price fluctuations have continued to be related among many coun-

---

*We would like to thank John Makin, Michael Bordo, David Laidler, and Michael Parkin for helpful comments on an earlier draft of this paper. We are also grateful to Bill Haraf for research assistance.

[1]The argument that foreign disturbances would be transmitted under flexible exchange rates via capital flows goes back to Mundell [10] and Fleming [5]. This point has also been emphasized by Cooper [2], Mussa [11], and Dornbusch and Krugman [4]. The implications of currency substitution have been discussed by Calvo and Rodriguez [1] and Miles [9]. Also, see Laidler [8] and Hamada and Sakurai [7], who use a Phillips curve type price setting mechanism to show that even in absence of capital flows, domestic and foreign outputs as well as prices could be interdependent under flexible rates.

EHSAN U. CHOUDHRI *is associate professor of economics, Carleton University.* LEVIS A. KOCHIN *is associate professor of economics, University of Washington.*

tries, even after the general abandonment of the fixed exchange rate system in the 1970s. However, most countries have not pursued independent monetary policies recently but rather have operated on the mixed system of managed float. It is, therefore, possible that the synchronous movements in output and prices across countries represent similar monetary policy behavior rather than a failure in the insulation capabilities of the flexible exchange rate system.

In this paper we present some evidence on this issue that is drawn from the experience of a number of European countries during the Great Depression. Our evidence deals only with small countries. From the point of view of small countries, the Great Depression was an external disturbance independent of domestic conditions in these countries. Thus, by focusing on small countries, we highlight the importance of the exchange rate system in the transmission of exogenous business cycle disturbances from abroad.

The centerpiece of our evidence is Spain, which, during the Great Depression, operated on flexible exchange rates combined with fairly stable monetary conditions while most of the world was committed to the gold standard. A comparison of Spanish experience in this period with the gold-standard countries provides a striking historical experiment on the insulation capabilities of the flexible exchange rate system. Some further evidence on this question is provided by the experience of some Scandinavian countries that started out on the gold standard but allowed their exchange rate to adjust in the middle of the depression.

The rest of the paper is organized as follows. In section 2, we discuss our sample of countries and present some background information on the operation of different exchange rate regimes. In section 3, we contrast the output and price behavior of different exchange rate regimes to test the insulation issue. The results are summarized in section 4.

2. THREE DIFFERENT CURRENCY EXPERIENCES DURING THE GREAT DEPRESSION

To examine the role of the exchange rate in the transmission of the Great Depression, we compare a number of small European countries that operated under different exchange rate regimes during the depression.[2] In choosing our sample, we have included all the small European countries for which output and price data was readily available and that did not use extensive exchange controls during the period in question.[3]

Our sample includes eight countries. In this sample, the most interesting case, for our purpose, is that of Spain, which remained on flexible exchange rates throughout the Great Depression. The flexible exchange rate system was not new to Spain. The Spanish peseta had been floating since several decades before the First World

---

[2] To minimize the possible influence of geographical differences, we considered only European countries.

[3] Our sample was selected from League of Nations, *Monetary Review* (1937), which provides a comprehensive discussion of the exchange rate policies pursued by each country during the Depression period. Excluding large countries (U.K., France, and Germany) as well as those where exchange transactions were restricted (see Table 3, p. 17 of the *Monetary Review*), we picked all the European countries for which output and price data was available from League of Nations, *Statistical Yearbook*.

War. After the war, several other countries also experimented with flexible exchange rates for short periods but all of these countries reverted to the gold standard by the late 1920s. Thus, at the onset of the Great Depression, Spain was the only major country operating on a flexible exchange rate system. During the depression, while Spain went through several changes in its government, the Spanish economy was largely unaffected by political turmoil until the Civil War several years later. The Spanish peseta remained flexible until March of 1934. (For a further discussion of the Spanish monetary experience see [3].)

Next, our sample includes four countries; the Netherlands, Belgium, Italy, and Poland, which stayed on the gold standard throughout the depression period. All of these countries except the Netherlands had experienced extreme price inflation and exchange rate depreciation in the 1920s, and this was perhaps an important consideration in their decision to keep their currencies pegged to gold [12, p. 357]. Whatever their motivation, these countries remained on unrestricted gold standard at their initial gold parities until 1935–36.

Finally, the three remaining countries in our sample are Denmark, Finland, and Norway. These three Scandinavian countries were on the gold standard as the Great Depression began. However, they suspended the gold standard soon after the United Kingdom decided to leave the gold standard in September of 1931. From this date up to January of 1933, the currencies of these countries were allowed to fluctuate more or less independently of sterling, and it was not until February of 1933 that the values of these currencies were again pegged to sterling.[4]

Figure 1 shows the behavior of the exchange rate (in terms of U.S. dollars) and money supply during 1928–33 in the three exchange rate regimes discussed above.[5] As the figure shows, the price of the Spanish peseta fell dramatically in this period, registering a depreciation of over 50 percent by 1932. The Spanish money supply behavior, on the other hand, remained reasonably stable except in the year 1931 when there was a sizable decrease in the money stock.[6] In a sharp contrast, the gold countries maintained fixed exchange rates with the United States up to 1932 (the U.S. dollar price of gold appreciated in 1933 as the U.S. left the gold standard in that year), but experienced a sustained decline in their money stock. The figure also shows that the experience of the Scandinavian countries falls in between Spain and the gold countries. The price of the Scandinavian currencies fell in 1931–32 but not as much as that of the peseta. The money supply also declined in these countries, but the decrease was smaller than that of the gold countries.

---

[4] Even in the floating period, the prices of Scandinavian currencies in terms of sterling did not fluctuate much (the range of variation was less than 10 percent).

[5] The data on exchange rates and money supplies (Fig. 1) and on industrial production and wholesale price indexes (Fig. 2 and Table 2) is from League of Nations, *Statistical Yearbook* (various issues). The money supply represents end-of-year data on notes plus commercial bank deposits (the definition of bank deposits varies from one country to another). The data on the share of manufactured exports and manufacturing production per head (Table 1) relates to the 1926–29 period and is from League of Nations, *Industrialization and Foreign Trade* (1945). As monthly (or quarterly) data was not available for some of the series, we present only annual data.

[6] The decrease in Spanish money supply reflects the effect of the European banking crisis that led to large-scale withdrawals of commercial bank deposits. The impact of the crisis on Spanish banks was most severe in the second and third quarters of 1931. For further details, see League of Nations, *Commercial Banking*, 1929–34.

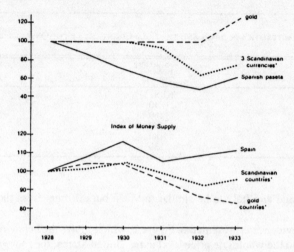

Fig. 1. The Behavior of Exchange Rates (Price in Terms of U.S. Dollars) and Money Supplies in the Three Exchange Rate Regimes (*Indicates an Unweighted Average)

3. THE TRANSMISSION OF THE GREAT DEPRESSION UNDER DIFFERENT EXCHANGE RATE REGIMES

A. Spain versus the Gold Countries

To highlight the difference between the flexible and fixed exchange rate systems, we begin this section by comparing the Great Depression experience of Spain with that of the gold countries. If flexible exchange rates insulate an economy from foreign disturbances, we would expect to observe that while output and prices fell in the gold countries during the Great Depression, Spanish output and prices remained unchanged in this period. On the other hand, if little or no insulation is available from the flexible exchange rate system, we would not expect to see much difference in the behavior of output and prices between Spain and the gold countries.

During the period in question, Spain was largely a rural economy with a small volume of trade in manufactured products. Some readers may argue that because of these characteristics, Spain would have been less exposed to the Great Depression regardless of its exchange rate policy. To explore this argument, Table 1 presents a comparison of Spain with the four gold countries in terms of the following two measures of industrialization and openness: (1) the value of manufacturing production per head and (2) the share of manufactured exports in total manufacturing. As the table shows, according to these measures, Spain was more industrialized and open than one gold country, Poland, and was not far behind another, Italy. Thus, if these characteristics are important in determining the sensitivity to foreign business cycles (and if the exchange rate system is unimportant), we would expect the be-

TABLE 1
SELECTED CHARACTERISTICS OF SPAIN AND THE GOLD COUNTRIES AT THE ONSET OF THE GREAT
DEPRESSION

Country	Manufacturing Production Per Head	Share of Manufactured Exports in Total Manufacturing
	(U.S. $)	(Percentage)
Spain	40	8.0
Netherlands	160	21.2
Belgium	240	23.6
Italy	80	12.2
Poland	30	5.4

SOURCE: See note 5.

havior of Poland and Italy to be similar to Spain but different from the Netherlands and Belgium.

The basic evidence is presented in Figure 2, which shows the behavior of industrial production and the wholesale price level in the United States, the four gold countries, and Spain during the depression. In this figure, we let the U.S. represent the rest of the world and focus on the 1928–32 period during which the dollar price of gold was fixed. The figure presents a striking contrast between the two exchange rate systems. All four gold countries experienced a severe decline in prices and output during 1928–32. It is remarkable that despite substantial differences in terms of industrialization and trade, the contraction in each gold country closely followed the U.S. pattern. In contrast, Spanish prices and output remained, for the most part, unaffected during the depression period. Indeed, the 1932 level of prices and production in Spain was not much different from the level in 1928.

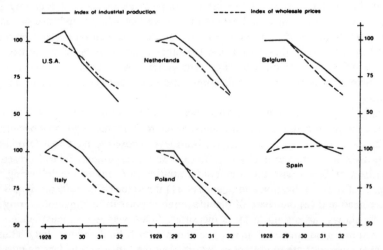

Fig. 2. The Behavior of Output and Prices During 1928–32: The Gold Countries and Spain Compared with the United States

Table 2 presents some formal evidence in the form of the following simple regressions for each of the five countries in question (the table also shows results for three Scandinavian countries that are discussed below):

$$X = a + b(XUS), \quad X = Y, P, \tag{1}$$

where Y and P represent the logs of industrial production and the wholesale price level for the small countries and YUS and PUS the logs of the same variables in the United States.[7] As the results in the table show, the effect of both the U.S. output and price level is insignificant for Spain but highly significant in the case of all four gold countries.[8] These results are thus consistent with the hypothesis that the flexible exchange rate completely insulates domestic output as well as prices from the influence of foreign output and price disturbances.

TABLE 2
THE OUTPUT AND PRICE REGRESSIONS: ANNUAL DATA, 1928–32

Country	The Output Regression $Y = a + b(YUS)$			The Price Regression $P = a + b(PUS)$		
	Intercept	Slope	R^2	Intercept	Slope	R^2
Spain	3.99*	0.13	0.32	4.76*	−0.04	0.31
	(0.47)	(0.11)		(0.19)	(0.04)	
Netherlands	1.10*	0.77*	0.97	−0.48	1.11*	0.99
	(0.34)	(0.08)		(0.19)	(0.04)	
Belgium	1.81*	0.61*	0.99	−0.74*	1.16*	0.99
	(0.13)	(0.03)		(0.20)	(0.05)	
Italy	1.71*	0.63*	0.95	0.56	0.88*	0.97
	(0.34)	(0.08)		(0.37)	(0.09)	
Poland	−0.17	1.04*	0.99	−0.04	1.01*	0.99
	(0.27)	(0.06)		(0.24)	(0.05)	
Denmark	4.17*	0.09	0.13	1.23	0.73*	0.86
	(0.64)	(0.15)		(0.77)	(0.17)	
Finland	2.86*	0.38	0.76	3.04*	0.34	0.59
	(0.54)	(0.12)		(0.73)	(0.16)	
Norway	3.86*	0.15	0.14	1.73*	0.62*	0.90
	(0.95)	(0.22)		(0.52)	(0.12)	

SOURCE: See note 5.
NOTE: Standard errors are shown in parentheses.
*Significant at 5 percent or less.

B. The Evidence from the Scandinavian Countries

As the evidence on the role of a flexible exchange rate in the Great Depression is based on the experience of only one country, some may dismiss this case as an

---

[7] In the case of the output regression, we also tried a weighted index of world production (calculated by the League of Nations) instead of the U.S. index but did not find any important differences in the results.

[8] If it is assumed that the distribution of the residual error in these regressions is the same for each country, the degrees of freedom could be increased, perhaps artificially, by estimating the regressions using pooled data for the five countries. We estimated such regressions, but the results of significance tests (on the slope coefficients) remained the same. As we used dummy variables in the pooled regressions to allow both the intercept and slope to differ across countries, the estimates of these coefficients for each country are the same as those reported in Table 2. The standard error of the slope as well as the intercept, however, is estimated from the pooled data and is the same for each country. The estimates of these

aberration.[9] To obtain further evidence on the effectiveness of exchange rate changes, we also examined the experience of three Scandinavian countries; Denmark, Finland, and Norway, which started out on the gold standard but switched to flexible exchange rates in 1931. If the exchange rate adjustment does not matter much in the transmission process, we would expect the output and price behavior of the Scandinavian countries to be not much different from the gold countries.

The results of output and price regressions for the three Scandinavian countries are also presented in Table 2. Looking first at the output regressions, it is clear that Scandinavian countries did not experience a strong impact of the Great Depression:[10] the effect of the U.S. output is negligible for Denmark and Norway, while for Finland it is noticeable (barely below the conventional 5 percent significance level) but small compared to the four gold countries. Turning to the price regressions, we find that the U.S. price did exert a significant effect on price levels in Denmark and Norway, but even for these two countries the size of the slope coefficient is small in relation to the gold countries.

The Scandinavian experience can be viewed as representing a mixed exchange rate regime that falls somewhere in between the pure flexible and pure fixed exchange rate systems of Spain and the gold countries. To test whether there are significant differences between the three regimes, we estimated the following regressions, which, using pooled data, restrict the slope coefficients to be the same for the three Scandinavian countries and for the gold countries.

$$P = 0.56^* \ (PUS) \ + \ 0.47^* \ (PUS)(DGO) \ - \ 0.60^* \ (PUS)(DSP)$$
$$(0.07) \qquad\qquad (0.09) \qquad\qquad\qquad (0.13)$$
$$+ \ 8 \ \text{country dummies}, \quad (2)$$

$$R^2 = 0.94, \ \text{D-W (Adj.)} = 1.54, \ \text{SEE} = 0.04, \ \text{No. Obs.} = 40 \ .$$

standard errors are shown below and can be combined with the values of coefficients given in Table 2 (for gold countries and Spain) to examine the results of the pooled regressions.

Summary of Selected Statistics from the Pooled Regression

| | The Standard Error of: | | D-W | |
	Intercept	Slope	(Adjusted)	R^2
The output regression	0.33	0.08	2.21	0.97
The price regression	0.25	0.06	2.65	0.99

[9] There is, in fact, another example of the working of the flexible exchange rate system during the Great Depression provided by Friedman and Schwartz [6, pp. 361–62]: China was on silver standard and as a result it had the equivalent of a flexible exchange rate system with respect to the gold standard countries. The Chinese economy was also not affected by the worldwide depression, at least until U.K.'s departure from the gold standard in 1931, apparently because of a depreciation of the gold price of silver.

[10] As U.K. was a major buyer of Scandinavian goods (in 1931–32, exports to U.K., as reported in L.N., *International Statistics*, accounted for 64.1 percent of total exports for Denmark, 44.7 percent for Finland, and 27.7 percent for Norway), it could be argued that output of these countries would be strongly related to U.K.'s output, and that these countries fared better in the Great Depression simply because U.K.'s experience was milder. To answer such an objection, it is interesting to note that two gold countries, the Netherlands and Belgium, also exported substantial amounts to U.K. (the share of these countries' exports to U.K. was 24.5 percent and 21.2 percent respectively) but did not find significant protection from the depression. Furthermore, regressing Scandinavian output on U.K. output, we find that the effect of U.K. output is insignificant except in the case of Finland (where the effect of U.S. output is also marked).

$$Y = 0.21^* \,(YUS) + 0.55^* \,(YUS)\,(DGO) - 0.08\,(YUS)\,(DSP)$$
$$(0.08)(0.10)(0.15)$$
$$+\ 8\ \text{country dummies}, \quad (3)$$

$$R^2 = 0.86,\ \text{D-W (Adj.)} = 2.11,\ \text{SEE} = 0.07,\ \text{No. Obs.} = 40,$$

where DGO and DSP represent dummy variables for the gold countries and Spain respectively (intercept terms are omitted to save space). (Note: standard errors are shown in parentheses and * indicates significance at 5 percent or less.)

The regressions are estimated in the form that facilitates testing whether the slope coefficient for the Scandinavian countries differs significantly from gold countries on the one hand and Spain on the other.[11] As the above tests show, the difference in the three regimes is especially marked in the price regression, which shows the interesting result that the slope coefficient for the Scandinavian countries is significantly smaller as compared to gold countries but significantly larger as compared to Spain. In the output regression, however, the Scandinavian slope coefficient is significantly different from gold countries but not from Spain.

The above tests can be extended to examine whether Scandinavian output and prices became less synchronized with the U.S. variables in the 1931–32 flexible exchange rate period as compared to the 1928–30 fixed exchange rate period.[12] Letting DSC2 denote the (interaction) dummy variable for observations representing both the Scandinavian countries and the years 1931 and 1932, the results of the extended tests are as follows:[13]

$$P = 1.21^*\,(PUS) - 0.17\,(PUS)\,(DGO) - 1.24^*\,(PUS)\,(DSP)$$
$$(0.19)(0.20)(0.21)$$

$$-\ 1.47^*\,(PUS)\,(DSC2) + 6.48^*\,(DSC2) + 8\ \text{country dummies}, \quad (4)$$
$$(0.28)(1.23)$$

$$R^2 = 0.97,\ \text{D-W (Adj.)} = 1.17,\ \text{SEE} = 0.03,\ \text{No. Obs.} = 40.$$

$$Y = -\ 0.04\,(YUS) + 0.80^*\,(YUS)\,(DGO) + 0.16\,(YUS)\,(DSP)$$
$$(0.23)(0.24)(0.26)$$

---

[11] In both regressions, the first term represents the estimate of the slope for the Scandinavian countries, the second term the difference in slopes between the gold and Scandinavian countries, and the third term the difference between Spain and the Scandinavian countries.

[12] We are indebted to an anonymous referee for suggesting this test. Note that because of our use of annual data, our distinction between the fixed and flexible exchange rate periods is only approximate.

[13] The coefficients in regression equations (4) and (5) can be interpreted as follows: The first term represents the slope estimate for the Scandinavian fixed exchange rate period (1928–30). The second and third terms represent, respectively, the slope difference of the gold countries and of Spain from the Scandinavian fixed rate period. Finally, the fourth and the fifth terms represent, respectively, the difference in slope and in intercepts beween the Scandinavian (1931–32) flexible and (1928–30) fixed rate periods (the intercept difference between the two periods is constrained to be the same for all three Scandinavian countries).

$$- 0.12 \ (YUS) \ (DSC2) + 0.37 \ (DSC2) + 8 \text{ country dummies}, \quad (5)$$
$$(0.32) \qquad \qquad (1.39)$$

$$R^2 = 0.88, \text{ D-W (Adj.)} = 1.85, \text{ SEE} = 0.06, \text{ No. Obs.} = 40 \ .$$

(Note: standard errors are shown in parentheses and * indicates significance at 5 percent or less.)

The price regression shows that in the Scandinavian countries, both the slope and the intercepts for the 1928–30 subperiod differ significantly from those for the 1931–32 subperiod. Interestingly, this regression also shows that during 1928–30, the Scandinavian countries behaved like the gold countries (note that the coefficient of the $(PUS) \ (DGO)$ term is insignificant), but in 1931–32 the Scandinavian behavior was akin to Spain (for the test that the slopes are the same for Spain during 1928–32 and the Scandinavian countries during 1931–32, the t-value is 1.04).

A different picture emerges from the output regression, which shows that the Scandinavian behavior did not differ significantly between the two subperiods. One possible explanation of this result would be that Scandinavian countries may have pursued a somewhat independent monetary policy in the period prior to the 1931 depreciation.[14]

4. CONCLUSIONS

In this paper we have argued that the experience of the Great Depression raises serious doubts about the currently popular view that flexible exchange rates are of little use in protecting a country from foreign business cycle disturbances.

Our case is based on the evidence for eight small European countries that followed three different types of exchange rate policies. Four of these countries (the Netherlands, Belgium, Italy, and Poland) operated on fixed exchange rates with the United States until (March) 1933. All of these countries suffered a severe contraction in both output and prices, which was strongly related to the contraction of these variables in the United States. In a striking contrast to the experience of these countries, Spain, which maintained a flexible exchange rate system, enjoyed fairly stable output and prices and thus virtually escaped the Great Depression. Furthermore, the three countries (Denmark, Finland, and Norway) that allowed their exchange rate to float in the middle of the depression, also enjoyed greater independence from the U.S. contraction in relation to the fixed exchange rate countries.

LITERATURE CITED

1. Calvo, Guillermo A., and Carlos A. Rodriguez. "A Model of Exchange Rate Determination with Currency Substitution and Rational Expectations." *Journal of Political Economy*, 85 (June 1977), 617–25.

[14]The evidence would suggest that under fixed exchange rates, while domestic and foreign prices are linked via arbitrage, the relationship between domestic and foreign output can be weakened, at least in the short run, by independent monetary actions (sterilization).

2. Cooper, Richard N. "Monetary Theory and Policy in an Open Economy. "*The Scandinavian Journal of Economics*, 78 (1976), 146–63.
3. Delaplane, Walter H. "The Spanish Peseta Since 1913." Unpublished dissertation, Duke University, 1934.
4. Dornbusch, Rudiger, and Paul Krugman. "Flexible Exchange Rates in the Short Run." *Brookings Papers on Economic Activity*, 3 (1976), 537–84.
5. Fleming, Marcus J. "Domestic Financial Policies under Fixed and under Floating Exchange Rates." *International Monetary Fund Staff Papers*, 9 (1962), 369–79.
6. Friedman, Milton, and Anna Schwartz. *A Monetary History of the United States 1867–1960*. Princeton, N.J.: Princeton University Press, 1963.
7. Hamada, Koichi, and Makoto Sakurai. "International Transmission of Stagflation under Fixed and Flexible Exchange Rates." *Journal of Political Economy*, 86 (October 1978), 877–95.
8. Laidler, David. "Expectations and the Behaviour of Prices and Output under Flexible Exchange Rates." *Economica*, 44 (November 1977), 327–36.
9. Miles, Marc. "Currency Substitution, Flexible Exchange Rates and Monetary Independence." *American Economic Review*, 68 (June 1978), 428–36.
10. Mundell, Robert. *International Economics*. New York: Macmillan, 1968.
11. Mussa, Michael. "The Exchange Rate, the Balance of Payments and Monetary and Fiscal Policy under a Regime of Controlled Floating." *The Scandinavian Journal of Economics*, 78 (1976), 229–48.
12. Yeager, Leland B. *International Monetary Relations: Theory, History and Policy*. Second edition. New York: Harper and Row, 1976.

[7]
The Gold Standard, Deflation, and Financial Crisis in the Great Depression: An International Comparison

Ben Bernanke and Harold James

2.1 Introduction

Recent research on the causes of the Great Depression has laid much of the blame for that catastrophe on the doorstep of the international gold standard. In his new book, Temin (1989) argues that structural flaws of the interwar gold standard, in conjunction with policy responses dictated by the gold standard's "rules of the game," made an international monetary contraction and deflation almost inevitable. Eichengreen and Sachs (1985) have presented evidence that countries which abandoned the gold standard and the associated contractionary monetary policies recovered from the Depression more quickly than countries that remained on gold. Research by Hamilton (1987, 1988) supports the propositions that contractionary monetary policies in France and the United States initiated the Great Slide, and that the defense of gold standard parities added to the deflationary pressure.[1]

The gold standard–based explanation of the Depression (which we will elaborate in section 2.2) is in most respects compelling. The length and depth of the deflation during the late 1920s and early 1930s strongly suggest a monetary origin, and the close correspondence (across both space and time) between deflation and nations' adherence to the gold standard shows the power of that system to transmit contractionary monetary shocks. There is also a high correlation in the data between deflation (falling prices) and depression (falling output), as the previous authors have noted and as we will demonstrate again below.

Ben Bernanke is professor of economics and public affairs at Princeton University and a research associate of the National Bureau of Economic Research. Harold James is assistant professor of history at Princeton University.

The authors thank David Fernandez, Mark Griffiths, and Holger Wolf for invaluable research assistance. Support was provided by the National Bureau of Economic Research and the National Science Foundation.

If the argument as it has been made so far has a weak link, however, it is probably the explanation of how the deflation induced by the malfunctioning gold standard caused depression; that is, what was the source of this massive monetary non-neutrality?[2] The goal of our paper is to try to understand better the mechanisms by which deflation may have induced depression in the 1930s. We consider several channels suggested by earlier work, in particular effects operating through real wages and through interest rates. Our focus, however, is on a channel of transmission that has been largely ignored by the recent gold standard literature; namely, the disruptive effect of deflation on the financial system.

Deflation (and the constraints on central bank policy imposed by the gold standard) was an important cause of banking panics, which occurred in a number of countries in the early 1930s. As discussed for the case of the United States by Bernanke (1983), to the extent that bank panics interfere with normal flows of credit, they may affect the performance of the real economy; indeed, it is possible that economic performance may be affected even without major panics, if the banking system is sufficiently weakened. Because severe banking panics are the form of financial crisis most easily identified empirically, we will focus on their effects in this paper. However, we do not want to lose sight of a second potential effect of falling prices on the financial sector, which is "debt deflation" (Fisher 1933; Bernanke 1983; Bernanke and Gertler 1990). By increasing the real value of nominal debts and promoting insolvency of borrowers, deflation creates an environment of financial distress in which the incentives of borrowers are distorted and in which it is difficult to extend new credit. Again, this provides a means by which falling prices can have real effects.

To examine these links between deflation and depression, we take a comparative approach (as did Eichengreen and Sachs). Using an annual data set covering twenty-four countries, we try to measure (for example) the differences between countries on and off the gold standard, or between countries experiencing banking panics and those that did not. A weakness of our approach is that, lacking objective indicators of the seriousness of financial problems, we are forced to rely on dummy variables to indicate periods of crisis. Despite this problem, we generally do find an important role for financial crises—particularly banking panics—in explaining the link between falling prices and falling output. Countries in which, for institutional or historical reasons, deflation led to panics or other severe banking problems had significantly worse depressions than countries in which banking was more stable. In addition, there may have been a feedback loop through which banking panics, particularly those in the United States, intensified the severity of the worldwide deflation. Because of data problems, we do not provide direct evidence of the debt-deflation mechanism; however, we do find that much of the apparent impact of deflation on output is unaccounted for by the mechanisms we

35   Financial Crisis in the Great Depression

explicitly consider, leaving open the possibility that debt deflation was important.

The rest of the paper is organized as follows. Section 2.2 briefly recapitulates the basic case against the interwar gold standard, showing it to have been a source of deflation and depression, and provides some new evidence consistent with this view. Section 2.3 takes a preliminary look at some mechanisms by which deflation may have been transmitted to depression. In section 2.4, we provide an overview of the financial crises that occurred during the interwar period. Section 2.5 presents and discusses our main empirical results on the effects of financial crisis in the 1930s, and section 2.6 concludes.

2.2 The Gold Standard and Deflation

In this section we discuss, and provide some new evidence for, the claim that a mismanaged interwar gold standard was responsible for the worldwide deflation of the late 1920s and early 1930s.

The gold standard—generally viewed at the time as an essential source of the relative prosperity of the late nineteenth and early twentieth centuries—was suspended at the outbreak of World War I. Wartime suspension of the gold standard was not in itself unusual; indeed, Bordo and Kydland (1990) have argued that wartime suspension, followed by a return to gold at prewar parities as soon as possible, should be considered part of the gold standard's normal operation. Bordo and Kydland pointed out that a reputation for returning to gold at the prewar parity, and thus at something close to the prewar price level, would have made it easier for a government to sell nominal bonds and would have increased attainable seignorage. A credible commitment to the gold standard thus would have had the effect of allowing war spending to be financed at a lower total cost.

Possibly for these reputational reasons, and certainly because of widespread unhappiness with the chaotic monetary and financial conditions that followed the war (there were hyperinflations in central Europe and more moderate but still serious inflations elsewhere), the desire to return to gold in the early 1920s was strong. Of much concern however was the perception that there was not enough gold available to satisfy world money demands without deflation. The 1922 Economic and Monetary Conference at Genoa addressed this issue by recommending the adoption of a gold exchange standard, in which convertible foreign exchange reserves (principally dollars and pounds) as well as gold would be used to back national money supplies, thus "economizing" on gold. Although "key currencies" had been used as reserves before the war, the Genoa recommendations led to a more widespread and officially sanctioned use of this practice (Lindert 1969; Eichengreen 1987).

During the 1920s the vast majority of the major countries succeeded in returning to gold. (The first column of table 2.1 gives the dates of return for the countries in our data set.) Britain returned at the prewar parity in 1925, despite Keynes's argument that at the old parity the pound would be overvalued. By the end of 1925, out of a list of 48 currencies given by the League of Nations (1926), 28 had been pegged to gold. France returned to gold gradually, following the Poincaré stabilization, although at a new parity widely believed to undervalue the franc. By the end of 1928, except for China and a few small countries on the silver standard, only Spain, Portugal, Rumania, and Japan had not been brought back into the gold standard system. Rumania went back on gold in 1929, Portugal did so in practice also in 1929 (although not officially until 1931), and Japan in December 1930. In the same month the Bank for International Settlements gave Spain a stabilization loan, but the operation was frustrated by a revolution in April 1931, carried out by republicans who, as one of the most attractive features of their program, opposed the foreign stabilization credits. Spain thus did not join the otherwise nearly universal membership of the gold standard club.

The classical gold standard of the prewar period functioned reasonably smoothly and without a major convertibility crisis for more than thirty years. In contrast, the interwar gold standard, established between 1925 and 1928, had substantially broken down by 1931 and disappeared by 1936. An extensive literature has analyzed the differences between the classical and interwar gold standards. This literature has focused, with varying degrees of emphasis, both on fundamental economic problems that complicated trade and monetary adjustment in the interwar period and on technical problems of the interwar gold standard itself.

In terms of "fundamentals," Temin (1989) has emphasized the effects of the Great War, arguing that, ultimately, the war itself was the shock that initiated the Depression. The legacy of the war included—besides physical destruction, which was relatively quickly repaired—new political borders drawn apparently without economic rationale; substantial overcapacity in some sectors (such as agriculture and heavy industry) and undercapacity in others, relative to long-run equilibrium; and reparations claims and international war debts that generated fiscal burdens and fiscal uncertainty. Some writers (notably Charles Kindleberger) have also pointed to the fact that the prewar gold standards was a hegemonic system, with Great Britain the unquestioned center. In contrast, in the interwar period the relative decline of Britain, the inexperience and insularity of the new potential hegemon (the United States), and ineffective cooperation among central banks left no one able to take responsibility for the system as a whole.

The technical problems of the interwar gold standard included the following three:

1. *The asymmetry between surplus and deficit countries in the required monetary response to gold flows*. Temin suggests, correctly we believe, that this was the most important structural flaw of the gold standard. In theory, under the "rules of the game," central banks of countries experiencing gold

37 Financial Crisis in the Great Depression

Table 2.1   **Dates of Changes in Gold Standard Policies**

Country	Return to Gold	Suspension of Gold Standard	Foreign Exchange Control	Devaluation
Australia	April 1925	December 1929	—	March 1930
Austria	April 1925	April 1933	October 1931	September 1931
Belgium	October 1926	—	—	March 1935
Canada	July 1926	October 1931	—	September 1931
Czechoslovakia	April 1926	—	September 1931	February 1934
Denmark	January 1927	September 1931	November 1931	September 1931
Estonia	January 1928	June 1933	November 1931	June 1933
Finland	January 1926	October 1931	—	October 1931
France	August 1926– June 1928	—	—	October 1936
Germany	September 1924	—	July 1931	—
Greece	May 1928	April 1932	September 1931	April 1932
Hungary	April 1925	—	July 1931	—
Italy	December 1927	—	May 1934	October 1936
Japan	December 1930	December 1931	July 1932	December 1931
Latvia	August 1922	—	October 1931	—
Netherlands	April 1925	—	—	October 1936
Norway	May 1928	September 1931	—	September 1931
New Zealand	April 1925	September 1931	—	April 1930
Poland	October 1927	—	April 1936	October 1936
Rumania	March 1927– February 1929	—	May 1932	—
Sweden	April 1924	September 1931	—	September 1931
Spain	—	—	May 1931	—
United Kingdom	May 1925	September 1931	—	September 1931
United States	June 1919	March 1933	March 1933	April 1933

Source: League of Nations, *Yearbook*, various dates; and miscellaneous supplementary sources.

inflows were supposed to assist the price-specie flow mechanism by expanding domestic money supplies and inflating, while deficit countries were supposed to reduce money supplies and deflate. In practice, the need to avoid a complete loss of reserves and an end to convertibility forced deficit countries to comply with this rule; but, in contrast, no sanction prevented surplus countries from sterilizing gold inflows and accumulating reserves indefinitely, if domestic objectives made that desirable. Thus there was a potential deflationary bias in the gold standard's operation.

    This asymmetry between surplus and deficit countries also existed in the prewar period, but with the important difference that the prewar gold standard centered around the operations of the Bank of England. The Bank of England of course had to hold enough gold to ensure convertibility, but as a profit-making institution it also had a strong incentive not to hold large stocks of barren gold (as opposed to interest-paying assets). Thus the Bank managed the gold standard (with the assistance of other central banks) so as to avoid both sustained inflows and sustained outflows of gold; and, indeed, it helped ensure continuous convertibility with a surprisingly low level of gold reserves. In contrast, the two major gold surplus countries of the interwar period, the United States and France, had central banks with little or no incentive to avoid accumulation of gold.

The deflationary bias of the asymmetry in required adjustments was magnified by statutory fractional reserve requirements imposed on many central banks, especially the new central banks, after the war. While Britain, Norway, Finland, and Sweden had a fiduciary issue—a fixed note supply backed only by domestic government securities, above which 100% gold backing was required—most countries required instead that minimum gold holdings equal a fixed fraction (usually close to the Federal Reserve's 40%) of central bank liabilities. These rules had two potentially harmful effects.

First, just as required "reserves" for modern commercial banks are not really available for use as true reserves, a large portion of central bank gold holdings were immobilized by the reserve requirements and could not be used to settle temporary payments imbalances. For example, in 1929, according to the League of Nations, for 41 countries with a total gold reserve of $9,378 million, only $2,178 million were "surplus" reserves, with the rest required as cover (League of Nations 1944, 12). In fact, this overstates the quantity of truly free reserves, because markets and central banks became very worried when reserves fell within 10% of the minimum. The upshot of this is that deficit countries could lose very little gold before being forced to reduce their domestic money supplies; while, as we have noted, the absence of any maximum reserve limit allowed surplus countries to accept gold inflows without inflating.

The second and related effect of the fractional reserve requirement has to do with the relationship between gold outflows and domestic monetary contraction. With fractional reserves, the relationship between gold outflow and the reduction in the money supply was not one for one; with a 40% reserve requirement, for example, the impact on the money supply of a gold outflow was 2.5 times the external loss. So again, loss of gold could lead to an immediate and sharp deflationary impact, not balanced by inflation elsewhere.

2. *The pyramiding of reserves.* As we have noted, under the interwar gold-exchange standard, countries other than those with reserve currencies were encouraged to hold convertible foreign exchange reserves as a partial (or in some cases, as a nearly complete) substitute for gold. But these convertible reserves were in turn usually only fractionally backed by gold. Thus, just as a shift by the public from fractionally backed deposits to currency would lower the total domestic money supply, the gold-exchange system opened up the

39 Financial Crisis in the Great Depression

possibility that a shift of central banks from foreign exchange reserves to gold might lower the world money supply, adding another deflationary bias to the system. Central banks did abandon foreign exchange reserves en masse in the early 1930s, when the threat of devaluation made foreign exchange assets quite risky. According to Eichengreen (1987), however, the statistical evidence is not very clear on whether central banks after selling their foreign exchange simply lowered their cover ratios, which would have had no direct effect on money supplies, or shifted into gold, which would have been contractionary. Even if the central banks responded only by lowering cover ratios, however, this would have increased the sensitivity of their money supplies to any subsequent outflow of reserves.

3. *Insufficient powers of central banks*. An important institutional feature of the interwar gold standard is that, for a majority of the important continental European central banks, open market operations were not permitted or were severely restricted. This limitation on central bank powers was usually the result of the stabilization programs of the early and mid 1920s. By prohibiting central banks from holding or dealing in significant quantities of government securities, and thus making monetization of deficits more difficult, the architects of the stabilizations hoped to prevent future inflation. This forced the central banks to rely on discount policy (the terms at which they would make loans to commercial banks) as the principal means of affecting the domestic money supply. However, in a number of countries the major commercial banks borrowed very infrequently from the central banks, implying that except in crisis periods the central bank's control over the money supply might be quite weak.

The loosening of the link between the domestic money supply and central bank reserves may have been beneficial in some cases during the 1930s, if it moderated the monetary effect of reserve outflows. However, in at least one very important case the inability of a central bank to conduct open market operations may have been quite destabilizing. As discussed by Eichengreen (1986), the Bank of France, which was the recipient of massive gold inflows until 1932, was one of the banks that was prohibited from conducting open market operations. This severely limited the ability of the Bank to translate its gold inflows into monetary expansion, as should have been done in obedience to the rules of the game. The failure of France to inflate meant that it continued to attract reserves, thus imposing deflation on the rest of the world.[3]

Given both the fundamental economic problems of the international economy and the structural flaws of the gold standard system, even a relatively minor deflationary impulse might have had significant repercussions. As it happened, both of the two major gold surplus countries—France and the United States, who at the time together held close to 60% of the world's monetary gold—took deflationary paths in 1928–29 (Hamilton 1987).

In the French case, as we have already noted, the deflationary shock took the form of a largely sterilized gold inflow. For several reasons—including a successful stabilization with attendant high real interest rates, a possibly undervalued franc, the lifting of exchange controls, and the perception that France was a "safe haven" for capital—beginning in early 1928 gold flooded into that country, an inflow that was to last until 1932. In 1928, France controlled about 15% of the total monetary gold held by the twenty-four countries in our data set (Board of Governors 1943); this share, already disproportionate to France's economic importance, increased to 18% in 1929, 22% in 1930, 28% in 1931, and 32% in 1932. Since the U.S. share of monetary gold remained stable at something greater than 40% of the total, the inflow to France implied significant losses of gold by countries such as Germany, Japan, and the United Kingdom.

With its accumulation of gold, France should have been expected to inflate; but in part because of the restrictions on open market operations discussed above and in part because of deliberate policy choices, the impact of the gold inflow on French prices was minimal. The French monetary base did increase with the inflow of reserves, but because economic growth led the demand for francs to expand even more quickly, the country actually experienced a wholesale price *deflation* of almost 11% between January 1929 and January 1930.

Hamilton (1987) also documents the monetary tightening in the United States in 1928, a contraction motivated in part by the desire to avoid losing gold to the French but perhaps even more by the Federal Reserve's determination to slow down stock market speculation. The U.S. price level fell about 4% over the course of 1929. A business cycle peak was reached in the United States in August 1929, and the stock market crashed in October.

The initial contractions in the United States and France were largely self-inflicted wounds; no binding external constraint forced the United States to deflate in 1929, and it would certainly have been possible for the French government to grant the Bank of France the power to conduct expansionary open market operations. However, Temin (1989) argues that, once these destabilizing policy measures had been taken, little could be done to avert deflation and depression, given the commitment of central banks to maintenance of the gold standard. Once the deflationary process had begun, central banks engaged in competitive deflation and a scramble for gold, hoping by raising cover ratios to protect their currencies against speculative attack. Attempts by any individual central bank to reflate were met by immediate gold outflows, which forced the central bank to raise its discount rate and deflate once again. According to Temin, even the United States, with its large gold reserves, faced this constraint. Thus Temin disagrees with the suggestion of Friedman and Schwartz (1963) that the Federal Reserve's failure to protect the U.S. money supply was due to misunderstanding of the problem or a lack of leadership; instead, he claims, given the commitment to the gold standard (and, presumably, the absence of effective central bank cooperation), the Fed had little choice but to let the banks fail and the money supply fall.

For our purposes here it does not matter much to what extent central bank choices could have been other than what they were. For the positive question of what caused the Depression, we need only note that a monetary contraction began in the United States and France, and was propagated throughout the world by the international monetary standard.[4]

If monetary contraction propagated by the gold standard was the source of the worldwide deflation and depression, then countries abandoning the gold standard (or never adopting it) should have avoided much of the deflationary pressure. This seems to have been the case. In an important paper, Choudhri and Kochin (1980) documented that Spain, which never restored the gold standard and allowed its exchange rate to float, avoided the declines in prices and output that affected other European countries. Choudhri and Kochin also showed that the Scandinavian countries, which left gold along with the United Kingdom in 1931, recovered from the Depression much more quickly than other small European countries that remained longer on the gold standard. Much of this had been anticipated in an insightful essay by Haberler (1976).

Eichengreen and Sachs (1985) similarly focused on the beneficial effects of currency depreciation (i.e., abandonment of the gold standard or devaluation). For a sample of ten European countries, they showed that depreciating countries enjoyed faster growth of exports and industrial production than countries which did not depreciate. Depreciating countries also experienced lower real wages and greater profitability, which presumably helped to increase production. Eichengreen and Sachs argued that depreciation, in this context, should not necessarily be thought of as a "beggar thy neighbor" policy; because depreciations reduced constraints on the growth of world money supplies, they may have conferred benefits abroad as well as at home (although a coordinated depreciation presumably would have been better than the uncoordinated sequence of depreciations that in fact took place).[5]

Some additional evidence of the effects of maintaining or leaving the gold standard, much in the spirit of Eichengreen and Sachs but using data from a larger set of countries, is given in our tables 2.2 through 2.4. These tables summarize the relationships between the decision to adhere to the gold standard and some key macroeconomic variables, including wholesale price inflation (table 2.2), some indicators of national monetary policies (table 2.3), and industrial production growth (table 2.4). To construct these tables, we divided our sample of twenty-four countries into four categories:[6] 1) countries not on the gold standard at all (Spain) or leaving prior to 1931 (Australia and New Zealand); 2) countries abandoning the full gold standard in 1931 (14 countries); 3) countries abandoning the gold standard between 1932 and 1935 (Rumania in 1932, the United States in 1933, Italy in 1934, and Belgium in 1935); and 4) countries still on the full gold standard as of 1936 (France, Netherlands, Poland).[7] Tables 2.2 and 2.4 give the data for each country, as well as averages for the large cohort of countries abandoning gold in 1931, for the remnant of the gold bloc still on gold in 1936, and (for 1932–35, when there were a significant number of countries in each category) for all gold standard and non–gold standard countries. Since table 2.3 reports data on four different variables, in order to save space only the averages are shown.[8]

The link between deflation and adherence to the gold standard, shown in table 2.2, seems quite clear. As noted by Choudhri and Kochin (1980), Spain's abstention from the gold standard insulated that country from the general deflation; New Zealand and Australia, presumably because they retained links to sterling despite early abandonment of the strict gold standard, did however experience some deflation. Among countries on the gold standard as of 1931, there is a rather uniform experience of about a 13% deflation in both 1930 and 1931. But after 1931 there is a sharp divergence between those countries on and those off the gold standard. Price levels in countries off the gold standard have stabilized by 1933 (with one or two exceptions), and these countries experience mild inflations in 1934–36. In contrast, the gold standard countries continue to deflate, although at a slower rate, until the gold standard's dissolution in 1936.

With such clearly divergent price behavior between countries on and off gold, one would expect to see similarly divergent behavior in monetary policy. Table 2.3 compares the average behavior of the growth rates of three monetary aggregates, called for short M0, M1, and M2, and of changes in the central bank discount rate. M0 corresponds to money and notes in circulation, M1 is the sum of M0 and commercial bank deposits, and M2 is the sum of M1 and savings bank deposits.[9] The expected differences in the monetary polices of the gold and non-gold countries seem to be in the data, although somewhat less clearly than we had anticipated. In particular, despite the twelve percentage point difference in rates of deflation between gold and non-gold countries in 1932, the differences in average money growth in that year between the two classes of countries are minor; possibly, higher inflation expectations in the countries abandoning gold reduced money demand and thus became self-confirming. From 1933 through 1935, however, the various monetary indicators are more consistent with the conclusion stressed by Eichengreen and Sachs (1985), that leaving the gold standard afforded countries more latitude to expand their money supplies and thus to escape deflation.

The basic proposition of the gold standard–based explanation of the Depression is that, because of its deflationary impact, adherence to the gold standard had very adverse consequences for real activity. The validity of this proposition is shown rather clearly by table 2.4, which gives growth rates of industrial production for the countries in our sample. While the countries which were to abandon the gold standard in 1931 did slightly worse in 1930 and 1931 than the nations of the Gold Bloc, subsequent to leaving gold these countries performed much better. Between 1932 and 1935, growth of industrial production in countries not on gold averaged about seven percentage points a year better than countries remaining on gold, a very substantial effect.

In summary, data from our sample of twenty-four countries support the

Table 2.2   Log-differences of the Wholesale Price Index

	1930	1931	1932	1933	1934	1935	1936
1. Countries not on gold standard or leaving prior to 1931							
Spain	−.00	.01	−.01	−.05	.03	.01	.02
Australia (1929)	−.12	−.11	−.01	−.00	.04	−.00	.05
New Zealand (1930)	−.03	−.07	−.03	.03	.01	.03	.01
2. Countries abandoning full gold standard in 1931							
Austria	−.11	−.07	.03	−.04	.02	−.00	−.01
Canada	−.10	−.18	−.08	.01	.06	.01	.03
Czechoslovakia	−.12	−.10	−.08	−.03	.02	.04	.00
Denmark	−.15	−.13	.02	.07	.09	.02	.05
Estonia	−.14	−.11	−.09	.02	.00	−.01	.08
Finland	−.09	−.07	.07	−.01	.01	.00	.02
Germany	−.10	−.12	−.14	−.03	.05	.03	.02
Greece	−.10	−.11	.18	.12	−.01	.02	.02
Hungary	−.14	−.05	−.01	−.14	.00	.08	.03
Japan	−.19	−.17	.05	.11	−.01	.04	.06
Latvia	−.16	−.18	.00	−.02	−.01	.05	.04
Norway	−.08	−.12	.00	−.00	.02	.03	.05
Sweden	−.14	−.09	−.02	−.02	.06	.02	.03
United Kingdom	−.17	−.18	−.04	.01	.04	.04	.06
Average	−.13	−.12	−.01	.00	.02	.03	.04
3. Countries abandoning gold standard between 1932 and 1935							
Rumania (1932)	−.24	−.26	−.11	−.03	.00	.14	.13
United States (1933)	−.10	−.17	−.12	.02	.13	.07	.01
Italy (1934)	−.11	−.14	−.07	−.09	−.02	.10	.11
Belgium (1935)	−.13	−.17	−.16	−.06	−.06	.13	.09
4. Countries still on full gold standard as of 1936							
France	−.12	−.10	−.16	−.07	−.06	−.11	.19
Netherlands	−.11	−.16	−.17	−.03	.00	−.02	.04
Poland	−.12	−.14	−.13	−.10	−.06	−.05	.02
Average	−.12	−.13	−.15	−.07	−.04	−.06	.08
5. Grand averages							
Gold standard countries			−.13	−.07	−.04	−.05	
Non-gold countries			−.01	.00	.03	.04	

Note: Data on wholesale prices are from League of Nations, *Monthly Bulletin of Statistics* and *Yearbook*, various issues. Dates in parentheses are years in which countries abandoned gold, with "abandonment" defined to include the imposition of foreign exchange controls or devaluation as well as suspension; see table 2.1.

Table 2.3   Monetary Indicators

	1930	1931	1932	1933	1934	1935	1936
1. Countries abandoning full gold standard in 1931							
M0 growth	−.04	−.02	−.07	.06	.05	.05	.08
M1 growth	.01	−.11	−.07	.02	.05	.04	.08
M2 growth	.03	−.08	−.04	.03	.05	.05	.06
Discount rate change	−0.8	0.4	−0.2	−1.2	−0.4	−0.1	−0.1
2. Countries still on full gold standard as of 1936							
M0 growth	.03	.07	−.06	−.02	.01	−.03	.03
M1 growth	.05	−.06	−.07	−.05	.01	−.06	.08
M2 growth	.08	−.00	−.02	−.02	.02	−.03	.05
Discount rate change	−1.4	−0.4	0.1	−0.4	−0.4	0.8	−0.3
3. Grand averages: Countries on gold							
M0 growth			−.04	−.03	.01	−.02	
M1 growth			−.09	−.04	−.01	−.06	
M2 growth			−.05	−.01	.01	−.02	
Discount rate change			0.2	−0.5	−0.4	0.7	
4. Grand averages: Countries off gold							
M0 growth			−.07	.05	.03	.06	
M1 growth			−.06	.01	.04	.05	
M2 growth			−.03	.02	.04	.05	
Discount rate change			−0.3	−1.0	−0.4	−0.2	

Note: M0 is money and notes in cirulation. M1 is base money plus commercial bank deposits. M2 is M1 plus savings deposits. Growth rates of monetary aggregates are calculated as log-differences. The discount rate change is in percentage points. The data are from League of Nations, *Monthly Bulletin of Statistics* and *Yearbook*, various issues.

view that there was a strong link between adherence to the gold standard and the severity of both deflation and depression. The data are also consistent with the hypothesis that increased freedom to engage in monetary expansion was a reason for the better performance of countries leaving the gold standard early in the 1930s, although the evidence in this case is a bit less clear-cut.

2.3 The Link Between Deflation and Depression

Given the above discussion and evidence, it seems reasonable to accept the idea that the worldwide deflation of the early 1930s was the result of a monetary contraction transmitted through the international gold standard. But this

45 Financial Crisis in the Great Depression

Table 2.4   Log-differences of the Industrial Production Index

	1930	1931	1932	1933	1934	1935	1936
1. Countries not on gold standard or leaving prior to 1931							
Spain	−.01	−.06	−.05	−.05	.01	.02	NA
Australia (1929)	−.11	−.07	.07	.10	.09	.09	.07
New Zealand (1930)	−.25	−.14	.05	.02	.13	.09	.14
2. Countries abandoning full gold standard in 1931							
Austria	−.16	−.19	−.14	.03	.11	.13	.07
Canada	−.16	−.18	−.20	.04	.20	.10	.10
Czechoslovakia	−.11	−.10	−.24	−.05	.10	.05	.14
Denmark	.08	−.08	−.09	.14	.11	.07	.04
Estonia	−.02	−.09	−.17	.05	.17	.10	.10
Finland	−.10	−.13	.19	.02	.03	.10	.09
Germany	−.15	−.24	−.24	.13	.27	.16	.12
Greece	.01	.02	−.08	.10	.12	.12	−.03
Hungary	−.06	−.08	−.06	.07	.12	.07	.10
Japan	−.05	−.03	.07	.15	.13	.10	.06
Latvia	.08	−.20	−.08	.31	.15	.05	.04
Norway	.01	−.25	.17	.01	.04	.10	.09
Sweden	.03	−.07	−.08	.02	.19	.11	.09
United Kingdom	−.08	−.10	−.00	.05	.11	.07	.09
Average	−.05	−.12	−.07	.08	.13	.10	.08
3. Countries abandoning gold standard between 1932 and 1935							
Rumania (1932)	−.03	.05	−.14	.15	.19	−.01	.06
United States (1933)	−.21	−.17	−.24	.17	.04	.13	.15
Italy (1934)	−.08	−.17	−.15	.10	.08	.16	−.07
Belgium (1935)	−.12	−.09	−.16	.04	.01	.12	.05
4. Countries still on full gold standard as of 1936							
France	−.01	−.14	−.19	.12	−.07	−.04	.07
Netherlands	.02	−.06	−.13	.07	.02	−.03	.01
Poland	−.13	−.14	−.20	.09	.12	.07	.10
Average	−.04	−.11	−.17	.10	.02	.00	.06
5. Grand averages							
Gold standard countries			−.18	.09	.03	.01	
Non-gold countries			−.06	.08	.12	.09	

Note: Data on industrial production are from League of Nations, *Monthly Bulletin of Statistics* and *Yearbook,* various issues, supplemented by League of Nations, *Industrialization and Foreign Trade,* 1945.

raises the more difficult question of what precisely were the channels linking deflation (falling prices) and depression (falling output). This section takes a preliminary look at some suggested mechanisms. We first introduce here two principal channels emphasized in recent research, then discuss the alternative of induced financial crisis.

1. *Real wages.* If wages possess some degree of nominal rigidity, then falling output prices will raise real wages and lower labor demand. Downward stickiness of wages (or of other input costs) will also lower profitability, potentially reducing investment. This channel is stressed by Eichengreen and Sachs (see in particular their 1986 paper) and has also been emphasized by Newell and Symons (1988).

Some evidence on the behavior of real wages during the Depression is presented in table 2.5, which is similar in format to tables 2.2–2.4. Note that table 2.5 uses the wholesale price index (the most widely available price index) as the wage deflator. According to this table, there were indeed large real wage increases in most countries in 1930 and 1931. After 1931, countries leaving the gold standard experienced a mild decline in real wages, while real wages in gold standard countries exhibited a mild increase. These findings are similar to those of Eichengreen and Sachs (1985).

The reliance on nominal wage stickiness to explain the real effects of the deflation is consistent with the Keynesian tradition, but is nevertheless somewhat troubling in this context. Given (i) the severity of the unemployment that was experienced during that time; (ii) the relative absence of long-term contracts and the weakness of unions; and (iii) the presumption that the general public was aware that prices, and hence the cost of living, were falling, it is hard to understand how nominal wages could have been so unresponsive. Wages had fallen quickly in many countries in the contraction of 1921–22. In the United States, nominal wages were maintained until the fall of 1931 (possibly by an agreement among large corporations; see O'Brien 1989), but fell sharply after that; in Germany, the government actually tried to depress wages early in the Depression. Why then do we see these large real wage increases in the data?

One possibility is measurement problems. There are a number of issues, such as changes in skill and industrial composition, that make measuring the cyclical movement in real wages difficult even today. Bernanke (1986) has argued, in the U.S. context, that because of sharp reductions in workweeks and the presence of hoarded labor, the measure real wage may have been a poor measure of the marginal cost of labor.

Also in the category of measurement issues, Eichengreen and Hatton (1987) correctly point out that nominal wages should be deflated by the relevant product prices, not a general price index. Their table of product wage indices (nominal wages relative to manufacturing prices) is reproduced for 1929–38 and for the five countries for which data are available as our table 2.6. Like table 2.5, this table also shows real wages increasing in the early

47   Financial Crisis in the Great Depression

Table 2.5   Log-differences of the Real Wage

	1930	1931	1932	1933	1934	1935	1936
1. Countries not on gold standard or leaving prior to 1931							
Spain			not available				
Australia (1929)	.10	.01	−.05	−.04	−.03	.01	−.03
New Zealand (1930)	.03	.00	−.00	−.05	−.01	−.01	.10
2. Countries abandoning full gold standard in 1931							
Austria	.14	.05	−.04	−.00	−.05	−.03	.06
Canada	.11	.15	.00	−.06	−.05	.02	−.01
Czechoslovakia	.14	.11	.08	.02	−.04	−.05	−.00
Denmark	.17	.11	−.03	−.07	−.09	−.01	−.04
Estonia	.16	.07	.02	−.06	−.01	.06	−.03
Finland			not available				
Germany	.12	.06	−.03	−.00	−.07	−.03	−.02
Greece			not available				
Hungary	.14	−.00	−.07	.09	−.06	−.11	−.00
Japan	.05	.21	−.04	−.12	.02	−.05	−.05
Latvia	.20	.18	−.15	−.05	.01	−.05	−.02
Norway	.08	.08	.02	−.02	−.01	−.03	−.02
Sweden	.17	.09	.01	−.02	−.06	−.01	−.02
United Kingdom	.17	.16	.02	−.02	−.03	−.03	−.03
Average	.14	.11	−.02	−.03	−.04	−.03	−.02
3. Countries abandoning gold standard between 1932 and 1935							
Rumania (1932)	.20	.14	−.10	−.05	−.02	−.15	−.12
United States (1933)	.10	.13	−.01	−.03	.04	−.03	.02
Italy (1934)	.10	.07	.05	.07	−.01	−.11	−.06
Belgium (1935)	.19	.10	.07	.04	.01	−.16	−.02
4. Countries still on full gold standard as of 1936							
France	.21	.09	.12	.07	.06	.09	−.06
Netherlands	.12	.14	.09	−.02	−.04	−.01	−.06
Poland	.11	.06	.05	.00	.01	.02	−.03
Average	.15	.10	.09	.02	.01	.03	−.05
5. Grand averages							
Gold standard countries			.05	.03	.01	.02	
Non-gold countries			−.02	−.03	−.03	−.04	

Note: The real wage is the nominal hourly wage for males (skilled, if available) divided by the wholesale price index. Wage data are from the International Labour Office, *Year Book of Labor Statistics*, various issues.

Table 2.6   Indices of Product Wages

Year	United Kingdom	United States	Germany	Japan	Sweden
1929	100.0	100.0	100.0	100.0	100.0
1930	103.0	106.1	100.4	115.6	116.6
1931	106.4	113.0	102.2	121.6	129.1
1932	108.3	109.6	96.8	102.9	130.0
1933	109.3	107.9	99.3	101.8	127.9
1934	111.4	115.8	103.0	102.3	119.6
1935	111.3	114.3	105.3	101.6	119.2
1936	110.4	115.9	107.7	99.2	116.0
1937	107.8	121.9	106.5	87.1	101.9
1938	108.6	130.0	107.7	86.3	115.1

Source: Eichengreen and Hatton (1987, 15).

1930s, but overall the correlation of real wage increases and depression does not appear particularly good. Note that Germany, which had probably the worst unemployment problem of any major country, has almost no increase in real wages;[10] the United Kingdom, which began to recover in 1932, has real wages increasing on a fairly steady trend during its recovery period; and the United States has only a small dip in real wages at the beginning of its recovery, followed by more real wage growth. The case for nominal wage stickiness as a transmission mechanism thus seems, at this point, somewhat mixed.

2. *Real interest rates.* In a standard IS-LM macro model, a monetary contraction depresses output by shifting the LM curve leftwards, raising real interest rates, and thus reducing spending. However, as Temin (1976) pointed out in his original critique of Friedman and Schwartz, it is real rather than nominal money balances that affect the LM curve; and since prices were falling sharply, real money balances fell little or even rose during the contraction.

Even if real money balances are essentially unchanged, however, there is another means by which deflation can raise ex ante real interest rates: Since cash pays zero nominal interest, in equilibrium no asset can bear a nominal interest rate that is lower than its liquidity and risk premia relative to cash. Thus an expected deflation of 10% will impose a real rate of at least 10% on the economy, even with perfectly flexible prices and wages. In an IS-LM diagram drawn with the nominal interest rate on the vertical axis, an increase in expected deflation amounts to a leftward shift of the IS curve.

Whether the deflation of the early 1930s was anticipated has been extensively debated (although almost entirely in the United States context). We will add here two points in favor of the view that the extent of the worldwide deflation was less than fully anticipated.

First, there is the question of whether the nominal interest rate floor was in fact binding in the deflating countries (as it should have been if this mechanism was to operate). Although interest rates on government debt in the United States often approximated zero in the 1930s, it is less clear that this

49 Financial Crisis in the Great Depression

was true for other countries. The yield on French treasury bills, for example, rose from a low of 0.75% in 1932 to 2.06% in 1933, 2.25% in 1934, and 3.38% in 1935; during 1933–35 the nominal yield on French treasury bills exceeded that of British treasury bills by several hundred basis points on average.[11]

Second, the view that deflation was largely anticipated must contend with the fact that nominal returns on safe assets were very similar whether countries abandoned or stayed on gold. If continuing deflation was anticipated in the gold standard countries, while inflation was expected in countries leaving gold, the similarity of nominal returns would have implied large expected differences in real returns. Such differences are possible in equilibrium, if they are counterbalanced by expected real exchange rate changes; nevertheless, differences in expected real returns between countries on and off gold on the order of 11–12% (the realized difference in returns between the two blocs in 1932) seem unlikely.[12]

3. *Financial crisis.* A third mechanism by which deflation can induce depression, not considered in the recent literature, works through deflation's effect on the operation of the financial system. The source of the non-neutrality is simply that debt instruments (including deposits) are typically set in money terms. Deflation thus weakens the financial positions of borrowers, both nonfinancial firms and financial intermediaries.

Consider first the case of intermediaries (banks).[13] Bank liabilities (primarily deposits) are fixed almost entirely in nominal terms. On the asset side, depending on the type of banking system (see below), banks hold either primarily debt instruments or combinations of debt and equity. Ownership of debt and equity is essentially equivalent to direct ownership of capital; in this case, therefore, the bank's liabilities are nominal and its assets are real, so that an unanticipated deflation begins to squeeze the bank's capital position immediately. When only debt is held as an asset, the effect of deflation is for a while neutral or mildly beneficial to the bank. However, when borrowers' equity cushions are exhausted, the bank becomes the owner of its borrowers' real assets, so eventually this type of bank will also be squeezed by deflation.

As pressure on the bank's capital grows, according to this argument, its normal functioning will be impeded; for example, it may have to call in loans or refuse new ones. Eventually, impending exhaustion of bank capital leads to a depositors' run, which eliminates the bank or drastically curtails its operation. The final result is usually a government takeover of the intermediation process. For example, a common scenario during the Depression was for the government to finance an acquisition of a failing bank by issuing its own debt; this debt was held (directly or indirectly) by consumers, in lieu of (vanishing) commercial bank deposits. Thus, effectively, government agencies became part of the intermediation chain.[14]

Although the problems of the banks were perhaps the more dramatic in the Depression, the same type of non-neutrality potentially affects nonfinancial firms and other borrowers. The process of "debt deflation", that is, the increase in the real value of nominal debt obligations brought about by falling prices, erodes the net worth position of borrowers. A weakening financial position affects the borrower's actions (e.g., the firm may try to conserve financial capital by laying off workers or cutting back on investment) and also, by worsening the agency problems in the borrower-lender relationship, impairs access to new credit. Thus, as discussed in detail in Bernanke and Gertler (1990), "financial distress" (such as that induced by debt deflation) can in principle impose deadweight losses on an economy, even if firms do not undergo liquidation.

Before trying to assess the quantitative impact of these and other channels on output, we briefly discuss the international incidence of financial crisis during the Depression.

2.4 Interwar Banking and Financial Crises

Financial crises were of course a prominent feature of the interwar period. We focus in this section on the problems of the banking sector and, to a lesser extent, on the problems of domestic debtors in general, as suggested by the discussion above. Stock market crashes and defaults on external debt were also important, of course, but for the sake of space will take a subsidiary role here.

Table 2.7 gives a chronology of some important interwar banking crises. The episodes listed actually cover a considerable range in terms of severity, as the capsule descriptions should make clear. However the chronology should also show that (i) quite a few different countries experienced significant banking problems during the interwar period; and (ii) these problems reached a very sharp peak between the spring and fall of 1931, following the Creditanstalt crisis in May 1931 as well as the intensification of banking problems in Germany.

A statistical indicator of banking problems, emphasized by Friedman and Schwartz (1963), is the deposit-currency ratio. Data on the changes in the commercial bank deposit-currency ratio for our panel of countries are presented in table 2.8. It is interesting to compare this table with the chronology in table 2.7. Most but not all of the major banking crises were associated with sharp drops in the deposit-currency ratio; the most important exception is in 1931 in Italy, where the government was able to keep secret much of the banking system's problems until a government takeover was affected. On the other hand, there were also significant drops in the deposit-currency ratio that were not associated with panics; restructurings of the banking system and exchange rate difficulties account for some of these episodes.

What caused the banking panics? At one level, the panics were an endogenous response to deflation and the operation of the gold standard regime.

51 Financial Crisis in the Great Depression

Table 2.7 **A Chronology of Interwar Banking Crises, 1921–36**

Date	Country	Crises
June 1921	SWEDEN	Beginning of deposit contraction of 1921–22, leading to bank restructurings. Government assistance administered through Credit Bank of 1922.
1921–22	NETHERLANDS	Bank failures (notably Marx & Co.) and amalgamations.
1922	DENMARK	Heavy losses of one of the largest banks, Danske Landmandsbank, and liquidation of smaller banks. Landmandsbank continues to operate until a restructing in April 1928 under a government guarantee.
April 1923	NORWAY	Failure of Centralbanken for Norge.
May 1923	AUSTRIA	Difficulties of a major bank, Allgemeine Depositenbank; liquidation in July.
September 1923	JAPAN	In wake of the Tokyo earthquake, bad debts threaten Bank of Taiwan and Bank of Chosen, which are restructured with government help.
September 1925	SPAIN	Failure of Banco de la Union Mineira and Banco Vasca.
July–September 1926	POLAND	Bank runs cause three large banks to stop payments. The shakeout of banks continues through 1927.
1927	NORWAY, ITALY	Numerous smaller banks in difficulties, but no major failures.
April 1927	JAPAN	Thirty-two banks unable to make payments. Restructuring of 15th Bank and Bank of Taiwan.
August 1929	GERMANY	Collapse of Frankfurter Allgemeine Versicherungs AG, followed by failures of smaller banks, and runs on Berlin and Frankfurt savings banks.
November 1929	AUSTRIA	Bodencreditanstalt, second largest bank, fails and is merged with Creditanstalt.
November 1930	FRANCE	Failure of Banque Adam, Boulogne-sur-Mer, and Oustric Group. Runs on provincial banks.
	ESTONIA	Failure of two medium-sized banks, Estonia Government Bank Tallin and Reval Credit Bank; crisis lasts until January.
December 1930	U.S.	Failure of Bank of the United States.
	ITALY	Withdrawals from three largest banks begin. A panic ensues in April 1931, followed by a government reorganization and takeover of frozen industrial assets.
April 1931	ARGENTINA	Government deals with banking panic by allowing Banco de Nacion to rediscount commercial paper from other banks at government-owned Caja de Conversión.

(continued)

Table 2.7 (continued)

Date	Country	Crises
May 1931	AUSTRIA	Failure of Creditanstalt and run of foreign depositors.
	BELGIUM	Rumors about imminent failure of Banque de Bruxelles, the country's second largest bank, induce withdrawals from all banks. Later in the year, expectations of devaluation lead to withdrawals of foreign deposits.
June 1931	POLAND	Run on banks, especially on Warsaw Discount Bank, associated with Creditanstalt; a spread of the Austrian crisis.
April–July 1931	GERMANY	Bank runs, extending difficulties plaguing the banking system since the summer of 1930. After large loss of deposits in June and increasing strain on foreign exchanges, many banks are unable to make payments and Darmstädter Bank closes. Bank holiday.
July 1931	HUNGARY	Run on Budapest banks (especially General Credit Bank). Foreign withdrawals followed by a foreign creditors' standstill agreement. Bank holiday.
	LATVIA	Run on banks with German connections. Bank of Libau and International Bank of Riga particularly hard hit.
	AUSTRIA	Failure of Vienna Mercur-Bank.
	CZECHOSLOVAKIA	Withdrawal of foreign deposits sparks domestic withdrawals but no general banking panic.
	TURKEY	Run on branches of Deutsche Bank and collapse of Banque Turque pour le Commerce et l'Industrie, in wake of German crisis.
	EGYPT	Run on Cairo and Alexandria branches of Deutsche Orientbank.
	SWITZERLAND	Union Financière de Genève rescued by takeover by Comptoir d'Escompte de Geneve.
	RUMANIA	Collapse of German-controlled Banca Generala a Tarii Românesti. Run on Banca de Credit Roman and Banca Romaneasca.
	MEXICO	Suspension of payments after run on Credito Espanol de Mexico. Run on Banco Nacional de Mexico.
August 1931	U.S.	Series of banking panics, with October 1931 the worst month. Between August 1931 and January 1932, 1,860 banks fail.
September 1931	U.K.	External drain, combined with rumors of threat to London merchant banks with heavy European (particularly Hungarian and German) involvements.
	ESTONIA	General bank run following sterling crisis; second wave of runs in November.

53 Financial Crisis in the Great Depression

Table 2.7 (continued)

Date	Country	Crises
October 1931	RUMANIA	Failure of Banca Marmerosch, Blank & Co. Heavy bank runs.
	FRANCE	Collapse of major deposit bank Banque Nationale de Crédit (restructured as Banque Nationale pour le Commerce et l'Industrie). Other bank failures and bank runs.
March 1932	SWEDEN	Weakness of one large bank (Skandinaviska Kreditaktiebolaget) as result of collapse of Kreuger industrial and financial empire, but no general panic.
May 1932	FRANCE	Losses of large investment bank Banque de l'Union Parisienne forces merger with Crédit Mobilier Français.
June 1932	U.S.	Series of bank failures in Chicago.
October 1932	U.S.	New wave of bank failures, especially in the Midwest and Far West.
February 1933	U.S.	General banking panic, leading to state holidays and a nationwide bank holiday in March.
November 1933	SWITZERLAND	Restructuring of large bank (Banque Populaire Suisse) after heavy losses.
March 1934	BELGIUM	Failure of Banque Belge de Travail develops into general banking and exchange crisis.
September 1934	ARGENTINA	Bank problems throughout the fall induce government-sponsored merger of four weak banks (Banco Espanol del Rio de la Plata, Banco el Hogar Argentina, Banco Argentina-Uruguayo, Ernesto Tornquist & Co.).
October 1935	ITALY	Deposits fall after Italian invasion of Abyssinia.
January 1936	NORWAY	After years of deposit stability, legislation introducing a tax on bank deposits leads to withdrawals (until fall).
October 1936	CZECHOSLOVAKIA	Anticipation of second devaluation of the crown leads to deposit withdrawals.

When the peak of the world banking crisis came in 1931, there had already been almost two years of deflation and accompanying depression. Consistent with the analysis at the end of the last section, falling prices lowered the nominal value of bank assets but not the nominal value of bank liabilities. In addition, the rules of the gold standard severely limited the ability of central banks to ameliorate panics by acting as a lender of last resort; indeed, since banking panics often coincided with exchange crises (as we discuss further below), in order to maintain convertibility central banks typically *tightened* monetary policy in the face of panics. Supporting the connection of banking problems with deflation and "rules of the game" constraints is the observation that there were virtually no serious banking panics in any country after aban-

Table 2.8   Log-differences of Commercial Bank Deposit-Currency Ratio

Country	1930	1931	1932	1933	1934	1935	1936
Australia	−.05	−.12*	.05	.01	.05	−.03	−.01
Austria	.17	−.40*	−.06	−.20*	−.07	−.01	−.02
Belgium	−.13*	−.22*	−.10*	.07	−.13*	−.27*	−.02
Canada	.07	−.01	.03	−.05	.00	.01	−.06
Czechoslovakia	−.11	−.08	.07	.02	.07	−.03	−.11*
Denmark	.08	−.03	.00	−.07	.02	.02	−.00
Estonia	.16	−.29*	−.02	−.05	.10	.05	.13
Finland	.09	−.05	.14	−.04	−.06	−.04	−.09
France	−.07	−.12*	−.01	−.10*	−.07	−.10	−.03
Germany	−.11*	−.40*	.05	−.09	−.01	−.08	−.02
Greece	.17	.07	−.27*	−.03	.06	−.04	.02
Hungary	.07	−.07	.10	−.03	−.08	−.05	−.03
Italy	.04	−.01	.05	.06	.01	−.20*	.08
Japan	.09	.03	−.12*	−.04	.03	−.00	.09
Latvia	.03	−.57*	.11	−.06	.12	.10	.45
Netherlands	.10	−.36*	−.05	−.06	−.05	−.08	.24
Norway	.04	−.15*	−.06	−.09	−.01	.03	−.23*
New Zealand	.04	−.11*	.03	.07	.15	−.08	−.32*
Poland	.07	−.29*	−.02	−.08	.10	−.06	.10
Rumania	.11	−.76*	−.05	−.11*	−.28*	.10	−.16*
Sweden	−.00	−.00	−.02	−.06	−.11*	−.08	−.07
Spain	.00	−.24*	.08	.03	.01	.06	N.A.
United Kingdom	.03	−.07	.10	−.07	−.02	.01	−.03
United States	.00	−.15*	−.26*	−.15*	.14	.05	.02

Note: Entries are the log-differences of the ratio of commercial bank deposits to money and notes in circulation. Data are from League of Nations, *Monthly Bulletin of Statistics* and *Yearbook*, various issues.
*Decline exceeds .10.

donment of the gold standard—although it is also true that by time the gold standard was abandoned, strong financial reform measures had been taken in most countries.

However, while deflation and adherence to the gold standard were necessary conditions for panics, they were not sufficient; a number of countries made it through the interwar period without significant bank runs or failures, despite being subject to deflationary shocks similar to those experienced by the countries with banking problems.[15] Several factors help to explain which countries were the ones to suffer panics.

1. *Banking structure.* The organization of the banking system was an important factor in determining vulnerability to panics. First, countries with "unit banking," that is, with a large number of small and relatively undiversified banks, suffered more severe banking panics. The leading example is of course the United States, where concentration in banking was very low, but a high incidence of failures among small banks was also seen in other countries (e.g., France). Canada, with branch banking, suffered no bank failures during

the Depression (although many branches were closed). Sweden and the United Kingdom also benefited from a greater dispersion of risk through branch systems.[16]

Second, where "universal" or "mixed" banking on the German or Belgian model was the norm, it appears that vulnerability to deflation was greater. In contrast to the Anglo-Saxon model of banking, where at least in theory lending was short term and the relationship between banks and corporations had an arm's length character, universal banks took long-term and sometimes dominant ownership positions in client firms. Universal bank assets included both long-term securities and equity participations; the former tended to become illiquid during a crisis, while the latter exposed universal banks (unlike Anglo-Saxon banks, which held mainly debt instruments) to the effects of stock market crashes. The most extreme case was probably Austria. By 1931, after a series of mergers, the infamous Creditanstalt was better thought of as a vast holding company rather than a bank; at the time of its failure in May 1931, the Creditanstalt owned sixty-four companies, amounting to 65% of Austria's nominal capital (Kindleberger 1984).

2. *Reliance of banks on short-term foreign liabilities.* Some of the most serious banking problems were experienced in countries in which a substantial fraction of deposits were foreign-owned. The so-called hot money was more sensitive to adverse financial developments than were domestic deposits. Runs by foreign depositors represented not only a loss to the banking system but also, typically, a loss of reserves; as we have noted, this additional external threat restricted the ability of the central bank to respond to the banking situation. Thus, banking crises and exchange rate crises became intertwined.[17] The resolution of a number of the central European banking crises required "standstill agreements," under which withdrawals by foreign creditors were blocked pending future negotiation.

International linkages were important on the asset side of bank balance sheets as well. Many continental banks were severely affected by the crises in Austria and Germany, in particular.

3. *Financial and economic experience of the 1920s.* It should not be particularly surprising that countries which emerged from the 1920s in relatively weaker condition were more vulnerable to panics. Austria, Germany, Hungary, and Poland all suffered hyperinflation and economic dislocation in the 1930s, and all suffered severe banking panics in 1931. While space constraints do not permit a full discussion of the point here, it does seem clear that the origins of the European financial crisis were at least partly independent of American developments—which argues against a purely American-centered explanation of the origins of the Depression.

It should also be emphasized, though, that not just the existence of financial difficulties during the 1920s but also the policy response to those difficulties was important. Austria is probably the most extreme case of nagging banking problems being repeatedly "papered over." That country had banking problems throughout the 1920s, which were handled principally by merging failing banks into still-solvent banks. An enforced merger of the Austrian Bodencreditanstalt with two failing banks in 1927 weakened that institution, which was part of the reason that the Bodencreditanstalt in turn had to be forceably merged with the Creditanstalt in 1929. The insolvency of the Creditanstalt, finally revealed when a director refused to sign an "optimistic" financial statement in May 1931, sparked the most intense phase of the European crisis.

In contrast, when banking troubles during the earlier part of the 1920s were met with fundamental reform, performance of the banking sector during the Depression was better. Examples were Sweden, Japan, and the Netherlands, all of which had significant banking problems during the 1920s but responded by fundamental restructurings and assistance to place banks on a sound footing (and to close the weakest banks). Possibly because of these earlier events, these three countries had limited problems in the 1930s. A large Swedish bank (Skandinaviska Kreditaktiebolaget) suffered heavy losses after the collapse of the Kreuger financial empire, and a medium-sized Dutch bank (Amstelbank) failed because of its connection to the Creditanstalt; but there were no widespread panics, only isolated failures.

A particularly interesting comparison in this regard is between the Netherlands and neighboring Belgium, where banking problems persisted from 1931 to 1935 and where the ultimate devaluation of the Belgian franc was the result of an attempt to protect banks from further drains. Both countries were heavily dependent on foreign trade and both remained on gold, yet the Netherlands did much better than Belgium in the early part of the Depression (see table 2.4). This is a bit of evidence for the relevance of banking difficulties to output.

Overall, while banking crises were surely an endogenous response to depression, the incidence of crisis across countries reflected a variety of institutional factors and other preconditions. Thus it will be of interest to compare the real effects of deflation between countries with and without severe banking difficulties.

On "debt deflation," that is, the problems of nonfinancial borrowers, much less has been written than on the banking crises. Only for the United States has the debt problem in the 1930s been fairly well documented (see the summary in Bernanke 1983 and the references therein). In that country, large corporations avoided serious difficulties, but most other sectors—small businesses, farmers, mortgage borrowers, state and local governments—were severely affected, with usually something close to half of outstanding debts being in default. A substantial portion of New Deal reforms consisted of various forms of debt adjustment and relief.

For other countries, there are plenty of anecdotes but not much systematic data. Aggregate data on bankruptcies and defaults are difficult to interpret because increasing financial distress forced changes in bankruptcy practices

57 Financial Crisis in the Great Depression

and procedures; when the League of Nations' *Monthly Bulletin of Statistics* dropped its table on bankruptcies in its December 1932 issue, for example, the reason given therein was that "the numerous forms of agreement by which open bankruptcies are now avoided have seriously diminished the value of the table" (p. 529). Perhaps the most extreme case of a change in rules was Rumania's April 1932 Law on Conversion of Debts, which essentially eliminated the right of creditors to force bankruptcy. Changes in the treatment of bankruptcy no doubt ameliorated the effects of debt default, but the fact that these changes occurred indicates that the perceived problem must have been severe. More detailed country-by-country study of the effects of deflation on firm balance sheets and the relation of financial condition to firm investment, production, and employment decisions—where the data permit—would be extremely valuable. A similar comment applies to external debt problems, although here interesting recent work by Eichengreen and Portes (1986) and others gives us a much better base of knowledge to build on than is available for the case of domestic debts.

2.5 Regression Results

In this section we present empirical results based on our panel data set. The principal question of interest is the relative importance of various transmission mechanisms of deflation to output. We also address the question, so far not discussed, of whether banking crises could have intensified the deflation process itself.

The basic set of results is contained in table 2.9, which relates the log-differences in industrial production for our set of countries to various combinations of explanatory variables. The definitions of the right-hand-side variables are as follows:

$\Delta \ln PW$: log-difference of the wholesale price index;
$\Delta \ln EX$: log-difference of nominal exports;
$\Delta \ln W$: log-difference of nominal wage;
DISC: central bank discount rate, measured relative to its 1929 value (a government bond rate is used for Canada; since no 1929 interest rate could be found for New Zealand, that country is excluded in regressions including DISC);
PANIC: a dummy variable, set equal to the number of months during the year that the country experienced serious banking problems (see below);
$\Delta \ln M0$: log-difference of money and notes in circulation.

Exports are included to control for trade effects on growth, including the benefits of competitive devaluation discussed by Eichengreen and Sachs (1986); and the wage is included to test for the real wage channel of transmission from deflation to depression. Of course, theory says that both of these variables should enter in real rather than in nominal terms; unfortunately, in practice the theoretically suggested deflator is not always available (as we noted in our discussion of the real wage above). We resolve this problem by supposing that the true equation is, for example,

(1) $\Delta \ln IP = \beta_e (\Delta \ln EX - \Delta \ln P_e) + \beta_w (\Delta \ln W - \Delta \ln P_w) + \text{error}$

where P_e and P_w, the optimal deflators, are not available. Let the projections of log-changes in the unobserved deflators on the log-change in the wholesale price deflator be given by

(2) $\Delta \ln P_i = \psi_i \Delta \ln PW + u_i \quad i = e, w$

where the u_i are uncorrelated with $\Delta \ln PW$ and presumably the ψ_i are positive. Then (1) becomes

(3) $\Delta \ln IP = -(\beta_e \psi_e + \beta_w \psi_w) \Delta \ln PW + \beta_e \Delta \ln EX + \beta_w \Delta \ln W + \text{new error}$

This suggests allowing $\Delta \ln PW$ and the nominal growth rates of exports and wages to enter the equation separately, which is how we proceed.[18] Putting $\Delta \ln PW$ in the equation separately has the added advantage of allowing us to account for any additional effect of deflation (such as debt deflation) not explicitly captured by the other independent variables.

The discount rate *DISC* is included to allow for the interest rate channel and as an additional proxy for monetary policy. Since $\Delta \ln PW$ is included in every equation, inclusion of the nominal interest rate *DISC* is equivalent to including the actual ex post real interest rate, that is, we are effectively assuming that deflation was fully anticipated; this should give the real interest rate hypothesis its best chance.

In an attempt to control for fiscal policy, we also included measures of central government expenditure in our first estimated equations. Since the estimated coefficients were always negative (the wrong sign), small, and statistically insignificant, the government expenditure variable is excluded from the results reported here.

Construction of the dummy variable *PANIC* required us to make a judgment about which countries' banking crises were most serious, which we did from our reading of primary and secondary sources. We dated periods of crisis as starting from the first severe banking problems; if there was some clear demarcation point (such as the U.S. bank holiday of 1933), we used that as the ending date of the crisis; otherwise we arbitrarily assumed that the effects of the crisis would last for one year after its most intense point. The banking crises included in the dummy are as follows (see also table 2.7):

1. Austria (May 1931–January 1933): from the Creditanstalt crisis to the date of official settlement of the Creditanstalt's foreign debt.
2. Belgium (May 1931–April 1932; March 1934–February 1935): for one year after the initial Belgian crisis, following Creditanstalt, and for one

year after the failure of the Banque Belge de Travail led to a general crisis.

3. Estonia (September 1931–August 1932): for one year after the general banking crisis.
4. France (November 1930–October 1932): for one year following each of the two peaks of the French banking crises, in November 1930 and October 1931 (see Bouvier 1984).
5. Germany (May 1931–December 1932): from the beginning of the major German banking crisis until the creation of state institutes for the liquidation of bad bank debts.
6. Hungary (July 1931–June 1932): for one year following the runs in Budapest and the bank holiday.
7. Italy (April 1931–December 1932): from the onset of the banking panic until the takeover of bank assets by a massive new state holding company, the Istituto por le Riconstruzione Industriale (IRI).
8. Latvia (July 1931–June 1932): for one year following the onset of the banking crisis.
9. Poland (June 1931–May 1932): for one year following the onset of the banking crisis.
10. Rumania (July 1931–September 1932): from the onset of the crisis until one year after its peak in October 1931.
11. United States (December 1930–March 1933): from the failure of the Bank of the United States until the bank holiday.

The inclusion of Austria, Belgium, Estonia, Germany, Hungary, Latvia, Poland, Rumania, or the United States in the above list cannot be controversial; each of these countries suffered serious panics. (One might quibble on the margin about the exact dating given—for example, Temin [1989] and others have argued that the U.S. banking crisis did not really begin until mid 1931—but we doubt very much that changes of a few months on these dates would affect the results.) The inclusion of France and Italy is more controversial. For example, Bouvier (1984) argues that the French banking crisis was not as serious as some others, since although there were runs and many banks failed, the very biggest banks survived; also, according to Bouvier, French banks were not as closely tied to industry as other banking systems on the Continent. For Italy, as we have noted, early and massive government intervention reduced the incidence of panic (see Ciocca and Toniolo 1984); however, the banks were in very poor condition and (as noted above) eventually signed over most of their industrial assets to the IRI.

To check the sensitivity of our results, we reestimated the key equations omitting first the French crisis from the *PANIC* variable, then the French and Italian crises. Leaving out France had a minor effect (lowering the coefficient on *PANIC* and its *t*-statistic about 5% in a typical equation); the additional exclusion of the Italian crisis has essentially no effect.[19]

As a further check, we also reestimated our key equations omitting, in separate runs, (i) the United States; (ii) Germany and Austria; and (iii) all eastern European countries. In none of these equations were our basic results substantially weakened, which indicates that no single country or small group of countries is driving our findings.

The first seven equations in table 2.9 are not derived from any single model, but instead attempt to nest various suggested explanations of the link between deflation and depression. Estimation was by OLS, which opens up the possibility of simultaneity bias; however, given our maintained view that the deflation was imposed by exogenous monetary forces, a case can be made for treating the right-hand-side variables as exogenous or predetermined.

The principal inferences to be drawn from the first seven rows of table 2.9 are as follows:[20]

1. Export growth consistently enters the equation for output growth strongly, with a plausible coefficient and a high level of statistical significance.

2. When wage growth is included in the output equation along with only wholesale price and export growth (row 5), it enters with the wrong sign.

Table 2.9   Determinants of the Log-difference of Industrial Production (dependent variable: $\Delta \ln IP$)

	Independent Variables					
Equation	$\Delta \ln PW$	$\Delta \ln EX$	$\Delta \ln W$	DISC	PANIC	$\Delta \ln M0$
(1)	.855					
	(.098)					
(2)	.531				−.0191	
	(.095)				(.0026)	
(3)	.406	.231				
	(.121)	(.043)				
(4)	.300	.148			−.0157	
	(.111)	(.041)			(.0027)	
(5)	.364	.231	.272			
	(.141)	(.046)	(.206)			
(6)	.351	.150	−.072		−.0156	
	(.128)	(.044)	(.197)		(.0029)	
(7)	.296	.103	−.119	−.0358	−.0138	
	(.123)	(.044)	(.189)	(.0102)	(.0028)	
(8)		.217*	−.015		−.0126	.405
		(.048)	(.189)		(.0031)	(.098)

Note: For variable definitions, see text. The sample period is 1930–36. The panel consists of twenty-four countries except that, due to missing wage data, Finland, Greece, and Spain are excluded from equations (5)–(8). Estimates of country-specific dummies are not reported. Standard errors are in parentheses.

*Export growth is measured in real terms in equation (8).

Only when the *PANIC* variable is included does nominal wage growth have the correct (negative) sign (rows 6 and 7). In the equation encompassing all the various channels (row 7), the estimated coefficient on wage growth is of the right sign and a reasonable magnitude, but it is not statistically significant.

3. The discount rate enters the encompassing equation (row 7) with the right sign and a high significance level. A 100-basis-point increase in the discount rate is estimated to reduce the growth rate of industrial production by 3.6 percentage points.

4. The effect of banking panics on output is large (a year of panic is estimated in equation (7) to reduce output growth by $12 \times .0138$, or more than 16 percentage points) and highly statistically significant (t-statistics of 4.0 or better). The measured effect of the *PANIC* variable does not seem to depend much on what other variables are included in the equation.

5. There may be some residual effect of deflation on output not accounted for by any of these effects. To see this, note that in principle the coefficient on $\Delta \ln PW$ in equation (7) of table 2.9 should be equal to and opposite the weighted sum of the coefficients on $\Delta \ln EX$, $\Delta \ln W$, and *DISC* (where the weights are the projection coefficients of the respective "true" deflators on $\Delta \ln PW$). Suppose for the sake of illustration that each of the projection coefficients equals one (that is, the wholesale price index is the correct deflator). Then the expected value of the coefficient on $\Delta \ln PW$ should be approximately .052; the actual value is .296, with a standard error of .123. Thus there may be channels relating deflation to depression other than the ones explicitly accounted for here. One possibility is that we are simply picking up the effects of a simultaneity bias (a reverse causation from output to prices). Alternatively, it is possible that an additional factor, such as debt deflation, should be considered.

As an alternative to the procedure of nesting alternative channels in a single equation, in equation (8) of table 2.9 we report the results of estimating the reduced form of a simple aggregate demand–aggregate supply (AD-AS) system. Under conventional assumptions, in an AD-AS model output growth should depend on money growth and autonomous spending growth (represented here by growth in *real* exports[21]), which shift the AD curve; and on nominal wage growth, which shifts the AS curve. In addition, we allow *PANIC* to enter the system, since banking panics could in principle affect both aggregate demand and aggregate supply. The results indicate large and statistically significant effects on output growth for real export growth, money growth, and banking panics. Nominal wage growth enters with the correct sign, but the coefficient is very small and statistically insignificant.

We have so far focused on the effects of banking panics (and other variables) on output. There is an additional issue that warrants some discussion here; namely, the possibility that banking panics might have themselves worsened the deflationary process.

Some care must be taken with this argument. Banking panics undoubtedly had large effects on the composition of national money supplies, money multipliers, and money demand. Nevertheless, as has been stressed by Temin (1989), under a gold standard, small country price levels are determined by international monetary conditions, to which domestic money supplies and demands must ultimately adjust. Thus banking panics cannot intensify deflation in a small country.[22] Indeed, a regression (not reported) of changes in wholesale prices against the *PANIC* variable and time dummies (in order to isolate purely cross-sectional effects) confirms that there is very little relationship between the two variables.

The proposition that bank panics should not affect the price level does not necessarily hold for a large country, however. In econometric language, under a gold standard the price level of a large country must be cointegrated with world prices; but while this means that domestic prices must eventually adjust to shocks emanating from abroad, it also allows for the possibility that domestic shocks will influence the world price level. Notice that if banking panics led to deflationary shocks in a large country and these shocks were transmitted around the world by the gold standard, a cross-sectional comparison would find no link between panics and the price level.

The discussion of the gold standard and deflation in section 2.2 cited Hamilton's (1987) view that the initial deflationary impulses in 1928–29 came from France and the United States—both "big" countries, in terms of economic importance and because of their large gold reserves. This early deflation obviously cannot be blamed on banking panics, since these did not begin until at least the end of 1930. But it would not be in any way inconsistent with the theory of the gold standard to hypothesize that banking panics in France and the United States contributed to world deflation during 1931–32.[23]

Empirical evidence bearing on this question is presented in table 2.10. We estimated equations for wholesale price inflation in the United States and France, using monthly data for the five-year period 1928–32. We included an error-correction term in both equations to allow for cointegration between the U.S. and French price levels, as would be implied by the gold standard. This error-correction term is the difference between the log-*levels* of U.S. and French wholesale prices in period $t-1$; if U.S. and French prices are in fact cointegrated, then the growth rate of U.S. prices should respond negatively to the difference between the U.S. price and the French price, and the French growth rate of prices should respond positively. Also included in the equations are lagged inflation rates (to capture transitory price dynamics), current and lagged base money growth, and current and lagged values of the deposits of failing banks (for the United States only, due to data availability).

The results are interesting. First, there is evidence for cointegration: The error-correction terms have the right signs and reasonable magnitudes, although only the U.S. term is statistically significant. Thus we may infer that shocks hitting either French or U.S. prices ultimately affected both price levels. Second, both U.S. base money growth and bank failures are important

63 Financial Crisis in the Great Depression

Table 2.10 Error-correction Equations for U.S. and French Wholesale Prices

	Dependent Variable	
	$\Delta \ln USAWPI$	$\Delta \ln FRAWPI$
Constant	.044 ($t = 3.81$)	$-.006$ ($t = 1.57$)
Log USAWPI $-$ log FRAWPI (lagged once)	$-.166$ ($t = 2.77$)	.071 ($t = 1.10$)
Four lags of own WPI growth	$-.530$ ($F = 1.57; p = .202$)	.320 ($F = 2.48; p = .057$)
Current and four lags of base money growth	1.412 ($F = 5.62; p = .0005$)	.519 ($F = 0.78; p = .569$)
Current and four lags of deposits of failing U.S. banks, in logs	$-.020$ ($F = 5.61; p = .0005$)	
R^2	.531	.307
D-W	1.62	1.87

Note: Deposits of failing banks are from the *Federal Reserve Bulletin*. USAWPI and FRAWPI are wholesale price indexes for the United States and France, respectively. Monthly data from 1928 to 1932 are used.

determinants of the U.S. (and by extension, the French) deflation rates; these two variables enter the U.S. price equation with the right sign and marginal significance levels of .0005.

With respect to the effect of banking panics on the price level, then, the appropriate conclusion appears to be that countries with banking panics did not suffer worse deflation than those without panics;[24] however, it is possible that U.S. banking panics in particular were an important source of *world* deflation during 1931–32, and thus, by extension, of world depression.

2.6 Conclusion

Monetary and financial arrangements in the interwar period were badly flawed and were a major source of the fall in real output. Banking panics were one mechanism through which deflation had its effects on real output, and panics in the United States may have contributed to the severity of the world deflation.

In this empirical study, we have focused on the effects of severe banking panics. We believe it likely, however, that the effects of deflation on the financial system were not confined to these more extreme episodes. Even in countries without panics, banks were financially weakened and contracted their operations. Domestic debt deflation was probably a factor, to a greater or lesser degree, in every country. And we have not addressed at all the effect of deflation on the burden of external debt, which was important for a number of countries. As we have already suggested, more careful study of these issues is clearly desirable.

Notes

1. The original diagnosis of the Depression as a monetary phenomenon was of course made in Friedman and Schwartz (1963). We find the more recent work, though focusing to a greater degree on international aspects of the problem, to be essentially complementary to the Friedman-Schwartz analysis.

2. Eichengreen and Sachs (1985) discuss several mechanisms and provide some cross-country evidence, but their approach is somewhat informal and they do not consider the relative importance of the different effects.

3. To be clear, gold inflows to France did increase the French monetary base directly, one for one; however, in the absence of supplementary open market purchases, this implied a rising ratio of French gold reserves to monetary base. Together with the very low value of the French money multiplier, this rising cover ratio meant that the monetary expansion induced by gold flowing into France was far less significant than the monetary contractions that this inflow induced elsewhere.

4. Temin (1989) suggests that German monetary policy provided yet another contractionary impetus.

5. There remains the issue of whether the differences in timing of nations' departure from the gold standard can be treated as exogenous. Eichengreen and Sachs (1985) argue that exogeneity is a reasonable assumption, given the importance of individual national experiences, institutions, and fortuitous events in the timing of each country's decision to go off gold. Strong national differences in attitudes toward the gold standard (e.g., between the Gold Bloc and the Sterling Bloc) were remarkably persistent in their influence on policy.

6. The countries in our sample are listed in table 2.1. We included countries for which the League of Nations collected reasonably complete data on industrial production, price levels, and money supplies (League of Nations' *Monthly Bulletin of Statistics and Yearbooks*, various issues; see also League of Nations, *Industrialization and Foreign Trade*, 1945). Latin America, however, was excluded because of concerns about the data and our expectation that factors such as commodity prices would play a more important role for these countries. However, see Campa (forthcoming) for evidence that the gold standard transmitted deflation and depression to Latin America in a manner very similar to that observed elsewhere.

7. We define abandonment of the gold standard broadly as occurring at the first date in which a country imposes exchange controls, devalues, or suspends gold payments; see table 2.1 for a list of dates. An objection to this definition is that some countries continued to try to target their exchange rates at levels prescribed by the gold standard even after "leaving" the gold standard by our criteria; Canada and Germany are two examples. We made no attempt to account for this, on the grounds that defining adherence to the gold standard by looking at variables such as exchange rates, money growth, or prices risks assuming the propositions to be shown.

8. In constructing the grand averages taken over gold and non-gold countries, if a

65 Financial Crisis in the Great Depression

country abandoned the gold standard in the middle of a year, it is included in both the gold and non-gold categories with weights equal to the fraction of the year spent in each category. We use simple rather than weighted averages in the tables, and similarly give all countries equal weight in regression results presented below. This was done because, for the purpose of testing hypotheses (e.g., about the relationship between deflation and depression) it seems most reasonable to treat each country (with its own currency, legal system, financial system, etc.) as the basic unit of observation and to afford each observation equal weight. If we were instead trying to measure the overall economic significance of, for example, an individual country's policy decisions, weighted averages would be more appropriate.

9. The use of the terms M1 and M2 should not be taken too literally here, as the transactions characteristics of the assets included in each category vary considerably among countries. The key distinction between the two aggregates is that commercial banks, which were heavily involved in commercial lending, were much more vulnerable to banking panics. Savings banks, in contrast, held mostly government securities, and thus often gained deposits during panic periods.

10. However, it must be mentioned that recent exponents of the real wage explanation of German unemployment invoke it to account for high levels of unemployment throughout the mid and late 1920s, and not just for the period after 1929 (Borchardt 1979).

11. In the French case, however, there may have been some fear of government default, given the large deficits that were being run; conceivably, this could explain the higher rate on French bills.

12. A possible response to this point is that fear of devaluation added a risk premium to assets in gold standard countries. This point can be checked by looking at forward rates for foreign exchange, available in Einzig (1937). The forward premia on gold standard currencies are generally small, except immediately before devaluations. In particular, the three-month premium on dollars versus the pound in 1932 had a maximum value of about 4.5% (at an annual rate) during the first week of June, but for most of the year was considerably less than that.

13. The effect of deflation on banks, and the relationship between deflation and bank runs, has been analyzed in a theoretical model by Flood and Garber (1981).

14. An important issue, which we cannot resolve here, is whether government takeovers of banks resulted in some restoration of intermediary services, or if, instead, the government functioned primarily as a liquidation agent.

15. In the next section we divide our sample into two groups: eleven countries with serious banking problems and thirteen countries without these problems. In 1930, the year before the peak of the banking crises, the countries that were to avoid banking problems suffered on average a 12% deflation and a 6% fall in industrial production; the comparable numbers for the group that was to experience panics were 13% and 8%. Thus, there was no large difference between the two groups early in the Depression. In contrast, in 1932 (the year following the most intense banking crises), industrial production growth in countries without banking crises averaged − 2%; in the group that experienced crises the comparable number was − 16%.

16. Although this correlation seems to hold during the Depression, we do not want to conclude unconditionally that branch banking is more stable; branching facilitates diversification but also increases the risk that problems in a few large banks may bring down the entire network.

17. Causality could run in both directions. For example, Wigmore (1987) argues that the U.S. banking panic in 1933 was in part created by a run on the dollar.

18. It has been pointed out to us that if nominal wages were literally rigid, then this approach would find no effect for wages even though changes in the real wage might

be an important channel for the effects of deflation. The reply to this is that, if nominal wages are completely rigid, the hypothesis that real wages are important can never be distinguished from an alternative which proposes that deflation has its effects in some other way.

19. In another sensitivity check, we also tried multiplying PANIC times the change in the deposit-currency ratio, to allow for differential severity of panics. The results exhibited an outlier problem. When Rumania (which had a change in the deposit-currency ratio of $-.76$ in 1931) was excluded, the results were similar to those obtained using the PANIC variable alone. However, inclusion of Rumania weakened both the magnitude and statistical significance of the effect of panics on output. The "reason" for this is that, despite its massive deposit contraction, Rumania experienced a 5% growth of industrial production in 1931. Whether this is a strong contradiction of the view that panics affect real output is not clear, however, since according to the League of Nations the peak of the Rumania crisis did not occur until September or October, and industrial production in the subsequent year fell by 14%. Another reason to downplay these results is that the change in the deposit-currency ratio may not be a good indicator of the severity of the banking crisis, as the Italian case indicates.

20. Results were unchanged when lagged industrial production growth was added to the equations. The coefficient on lagged production was typically small and statistically insignificant.

21. Deflation is by the wholesale price index.

22. A possible exception to this proposition for a small country might be a situation in which there are fears that the country will devalue or abandon gold; in this case the country's price level might drop below the world level without causing inflows of reserves. An example may be Poland in 1932. A member of the Gold Bloc, Poland's wholesale price level closely tracked that of France until mid 1931, when Poland experienced severe banking problems and withdrawals of foreign deposits, which threatened convertibility. From that point on, even though both countries remained on the gold standard, money supplies and prices in Poland and France began to diverge. From the time of the Polish crisis in June 1931 until the end of 1932, money and notes and circulation dropped by 9.1% in Poland (compared to a gain of 10.5% in France); Polish commercial bank deposits fell 24.5% (compared to a 4.1% decline in France); and Polish wholesale prices declined 35.2% (compared to a decline of 18.3% in France). Despite its greater deflation, Poland lost about a sixth of its gold reserves in 1932, while France gained gold.

23. This hypothesis does not bear on Temin's claim that there was little that central banks could do about banking crises under the gold standard; rather, the argument is that if, fortuitously, French and U.S. banking panics had not occurred, world deflation in 1931–32 would have been less severe.

24. Indeed, if banking panics induced countries to abandon gold, they may have indirectly contributed to an eventual rise in price levels.

References

Bernanke, Ben. 1983. Non-monetary effects of the financial crisis in the propagation of the Great Depression. *American Economic Review* 73: 257–76.

——. 1986. Employment, hours, and earnings in the Depression: An analysis of eight manufacturing industries. *American Economic Review* 76: 82–109.

Bernanke, Ben, and Mark Gertler. 1990. Financial fragility and economic performance. *Quarterly Journal of Economics* 105: 87–114.

Board of Governors of the Federal Reserve System. 1943. *Banking and monetary statistics, 1919–41.* Washington, DC: Government Printing Office.
Borchardt, Knut. 1979. Zwangslagen und Handlungsspielraume in der grossen Wirtschaftskrise der fruhen dreissiger Jahren: Zur Revision des uberlieferten Geschichtesbildes. *Jahrbuch der Bayerische Akademie der Wissenschaften,* 87–132. Munich.
Bordo, Michael, and Finn Kydland. 1990. The gold standard as a rule. Typescript, Rutgers University and Carnegie-Mellon University.
Bouvier, Jean. 1984. The French banks, inflation and the economic crisis, 1919–1939. *Journal of European Economic History* 13: 29–80.
Campa, Jose Manuel. Forthcoming. Exchange rates and economic recovery in the 1930s: An extension to Latin America. *Journal of Economic History.*
Choudhri, Ehsan U., and Levis A. Kochin. 1980. The exchange rate and the international transmission of business cycle disturbances: Some evidence from the Great Depression. *Journal of Money, Credit, and Banking* 12: 565–74.
Ciocca, Pierluigi, and Gianni Toniolo. 1984. Industry and finance in Italy, 1918–40. *Journal of European Economic History* 13: 113–36.
Eichengreen, Barry. 1986. The Bank of France and the sterilization of gold, 1926–1932. *Explorations in Economic History* 23: 56–84.
———. 1987. The gold-exchange standard and the Great Depression. Working Paper no. 2198 (March). Cambridge, Mass.: National Bureau of Economic Research.
Eichengreen, Barry, and T. J. Hatton. 1987. Interwar unemployment in international perspective: An overview. In *Interwar unemployment in international perspective,* ed. B. Eichengreen and T. J. Hatton, 1–59. Boston: Kluwer Academic Publishers.
Eichengreen, Barry, and Richard Portes. 1986. Debt and default in the 1930s: Causes and consequences. *European Economic Review* 30: 599–640.
Eichengreen, Barry, and Jeffrey Sachs. 1985. Exchange rates and economic recovery in the 1930s. *Journal of Economic History* 45: 925–46.
———. 1986. Competitive devaluation in the Great Depression: A theoretical reassessment. *Economic Letters* 21: 67–71.
Einzig, Paul. 1937. *The theory of forward exchange.* London: Macmillan.
Fisher, Irving. 1933. The debt-deflation theory of great depressions. *Econometrica* 1: 337–57.
Flood, Robert P., Jr., and Peter M. Garber. 1981. A systematic banking collapse in a perfect foresight world. NBER Working Paper no. 691 (June). Cambridge, Mass.: National Bureau of Economic Research.
Friedman, Milton, and Anna J. Schwartz. 1963. *A monetary history of the United States, 1867–1960.* Princeton: Princeton University Press.
Haberler, Gottfried. 1976. *The world economy, money, and the Great Depression.* Washington, DC: American Enterprise Institute.
Hamilton, James. 1987. Monetary factors in the Great Depression. *Journal of Monetary Economics* 19: 145–69.
———. 1988. The role of the international gold standard in propagating the Great Depression. *Contemporary Policy Issues* 6: 67–89.
Kindleberger, Charles P. 1984. Banking and industry between the two wars: An international comparison. *Journal of European Economic History* 13: 7–28.
League of Nations. 1926. *Memorandum on Currency and Central Banks, 1913–1925.* Geneva.
———. 1935. *Commercial banks, 1929–1934.* Geneva.
———. 1944. *International currency experience: Lessons of the inter-war period.* Geneva.
Lindert, Peter. 1969. Key currencies and gold, 1900–1913. *Princeton Studies in International Finance,* no. 24.
Newell, Andrew, and J. S. V. Symons. 1988. The macroeconomics of the interwar

years: International comparisons. In *Interwar unemployment in international perspective*, ed. B. Eichengreen and T. J. Hatton, 61–96. Boston: Kluwer Academic Publishers.

O'Brien, Anthony. 1989. A behavioral explanation for nominal wage rigidity during the Great Depression. *Quarterly Journal of Economics* 104: 719–35.

Temin, Peter. 1976. *Did monetary forces cause the Great Depression?* New York: W. W. Norton.

——. 1989. *Lessons from the Great Depression*. Cambridge, Mass.: MIT Press.

Wigmore, Barrie. 1987. Was the Bank Holiday of 1933 a run on the dollar rather than the banks? *Journal of Economic History* 47: 739–56.

Financial flows across frontiers during the interwar depression

By HAROLD JAMES

In explaining the interwar depression, a new scholarly orthodoxy, dominated by 'a striking degree of consensus', has recently emerged.[1] In large part it is a modern restatement of the widely held contemporary view that after 1922 the operation of the restored international gold standard (or, more properly, a new gold exchange standard) created a pattern of linkages that left the world's economies vulnerable to deflationary shocks emanating from the restrictive monetary policies of France and the US.[2] The gold 'sterilization' of these countries in response to gold and exchange inflows restricted domestic monetary expansions which might have balanced the contractions that were taking place elsewhere.[3] Through their policies France and the US prevented the realization of any effective international cooperation, and crippled the international financial system. Removing the shackles of the gold standard thus became the most important prerequisite for world recovery.

The primary transmission mechanism for these shocks was international financial mediation. Money flows transferred deflation across frontiers, and thus dramatically reduced purchasing power in other economies.[4] This in turn led to the collapse of international trade, to which the worldwide movement to increase tariffs and otherwise restrict trade through the implementation of quota systems was merely a response (rather than being a primary cause of the international depression). This new history of depression is, in its account of causation, above all a monetary history.

The central part of this explanation lies in the financial shocks of 1931 and 1932 which intensified the deflationary spiral. There are two major puzzles in both the traditional and the modern accounts. First, the international simultaneity of the shock to different national monetary systems requires explanation. What constituted the linkage? Secondly, what forces prevented the international monetary system from returning to equilibrium? This is a question about investors' attitudes and the effects they had in limiting the options available to policy-makers. In classic accounts of the gold standard, interest rates provided the central adjustment device, yet in the interwar period rate rises often failed to attract new flows, and instead worked as a negative signal. The Governor of the Banque de France, Clément Moret, put the point clearly when he stated: 'There is a psychological factor

---

[1] Eichengreen, 'Origins and nature', p. 213.
[2] See for instance Henry Strakosch, supplement to *Economist*, 9 Jan. 1932.
[3] Eichengreen, 'The Bank of France'; Eichengreen and Sachs, 'Exchange rates'; Temin, *Lessons*, pp. 21-3.
[4] Friedman and Schwartz, *Monetary history*, pp. 359-60.

that entirely escapes the action of the Banque. Movements of capital are today determined, less by differences in interest rates than by the greater or lesser security they offer.'[5] When capital movements occurred, 'motivated by the desire to profit by, or avoid loss from, expected exchange movements', the effect on the world economy was, as Haberler pointed out, severely deflationary: 'While the flow of funds will cause a considerable reduction in investment in the countries from which it comes, it will be largely sterilized in those to which it goes.'[6]

Both these problems about the operation of the interwar gold standard have in the past been answered, in a cavalier manner, with a single word: 'confidence'. In the modern literature, 'confidence' is merely replaced by another term: 'credibility'. 'Credibility' concerns the ability of policy-makers to act in accordance with their stated policies and with an underlying policy regime. In the context of the 1920s, that regime was the restored international gold standard, the measure of 'credibility' was 'confidence', and the indicator of the failure of 'credibility' financial panic.

The purpose of this article is to investigate the nature of the interconnectedness of European economies. What role did investor psychology play? And what were the circumstances which moulded it?

I

In Europe after 1931, financial and banking crises spread across national frontiers, demonstrating an apparent degree of coordination that surprised and puzzled many commentators.[7] The transmission mechanism involved was rarely direct capital links. In the most famous case, the Austrian crisis around the Creditanstalt in May 1931 is supposed to have provoked the German bank collapse of June-July, although the extent of German financial involvement in Austria was very limited, and it would be impossible to argue that the Austrian developments directly weakened German institutions.[8]

Several alternative hypotheses suggest themselves, the first is a rational, but non-monetary explanation. Bank crises were responses to general macroeconomic conditions. The worldwide price decline for many commodities after the mid 1920s affected financial institutions because it reduced the value of banks' collateral. In this case, the primary origins of depression lie clearly outside the financial sector.

The second hypothesis draws on the psychological theories of investment behaviour current at the time. There existed an international psychology of crisis which provided the transmission mechanism. This was the language familiarly used at the time: financial stability depended on a 'confidence' or market sentiment, which governments were unable effectively to control or manipulate. Such a psychology might undermine government attempts at monetary stabilization. In 1933 Keynes, while appealing for greater 'national self-sufficiency', acknowledged this as the principal difficulty in making

---

[5] Banque de France (B.d.F.), Paris, Conseil Général Procès-Verbaux, 27 Nov. 1930.
[6] Haberler, *Prosperity and depression*, p. 441.
[7] See Bernanke and James, 'The gold standard'.
[8] See Kindleberger, *World in depression*, p. 148.

contra-cyclical policy: 'Advisable domestic policies might often be easier to compass, if, for example, the phenomenon known as the "flight of capital" could be ruled out.'⁹ The gold standard depended above all on the assumption of 'confidence', but the panic psychology it generated in the 1920s made this an ever more elusive quest.

The third alternative is a modern variant of the second, and concerns an explanation of the motives involved in panic. Specifically, the gold standard encouraged large speculative movements once a fear became prevalent among investors that there might be a departure from gold. 'Credibility' meant ensuring that a commitment to a specific market parity was convincing to market psychology by limiting the scope for policy actions to those measures possible within the gold standard regime. In this setting, exchange rates, and an assessment of the probability of their alteration, would matter much more than relative interest rates, and the classical steering mechanism of the gold standard (discount rate changes) would become ineffective.

Here a fourth explanation is suggested—that interpretation of the domestic budget positions of gold standard countries held the key to calculations about 'confidence' and exchange rate structures. Budget deficits threatened a likely departure from gold, not just because there may have been a fear of the repetition of the inflations and hyper-inflations that had ravaged Europe in the immediate postwar period, but because investors and portfolios had not adjusted to a fundamental shift in the character of indebtedness. In particular, increased public deficits could not be accommodated easily by financial markets. The results was to increase the volatility of these markets.

II

This point becomes clearer by means of a comparison between the extent of interwar international capital movements and those of the pre-1914 period. It was not so much that new or unprecedentedly large capital movements were taking place in the 1920s. In absolute terms, the flow was actually reduced in comparison with the prewar years, but it responded in a newly volatile fashion.

This phenomenon was often described as flight of capital. 'Capital flight' is a fundamentally political term, and one man's concept of flight may be interpreted by another as simply a normal capital export.¹⁰ Looking at the interwar period in a longer term perspective, its capital flows scarcely justify the more emotive descriptions of orgies of lending and massive debt problems. The overall flows of the 1920s were smaller rather than greater than the prewar movements: for 1911-3, the average annual capital export of Britain, France, Germany, and the US to the rest of the world was $1,400 million. In the period 1924-8, when capital flows were at their greatest, the annual figure was $860 million (or $550 million in prewar prices).¹¹

There is a dramatic contrast between the prewar world, in which short-

---

⁹ Keynes, 'National self-sufficiency', p. 236. For the relationship of market psychology and Keynesian thought, see Middleton, *Towards the managed economy*, p. 162.
¹⁰ Machlup, 'Die Theorie der Kapitalflucht'.
¹¹ Lewis, 'World production', p. 130; United Nations, *International capital movements*, p. 25.

term capital movements were still primarily concerned with the financing of trade, and the larger movements of the postwar world. There are no reliable estimates for prewar global short-term indebtedness, but the figures available for individual countries indicate much lower levels than for the 1920s. Britain, by far the largest short-term creditor, had assets of $1,715 million, while Germany had $240 million and the US $450 million in liabilities.[12] For 1930, the Bank for International Settlements estimated the total world short-term indebtedness as 70,000 million Swiss francs or $13,500 million, of which Germany accounted for $3,900 million, the US for $2,700 million, and the UK for $1,900 million. Of this total, only $4,300 million related to strictly commercial transactions: the implication left by the B. I. S. figures was that the rest was 'hot money', that reacted to political crises.[13]

The high short-term indebtedness of the US and Britain, despite their overall status as creditors, reflected their attractions as a haven for deposits, often originating from the major capital importing countries. This development represented a counterflow, in which capital exports to central Europe, Germany, or South America were re-exported by the borrowers.

Contemporary calculations of hot money flows—based largely on guesswork built around rather unreliable figures for trade and reported capital flows—seem at first rather high. In Germany in 1930, capital moved out since 1926 was estimated at 9,000 million marks, representing around one-eighth of NNP or twice the volume of the German note issue. For France in 1938, capital flight constituted an estimated one-quarter of national income, or 88 per cent of currency in circulation. Even for the much larger US, the estimates of capital flight in 1933 in the aftermath of the dollar's departure from gold suggest 18 per cent of note issue.[14] It is scarcely surprising that figures of these magnitudes alarmed contemporaries, and led in Germany, France, and the US to political movements built around opposition to alleged capitalist conspiracies.

The political motivation of interwar capital movements has become a familiar part of the literature. In 1924, the French government blamed pressure on the franc on German speculation. The German government and the German Central Bank believed that the runs on the mark during the Paris experts' conference in spring 1929, and again after the September 1930 parliamentary elections, were the result of French intrigue. The political crisis of August 1931 in Britain was interpreted as a 'bankers' ramp' mounted by American financial institutions in league with the City. The French press, as well as the French intelligence service, believed that Germany was behind the repeated runs on the franc after 1933.[15]

[12] Bloomfield, *Short-term capital movements*, pp. 71-82.
[13] Bank of England (B.o.E.), London, OV50/6, Oct. 1936, F. G. Conolly (B.I.S.) memorandum, 'International short term indebtedness'.
[14] These estimates of 'capital flight' are taken from contemporary sources: for Germany, James, *German slump*, p. 298; for the US, Federal Reserve Bank of New York (F.R.B.N.Y.), New York, Harrison papers 2010.2, 22 Nov. 1933, Crane memorandum on telephone conversation between Harrison and Roosevelt; B.o.E., OV31/23, 25 Sept. 1933, Sprague memorandum for Clay; 12 Dec. 1933, Jacobsson to Niemeyer; for France, Drummond, *London*, pp. 45-6
[15] Philippe, *Le drame financier*; Frayssinet, *La politique monétaire*; Schuker, *End of French predominance*, pp. 55, 94; James, *Reichsbank*, p. 77; Williamson, 'A bankers' ramp?'; on France in the 1930s, French Ministry of Finance, Paris, B18675, 2 Apr. 1936, memorandum of État Major de l'Armée, 2ᵉ bureau.

In each case, the element of truth in these over-politicized interpretations lay in the belief of the financial community that government budget deficits—even of a comparatively modest size—provided the critical signal of serious underlying economic difficulties. This was in part a lesson learnt as a result of the inflationary and hyper-inflationary experiences of the early 1920s, when the running of deficits and their financing through monetary expansion appeared to be 'a sort of post war Finance Minister's drug habit'.[16]

The threat to stability could come in two forms: either that there would be a buyers' strike in the bond market and an inability of government authorities to roll over the substantial volumes of their outstanding short-term debt; or that the government would preempt the first threat by expanding the money supply and resorting to inflationary finance. Either of these developments threatened policy makers' ability to continue to act in accordance with the requirements of their policy regime, and in this way undermined 'credibility'. The first of these explanations has been developed as a theoretical model for debt crises by Alesina, Prati, and Tabellini, and applied in the case of France in the 1920s by Prati. A similar mechanism has been used by Balderston to explain the limitations on German fiscal room for manoeuvre in the later 1920s.[17] This approach has a particular applicability where capital markets were destabilized by recent experience of inflation.

The interpretation of the size of acceptable public sector deficits influenced the rest of the financial structure. Initially this was the mechanism of propagation of financial crisis in central Europe, where as a result of capital inflows to promote reconstruction after inflation, business debt had expanded. From 1926 to 1930, the indebtedness of business corporations as a proportion of owned capital remained steady or fell in the US (from 65.9 to 60.9 per cent) and in Britain (from 58.0 to 50.3 per cent), while these ratios increased dramatically in central Europe. The Hungarian ratio rose from 69.3 to 80.3 per cent, and the German ratio from 65.1 to 81.9 per cent.[18] Rising business indebtedness did not attract substantial adverse comments, investor worries, or a panic psychology. Government deficits, however, did; and the behaviour of public sector debt profoundly affected, through the panic mechanism, the market for private debt. Budget deficits rose inevitably in the depression, as tax and other revenues fell off, and as social spending requirements rose. The fiscal response to depression proved to be a major source of financial instability, which in turn intensified the depression.

In the course of that panic, a fundamental and very rapid liquidation of short-term debt occurred. In 1930 the B. I. S. had estimated short term indebtedness as 70 billion Swiss francs. Its later calculations showed total international short-term indebtedness to have fallen to 45 billion Swiss francs at the end of 1931 and 32 billion at the end of 1933 (and its contemporary

---

[16] League of Nations (L.o.N.), Geneva, Salter papers S123, April 1924, 'Notes on currency questions'.
[17] Alesina, Prati, and Tabellini, 'Public confidence'; Prati, 'Poincaré's stabilization'; Balderston, 'German capital and labour markets'.
[18] League of Nations, *World economic survey, 1932-3*, pp. 137-8.

figures demonstrated an even more dramatic decline: to 30 billion by the end of 1931).[19]

III

The interaction of fiscal and debt crises became clear with the episode that led to the general European, and then world, panic: the failure in May 1931 of the largest Austrian bank, the Vienna Creditanstalt. It failed for two fundamental reasons: its bad debts, and the fall during the depression of the value of its security portfolio.[20] As it was by far the largest Austrian bank and had become in effect a holding company for the Austrian economy, its difficulties inevitably had far reaching implications. In a narrow sense, the problems of the Creditanstalt had nothing to do with the difficulties of financing government in Austria during an economic downturn, but the Austrian banking crisis became a general crisis of 'confidence' because of the implications of the Creditanstalt affair for the national budget.

The losses of the bank were underestimated in May 1931, and calculations of the total continued to mount throughout the year. The accounts published on the night of 11 to 12 May revealed losses of 140 million Austrian schillings; by mid June the figure was 500 million, and at the end of the year it had risen further to 923 million (or two-thirds of the Austrian budget for that year).[21] These sums were to be covered by purchases of Creditanstalt paper by the National Bank with a government guarantee. Thus the Creditanstalt's losses would widen the government's budget deficit. Rescuing the banking sector involved the 'socialization of debt'—the transfer of liabilities from the private to the public sector. Given the example and the precedent of the early 1920s inflation, such a transfer destabilized the markets. This new debt could not be absorbed by the domestic market unless it further liquidated commercial credit, which would obviously be highly counter-productive as a way of salvaging the financial system. Only money creation appeared as an alternative to default on both foreign and domestically held debt. The possibility that Austria might be pushed off the gold standard became a self-fulfilling threat. Withdrawals from Austria took place across the exchanges, and threatened the entire banking structure (not just banks with a weak reputation) as well as the country's ability to transfer exchange and thus its commitment to the gold standard.

Even in early May 1931, before the Creditanstalt's difficulties became public knowledge, leading financial opinion makers such as the house of J. P. Morgan in New York were alarmed by the predictions of a large Austrian budget deficit for 1931. In France, one of Austria's major creditors, even socialist newspapers complained about the inflated size of the 'hypertrophied' Austrian state, and all French investors became more nervous.[22] French, but also central European, funds were moved internationally. France

---

[19] B.o.E. OV50/6, Conolly memorandum; B.I.S., *Third annual report*, p. 11.
[20] See Nötel, 'Money, banking and industry', p. 162; most recently, Stiefel, *Finanzdiplomatie*.
[21] The audited account: L.o.N. C88, 3 Oct. 1931, Deloitte Plender Binder to Austrian Minister of Finance.
[22] Kunz, *Battle for Britain's gold standard*, p. 47: *L'Avenir*, 10 May 1931.

became a major centre for funds moving out of central Europe: some indication of the extent to which the French market became a shelter for flight capital is given by the rise in private deposits at the Banque de France during the central European panic: from 11,884 million French francs on 27 March 1931 to 15,187 million francs in July.[23] The rise represents an addition of $128 million: by coincidence, almost exactly the amount of the international B. I. S. and Central Bank credits given to support the Hungarian and German central banks ($125 million).

Could greater international cooperation have stopped the Creditanstalt crisis? Such cooperation would have involved the allocation of foreign funds to the Austrian state or to its central bank, and alleviated the exchange position but at the same time allowed the run on the Creditanstalt and the transfer out of private funds to continue for longer. It would thus have increased the problems of the Austrian authorities in dealing with the domestic situation. Cooperation without a complete overhaul of Austria's financial system was consequently believed to be ineffective. The eventual resolution of the Creditanstalt crisis involved two parallel processes, both directed by foreigners as representatives of the creditor countries. While the Dutchman Adrianus van Hengel supervised the reconstruction of the Creditanstalt, another Dutchman, Rost van Tonningen, was appointed by the Financial Committee of the League of Nations to control the Austrian budget and ensure the implementation of a harsh austerity programme.

The lesson of the Creditanstalt collapse was that budget deficits and bank collapses were causally linked, and that withdrawals across the exchange posed a double threat, to internal financial stability and to gold standard maintenance. The logic of Austria became that of other crisis bound central European countries. In Hungary, which like Austria had been the subject of a stabilization imposed by the League, the budget had been strained by the institution of a rebate ticket scheme on agricultural products, the *boletta*, designed to maintain wheat prices in the face of the worldwide collapse, as well as a wheat buffer stock programme, the *futura*. As the President of the Hungarian National Bank confessed, some time before the beginning of the banking crisis: 'the fact that such a situation could remain undisclosed until so late a stage argued a lack of financial control and administrative organization which could not be denied.'[24] In addition, there were huge deficits in the accounts of publicly owned enterprises.

The budget difficulty, as interpreted by investors, led to a movement of funds out of Hungary. This run was tackled by the Hungarian authorities in a rather more imaginative way than in Austria, in part because it was recognized from the first movements of money that a general crisis of confidence was involved. There were signs of similar developments to those which had shaken the Vienna banks, as current accounts in the major Budapest banks fell and banks consequently started to withdraw credits to their major customers, pushing up the bankruptcy rate.[25] The run on

[23] B.d.F. Conseil Général Procès-Verbaux.
[24] B.o.E. OV 33/79, 9-10 Feb. 1932, H. A. S[iepmann] note on conversation with Dr Popovics.
[25] B.d.F. Hungary 22 June 1931, McGarrah to Moret; B.o.E. G1/306, 6 June 1931, Popovics cable to Norman.

Budapest banks had less to do with specific weaknesses in their portfolios than with a general fear of the reaction that would be produced by the publicity surrounding the budget deficit. In that sense, it was not purely a banking problem. The Hungarian National Bank kept its commercial banking sector liquid by a generous policy of discounting bank bills. The result was that the outflow of funds from Hungarian institutions could continue across the exchanges, so that the major part of the strain fell on the external exchange rather than on the Hungarian institutions. This prompted foreign creditors to agree to a standstill, or voluntary debt freezing agreement, for Hungarian debt.

The fear of public insolvency played a significant part in the German banking crisis of June and July 1931. Again, as in Austria, there was mixture of specific worries about particular banks (especially the losses resulting to the Darmstädter- und Nationalbank as a result of its lending to Nordwolle) with a wider reaching calculation. A fear that the government was unable to finance its (relatively small) deficit and its problems in making cash payments, together with difficulties in local and state governments, prompted a run on deposits, which forced the closure of Germany's leading banks.[26] The run on deposits took the form of withdrawals across the exchanges, and the rapid depletion of the Central Bank's international reserves.

Germany had a large share of the world's cross-national short-term deposits. After Germany, the international panic spread to those other countries with large short-term liabilities, Britain and the US. Though the history of the capital markets in Britain and the US was completely different from those in Germany, and though there had been no traumatic Anglo-Saxon postwar inflations, the reactions and the arguments about the origins of weakness that resulted from the panics show a substantial similarity to the earlier drama of central Europe. Once again, it was the budget and the question of how it might be balanced that preoccupied financiers.

In Britain, the extent of the likely budget deficit had been at the centre of public debate at least by the time of the German crisis, which further increased awareness of the destabilizing effects of budget deficits. In early 1931, the House of Commons Public Accounts Committee had already been warned that the central budget was severely unbalanced.[27] The result was the appointment of a committee on national expenditure, the May Committee, which reported on 31 July. A memorandum written in late July by Sir Richard Hopkins, the Controller of Finance and Supply Services in the British Treasury, stated:

> We cannot control that we are in the midst of an unexampled slump, nor the fact that Germany is bankrupt, that great assets of ours are frozen there, and that foreign nations are drawing their credits from there over our exchanges. Nor can we control the fact that foreign nations have immense sums of money in London and will try to get them away if distrust of the pound extends . . . . The first thing at which foreigners will look is the budgetary position.[28]

---

[26] James, 'Causes of the German banking crisis'.
[27] See B.o.E. G15/28, 20 Sept. 1943, H. C. Mynors, note of a talk with Sir Horace Wilson.
[28] Cited by Cairncross and Eichengreen, *Sterling in decline*, p. 64.

In particular, foreign opinion interpreted the report of the Macmillan Committee (published, by coincidence, on the date of the general German bank closure, 13 July) as a plea for inflationism. The Committee had recommended measures to halt 'the violent downturn of prices, the effects of which upon political and social stability have already been very great', and it criticized the choice of parity at which Britain had returned to the gold standard in 1925.[29] The Governor of the Banque de France believed the Macmillan report to be a plea for 'a managed inflation, in the form of authorization of the Bank of England to increase the note issue'.[30] Foreign investors apparently shared this opinion, and the withdrawals started immediately. Whereas in early July, movements of gold from Germany had stayed in London, after 13 July London too was affected. In the period 12-22 July, according to the Banque de France, Britain lost £20 million, of which half went to France, £6 million to the Netherlands, and £4 million to Switzerland (other traditional safe havens for capital flight).[31]

Concern about the British budget raised the issue of Britain's role as a global financial intermediary, and sterling's position as a unit of account. As in central Europe, two related issues were involved: the stability of a currency facing international drains, and the stability of banks threatened both by a run on deposits and by the freezing of their assets. As in the previous crises of 1931, the double dilemma required not simply a measure that would allow banks to continue in business, but a remedy to halt the external drain that also threatened the position of the banks.

The major investments of French banks in central Europe, for instance, went through the City of London. Between 1928 and 1931, the four leading French banks had accumulated total foreign balances of between 5,000 and 6,000 million French francs ($200-230 million), of which an estimated two-thirds were in sterling. But the Bank of England's internal investigation of the distribution of French funds in London concluded that of the French sterling balances, only 10 per cent were actually invested in the short-term London market, and the rest were re-lent to central Europe.[32] As early as May 1931, the New York market had been swept by rumours about the difficulties of major London banks (the Governor of the Federal Reserve Bank explicitly named Barclays, Schroders, and Rothschilds). After July, Lazards, Barings, and Schroders were close to bankruptcy, and Lazards needed a credit line from the Bank of England.[33]

The double necessity of defending banks and protecting sterling explains the highly peculiar path of British official policy prior to devaluation. Although the Bank of England helped to arrange in August a privately financed credit for the British government through J. P. Morgan New York (a loan whose conditions brought down the Labour Government) the Bank did not use the additional reserves, it had gained in this way in any attempt

---

[29] *Committee on Finance and Industry*, p. 92.
[30] B.d.F. Conseil Général Procès-Verbaux, 16 July 1931.
[31] Ibid., 23 July 1931.
[32] B.o.E. OV 45/81, 12 Dec. 1930, H. A. S[iepmann] memorandum for Mr Powell.
[33] B.o.E. OV32, 18 May 1932, Harrison cable to Norman. See also Diaper, 'Merchant banking', pp. 69-71; Boyce, *British capitalism*, pp. 344-5.

at a defence of sterling in September. Neither did it raise the bank rate in early September, as it should have done under the conventions of the gold standard, and as French and American creditors had urged.

The combination of these two official inactivities, over the use of the exchange from the Morgan credit and over the bank rate, made the Bank of England's policy look alternately incoherent or defeatist. One recent analyst concluded that the only explanation must be that the abandonment of the gold standard had been secretly prepared well in advance by the Bank.[34] But there is no direct evidence to support this suggestion. The eventual depreciation of sterling on 21 September 1931 was indeed the necessary result of a systematic inertia, but its motivation was different. The experience of central Europe had showed the impotence of discount rate policy in halting an external run. More importantly, this was also a potential banking crisis. Using the foreign exchange from the Morgan credit would have allowed the withdrawals of short-term deposits from London banks to continue without affecting the exchange, and would have led to a situation in which a massive and politically embarrassing support operation for the affected London banks would become necessary.

Already on 27 July, Hopkins had told the Bank of England's policy-making body, the Committee on Treasury, that the City faced the danger of a run. At this meeting, the views of the British clearing banks were also reported: they opposed any foreign Central Bank credit to the Bank of England which would allow the Bank of England to continue to make gold shipments that would be financed from the withdrawal of deposits in London banks.[35] Although eventually foreign credits were taken, they were not used, an inactivity that was in full accordance with the spirit of the clearing banks' observations and requests.

Devaluation appeared to be a way of stopping the external drain on British banks. This was the immediate rationale, rather than a response to the general problems of depression or an attempt to deal with Britain's trading position. By letting the currency depreciate, and at the same time maintaining the commitment to a balanced budget, the one-way possibility of a large *future* fall in the sterling parity would be removed and replaced by the possibility of a rise or a fall, or of greater stability. There would no longer be an attraction in liquidating sterling deposits in British banks in order to move funds across the exchange. Without the devaluation, drains on the banks would have continued until the outbreak of a major banking crisis.

The effect of British depreciation in September 1931 involved the exporting of the confidence problem. The US was now clearly the outstanding international short-term debtor left on the gold standard. It faced the threat of a withdrawal of deposits. Despite its favourable trade balance in the depression, a risk of an attack on the dollar emerged. With this, the same combination of a potential threat to the currency and an actual threat to the banking system (as deposits were withdrawn) had the same repercussions in the US as it had had in continental Europe.

[34] Kunz, *Battle*, pp. 132-4, 185-8.
[35] B.o.E. G14/316, 27 July 1931, minutes of Committee on Treasury.

In late 1931 and 1932, a new wave of bank panics hit the US, as the numerous internal weaknesses of the banking structure were amplified by an international drain. What happened is shown clearly by the weekly gold statements prepared, but not published, by the Federal Reserve Bank of New York (F.R.B.N.Y.). There were some outflows in July 1931, as the extent of American banks' involvement overseas became apparent, but the large outflows started with the intensification of the sterling crisis of September. Gold was earmarked for European central banks in the week ending 21 September, and in October big outflows occurred: in successive weeks $61.5 million in gold was shipped to France (in the week ending 5 October), then $89 million, $42.6 million, and $53.9 million. The 1 per cent discount rate increases imposed by the F.R.B.N.Y. on 9 October and 16 October had little effect in stopping the drain, but contributed significantly to the worsening of domestic business conditions.[36] The lesson of Europe, that discount rate changes were not an effective policy instrument, was being absorbed in the US.

There was a new round of drains in January and February, then a brief lull until April, when the outflows were resumed at the same time as a major group of bank failures occurred in the midwest. The Federal Reserve System's initial answer to the panics of 1932 was to inject new liquidity through open market purchases. It was an approach similar to that adopted by the Hungarian authorities in 1931: that the domestic banking system should be saved, even if this meant providing the resources which would let the external run continue. By April 1932 increased liquidity had become the explicitly acknowledged programme of Governor George Harrison of the F.R.B.N.Y. [37] As a strategy for fighting credit deflation, however, it was dramatically unsuccessful: the bank collapses continued in an explosive crescendo until March 1933.

The generally accepted explanation of the ineffectiveness of the open market programme emphasizes the institutional resistance to Governor Harrison's programme within the Federal Reserve System.[38] A more compelling cause of the failure lay in the expectations of the international market, which interpreted the purchases of government securities as inflationary, and as a signal to continue the run. Unlike the Hungarian case, there was no immediate *de facto* departure from gold in response to the new policy through a mix of capital controls and bank standstill agreements; and neither was there a devaluation. But the threat was clear. In January 1932, a former Federal Reserve banker, economics professor, and popular journalist, Parker Willis, circulated reports of American fiscal irresponsibility in the influential periodical *Agence Economique et Financière*. The reaction was that major American institutions started to 'bear the dollar', and by June 1932 the Bank of England struggled with private Americans sending gold to London for safe keeping.[39]

[36] The gold outflows are reported in F.R.B.N.Y., 'Japan' country file.
[37] F.R.B.N.Y. C261, 13 April 1932, Harrison cable to Norman.
[38] Most systematically set out in Friedman and Schwartz, *Monetary history*, pp. 347, 384-8.
[39] F.R.B.N.Y. C261, 27 May 1932, Knoke-Kay telephone conversation; 4 June 1932, Harvey cable to Harrison.

FINANCIAL FLOWS DURING THE INTERWAR DEPRESSION 605

In fact there appeared to be powerful analogies between the position of the US and the by now painfully familiar imbroglio of central European finance. The nervousness about public finance started in 1931, when Congress overrode a presidential veto to pass the Veterans' Bonus Bill, with the explicit purpose of injecting an additional purchasing power of $1,200 million. This expenditure appeared in the budget, and 1931 was consequently one of the most expansionary accounts in the whole interwar period, with the differences between government revenues and expenditures running at some 5 per cent of GNP (or 3.6 per cent of full employment GNP).[40] Throughout the summer of 1931, estimates of the federal deficit rose. By autumn, the consequences of government debt issue for the securities market had become a part of the explanation for bank weakness. This was the message delivered in December 1931 by the Committee on Progress of Public Works of the President's Organization on Unemployment Relief: new issues of government bonds would 'cause serious declines in the market values of the present outstanding low-yield issues .... It may well be that one result would be a considerable number of additional bank failures.'[41] The panic of April-May 1932 focused specifically on the raised projections for the 1932 deficit (announced on 3 May),[42] and a budget balancing bill in June calmed the panic, but only temporarily.

Immediately after the presidential campaign of 1932, the effect of Democratic campaign promises to balance the Federal budget meant substantial gold inflows, but by the beginning of the new year, the fear that the US might abandon gold prompted a new series of outflows. Between 1 February and 14 March 1933 the F.R.B.N.Y. lost three-fifths of its gold reserves. Since it was US banks that were losing deposits, and since domestic depositors reacted to the news, a fresh round of bank failures resulted.[43] This predicament was the major theme of foreign advice and warning. In February, the Governor of the Bank of England called the Federal Reserve's attention to the 'flood of dollar offerings' in London. By early March, the London market interpreted the run and the need for the bank holiday as a sign that 'we [the USA] were already off or else we were going off the gold standard'.[44] The result was a pronounced outflow of capital, a substantial proportion of which went to France.

Immediately on assuming office, Roosevelt needed to decree a banking holiday. The quick answer to bank panics lay less in institutional banking reform—which would take time—than in the deliberate use of uncertainty about the dollar's value to reduce the level of speculative flows. This stance provided the 'bombshell' of 3 July 1933, in which Roosevelt announced that the US had no intention of stabilizing the dollar. The presidential message quite deliberately destroyed the chances of international economic cooperation on exchange matters at the 1933 London World Economic Conference.[45] Its

[40] Brown, 'Fiscal policy', pp. 865-6.
[41] Barber, *From New Era*, p. 120.
[42] F.R.B.N.Y. Harrison papers 3117.2, 20 May 1932, Hambro-Harvey telephone conversation.
[43] This case is argued convincingly in Wigmore, 'Bank holiday'.
[44] F.R.B.N.Y. 3115.4, 24 Feb. 1932, Harrison-Norman telephone conversation; C261, 6 March 1932, Hambro-Crane conversation.
[45] Kindleberger, *World in depression*, p. 216.

aim was not only to increase US domestic prices, but also to reduce capital movements by creating greater uncertainty, as a central element of the new policy became the view that the world's problem lay in excessive capital movements.

The main lesson of the depression and of the outflows of 1933, according to the American interpretation, was that capital flows and international lending weakened the US economy and limited the room for manoeuvre in budgetary policy. Ending this constraint required a reduction of the capital flows that made the international economy so sensitive. The point was very emphatically made already in late 1932 by the Harvard economist John H. Williams, the US representative on the Financial Subcommittee of the Preparatory Commission for the World Economic Conference, and a committed advocate of the gold standard and fixed parities:

> The United States are [sic] not economically a creditor country: there is an adverse balance in the invisible item of the US balance of payments (tourist traffic and immigrant's remittances). The US became a creditor country as a result of the War: but the massive exports of capital were a mistake, and it may be anticipated that exports of capital in the future will be on a limited scale.[46]

Responses to crisis in central Europe and then in Britain and the US all involved the same calculation, which required belief in a limitation of the scope for money and capital movements to destabilize domestic economies. And as fewer countries remained open to capital movements, those countries felt the destabilizing effects more profoundly.

US policy deliberately shifted attention to France, and to the French budget. Roosevelt was quite proud of this new turn in the direction of international financial nervousness, which he attributed to US dollar policy. It was, he said of the French, 'their own fault inasmuch as they had not balanced their budget for three years and that it was unavoidable that because of their budgetary situation something of this sort would have had to develop'.[47] In 1931 and 1932 France, with a gold currency backed by massive reserves, appeared to offer what the Governor of the Banque de France had already in 1930 termed 'a currency of refuge'.[48] But this led to considerable problems for French monetary policy. The increased gold reserves that had resulted from the big inflows of 1931 and 1932 could not be used as a basis for domestic expansion, because there existed a strong likelihood that the sums would be moved out again. What would occur should the capital flows be reversed, and French banks be affected by massive withdrawals by foreign depositors? At the same time the monetary surplus could be interpreted as offering a temptation of responding to the world economic crisis by expanding; and this was exactly the kind of belief that would destabilize markets. Such a reverse flow had already begun in December 1932, and after this all the major banks lost deposits, were threatened by illiquidity, and survived only by discounting paper at the Banque de France.

---

[46] L.o.N. R2672, 4 Nov. 1932, minutes of meeting of financial sub-committee.
[47] F.R.B.N.Y. Harrison papers 2010.2, 22 Nov. 1933, memorandum on 21 Nov. 1933 Harrison-Roosevelt telephone conversation.
[48] B.d.F. Conseil Général Procès-Verbaux, 27 Nov. 1930.

The large French budget surpluses following the franc stabilization of 1926 also helped to create the impression that there were plentiful funds available for new spending projects. By the budget year 1930-1, there was a small deficit; and it grew larger during 1931. By late 1932, the budget was the subject of fiercely politicized debates in the French Assembly. The difficulties of borrowing in the long-term market forced the French government to resort to the issue of Treasury bills, which increasingly were not taken by the public or the banks, but instead needed to be rediscounted by the Banque de France.[49]

The deposits of the four large French banks, which fell between 1932 and 1936 from 21,000 million francs to 15,300 million, again give an indication of the extent not so much of French domestic problems as of the external drains facing France.[50] When bank deposit withdrawals threatened the French credit structure, the Banque de France increased its rediscounting in order to keep the French banks liquid: but this made resources available for outward movements over the exchanges. In this way, the Banque, while propping up the French banking structure, actually fostered the flight of capital from the country.

The only response to this dilemma was to attempt to remove the source of the speculation by promoting confidence, and this required reducing the budget deficit. But soon this policy of deflation, followed with more or less rigour by all the governments between 1932 and 1936 (with the partial exception of the Flandin ministry in 1935), also had its perverse effects on economic stability.[51] Observers soon realized that political attempts to stabilize the budget were contentious and divisive, and that deflation, by undermining political stability, also reduced confidence in the franc. By 1935, this interpretation had gripped the foreign exchange markets: 'London circles were explaining the softness of the French franc as due to the drastic measures which the French cabinet proposed to take in connection with its supplementary budget and which might well lead to a split in the cabinet.'[52]

The previous reaction to financial panics had been the belief that deficits needed to be avoided because they caused capital flight, which threatened the commitment to gold and also internal financial stability. Now it appeared that avoiding budget deficits produced the same effects on market psychology. With this, the last argument for gold in the last bastions of the gold standard crumbled.

IV

Uncertainty about public budgets thus played a central role in undermining the stability of the interwar financial system. During the depression, a vicious circle had emerged, linking budget deficits to assessments of exchange rate stability, the resulting capital flows to withdrawals of deposits from banks, and subsequent bank failures and crises in turn to budget problems. It is

---

[49] Mouré, *Managing the franc*, pp. 166, 190.
[50] *Mouvement économique*, p. 203.
[51] See in general Jackson, *Politics of depression*.
[52] F.R.B.N.Y. 261, 16 May 1935, Knoke-Cariguel telephone conversation.

important to note that this effect was not only visible in countries with harsh experiences of inflation or hyper-inflation in the aftermath of the First World War. It was equally evident in countries such as Britain or the US which had not suffered this particular postwar trauma. This suggests that the origins of the problem do not lie in particular political cultures which reacted allergically to the prospect of a repetition of inflation. At first this conclusion is extremely puzzling. Why should exactly the same calculation apply in France, the US, and Britain, where capital markets existed which should have been perfectly capable of financing government deficits in the depression, as in countries in Latin America and central Europe, where capital markets were either inadequately developed or had been destroyed by inflation?

France and the US ran what were by contemporary standards very high central budget deficits under a gold standard regime during the depression: the US in 1931 and France from 1932. Britain, on the other hand, despite the intense political debate of 1931, in an international comparison looked highly responsible and even restrictive (table 1). Worries about a potentially expansive budget in a gold standard regime were enough to cause the major crisis of August-September 1931, but no actual bank collapses of the kind experienced in the US, France, or in the other gold standard countries, Belgium and Switzerland.

Table 1. *Central state surpluses/deficits as a proportion of GNP (per cent)*[a]

	Austria	Belgium	France	Germany[b]	Hungary	Italy	UK	US
1928[c]	−0.7		+1.6	−1.2	+0.2	0.0	+0.4	+0.8
1929	+0.2		+1.6	−1.6	−0.5	−0.3	−0.3	+0.7
1930	−2.2		−0.1	−2.1	−3.6	−3.4	−0.5	−0.5
1931	−3.1	−4.4	−0.9	−0.1	−3.2	−4.5	0.0	−3.2
1932	−0.2		−2.9	−0.4	−2.2	−3.8	−0.7	−2.3
1933	−2.6		−5.3	−0.2	−1.5	−8.7	−0.4	−3.6
1934	−2.5	−2.6	−4.5	−1.0	−1.5	−2.3	+0.2	−4.0

Notes: [a]NNP for Belgium and Hungary; national income for France
[b]Net increases in central government debt, from *Konjunkturstatistisches Handbuch 1936*, p. 171. This series does not include tax certificates (after 1932) or Mefo-Bills (after 1933), for which, however, there existed no formal market.
[c]For Austria, Belgium, and also for France until 1929 and after 1933, the budget year coincided with the calendar year. For Germany, the UK, and France in 1930/1 and 1932/3 the budget year ran from 1 April to 31 March. For Hungary, Italy, and the US, the budget year ran from 1 July to 30 June.
Sources: League of Nations, *Public finance, 1928–1935;* GNP from Mitchell, *European historical statistics; Annuaire statistique de la France.*

An explanation of the increased vulnerability of finance to politics lies in the overall expansion of public debt relative to the prewar era. One dramatic difference between the pre- and postwar worlds was the extent to which debt structures were dominated by public sector liabilities.

The primary cause of the relative rise of public sector debt was the war. Absolute figures for public sector debt rose dramatically: in the UK, for instance, unredeemed public debt increased more than tenfold between 1914 and 1920 (table 2). These rises were particularly dramatic where there was no substantial inflation to reduce the real value of government liabilities.

In other countries, especially in central Europe, the value of the public debt was reduced by the effects of monetary inflation. But even in these

FINANCIAL FLOWS DURING THE INTERWAR DEPRESSION 609

cases, the same effects reduced the worth of private liabilities (notwithstanding the fact that in legal stabilization settlements, different rates of revaluation were often applied to private and public liabilities). The public/private mix also showed a fundamental shift, albeit not as great a movement as in the case of non-inflationary economies.

Table 2. *Public debt as a proportion of nominal capital of joint stock companies (per cent)*

Year	UK	Germany
1914	622	189
1930	6,764	221

Source: calculated from Mitchell and Deane, *Abstract*, p. 203; Balogh, *Studies*, p. 281; *Deutsches Geld- und Bankwesen*, pp. 294, 313.

The increased share of public sector debt in the liability structure thus occurred everywhere (though to different extents), despite previous experience of inflation, and the markets responded in similarly nervous ways to these shifts. The need to finance government debt payments also affected the new issues market, which frequently determined market expectations much more directly than the absolute quantities of circulating debt. Absorbing new debt issues posed difficulties because of the reduced savings ratios that resulted in part from the redistribution of wealth and savings of the war and postwar periods, and in part, in those countries with experience of inflation, from the memory of the past losses.

If the new public debt could not be absorbed by the long-term market, larger amounts of short-term debt would circulate. These created considerable problems, and directly caused the peculiar reactions of 1920s markets to central bank discount rate changes (subsequently, fear of devaluation played a greater role). Increasing discount rates as a protective measure at a time of exchange rate difficulties would depress the value of financial issues. If this reduction was anticipated by foreign or domestic markets, they would attempt to move their funds from securities into bank deposits. In selling government securities, they would oblige the central bank to absorb the government paper. This would make sums available for the purchase of foreign exchange, intensifying rather than alleviating the exchange problem. This was the phenomenon that was subsequently interpreted and denounced as capital flight.[53] It affected the Bank of England after the return to the gold standard in 1925, but also the policy of the Banque de France.

The French case shows clearly how during the first half of the 1920s, and again in the depression, after 1931, public debt dominated the new issues market (table 3). This was interpreted, not as a signal for confidence, but rather as the opposite. It became more difficult to sell public sector debt, and the risk premia increased. By contrast the stabilization period, between 1926 and 1931, was stable precisely because of the reduced claims made on the market by the public sector.

[53] For a discussion of this process, see Cairncross and Eichengreen, *Sterling in decline*, pp. 50-1.

Table 3. *France: share of public debt in total new issues (per cent)*

1919	89.0	1928^a	58.9
1920	89.4	1929	—
1921	74.4	1930	—
1922	78.5	1931	—
1923	75.7	1932	48.0
1924	47.0	1933	54.6
1925	82.3	1934	57.4
1926	34.7	1935	67.6
1927	51.3	1936	80.7

Note: ^aAfter 1928, the figures include debt withdrawals; from 1929 until 1931 there were no net debt issues.
Sources: Indices généraux, p. 134; *Mouvement économique*, p. 201.

The French data show a considerable narrowing of the gap between yields on public and on private bonds after the war. Public bond prices fell relative to industrial or railway issues: thus a 3 per cent *rente* was quoted in 1927 at 65.1 per cent of its 1913 price, while 3 per cent railways were 74.4 per cent and industrials 76.5 per cent. By 1931 the prices had moved much closer to the 1913 relationship, and then—after the onset of depression—*rente* prices rose relative to industrials and railways. A similar fall in the price of state bonds relative to mortgage bonds occurred in Germany, and is usually explained by a sharp fall in the willingness of the German domestic investing public to purchase these bonds.[54] The difference between the rates is an indicator of the degree of financial nervousness: in 1924 industrial and private mortage bonds yielded less than state paper, but by 1929 state bonds had recovered. In the crisis of 1931, the yield on mortgage bonds was again substantially below that on state bonds (8.73 per cent and 9.23 per cent respectively on 9 September).[55]

Difficulties in selling government debt arose in part out of market conditions, and from the increased supply of debt. But there was also a much more politicized aspect of the uncertainty: worry about public sector finance raised questions about social distribution. The politics of spending and taxation became much more contested in the interwar years than had been the case earlier. Would tax increases be forthcoming to service the ever more expensive debt? Or would increased taxes raise demands for more extensive redistribution to combat social inequalities, and in this way further politicize the fiscal process?

V

The supposition that interwar monetary and financial problems originated primarily from the growth in government debt and the vulnerability of the debt structure to political processes and decisions was sufficiently widely accepted to figure prominently in contemporary attempts to formulate responses to depression.

A first obvious reaction to a trauma that affected financial markets that

---

[54] *Indices généraux*, p. 130; *Mouvement économique*, p. 199; Balderston, 'Origins', p. 510; *idem*, 'German capital and labour markets', p. 161.
[55] Döring, 'Kreditmärkte', p. 395.

were highly integrated across national frontiers was to limit the extent of international linkages. Devaluation alone was often insufficient to achieve such an uncoupling, and capital controls, frequently associated with voluntary freezings of debt, were required to break the tie with the world economy, and to institute what Hayek termed 'monetary nationalism' ('the doctrine that a country's share in the world's supply of money should *not* be left to be determined by the same principles and the same mechanism as those which determine the relative amounts of money in its different regions or localities').[56]

A second response involved limiting international linkages as a method of restricting the usable information available to those moving capital. A far more drastic—and apparently quite successful—approach led simply to the suppression of usable financial information. it has recently been pointed out just how effective an anti-cyclical strategy this proved to be in Mussolini's Italy. Italian banking, as a mixed or universal system, was in many contemporary judgements[57] as vulnerable as the structures of Austria, Hungary, or Germany. Mussolini's government responded in a manner possible only under an authoritarian regime: the suspension of publication of regular accounts of balances and assets, coupled with capital controls, prevented the outbreak of an Italian banking crisis in 1931-2.[58] Even extraordinarily large public deficits (which in 1933 reached 8.7 per cent of GNP) could not shake the banking system.

A third, and potentially even more far-reaching method of responding to the peculiar nature of the interwar crisis was to attempt to instil confidence by removing the state and its budget from public debate and criticism. This approach aimed at the creation of a consensus about the desirability of state activity. A national community, motivated by suitable propaganda, would provide a more enthusiastic acceptance of public debt. This was the intention of authoritarian regimes and dictatorships of the radical right, which believed that national community would solve the economic problem. In Germany, the National Socialists in the 1930s explicitly regarded the willingness of the German public to buy government securities either directly or through banks as a plebiscite on the regime. Alternatively, in a different, and progressive, version of the same strategy, a new consensus could be created by the expansion of the state's activity to build a new and better social community. This was the approach of the Belgian socialist Henri de Man, as well as the stance of the French Popular Front.

VI

The diagnosis frequently made of the interwar period involved the assertion that there was too much international capital movement. This was highly misleading as analysis, and the political theory and economic doctrine

---

[56] Hayek, *Monetary nationalism*, p. 4.
[57] For instance, the Swiss banker Felix Somary, who believed that the world economy could not recover before the pound left gold, and before the German and Italian banks collapsed: Institut für Zeitgeschichte, Munich, Hans Schäffer diary, entry for 27 Jan. 1931.
[58] Toniolo, *L'economia*, pp. 228-33.

generated as a response provided the basis for political authoritarianism and economic nationalism. The problem should better be understood as lying in a changed debt structure that made it much more difficult to accommodate international capital movements. The vulnerability affected not only economies with extreme inflationary experiences, but also—and more destructively from the standpoint of international stability—the major centres of international finance in London, Paris, and New York. Between 1931 and 1933 they were thus open to a fundamental shock that brought down the world financial system and all hopes for international cooperation.

Princeton University

Footnote references

Official publications
Bank for International Settlements, *Annual reports* (Basle, 1931-).
Committee on Finance and Industry, *Reports and minutes of evidence*, 1931.
Deutsche Bundesbank, *Deutsches Geld- und Bankwesen in Zahlen, 1876-1975* (Frankfurt, 1976).
Indices généraux du mouvement économique en France de 1901 à 1931 (Paris, 1932).
Institut National de la Statistique et des Études Économiques, *Annuaire statistique de la France* (Paris, 1966).
Konjunkturstatistisches Jahrbuch, 1933, and *1936* (Berlin, 1933 and 1935).
League of Nations, *World economic survey, 1932-3* (Geneva, 1933).
League of Nations, *Public finance, 1928-1935* (Geneva, 1936-7).
Mouvement économique en France de 1929 à 1939 (Paris, 1941).
United Nations, *International capital movements* (Lake Placid, N.Y., 1949).

Secondary sources
Alesina, A., Prati, A., and Tabellini, G., 'Public confidence and debt management: a model and a case study of Italy', in R. Dornbusch and M. Draghi, eds., *Public debt management: theory and history* (Cambridge, 1990), pp. 94-118.
Balderston, T., 'The origins of economic instability in Germany, 1924-1930: market forces versus economic policy', *Vierteljahrschrift für Sozial- und Wirtschaftsgeschichte*, 69 (1982), pp. 488-514.
Balderston, T., 'The beginning of the depression in Germany, 1927-30: investment and the capital market', *Econ. Hist. Rev.*, 2nd ser., XXXV (1983), pp. 395-415.
Balderston, T., 'Links between inflation and depression: German capital and labour markets, 1924-1931', in G.D. Feldman, ed., *Die Nachwirkungen der Inflation auf die deutsche Geschichte, 1924-1933* (Munich, 1985), pp. 157-85.
Balogh, T., *Studies in financial organization* (Cambridge, 1948).
Barber, W. J., *From New Era to New Deal* (Cambridge, 1985).
Bernanke, B. and James, H., 'The gold standard, deflation and financial crisis in the Great Depression: an international comparison', in R. G. Hubbard, ed., *Financial markets and financial crises* (Chicago, 1991), pp. 33-68.
Bloomfield, A. I., *Short-term capital movements under the pre-1914 gold standard* (Princeton, 1963).
Borchardt, K., *Perspectives on modern German economic history and policy* (Cambridge, 1991).
Boyce, R. W. D., *British capitalism at the crossroads* (Cambridge, 1987).
Brown, E. C., 'Fiscal policy in the 1930s: a reappraisal', *Amer. Econ. Rev.*, 46 (1956), pp. 857-79.
Brown, W. A., *The international gold standard reinterpreted, 1914-1934*, 2 vols. (New York, 1940).
Cairncross, A. and Eichengreen, B., *Sterling in decline* (Oxford, 1983).
Capie, F., Mills, T., and Wood, G. E., 'What happened in 1931?', in F. Capie and G. E. Wood, eds., *Financial crises and the world banking system* (1986), pp. 120-48.
Clarke, P., *The Keynesian revolution in the making* (Oxford, 1988).
Diaper, S., 'Merchant banking in the interwar period: the case of Kleinwort Sons & Co.', *Bus. Hist.*, 28 (1986), pp. 55-76.
Döring, D., 'Deutsche Aussenwirtschaftspolitik, 1933-1935: die Gleichschaltung der Aussenwirtschaft in der Frühphase des nationalsozialistischen Regimes' (unpub. Ph.D. thesis, Univ. of Berlin, 1969).
Drummond, I., *London, Washington, and the management of the franc, 1936-39* (Princeton, 1979).
Eichengreen, B., 'The Bank of France and the sterilization of gold', *Exp. Econ. Hist.* 23 (1986), pp. 64-87.
Eichengreen, B., 'The origins and nature of the great slump revisited', *Econ. Hist. Rev.*, XLV (1992), pp. 213-39.

FINANCIAL FLOWS DURING THE INTERWAR DEPRESSION

Eichengreen, B. and Sachs, J., 'Exchange rates and economic recovery in the 1930s', *J. Econ. Hist.*, 45 (1985), pp. 925-46.
Eichengreen, B. and Wyplosz, C., *The economic consequences of the franc Poincaré* (1986).
Frayssinet, P., *La politique monétaire de la France, 1924-1928* (Paris, 1928).
Friedman, M. and Schwartz, A. J., *A monetary history of the United States, 1867-1960* (Princeton, 1963).
Haberler, G., *Prosperity and depression: a theoretical analysis* (Lake Success, N.Y., 1946).
Hayek, F., *Monetary nationalism and international stability* (1937).
Jackson, J., *The politics of depression in France, 1932-1936* (Cambridge, 1985).
James, H., 'The causes of the German banking crisis of 1931', *Econ. Hist. Rev.*, 2nd ser., XXXVII (1984), pp. 68-87.
James, H., *The Reichsbank and public finance in Germany, 1924-33* (Frankfurt, 1985).
James, H., *The German slump: politics and economics, 1924-1936* (Oxford, 1986).
Keynes, J. M., 'National self-sufficiency', in D. E. Moggridge, ed., *The collected writings of John Maynard Keynes*, XXI, *World crisis and policies in Britain and America* (1982), pp. 233-46.
Kindleberger, C. P., 'Banking and industry between the two wars: an international comparison', *J. Eur. Econ. Hist.*, 13 (1984), pp. 7-28.
Kindleberger, C. P., *The world in depression* (Berkeley, 1986).
Kunz, D. B., *The battle for Britain's gold standard in 1931* (Beckenham, 1987).
Lewis, W. A., 'World production, prices and trade, 1870-1960', *Man. School*, 20 (1952), pp. 105-38.
Machlup, F., 'Die Theorie der Kapitalflucht', *Weltwirtschaftliches Archiv*, 36 (1932), pp. 512-29.
Middleton, R., *Towards the managed economy* (1985).
Mitchell, B. R., *European historical statistics, 1750-1970* (1978).
Mitchell, B. R. and Deane, P., *Abstract of British historical statistics* (Cambridge, 1962).
Moggridge, D. E., *British monetary policy, 1924-1931: the Norman conquest of $4.86* (Cambridge, 1972).
Mouré, K., *Managing the franc Poincaré: economic understanding and political constraint in French monetary policy, 1928-1936* (Cambridge, 1991).
Nötel, R., 'Money, banking and industry in interwar Austria and Hungary', *J. Eur. Econ. Hist.*, 13 (1984), pp. 137-202.
Philippe, R., *Le drame financier de 1926-1928* (Paris, 1931).
Prati, A., 'Poincaré's stabilization: stopping a run on government debt', *J. Monetary Econ.*, 27 (1991), pp. 213-39.
Schuker, S. A., *The end of French predominance in Europe: the financial crisis of 1924 and the adoption of the Dawes Plan* (Chapel Hill, 1976).
Stein, H., *The fiscal revolution in America* (Chicago, 1969).
Stiefel, D., *Finanzdiplomatie und Weltwirtschaftskrise: die Krise der Credit-Anstalt und ihre wirtschaftlich-politische Bedeutung* (Frankfurt, 1989).
Temin, P., *Lessons from the great depression* (Cambridge, Mass., 1989).
Toniolo, G., *L'economia dell'Italia fascista* (Rome and Bari, 1980).
Wigmore, B. A., 'Was the bank holiday of 1933 caused by a run on the dollar?', *J. Econ. Hist.*, 47 (1987), pp. 739-55.
Williamson, P., 'A bankers' ramp? Financiers and the British political crisis of August 1931', *Eng. Hist. Rev.*, 99 (1984), pp. 770-806.

Empirical Studies of the European Interwar Economy

The transmission of the Great Depression in the United States, Britain, France and Germany*

James Foreman-Peck
St. Antony's College, Oxford University, UK

Andrew Hughes Hallett
Strathclyde University, Glasgow and CEPR, London, UK

Yue Ma
Strathclyde University, Glasgow, UK

1. Introduction

Macro-economic experience between the World Wars was dominated by the post-1918 boom and slump and by the Great Depression beginning 1929. Most national economies recovered from the first recession but the second was more persistent, precipitating the disintegration of the liberal economic order and the rise of political extremism. By the 1930s all industrial countries were concerned with policy measures to combat widespread unemployment. Public works, wage cuts, changes in exchange rate regime and trade restrictions were widely discussed and often implemented. The following two papers, by Dimsdale and Horsewood, and by Ritschl and Borchardt, assess the effectiveness of these policies in Britain and Germany. The present paper addresses the international spread of the Great Depression, attempting to distinguish the relative contributions of internal and external factors for the four largest market economies. Whereas Dimsdale and Horsewood, and Ritschl and Borchardt, examine the effectiveness of policies that might have been pursued, we restrict ourselves to the impact of policies, events and institutions that actually occurred. Earlier models have emphasized United States' income and asset effects on Germany and Britain [Sommariva and

*Financial assistance from the ESRC is gratefully acknowledged.

Tullio (1987, pp. 182–90), Broadberry (1989)] although gold movements between 1929 and 1931 show that other countries as well as the U.S. must have played a significant role [Fremling (1985)]. The spread of the 1931 financial crisis from Germany to Britain and the impact of Sterling depreciation on France [Patat and Luttala (1990, p. 70)] are obvious international disturbances. The commitment of the major industrial countries to the gold standard has also been identified as a structural cause of depression [Eichengreen (1990), Temin (1989)]. But none of these studies have been able to consider international transmissions in a multi-country model. That is our contribution.

2. A model of interactions between the interwar economies

The simulations in this study have been conducted on a small four country model, containing 94 equations estimated on monthly data from January 1927 to December 1936 using ordinary least squares and cointegration techniques. Monthly data is particularly appropriate for modelling financial disturbances in which events move very quickly.

Each national model has the highly aggregated specification of 4 markets (goods, money, labour, foreign trade) and 4 sets of agents (consumers, producers, labour and banks). In contrast to the national models of our companion papers, domestic absorption is modelled using the simplest structure capable of answering the questions we have posed. Governments or central banks appear when we allow policy responses, but the money supply is driven by the commercial banks, making advances on a given monetary base according to the level of the discount rate set by the central bank. The monetary base itself is allowed to vary to some extent independently of the gold stock, under a gold exchange standard. An alternative flexible exchange rate regime is also available. Bilateral trade-flows and multilateral capital/gold flows complete the links between countries. We control for legislative and institutional changes via dummy variables. For each country the specification is as follows:[1]

$m^d/p = \alpha_{11} y - \alpha_{12} r - \alpha_{13} \Delta p - \alpha_{14}\, \text{risk}$ (LM, incl. precautionary terms)

$m^s = \alpha_{21} gm + \alpha_{22} m_0 + \alpha_{24}(rd - r) - \alpha_{25} bf$ (money supply, incl. bank deposits and liquidity constraints)

$a = \alpha_{31} r + \alpha_{32} y - \alpha_{33}(p - p^* e) - \alpha_{24} \Delta p + \alpha_{35} s + \alpha_{36} g$ (domestic absorption, IS curve)

$p = \alpha_{41} w + \alpha_{42} prod + \alpha_{43} pm$ (prices, Dimsdale–Nickell, 1989)

$w = \alpha_{51} p + \alpha_{52} emp + \alpha_{53} prod - \alpha_{53} u$ (wages, Dimsdale–Nickell)

$y = a + tb/p$ (GDP definition)

[1] A full derivation, estimates and data sources are available from the authors.

$cf = \alpha_{61}(e_{+1}-e) + \alpha_{62}(r-r^*) - \alpha_{63}\text{risk}$ (capital inflows, covered interest parity)

$tb_i = \sum_{j \neq i} im_{ji} - \sum_{j \neq i} im_{ji}$ (trade balance, includes invisibles)

$gm = cf + tb$ (definition of gold inflow)

$im_{ij} = \alpha_{71} y + \alpha_{72}(p+p^*e) + \alpha_{73}\text{tariffs}$ (bilateral imports, $j = 1, \ldots, 4, j \neq i$)

Key:
- bf = bank failures
- s = stock exchange turnover
- pm = price of raw materials
- m_0 = notes and coins
- rd = discount rate
- r = short term interest rate
- im_{ij} = real imports into i from j
- g = index of fiscal stance
- p^* = foreign price index
- $prod$ = labour productivity
- emp = employment level
- u = unemployment rate

For the floating exchange rate regime, capital flows are replaced by

$$e_t = e_{t+1} + (r_i - r_j) + \alpha_{81} cf_i - \alpha_{82} cf_j - \alpha_{83}\text{risk}^*,$$

where e_t is the $i-j$ bilateral exchange rate, e_{t+1} is the forward rate, and risk* comprises 'reset' terms in uncovered interest parity.

3. Simulation results

In the table in the appendix all results are given as percentage deviations from historical values, calculated over the period October 1929 to December 1933. A positive sign indicates a rise in that variable compared to the level to which it had fallen during the depression period. The simulations were designed to decompose the contributions to the recession by source, either directly or by transmission.

(a) *The contributions of national output decline and trade restrictions.* How and when the Great Depression began remains a matter of controversy. The enormous size of the United States suggests that economy was more likely to be a source than a recipient of internationally transmitted disturbances. All three European economies were smaller (with GNPs of less than 25% of the U.S.), and more open (with trade at about 20% of GNP, compared with 5% for the U.S.). Since we do not know what triggered the domestic downturn in the U.S., we cannot control that element. We therefore begin by investigating whether the massive fall in U.S. output during the early 1930s was an important contributor, if not the chief transmitter of world recession. We do that by exogenising U.S. production at its 1929 peak level. Agents are assumed to believe that this would be sufficient to preserve the Gold Standard (and the U.K.'s membership). Exogenising U.S. output cannot reveal what triggered the fall in output and hence cannot distinguish between internal shocks and external effects feeding back from Europe or from unfortunate domestic policy reactions, nor what interventions would have put things right. But it can show how much damage was done to other variables, and how much of that downturn was transmitted to other countries.

Simulation A1 shows that, of all the results reported here, the collapse in U.S. output was the largest single contributor to the depression. The U.S. regains most (40% points) of its 45% loss in GDP.[2] This is achieved with a fall in the trade balance and gold stocks: the figures for 1931–32 represent a trade balance deterioration of 1.6% of the pre-crash GDP level and a monthly loss of 4% of its gold stock. However, prices and wages rise 18% and 85% by 1933, reversing about half of their historical decline. The U.S. is therefore forced to tighten monetary conditions compared to the recession; interest rates rise by 4% points, and money/bank assets contract by a few per cent each month, to contain inflation and capital outflows.

The effects of this simulation on other countries are also larger than in other simulations, although it is clear that this is because the impulse to U.S. production is so large and not because the spillovers are particularly strong. To illustrate; suppose country i has target y_i and country j suffers a disturbance in x_j. Then we are simulating $dy_i = (\delta y_i/\delta x_j) dx_j$, with domestic effects if $i=j$ and spillover effects when $i \neq j$. The decline in U.S. production is important because dx_j is larger when $j=$U.S., and not because $\delta y_i/\delta x_j$ is larger. In fact separate calculations showed that the multipliers were much the same for all 4 countries: the spillovers between France and Germany were a little larger than elsewhere, and the U.S. domestic multipliers a little more persistent. Moreover with domestic output multipliers of around 1.3, and spillover multipliers about 10–15% of that, these results are entirely consistent with modern empirical exercises [Hughes Hallett (1986, 1987)]. But the U.S. economy is 4 times larger than the largest European economy, so dx_j is 4–6 times larger than equiproportional French, German or U.K. figures. Hence we find that the European economies could have avoided as much as a quarter of their historical losses had the U.S. maintained its production levels; together with improving trade balances and variable gold inflows, but little change in monetary policy (Germany excepted). Note that the U.S. economy responds by late 1929, the U.K. by mid-1930, and France and Germany in 1931. In other words, any counter recessionary policies in the U.S. would have taken up to 2 years to have some impact in Europe.

Would boosting European production back to its 1929 peak have similarly prevented recession and transmitted a strong impulse to the U.S.? Simulation A2 shows the European countries would get almost as large a boost in GDP

---

[2]If the figures in table A1 appear large, recall that 67% gain on historical values is the same as a 40% fall from the 1929 peak; and that U.S. production fell 50% between 1929 and 1933, while the U.K., French and German falls were 20%, 40% and 60% respectively.

as the U.S. did. France and Germany recover three-quarters of their historical losses of 40% and 60%, but the U.K. regains only half of its 19% fall in output. All 3 countries have worsening trade balances. But the biggest changes are in the gold movements: Germany decumulates then accumulates gold rapidly, while France accumulates and the U.K. decumulates fast. Germany has to tighten monetary policy very sharply to stem its outflow, but France and Britain take no action before 1933. Finally the U.S. derives a much smaller spillover from this scenario than Europe did from A1 (recovering just 11% of its lost output), but with no cost to its trade balance.

Perhaps the salient point is that by acting together the 3 European countries could have had nearly as much success in countering the recession as the U.S., albeit with smaller transmission effects to the U.S. than vice versa. But none of them acting individually (results not reported here) could have done so. Finally the availability of U.S. assets would be important because U.S. gold movements play a role when the U.S. expands. However, as Fremling (1985) argued, other countries also contribute since some of the gold flows in simulation A1, and nearly all of them in A2, come from the rest of the world.

Did the Smoot–Hawley tariff and the British, French and German trade restrictions deepen the recession? Simulation A3 shows the results of removing the tariffs and trade barriers from the model's historical tracking exercise. Output is slow to pick up but shows substantial gains for France and Germany (with gold and monetary expansions to match) but significant losses for the U.K. and U.S. Spending and the trade balances follow the same pattern. Thus trade liberalisation might have boosted trade and output overall, but with positive effects in those countries bound to the gold standard and negative effects elsewhere. In other words, the income effects of removing trade barriers outweigh the substitution effects, *except* where devaluation weakens the tendency for prices to fall. But the effects would be small compared to measures designed to maintain production levels.

(b) *European bank failures and German deflation.* The second phase of depression began with the collapse of the Austrian Credit-Anstalt in May 1931 and the ensuing Austro-German financial crisis. Earlier monetary contraction in Germany, because of Chancellor Brüning's deflationary policy, undoubtedly set the scene for the crisis. Simulations C1 and C2 show that deflation and bank collapses had quite a strong recessionary impact on Germany, some impact on the U.K., but rather little spillover onto France or the U.S. In Germany, deflation cut 2% from growth and 5% from spending to give some mild (but much needed) improvements in the trade balance (simulation C1). Monetary policy was tightened, but not strongly. The bank failure/liquidity squeeze simulation (C2) shows a similar pattern but with smaller figures. The spillover effects, however, are more clearly differentiated because the deflation programme spread recession to other countries whereas the bank failures did not. Growth in the U.K., where loans to the German banking system were organised, was reduced with the loss of liquidity, but France and the U.S. were hardly affected, and none of the trade balances were disturbed.

(c) *The choice of regime.* The German financial crisis spread to Britain, helped by international concern about British public finance. A run on sterling pushed Britain off the gold standard in September 1931. Did that push other countries into recession? Or was the gold standard itself responsible for the depth of the recession, implying a free float would have been preferable? Those questions are of interest today because the resilience of the European Exchange Rate Mechanism (and monetary union) has not been tested in periods of financial instability.

Preventing sterling's 30% devaluation (simulation B1) is beneficial to France, Germany and the U.S. – but depresses the U.K. considerably. In terms of growth and spending, Germany and the U.S. benefit more than by removing trade restrictions but less than if production levels were maintained; for France the benefits are smaller than either supporting production or removing trade barriers. Germany does better because preventing sterling's devaluation expands Germany's exports, even if later its debt burden becomes heavier. France and the U.S. see little improvement in their trade balances.

The U.K.'s decision to leave the gold standard may have been its best *unilateral* move. It raised output and spending by more than the imposition of tariff barriers (but by less than maintaining output levels) while improving the trade balance and avoiding further monetary restrictions. The cost of supporting the gold standard would have been large. Gold inflows of about £12m per month in 1932 and £35m per month in 1933 represent about $1\frac{1}{2}$% of U.S. *or* French gold stocks in 1932, and 4%–6% of their 1933 stocks. Who might have provided those gold flows? The Bank for International Settlements was the most likely supplier, perhaps by recycling French and American stocks which represented 60% of the world's official reserves in 1929 [Foreman-Peck (1991)]. We tested that proposition by obliging France and the U.S. to lend 10% of their average 1932–33 gold stocks each month to the U.K. and Germany equally (detailed results not reported here). In fact recycling had little impact on U.S. growth, trade or monetary stance. France would benefit a little from the increase in intra-European trade, but spending falls overall because monetary policy is forced to tighten. Germany also enjoys some extra growth. Only the U.K. benefits significantly; with stronger growth in output and spending, and an improving trade position. So for the U.K., recyling would have been an attractive option. But for the others it would be unattractive, except as an easy way of supporting sterling and the Gold Standard.

Would countries have weathered the storm better with adjustable exchange rates? Simulation B2 shows that the depth of the recession can, in part, be blamed on the decision to maintain the gold standard regime beyond July 1931. All four countries would have had higher output and spending had they all abandoned the scheme at that point, although the gains over history are relatively small. German GDP recovers one-fifth of what was lost during the recession, but that has to be set against increased debt service payments. France and the U.S. recover only one-tenth and one-eighth of their losses. And Britain records tiny figures here because she was already floating; her gains are purely spillovers from improvements elsewhere. All of this is achieved without any significant trade balance problems, very little inflationary pressure and no changes in monetary policy (Germany excepted). So the commitment by the U.S., France and Germany to the gold standard deepened the recession (for them), but not by so very much.

4. Conclusions

The simulations explain why effective cooperative strategies were so difficult to formulate in this period. Some national economies gained and others lost from the policies implemented – trade restrictions, sterling depreciation, gold recycling and general floating rates – even when all their repercussions are taken into account. 'Beggar thy neighbour' was the rule. As far as the magnitudes of the policies, events and institutions are concerned, each one only appears to have a small impact. But the events themselves were related and, taken together, important. The German monetary squeeze, and U.S. and French gold hoarding, created conditions which led Britain to abandon the gold standard. And the decline in American demand precipitated trade protection to defend national balances of payments or domestic producers. Cumulatively they account for 4% of U.S. GDP, 16% of German GDP and 24% of French GDP in 1932.12, excluding the direct impact of the U.S. downturn. Britain by contrast would have been worse off in total under the simulated scenarios. Thus France emerges as the principle victim of world policies. The other countries either generated a larger proportion themselves (Germany and the U.S.) or pursued more appropriate policies (Britain). In addition those policies indicate that, in the face of a downturn of the magnitude of the Great Depression, any attempt to maintain a European exchange rate mechanism or monetary union would, by analogy, be extremely painful.

Appendix

References

Broadberry, S., 1989, Monetary interdependence and deflation in Britain and the United States between the wars, in: M. Miller, B. Eichengreen and R. Portes, eds., Blueprints for exchange management (Academic Press, New York).

Appendix

Table A.1
Results.[a]

	GDP				TB				GM				M3			
	30.12	31.12	32.12	33.12	30.12	31.12	32.12	33.12	30.12	31.12	32.12	33.12	30.12	31.12	32.12	33.12
Simulation A1: U.S. Production held at its 1929 peak (compared to history)																
U.K.	4.0	7.6	14.1	10.6	2.7	4.7	7.8	4.8	5.2	12.9	19.9	12.8	0.6	1.8	5.1	9.9
U.S.	47.6	69.8	87.8	66.5	−1.8	−2.8	−2.8	−2.5	−11.0	−15.6	−20.8	−16.5	0.3	−1.9	−3.1	−10.3
Fr	3.0	6.2	10.2	10.9	1.3	2.1	2.3	2.2	34.2	60.7	54.0	−96.6	1.1	5.7	14.1	14.4
Ger	1.6	5.9	10.2	9.3	1.4	2.7	−3.9	−1.9	15.6	38.0	−3.5	−0.1	4.8	24.3	48.1	54.6
Simulation A2: Production in the 3 European countries held at 1929 peak values																
U.K.	13.9	16.9	24.0	10.4	−0.7	−5.9	−6.6	−12.4	−5.8	−30.0	−49.3	−70.8	−0.2	−2.5	−8.6	−16.6
U.S.	0.2	2.8	8.1	3.8	0.1	0.9	1.3	1.4	−0.7	1.0	3.5	8.1	0.0	−1.4	−2.7	−1.8
Fr	7.6	29.6	49.4	34.5	3.2	2.6	−5.9	−3.0	84.0	187.3	249.1	185.3	2.3	14.8	46.9	97.4
Ger	51.0	78.3	83.3	47.7	−4.6	−2.0	−1.9	8.5	−42.4	−40.5	40.9	30.1	−17.0	−40.0	−61.0	−74.0
Simulation A3: The result of removal of all trade restrictions from 1930 onwards																
U.K.	0.9	0.0	−5.2	−3.8	0.7	−0.6	−3.6	−1.5	1.2	0.5	−1.9	−0.4	0.1	0.3	0.2	−0.2
U.S.	−0.4	−0.5	−1.1	−1.3	−0.4	−0.3	−0.4	−1.1	−2.4	−1.7	−1.6	−7.7	0.0	−0.4	−0.9	−1.6
Fr	0.1	0.4	19.3	11.4	0.0	0.8	7.8	4.4	1.1	−0.1	145.0	306.3	0.0	0.2	2.5	30.0
Ger	0.3	1.7	4.4	4.5	0.3	1.4	2.3	0.6	2.4	11.1	22.0	41.9	0.5	4.4	16.6	53.2
Simulation B1: No sterling devaluation in 1931 (the gold standard is maintained)																
U.K.	0.0	−2.3	−5.2	−4.2	0.0	−0.5	0.9	3.3	0.0	2.5	12.4	34.9	0.0	0.1	1.2	4.9
U.S.	0.0	0.4	4.0	1.2	0.0	0.4	0.1	−0.4	0.0	1.6	1.1	−1.2	0.0	0.0	0.2	0.6
Fr	0.0	0.9	3.8	3.7	0.0	0.6	−0.4	−0.7	0.0	3.1	11.3	−6.9	0.0	0.0	0.6	1.2
Ger	0.0	3.6	5.1	7.7	0.0	2.6	1.4	−1.6	0.0	8.8	22.6	13.0	0.0	1.0	11.3	26.9
Simulation B2: All float vs. history																
U.K.	0.0	0.2	0.2	0.5	0.0	−0.1	−0.2	−0.2	0.0	0.0	0.0	0.0	0.0	0.0	0.0	0.0
U.S.	0.0	0.6	6.1	3.5	0.0	0.4	0.1	−0.4	0.0	0.0	0.0	0.0	0.0	0.0	0.2	0.6
Fr	0.0	1.0	3.9	3.5	0.0	0.7	−0.4	−0.7	0.0	0.0	0.0	0.0	0.0	0.0	0.6	1.2
Ger	0.0	11.6	5.8	5.4	0.0	13.6	2.0	−1.2	0.0	0.0	0.0	0.0	0.0	1.1	11.4	26.9

Simulation C1: German deflation policies removed																
U.K.	0.1	1.0	3.3	2.4	0.1	0.7	2.0	1.0	0.5	4.7	8.9	4.9	0.0	0.4	1.6	3.2
U.S.	0.1	0.1	0.2	0.2	0.1	0.1	0.1	0.2	1.0	0.6	−3.3	1.6	0.0	0.1	0.2	0.1
Fr	0.0	0.2	0.9	1.3	0.0	0.1	0.4	0.5	0.0	1.1	9.4	24.5	0.0	0.0	0.3	2.7
Ger	−0.3	1.1	2.7	0.1	−0.3	−1.2	−3.3	−2.5	8.1	7.2	7.2	7.2	5.8	11.3	19.6	27.4
Simulation C2: Central European banking crisis (May 1931) removed																
U.K.	0.0	0.3	1.4	0.7	0.0	0.3	0.9	0.1	0.0	2.9	4.6	0.4	0.0	0.1	0.7	1.5
U.S.	0.0	0.1	0.0	0.1	0.0	0.1	0.0	0.1	0.0	0.8	−0.6	−0.3	0.0	0.0	0.2	0.1
Fr	0.0	0.0	0.4	0.7	0.0	0.0	0.2	0.3	0.0	0.2	2.6	10.5	0.0	0.0	0.1	1.0
Ger	0.0	−0.5	2.4	1.8	0.0	−0.5	−1.4	−0.7	0.0	−4.4	−19.2	−8.9	0.0	8.4	2.3	−4.9

ªGDP: real GDP (% deviation from hist. values). TB: real trade balance (deviation from hist. values). GM: current gold inflow (difference from hist. values). Tens of millions of dollars for U.K. and U.S.; hundreds of millions of francs for France; tens of millions of marks for Germany. M3: money supply M3 (% deviation from hist. values).

References

Broadberry, S., 1989, Monetary interdependence and deflation in Britain and the United States between the wars, in: M. Miller, B. Eichengreen and R. Portes, eds., Blueprints for exchange management (Academic Press, New York).

Dimsdale, N., S. Nickell and N. Horsewood, 1989, Real wages and unemployment in Britain during the 1930s, The Economic Journal 99, 271–292.

Eichengreen, B., 1990, Elusive stability: Essays in the history of international finance 1919–1939 (Cambridge University Press, Cambridge and New York).

Foreman-Peck, J., 1991, The gold standard as a European monetary lesson, in: J. Driffill and M. Beber, eds., A currency for Europe (Lothian Foundation Press, London).

Fremling, G.M., 1985, Transmission of the Great Depression, American Economic Review 75, 1181–1185.

Hughes Hallett, A.J., 1986, Autonomy and the choice of policy in asymmetrically dependent economies, Oxford Economic Papers 38, 516–544.

Hughes Hallett, A.J., 1987, The impact of interdependence on economic policy design: The case of the US, EEC and Japan, Economic Modelling 4, 377–396.

Patat, J.-P. and M. Luttala, 1990, A monetary history of France in the twentieth century (Macmillan, London).

Sommariva, A. and G. Tullio, 1987, German macroeconomic history 1880–1979 (Macmillan, London).

Temin, P., 1989, Lessons from the Great Depression (MIT Press, Cambridge, MA).

Part II
The Response to Crisis

Tariffs and Exchange Control: the Struggle to Escape.
By H. V. Hodson.

(a) INTRODUCTORY

1931 was the year of financial crisis. From the collapse of the Credit-Anstalt in May to the relinquishment of the Gold Standard by Great Britain four months later, the world was subjected to a series of disasters, in the field of finance and foreign exchange, which entirely prevented any commercial recovery, and indeed accelerated the decline of production and the drying-up of international trade. But by the end of the year the thunder of these explosions had died away and only the echoes reverberated still. The banking system of Germany had been restored to solvency if not to strength. Artificial supports of one kind or another were propping up the financial systems of Central and Eastern Europe so that no further spectacular collapse was threatened. The pound sterling had reached what appeared at that time, at least, to be a natural level, and a fairly well-defined group of currencies had attached themselves to it, in distinction not only from the few remaining Gold Standard countries, and the countries which maintained their exchanges nominally at parity with gold by all kinds of restrictive devices, but also from those whose money was out of fixed or *de facto* relation either with sterling or with gold.[1]

The extraordinary 'toughness' of the capitalist system had been tested and proved. In spite of all those shocks, the main structure of the system still stood, supported though it was by every kind of

[1] See the *Survey for 1931*, p. 237, for a classification of the world's currencies in April 1932. Between that date and the end of 1932, Siam, Peru and South Africa abandoned the Gold Standard; and Rumania and Persia introduced foreign exchange restrictions which rendered the Gold Standard ineffective.

makeshift scaffolding, and partially supplanted as it was in many countries by further and further encroachment of government activity into the former field of private enterprise in production, trade, and banking. Its condition, as was said of affairs in Austria at the time, was 'always grave but never serious'. Firms and individuals, aided by the decline of costs either through legislative action or through more natural processes, and spurred on by the normal incentives of capitalist trade and industry, were still finding means of curtailing their losses or of making profits, while most Governments were facing their fiscal problems with determination and reducing their deficits, even though scarcely any of them could achieve surpluses. 1932, indeed, may be described as the first year of attempt, by national and international action, to escape from the world economic crisis. The attempt had been far from successful at the end of the year, and an observer regarding the enormous and still swelling army of unemployed, the miserable trickle of international trade, the failure to settle international political problems, the disturbing fluctuations of international exchanges, the vast height of tariff barriers and the unmitigated strangulation of trade and finance by direct control of the exchanges, all of which characterized the latter days of 1932, might have been inclined to scoff at such a description of the year. But equally no one who recalled the Lausanne settlement, the relaxation of monetary conditions, the definite assault on the War Debts problem, the eager preparations for the World Economic Conference, the Austrian loan agreement, the attempt (whether well or ill advised) at Ottawa to revivify trade within the British Commonwealth, and the attack by the Stresa Conference and the League's Financial Committee on the problem of exchange blockade in Europe, could deny altogether that the attempt had been made.

(b) THE UNIVERSAL TARIFF WAR

With scarcely an exception, tariffs were rising throughout the world in 1932. In Australia, with the advantage of exchange depreciation, the Government in office was pledged to cut down the tremendous protective tariff associated with the name of Mr. Scullin; but even there little effective reduction was achieved before the end of the year. In the United States, the Democratic Party, officially pledged to reduction of the Hawley-Smoot tariff, already held the balance of power in Congress, and the presidential election held out the promise of better things to come, but the only significant alteration of the American tariff in 1932 was the addition of high import duties on copper, lumber, and oil, in the course of the passage of the

Tax Bill—this with the aid of Democratic votes. The most notable addition to the tariffs of the world was, of course, the British Import Duties Act. After a brief experiment with a temporary tariff, concentrated on certain luxuries or non-essential goods and in many cases intended to be practically prohibitive, Great Britain stepped on the 1st March, 1932, into the ranks of the moderate tariff countries of the world. A general 10 per cent. tariff (subject to certain exceptions, mostly staple foodstuffs and raw materials) was to be augmented by a series of more or less protective duties on manufactured goods, ranging up to a total duty of $33\frac{1}{3}$ per cent. *ad valorem*, on the initiative of an independent tariff board with wide terms of reference adverting to the 'advisability in the national interest of restricting imports into the United Kingdom'. None of these duties was to apply to imports from other parts of the British Commonwealth, but this provision was of minor importance in relation to manufactured goods. As the year wore on, more and more duties were added by successive recommendations of the tariff committee.

It is impossible to compute how far the imposition of the British tariff was responsible for subsequent increases of tariffs elsewhere, and indeed this is no place for such a speculative discussion, but that event can definitely be described as an episode in the universal tariff war that was raging throughout this phase of the world crisis. In the first place, the popular demand for a tariff in Great Britain was influenced, beyond question, by the growth of tariffs on British goods entering foreign countries, and by the feeling not only that a free trade policy was incompatible with such restriction of British exports, but also that a tariff was necessary as a bargaining instrument to secure the reduction of foreign duties. In the second place, the depression was certainly deepened (if not caused) by the sudden reduction of international lending, which compelled debtor countries to achieve outward balances of trade, partly by stimulating exports and partly by restricting imports; if, then, further obstacles were to be opposed to their exports by creditor countries, they had no alternative but to enhance their restrictions upon imports. In the third place, in certain instances there is evidence of definite retaliation.

It was, no doubt, accidental though it was unmistakable that the British tariff pressed particularly hardly on German products. A table published by the *Economist*,[1] based on 1930 import figures, showed that whereas in 1930 over 89 per cent. of imports from Germany came in free of duty, after the ratification of the Ottawa schedules 24·2 per cent. of such imports would be subject to 10 per cent. duty, 49·7 per

[1] Supplement to the issue of the 22nd October, 1932.

cent. to duties ranging from 11 to 20 per cent. *ad valorem*, and 10·9 per cent. to duties exceeding 20 per cent. *ad valorem*, leaving only 4·5 per cent. of the imports free of tax. These figures for Germany may be compared with the following for imports from all foreign countries: in 1930, free 83 per cent. and taxed 17 per cent.; after Ottawa, free 25·2 per cent.; subject to 10 per cent. duty, 28·3 per cent.; subject to 11–20 per cent. duty, 21·8 per cent.; subject to over 20 per cent. duty, 7·7 per cent. The achievement of an outward balance of trade by Germany—sufficient to pay her obligations for interest and long-term capital amortisation, though it left nothing over for Reparations—was one of the most remarkable features of international economic life in the first three years of the slump. In 1929 Germany's imports totalled over £670,000,000, exceeding her exports by £40,000,000. Yet in 1930 her exports, at £610,000,000, exceeded her imports by £80,000,000, and in the following year the outward balance had been increased to £140,000,000, in spite of a reduction of exports to only £485,000,000.[1] As a result, however, of the growth of tariffs elsewhere and the depreciation of exchanges against the mark, along with the general decline of international trade, this balance showed signs of serious diminution before 1931 was out, and the British tariff further gravely aggravated Germany's difficulties.[2]

Therefore it was not surprising to find the German Government referring to the British duties when they replied to an official protest against the restrictions laid upon imports of British coal into Germany by means of the quota system. As late as 1931, imports of British coal and coke into Germany had totalled 3,900,000 tons, including some 850,000 tons delivered in free port areas for bunkers, this category not being subject to quota regulation; under the quota order of March 1932 imports within the quota scheme were to be reduced from 3,100,000 tons to 1,500,000 tons in the year 1932. The system of quota regulation in the coal trade was of old standing in Germany, and it was not against the principle of it that the British Government were protesting, but against alleged violation of most-favoured-nation rights assured to Great Britain under the Anglo-German commercial treaty of 1924; it was claimed that the quotas allotted to other countries had not been proportionately reduced because Germany had special agreements with them relating to reciprocal quotas.

---

[1] Except where otherwise stated, all conversions from foreign currencies in this chapter have been calculated at gold parity.

[2] Germany's exports fell in 1932 to £281,000,000 (gold), and her surplus of exports over imports to £53,000,000.

TARIFFS AND EXCHANGE CONTROL

Later it became known that there was also in existence a document not taking the form of a treaty, but containing a unilateral undertaking on behalf of the German Government not to alter for the worse their regulation of the coal trade during the currency of the Anglo-German trade treaty. The reply of the German Government to the British protests was to the effect that the whole basis of the treaty had been fundamentally altered by the imposition of the British tariff; they requested a discussion of the latter duties in so far as these bore specially hardly on German exports, by way of verbal negotiations as the treaty provided; but the British Government, while accepting the principle of arbitration on the quota issue, refused to allow their tariff policy to be called in question. This attitude was modified after the Ottawa Conference, and during December 1932 discussions took place in Berlin between delegations representing the British and German Governments concerning on the one hand the British tariff on certain articles of special interest to German trade, and on the other the German quota on British coal. Only a preliminary exchange of views was completed by the end of the year, but later a limited agreement embodying mutual concessions was initialled and duly ratified, not without protest from those British industries whose measure of protection had been thereby curtailed.

The coal quota was not by any means the only addition to existing restrictions on trade imposed by the German Government during 1932, nor the only one to arouse international antagonism. In January a decree was promulgated empowering the Government in cases of urgent necessity to impose a compensating surcharge on goods coming from countries whose exchanges had fallen below gold parity, and to impose increased customs duties on goods coming from countries with which Germany had no commercial treaty or from which Germany did not receive most-favoured-nation treatment. The primary object of the decree was apparently to stop abnormal imports of butter from Denmark, who had been given a considerable advantage in the German market by the depreciation of the krone. This action aroused deep resentment in Denmark, but it was not until October that a new tariff was imposed by the Danish Government, involving large increases of duties upon foodstuffs as well as industrial articles, especially silk and rayon and manufactured clothing, and frequently changing *ad valorem* into specific duties—the protective effect of the former (as many another country found) having progressively diminished as the general level of prices fell. While this tariff was felt sharply by German exporters, its declared purpose was simply to right Denmark's failing balance of trade. In February 1933 another round of this bout between the two countries was begun. The Reich Government (in which Herr Hugenberg was Minister for Food and Agriculture and for Economic Affairs) raised the protective duties on live stock, meat, and lard, in many cases to at least double their former level. The new duties were to come into operation on the 15th February, upon the expiry of the German-Swedish trade treaty, in which Germany had forsworn any increase of the duty on lard beyond Rm. 10 per 100 kgs., whereas under the new dispensation it was to be Rm. 50. Apart from their effect on other countries, these drastic measures threatened to reduce Danish exports to Germany to a mere fraction of their former value, and in retaliation the Danish authorities responsible for the allotment of foreign exchange proceeded equally drastically to prune Germany's exports to Denmark.

The chief countries affected by Germany's new 'super-tariff' against countries with whom she had no commercial treaty were Canada and Poland, with the latter of whom Germany had for long been engaged in a devastating tariff war. With Canada, negotiations for the conclusion of a treaty were soon begun, and eventually met with success. On the 1st September, again, the German Government further increased the duties payable on many industrial and agricultural products. These changes appeared to be directed principally against British goods, for duties on many categories of textiles and clothing, being British specialities, were raised considerably, some of them trebled. Other imports to suffer were American machinery and important Czechoslovak products. A month later, in response to persistent agrarian agitation, a score of import quotas was imposed on agricultural products, including butter, lard, bacon, and many market-gardening products. In February 1933 the Reich Government added to the restrictions already mentioned (including the raised duties on live stock, meat, and lard), a series of measures designed to eliminate all German imports of cereals except such as were balanced by an equivalent export of cereals. By this time industrial and financial interests were seriously alarmed by the bad will, and in some cases explicit retaliation, engendered abroad by these restrictions; indeed, the conflict of interest between town and country, as manifested in these issues of tariffs and quotas, had become one of the most vital internal issues that any German Government had to face.

The quota system was widely used by France, too, as a means of protection for her industry and agriculture, and of arresting the steady change of her external balance of commodity trade from a

TARIFFS AND EXCHANGE CONTROL

surplus to a deficit, which had been going on ever since 1928. During 1932 the system was widely extended. In the course of an unofficial exchange of protests initiated by the British Chambers of Commerce, the British tariff and propaganda in Great Britain against the purchase of foreign goods were mentioned as contributory reasons for the reduction of France's imports by quotas. In a public statement explaining the system, Monsieur Rollin, Minister of Commerce in the Tardieu Government, said that to have increased tariffs alone would have been useless, for in the period of a crisis no tariff wall, unless fantastically high, could prevent the movement of enormous accumulated stocks. Moreover, nearly three-quarters of France's tariff duties had been consolidated under commercial agreements between 1927 and 1928, and the Government could not alter them. It was soon found, however, that the effect of restrictive quotas was a great rise in the cost of living, indeed occasionally acute shortage of certain goods, including some foodstuffs, besides the retaliatory measures of other countries; and from the 1st July the system was relaxed, in preparation, it was officially said, 'for a progressive return to a greater liberty of international exchange'. The majority of the quotas were enlarged, the increase of the coal quota being of special advantage to Great Britain. On the other hand, the navigation laws of the eighteenth century were recalled by the decision of the French Government to compel French importers of coal, as from the 1st September, to ship 50 per cent. of their coal in French bottoms.

At the beginning of June 1932 the Economic Committee of the League of Nations reported[1] that since the beginning of 1930 practically every country had remoulded its customs tariff on a more or less extensive scale, or had increased its import duties on particular products; and that in the past few months alone, for example, Belgium, Denmark, Estonia, Italy, Latvia, Lithuania, the Netherlands, Poland, Portugal, Rumania, Sweden, Bolivia, Brazil, Siam, the Union of South Africa and—'most striking development of all'— the United Kingdom, had increased their duties in some cases on important categories of goods, or even the whole of their tariffs. Moreover, measures for the direct regulation of trade had been widely adopted, of which the most frequent were measures to establish import quotas or to institute import licenses or permits. Austria, Belgium, Czechoslovakia, Denmark, Estonia, France, Germany, Greece, Hungary, Italy, Latvia, Norway, Poland, Rumania, Spain, Switzerland and Turkey were the chief countries in Europe which had introduced such measures. While these regulations were applicable

[1] League of Nations Document *C. 516. M. 255. 1932. II B.*

—in Belgium, Denmark, Germany and Rumania, for example—only to certain groups of goods, or (as in Italy) were strictly limited to goods specified as coming from particular countries, they had been continuously intensified in France, Estonia and other countries, and actually extended in Latvia and Turkey to the whole volume of imports. Certain countries, such as Estonia and Persia, had preferred the system of import monopolies to the system of import quotas or permits, while others, such as Spain, Portugal and Colombia, had rigidly prohibited the importation of particular products. A number of countries, furthermore, had not restricted these regulative measures to the import trade, but had adopted a system of permits for the export of particular products (as in Denmark and Spain) or for all exports (as in New Zealand).

It is quite impossible to review comprehensively the various aggravations of trade restriction, occurring all over the world, in creditor and debtor countries, in retaliation one towards another and in a general attempt to secure that elusive and illusory trophy, an outward balance of trade. All that can be done here is to mention a few instances of illustrative importance. The Chinese Government imposed heavy duties on the import of luxury articles, medicines, and toys, that is to say, goods bought chiefly by foreigners, but the principal reason was apparently the need for greater revenue, and this was a motive which operated in other countries, including Great Britain herself. In India, the influx of Japanese cotton goods through the depreciation of the yen forced the Government to refer the question of further protection for local industry to the Tariff Board, on whose recommendation import duties on cotton piece goods not of British manufacture were raised on the 30th August, generally, from 20 per cent. to 50 per cent., less the existing $11\frac{3}{4}$ per cent. surcharge, the net increase being thus $18\frac{1}{4}$ per cent. *ad valorem*; but as the Board's calculations were based on an exchange rate of Rs. 106 to 100 yen, and the actual rate was Rs. 86 to 100 yen, the Japanese manufacturer continued to enjoy a substantial advantage.[1] Here again was a motive which operated very generally, both in Europe and in the New World. In view of the attitude of the German Government towards British complaints about their own quota on coal imports, it is interesting that they were reported, in August, to be appealing

[1] On the 6th June, 1933, the Government of India announced that, the yen having remained for six months at approximately Rs. 82 to 100 yen, the import duties on cotton piece goods not of British manufacture would be raised to 75 per cent. *ad valorem* (or, in the case of plain grey piece goods $6\frac{3}{4}$ annas per lb., whichever was the higher). Discrimination against Japan was precluded by a trade convention between the two countries.

to the most-favoured-nation clause in a dispute with Belgium over the latter's progressive reduction of quotas on imports of coal. Finally, there must be mentioned the new Uruguayan tariff promulgated in August, for it embodied a principle frequently championed in public controversy over tariffs, in spite of the obvious economic fallacies inherent in it. Duties were to be reduced on goods imported from countries with which Uruguay had a favourable balance of commodity trade exceeding 1,000,000 pesos per annum, while an additional tariff was to be imposed on goods from other countries in proportion to the adverse balance of Uruguay's trade with them. It may be noted that this measure promised to award valuable preference to Great Britain, but that its full implementation was prevented by the existence of most-favoured-nation treaties.

(c) Exchange Control

Restriction of trade and financial intercourse through control of exchange operations was almost as universal as the heightening of tariffs. In a few cases, however, there was actually a relaxation of such control. In Great Britain there never had been any general supervision of transactions involving the sale of foreign exchange, but a ban was placed upon new capital issues for other countries—indeed upon all new issues during the process of National Debt conversion. This was slightly relaxed on the 1st October, 1932, when a Treasury notice stated that no further restrictions in the way of new issues were required, except (until further notice) (a) issues on behalf of borrowers domiciled outside the Empire or issues the proceeds of which would be remitted abroad, and (b) the optional replacement of existing issues by new issues involving either underwriting or an invitation to the public to subscribe new cash. Early in 1933, the Treasury, in accordance with these regulations, banned the issue of securities to the public to provide funds for the repurchase from American interests of a controlling block of shares in Messrs. Boots Ltd., the multiple chemists.[1] In Sweden and Finland exchange control was removed in December 1931. In Portugal and Spain the difficulties in the way of exchange transactions were reduced in the course of the year, while in Venezuela the rationing system adopted by the banks was removed. In reply to a parliamentary question on the 13th June, the Secretary to the Overseas Trade Department of the Board of Trade said that the countries in which restrictions upon exchange transactions were operative were as follows: Austria,

---

[1] See the Treasury Order of the 17th May, 1933, for the exact terms of the ban.

Bulgaria, Czechoslovakia, Denmark, Estonia, Germany, Greece, Hungary, Iceland, Latvia, Portugal, Rumania, Spain, Turkey, Jugoslavia, Portuguese East Africa, Portuguese West Africa, Portuguese Guinea, Argentine, Bolivia, Brazil, Chile, Colombia, Costa Rica, Ecuador, Nicaragua, Salvador, Uruguay. In three countries —Italy, Lithuania and Norway—registration or supervision was undertaken by the banks.

Germany was the foremost exponent of exchange control, and in the course of 1932 the restrictions which she imposed were tightened progressively in view of the failing export balance achieved. In 1931 the average monthly excess over imports was more than Rm. 200,000,000, whereas in only two months of 1932, March and September, did the monthly surplus exceed even Rm. 100,000,000. The various means of evasion (for instance the tender of German securities by foreign firms as payment for goods supplied, in lieu of foreign exchange) were stopped one after another. By April the quotas of exchange allotted to importing firms had been limited to 25 per cent. of their foreign exchange requirements in October 1930. The total imports, however, were not restricted in quite the same proportion, largely because importers made use of foreign credit lines becoming available through the agreed liquidation of credits under the standstill arrangement.[1] Other points of interest in connexion with German exchange control were the decision to place the contribution to the finances of the League in a blocked account (August), and the prohibitive export duty (Rm. 8 per kg.) placed on the export of used machines and parts, in order to prevent the setting up of businesses abroad by German firms seeking to escape the high costs of production at home and protective tariffs abroad. Thus move and countermove followed in rapid succession in the suicidal game of trade-snatching. An incident of the game was the cancellation by Germany of the concessionary arrangement with Italy whereby the latter paid for imports from Germany out of blocked accounts in marks. Italy responded by paying net mark debts as to three-quarters in blocked lire; and after three and a half months of tension Germany capitulated, the former arrangement being renewed.

In some countries management of exchange transactions was reinforced or replaced by direct control of imports. This was so in Austria, for instance, where a system of import control over a wide list of commodities, including foodstuffs, textiles, motor cars and a great many other manufactures, was imposed on the 1st May. Another country to use the method of direct import control was

---

[1] See the *Survey for 1931*, pp. 217–18, 238–9.

Sect. ii   TARIFFS AND EXCHANGE CONTROL

Denmark. Upon the abandonment of the Gold Standard by Great Britain, 'as a means of facilitating trade and controlling currency, a foreign exchange committee was established under the aegis of the National Bank, who could, on the one side, direct Danish imports to the countries who were the principal receivers of Danish exports, and, on the other side, curtail the import of luxury goods which Denmark at a time of crisis could ill afford. This arrangement proved to be very much in favour of England.'[1] On the 10th October it was announced that the currency restrictions then in force were to be abolished, and in place of the foreign exchange committee there would be instituted a special board for all foreign trade; at the same time a series of tariff increases was submitted.[2]

One of the worst features of import control through tariffs and exchange restriction in Central and Eastern Europe was the recrimination and retaliation that they engendered, resulting in an ever tighter strangulation of trade. Thus, in Rumania a bill was passed in February to regulate dealings with countries where currency restrictions were in force; all payments for imports from such countries were to be made through a special compensation department of the National Bank. In May this system was made more rigorous, the export of currency being prohibited and all exchange operations being centralized at the National Bank. When Hungary's trade treaty with Austria expired and the latter proceeded to put on a tariff which severely injured Hungary's seasonal export of fruit and vegetables, specific action was taken to restrict the sale of Austrian schillings.

> The effect of all these forms of restriction on commercial relations can easily be imagined. Every import is necessarily an export in another country; thus, there developed a process by which these foreign exchange restrictions produced, by their cumulative effect, a disastrous influence on the trade of those countries, both with each other and with third countries, at a time when international trade was so badly hit by the world crisis.
>
> Naturally, means were sought for attenuating these consequences, more particularly by agreements essentially involving exchanges of goods. The international clearing conventions belong to this group. Without going into details, it may be noted that these clearing conventions did not yield appreciable results, except when the monetary situation of the two contracting countries was practically equivalent.
>
> Each state has tried to protect itself by shifting to others the consequences of a general situation; each has tried to push its exports and to reduce its imports to a minimum, this being indeed essential if it was

[1] Statement of the Danish Legation in London, 8th June, 1932.
[2] See p. 7 above.

to be able to ensure the service of the external debt. This policy might have produced results if it had been pursued by one country alone and if the others had accepted the situation. But, as each country was taking identical measures on a national basis, these measures neutralized one another. The result was—experience on this matter is conclusive—not only nil, but negative; it seriously increased the difficulties which it was desired to remove. In no case was the individual problem solved.[1]

Representatives of the national committees of the International Chamber of Commerce, meeting in Paris on the 7th March, 1932, to inquire into the operation of foreign exchange restrictions, denounced them not only as restricting trade, but also as leading to an alarming and dangerous degree of state interference with private trading. The report particularly condemned bilateral clearing arrangements as an inadmissible form of indirect preference. The committee were of opinion that if choice had to be made between direct but temporary restriction of imports and their indirect restriction through exchange control the former was the lesser of the two evils.

(d) BARTER

The break-down of the ordinary processes of international trade, and the inability of the credit system at this period of crisis to solve the paradox of excess in producing countries side by side with want in consuming countries, forced the world to turn in despair to primitive barter. Several instances of international barter through governmental agency occurred during 1932. Naturally, the Soviet Government were in the best position to act in this way, and several barter agreements were negotiated for the exchange of Russian oil and other products for goods of which the Soviet Union had need. One of the most notable instances was the undertaking of the Aluminum Company of Canada to dispose of a quantity of Russian oil taken in exchange for large shipments of aluminium. A ban on certain Russian imports was in force in Canada and for some time it was doubtful whether the Canadian Government would allow the clearance of the oil cargoes, especially in view of the strong stand that they had taken over trade with the Soviet Union in their negotiations with the United Kingdom Government at the Ottawa Conference; but the threat of losing an order involving the employment of several hundreds of men was apparently sufficient to outweigh scruple. Towards the end of the year negotiations were afoot for a similar exchange of Russian coal and oil for Canadian cattle and hides. Another notable

---

[1] Report of the Stresa Conference for the Economic Restoration of Central and Eastern Europe (League of Nations Document *C. 666. M. 321. 1932. VII*), pp. 9 and 11.

example of barter was the agreement between a group of Bremen cotton firms, on the one hand, and the Banque Misr of Cairo and the Agricultural Credit Bank of Egypt, on the other, for the exchange of 20,000 bales of Egyptian cotton against an export of German nitrate; there was no transfer of foreign currency, the Bremen cotton merchants merely crediting a sum in marks to the nitrate manufacturers. A further German effort on the same lines was the contract concluded between a coal-mining company of Duisberg-Ruhrort and the Brazilian Government for the delivery to the Brazilian State Railways of 350,000 tons of coal in the course of some six months, to be taken in direct exchange against additional German imports of Brazilian coffee. But a few isolated instances of barter, on however large a scale, could scarcely affect the whole body of international trade, with its complications and specialization, in a significant measure.

More important than these individual contracts were the numerous inter-governmental agreements, among European countries employing or suffering from measures of import control, for the exchange of particular commodities in specified amounts. Agreements of that kind had been concluded, up to the middle of 1932, between Germany and Hungary, Austria and Rumania, Bulgaria and Greece, Bulgaria and Switzerland, France and Latvia, Norway and the U.S.S.R., Poland and Austria, Hungary, Bulgaria, Estonia and Jugoslavia. With these might also be grouped the various compensation or clearing agreements, since their purpose was likewise to avoid direct payment for the goods exchanged.

(e) Bilateral Agreements

In every year since the War, but especially after the restoration of Central European finances and the arrest of inflation, there was in Europe and elsewhere a large or small crop of bilateral trade treaties. Even 1932 was not without its harvest, though trade treaties of the ordinary kind were outnumbered by the special clearing agreements made by countries who were subjecting foreign exchange transactions to government control. The principle of such agreements was generally that exchange credits for the purpose of imports would be allotted by a joint clearing house in equal proportions to each of the two countries concerned, so that imports and exports between them would always just balance; but there were numerous variations from the type. It was the policy particularly of Austria and Hungary to conclude these compensation or clearing agreements; thus the former signed agreements with France, Germany, Hungary, Italy, the Netherlands, Switzerland and Jugoslavia; while Hungary signed agreements with Austria, Belgium, France, Germany, Italy and Switzerland. The last-named, and France, were among the countries who concluded agreements of this kind besides those already mentioned. The unsatisfactory working of clearing agreements, in that they hindered the ordinary processes of commerce and prevented the establishment of normal balances of trade in one direction or the other, was the cause of comment by the League's Financial Committee and by the Stresa Conference.

France was generally regarded at this period as one of the chief exponents of economic nationalism, and certainly the emergency quota restrictions, to which she resorted as a means of combating the fall of world prices and the depreciation of foreign currencies, formed a new and severe restraint upon her trade with other countries; yet during 1932 she negotiated, or attempted to negotiate, important agreements for the mitigation of the general tariff war. It must be recalled that her post-war tariff policy, dictated first by the menacing adverse balances of trade that she incurred up to 1925, was maintained and reinforced largely because her internal price level became further and further out of harmony with the world price level (partly, indeed, as a result of the tariffs themselves). While world prices were falling sharply, French price indices, especially indices of the cost of living, showed even a contrary tendency. This naturally caused extreme difficulties among the producers of goods like cereals and other farm products which were peculiarly exposed to the world price-deflation; and measures were accordingly taken to protect them. This, however, only created a new disequilibrium, for it raised the cost of living still further; hence manufacturers, faced with acute price-cutting in foreign markets, found their costs actually rising, and their employees clamouring for higher wages when wages elsewhere were being cut. The disequilibrium was tolerable so long as unemployment in France was negligible, and French industries, with the advantage of up-to-date plant and strong finances, were holding their own in world markets. By the beginning of 1932, however, neither of those conditions still held; exports had fallen disastrously, and unemployment was assuming threatening proportions. Hence a move to mitigate the tariffs and quotas that were strangling France's foreign trade steadily gathered force, and clearly affected government policy. In October the President of the newly formed French Union of Exporting Industries addressed a memorial to the Prime Minister, calling for reciprocal reduction of trade barriers by agreement with other countries, and especially denouncing the typically French policy of import quotas.

Sect. ii   TARIFFS AND EXCHANGE CONTROL   17

Some of the extreme cases of trade restriction (for instance, the quota on British coal) were, in fact, modified unilaterally from time to time by the French Government, and in August 1932 special agreements for the abatement of restrictions recently imposed on French goods, in return for equivalent concessions, were concluded with Belgium, Spain and Italy; but the most important efforts of France towards a new tariff policy in 1932 were made in relation to Germany and the United States. Negotiations on the question with the latter country were begun in 1931, and continued in a desultory fashion throughout 1932, with no very tangible result except an understanding that in fixing future quotas for the products of the United States the French Government would first ascertain the views of the American industries affected. In August 1932 matters were brought to a head when Mr. Walter Edge, the United States Ambassador in Paris, presented an *aide-mémoire* requesting the modification of existing quotas, and especially protesting against features of the recent Franco-Belgian agreement which the United States Government regarded as constituting unfair discrimination. The negotiations began to take a more realistic turn, but they were baulked by a fundamental difference between French and American trade policies which gave the episode its greatest interest to the outside world. The French tariff, consisting of a general tariff and a minimum tariff (the latter accorded only to countries which had granted French exports advantageous treatment), was designed for the conclusion of discriminatory trade treaties; whereas the United States tariff law made no provision for any rate of duty below the general rate, only for an increase in the case of countries discriminating against American goods. This difference prevented the negotiations between the two countries from achieving any success in 1932, but the advent to power in the United States of the Democratic Party, with its specific policy of reciprocal trade agreements, gave grounds for hope that they would not eventually be abortive.

In February 1932 the commercial relations sub-committee of the Franco-German Economic Commission, which was set up under the terms of the trade treaty of 1927, negotiated a series of agreements for the more liberal operation of the quota system as between the two countries. This, however, was but the prelude to a general review of the 1927 treaty, which was begun in Berlin on the 21st November. There were two main reasons prompting the French Government to make this move: first, in the absence of Reparations the balance of trade in Germany's favour was considered excessive, and, second, the whole system of trade relations needed revision in the light of the abnormal barriers other than tariffs that had been erected. Both countries wished, further, to secure the maximum of tariff freedom in view of their forthcoming, or possible, negotiations with other countries. The agreement, which was initialled on the 21st December, made certain modifications of tariffs and quotas, and established an exchange clearing arrangement, but its chief interest here lies in the modification effected in the most-favoured-nation clause. Most-favoured-nation treatment would be maintained in principle, along with fixed maximum charges on a number of tariff items, automatically accruing to other most-favoured nations. In future, however, either country might cancel any such fixed maximum charge at fourteen days' notice, and thus the signatories secured almost complete freedom in relation to each other or to other countries. In a statement on the agreement Monsieur Durand, the French Minister of Commerce, said that the most-favoured-nation clause would no longer hinder France in trade negotiations. Most-favoured-nation treatment would be granted only in individual cases and on a reciprocal basis. It was understood that the French Government had particularly in mind the application of discriminatory duties against countries with depreciated currencies.

Germany was engaged in other bilateral trade negotiations in the course of 1932, though not always with success. An attempt to end the long tariff war with Poland to the mutual advantage of the two countries failed,[1] as did negotiations with Sweden for the replacement of the trade treaty which was shortly due to expire;[2] it was reported that feeling in the Scandinavian countries was extremely resentful at the progressively more rigorous restrictions placed on their products in the interests of German agriculture, and hence was reluctant to accord most-favoured-nation treatment to Germany. The latter herself, in December 1932, declared her refusal further to accord most-favoured-nation treatment to Argentina in spite of the existence of a long-standing treaty between them, on the ground that Argentina had granted a number of tariff reductions to Chile, which she extended to Great Britain and other countries possessing most-favoured-nation treaties with her, but not to Germany, and that this was the deliberate policy of the Argentine Government. Attempts to reach a new trade basis with Great Britain did not achieve success until April 1933, when a temporary arrangement providing for reciprocal concessions on specific items was initialled. In January 1932 the Reich Government promulgated a decree

---

[1] See the present volume, Part IV, section (ii) (c).
[2] See p. 8 above.

authorizing the imposition of additional duties on goods coming from countries with whom Germany had no most-favoured-nation treaty. Among the countries in this category was Canada, with whom, at the end of the following December, a temporary agreement was signed, providing for mutual most-favoured-nation treatment for an initial period of three months. Canada would grant German goods the benefit of the intermediate tariff rates, while Germany would accord to Canada her conventional tariff, or the general tariff where no conventional rates existed.

This account of bilateral trade treaties in 1932 is far from inclusive, its intention having been merely to illustrate the trend of events. Perhaps the first observation to be made is the importance of the most-favoured-nation clause. Even if it did nothing else, the clause sufficed to prevent excesses of tariff restriction which might otherwise have been committed, and it therefore seemed irksome to countries anxious to heighten trade barriers or to indulge in discriminatory tariff warfare. Yet no most-favoured-nation clauses, and no bilateral tariff treaties of the traditional kind, could do much to stem the tide of economic nationalism, driven on by the effects of falling prices; for such agreements were almost undone by the imposition of prohibitive tariffs, by the addition to ordinary tariffs of anti-exchange dumping duties and surcharges, and most vitally by the employment of quota systems and exchange control, which made the former straightforward tariffs of Europe seem liberal by comparison. Thus new bilateral trade treaties, with or without most-favoured-nation clauses, had but a slight effect on the course and volume of world trade in 1932, nor in them alone could be found much hope for the immediate future.

(f) Agrarian Preference: the Stresa Conference

The question of preference for the products of the agrarian countries of Europe has a history of several years' duration. It is unnecessary here, however, to go back further than the Second International Conference on Concerted Economic Action,[1] of the 17th to the 28th November, 1930, at which a committee was appointed to 'consider the question of negotiations regarding the trade of the agricultural states of eastern Europe with the states of central and western Europe'. What in fact the committee discussed was a joint proposal by the Governments of Bulgaria, Hungary, Poland, Rumania and Jugoslavia for the accordance of preference for their exports of grain by other European countries. The committee took no decision

[1] See the *Survey for 1930*, Part VI, section (ii).

on the question of principle involved or on the possibility of the application of the scheme, but reported its agreement on the following points.

(a) The system of preferences would have to be regarded as a conditional, exceptional and limited derogation to the most-favoured-nation clause, which must characterize the normal régime of international trade. It could only be established in agreement with countries enjoying most-favoured-nation treatment.

(b) Preferences would be accorded only for cereals and their derivatives.

(c) Preferential treatment should not harm the interests of overseas exporting countries, in as much as the latter were bound to be always the main providers of Europe.

(d) The preferential régime must not in any way endanger the protection of the agricultural interests of the importing countries, and should not in any case cause any injury to agriculturalists in European importing countries.

(e) The preferential régime would only be accorded for quantities to be limited by quotas or other methods.

(f) The demand for preference would not be made of those European countries which admitted cereals free of duty nor of those countries whose import duties were insignificant.

(g) If European countries, on being approached with a view to giving preference to cereals, were to demand an off-setting advantage amounting likewise to a customs preference, such preference would not be admissible without the consent of the interested countries enjoying most-favoured-nation treatment.

The Italian delegation, while noting these specifications for the preferential régime, affirmed their definite opposition to such a plan. It will be observed that the conditions, including the ban on injury to the agricultural interests either of the importing countries or of the extra-European exporting countries, would virtually nullify the effect of any proposed preferences, unless the cunning employment of quotas were somehow to overcome the inherent conflict of interests.

In execution of a resolution adopted by the Commission of Inquiry for European Union during its second session (16th to 21st January, 1931), a Conference of the grain-exporting countries of Central and Eastern Europe and of certain European importing countries was held on the 23rd February, 1931, to 'make a common effort to find means of disposing of the grain surplus' actually available in Europe. The Final Act of this Conference, signed by seventeen countries, noted that both the representatives of the countries which normally bought foreign wheat and those of the countries which did not import wheat, or did not usually import wheat from the countries under

Sect. ii TARIFFS AND EXCHANGE CONTROL 21

consideration, were willing to participate to the utmost possible extent in the purchase of the available stocks. The Conference would not take upon itself to prescribe any practical solution, but 'the signatories, being prepared to reserve a certain proportion of their imports of foreign wheat for wheat originating in the countries under consideration, undertook to initiate, without delay, the negotiations necessary to enable those transactions to be carried out'. The importing countries were prepared to act likewise in regard to maize and barley, but the Conference reserved the examination of the question of rye and oats. What had thus been achieved was the acknowledgement of the principle of preference for European wheat, maize, and barley by the importing countries as well as by the clamorous exporters.

The Commission of Inquiry for European Union also set up a committee to consider the problems of the export of future harvest surpluses. This committee, which met on the 26th February, 1931, 'recognized that the disposal of surplus European cereals was not merely a European but a world problem, and that a wholly satisfactory solution could be reached only by an understanding between all the parts of the world concerned'. 'There is no over-production in Europe,' wrote the committee; 'there is over-production in the world as a whole.' On the subject of the preferential privileges requested by the exporting countries, the committee reported that the conclusions of the committee of the Conference on Concerted Economic Action (reported above) were still valid, and noted that practical attempts on the lines in question were shortly to be made by several European countries. The committee also turned its attention to other measures calculated to facilitate the regular disposal of the surplus cereals in question by improving the conditions of sale, in the fields of finance, organization, statistics, quality and transport.

The next events in the story, chronologically, were the International Wheat Conferences held in Rome on the 26th March, 1931, and in London on the 18th May. These Conferences failed to achieve their aim of securing a world-wide agreement on the production and marketing of wheat. At the London Conference a plan for the curtailment of production met with approval in principle from the leading delegations except that of the Soviet Union, whose policy was declared to be opposed to limitation of production though favourable to a system of export quotas; the latter project, however, did not meet with the consent of other important delegations.

But certain action had been taken bilaterally meanwhile. The Co-ordination Sub-committee of the Commission of Inquiry for

European Union, reporting in September 1931, affirmed once more the principle that bilateral agreements involving customs preference for grain should have the character of temporary and limited exceptions to the most-favoured-nation clause. The sub-committee, having examined the preferential arrangements agreed upon in the German-Rumanian Commercial Agreement of the 27th June, 1931, and the German-Hungarian Commercial Agreement of the 18th July, 1931, expressed the opinion that these were in keeping with the principles that had been laid down and that they fulfilled the specified conditions. The Greek Government submitted to the sub-committee a memorandum advocating the extension of special facilities to agricultural products other than grain. The ideas set forth in the memorandum were supported by a number of delegations, who also asked for the extension of the system to other products.

The Danubian customs preference plan, associated with the name of Monsieur Tardieu, was not designed purely, or even perhaps primarily, to assist the marketing of the agricultural surpluses of Central and Eastern Europe, but that was one of its aims, so that a brief account of it must be included in this section. Discussions with a view to relieving the plight of the successor states of the Austrian Empire by joint action had been going on among the Great Powers for some time, and it is difficult to assign the initiative to any one event or country. The discussions, however, took a more definite turn when on the 5th March, 1932, the French Government delivered to the British delegation at Geneva a memorandum containing suggestions for economic and financial reconstruction in the area in question. On the 16th February the Austrian Chancellor had warned the assembled Ministers of Great Britain, France, Germany and Italy that, while his Government were prepared to enter into negotiations with all countries for an economic *rapprochement*, they felt compelled to restrict imports as the only means of preventing inflation. The French proposal did not at this stage contain any cut-and-dried scheme, but when a Conference of the four Great Powers concerned was held in London at the beginning of April, Monsieur Tardieu put forward the following plan. The five 'Danubian' states—Austria, Czechoslovakia, Hungary, Jugoslavia and Rumania—should establish reciprocal preferences to the extent of one-tenth of existing tariffs. Certain other countries, including Germany and Italy, should grant the Danubian countries preferential entry for their agricultural products, without any direct compensation by way of counter-preferences. Third, a loan of $50,000,000 should be raised on the guarantee of the countries in whose centres it was issued, and spent, under international authority, for the protection of the budgets and the exchanges of the Danubian group.

This plan was rejected, and the London meeting proved altogether abortive, for a number of reasons. Neither Germany nor Great Britain viewed with favour a sacrifice of their most-favoured-nation rights without compensation in the way of more favourable terms of entry for their own manufactured products. Germany, still smarting from the sting of having to abandon the scheme for economic *Anschluss* with Austria, disliked a proposal which would have brought the latter more closely into another economic orbit, that of Czechoslovakia and the Little Entente. The British Government had to refuse agreement to any plan involving financial contribution or guarantee. Italy also, resenting in some measure the political implications of the plan, adhered to her preference for bilateral treaties. Nor were the Danubian countries themselves unanimous in their support for the plan. Austria in particular felt that too much favour was being shown to the agricultural as compared with the manufacturing countries in the group. In these circumstances any such device as the Tardieu plan was bound to be a failure.

Further bilateral agreements for preferences on cereals were entered into, however, though their entry into force was sometimes delayed by the opposition of third states enjoying most-favoured-nation treatment. Moreover, as the Stresa Conference rather ingenuously remarked, 'even if all these agreements were in force they would probably fail to achieve the most important result—namely, an increase in the home price in the producing countries'.

The Stresa Conference was the result of the appointment by the Lausanne Reparations Conference of a special committee

> with the duty of submitting to the Commission of Inquiry for European Union at its next session proposals as to measures required for the restoration of the countries of Central and Eastern Europe, and, in particular:
>
> (a) Measures to overcome the present transfer difficulties of those countries and to make possible the progressive suppression, subject to the necessary safeguards, of the existing systems of exchange control.
>
> (b) Measures to revive the activity of trade, both among those countries themselves and between them and other states, and to overcome the difficulties caused to the agricultural countries of Central and Eastern Europe by the low price of cereals, it being understood that the rights of third countries remain reserved.

The committee sat at Stresa from the 5th to the 20th September, 1932, under the chairmanship of Monsieur Georges Bonnet. The following countries were represented by delegations: Austria, Belgium, the United Kingdom, Bulgaria, Czechoslovakia, France, Germany, Greece, Hungary, Italy, the Netherlands, Poland, Rumania, Switzerland and Jugoslavia; while Latvia sent an observer.

The Stresa meeting was preceded by a Conference at Warsaw of the delegates of the eight agrarian countries of Central and Eastern Europe—Bulgaria, Estonia, Hungary, Latvia, Lithuania, Poland, Rumania and Jugoslavia. Agreement was reached there on the following points: (i) the progressive suppression of the obstacles to international trade; (ii) the assignment by the creditor states to the debtor states of import quotas sufficient to allow the latter to discharge their debts; (iii) customs preference in favour of the agricultural products of the eight states; (iv) the raising of the prices of agricultural products by means of an improved organization of the consuming markets. This epitomized the policy eventually put forward by the agrarian states at Stresa. Early in the course of the Conference the Polish delegates elaborated their proposals, adumbrating (i) the complete abolition of import and export restrictions and prohibitions, the abolition to be essentially associated with the grant of supplementary quotas to debtor countries; (ii) preferential treatment for cereals and live stock, in the form of a considerable reduction of customs tariffs; (iii) creation of a special fund for the liquefaction of bills 'frozen' owing to the difficulties of agriculture and connected industries.

Objection to these proposals arose mainly on three counts, namely, the demand of industrial states like Czechoslovakia and Austria that their products should be no less favourably treated than those of their agricultural neighbours; the insistence of certain of the importing countries, notably Great Britain and Italy, upon the retention of most-favoured-nation rights; and the refusal of the British delegates to subscribe to any plan for an international stabilization fund. The French, Italian and German delegations all laid schemes before the Conference. The French project, which was to take the form of a multilateral convention, included the grant of customs preference for cereals imported from the Danubian countries, and the establishment of a fund to which each importing state should contribute in proportion to the amount of its imports, with the aim of improving the market value of the cereals concerned. The introduction of the preferential system would have to be considered, first of all, by the oversea exporters of grain enjoying most-favoured-nation treatment. Italy, on the other hand, proposed a system of bilateral agreements for the purchase of grain from the Danubian countries. Each exporting country would receive, as a temporary measure, a subsidy pro-

Sect. ii   TARIFFS AND EXCHANGE CONTROL   25

portionate to its average export of cereals in the past three years, to be provided by a toll levied upon every European country on the basis of its total foreign trade. The grain-exporting countries in question would lower their customs tariffs to assist imports from other European countries and from the oversea countries. The German delegation agreed in principle to the French plan, but put forward an alternative in case the latter should be rejected. The German plan provided for a convention to be concluded between Germany, France, Italy, Austria and Czechoslovakia for the purchase of wheat, barley, forage and maize, under a preferential system involving reductions of tariffs, from Bulgaria, Hungary, Rumania and Jugoslavia, with whom they would make bilateral agreements. The agreements would be examined, and might be modified, by an international committee.

Ultimately, the Economic and Agricultural Committee of the Conference drew up a report which was unanimously accepted by the Conference in plenary session. The United Kingdom delegation, however, while in general approving the recommendations made, and in particular those which represented a step in the direction of removing obstacles to trade, drew attention to the special position of those countries, such as the United Kingdom, whose commercial policy did not include the imposition of quotas or heavy import duties on cereals; and they made reservations on behalf of His Majesty's Government in regard to participation in proposals involving financial contributions or guarantees. The committee's report was based on a draft multilateral convention, aimed at improving the price of cereals by a combination of the grant of preferences in bilateral treaties (subject to the rights of third states) and financial contributions to a special fund. The draft limited the preferences to be granted by the bilateral treaties or by collective action to the average quantities exported during the three years 1929–31. This limitation, the committee observed, was of great importance because it laid down acceptable limits to the concessions asked of European countries, while giving oversea countries an assurance that the production of cereals in Central and Eastern Europe would not increase behind the shelter of an unlimited preferential régime. Article 1 of the draft convention stated that signatory countries which were exporters of wheat, barley for fodder, maize, rye, barley for brewing, and oats, should 'receive facilities for their exports' within specified limits as above. Article 2 laid down that an aggregate sum of 75,000,000 gold francs (£3,125,000 gold) should be taken annually from the proceeds of contributions by the adhering states (as provided for in the report of the Financial Committee of the Conference)[1] towards a general fund for the economic and financial reconstruction of Central and Eastern Europe, and should be used to promote the revalorization of cereals. The share to be contributed by each state would be reduced in proportion to the effective operation of whatever advantages it had granted to selling countries, by means of bilateral treaties for the importation of the above-mentioned cereals. (Germany would acquit herself altogether of her contribution through such bilateral treaties.) Article 3 provided for the setting up of a committee representing the adhering states, whose principal duty would be the award of shares in the aggregate sum to the different beneficiaries, according to the results of their harvests and the effective advantages they received under bilateral agreements. Article 4 dealt with arbitration. Article 5 declared that in compensation for these favours the beneficiary countries, 'desiring to co-operate with the other countries in introducing a liberal commercial policy and a moderate tariff policy', undertook to grant adequate concessions to the contributing countries by bilateral agreements, so far as compensation had not already been given. The advantages thus granted would in no case affect the rights derived by third countries from the most-favoured-nation clause, and would extend to all signatory states. Article 6 dealt with ratification; the convention would not be binding upon any signatory until it had been possible to put into force the various bilateral treaties. Article 7 provided that the convention should remain in force until the 31st October, 1935, unless world prices had previously reached a remunerative level.

When these proposals came before the Commission of Inquiry for European Union, at its session of the 1st October, under the chairmanship of Monsieur Herriot, their practical acceptance did not seem very probable. The British delegate once more expressed his Government's refusal to participate in financial guarantees, while opposition to the plan for the revalorization of cereals was also expressed by Monsieur Litvinov, for the Soviet Union, and by the representatives of most of the Northern European countries. The report of the Stresa Conference was then passed to the Council of the League, with a request for expert examination; three reservations were attached, one reserving the rights of third parties, a second releasing Governments from final decisions until definite schemes should be submitted to them, and a third incorporating with the minute to the Council all the other reservations that had been made in the course of the discussion. For good or ill, the plan for the

[1] See p. 93 below.

revalorization of cereal exports from Central and Eastern Europe was still bogged in the quicksand of committees and conferences at the end of 1932.

One of the obstacles, as has already been mentioned, was the resentment of countries not producing cereals at the special favour accorded to those products. The demand for the extension of preferential treatment to other agricultural products was repeated at Stresa. The Conference, however, while recognizing the 'primordial importance' of the crisis in the live stock and timber trades, felt bound for the moment to confine itself to cereals in order to give this experiment time to develop and prove its value. The conviction was also expressed that the Oriental tobacco question had assumed a particularly urgent character, but no recommendations were made cognate to those for cereals. Lastly, ran the report, there still remained the particularly important problem of Austria, whose exports were not mainly agricultural and who had to cope with particularly serious marketing difficulties.

(g) THE OTTAWA CONFERENCE

It does not beg any questions about the value of the Ottawa Conference in promoting or deferring world trade recovery to include the Conference among the efforts to escape from the toils of ever-rising tariffs. Undoubtedly in the popular mind, and explicitly in the mind of the Government, one of the chief reasons for the imposition of the British tariff was the need for a weapon with which to secure more liberal treatment abroad for Great Britain's exports; and what more favourable field for the exercise of such persuasion could there be than the British Commonwealth, in which pleas of commercial advantage could be reinforced with appeals to imperial sentiment? Imperialists of the narrower school demanded, in effect, preference for preference's sake, but by reason both of her political history in tariff matters, and her obvious economic interest, Great Britain, as a nation, sought at Ottawa an extension of preference from the Dominions essentially by means of a reduction of the latters' tariffs against British goods rather than by means of an enhancement of their tariffs against foreign goods.

This point of view was emphatically expressed by Mr. Baldwin, who led the United Kingdom delegation, both in his opening speech to the Conference and in a supplementary statement which was issued after Mr. S. M. Bruce had declared that the Australian people regarded the British preferences granted under the Import Duties

Act 'as a somewhat tardy response for the benefits from Australia long enjoyed by British industry'.

> What then [asked Mr. Baldwin] should be the first aim of this Conference? It should be to clear out the channels of trade among ourselves. . . . There are two ways in which increased preference can be given—either by lowering barriers among ourselves or by raising them against others. The choice between these two must be governed largely by local considerations, but, subject to that, it seems to us that we should endeavour to follow the first rather than the second course. For, however great our resources, we cannot isolate ourselves from the world. No nation or group of nations, however wealthy and populous, can maintain prosperity in a world where depression and impoverishment reign. Let us therefore aim at the lowering rather than the raising of barriers, even if we cannot fully achieve our purpose now, and let us remember that any action we take here is bound to have its reactions elsewhere.
>
> It is [he said in his supplementary statement] necessary to bear in mind that the percentage of duty charged on the value of the article is of great importance in assessing the value of a preference. A preferential rate of duty, if the preference is to be of material assistance, must not be so high as, in effect, seriously to restrict importation: and the United Kingdom delegation would urge upon the Dominions that the rates of duty charged should be so graduated as to give the products of the United Kingdom a reasonable chance of competing on equal terms, and that the rate of duty against United Kingdom products should be fixed for protective purposes no higher than is necessary to give a reasonably efficient industry in the Dominion a fair chance. In this connexion they desire to draw attention to the favourable tariff treatment which they have hitherto accorded to imports from the Dominions which compete with goods produced in the United Kingdom.

Indeed, in its sole general statement of principle the entire Ottawa Conference recorded its conviction:

> That by the lowering or removal of barriers among themselves provided for in [the] Agreements the flow of trade between the various countries of the Empire will be facilitated, and that by the consequent increase of the purchasing power of their peoples the trade of the world will also be stimulated and increased.

From the international point of view, the results of Ottawa must be treated in relation to two questions, namely, how far did the agreements lower or remove the barriers against trade within the Empire, thereby justifying the above claim, and how far did they increase tariffs against the rest of the world, or threaten such diversion of trade from the rest of the world as would exacerbate the existing tendency to raise tariffs competitively in the scramble for trade. These questions the reader himself must answer, on the basis of the following summary of the agreements.

The agreements between the United Kingdom and the Dominions were to run for five years; that with India was made terminable on six months' notice given by either party. It may be noted that in the field of international commercial agreements five years is an exceptionally long term of currency without the possibility of denunciation. Great Britain undertook (a) to continue free entry for all Empire products already admitted free, (b) to impose fresh duties (i.e. to put on duties where none existed, or to increase actual duties, or to consolidate *ad valorem* into specific duties) on certain imports from foreign countries, notably wheat, maize, butter and cheese, canned and dried fruits, a number of raw fruits, copper, linseed and rice; (c) to regulate quantitatively imports of chilled and frozen beef and frozen mutton and lamb and (when the Commission on the reorganization of the pig industry should have reported) bacon and ham, with the aim of raising the wholesale price of meat in the British market to such a level as would maintain efficient production at home and in the Dominions, and of giving the latter an expanding share of British imports of meat; (d) to maintain certain existing preferences, i.e. by not reducing the existing duties on foreign imports of the commodities concerned; and (e) to perform certain other undertakings, chiefly regarding the consolidation of preferences on tobacco, South African wine and coffee, but including also an undertaking given to Canada that if the preferences granted or guaranteed at Ottawa appeared likely to be frustrated in whole or in part through state action on the part of any foreign country, the United Kingdom Government would exercise their powers to prohibit the import of such commodities from the country in question for so long as was necessary to make the preferences effective. In pursuance of this undertaking, the British Government on the 17th October gave six months' notice of denunciation of the 1930 commercial agreement with the U.S.S.R., which granted the latter most-favoured-nation rights.[1] The incidence of the new duties imposed on foreign imports under the Ottawa Agreements is shown first by the fact that the proportion of imports from foreign countries admitted free, which

[1] In April 1933, during the course of the trial of a number of British subjects on charges of counter-revolutionary activities in Russia, the British Government imposed an embargo on imports of the following commodities from the Soviet Union: butter, wheat, barley, oats, maize, poultry and game, raw cotton, petroleum and timber. The embargo was removed on the 1st July, 1933, on the release of the two British subjects who had been imprisoned as a result of the trial. The counter-embargo which had been imposed by the Soviet Government was withdrawn simultaneously, and negotiations for the conclusion of a fresh commercial treaty between the two countries were thereupon resumed.

was 83 per cent. before the various tariff measures were passed by the National Government, fell as a result of the Ottawa Conference from 30 per cent. to 25 per cent.; and second by the following table prepared by *The Economist*.[1]

Protective Duties before Ottawa Percentage of Foreign Imports Taxed at			*Protective Duties after Ottawa* Percentage of Foreign Imports Taxed at		
10%	11–20%	Over 20%	10%	11–20%	Over 20%
32·9	15·3	4·6	28·3	21·8	7·7

The countries on whom the new duties fell particularly onerously were Denmark, Holland, Belgium, Sweden, Italy, Finland, Poland and Chile, while Argentina stood to lose most trade through the regulation of meat imports.

The concessions granted by the Dominions and India in exchange for these favours differed in each case, but at the outset mention must be made of the common undertaking entered into by Canada, Australia and New Zealand. They promised, first, to give tariff protection only to those industries which were reasonably assured of sound opportunities of success, and, second, to keep or reduce protective duties to a level which would give United Kingdom producers full opportunity of reasonable competition on the basis of the relative costs of economical and efficient production, provided that special consideration might be given to the case of industries not fully established. In Canada and Australia these conditions would form the terms of reference to independent tariff boards, before whom British producers should henceforward have the right of stating their case, while in New Zealand the agreement would be implemented by the Government directly, British producers again being given a hearing. The above principle of the 'compensatory tariff', which incidentally was the theoretical basis of the United States tariff schedule, was regarded by some as the most important feature of the Ottawa Agreements and as the one most calculated to secure a liberation of trade by reducing Dominion tariffs, despite the obvious fact that if it were rigorously carried out it would consume the mutual advantage of international trade altogether, rendering the latter redundant and impossible except in cases of dumping. Certain commentators pointed out that the application of the same general terms to three Dominions with varying scales of tariffs would tend to bring about a reduction of duties, since the Dominion with the lowest existing rate of duty would establish a criterion of economical and efficient production for the others. The further principle,

[1] Ottawa Supplement, 22nd October, 1932, p. 7.

that exporters should be heard before a revision of a tariff was carried out, was also of considerable general importance in connexion with international trade relations. However, even by the middle of 1933, no general review of the tariff in accordance with the terms of the agreement had been accomplished in any of the three Dominions.

All that can be related here concerning the specific changes in Dominion tariffs is the measure in which they involved a raising of tariffs against foreign countries. Australia undertook to apply a general formula for the guarantee of minimum British preferential margins, rising to 20 per cent. *ad valorem* preference where the duty on United Kingdom goods was over 29 per cent. *ad valorem*; the application of this formula resulted in the majority of cases in an increase of the general tariff. The Lyons Government was in any case pledged to the removal of the prohibitions and the grosser features of high protectionism that characterized the Scullin tariff. On 132 items in the Canadian schedule, which covered 215 items in all, there would be a reduction of the duties on United Kingdom goods (accompanied in some instances by a simultaneous raising of the foreign duty), while in respect of the remainder increased margins of preference were to be secured for the United Kingdom by means of advances of the general tariff.

It has been estimated, on the basis of 1931–2 imports into Canada, that the British preferential tariff would be reduced to zero in categories of which total imports were $31,200,000, including $8,300,000 of British goods; that the preferential tariff would be otherwise lowered in categories of which total imports were $58,900,000, including $37,400,000 British; and that the foreign tariff would be raised in the case of $35,100,000 of total imports, including $8,800,000 British. The total trade affected by the schedules was thus $70,700,000 of foreign goods and $54,500,000 of United Kingdom goods in 1931–2, representing roughly 22 per cent. of Canada's total imports. To estimate how much trade might be diverted as a result of these changes—a point on which there was considerable dispute during the course of the Conference itself—would be merely to guess, but the diversion might be put at a maximum of one-third of the foreign trade affected, namely, $24,000,000 odd, the United States being of course the chief loser.

The specific changes in the New Zealand tariff related only to four items, confectionery, clothing, hosiery, and silk and rayon piece goods, on all of which the British preferential duty would be reduced. South Africa undertook (*a*) to grant new or increased preferences on a brief list of manufactures, in most cases partially at least by means of an increase of the general tariff, (b) to impose new duties on certain foreign piece goods of cotton and rayon, and underclothing, leaving the existing British preferential tariff unchanged, and (c) not to lower existing margins of preference on a lengthy list of British manufactures. Newfoundland, whose tariff was primarily revenue-producing and not protective, promised a preference of 10 per cent. on 61 classes of goods, with the qualification that the preference might be reduced if it resulted in a loss of revenue. The Indian Government undertook to give a $7\frac{1}{2}$ per cent. preference on motor-cars, omnibuses, and accumulators, and to give a 10 per cent. preference on a long list of manufactured goods, to be secured either by an increase of duty on foreign goods or by a reduction of duty on British goods, or by a combination of both. It has been estimated that in 1930–1 the volume of imports in the categories affected by this undertaking amounted to £32,000,000, of which £12,700,000 were already imported from Great Britain. Southern Rhodesia promised increased margins of preference on electrical and radio material, typewriters, cutlery and glassware (in some cases inevitably by dint of an increase of the foreign tariff), as well as minimum specific duties on foreign cotton, silk and rayon piece goods.

Perhaps the most satisfactory feature of the Dominions' concessions, from the point of view of liberation of trade, was the undertakings in respect of surcharges and other abnormal hindrances to British trade. Australia promised to repeal as soon as possible the proclamation of May 1932, prohibiting certain imports, to remove as soon as practicable the surcharges imposed at that time, and to reduce or remove the primage duty as soon as the finances of the Commonwealth would allow. Canada promised to ensure a minimum of uncertainty, delay, and friction in connexion with tariffs, and to provide machinery for the prompt and impartial settlement of disputes; to abolish surcharges on United Kingdom imports as soon as possible and to consider the ultimate abolition of the exchange dumping duty on United Kingdom products. New Zealand undertook not to increase the existing primage duty of 3 per cent. on United Kingdom goods which were otherwise duty free, and to remove it as soon as financial conditions permitted.

Without attempting to compute the extent of each factor, we may observe that the Ottawa Agreements resulted in a certain measure of liberation of trade within the British Commonwealth, a certain measure of increase of British tariffs against the rest of the world (including an aggravation of the United Kingdom tariff), and some diversion of trade from outside to within the British Commonwealth.

TARIFFS AND EXCHANGE CONTROL

The effects of these phenomena on international trade and commercial relations generally could only be judged after lengthy experience of the actual operation of the agreements; but it is possible to make some comment on the reaction of Ottawa upon Great Britain's potential ability to use her tariff to secure the reduction of foreign tariffs. That this use was, from the first, officially contemplated was shown by the terms of Clause 7 of the Import Duties Act, which provided for the reduction of duties, upon the recommendation of the Board of Trade, on the goods of any specified country, presumably one which accorded reciprocal advantages to the United Kingdom. Now under the Ottawa Agreements the concessions that Great Britain could make for the benefit of foreign countries (except, of course, an undertaking not to increase existing duties) were limited for a period of five years in respect of all commodities for which the agreements provided a minimum general rate of duty or a minimum rate of preference where the preferential rate was already zero. This list of commodities included several, such as butter and timber, which were of particular interest to countries most likely, on account of the closeness of their trading relations with Great Britain, to offer her advantageous reciprocal terms. Further, the Ottawa Agreements would certainly prevent the entry of Great Britain into a free trade or very low tariff group, or any agreement like the Belgo-Dutch Convention for the progressive reduction of mutual tariffs to a low level. The admission of foreign countries to the whole preferential system enjoyed by members of the Commonwealth would be ruled out by a resolution of the Ottawa Conference affirming that while each Government would determine its particular attitude in its treaty relations towards other countries, the different delegations recorded their policy 'that no treaty obligations into which they might enter in the future should be allowed to interfere with any mutual preferences which Governments of the Commonwealth might decide to accord to each other, and that they would free themselves from existing treaties, if any, which might so interfere'. In accordance with this resolution the South African trade treaty with Germany, which promised the latter the benefit of any preferences that might be subsequently granted to Great Britain, was abrogated at the instance of the South African Government.

Finally, the Conference deliberated the policy to be adopted by nations of the British Commonwealth towards the most-favoured-nation clause in commercial treaties, and decided that whereas each participant would still act independently in its relations with foreign countries, and on its own judgment, their unanimous policy was that most-favoured-nation rights must be strictly upheld, against the tendency to modify them in respect of limited preferential groups, but that no claim could be countenanced to participate in the mutual preferences within the British Commonwealth, on the part of a foreign country pleading its most-favoured-nation rights.

(*h*) OTHER MULTILATERAL ACTION: THE BELGO-DUTCH CONVENTION

After the World Economic Conference of 1927 gave warning of the pressing need for a reduction of tariffs throughout the world, attempts to carry out its resolutions took two main forms, multilateral or universal negotiations (the International Conferences on Concerted Economic Action) and bilateral commercial agreements. It could assuredly be claimed that the World Economic Conference, the work of the Economic Committee, and other efforts under the auspices of the League of Nations had encouraged a more far-seeing and more internationalist attitude among the nations of Europe than they would otherwise have had in their commercial relations, but a glance at the world's tariff systems in 1932—or even before the acute financial crisis drove country after country to emergency measures of trade restriction—proves that the attempts were on the whole a failure. The abortive efforts of the Conference on Concerted Economic Action to establish a 'tariff truce' have already been described in this series.[1] For the failure of bilateral treaties, based, as the World Economic Conference recommended, on the most-favoured-nation clause, to achieve any appreciable general reduction of tariffs, a number of reasons must be adduced. First of all came all those obstacles inherent in the nature of protective tariff systems—the vested interests sheltering behind them and the difficulty of exchanging the advantage of one industry, manufacturing principally for the home market, for that of another industry seeking larger markets abroad. Then there were political reasons—the widespread fear of war or blockade which rendered the countries of the world unwilling to sacrifice economic independence, however dearly bought; as well as the political antagonisms between pairs or combinations of countries (Germany and Poland, for instance) which hindered the conclusion of commercial treaties among them. Possibly, too, as the sub-committee of economic experts mentioned below suggested, another reason was the want of any clear conception of the ultimate goal. 'In the absence of such a conception to act as a guide as well as an encouragement, tariff reduction, whether by general agreement or by means of bilateral treaties, appeared in the light of a bargaining

[1] See the *Survey for 1930*, Part VI, section (ii).

Sect. ii   TARIFFS AND EXCHANGE CONTROL

arrangement and not of a step towards a new and better system of international economic life.' As far as Europe was concerned—and that was the limit of its terms of reference—the sub-committee declared that 'the ultimate goal must be the widest possible collaboration of the nations of Europe in the sense of making Europe a single market for the products of any and every country in it'. Finally, the most-favoured-nation clause itself acted as a brake, since countries were reluctant to enter into reciprocal arrangements one with another for the mutual reduction of tariffs, knowing that the advantage of any such reduction would also be enjoyed by third parties who had granted no counter-concession, by virtue merely of their possessing most-favoured-nation rights. Thus, while the general application of the most-favoured-nation clause acted as a brake on the upward movement of tariffs and checked tendencies towards catastrophic tariff wars, it certainly was a hindrance to the conclusion of limited arrangements for the reduction of tariffs among groups having some geographical and economic unity—a risky procedure in normal times, but one which offered some hope in the days of ever-growing restrictions on international trade during the world depression.

This question was the one that most exercised the sub-committee of economic experts, appointed in accordance with a resolution of the 28th May, 1931, of the Commission of Inquiry for European Union, 'to examine in complete freedom and in a spirit of liberal understanding all means which might seem calculated to bring about closer and more profitable co-operation between the different countries with a view to improving the organization of production and trade'. The sub-committee held two series of meetings under the chairmanship of Dr. Trip (Netherlands), and signed its report on the 29th August, 1931. The experts affirmed that they did not wish in any way to modify 'the general basis of the most-favoured-nation clause, which must remain the essential safeguard of normal commercial relations between the nations', adding that if any of the agreements which they contemplated were in any way to affect the rights of third parties under that clause, such agreements could not come into force until an understanding had been reached with those non-contracting parties. They thought, however, that cases might arise in which European or non-European countries which were not parties to the agreements in question might, without prejudice to their individual interests, be willing to agree to some modification of their rights in view of the benefits likely to accrue to the world in general from the growing prosperity of Europe as a whole which such agreements were designed to promote. What was clearly in their mind was a limited preferential agreement for the mutual and perhaps progressive reduction of tariffs, most probably among low-tariff countries.

From the economic point of view, they agreed, the *rapprochements* which they envisaged should be subject to the following conditions:

> (a) The groups of countries which they affected should be such as to ensure that they were in conformity with the general interest and contributed to the general progress of Europe. (This was really a reservation intended to rule out disturbing semi-political accords. The sub-committee was working under the shadow of the Austro-German customs union dispute, which affected the attitude of several of the delegations.)
>
> (b) They must not injure the interest of other countries, but must, on the contrary, tend to encourage economic intercourse with them.
>
> (c) They must as far as possible include the free movement of individuals, goods and capital, and indeed all forms of economic activity, so that a fair balance might be established between sacrifices and advantages.
>
> (d) If they were to lead to treaties or agreements different from the ordinary commercial treaties:
>
>> (1) These must be open to accession by all countries prepared to conform with the obligations which such treaties or agreements entailed.
>>
>> (2) They must provide for the granting of the stipulated advantages to non-signatory countries which should accord equivalent advantages, whether by treaty or by virtue of their own autonomous policy.

The sub-committee added that the peril implicit in the diversion of trade through the conclusion of any economic agreements could be avoided only if they were such as to initiate a movement for the reduction of tariff barriers generally. Moreover, they should be as far as possible of a permanent character.

If, said the economic experts, the understandings envisaged were to take the form of customs unions, then they would achieve the desired results only if they took into account the situation of countries not prepared to participate. Among the latter (to paraphrase the report) would be countries whose tariffs were too high and those whose tariffs were too low—the former being unwilling to abolish their tariffs on the products of the participating countries, and the latter being unwilling to raise their tariffs against the rest of the world to the level established by the customs union. As for the first group, progress must be sought either by an extension and improvement of the actual system of commercial treaties, or by the conclusion of general agreements for preventing the increase of trade barriers, such as the abortive Tariff Truce. As regards the second group (the sub-committee plainly having its eye on Great Britain, where a few days previously the first National Government had been formed, and a 'revenue tariff' seemed a probable contingency), it was wrong that they should be denied the chance of participating in agreements for the abolition of mutual tariffs in Europe, or that the price of their participation should have to be the increase of their tariffs to the level of the other participants. Clearly, indeed, their present liberal policy might 'serve as a basis upon which greater freedom for international commerce throughout the world as a whole could be built'—perhaps a desperate prayer to the British Government. It was therefore desirable that any European group or nation which was willing to extend the freedom of its market by the inclusion of free-trade or low-tariff countries should be permitted to do so, subject to agreement in regard to the fiscal duties of the parties concerned (in other words, they might be allowed to retain duties at a level and of a kind intended for the production of revenue).

The experts went on to consider the place of international industrial agreements (cartels) in the furtherance of trade, and elaborated their advantages and their dangers, which it was the duty of individual states to obviate. Subject to certain conditions, industrial combines might lead to a community of interests which would tend to create a favourable atmosphere for commercial negotiations, 'and to bring about that reconciliation for which the public in all countries is so eager'. Some of the delegates expressed the view that agreements among producers might one day come to transcend and obviate tariff barriers generally. It may be noted here that the policy of direct industrial co-operation (rationalization, or complementary production) was powerfully advocated by British industrial interests, preparatory to the Ottawa Conference, as the best means of enlarging and improving trade within the British Commonwealth, and that an understanding between the iron and steel producers of the United Kingdom and Canada—the 'Montreal Pact'—was the basis of the new Canadian tariff schedule in the iron and steel sections as incorporated in the Ottawa Agreements.

Considerable space has been devoted to the work of the sub-committee of economic experts because it represents the considered and unanimous opinion of a group of economists, bankers, business men and others representing the countries of Europe, upon a new or growing tendency in international commercial relations, and their guidance towards what seemed the most hopeful method of securing a liberation of European (and by the same token world) trade, having regard to the failure in practice of other means. Their views, however, were not in every case precisely in accord with those of their respective Governments. The British Government, in their published commentary on the report, declared that they had always held that customs unions proper must necessarily constitute an exception from the most-favoured-nation clause, but that, as for economic *rapprochements* not amounting to complete customs unions, such as regional tariff preferences, they remained of the view that it would cause conflict with the whole spirit of the most-favoured-nation clause if it were open to any countries to conclude arrangements with each other which they did not extend to other countries. This difference of opinion was the cause of the resignation of Sir Walter Layton from the preparatory committee for the World Economic Conference, in October 1932, for Sir Walter, who had been the British delegate to the meeting of economic experts, found himself too much at variance with the Government's conservative attitude towards the most-favoured-nation clause (except, of course, as concerned preferential agreements within the British Commonwealth) to continue as his country's representative on the preparatory committee.

The British Government had had occasion, meanwhile, to give practical expression to their attitude in this matter. The possibility of an understanding among the low-tariff countries of Northern Europe for mutual reductions of tariffs had been exposed by the conclusion of the Oslo Convention of December 1930 (entering into force on the 7th February, 1932), whereby Norway, Sweden, Denmark, Holland, Belgium and Luxembourg (who was in customs union with Belgium) undertook for one year not to raise their mutual tariffs without first consulting each other,[1] but it was generally recognized that the strained financial conditions of 1931 and 1932 greatly handicapped further progress in that direction. It was something of a surprise, therefore, to the outside world when it was announced, on the 20th June, 1932, in the course of the Lausanne Conference on Reparations, that the Governments of Belgium, Luxembourg and the Netherlands had initialled a Convention for the progressive reduction of the tariffs on each other's goods by 10 per cent. of their amount per annum. The conversations which led up to the signature of this agreement had included the other participants in the Oslo Convention, but the Scandinavian countries, all of whom had suffered exchange depreciation since Great Britain's relinquishment of the Gold Standard, preferred to postpone any action until economic conditions were more settled—perhaps until they had investigated the possibilities of a

[1] See the *Survey for 1931*, p. 154, footnote 2.

tariff understanding with Great Britain. In a covering statement, the Belgian delegation to the Lausanne Conference stated that the Convention was based upon principles formulated on various occasions by the League of Nations—presumably those embodied in the report of the economic experts' committee quoted above. In particular, while the advantages accorded by the Convention were reserved to the states taking part in it, any other state might adhere to it on a footing of equality with the three signatories. The announcement was accompanied by the publication of a vigorously worded appeal by the King of the Belgians for the reduction of barriers to trade throughout the world.

The text of the Convention of Ouchy-Lausanne was not published until the 3rd August. According to Article 1, the contracting parties pledged themselves not to increase customs duties existing between them above their actual level, nor to establish duties not already existing. They further agreed not to proceed to any protective increase of their customs duties, nor to any establishment of new protective duties applying to the merchandise of third states to whom they were bound by commercial conventions, unless those states, by a further raising of customs barriers or obstacles to trade, should cause serious prejudice to the signatories. Article II provided for the progressive reduction of customs duties, in the signatories' reciprocal relations, by 10 per cent. of their existing rate per annum, beginning with an immediate cut of 10 per cent. and ending four years later, by which time the duties would be one-half their former rates. Duties would in no case be reduced below a rate corresponding to 4 per cent. *ad valorem* for semi-manufactured products and 8 per cent. *ad valorem* for entirely manufactured products. While reserving the right to make certain exceptions, the contracting parties undertook in Article III not to apply between them any new prohibition or restriction to import or export, or any new measure of regulation which would have the effect of hampering their reciprocal exchanges. But should those exchanges be seriously disturbed by abnormal circumstances, each of the parties would have the right to limit its exports or imports, provided the quota fixed should be not less than 100 per cent. of the average quantities exported or imported during normal years. Further, the contracting parties agreed to abolish, as soon as circumstances should permit, in their reciprocal relations, all existing measures of prohibition, restriction, or regulation, with specified exceptions. By Article V they undertook to apply to their reciprocal exchanges the unconditional and unlimited régime of the most favoured nation. The Convention was concluded for a period of five years (Article VII); thereafter it would remain in force, for those who had not denounced it, from year to year. Article VIII laid down that any third state would have the right to adhere to the Convention, on a footing of equality with the signatory states, and moreover that so long as third states, without adhering to the Convention, nevertheless observed its provisions in fact, they would be admitted to the benefit of the conventional régime.

Not merely was the Convention favourably received by public opinion in the participating countries, but it was followed by an agitation for the establishment of a complete customs union among them. A referendum on the subject was held by the Netherlands Chamber of Commerce in Belgium, and, out of nearly 1,100 replies received from Chambers of Commerce and other representative institutions, industrialists, merchants and bankers in Belgium and Holland, no less than 87 per cent. were favourable to a tariff union, support being almost equally divided between the two countries.

The official attitude of the British Government towards the Convention was that their own policy in respect of their commercial treaty relations with foreign countries must await the outcome of the Ottawa Conference, but that meanwhile they must insist on the preservation of their most-favoured-nation rights unimpaired. This insistence, which would, if generally followed, have defeated the purpose of the Convention altogether, was not pressed in practice, in spite of its reaffirmation, as recorded above, at the Ottawa Conference. There was no hint that the British Government contemplated entering into any such multilateral, or even bilateral, agreement with foreign countries; and when it was announced, on the 17th October, that they had invited the Danish, Norwegian and Swedish Governments to open conversations in London on tariff matters it was semi-officially reported that no question of treaty revision would be raised, but that agreements would merely be sought within the framework of present trade treaties. The agreements concluded early in 1933, indeed, entailed no alteration of principle in Great Britain's trade relations with the Scandinavian countries, but provided only for adjustments, generally in the way of greater freedom of trade, on a limited number of items. It may be observed that the use of the quota system to regulate British imports of certain foodstuffs enabled the British Government to grant exclusive concessions to a few countries without violating most-favoured-nation treaties, at any rate according to a strict interpretation of their terms.

[11]

THE GREAT TRADE WAR.

The heavy contraction of international trade is one of the outstanding features of the present depression. The value of world trade in 1932 was less than 40 % of that in 1929. It is true that this decrease is due partly to the reduction in the level of prices of the goods exchanged, amounting to nearly one-half of the prices in 1929; but the volume of trade during the three-year period has also decreased by about 25 % — a disquieting circumstance, particularly in view of the fact that the rate of decline has been accelerating. According to the latest issue of the Review of World Trade just published by the League of Nations, the quantum of world trade was 7 % less in 1930 than in 1929, 9 % less in 1931 than in 1930 and 11—12 % less in the first half of 1932 than in that of 1931.

As everybody knows, this reduction — which far exceeds the decline in world production — is due largely to deliberate action on the part of the various countries of the world. In a period when economic and financial conditions are bad and industrial activity is declining, there is obviously no expedient that seems to be cheaper and more ready to hand than a restriction of imports in favour of domestic production. When systematized, however, such restrictions imply a general deterioration of export industries in all countries. It is true that food exports from the main producing countries are in many cases being maintained at the same quantities as a few years ago, or in certain cases have even increased; but the prices of food products on the world market have fallen to a level that has rendered it necessary for the exporting countries to reduce heavily their import of industrial products. Moreover, the exchange of such products between industrial countries has shrunk rapidly, as, naturally, the trade also in most industrial raw materials.

The table on the following pages, comprising countries representing together nine-tenths of the total world trade, aims at giving a bird's eye view of the measures taken during one of the darkest periods in the history of international trade, namely, that from the abandonment of the gold standard by the United Kingdom in September, 1931, to the end of 1932. Trade barriers have, it should be remembered, been tending to increase for several years, some of the most important restrictive measures being the increase in agricultural protection in certain European countries during 1928—29 and the increase in duties on industrial products in the United States by the introduction of the Hawley-Smoot tariff in the middle of 1930. The movement accelerated during the early part of the economic depression, and from the summer and autumn of 1931 it assumed unprecedented proportions.

During the period of little more than a year that has elapsed since then, over twenty States, headed by the United Kingdom, have abandoned the gold standard and allowed their currencies to depreciate, thereby accelerating the downward movement of prices in terms of gold on the world market. A similar number of countries — all debtor countries — have introduced a central control of their foreign currency transactions, in the majority of cases employing this control also for checking the imports of goods. Even where these countries still maintain the exchange rates of their currencies at par, the control has in fact implied a departure from the free working of the gold standard. A really effective gold standard — in the sense that no exchange restrictions are in force — accordingly exists to-day in only a few countries: the United States, France, Belgium, Holland and their oversea colonies and protectorates, Switzerland, Lithuania, and possibly also Poland and two or three Central American countries whose monetary systems are linked to the United States dollar.

Combined with the exchange control is the system of clearing agreements (like other bilateral measures not shown in the table), based upon the idea — in contrast to that of so-called »triangular trade» — that business transactions between the two countries concerned are allowed only in so far as their mutual payments balance. The idea has often proved, both in theory and in practice, to be divorced from the reality of trade relationship; nevertheless a network of clearing agreements has now been established over a large part of Europe, particularly in the Succession States, as also in the Balkan States; and a few such agreements have likewise been concluded between countries in Europe and countries in other parts of the world.

All countries have raised their Customs duties during the period under review, and, as the table shows, several of them have once or twice raised the duties on all the items in their tariff simultaneously. Factors of primary importance are: the introduction of Customs duties on the bulk of United Kingdom imports and the preferential treatment of goods imported by the United Kingdom from the British Dominions and Colonies, followed in the last quarter of 1932 by the carrying out of the Ottowa Agreements, the consolidation and extension of this preferential treatment in the United Kingdom and the establishment or increase of the margin of preference for British goods in the Dominions, largely by means of increases in the duties levied there on non-British goods.

The table shows next the enormous development of what is generally called quantitative restrictions on imports — quotas, prohibitions, permit systems etc. A year ago it was still possible to make a clear distinction between the different systems of this kind, but with the recent development of the »technique» many countries have invented very ingenious systems combining quotas with prohibitions and licensing systems, allowing a high degree of administrative arbitrariness and often disabling existing commercial treaties and agreements. In certain creditor countries, such as France and Switzerland, quantitative restrictions are to-day undoubtedly the most effective of trade barriers. The importance of more special forms of such restrictions, such as import monopolies and mixing and milling regulations, is also growing rapidly.

Available space has not permitted any indication of the kinds of goods affected by the increases in Customs duties and other import restrictions, but if the long list of dates does not give a clear idea of the real significance of the measures, it at least shows the concentration of activity in the field of trade barriers and hints at the uncertainty and risk to which importers and exporters are exposed in arranging for future business transactions, even where existing trade barriers are not prohibitive.

The zeal manifested within the field of export regulations has been less active; as the aim of recent regulations has largely been to check imports and favour exports, a number of export duties and prohibitions have been reduced or abolished (shown in heavy type in the table). On the other hand, a considerable number of new export premiums are recorded.

The last four columns show some of the most tangible results of the destruction of trade: on the one hand the moratoria and defaults in respect of the foreign commitments of a number of debtor countries whose financial position has been rendered increasingly difficult by the unwillingness of creditors to receive payment in the form of goods and by the falling-off in the investment of foreign capital, on the other hand the percentage reduction of trade values as compared with 1930 and 1931.

The distress of the agricultural countries during the early part of the depression caused larger quantities of their products — foodstuffs and raw materials — to be thrown on the market, resulting in a disastrous fall in the prices of these products and entailing a reduction in the prices of industrial commodities. Most industrial countries have tried to escape the effects of the downward price movement by means of import barriers, though this policy has to a certain extent involved the sacrifice of their export industries. The agricultural countries have then had to reduce still further the prices of their staple articles; but the demand for these has not increased proportionately, as the consumers in the importing countries have had to pay the price inflated by trade barriers.

A lowering of trade barriers all over the world would probably result in a general increase in prices on the world market, beginning with those of primary products, and thus lead to the improvement in business that all are so eagerly awaiting. The importance for a suffering world of concerted action against trade barriers is thus very great; but unfortunately even the gods may fight in vain against such evil forces as narrow-minded rivalry, jealousy and lack of confidence. One is nowadays constantly being reminded of the old maxim: »Mir nichts und dir nichts, so haben wir alle beide nichts».

SUMMARY OF TRADE EVENTS SINCE SEPTEMBER 1931.

The following list excludes the Soviet Union (where foreign trade is strictly controlled by the Government) and a number of smaller countries, colonies, protectorates, etc.

It excludes most measures of a purely bilateral nature (e. g., clearing agreements, quotas and customs duties affecting the trade with one country only) as well as purely temporary changes in duties, changes in established quotas and in mixing regulations, prohibitions introduced for prophylactic and similar reasons, and a number of measures which only affect trade in articles of small importance.

Dates in lean type indicate new measures introduced, or a tightening up of existing regulations; (increases in customs duties, etc.) those in heavy type indicate the abolition or mitigation of existing regulations (reductions of customs duties, etc.).

Import monopolies and milling regulations introduced between the autumn of 1929 and September 1st, 1931, are indicated in square brackets [ ] in the columns concerned; otherwise

Country	Gold standard abandoned	Exchange control introduced	Customs duties		Import quotas, prohibitions, licensing systems and similar quantitative restrictions on certain articles or groups of articles
			general increases	increases on individual items or groups	
Countries that have abandoned the gold standard since September 21st, 1931.					
United Kingdom	'31: 21/9	—	'32: 1/3	'31: 25/11, 4/12, 19/12. '32: 5/1, 1/3, 1/4, 20/4, 26/4, 11/5, 13/6, 14/6, 8/7, 13/7, 15/7, 28/7, 1/9, 6/9, 21/10, 9/11, 17/11¹, 29/12	'32: 22/11 (meat & pork)
Palestine	'31: 21/9	—	—	'32: April, 22/7	—
Colombia	'31: 21/9	'31: 21/9	—	'31: 29/9, 10/12. '32: 14/6, 30/6	'31: 16/10, 7/12, 20/12. '32: 1/1
India	'31: 21/9	—	'31: 30/9	'31: 30/9, 12/12. '32: 12/3, 2/4, 30/8, 30/8, Sept., 21/11. 33: 1/1⁵	—
Straits Settlements	'31: 21/9	—	—	'32: 21/3, 15/4, 13/5, 14/10, 29/10	—
Bolivia	'31: 25/9	'31: 3/10	—	'31: 28/11. '32: 23/3	—
Egypt	'31: 26/9	—	'32: 12/5, 1/6⁷	'32: 31/3, 11/5, 12/5, 2/6, 11/6, 7/7, 19/7, 22/7, 13/9, 12/12	—
Irish Free State	'31: 26/9	—	—	'31: 31/12. '32: 1/1, 19/3, 23/3, 13/4, 22/4, 25/4, 29/4, 3/5, 6/5, 11/5, 19/5, 2/6, 7/6, 7/7, 25/7, 26/7, 1/8, 30/8, 31/8, 27/9, 28/9, 20/10, 2/11, 11/11	'32: 1/9, 2/11
Norway	'31: 27/9	'31: 17/10 (unofficial)	'32: 13/1	'32: 29/6, 2/7, 24/9	'32: 18/3 (sawn wood, provisional since 17/7 1931), 29/4, 28/10
Sweden	'31: 27/9	—	—	'32: 31/1, 1/4, 1/5, 15/5, 1/7, 1/7	—
Denmark	'31: 28/9	'31: 18/11⁸	—	'31: 19/10, 27/11. '32: 22/6, 15/10	'31: 27/11 (wines, etc.). '32: 1/2, 1/9
Salvador	'31: 8/10	—	—⁹	'31: 15/11. '32: 7/1, 19/1, 25/5, 2 6, 9/6, 18/7, 27/7, 7/9, 7/9	'32: 1/9
Finland	'31: 12/10	—	—	'31: 14/11. '32: 1/1, 12/2, 1/4, 21/4, 21/4, 1/10, 25/10, 14/11, 14/11	—

N. B. For foot-notes, see pp. 12—13.

(Continued overleaf)

SUMMARY OF TRADE EVENTS SINCE SEPTEMBER 1931.
(Continued)

measures taken before the latter date are not indicated, except in the columns »Gold standard abandoned», »Exchange control introduced» and »Moratoria».

Attention should be paid to the fact that the mitigation of certain trade restrictions is often offset by a tightening up of others. Thus, for example, when, as in the case of a few countries certain quota regulations and prohibitions were abolished in the summer and autumn of 1932, the customs duties on the goods affected were increased.

Payments in the service of private foreign debts have been restricted not only by the moratoria indicated below but in certain countries also by official exchange control and numerous private defaults.

The percentage reduction in the foreign trade as shown in the last two columns refers to the value of total trade (imports plus exports) in terms of gold.

Import monopolies	Milling, mixing, etc. regulations	Export regulations		Moratoria on foreign debt service		Percentage reduction in foreign trade during first half of 1932 as compared with first half of:		Country
		premiums	duties or prohibitions	Public debt	Private debts	1930	1931	
Countries that have abandoned the gold standard since September 21st, 1931.									
—	—	—	—	—	—	51.9	34.0	United Kingdom
—	—	—	—	—	—	14.3	+11.2²	Palestine
—	—	'32: 7/3 (coffee)	'31: 18/12 (bananas)	'32: 12/2³	—	—⁴	—⁴	Colombia
—	—	—	—	—	—	60.7	38.0	India
—	—	—	—	—	—	65.8	44.5	Straits Settlements
—	—	—	'32: 3/2, 25/7 (tin)	'31: Jan.⁶	—	—⁴	—⁴	Bolivia
—	—	—	'32: Oct. (eggs)	—	—	53.4	23.8	Egypt
—	—	'32:21/4, 17/9, 26/9, 5/10, 12/10, 1/12	—	—	—	43.2	32.3	Irish Free State
['29: 1/7 (grain)]	'31: 1/11 (margarine)	—	—	—	—	51.2	33.9	Norway
['31: 1/6 (wheat & rye)] '32: 1/3 (sugar)	['30: 13/6 (wheat & rye flour)]	—	—	—	—	55.1	40.8	Sweden
—	—	—	—	—	—	49.8	39.4	Denmark
—	—	—	'32; 9/6 (coffee)	'32: 12/3	'32: 12/3	—⁴	—⁴	Salvador
'32: 5/4 (alcoh. beverages)	'31: 1/10 (rye flour, oats)	—	'32: 1/1 (pulpwood, etc.)	—	—	55.1	36.9	Finland

Disintegration of the World Economy Between the World Wars II

Country	Gold standard abandoned	Exchange control introduced	Customs duties		Import quotas, prohibitions, licensing systems and similar quantitative restrictions on certain articles or groups of articles
			general increases	increases on individual items or groups	
Canada	'31: 19/10	—	—	'31: Nov., 12/12. '32: 25/4, 18/7, 3/10, 13/10 [10]	—
Japan	'31: 13/12	'32: 1/7	'32: 16/6	'32: 10/6	'31: 8/12
Portugal	'31: 31/12	1924	'32: 27/2	—	'31: 5/11. '32: 3/3, 4/3
New Zealand	'32: 1/1 [11]	—	—	'31: 3/11, 15/12. '32: 1/1, Feb., 1/10, 14/10 [12]	—
Ecuador	'32: 9/2	'32: 30/4	—	'31: 16/11, 11/12	'31: 6/11
Chile	'32: 20/4	'31: 30/7	—	'31: 28/12. '32: 26/2, 18/4, 5/3, 30/5, 16/6, Aug., 21/9, 21/9, 1/10	'32: 5/7, 10/10 [13]
Greece	'32: 26/4	'31: 28/9	'32: 5/12	'31: 19/12. '32: 2/2, 22/5, 25/5	'32: 1/5, 15/5
Siam	'32: 11/5	—	'32: 22/2	—	—
Peru	'32: 18/5	—	—	'32: 3/8, 16/11	—
Union of S. Africa	'32: 27/12	'31: Nov. (unofficial)	'31: 30/10 '32: 23/3	'32: 24/3, 12/5, 26/8, 13/10 [16]	'32: 20/4, 2/6

Other Countries (alphabetical order).

Argentina	'29: 16/12	'31: 10/10	'31: 8/10	'31: 21/9, [17] 15/10, 15/11. '32: 25/1, 10/2	—
Australia	'29: 17/12	—	'32: 25/2, 14/10 [18]	'32: 14/1, 25/2, 18/3, 4/5, 4/5, 21/5, 14/6, 31/8, 2/9	'32: 25/2, 19/5, 2/6, 2/9 [10]
Austria	— [20]	'31: 9/10	—	'31: 26/10. '32: 15/1, 22/1, 12/2, 12/2, 25/2, 17/3, July, 1/8, 3 8, 25/8, 30/8, 6/12	'32: 29/4, 2/5, 29/6, 15/7, 3/8, 25/8, 30/8
Belgium	—	—	'32: 27/3	'31: 27/11. '32: 3/2, 5/3, 1/4, 18/5, 18/5, 30/5, 1/8, 9/9	'31: 1/10. '32: 26/3, 10/4, 26/4, 12/5, 1/6, 9/6, 14/6, 25/6, 30/6, 21/7, 23/7, 20/8, 26/8, 28/8, Sept., 28/9, 29/9,
Brazil	— [22]	'31: 18/5	'31: 4/12	'32: 24/2, 26/4, 10/5, 1/7, 1/7, 19/7	'31: 5/10
Bulgaria	—	'31: 15/10 [25]	—	'31: 25/11. '32: 30/3, 3/5, July, 2/8	—
China	— [22]	—	'31: 1/12	'32: 1/4, 4/8	—
Czechoslovakia	—	'31: 3/10	—	'31: 10/12. '32: 10/1, 1/3, May, 12/7, 29/8, 1/9, 10/10, 10/11	'31: 13/11, 26/11, 29/11, 4/12, 6/12, 8/12, 23/12. '32: 17/1, 18/1, 25/1, 15/2, 1/3, 7/3, 2/4, 4/4, 6/5, 15/5, 1/0, 5/6, 14/6, 25/6, 2/7, 12/7, 1/8, 29/8
Dutch East Indies	—	—	'32: 1/1, 15/6	'32: 16/4	—

N. B. For foot-notes, see pp. 12—13.

(Continued overleaf)

Import monopolies	Milling, mixing, etc. regulations	Export regulations		Moratoria on foreign debt service		Percentage reduction in foreign trade during first half of 1932 as compared with first half of:		Country
		premiums	duties or prohibitions	Public debt	Private debts	1930	1931	
—	—	—	—	—	—	58.4	36.6	Canada
—	—	—	—	—	—	46.8	29.6	Japan
—	'32: 3/3 (flour)	—	—	—	—	46.7	23.1	Portugal
—	—	—	—	—	—	55.8	32.0	New Zealand
—	—	—	—	—	—	—[4]	—[4]	Ecuador
'32: 10/9 (petroleum products).	—	'32: 20/4 (sulphur)	'32: 19/8, 14/9	'31: 1/7	'32:20/6[14]	78.7	70.2	Chile
—	—	—	'31: 1/9 (currants)	'32: 1/4[16]	—	42.4	30.5	Greece
—	—	—	—	—	—	50.6	21.1	Siam
—	—	—	—	'31: 29/5	—	63.7	39.1	Peru
—	—	'31: Oct., 1/12 '32: 22/1, 23/3	—	—	—	32.2	22.0	Union of S. Africa
—	—	—	—	—	—	53.8	34.1	Argentina
—	—	—	—	—	—	54.4	24.3	Australia
—	'32: 8/6 (coal)	—	—	'32: 23/6	'32: 23/6[21]	50.9	35.9	Austria
—	'31: 22/9 (wheat flour)	—	—	—	—	46.5	33.6	Belgium
—	—	—	'31: 11/12, '32: 1/1 (bananas)	'31:Sept.[23]	—[24]	55.3	27.2	Brazil
'31: Oct. (wheat, rye) '32: 20/7 (wheat)	'32: 30/3 (hemp goods)	'32: 28/2 (maize)	—	'32: 20/4[26]	—	34.2	35.9	Bulgaria
—	—	—	'32: 27/5, (silk), 1/9 (silk goods)	—	—	—[4]	—[4]	China
'32: 29/7 (cereals)	['30: 7/11 (wheat & rye flour Jan. (rye flour) 1/9 (motor fuel)	—	—	—	—	64.2	36.4	Czechoslovakia
—	—	—	—	—	—	—[4]	—[4]	Dutch East Indies

Country	Gold standard abandoned	Exchange control introduced	Customs duties		Import quotas, prohibitions, licensing systems and similar quantitative restrictions on certain articles or groups of articles
			general increases	increases on individual items or groups	
Estonia	—	'31: 18/11	—	'31: 21/11, 12/12. '32: 3/2, 26/2, 1/4, 2/6, 14/7, 19/8, 3/10	'31: 5/11, 10/11, 11/11, 16/12. '32: 20 1, 16/2, 11/3, 4/4, 8/4, 12/4, 13/4, 2/6, 20/6, 17/8, 31/8, Oct.
France	—	—	—	'31: 12/11, 1/12. '32: 7/1, 9/1, 15,2, 2/3, 4/3, 21/3, 22/3, April, 8/4, 9/4, 20/4, 3/6, 24,6, 7/7, 13/7, 20/7, 19/8, 17/9, 27/9, 1/10, 16/11, 19/11, 22/11	'31: 30/9, 1/10, 6/10, 31/10, 31/12. '32: 7/1, 13 1, 14/1, 20/1, 26/1, 3/2, 4/2, 7/2, 10/2, 15/2, 18/2, 29/2, 2/3, 9/3, 17/3, 18/3, 19/3, 26/3, 28/3, 1/4, 5 4, 14/4, 20/4, 23/4, 1/5, 17/5, 19/5, 20/5, 25/5, 30/5, 31/5, 1/6, 4/6, 18/6, 29/6, 1/7, 29/7, 1/8, 12/9, 16/9, 23/9, 29/9, 1/10, 9/10, 26/10
Germany	—	'31: 13/7	—	'32: 18/1, 5/2, 15/2, 30/4, 14/6, 30/6, 5/7, 1/8, 6/9, 19/9, 14/11	'32: 16/1, 1/2, 1/3, 27 14/11
Guatemala	—	—	—	'32: 17/8, 19/5, 23/8	—
Holland	—	—	'32: 1/1 30	'32: 1/1, 1/4, 1/6, 29/9	'32:16/1, 24/1, 6/2, 16/2, 15/3, 18/3, 24/3, 26/3, 19/4, July, 1/8, 25/8, 1/10, 1/11 (el. bulbs)
Honduras	—22	—	—	'32: 3/2, 4/2, 26/2 3/3, 26/3, 4/4, 14 4	—
Hungary	—	'31: 17/7	—	'32: 18/1, 7/9, 7/9, 15/11	'31: 1/10, 2/10, '32: 23/1, 5/3, 17/4, 25/4, 19/5, 13/6, 21/7, 6/11
Italy	—	—32	'31: 25/9	'32: 12/2, 29/2, 4/3, 1/4, 2/5, 14/5, 26/5, 26,5, 16/6, 2/7, 8/8, 19/8, 28/8, 2/9, 12/9, 29/10, 2/11	'31: 16/12. '32: 18/2, 22/2, 1/4, 15/7, 15/8
Latvia	—	'31: 8/10	'32: 12—14/7, Sept.	'32: 14/7 33	'31: Oct. '32: 11/2, 18/2 (general), 4/3, April, 14/7, Sept.
Lithuania	—	—	'31: 15/10	'31: 23/12. '32: 1/2, April, 12/6, 12/6, 28/6, 19,8, Sept.	—
Mexico	'31: 25/7	—	—	'32: 6/2, 16/2, 9/3, 28/3, 7/4, 20/4, 9/5, 10/6, 26/7, 5/8, 12/8, 16/8, 24/8, 8/9, 22/9, 18/10, 22/10, 24/10	'32: 1/1, 11/2, 7/3, 26/3, 30/7, Aug.
Nicaragua	—	'31:13/11 36	'32: 5/10	—	—
Panama	—	—	—	'31: 21/11. '32: 1/4, 1/7, 1/11	—
Persia	—22	'32: 27/5	'32: Febr.	—	'32: 21/2, 1/6, 1/9
Poland	—	—	—	'31: 24/9, 20/11, 19/12, 22/12. '32: 1/1, 1/1, 14/1, 19/2, 15/3, 31/3, 26/3, 14/9, 15/9, 8/11, 22/11	'32: 1/1, 27 11/2, 7/3, 26/3, 30/7, Aug.

N. B. For foot-notes, see pp. 12—13.

Import monopolies	Milling, mixing, etc. regulations	Export regulations		Moratoria on foreign debt service		Percentage reduction in foreign trade during first half of 1932 as compared with first half of:		Country
		premiums	duties or prohibitions	Public debt	Private debts	1930	1931	
—	—	—	—	—	—	60.0	37.5	Estonia
—	['29: 1/12 (wheat flour)]	—	—	—	—	48.7	35.3	France
—	['29: 4/7 (wheat flour)]	'31: 25/11 [28]	'32: 27/3, 1/5, 25/6	—	'31: 17/9 [29]	54.3	36.3	Germany
—	—	—	'32: 8/6 (chicle)	—	—	—[4]	—[4]	Guatemala
—	['31: 1/7 (wheat flour)] '32: May (margarine)	—	—	—	—	49.3	34.2	Holland
—	—	—	—	—	—	—[4]	—[4]	Honduras
—	'31: 20/10 (coal)	—	—	'31: 23/12	'31: 23/12 [31]	62.9	44.0	Hungary
—	['31: 10/6 (wheat flour)] '32: 24/1 (motor fuel)	'31: 15/10	—	—	—	50.2	32.0	Italy
'32:5/1(sugar) April (pharm. prep.) 15/6 (cereals)	'31: 7/12 (motor fuel). '32: 15/10 (techn. fats)	—	'31: 5/12 (timber). '32: 16/4, 7/10(bacon, hogs), 22/11, 25/11	'32: April	—	66.0	50.0	Latvia
—	—	'32: 1/8	—	—	—	37.9	30.8	Lithuania
—	—	—	'32: 28/5	—[34]	—	52.3	25.2	Mexico
—	—	—	—	'32: 1/1 [36]	—	—[4]	—[4]	Nicaragua
—	—	—	—	—	—	—[4]	—[4]	Panama
'31: Sept. (general)	—	—	'32: 23/7	—	—	—[4]	—[4]	Persia
—	—	'31: 1/10, (bacon, meat), 1/11 (coal). '32: 1/1, 30/9	'31: 1/12 '32: 15/3, 28/5, 31/8, 1/10	—	—	59.3	44.7	Poland

Country	Gold standard abandoned	Exchange control introduced	Customs duties		Import quotas, prohibitions, licensing systems and similar quantitative restrictions on certain articles or groups of articles
			general increases	increases on individual items or groups	
Rumania	—	'32: 17/5	—	'31: 24/10. '32: 1/2, 21/2, 30/5, 10/8, 12/9	'31: Nov. '32: 1/3, 6/12 (130 items)
Spain	—[22]	'31: 31/5 [35]	—	'32: 19/3, 1/4, 1/4, 26/5, 21/9	'31: 3/10, 23/12. '32: 26/5, June —Aug., 4/12 (newsprint)
Switzerland	—	—	—	'31: 15/12, 22/12. '32: 14/1, 5/2, 1/3, 1/3, 23/3, 27/3, 25/4, 26/4, 25/5, 1/6, 6/6, 29/6, 5/7, 1/8, 6/9, 21/9, 4/10, 18/10, 17/11, 22/11	'32: 18/1, 25/1, 5/2, 9/2, 15/2, 1/3, 12/3, 23/3, 1/4, 21/4, 30/4, 30/4, 6/5, 12/5, 24/5, 3/6, 10/6, 4/7, 10/7, 15/7, 10/8, 24/8, 6/9, 21/9, 12/10, 22/11
Turkey	—[22]	'30: 26/2 [88]	—	—	'31: 16/11. '32: 1/1, 20/2, May, 1/6, 1/9, Sept.
Uruguay	—[22]	'31: 14/10 [86]	—	'31: 10/9, 27/9, 15/11. '32: 24/4, 29/6, 30/6, 4/8	
U. S. A.	—	—	—	'32: 21/6, 10/9, 17/9	—
Venezuela	—[42]	—	'32: 2/3	'32: 4/2, 2/3, 27/4, 29/6, 9/8	
Yugoslavia	—[43]	'31: 7/10 [35]	—	'31: Dec. '32: 25/1, 11/2, 17/2, 29/6, 16/8, 25/8, 31/10	'31: 9/11

1 United Kingdom: Increase in the duties levied on certain goods from non-British countries (according to the Ottawa Agreements).

2 Palestine: *Increase* 11.2 %.

3 Colombia: Amortization of the Government debt suspended on 12/2 1932 (total service of municipal and departmental foreign debt was suspended already on 8/12 1931).

4 Colombia, Bolivia, Salvador, Ecuador, China, Dutch East Indies, Guatemala, Honduras, Nicaragua, Panama, Persia, Venezuela: Half-yearly figures showing the foreign trade of these countries are not available.

5 India: Customs duties increased for certain non-British goods, but reduced for certain British goods 1/1 1933.

6 Bolivia: Government loans in default since January 1931.

7 Egypt: Supplementary duty of 1 % ad. val. introduced 12/5 1932; increases in the duties on most of the items in the tariff 1/6 1932.

8 Denmark: Exchange control for the restriction of foreign trade mitigated 27/8 1932. — New exchange regulations in force 1/1 1933.

9 Salvador: Fee for consular visas raised to 6 % of the value of imported goods, 16/3 1932.

10 Canada: Increase in the ›intermediate‹ tariff for a considerable number of items (simultaneously reduction or removal of the existing British preferential duties for certain other items), 13/10 1932.

11 New Zealand: The currency depreciation began already in 1930.

12 New Zealand: Customs surtaxes of 22 1/2 % or 5 % abolished for dutiable British goods, 14/10 1932.

13 Chile: quota system introduced for all goods, 10/10 1932.

14 Chile: Moratorium for purely commercial foreign obligations, which were to be paid in quotas of 10 % during each period of three months, 20/5 1932.

15 Greece: Suspension of amortization, and reduction of the transferred portion of interest payment on the public foreign debt to 30 % as from 1/4 1932.

16 Union of South Africa: Increases in the tariff applied to non-British goods, 13/10 1932.

17 Argentina: The increase in customs duties that came into force on 21/9 1931 affected about 400 articles.

18 Australia: The tariff increase on 14/10 1932 affected the ›general‹ rates for about 400 products or classes of goods (involving increased margin of preference for British products).

19 Australia: All import prohibitions were abolished 2/9 1932.

20 Austria: Since the early part of 1932, most of the foreign transactions of Austria have been based on the depreciated rate of the schilling in the free market.

21 Austria: Standstill agreement with foreign creditors for short-term banking debts since 16/6 1931.

22 Brazil, China, Honduras, Persia, Spain, Turkey, Uruguay have since the war not adhered to the gold standard.

Disintegration of the World Economy Between the World Wars II

| Import monopolies | Milling, mixing, etc. regulations | Export regulations | | Moratoria on foreign debt service | | Percentage reduction in foreign trade during first half of 1932 as compared with first half of: | | Country |
		premiums	duties or prohibitions	Public debt	Private debts	1930	1931	
—	—	—	'31: 18/3 (pyrites). '32: 14/3 (soda), 12/5, 6/6. '32: 24/4 (copper ore)	—	—	49.7	33.3	Rumania
—	—	—		—	—	62.6	27.4	Spain
—	'32: April (shoes)	—	'32: 22/3, 22/11	—	—	39.0	26.9	Switzerland
—	—	—	—	—[39]	—	41.2	33.3	Turkey
'31: 5/10 (fuel, alcohol, cement)	—	—	'31: 22/10	'32: 20/1[40]	'31: 7/9[41]	73.7	55.2	Uruguay
—	—	—	—	—	—	59.4	34.5	U.S.A.
—	—	—	—	—	—	—[4]	—[4]	Venezuela
['31: 27/6 (wheat, rye, wheat flour)] '32: 20/7 (journals etc.)	'32: 10/10 (motor fuel)	—	'32: 1/4	'32: 1/11[44]	—	59.8	43.7	Yugoslavia

[23] Brazil: Amortization of the public debt suspended in September 1931, interest payments in October 1931. For a period of three years payments will be made in interest-bearing scrip.

[24] Brazil: 60 days moratorium for foreign commercial debts from the beginning of Nov. 1931. In the second half of 1932 regulations have been made for the payment of foreign currency bills in monthly instalments.

[25] Bulgaria: Exchange control tightened in December 1931 and May 1932.

[26] Bulgaria: Suspension of the transfer of 50 % of the payments in the service of foreign public debts.

[27] Germany: quota for British coal 1/3 1932.

[28] Germany: The system of import certificates (Einfuhrscheine) was reintroduced for malt and certain milling products of barley and oats on 25/11 1931.

[29] Germany: Standstill agreement with foreign banks for short-term debts due to them in force from 17/9 1931, prolonged in February 1932 (to the end of February 1933).

[30] Holland: The increase in the customs duties that came into force on 1/1 1932 affected all dutiable goods but was relatively small (from 8 to 10% and from 5 to 6 % ad valorem.)

[31] Hungary: Transfer moratorium declared on 23/12 1931. On 8/11 1932 a Standstill agreement for short-term debts was concluded with American and British creditors.

[32] Italy: An unofficial exchange control is exercised by the Italian Federation of Credit and Insurance.

[33] Latvia: The tariff increase on 14/7 1932 affected about 300 tariff items.

[34] Mexico: The service of the Government foreign debt suspended for several years past.

[35] Nicaragua, Spain, Uruguay, Yugoslavia: The exchange control has not been exercised for the restriction of imports.

[36] Nicaragua: Amortization of the Government foreign debt suspended on 1/1 1932.

[37] Poland: The import restrictions of 1/1 1932 (prohibitions) affected about 200 tariff items.

[38] Turkey: Exchange control tightened in May and August 1932.

[39] Turkey: The service of the Government foreign debt was suspended already on 25/11 1930.

[40] Uruguay: Amortization of the Government foreign debt suspended 20/1 1932.

[41] Uruguay: Moratorium on commercial debts 7/9 1931, renewed and extended by law of 12/7 1932.

[42] Venezuela: The gold standard was abandoned de facto in 1930, when the currency began to depreciate.

[43] Yugoslavia: Currency depreciation since June 1932 without formal abandonment of the gold standard.

[44] Yugoslavia: Suspension of the transfer of the service of Government foreign debts on 1/11 1932.

[12]
Breaking with orthodoxy: the politics of economic policy responses to the Depression of the 1930s Peter Alexis Gourevitch

When the Great Depression rippled around the world in 1929, most countries responded with the same economic policy, deflation. This was the "orthodox" response prescribed by orthodox analyses, but it did not work. After some two to four years of failure, most countries broke with orthodoxy to try "neo-orthodoxy"—devaluation of the currency, tariffs, and some corporatistic regulation of domestic markets. Some countries broke more drastically, either immediately or after a few years of neo-orthodoxy, to try more unusual departures from standard views—demand stimulus through deficit spending, known after the war as Keynesianism, or more drastic forms of state-dominant corporatistic regulation of the domestic economy.

How can this policy sequence be understood; in particular, how can we explain the divergence of countries after the initial similarity in their policy moves? Why did some countries remain with "conventional" breaks from orthodoxy while others experimented more radically? The answers to these questions may shed light on the politics of economic policy. They may also have implications for other outcomes, for the timing of great shifts in policy and great shifts in politics is too close for coincidence. To understand the connections between breaking with economic orthodoxy and the destruction of constitutional government by fascism (Germany), the critical realignment elections (Sweden and the United States), the Popular Front and its demise, the disruptions of the Labour Party and the ascendancy of the Conservatives might be to understand the connection between *economic experimentation* and *political experimentation*.

The answers given to these questions address current controversies over

---

So many have helped, it is impossible to cite everyone. I wish to thank particularly the reviewers of this journal, many colleagues at the University of California at San Diego, Cornell University, Harvard University's Center for European Studies, and several Swedish universities; James Kurth and the participants at a special meeting held at Swarthmore College, Albert Hirschman, and Roger Haydon; the National Endowment for the Humanities, and the UCSD Committee on Research.

the 1970s and 1980s. Both periods raise conceptual questions concerning the relationship among international economic crisis, the evolution of the international division of labor in different sectors or branches ("the product cycle"), the development of political coalitions among different producer groups within particular countries, the content of government policy, and the character of political forms.

The policy debate around the current crisis challenges a set of political and policy arrangements whose historical origins lie in the earlier crisis—which was, in turn, a challenge to arrangements that had been derived from the economic dislocations of the last quarter of the 19th century. In very general terms, the 1930s disrupted a particular set of producer group relationships. The 19th century's enmity between agriculture and labor over tariffs and other quarrels turned into farmer-labor alliances, albeit of kinds that differed from place to place. The relationship of labor and agriculture to different types of business (some sharply antagonistic, others more cooperative) underwent acute shifts as well.[1]

In several countries where constitutional government survived, particularly Sweden and the United States, the outlines of a pattern were emerging by the late 1930s, one that would spread over most of Western Europe in the postwar period. Involving mutual accommodation among elements of labor, business, and agriculture, this pattern is commonly labeled "social-democratic," after the European parties that played a key role in it, or "Scandinavian," after the region that embodies it most clearly. It is built around a set of economic policies that combine Keynesian demand management, an open international economy, trade union autonomy in labor markets, private control of capital in both investment and management, and subsidies for agriculture.[2] It is this social-democratic compromise which is now under sharp challenge: the victories of Reagan and Thatcher represent the unraveling of political relationships built around economic policies dating back to the 1930s, and the many shifts in political majority of recent European elections (Mitterrand, Papandreou, Kohl, Gonzalez, Palme) show the political ramifications of current economic disruptions. Unraveling the older pattern is thus instructive both for testing types of explanation for a particular period and for specifying which relationships are now under stress.

1. For an overview of the policy debate in the 1930s, see H. W. Arndt, *The Economic Lessons of the Nineteen-Thirties* (Oxford: Oxford University Press, 1944); David S. Landes, *The Unbound Prometheus: Technological Change and Industrial Development in Western Europe from 1750 to the Present* (Cambridge: Cambridge University Press, 1969); W. Arthur Lewis, *Economic Survey, 1919–1939* (London: Allen & Unwin, 1960).

2. On the postwar compromise, the literature is large; see Andrew Shonfield, *Modern Capitalism* (London: Oxford University Press, 1969). For a view from the standpoint of the role of the labor movements, see George Ross, Peter Lange, et al., *Unions, Change and Crisis: French and Italian Union Strategy and the Political Economy* (Winchester, Mass.: Allen & Unwin, 1983). For a view exploring the political-economic origins of postwar consociationalism and democratic corporatism, see Peter Katzenstein, *Corporatism and Change* (Ithaca: Cornell University Press, forthcoming).

Social science is, of course, full of possible explanations for the economic policy outcomes of the 1930s. My focus will be on the "political sociology of political economy"—on the pattern of alliances among social actors whose interactions shape patterns of policy. Certain features of some such alliances are well-known. For example, the iron and rye coalition of late 19th century Germany linked industrialists producing "heavy" goods (iron and steel) with grain growers. Together they supported high tariffs in opposition to finished consumer goods manufacturers using advanced technology, meat and dairy farmers, and consumer-oriented labor, all of whom opposed tariffs.[3] At about the same period, after many years of free trade, Britain experienced a resurgence of sympathy for protectionism, particularly among the metal producers of Birmingham and grain farmers. They opposed the continued economic liberalism of the great finance-shipping-insurance grouping symbolized by the City and allied with labor concerned with cheap food.[4] American history notes "Gold Democrats," free–trade-oriented merchants and bankers pushed toward the Democratic Party in opposition to their protectionist brethren in the Republican Party. In the post 1945 era, the differences in sectoral preference toward commercial policy have become increasingly obvious: free-trade automobile makers turned protectionist when that industry went into crisis, joining the makers of televisions, shoes, steel, and other products. In America, the internationalism of free trade has historically had some association with Eastern financial circles, while isolationism and economic nationalism have been associated with the manufacturing mid-West.[5] These "sectoral" proclivities are known, and some political scientists have found them worthy of interpretation.[6]

In this essay I assume that something can be learned about the 1930s by exploring further the relationship implied by these well-known cases. But I also assume that in analyzing the political and policy relationships among capital, labor, and agriculture, these terms must be disaggregated into sectors, or branches, that have identifiable characteristics. What the industries produce and how, who buys their products, their capital requirements, their labor

---

3. The classic study of German tariff conflicts is Alexander Gerschenkron, *Bread and Democracy in Germany* (1943; rpt., New York: Howard Fertig, 1966). See also Ivo Lambi, *Tariffs and Protection in Germany* (Weisbaden: Steiner, 1963).

4. On British tariff controversies see Benjamin Brown, *The Tariff Reform Movement in Britain, 1884–1895* (New York: Columbia University Press, 1943); D. H. Aldcroft and H. W. Richardson, *The British Economy, 1870–1939* (London: Macmillan, 1969).

5. U.S. tariff policy has had numerous treatments from different sorts of specialists. For emphasis on politics, see E. E. Schattschneider, *Politics, Pressure and the Tariff* (Hamden, Conn.: Archon, 1963); W. A. Williams, *Roots of the Modern American Empire* (New York: Random House, 1969) as well as his other books. On economics, see Frank Taussig, *A Tariff History of the United States* (New York: A. M. Kelley, 1967). For a work that argues against the importance of producer-group interests, see Raymond Bauer, Ithiel de Sola Pool, and L. A. Dexter, *American Business and Public Policy* (Chicago: Aldine-Atherton, 1967).

6. See particularly James Kurth, "The Political Consequences of the Product Cycle: Industrial History and Political Outcomes," *International Organization* 33 (Winter 1979): 1–34.

component, organizational characteristics, international competitiveness, and so on—these elements of a sector shape its *situation*. Situation influences a sector's policy preferences, which in turn affect its political behavior, which ends by affecting politics and policy outcomes.

This is not a new theory. It is a familiar mixture of the interest-group approach, social forces analysis, structural Marxism, rational choice, and old-fashioned liberalism derived from Bentham, Smith, and Mill. The distinctive features of its use here are fourfold. First, I stress sectors, rather than firms or specific organizations. Second, I emphasize the international situation in shaping group behavior; sector policy goals are influenced by location in an international division of labor. Third, I am concerned with the substantive content of sectoral "alliances," which is to say the terms of trade of alliances with other actors. Finally, I focus attention on the importance of politics not as formal institutions but as the forging of coalitions out of social components.

The interest-group and social forces approaches have had many valid criticisms leveled against them. The journey from the first step (group situation) to the last (policy or other outcomes) can be quite long, and there are certainly intervening variables (ideology, institutions, leadership, and security issues, to name but a few) that affect the interplay of situation, preference, and political outcomes.

Knowing "interests," whether of an individual, a group, or a class, poses its own problems. To say that a group takes a particular position because "it is objectively in its interest to do so" is a form of proposition requiring its own sort of justification. In this article, however, I mean to explore a sociological proposition, not a philosophical one. From knowing a group's situation, we may generate an expectation about various behaviors (policy preferences and political alignments) and thereby gain leverage to explain policy outcomes. I assume that groups frequently pursue policies that are not optimal, that reality is sufficiently ambiguous as to provide a multitude of calculi from which a variety of behaviors could be drawn that would be "in a group's interests." Yet this is less true in a sociological sense: group preferences and behaviors follow patterns that can to some degree be related to group positions, even if they lead to miscalculation in relation to group "interest."[7]

Despite its problems, the interest approach deserves pursuit. It seems odd to imagine one could examine the politics of economic policy without asking *qui bono* and without considering that benefit might shape behavior. Politics and interest interact strongly. Politicians seeking to get and keep power have to fashion coalitions, not just electoral majorities but governing coalitions, combinations of social forces that have producer-group power and whose

---

7. For a very interesting treatment of the way power, preferences and interests can be interpreted, see John Gaventa, *Power and Powerlessness in Appalachia* (Oxford: Clarendon Press, 1980).

compliance or even enthusiasm is essential to attaining goals. At a minimum, interest groups and social forces are the raw materials, the essential components from which such coalitions are constructed. In this context, crises are interesting—a curse for the Chinese, a subject for the social scientist, an opportunity or a constraint for politicians. Crises pry open the political scene, throwing traditional relationships into flux. Groups, institutions, and individuals are torn loose from their moorings, their assumptions, their loyalties, their "cognitive road maps." Circumstances become less certain, and solutions less obvious. Crises thus render politics more plastic. Political actors have choices to make; they can forge new coalitions, or they can revive old ones. In this process of construction, the structure of the group situation provides political entrepreneurs with both constraints and opportunities. Thus, even to evaluate the limits of interest in explaining an outcome and to identify where other variables mediate it, we need some portrait of the structure of interests. Here, an account of how the production profile of each country fits into the international division of labor proves instructive.

Those who seek policy goals (interest groups) have a need for a politics that will help fulfill their policy. Conversely, those who seek power, whose goals are political, need a policy approach that will suit their politics. This article is about that interaction, worked out through the great crisis of the 1930s. The first section briefly defines the major policy alternatives available for coping with the Depression, and the categories of social forces whose preferences are relevant. The second section explores the policy debate in Germany, the United States, Sweden, Britain, and France. The final section interprets these findings.

The options and their political ramifications

The striking innovation in economic policy during the 1930s was demand-stimulus policy, known in the postwar period as Keynesianism. It is familiar as a countercyclical policy that seeks to correct the deficiency of inadequate demand through deficit spending by governments. Demand-stimulus policy, it has been claimed, saved constitutional government in the capitalist economies by changing the political struggles over economic policy from a zero-sum game to a mixed game. The zero-sum alternatives were posed by the policy programs of the orthodoxies that prevailed in the 1930s, those which were debated at the time and which preceded the innovation of demand stimulus.

The first was *orthodox deflation*, which involved cutting down on costs through lower wages, lower taxes, and less government spending in order to cheapen costs and thereby to attract buyers at home and abroad. It required a defense of the value of the currency and, in that period, its fixed relation to gold.

The second was *the socialization of investment*. The major critique of orthodox deflation at the outset of this period was socialist orthodoxy, which argued that private investment could not sustain a full-employment economy. The only way to avoid the frightful costs of the business cycle was to socialize investment and planning, thereby freeing employment-generating decisions from the interests of a specialized group within the economy, the private investors of capital.

These two alternatives were seen as "zero-sum" in that each requires sacrifices from a major segment of the population. The deflation school insists that high wages and high taxes for transfer payments (unemployment compensation and other benefits) threaten profitability. The owners of capital are discouraged from investing, or even producing, with existing capacity because wages and taxes eat up profits. Wages and wage-sustaining taxes must therefore be cut. Conversely, the socialization of investment school leads to the elimination of the owners of capital. If the private owners of capital are unwilling to lower unemployment, they must be replaced by mechanisms that will.

Each position has a dramatic political implication as well: to attain the economic end, it may be necessary to destroy the constitutional system. The deflationists may be tempted to try authoritarian government as a way of destroying labor's ability to resist wage cuts and welfare reductions through strikes and the ballot box. Conversely, the socializers may seek authoritarian government as a way to break private capital's hold on the economy (in particular, its ability to engage in a "capital strike") and to forestall possible political moves by capital against labor organizations.

The alternatives to these two poles of policy were "mixed games" in the sense that they blurred the effects of policy across different segments of the population and the nature of the sacrifices demanded of each.

Neo-orthodoxy was the "orthodox" break with orthodoxy in that it was derived intellectually from remedies for disorder suggested by classic economic theory, and it preserved private property. Nonetheless, it remained both intellectually and politically controversial. It involved devaluation of the currency, which allows the relaxation of deflation policies since it is no longer necessary to curb imports in defense of the currency via restraint of spending and purchasing; tariffs, which protect industry from imports; and cartelization, which helps share out markets and maintain prices, either officially through government-sponsored agreements or unofficially through private arrangements.

Demand stimulus, or the "unorthodox" break with orthodoxy of either kind, departed intellectually as well as politically from existing traditions. In substance it meant boosting demand through deficit-financed public works or transfer payments, or both. This would prove to be the new scheme of the 1930s. It may have occurred earlier, through unintended deficits or through specialized spending, but it was not deliberately tried until the 1930s, and even then only sparingly.

Reality, of course, is more confusing than the simplification that generalization requires. Real countries did a mixture of things; some said they were doing one thing and actually did another. The boundaries among actual behaviors blur easily: recent interpretations of the Swedish case, for example, argue that the actual effect of its supposed demand-stimulus policy was far less striking than the common image allows. The United States did not really try demand stimulus until late in the decade, in 1938. Nazi Germany was the most extensive experimenter in the 1930s, and the most successful. Demand stimulus would only come of age after World War II. Nonetheless, reflation through public spending was proposed in many countries even before Keynes published his famous book; attempts were made, experiments were tried, doctrines developed, alliances forged. The postwar pattern took form in the 1930s.

These alternative policies changed the political struggle because they made it possible to attract people across the boundaries defined by the two orthodoxies. With neo-orthodoxy, tariffs helped draw together producers of different sorts—business and agriculture, plus labor in the protected sphere for the end of deflation policy reduced the pressure to cut wages. Demand stimulus altered the game because wages and profits could rise together rather than inversely.[8]

What accounts for the choice of one policy option over others in this period? And what connection was there between the struggle over policy choice and the struggles over political system and political coalitions that occurred at the same time? I seek to explicate the political preconditions of breaking with orthodoxy, and the character of political support that mobilized on behalf of policies in different countries. Why did some countries stop the policy sequence with neo-orthodoxy while others went on to demand stimulus? Descriptively, this means examining what the support coalitions of Nazi Germany, social-democratic Sweden, and New Deal America have in common that enabled more extensive breaks with orthodoxy than occurred in France (save for a few months of the Blum government) and the United Kingdom.

It may at first blush appear that their policy coalitions have nothing in common and that there is no connection between politics and economic policy. What, after all, could be further apart than social-democratic Sweden and Nazi Germany, or Nazi Germany and the United States of the New Deal? Though demand-stimulus policies may in the long run have contributed to the strengthening of democracy at that historical juncture, by helping

---

8. On the relation between Keynesianism and political struggles, see Robert Skidelsky, "The Decline of Keynesian Politics," and Colin Crouch, "The State, Capital, and Liberal Democracy," in Crouch, ed., *State and Economy in Contemporary Capitalism* (London: Croom Helm, 1979).

TABLE 1. *Economic policies, coalitions, and regimes*

Policy Sequence for Crisis	Regimes and Support Coalitions	
	Constitutionalist	Authoritarian
1. Orthodox Deflation (defend currency; cut spending; push down wages) Procyclical.	UK to 1931 (PLP, business liberals)[a] Germany to 1933 (mixed; e.g., SDP, Catholics, etc.)[b] Sweden to 1931 (business, agriculture) U.S.A. to 1933 (business, agriculture)[c] France to 1936 (business, agriculture) & post 1937	
2. Socialist Orthodoxy (socialize investment through nationalization, plus planning) Not pursued.	Supported only by Communists at times; unions and Socialist parties use it rhetorically, but actually endorse deflation combined with resistance to wage and welfare cuts, 1930–32	
3. Neo-orthodoxy (devalue currency; use tariffs and official or private cartels)	UK post 1931 (all but unions, PLP) U.S.A. 1930–31, 1933–35/7 (business, agriculture) Sweden 1931–32 France post 1937	
4. Demand Stimulus (deficit spending through public works, transfer payments, etc.) Countercyclical.	Sweden post 1936 (farmer-labor, part business)[d] U.S.A. post 1936 (farmer-labor, part business)[d] France 1936–37 (farmer-labor, part business)	Germany post 1933 (agriculture, domestic business, nonunion labor)

a. Parliamentary Labour Party. b. German Social-Democratic Party. c. Except for tariffs.
d. Partial moves only.

constitutional regimes deal more effectively with the economic crisis, they were by no means the monopoly of constitutional regimes. Indeed, Germany used such policies more extensively than anyone else in the period and brought the unemployment rate of workers and underutilized capacity down faster than anyone else. With this in mind, we might conclude that since different political systems pursued the same policies, and similar political systems pursued different ones, there is no connection between the two and economic policies are polymorphous—anyone can take up any policy through any political system, so no linkages can be established.

Economic policies are, however, *not* completely polymorphous. Not just anyone supported one or another policy; this was not a randomly distributed set of preferences. Farmers were critical of the market everywhere, while business interests uniformly denounced socialism. In work on the international economic crisis of 1873, I found that the preferences of various groups played a considerable role in explaining the choice of policies in different countries. In exploring the behavior of similar groups during the next great crisis, I see the glimmers of some regularities in these preferences, at the level of interest groups. In the various countries, it may be possible to specify the support base for the alternative policies, the alliances that occurred, and the trade-offs. Furthermore, by specifying what alliances with what terms of trade were possible but were not tried, or were tried and failed, we may explore the similarities among interest groups that, however, express themselves politically in different ways.

Actors and situations

Let us use a rather crude model of the interest groups that constitute society, adapted from Alexander Gerschenkron's excellent *Bread and Democracy in Germany*.[9] The outstanding feature of Gerschenkron's classification is a disaggregation into three major groupings (agriculture, industry, and labor), each divided into two main camps according to situation in the international economy. Agriculture thus involves large-scale grain-growing estates (Junkers), and small proprietors who used cheap foreign grain as inputs. Industry is

9. Gerschenkron, *Bread and Democracy*. In considering the importance of producer groups in politics, the relation between producer groups and the historical sequences of the industrial revolution, and the international elements of the product cycle, I have been strongly influenced not only by Gerschenkron but by Barrington Moore Jr., *The Social Origins of Dictatorship and Democracy* (Boston: Beacon Press, 1966); Kurth, "Political Consequences"; Landes, *The Unbound Prometheus*; and Raymond Vernon, *Sovereignty at Bay* (New York: Basic Books, 1971). My own views on some of these issues can be found in Gourevitch, "International Trade, Domestic Coalitions and Liberty: Comparative Responses to the Crisis of 1873–96," *Journal of Interdisciplinary History* 8 (Autumn 1977): 281–313. See also Gourevitch, "The Second Image Reversed: The International Sources of Domestic Politics," *International Organization* 32 (Autumn 1978): 881–912.

split into heavy industry (iron, steel, coal) with very high capital requirements, very strong international competitive pressures, and a need for stable markets; and finished goods manufacturers for whom heavy industry was an input, with high technology, a strong position in international markets, and considerable reliance on consumers as markets. As for labor, Gerschenkron focuses on the German Social-Democratic party (SPD) as a bloc. But labor could also be disaggregated, into unionized and nonunionized labor, each caught among frequently conflicting pressures as producers and consumers. Gerschenkron gives some consideration to other groups such as banking, merchants, and shippers, professionals, shopkeepers, and other middle-class strata. In the case he examines, these groups appear not to have separated out with distinctly different positions. Banks, for example, had close relations with different industries and tended to express the needs of their clients (heavy or finished, accordingly); shippers favored policy that would promote trade, lawyers the policies of their clients, and so on.

The situational features of different sectors most likely to account for their varying propensities to ally with labor are international competitiveness (position of the domestic industry in the international division of labor of the product cycle), labor component (labor costs as a percentage of value added), type of market for product (consumer vs. capital goods, including the military dimension and the government as possible buyer), technology (degree of stability), and investment features (minimum capital requirements). The possible combinations of these dimensions are many, but they can be simplified as constituting components of a single variable—international competitiveness.

There are many qualifications and adjustments necessary for this model of social groups, but the country cases will permit us to explore how different groups behaved in relation to the economic policy alternatives for responding to the Depression that were available to the political systems of the day.

The demand-stimulus coalitions of Sweden, the United States, and Germany were, in sum, *cross-sector, cross-class* alliances of groups whose patience with market solutions had run out. In each case farmers made de facto or explicit alliances with certain sectors of business who were themselves seeking help to break from economic orthodoxy, and with certain elements of labor willing to alter old habits to bring about change. In Sweden and the United States, the labor component of this alliance was provided by the labor organizations themselves. In Germany, of course, it was not, as the union movement was crushed.

Germany

The interwar debate over German economic policy, as well as quarrels over the constitution, social structure, foreign policy, and many other issues, can be seen as the continuation of a complex set of quarrels within German society reaching back to the origins of the German Empire forged by Bismarck in 1871. The marriage of iron and rye in the tariff of 1879 is one of the best-known examples of domestic horsetrading among sectors of the national economy.[10] Heavy industry, the Junkers and smaller farmers, elements of the civil service, banking, and other social groups formed the social base of the coalition that dominated German politics through the end of World War I. It pursued a policy package of protectionism in commercial relations, authoritarianism in politics, naval building, and militarism in foreign policy. Germany did have its counterpart to the British business-labor alliance in support of the cheap loaf and free trade: it contained finished goods manufacturers and high-technology industries strongly oriented toward export, and labor concerned about cheaper food and lower costs. But before 1914, the conservative bloc prevailed.

Military defeat fractured these alignments. Fitfully, and with many obstacles (among them the Kapp putsch, the Ruhr occupation, and hyperinflation), the Social Democrats and the progressive elements of business managed to wriggle away from the iron-rye bloc to form a de facto accommodation, the "Weimar coalition," built around an internationalist economic orientation, democratized labor relations and politics at home, high social insurance benefits, and acquiescence in the post-Versailles international system. The economic collapse of 1929 destroyed the Weimar coalition, opening the way for the resurgence of the old bloc in new, more virulent form.[11]

The international economy throughout played a great role in shaping the fate of political alignments. As in the prewar period, a major issue of postwar domestic politics was Germany's relationship to the world. Germany again faced two broad alternatives for foreign economic policy, each linked to a particular posture in international relations, domestic constitutional arrangements, and domestic social policy. On the one side was the integration of Germany into an intensified international division of labor, accepting an open economy and the various post-Versailles arrangements. On the other side was resistance to internationalism, shielding Germany from world market forces and possibly using government to prepare the ground for revision of Versailles.

Between these two end points were a variety of combinations. The struggle

10. From the vast literature on Germany before World War I, see Gordon Craig, *Germany 1866–1945* (Oxford: Clarendon Press, 1978), and Craig's *The Politics of the Prussian Army, 1640–1945* (New York: Oxford University Press, 1964); Hans-Ulrich Wehler, "Bismarck's Imperialism," *Past and Present* 48 (1970): 119–55; Helmut Bohme, "Big Business Pressure Groups and Bismarck's Turn to Protectionism, 1873–79," *Historical Journal* 10 (1967): 218–36. For a view critical of these and mine, see Ronald Rogowski, "Iron, Rye, and the Authoritarian Coalition in Germany after 1879" (Paper delivered at the APSA meeting, Denver, September 1982).

11. David Abraham, *The Collapse of the Weimar Republic* (Princeton: Princeton University Press, 1981); this contains an extremely useful and interesting account of the substantive policy goals of different interest groups and the possible combinations of them. See also Gerald Feldman, *Iron and Steel in the German Inflation, 1916–23* (Princeton: Princeton University Press, 1977).

over economic policy, and the whole shape of German politics and society, turned on the pattern of alignments and coalitions among social actors. Much depended on the relations of different fractions of business to one another, to labor, and to agriculture. While labor and capital were in conflict everywhere over a number of issues, some accommodation was possible and did occur.[12]

In Germany, as elsewhere, certain elements of capital were more likely than others to work with labor. Foreign economic policy issues drove elements of German industry into conflict with one another. No element was strong enough by itself to prevail, and so each sought allies. Export industry and labor supported elements of what can be called an "understanding"—there was no formal agreement, such as the Saltsjobaden accord reached in Sweden in 1938, but there was a willingness to accept each other's policies. While all Germans disliked the Versailles Treaty, the export industries and labor were willing to accommodate themselves to it as the price for Germany's integration into a stable international order. After the hyperinflation, industry desperately needed capital to finance the revival of production, and these elements supported the Dawes plan. Integration into an open world economy, access to foreign capital, mass civilian purchasing power, restraint on the drain of inefficient sectors, modernization and rationalization at home—these were the goals of the electrotechnical and chemical industries, symbolized by Siemens and I. G. Farben and individuals such as Carl Duisberg and Walter Rathenau. Fritz Ebert symbolizes the social-democratic side of the Weimar coalition's exchanges: control of the radical elements on the Left, a constitutionalist polity, trade union rights in collective bargaining, full employment, and social insurance programs. Export industry needed labor for political support in resisting autarchy and, economically, as customers for mass consumption's products. And, compared to less efficient business, export industry could (relatively speaking) afford the accommodation, for wages were a smaller proportion of its costs.

In opposition to these internationalists were the members of the prewar iron-rye coalition. Given considerable worldwide expansion of industrial capacity during the war, iron and steel were now in worse shape than before; while German heavy industry remained comparatively efficient, it could not cope with worldwide overproduction. In agriculture, there had been a similarly considerable expansion of production, and the fall of prices marked an agricultural crisis several years before the crash of 1929. While revision of Versailles appealed to nationalists occupying all sorts of "objective" situations, there continued to be some "sociological" basis to it among these economic

---

12. In his very important recent book on the political economy of Weimar, *Collapse of the Weimar Republic*, David Abraham has mapped out the pattern of different social groups' preferences on a range of issues, economic and other, showing the terms of trade along which alliances could occur. His work resonates strongly with the approach taken here and with the modeling in Thomas Ferguson's "From Normalcy to New Deal," *International Organization* 38 (Winter 1984).

interests. Heavy industry and agriculture remained more protectionist, more autarchic in policy preferences, and more resistant to accommodation with the trading community abroad and with labor at home.

So long as the world economy was healthy, the pressures for autarchy could be resisted. Exports generated the profits to make an alliance of high technology and labor possible. Foreign loans provided the capital to make the goods that could be sold abroad to earn the foreign exchange that would pay reparations, loans, and wages. But when the world economy collapsed, the alliance came unstuck. The costs and benefits of domestic coalitional behavior changed considerably. Electoral research has documented these shifts at the level of the mass electorate, which abandoned the system's parties for more extreme formations.[13] These shifts occurred within a context that has been less clearly explored, the conflict over economic and other policies, strongly shaped by interest groups and the structural situation in which they operated. The flight from the system's parties was a response to the deadlock among them and among the interest groups struggling over different conceptions of policy.

Within the Weimar coalition, the deterioration of the international economy eroded the coalition between labor and the dynamic manufacturers. As exports plummeted, industry's ability to pay the costs of the labor alliance dropped. Without strong markets, high wage bills and transfer payments were too costly. The assertions of heavy industry groups now sounded more plausible to the exporters: a revival of sales required lower prices, which required lower costs, which required lower wages and taxes. In the language of the current Euro-American argument, this was a "supply-side" argument. The export sector had been advocating a demand-side view: higher wages helped higher consumption. In the business associations, the export group was weakened, and heavy industry leaders replaced them as spokesmen. Export and heavy industry both initially supported deflation as a way of cutting costs. Elements of both sectors were soon to turn toward other policies, such as reflation, armaments and exchange controls, corporatism and structured markets. But in both branches the Depression immediately led to sharp conflict with labor.

Labor found itself caught in an increasingly tight pincer, between its preferences for economic policy and its preferences for the maintenance of a constitutionalist coalition. The trade unions and SPD opposed the deflationary content of Bruning's policy but sustained the government in office in order to preserve the republic and bar the way to the far Right. As defenders of labor in the market, the party and unions opposed the reduction of un-

---

13. In addition to the classical treatments of the mass electorate (S. M. Lipset, *Political Man* [Garden City, N.Y.: Doubleday, 1963], and Rudolf Haberle, *From Democracy to Nazism* [Baton Rouge: Louisiana State University Press, 1970]), see Richard Hamilton, *Who Voted for Hitler* (Princeton: Princeton University Press, 1982), for a treatment stressing the social diversity of the Nazi electorate and the importance of Nazi organizational skills.

employment benefits, the pressure against wages, and the rollback of state expenditures (in the last they were particularly constrained as the representatives of large numbers of civil servants). To defend labor rights won in the political arena, the SPD felt compelled to support a prosystem government even when that government pursued economic policies contrary to social-democratic goals in the labor market.

SPD leaders, particularly Rudolf Hilferding, the finance minister and leading party intellectual in matters of economic theory, were sharply constrained politically by their economic ideas. They saw no alternative other than full socialization of the economy, for which they had no electoral majority, or operation of the capitalist economy by its own logic, which Hilferding understood according to the same orthodoxy as the prodeflation economists. Hilferding completely rejected the demand-stimulus ideas that were circulating in Europe. The trade union movement had been persuaded to adopt such a program, the WTB plan, named after Woytinski, a Russian emigré social-democratic economist, Tarnow, a trade union official, and Baade, an agriculture expert. The plan called for deficit-financed public works. In a showdown between union and party leaders, Woytinski and his colleagues were unable to overcome Hilferding's commitment to an orthodox capitalist interpretation of capitalism.[14]

The SPD thus lost an opportunity that was as much political as economic. By 1932, when the debate took place inside the SPD, there was considerable dissatisfaction with economic orthodoxy in all circles of German society, including the varying wings of industry. Among the heavy industrialists there had always been misgivings about the deflationist line. Market mechanisms had not worked well for steel and iron producers in the 1920s. In crisis, they turned readily and rapidly back to familiar policy instruments: tariffs and other forms of autarchy, and government spending, particularly on capital goods such as military items. While demand stimulus per se had no particular theoretical basis among the heavy industrial circles, government assistance in economic development did.

In the context of severe contraction in the world economy, domestic business had a greater affinity for demand-stimulus thinking than did export business. For companies seeking to tap the world market, reflating the domestic market is too limited a response; they are likely to seek a revival of international trade. Companies concentrating on the domestic market because of international competitive conditions have already foregone that alternative.

Thus, an acute international depression creates the conditions for a reversal of the previous relations between labor and business. Internationally oriented businesses shift away from support of high labor purchasing power toward cheaper labor costs, and thus toward the concerns of heavy industry. Labor turns away from consumer concerns of supporting free trade toward producer

14. Vladimir Woytinski, *Stormy Passage* (New York: Vanguard, 1961).

concerns of preserving jobs, and hence toward heavy industry. The different wings of agriculture draw together to seek market intervention, and hence toward heavy industry. While the issues of conflict (wages and benefits, union rights, social insurance, foreign economic policy) between heavy industry and other groups remain, new possibilities arise for a different combination of groups around other policies.

International crisis may also move an industry or a company from one bloc to another. While autarchy was generally an unsatisfactory solution for sectors seeking world markets, one very large company in the export bloc found itself in such deep trouble in 1932 that autarchy seemed attractive. The huge chemical trust I. G. Farben, as James Kurth has noted, had heavily invested in coal gasification. When oil prices dropped sharply in 1931 after the East Texas oil fields came on line, the company desperately sought aid. In the maneuverings of late 1932, Farben preferred the Schleicher variant of intervention (demand-stimulus corporatism with labor participation) over the Hitler version (which excluded labor). Farben leaders did not play an active role in bringing Hitler to power, but they would rally to his policies and, in the end, play a greater role than any other company or industry in the Nazi regime, down to synthetic rubber plants at Auschwitz.[15]

In the conflict over economic policy, the behavior of agricultural interests (voters, interest groups, and parties) was vital. German agriculture rebelled against bourgeois economic orthodoxy thoroughly and rapidly. None of the system's parties showed much responsiveness to the countryside's plight. The bourgeois parties defended the market against rural holders' pleas, and the Left saw no reason to help private property, in particular a property-owning segment that never gave evidence of willingness to cooperate with labor. There were individuals within the SPD, the bourgeois parties, and the farmers' parties who sought to promote alliances, but they made no headway.

It is not hard to find ample reason for conflict between farmers and workers; indeed, 19th and 20th century history is full of examples. But farmer-labor alliances did occur in the 1930s, in Sweden and in the United States. There is no end of possible explanations for the absence of such alliances in Germany—political culture, interest-group organization, political party structures, market organization, market situation. The approach taken here points toward the weakness of economic modernization in the German countryside, which increased agriculture's dependence on state intervention and inhibited a convergence of interests with efficient industry and labor, as happened in other countries. What is certainly clear is the importance of the relations between labor and agriculture in affecting outcomes.

By 1932, three economic packages were under debate in Germany. The first was a continuation of Bruning's economic orthodoxy. This might have

---

15. Kurth, "Political Consequences"; Joseph Borkin, *The Crime and Punishment of I. G. Farben* (New York: Free Press, 1978).

worked to some degree, since the world economy did improve in 1933 and the Bruning government might well have received some credit for improvements. By late 1932, however, the political support for waiting it out had crumbled. A second possibility was to abandon deflation in favor of neo-orthodoxy: devaluation, tariffs, and agricultural price supports, what the United Kingdom did after 1931 and the United States did in separate steps in 1931 and 1933. In Germany, however, devaluation still seemed abhorrent in 1932, and mild neo-orthodoxy seemed too passive to many segments of German society.

The third package involved demand stimulus through deficit-financed spending. It came in two versions, parliamentary and authoritarian. Schleicher tried to organize a quasi-parliamentary version of demand stimulus, and failed. Unlike the American and Swedish experimenters, he excluded agriculture and threatened the special advantages of the Junkers, thereby angering the camarilla around Hindenburg. Labor and business could not agree on a package, because labor was unwilling to shoulder the costs as business demanded. In the United States and Sweden, where business came to accept demand stimulus, it did so only when the labor-farmer alliance showed sufficient political strength to force some sectors of business to become more accommodating. In Germany, the attempt was quite different: agriculture was excluded from the Schleicher discussion, which tried to effect a direct bargain between the two actors with the historically deepest antagonism, labor and heavy industry.[16]

Instead of explicit social bargaining among major social groups within a modified constitutionalism—Schleicher's attempt—Hitler mixed explicit bargaining with certain actors (business and agriculture) with direct mobilization of individuals and the exclusion of their institutionalized representatives (particularly unions and the SPD but some elements of agriculture, white-collar workers, and business as well). Direct accommodation among agriculture and business elites (Von Papen's attempt with the Cabinet of Barons) could not work because it lacked mass support. Hitler could provide just that, tapping unemployed workers who were not unionized, farmers, salaried personnel, and property owners small, medium, and large. Indeed, the social diversity of the Nazi vote is more complex than the traditional stress on the "middlestand" allows. Hitler combined rejection of the orthodox economic alternatives (socialization and the market) with nationalism, a combination that appealed to many different elements of society and did

---

16. On business see Gerald Feldman, "The Social and Economic Policies of German Big Business, 1918–29," *American Historical Review* 75 (October 1969): 47–55; and several works by Henry Ashby Turner Jr.: "Big Business and the Rise of Hitler," *American Historical Review* 75 (October 1969): 56–70; "Emil Kirdorf and the Nazi Party," *Central European History* 1 (December 1968): 324–44; "Hitler's Secret Pamphlet for Industrialists, 1927," *Journal of Modern History* 11 (September 1968): 348–74; "The Ruhrlade, Secret Cabinet of Heavy Industry in the Weimar Republic," *Central European History* 3 (September 1970): 195–228; and *Stresemann and the Politics of the Weimar Republic* (Princeton: Princeton University Press, 1963).

worst with those strongly integrated into alternative interpretations of the world—unions, the Marxist parties, and the Catholic center. But settling the controversy over the Nazi vote will not by itself completely explain either the *Machtergriefung* or the content of policy. After all, in the last normal election, November 1932, Hitler did not exceed 34 percent of the vote. To take power required help from other sources. He got it from the conservatives within agriculture and business who sought a deal—the chancellery for control of labor.

This political bargaining for economic policy is significant. By themselves the economic elites would not have undertaken what Hitler did in economic policy after January 1933, however much they liked the economic results and, at least until the late 1930s, the political ones as well. Neither the economic results nor the political outcomes were the result of the desires of any single group. They emerged from an interaction. Everyone had reasons to prefer some other, "purer" policy and political choice. In this point lies the weakness of many social explanations of fascism, the notion that fascism derives from big business, or the Junkers, or the petty bourgeoisie. Big business in fact preferred the Cabinet of Barons, as did the Junkers; the petty bourgeoisie did not like the bargains fascism struck with big business and the Junkers. Nonetheless, the process that produced the fascist triumph did have a social basis, which cannot be rejected in favor of heavily institutional, individualist, culturalist, or psychological explanations. Thus the heavy industrialists may have preferred the Cabinet of Barons, but they accepted Hitler as preferable to still other alternatives. And while they may have preferred the Cabinet of Barons politically, in economic terms the cabinet had become too conservative and too orthodox for them.

The break from economic orthodoxy required political help. Property owners everywhere were finding it difficult to reconcile a variety of contradictions in their attitudes, preferences, and political behaviors. They wanted defense of property, restraint of labor pressures, and limits on state interference in appropriate ways. Many wanted state aid for an emergency but were reluctant to pay the price of social insurance and state aid for employment. Ordinary "bourgeois" politicians had trouble integrating these various goals in politically effective ways. They appeared to defend capital at the expense of the masses. Hitler had mass support, and a coalition between Nazis and certain social forces gave the government autonomy to try a blend of policies.

The Nazis proved better able than policy makers in other countries to bring down unemployment (and this was true even *before* the upswing in military spending). With extensive public works and government purchasing, Germany ran deficits and infused purchasing power into the economy. Exchange controls and trade restrictions curtailed imports and effectively devalued the mark while maintaining its nominal value. By the end of 1934, unemployment had dropped, and more sharply than anywhere else. In Sweden and the United States, the other countries where some job creation was attempted in this period, actual demand stimulus was far less ample than in Germany and had less effect. Revival in these countries had far more to do with the boost to exports from devaluation, the boost to investment from cheap interest rates, and an upturn in worldwide demand. Thus the first country to try demand stimulus and make it work was, sad to say, Germany under the Nazis.[17] (Japan experimented with this policy as well, also at the time the regime was becoming increasingly fascist, but that case is outside the framework of this article.)[18]

The German case exhibits the impact of international economic crisis on domestic alignments of social forces around economic policies and politics. An important predictor of alliance behavior is the relationship of social groups to the international economy, which is in turn a function of its location within the product cycle: efficient, competitive industries, at the cutting edge of the international distribution of labor, tended to have policy preferences and alliance propensities different from those of industries that found themselves less well positioned, if not in efficiency then in the structure of demand and costs. The crash of 1929 undermined the agreements among social groups that sustained Weimar. As the Depression worsened, demands for policy shifts grew. Situation in the international economy helps predict the direction of these policy shifts, and the structure of policy preferences helps in turn to define the situation within which other variables—political leadership, circumstance, ideology—play a role. The pattern of group support for breaking with orthodoxy in Germany had some remarkable similarities with those of other countries. The sharp difference was the political formula.

The United States

As Ferguson shows, situation in the international economy affected policy preference and alliance propensities in the United States as well as in Europe.[19] Conflict over foreign economic policy is one of the oldest and most durable issues in American politics. As elsewhere, the conflict can be simplified into a debate between "internationalists" (advocating low tariffs and America's more intense involvement in the international division of labor) and "nationalists." (In U.S. discourse the latter were known for many years as "isolationists," seeking some degree of insulation from the vagaries of the international economy, principally through tariffs.) Core support for the nationalist position came from the large-scale heavy industry of the mid-West—

17. John D. Heyl, "Hitler's Economic Thought: A Reappraisal," *Central European History* 6 (March 1973): 83–96; Arndt, *Economic Lessons of the Nineteen-Thirties*; Alan S. Milward, "Fascism and the Economy," in Walter Laqueur, ed., *Fascism, A Reader's Guide: Analyses, Interpretations, Bibliography* (Berkeley: University of California Press, 1976).
18. See Charles Kindleberger, *The World in Depression, 1929–1939* (Berkeley: University of California Press, 1973).
19. Because Ferguson's "From Normalcy to New Deal" analyzes the U.S. case in detail, treatment here will be brief. The two articles reinforce each other.

steel was protectionist here as everywhere else in the world. Core support for the internationalist position came from shippers, trade-oriented bankers, and high-technology industries at the export phase of the product cycle.

One conspicuous difference from Europe lies in the situation of agriculture and the related situation of labor. This is, however, a difference not in the explanatory importance of international situation but in its actual content in differing countries. American agriculture was quite efficient; indeed, it was a major source of Europe's problems. The supply of cheap food was therefore not a policy problem either for labor or for industries worried about keeping down costs. In Europe, grain growers were protectionist, while the producers of higher-quality foodstuffs (meat, dairy, etc.) were more likely to favor free trade. In the United States, this policy proclivity of products was reversed. The quality food producers had plenty of cheap domestic grain to use as inputs in their production and for their own consumption. Since the consumers of these quality foodstuffs were urban residents and industrial workers, whose consumption rose as their incomes rose, this part of the countryside had some interest in promoting the health of domestic industry. Conversely, commodity producers (grain, cotton) sold on world markets; they could not increase their sales by protecting and promoting American industrial growth, but had to export.

The situation of the quality food producers in relation to other groups facilitated their entry into a protectionist coalition. With cheap food assured, members of the labor movement could follow their interests as industrial producers. The Republican bloc fused in the 1890s thus linked elements of labor, agriculture, and industry around industrial protectionism, in conflict with the internationalist groups drawn from export industry and export agriculture, focused on the Democratic party.[20]

The Depression of 1929 ruptured these relationships. Franklin Roosevelt's victory in 1932 put back together what the election of 1896 had ripped asunder—agriculture and labor, both driven away from the GOP by the desire for government action in response to economic distress. In the face of sharply falling prices, the different elements of agriculture converged in clamoring for some sort of corporatistic organization of markets. The large chunks of ethnic working-class electors that had voted Republican now joined up with those workers who had always voted for the Democrats. To that core of electoral and interest-group support came elements of business. The label "business" itself is, however, insufficient: the content, the *types* of business involved, changed over time, as did economic policy.

The first New Deal marked a heavy defeat for internationalists. The United States went off gold, broke up the London Conference, set up the Agricultural Adjustment Administration (AAA) to help agriculture via production controls,

---

20. Walter Dean Burnham, *Critical Elections and the Mainsprings of the American Party System* (New York: Norton, 1970).

marketing arrangements, and price supports, and passed the National Recovery Administration (NRA) to do the same for industry. In place of world markets, the domestic economy would be parceled out among existing producers. Demand-stimulus suggestions existed, but they were marginal to policy discussions. While labor and agriculture provided much of the energy for this approach, it was hardly done in opposition to business. On the contrary, it represented just what a very large portion of American industry increasingly thought had to be done.[21]

Yet the coalition behind the first New Deal was itself riddled with fault lines. As policy failed to produce effective results, internal stresses cracked the coalition open. There were acute conflicts within sectors, among sectors, and between business and other groups. Within sectors, fighting increased over the content of the NRA codes. The characteristically conservative notion that self-administration by businessmen freed of politics would overcome conflict proved illusory. Differently situated firms proposed different codes. Compliance without coercion was impossible, and coercion itself was opposed. By the time the Supreme Court found the NRA unconstitutional, business had abandoned it, thereby bringing into the open conflict over what economic policy to follow instead. Within business, the partial revival of the world economy exacerbated disagreement about foreign economic policy: internationalists wanted to escape from the Smoot-Hawley tariff and to restore a stable international payments and trading system. At the same time, business and labor fought ever more sharply over the labor relations provisions of the NRA.

These tensions, bursting open the coalition of the first New Deal, reopened various possibilities for policies and politics: a return to deflation, cautious forms of neocorporatism such as the British Conservatives were trying, or more experimentation toward what became the social-democratic model. As in any complex crisis, leadership played a role: Roosevelt took the third route, with significant consequences. The options, and the ingredients of the support coalitions for each option, were profoundly shaped by the economic situation of various actors.

The Second New Deal produced an interrelated set of policies: the Wagner Act, Social Security, continuation and extension of the AAA, pursuit of

21. The literature on the New Deal is, of course, immense. In addition to the well-known materials, I have found particularly useful some newer work by Thomas Ferguson: "From Normalcy to New Deal," and his *Critical Realignment: The Fall of the House of Morgan and the Origins of the New Deal* (New York: Oxford University Press, forthcoming); and by Theda Skocpol, who has coauthored several articles with a stress on institutions; see "Political Responses to Capitalist Crisis: Neo-Marxist Theories of the State and the Case of the New Deal," *Politics and Society* 10, 2 (1980); Skocpol and Kenneth Finegold, "State Capacity and Economic Intervention in the Early New Deal," *Political Science Quarterly* 97 (Summer 1982): 255–78; Skocpol and Margaret Weir, "State Structures, Political Coalitions, and the Possibilities for Social Keynesianism: Responses to the Great Depression in Sweden and the United States" (forthcoming).

reciprocal trade negotiations, the Tripartite Monetary Agreement, and conscious demand stimulus in response to the tremendous slump of 1938 (which came from balancing the budget in 1937). This combination of policies entailed exchanges: labor accepted higher food costs in exchange for agriculture's support of a new industrial relations system and social insurance. As Ferguson's modeling predicts, the economic elites from the business side most willing to accept the costs of this exchange were those particularly interested in foreign trade and able to bear higher labor costs.

In policy terms, there was a shift in the political location of demand-stimulus experimentation. It began life as part of an inward-looking, nationalist impulse, an attempt to rescue domestic economies from the ruin of the international one. It was so proposed in Europe and America in the early 1930s and was used that way by the Nazis. Where constitutionalist politics continued, however, demand stimulus was free to seek other sponsors. It took a certain amount of learning—economic, intellectual, and political—to produce acceptance of the faltering steps of prewar Keynesianism. The learning involved sequences of trial and error, policy attempts and policy failures. The full use of demand stimulus did not occur until after 1945, but in the Second New Deal we see the postwar social-democratic model: an open foreign economic policy, full employment fiscal policy, social insurance transfer payments, trade union rights in collective bargaining, high wages, and stable monetary policy.

Sweden

Three Scandinavian countries formed farmer-labor alliances in the 1930s: Denmark in 1932, Sweden later that year, and Norway in 1935. In each country, these "cow trades" represented dramatic breaks with earlier political patterns and also involved dramatic breaks in economic policy. Since the Swedish experience figures so prominently in social science discussions of 20th century political economy, I concentrate on that case.

The alliance pattern of Swedish economic actors bears strong parallels with that of other countries. The quarrel between protection and free trade split Sweden through World War I. As in Germany, grain growers and locally oriented industries were protectionists, while the producers of high-quality foodstuffs, workers, and the high-technology export industries for which Sweden became famous preferred free trade. The first coalition was politically conservative, the second politically liberal. In foreign policy, the former pursued a pro-German policy during World War I, provoking a British blockade. The second alliance overthrew the conservative government under Hammarskjöld, switching Swedish policy dramatically: the pro-British policy allowed the revival of foreign trade and lowering of food costs, suffrage was broadened, and constitutional dominance of the parliament over the crown was established. This "progressive" alliance linked the Social Democrats of labor with export-oriented business (Liberals) and grain-consuming farming.[22]

In the 1920s, labor went back to relative isolation, though they did participate in some governing coalitions. High valuation of the currency induced strong pressure to drive down industrial wages. The Agrarian party, among others, showed very strong animosity toward the Social Democrats, while the Liberals and other business groups saw no need to seek labor assistance for policy goals. When the Depression began, the Social Democrats had one major advantage compared to their English and German counterparts—they had been out of power for a number of years.

Sweden's first response to the Depression was orthodox, deflation and no devaluation. When Britain devalued sterling in 1931, the run against the Swedish krona forced a policy switch. As the world economy continued to deteriorate, the competitive advantage of devaluation proved limited. Domestic dissatisfaction with market solutions heightened. Farmers sought aid through marketing boards and price supports. The Social Democrats demanded better unemployment compensation and began explicitly to propound deficit-financed public works. While the farmers mobilized bourgeois support for their schemes, at least in piecemeal fashion, that support seemed unstable. Business interests were reluctant to support higher food costs and government intervention in markets, and the bourgeois parties were all reluctant to accept labor's demands. The cow trade between the Swedish SDP and the Agrarian party overcame the political obstacles. The surprise at the time was that workers would accept higher food costs and farmers higher worker wages, since that particular trade had never occurred before. After the fact, it seems clear, and not surprising, that these two groups would be the least committed to economic orthodoxy and the most willing to experiment in times of stress.[23]

The business history of the period is not sufficiently detailed to permit careful exploration of differential capacity to accept the costs of participating in such a coalition. Some evidence, however, fits the pattern outlined earlier. Before the Depression, the high-technology export industries and their banking allies, the Wallenbergs, had been the most likely to ally with labor. At the bottom of the Depression, the tension between the two was great: the internationalists wanted to lower wage costs, not to raise them as the cow trade would. Yet size makes a difference: the fortress within which economic nationalism protected domestic demand in the United States and Germany was large; in Sweden, it would have been hopelessly small for Electrolux, Swedish ballbearings, Erickson, and the other firms reliant on international

22. Steven Koblik, ed., *Sweden's Development from Poverty to Affluence*, trans. by Joanne Johnson (Minneapolis: University of Minnesota Press, 1975).
23. The controversy about whether their ideas were derived from the British discussion of the late 1920s, led by Keynes, or were a native product derived from socialist concepts of underconsumption and Swedish economists is not relevant here.

markets. The smaller firms of relatively low technology (building, cement, etc.) were, conversely, sympathetic to the stimulation of domestic purchasing power.[24]

Prior to 1936, the "rejectionist" elements of Swedish industry hoped to break up the cow coalition. When the election of 1936 strengthened it, they sought an alliance instead. The understanding embodied in the Saltsjobaden agreement of 1938 traded business acceptance of social-democratic government, high labor costs (wages and the welfare state), full-employment fiscal policy, and government activism for social services in exchange for labor peace in labor markets (no strikes), continuation of private control over property and capital markets, and openness in relation to the world economy. This pattern has prevailed in Sweden to the present time. The bourgeois coalition that has held office since 1976 has been unable to alter the power relationships that compel the overall policy pattern.

While the new fiscal policy of demand-stimulated employment aroused much attention in Sweden, it would not have much effect on Swedish economic life until after World War II. Sweden's recovery in the 1930s was due much more to the revival of the international economy for reasons completely beyond local control (policies pursued in the major markets of Germany, the United States, and the United Kingdom) and to Swedish policy decisions that took advantage of that revival—the devaluation of 1931 (which was in fact beyond Swedish control as well), low interest rates that stimulated building and investment, and considerable private restructuring of industry.[25] Even in Sweden the improvement remained limited until the war stimulus wiped out unemployment. Demand stimulus and government economic intervention became politically and intellectually respectable in the 1930s, even if their real effects were then limited to agriculture, insurance schemes, and some leadership of direct investment (rural electrification). The gradual economic improvement worked to the benefit of the Social Democrats; in this case incumbency was a benefit, allowing the Social Democrats to lock in the coalition's members and the ideas used to launch it.[26]

---

24. Erik Dahmen, *Entrepreneurial Activity and the Development of Swedish Industry, 1919–1939*, trans. by Axel Leijonhvud (Homewood, Ill.: Richard D. Irwin, 1970). This is a particularly interesting economic history for the purposes of the approach taken here, because it is one of the few that disaggregates by industrial sector.

25. For critical evaluations of the course of Swedish policy in the 1930s, see Bo Gustafson, "A Perennial of Doctrinal History: Keynes and the 'Stockholm' School," *Economy and History* 16 (1973): 114–28; T. A. Tilton, "A Swedish Road to Socialism: Ernst Wigforss and the Ideological Foundations of Swedish Social Democracy," *American Political Science Review* 73 (June 1979): 505–20; Donald Winch, "The Keynesian Revolution in Sweden," *Journal of Political Economy* 74 (April 1966): 168–76; Carl G. Uhr, "The Emergence of the 'New Economics' in Sweden: A Review of a Study by Otto Steiger," *History of Political Economy* 5 (Spring 1973): 243–60; and various articles by Lars Jonung based on his current research: "Knut Wicksell's Norm of Price Stabilization and Swedish Monetary Policy in the 1930s," *Journal of Monetary Economics* 5 (1979); and "The Depression in Sweden and the United States: A Comparison of Causes and Policies," in Karl Brunner, ed., *The Great Depression Revisited* (Boston: Martinus Nijhoff, 1981).

26. From the large literature on Sweden in this period, note: Andrew Martin, "The Dynamics

The United Kingdom

Sweden saw constitutionalist demand stimulus, Germany nonconstitutionalist demand stimulus, and the United States an export business adaptation to demand stimulus. The United Kingdom experienced a constitutionalist rejection of demand stimulus. The rejection of both socialist orthodoxy and demand stimulus did not (as the "gaming" model referred to above supposed) inexorably lead either to further economic degeneration or to the destruction of constitutional government. Britain shows it was possible to stop with the neo-orthodox moves away from the old ways, without driving labor to rebellion or crushing it with police terror. Nor, indeed, could the mixed-market solution of cheap money in the context of a devalued pound, higher tariffs, and cartelization be called a complete failure.

The common image is that, by sticking to market-oriented orthodoxies, Britain continued to sink and stagnate. It proves to be at least exaggerated, if not quite false. Some recovery occurred, and Britain did better in the 1930s than before (partly a comment on how badly it did in the 1920s). Some historians attribute the improvement to the impact of new inventions—rayons, electrical goods, autos—as the product cycle moved across the Atlantic. The interesting argument, however, concerns not whether some improvement occurred in Britain but whether the strategy pursued was suboptimal and whether labor lost a major opportunity to establish political hegemony like their Swedish counterparts. Unemployment never sank below 10 percent across the decade. Could Britain have done better with demand stimulus? H. W. Arndt and many other economic historians think so; the neoclassicists think not.[27]

---

of Change in a Keynesian Political Economy: The Swedish Case and Its Implications," in Crouch, *State and Economy*; Koblik, *Sweden's Development*; Dahmen, *Entrepreneurial Activity*; Eli F. Heckscher, *An Economic History of Sweden*, trans. by Goran Ohlin (Cambridge: Harvard University Press, 1954); Walter Korpi, *The Working Class in Welfare Capitalism: Work, Unions, and Politics in Sweden* (London: Routledge & Kegan Paul, 1978); Leif Lewin, Bo Jansson, and Dag Sorbom, *The Swedish Electorate, 1887–1968* (Stockholm: Almquist & Wiksell, 1972); Assar Lindbeck, *Swedish Economic Policy* (London: Macmillan, 1975); Arthur Montgomery, *How Sweden Overcame the Depression, 1930–1933* (1938; rpt., New York: Johnson, 1972); Sven Anders Soderpalm, *Direktorsklubben-Storindustrin i svensk politik under 1930- och 40 - talen* (Zenit: Raben & Sjorgen, 1976); Herbert Tingsten, *The Swedish Social Democrats: Their Ideological Development*, trans. by Greta Frankel and Patricia Howard-Rosen (Totowa, N.J.: Bedminster Press, 1973); Olle Nyman, *Svensk parlamentarism 1932–1936: Fran minoritets parlamentarism till majoritetskoalition* (Uppsala: Almquist & Wiksell, 1947).

27. Arndt, *Economic Lessons of the Nineteen-Thirties*; Derek H. Aldcroft and Harry W. Richardson, *Building in the British Economy between the Wars* (London: Allen & Unwin, 1968); Harry W. Richardson, *Economic Recovery in Britain, 1932–39* (London: Weidenfeld & Nicolson, 1967); Alexander Youngson, *The British Economy, 1920–57* (Cambridge: Harvard University Press, 1960); Donald Winch, *Economics and Policy: A Historical Study* (New York: Walker, 1969); Keith J. Hancock, "Reduction of Unemployment as a Problem of Public Policy, 1920–29," *Economic History Review*, 2d ser., 15 (December 1962): 328–43, and "Unemployment and the Economists in the 1920s," *Economica*, n.s., 27 (1960): 305–21; Alfred Kahn, *Great Britain in the World Economy* (New York: Columbia University Press, 1946); Susan Strange, *Sterling and British Policy* (London: Oxford University Press, 1971).

There was less policy experimentation in the United Kingdom in the 1930s than in other countries, and a Liberal-Labour (Lib-Lab) coalition pursuing Keynesian policies failed to develop. Examining the relationship of British economic interest groups to the international economy may help account for the specificity of the British case. Two features of the British economy are particularly striking: the finance-trading complex identified with the City, and the relatively small and modernized agricultural sector. The strength of the former reinforced British attachments to orthodoxy and resistance to the inward-looking status of Keynes's ideas in the early 1930s. The weakness of the latter deprived labor and dissident business elements of small-holding property owners as political allies with whom to challenge that orthodoxy.

Despite images of British consensus to the contrary, there had been disagreement about British economic policy for many years. Joseph Chamberlain led Birminghan-centered steel and other industries menaced by the new trading conditions of the post 1873 era to clamor for tariffs. Despite some agricultural and labor support, he failed. The conflict continued in the 1920s. The international banks and their allies (shipping, insurance) pressed for a rapid return to convertibility, and at a high rate; industry feared that a high rate would price its goods out of foreign markets and force deflationary policies, cutting into domestic markets. The bank view prevailed, forcing sharp deflationary pressure that led to the General Strike of 1926 and a major defeat for labor. It is in this context that Ramsay MacDonald came to power in 1929. The defeat of 1926 undermined Labour's willingness to challenge the internationalist orthodoxy, and contributed to that immense concern for the approval of the City which seems characteristic of Labour party politicians (though not union leaders) from MacDonald to Wilson and Callaghan.

The trade unions did press for public works and deficit spending. While serving on the Macmillan Committee, whose mandate was to explore the country's economic plight, Ernest Bevin had been deeply impressed by the failure of the banking-Treasury world to consider the implications of exchange and interest-rate policy for industry and employment. Fighting unemployment by getting factories to produce again appealed to his pragmatic mind, and he led the Trades Union Congress (TUC) to accept the new idea. Some figures in the Labour party supported the notion as well, most notably Oswald Mosley. The two top party officials, MacDonald and Philip Snowden, remained resolutely orthodox.[28]

As the Depression deepened, criticism rose not only in labor ranks but also in the opposition. The Conservatives accepted deflation but wanted tariffs as well, though not devaluation. It was the Liberals who pressed hardest on behalf of public works and deficit budgets, to accompany tariffs or de-

---

28. Alan Bullock, *The Life and Times of Ernest Bevin*, vol. 1 (London: Heinemann, 1960); Robert Skidelsky, *Politicians and the Slump* (London: Macmillan, 1967).

valuation or both. Almost a decade before the publication of *The General Theory*, Keynes and other economists helped work out for the Liberals a "Programme of Expansion" (its slogan was "We Can Beat Unemployment"). These programmatic statements criticized the stress placed on the pound, arguing that the currency should serve productivity and employment, not the reverse. Keynes and the Liberals accepted devaluation of the pound. Though historically the Liberals were free traders, and continued to criticize the Conservative push for tariffs, Keynes and the Liberals were willing to contemplate devaluation, which has a protectionist effect.

It is by no means easy to explain why it should have been the Liberals who in the late 1920s took up this Chamberlainian theme in the new intellectual guise developed by Keynes. The Liberal social base seems still to have been free–trade-oriented elements of industry and agriculture. The sorts of industries that had sustained critiques of banking and free-trade orthodoxy, and complained constantly during the 1920s to various committees, had Conservative party ties, not Liberal ones, and could be pulled over toward the more cautious tariff-cartel version the Tories preferred.

The answer may lie in the dynamics of party rivalry and leadership. The Liberals were, after all, in deep political trouble, and they needed political "product differentiation," arguments with mass appeal. Unemployment was certainly of immense political significance; attacking both Labour and the Conservatives as wrong-headed made political sense, and the solution proposed had the political virtue of being neither clearly protectionist (so as not to offend the powerful "cheap loaf" stance of laboring-class voters) nor orthodox socialist (so as not to offend the middle-class electorate). Leadership also mattered: Lloyd George was a risk taker, looking for arguments for a comeback, and smart enough to be convinced by the reasoning of smart men like Keynes. His behavior contrasts sharply with the intellectual rigidity of Snowden, MacDonald, and Stanley Baldwin.[29]

Hitching Keynes to the Liberal party base aggravated an already strained situation. As Labour resisted the proffered Lib-Lab alliance, the Liberals crumbled under the pull of competing policy programs. By 1931, so many had defected that it was no longer clear that there remained a large enough "Lib" to construct a working majority even if MacDonald were finally to try for one.

Since the Liberals were the third party, the interpretation of policy debates in the period cannot end with speculation about why they took up Keynes. Breaking with deflationist orthodoxy required help from other social forces and party formations. Elements of the Conservative party were sensitive to the needs of manufacturing industry as distinct from the banking-shipping

---

29. Dennis A. Kavanagh, "Crisis and Management and Incremental Adaptation in British Politics: The 1931 Crisis of the British Party System," in Gabriel Almond et al., ed., *Crisis, Choice, and Change: Historical Studies of Political Development* (Boston: Little, Brown, 1973).

wing. Such people provided support for some break from the old orthodoxy, but not enough to go the next step. As in America, the major debate in business circles was between classical "free trade-deflation-defense of the pound" orthodoxy and "protectionism-cartelization" deviations. The elements interested in more activist, government-led schemes could not persuade their business compatriots to go along. This is not surprising; elsewhere, firms interested in demand stimulus did not get it by convincing their business brethren of its merits but by allying with other groups intensely dissatisfied with the market mechanisms (labor and agriculture).

In the United Kingdom, the "steel-syndrome" bloc of businesses had some "positional" disadvantages compared to their counterparts in other countries. First, in no other country did industry face such a large bloc of interests tied to international trade and payments.[30] As I have suggested, demand stimulus in the first phase appealed primarily to domestically oriented elements of the economy. But no other country at the time had so many interests living off remittances, loans, shipping, and the like; the United States, Germany, and Sweden had fewer foreign investments and did not manage a reserve currency. To some degree, this internationalism inhibited militarism: autarchy could not be appealing to those who lived off international trade and hence militarism lacked an important legitimizing force. Furthermore, agriculture as a sector was smaller in Britain than anywhere else, also the consequence of having been the first industrializer. This meant fewer potential allies for the attack on money, banks, and internationalism. Finally, British labor was very deeply wedded to the cheap loaf, making the construction of a protectionist alliance including labor that much harder. (Though, as the experience of Joseph Chamberlain shows, workers as electors could be won over to protectionism more easily than their representative organizations.)

The most puzzling question of all is why the Labour party did not take up demand stimulus. There is every likelihood that had Labour done so, it could have concluded an alliance with the Liberals. Credit for the post 1932 recovery (a probability whatever the government actually did) would have gone to them, not to the Conservatives. British politics might have looked more like the Swedish variety, dominated by labor for a couple of generations. The interpretative problems are quite similar to those raised when the same question is applied to the German Social Democrats. Snowden, like Hilferding, did not believe in the demand-stimulus arguments; he was operating a market economy, with orthodox rules. MacDonald seems to have been heavily influenced by "good elite opinion," which excluded Keynes and Lloyd George. Thus the top party leadership was socialized into the British "orthodoxy."

30. Frank Longstreth, "The City, Industry and the State," in Crouch, *State and Economy*; Robert Gilpin, *United States Power and the Multinational Corporation* (New York: Basic Books, 1975); Stephen Blank, "Britain: The Politics of Foreign Economic Policy," in Peter Katzenstein, ed., *Between Power and Plenty* (Madison: University of Wisconsin Press, 1977); Samuel H. Beer, *British Politics in the Collectivist Age* (New York: Alfred A. Knopf, 1965)."

As in Germany, the trade union leadership may have been more open to new arguments because of a greater pragmatism born of closeness to labor-market conditions. But Bevin could not persuade MacDonald; MacDonald talked endlessly with the Liberals, but failed to make the agreement. In 1931 the Labour party was unified in opposing Snowden and MacDonald, though the issue was cutting unemployment benefits, not a program of public works. It seems highly likely that had the party leadership formed the Lib-Lab alliance around a demand-stimulus scheme, both the TUC and the parliamentary Labour party would have supported it. The subsequent evolution of British policy and politics would then have been quite different.

The actual story is well known and needs no lengthy discussion: MacDonald tried to save the pound through the further deflationary move of cutting unemployment insurance, was expelled from the Labour party, and formed a new government excluding most of the party. The pound quickly proved undefendable. When the financial circles most deeply wedded to a strong currency realized this, MacDonald devalued. Soon afterwards Britain adopted its first significant peacetime tariffs since the Corn Laws. The Conservatives quickly came to dominate the National Government and were swept into power at the next election. Under the impact of tariffs, very low interest rates, innovations, and the revival of demand in other countries, the British economy did improve. Low interest rates plus automobiles and electrification helped spur shifts in residential patterns, and a housing boom ensued. The government helped with electrification, and eventually via military purchases, but demand stimulus per se did not occur until after World War II.

The British case shows well the interaction between political choice and sectoral constraints. The contours of alternative coalitions supporting different policy options can be detected and appear plausible, but they faced obstacles that, while not insurmountable, appear large. The unique role of the City, the smallness of the agricultural sector, the orientation of labor toward the cheap loaf, and the cultural hegemony of economic orthodoxy in the first nation to have industrialized—these constraints, in the absence of political imagination in the right place (with the Liberals instead of Labour) and with the historical accident of a Labour government in office at the onset of the Depression, proved insurmountable.

France

An extremely cursory glance across the Channel shows promising similarities between France and the other cases. An undervalued franc helped keep the Depression at bay for several years. Products flowed out, gold flowed in, and prosperity prevailed. After 1931, currency devaluations all over the world reversed the relationship, and finally brought the Depression to France. Conservative governments tried the classic deflationary remedy by cutting budgets and pressing on wages. The conservative cabinets drew for support on agriculture, business, and conservative (Catholic) workers, to the exclusion of the labor unions and labor-connected parties. After the march on the Palais Bourbon in 1934, an alterntive coalition gradually took shape. The elections of 1936 changed both economic policy and governing coalition. The Popular Front linked together the labor formations, elements of agriculture, and the "republican" bourgeoisie. Léon Blum attempted elements of the social-democratic package being worked out in Sweden and the United States: social insurance, higher wages, and deficit spending. Economic policy, however, was but one of a number of extremely controversial issues weighing down the French polity, and but one of the issues that brought down the Popular Front a year later. For my purposes, the important element of the case is the politics of the break with deflation: what groups supported that attempt, and through what political formula? To win the election of 1936, to govern, and to shift economic policy, the Socialists had to construct and to manage a very diverse alliance, from Communists *téléguidé* by Stalin to the highly bourgeois constituency of the Radical party. What sorts of farmers, what sorts of bourgeois were willing to link up with elements of labor in such a coalition?[31]

Labor's criticism of orthodoxy was made easier than in Germany and Britain by the exclusion of labor-related organizations from governing coalitions as France entered the Depression. Like any opposition, the Socialists, Communists, and trade unions could mobilize discontent without being judged on actual performance and without being very clear about what compromises each would accept if actually in power. In theoretical terms, the Socialists and Communists interpreted the Depression as a crisis of capitalism to be solved only by socialization of the economy. In the political reality of the mid 1930s, however, socialization was not possible within a constitutionalist framework. The Socialists had long since become defenders of the Republic; the Communists switched to that stance after the Nazi seizure of power in Germany. In formulating a program for labor, both parties sought to accommodate the demands of other groups (agriculture and elements of business) and parties (the Radicals).

As in other countries, agriculture was a major source of discontent with orthodox deflation. As in other countries, bourgeois governments did relatively little to help the countryside deal with plunging prices. Whatever their partisan attachments, farmers agitated for some sort of assistance, be it price supports, government purchases, or marketing agreements. In their discontent with deflation, farmers moved politically in different directions: some to the Right (Dorgères, for example), others to the Left (particularly to the Communists, who gained the most votes among the three parties of the Popular Front coalition). Electoral sociology on what sort of farmer moved which way focuses on certain demographic characteristics of farmers (size of holding,

---

31. François Goguel, *La politique des partis sous la IIIe République* (Paris: Seuil, 1946).

location, religion). But it has omitted various situational features: the product raised, the nature of the farm's relationship to markets, recent experience with government policies. In short, rural discontent with orthodox deflation appears clearer than the mechanisms by which that discontent was translated into political action. Large blocs of farmers appear to have been available to support programs of state intervention in the rural economy—not socialization, but corporatism (neo-orthodoxy).[32]

In France, as elsewhere, a farmer-labor alliance was not enough. Support from at least some elements of the bourgeoisie was vital, but it materialized only to a limited degree. Bourgeois support for the Popular Front was strong enough to win the election of 1936, sustain defense of the Republic for a few years, and to work out and ratify the Matignon accords as a solution to the sit-down strikes. It was not strong enough to sustain the Blum government in office, to continue the economic program begun in 1936, and in the long run generate a cross-class program of national self-defense. As one of the leading historians of the Popular Front, Georges Dupeux, has written, the moderate social-democratic policy stance of Léon Blum failed because it lacked a necessary partner—a moderate business bourgeoisie.[33]

A situational interpretation of this absent partner would stress the relative weakness in the French economy of strong, internationally competitive, high-technology, low labor-component industries and firms. "Progressive" ideas about business-labor relations received a hearing in France during the interwar years, and Ernest Mercier and Auguste Detoeuf are perhaps the best-known French equivalents to Carl Duisberg. Their industry was electrical equipment. But these figures and industries are strikingly atypical of French economic history from 1870 to 1940, which is full of the destruction of economic pioneers rather than of their success. The men who represented business in the Matignon agreements came from the largest companies, particularly in metallurgy. They were bitterly attacked by the smaller, more backward companies and forced out of offices in the employers' association.[34] Most French industry was small, labor-intensive, and overwhelmingly protectionist. Few businessmen were in the market for allies to create an open, internationalist strategy.

Small property owners, however, were by no means unanimous defenders of orthodox deflation. In France as elsewhere smallholders were cross-pressured: fearful of labor radicalism, fearful of big business and untrammeled competition. Attacks against *les gros*, the *deux cent familles*, the *mur d'argent*

32. Michel Auge-Laribe, *La politique agricole de la France* (Paris: PUF, 1950); Charles K. Warner, *The Winegrowers of France and the Government since 1875* (New York: Columbia University Press, 1960).
33. Georges Dupeux, *Le Front populaire et les élections de 1939* (Paris: Armand Colin, 1959).
34. Henry Ehrmann, *Organized Business in France* (Princeton: Princeton University Press, 1957); Richard Kuisel, *Ernest Mercier: French Technocrat* (Berkeley: University of California Press, 1967).

resonated loudly, and were by no means the monopoly of the Left. The Radical party electorate had little sympathy for nationalization and deep hostility to devaluation, but it did have some sympathy for an effort to break free of deflation.

These conflicting pressures from diverse constituencies put the Blum government into a bind from which, interestingly, "demand-stimulus" experimentation was an easier next move than "neo-orthodoxy." Despite the prior experience of other countries that had vainly sought to defend the currency, virtually all segments of the French public remained attached to the defense of the franc Poincaré. Only one politician of any significance, Paul Reynaud, pleaded for devaluation, and he was scorned for his efforts. The Left parties proposed exchange controls instead of devaluation, but this was unacceptable to the Radicals.

Thus orthodoxy had been tried and found wanting, and socialization of the economy and currency devaluation were both unacceptable.[35] Reflating the economy through some sort of demand stimulus was the only possibility left. Quite uninfluenced by Keynes, the Socialists drew upon an old tradition in Left thinking about the economy: underconsumption theory. The central predicament of capitalism in this view was the tension between production and consumption: the capitalists' squeezing of the surplus prevented workers from having enough money to buy the output. Higher wages for workers and higher prices for farmers would reflate the economy through higher demand. Through the Matignon agreements and subsequent legislation the Socialists increased wages, constructed a national retirement system, a limited work week, paid vacations, and trade union rights. For agriculture, the Popular Front extended corporatistic marketing arrangements through the Office du Blé.

The effort to resist devaluation failed. Blum refused to do it upon taking office, but by September runs on the franc proved unstoppable, and, as in the United Kingdom, a Labour-type government finally gave up monetary orthodoxy when the guardians of that orthodoxy (the bankers, elite economic opinion) said it had to be done.[36]

35. Jean Bouvier, "Un débat toujours ouvert: la politique économique du Front populaire," *Le mouvement social* no. 54 (January–March 1966): 175–81; Daniel Guérin, *Front populaire, révolution manquée*, rev. ed. (Paris: Maspéro, 1970); M. Kalecki, "Lessons of the Blum Experiment," *Economic Journal* 48 (March 1938): 26–41; Georges Lefranc, *Histoire du Front populaire*, 2d ed. (Paris: Payot, 1974); Robert Marjolin, "Reflections on the Blum Experiment," *Economica*, n.s., 5 (May 1938): 177–91; Alfred Sauvy, *Histoire économique de la France entre les deux guerres* (Paris: Fayard, 1967), vol. 2: *1931–39*, and also some interesting articles in vol. 4.

36. Daniel Brower, *The New Jacobins: The French Communist Party and the Popular Front* (Ithaca: Cornell University Press, 1968); Louis Bodin and Jean Touchard, *Le Front populaire de 1936* (Paris: Armand Colin, 1961); Nathanael Greene, *Crisis and Decline: The French Socialist Party in the Popular Front Era* (Ithaca: Cornell University Press, 1969); Pierre Broué and Nicole Dorey, "Critiques de gauche et opposition révolutionnaire au Front populaire (1936–38)," *Le mouvement social* no. 54 (January–March 1966): 91–133; Joel Colton, *Léon Blum* (New York: Alfred A. Knopf, 1966); Henry Ehrmann, *French Labor from Popular Front to Liberation* (New York: Oxford University Press, 1947); Jean Lacouture, *Léon Blum* (Paris: Seuil, 1977).

In France neither break with orthodoxy (the full break of demand stimulus, tried first, and the partial break of devaluation, tried second) helped the economy very much. Capital fled the country, inflation was sharp, and production did not increase. Within a year the government fell. New coalitions swung rightward, and unraveled much of the Popular Front's reforms: the work week was lengthened, real wages sank, and unions were ignored or brushed aside. While the coalition of interests that supported the Popular Front looked a lot like those who supported the crisis coalition in Sweden (agriculture, labor, and some elements of business), the solidity of the latter proved far greater than the former's. France thus saw the weakest and least successful demand-stimulus coalition in a parliamentary system.

In exploring these questions, I do not mean to brush aside the other forces that shaped voting and alliances: the existence of a strong Republican, revolutionary, and anticlerical tradition in France among farmers, businessmen, teachers, professionals, and civil servants certainly affected Popular Front politics; so did the example of the collapse of Weimar, which galvanized Republican defense and helped get the Communists to switch over. The coalition may have come into being to save the Republic, but the coalition formed for that purpose also had capabilities in economic policy different from those of the previous (or succeeding) coalitions.

Conclusion

What generalizations does this all-too-rapid tour d'horizon sustain? There appears to be some consistency across countries in the "marginal propensity" of various groups to support, or fail to support, demand-stimulus policies in the 1930s. The patience of various actors with orthodoxy and neo-orthodoxy was not uniform. At the level of interest groups (or, in a different usage, social forces) trade unions, agricultural associations, and domestically oriented heavy industry were the first to find appeal in policies that went beyond the market mechanism in general terms, and, more specifically, policies involving government pump priming, and job and demand creation.

At the height of the Depression, in 1932–33, these were the groups most likely either to press for or to support state-led solutions to the crisis. The opponents of such moves were likely to be the international wings of the various economic sectors: international (though not domestic) banking, export industries, export-oriented agriculture, and perhaps export-related labor. Later, as economies revived and other issues changed, the politics of demand stimulus changed as well. Conflicts within the reflation coalition over wages, welfare, industrial relations, and foreign economic policy reopened the political struggle (where the survival of constitutional government allowed it), leading to the formation of a new coalition linking internationalism in economic policy to the promotion of demand at home, through fiscal policy, social insurance, and wages.

By and large, this is consistent with the hypothesis that policy preferences toward the Depression can best be explained as a function of a group's "situation" in the economy, where situation is defined as a composite of international competitiveness, labor component, technology, and so on. Situations change—the international distribution of labor, business cycles (long and short), technological innovation, and events are of course constantly in motion. Big changes in situation induce reexamination of policy preferences and of political needs. Actors try one alternative, then if need be another, and we observe *policy sequences*—economic actors move to different policies in response to changing economic circumstances and changing political circumstances.

Deflation was an internationalist strategy. It aimed at beating down domestic costs of production to lower prices, in order to revive foreign and domestic sales. Neo-orthodoxy marked a step toward a nationalist strategy. It funneled domestic demand toward domestic products, given the inadequacy of international demand, and shared out production among existing domestic producers.[37] Demand stimulus entered this policy sequence as an accentuation of economic nationalism, then shifted quite rapidly to association with internationalism. In the 1980s this historical link of demand stimulus to internationalism is under strain, and the strategy is increasingly associated with nationalistic tendencies. Demand stimulus may then have one political meaning in a worsening economic environment, another when things are improving—when the high-technology, lower labor-component, export-oriented industries have an internationalism to sell.

Shifts in policy correspond to shifts in politics, which correspond to shifts in group demands, which in turn correspond to changes in the international economy. A given policy preference is not necessarily in the "interest" of the actor. On the contrary, it is possible to posit a calculus or frame of reference that could make a range of conflicting policies reasonable from the standpoint of different strategies. Thus by one strategy international business should support demand stimulus in 1933, by another it should oppose it. The way out of this interpretative trap is to be sociological, to ask what sorts of strategy various groups actually did prefer. Some groups may tend to evolve certain visions, or shift group preferences, more readily or rapidly than others. When we find such patterns, we can reason backwards to ask what logic underlies these different responses. As I have noted, I am exploring the extent to which that logic may be "situational." This will inevitably sound as if I argue "they had to do it because it was in their interests, and

---

37. On economic policy and nationalism in the 1930s, see Albert Hirschman, *National Power and the Structure of Foreign Trade* (Berkeley: University of California Press, 1945); David Kaiser, *Economic Diplomacy and the Causes of the Second World War* (Princeton: Princeton University Press, 1980).

they could do nothing else." But what I wish to convey is "they did it because people occupying that situation were likely to think that way." An adequate critique of the argument, therefore, is not that the reader can think of an alternative strategy which a particular group could in principle have followed. Rather, it would be that a particular group did not follow the expected course; or that some other logic underlies the pattern observed; or that there is no pattern at the level of groups.

Is "situation" the only explanation, or the best one? Alternative interpretations are possible, and I have suggested some of their strengths and limitations. I find it significant, and surprising, that while there are plenty of alternative explanations of the *politics* of the period (fascism, constitutionalism, etc.) there are no alternative explanations of the *policies* of the period. The political culture, political leadership, party system, bureaucratic politics, economic ideology, and international-system explanations of the adoption and rejection of economic policies on a *comparative* basis in the 1930s remain to be constructed. Such explanations—as types—are familiar, but they are familiar because of their use regarding outcomes other than economic policy.[38]

Discussion of the "best" explanation often stresses too heavily the choice among alternatives rather than the piece of the whole, or the function, that each handled. For example, it is not a question of whether leadership mattered but of what materials leadership could use—what constraints or opportunities were provided by group situation. Thus the classic criticism of Bentleyism—a statement of the groups does not state everything—is correct but incomplete. Such a statement specifies the constraints and opportunities of leadership and other forces. It clarifies the material with which politicians have to work, the structural conditions on which ideologies, earlier experiences, institutional attachments, defense issues, and so on have to work. It suggests the forces that contribute to group strategies. And in a world of complex situations, we need more ideas about how groups operate, not fewer.[39]

The same point can be made in relation to other causal variables favored in other discourse. I am not a priori opposed to institutional or political culture arguments. Institutions obviously affect the struggle for power: for a specified production profile, different institutional arrangements promote different outcomes. Weimar remains the locus classicus. Similarly, culture matters: actors rarely understand a situation solely of itself. Prior experiences and analytic approaches shape current analysis. German steel's preference for military over civilian modes of government aid is but one example. But

38. See the many interesting chapters in Suzanne Berger, ed., *Organizing Interests in Western Europe* (New York: Cambridge University Press, 1981).

39. For an interpretation of postwar economic policy that stresses the structure and number of interest groups (as opposed to their specific substance) see Mancur Olson, *The Rise and Decline of Nations* (New Haven: Yale University Press, 1982). For an interpretation of links between the general approach to policy and the social implications of technology, see Michael Piore and Charles Sabel's forthcoming book, tentatively entitled "The Industrial Divide: Technology and the Institutions of Coordination and Stabilization in Advanced Industrial Capitalism."

these variables cannot be lifted out of social context and fired off as explanatory cannon. How the institutions matter depends on who is trying to use them. How a particular ideology about political economy affects an actor depends on the actor's situation. The same ideology or institution may produce different outcomes according to the actors on whom they operate.

The contribution of this article (and of the approach it uses) is to structure more carefully the relationship between society and mediating variables by insisting on the importance of the former in making sense out of the latter. To note that at this or that point leadership, or institution, or culture is being used as part of the explanation is no criticism of the argument, since my goal has been from the beginning to see just where these variables might matter. Thus, in the British case, I stress not that leadership was unimportant, but that whatever leader sought to break with orthodoxy would have drawn support (and resistance) from identifiable sources. Looking at why these sources were weaker or stronger in the United Kingdom than in other places tells us something about the likelihood of a particular outcome.

Much of this article has considered whether other policies were possible in each country. But were other *politics* possible, either connected with the actual policy followed or with another policy? My line of inquiry has brought out the importance of a variable neglected in current discourse on political outcomes: the significance of economic policy in shaping preferences for leaders, parties, cabinets, and regimes. The capacity of different political formulae to accommodate various policies can be explored by testing out alternative combinations of support. In some cases the obstacles seem only moderate, for example a Lib-Lab coalition in Britain. In others, the obstacles seem formidable, though not totally impossible, for example in Germany a neo-orthodox policy shift under a moderate constitutionalist (Muller of the Center party) or a military dictator (Schleicher); or in the same country, a demand-stimulus break under a moderate constitutionalist (Stressman) or a military dictator (Schleicher). There was nothing inevitable about the cow coalition in Sweden, or a Republican incumbency in 1929 helping a Democratic counterattack. Alternative outcomes were thus possible, though only within specific limits whose patterns this article has sought to establish.

The patterns that emerged in the 1930s, and were consolidated in the postwar years, are now under considerable stress. Argument over how to interpret the 1930s is an argument over how to interpret the 1980s, how to predict what is likely to happen, and how to prescribe it. The stretchmarks of previous booms and busts remain, not only in the reality of political conflicts but in the minds of those who fight over interpretation and explanation. Intellectual and political tasks intertwine: the ability to imagine alternatives in both policy options and political formulas may well have a bearing on which solutions succeed. The 1930s were too costly for us not to think about what we can learn from them for the present.

[13]
International industrial cartels, the state and politics: Great Britain between the wars

CLEMENS A. WURM

For an understanding of multinational enterprise it is necessary to include an analysis of international cartels. Between the wars they formed an important structural characteristic of the world economy. According to contemporary reckoning in the 1930s between 30% and 50% of world trade was controlled or influenced by international agreements or 'loose associations'. Up until the early years after the Second World War they held the attention of scholars, journalists and politicians in the same manner as the multinational concerns have since the 1960s. And like the latter they have been judged in highly differing, or contradictory manners.

International cartels performed a number of functions, which are fulfilled today by multinational enterprises. In individual cases an international cartel could even become a multinational concern[1]; occasionally it is described as a 'forerunner' of multinational enterprise. International cartels are generally less stable and their resources more limited than those of multinational concerns or national cartels, although they can, as Alice Teichova has pointed out, react to changes swiftly and with flexibility, and represent a more effective instrument of economic penetration than direct investment.[2] Mainly – although not always – large enterprises were the driving force in the formation of international cartels. They preferred, according to region and product, to secure the market by direct investment or an agreement with competitors.

International cartels do not abolish competition. They shift the arena and change the rules according to which it takes place. They are economic creations; in general, they owe their formation to private initiative. During the inter-war period, however, the state was also involved in their creation; the government of the day was more often the driving force than was industry. Their promotion became a 'tool of politics',[3] a means by which to strengthen the position of national groups on the world market or to suppress the activity of rivals. In a period which was characterised by extreme economic nationalism and increasing concentration of political and economic power, the massive intervention of practically all governments in foreign trade and the protection of the flank by the state formed – next to classical factors like competitiveness and technical know-how – a decisive element in the negotiating strength and capacity of firms to maintain their hold on world markets.

The following sections examine the co-operation, or lack of co-operation, of British industry and government in the formation of cartels in the country's 'old' industries. They refer principally to the iron and steel industry, the cotton industry and coal mining. They proceed methodically from the premise that international cartels can only be suitably analysed if the widely diverging questions of economic and political historiography are brought closer together. In contrast, for example, to the chemical industry, which, from 1926, was dominated by a single firm, the branches considered here are composed of an abundance of firms, highly differentiated in size, structure, technology and market position. They are sectors in which national production methods were decisive. In the steel industry alone and for some of the products of its rolling mills, multinational enterprises played a big role (Stewarts & Lloyds; Dorman Long & Co.; Guest, Keen and Nettlefolds etc.). Historically determined structural conditions and the lack of modernisation made them dependent on political action to an extraordinary degree.

I

To improve our understanding it is necessary to introduce briefly the essential facts about the international cartelisation of the industries under consideration. In iron and steel, the European Steel Cartel (Internationale Rohstahlgemeinschaft (IRG)) was created in 1926 by the most important continental producer countries (Germany, France, Belgium, Luxemburg as well as the Saar). The British industry remained apart from this institution. However in 1935–6 they did join the successor organisation, the International Steel Cartel (Internationale Rohstahlexportgemeinschaft (IREG)) and its marketing association, which were formed in 1933. There was a whole series of cartels for special products like rails, pipes and tinplate, in which British industry was involved to a large extent. In coal mining, the Anglo-Polish Agreement, signed in December 1934, limited Polish seaborne coal exports to 21% of the British. In 1937, after the creation of several smaller cartels between national groups from Germany, Britain, the Netherlands, Belgium and Poland, a comprehensive agreement was signed to cover the price, market share and sales conditions for coke. The coal agreement signed in January 1939 between the Mining Asociation of Great Britain and the Rheinisch-Westfaelisches Kohlensyndikat, according to which Britain got 46.27% and Germany 32.08% of total European exports, did not come into effect before the outbreak of the war. The British attempt, in 1933–4, to divide up the world cotton textile market with the Japanese failed because of Japanese resistance.

II

Even before the First World War British industry had made various international agreements. According to the estimates of P. T. Fischer and H. Wagenfuehr, in 1929 it was involved in 'at least 40 international cartels'.[4] Examples are the chemical, artificial silk and copper production industries, as well as aluminium and linoleum manufacturing. However the degree of participation in the 1920s should not be over-estimated. In important branches like steel, the British stayed out of agreements (although admittedly British companies did play an important role in the refounding of the rail cartel). In coal mining, their disapproving attitude was viewed – whether rightly or wrongly – as the main obstacle to the international cartelisation of a complete industrial branch. 'England', judged G. von Haberler at the beginning of the 1930s, 'is not a member of most international cartels.'[5]

The reasons for the British restraint are very complex. Contemporary observers have, by way of explanation, referred to the peculiarities of English law, the individualism of the entrepreneurs and the continued effect of 'Manchester-liberal' opinions. Research has shown the decisive reason to be organisational deficiencies and a lack of inner unity amongst British industry. Also the government, the Civil Service, influential bankers like R. McKenna (Midland Bank) or R. H. Brand (Baring Bros), representatives of leading concerns in the 'new' branches like Sir Alfred Mond (ICI) or Sir Hugo Hirst (General Electric Co.) and important press organs like *The Times* or *The Economist*, all viewed collaboration in national associations as an indispensable precondition for successful international negotiation and co-operation: only united national industries were able to hold their own with highly-organised foreign concerns. As Sir Hugo Hirst told steel industrialists in 1925, 'You cannot make international agreements unless you are united at home.'[6]

Without doubt fragmentation and the low degree of concentration were a serious handicap to successful cartel formation. However it remains to be seen whether other factors were not more important in individual cases. The continued faith of the government in free trade – not organisational deficits – was the decisive reason that the British steel industry remained apart from the European Steel Cartel (Rohstahlgemeinschaft) in the 1920s.[7] For a long time the British pit owners rejected the majority of international agreements absolutely. They wanted to reconstruct the competitiveness of their industry with wage cuts and win back lost market shares *before* any negotiations, in order to be better armed for the battle over quotas. Only from about

1928 – and then only gradually – was a stronger degree of support given to the view, 'that, in the future, international arrangements would be necessary'.[8]

Very little is known of the position of the cotton industrialists during the 1920s. It appears that in this period, international cartel agreements did not play a big role in their deliberations. An attempt at the end of 1929 by the Lancashire Cotton Corporation, made with the consent of the Governor of the Bank of England, to open talks with Japanese industry, met with little accommodation amongst manufacturers of the Far Eastern Empire and came to nothing.

The world economic crisis formed an important date in the inter-war cartel movement. The changes which it brought about in the politics, economy and society of Britain, created new conditions for British cartel policy. With the protective tariff, industry found the instrument that made it possible to speak as equals to foreign competitors. The devaluation of the Pound Sterling improved its competitiveness; in individual cartels this led quickly to higher quotas for British companies. Traditional obstacles to international cartels, such as the fear of exploiting the consumer or the gradual erosion of liberal economic principles, which still played a role in the 1920s, no longer determined the limits to action. Changes of view on economic policy and the widely held opinion that unregulated competition had worsened the depression by causing price falls allowed an economic order to develop, which, compared with the prewar years, was new and whose features were fixed prices, production and competition control, and a tendency to suspend the market as a regulative force.

In the strategy of individual branches or large concerns, international cartels took up a more important place than before. Market arrangements supplemented or took the place of direct investment. A study carried out for the British government during the Second World War on British participation in private international industrial agreements showed what a high proportion of the country's exports and total manufacturing at the end of the 1930s had been gained by internationally cartelised products. The study came to the conclusion that for 1938, the proportion of the export trade directly affected by international arrangements of various sorts can be put roughly at three-tenths of the total value of the exports of goods wholly or mainly manufactured. For the total gross output [in value] of the United Kingdom factory trades in 1935, the figure was around 16%. An estimate based on employment shares came to the same result.[9]

There is much to be said for the view of Geoffrey Jones, that the reduction in direct British investment abroad in the 1930s, in comparison with the 1920s has a lot to do with the fact that firms attempted to defend or win markets through agreement. 'The mirror image of the decline of multinational activity was the increased participation by British companies in international cartels.'[10] International cartels were also of importance for the geographical direction of British exports: the increased movement of British goods to the Commonwealth is, besides the Ottawa Agreements and the advantages of the Sterling Area, attributable to the preference of many – although not all – international cartels to allocate Empire markets to British firms. Finally, in many cases the existence or lack of cartel agreements was a decisive factor for company profits in individual markets. 'British companies prospered where market sharing or other arrangements were in existence and experienced difficulties where they were not.'[11]

If in the 1920s the government limited its activity in connection with international cartels to classical state functions, then in the 1930s it encouraged the participation of industry in international agreements through direct measures. Not the least of its objectives in fostering the internal cartelisation of individual branches such as coal and steel was to make possible its successful collaboration in agreements. The Import Duties Advisory Committee (IDAC), which was created in 1932 – convinced 'that the regulation of trade by international agreements is of advantage to industry in this country'[12] – recommended several times the raising of tariffs, in order to improve the negotiating position of the British group, and to secure the continued existence or make possible the re-establishment of an agreement. The best-known example is the iron and steel industry and its 'General Agreement' with the International Steel Cartel (Internationale Rohstahlexportgemeinschaft (IREG)) in 1935: the raising of the tariff to the prohibitive level of 50% forced continental firms which were dependent on the British market (according to a Treasury official) to capitulate and secured for British industry a long-term agreement to their conditions. In the case of the coal industry, the British government used its strong position in trade negotiations with Poland – which needed the British market for its agricultural produce – in order to bring about an agreement between the Mining Association of Great Britain and the Polish industry in December 1934. This established not only prices, but a fixed relationship between the total quantity of British coal exports, and Polish sea-borne exports and local border deliveries to Germany. The Scandinavian market especially was relieved of Polish price pressure through this agreement.[13] Finally, in the case of the cotton industry, the Board of Trade took the initiative, without either the knowledge or prior agreement of most of the industry, in the unsuccessful talks which the English manufacturers had with Japanese textile magnates over division of the world market. 'Lancashire', according to the deputy chairman of the LCC, John Grey, 'had been pushed into the Japanese conversations.'[14]

During the international negotiations, Whitehall and the representatives of industry kept in close contact with each other. The widespread notion that

British industrialists, in contrast to French or German, carried out their negotiations autonomously or independent from the government, is – at least in so far as it concerns the branches dealt with here – a myth. The steel industry and the IDAC were in regular contact during the talks with continental firms. The Board of Trade was informed promptly – occasionally by telephone – by British industry, over the course of important meetings with continental groups. The import quota, which the British Iron and Steel Federation (BISF) offered the international steel cartel for the provisional agreement, corresponded to the ideas of the IDAC, not the BISF. The trade conference between delegates from Lancashire and Japan from 14 February 1934 to 14 March 1934, in which the English delegation sought to win from the Japanese cotton industry a strict limitation and regulation of their exports (against the prospect of higher prices), took place in the rooms of the Board of Trade. The British manufacturers wanted this on 'psychological grounds', but it appeared that, in view of the superior competitiveness of their rivals, the power of the state was the only instrument capable of making the Japanese give way. Although the British side, in contrast to the Japanese, did not send an official observer to the talks, Sir Horace Wilson, the government's chief industrial adviser, was kept constantly informed of their progress. In the last phase of the discussion the course of proceedings was worked out in close consultation between the Board of Trade and the Lancashire delegates.

Whitehall exercised influence not only in the run-up to new agreements on quotas and in negotiations, but in individual cases Ministries pressed for higher shares in existing agreements or the reservation of particular markets for British companies. For example, officials of the Department of Overseas Trade (DOT) and the Foreign Office pointed out to the Secretary of the British group at the International Railmakers Association (IRMA), R. Lyttleton of GKN, that Britain claimed a 'considerably higher share' of the total quota (the share amounted to 23.8%), because devaluation, protective duties and bilateral trade negotiations had strengthened her position in the meantime. The exercise of direct political influence on international cartels, often complained of by contemporaries, was therefore by no means, as generally assumed, restricted to the dictators of National Socialist Germany, although the influence exercised there was more direct, more comprehensive and more decisive.

III

The motives of the government for its active role varied from case to case and do not permit generalisations. Considerations of an economic and general political nature stand in the foreground, such as the need to improve the country's balance-of-payments through the encouragement of exports (hence the pressure for higher export quotas) and to reduce unemployment, or generally the desire to stabilise market and sales conditions, and increase returns to the companies. The agreement of the BISF with the IREG, for example, formed an important element, in the view of the government, of the IDAC-determined policy which it had been following since 1932, the object of which was to revitalise the iron and steel industry.

The goals of government and industry were by no means always identical. W. Runciman of the Board of Trade wanted to raise exports by joining the International Steel Cartel; it sought the highest possible British export share against concessions on imports. In contrast, the primary matter of concern to the manufacturers was 'to put their own house in order' and that of the world steel market, as well as to achieve better prices. They gave precedence to the security of the domestic market. For them the agreement with the IREG represented the keystone in a building which effectively – indeed more effectively than customs duties – safeguarded the monopoly position of manufacturers in the domestic market. The government satisfied itself with the pricing policy undertakings of the BISF, which was not even responsible for pricing policy according to the association statutes, but represented instead a moral self-restraint on the part of the companies, which could not have stopped the later, much-criticised price rises (above all, the increase of May 1937).

Various estimates and priorities existed, especially where the government exercised pressure on industry to join an international agreement (for example, mining) or where it seized the initiative itself in the negotiations. The British government, in contrast to the pit owners, was convinced that an agreement was more necessary for them than for the Polish competitors, who since the middle of the 1920s had increasingly pushed British coal out of its markets with low prices, particularly in northern Europe. At the same time it was convinced that British mining, because of structural deficiencies (for example, lack of control of the export trade) was not in a position to realise an effective international cartelisation and – more important – was not even ready to take a serious initiative in that direction, since a portion of the coal owners had not given up the hope of beating the competition out of its own resources, because Poland, according to their estimates, was 'financially near breaking point' and Polish industry could not withstand the price war much longer. Also some pit owners believed they detected some easing of German competition. 'It must be anticipated therefore', Whitehall felt, 'that no serious move will be made by the British coal owners towards an international agreement with the other producing countries unless very strong pressure is exerted upon them by the government.'[15] By pushing towards market agreements, the government believed it knew the 'real' interests of the coal mining industry better than the industrialists themselves.

The example of the cotton industry shows that it was by no means just economic considerations that played a role with the political leadership. Lancashire called loudly for drastic state intervention to stop the progress of Japanese competition on the world market: 'whatever the trade might do internally, it would be absolutely impossible to bridge the gap between the English and the Japanese prices'.[16] However, in a situation of political crisis (the conflict in Manchuria), the government did not want to worsen further its relations with the Far Eastern country through action on trade, but on the contrary wanted to signal accommodation to the offer of talks. The cartel venture of the government was launched not the least out of foreign policy considerations. This example illustrates also that it would be false to deduce too quickly from the government's cartel initiatives a high degree of readiness to state intervention. Often the opposite was the case: direct negotiations between the parties concerned relieved the government of the necessity to be active itself on behalf of industry.

IV

The Coal Agreement between the Polish and British pit owners reduced competition in northern Europe and led to higher prices in a series of markets. However altogether it was an agreement of limited range. The hopes, harboured on both sides, that the agreement would lead the way to a comprehensive international cartel with the participation of all exporting nations, did not fulfill themselves.[17] Whether the agreement with Polish industry had helped British coal exports or merely caused a diversion in trade direction – the coal forced out of the Baltic and Scandinavian markets now made more competition for British goods in West Europe and the Mediterranean – is hard to judge and disputed in historiography.[18] On the other hand, it is certain that the agreement created an advantage for the English pit owners of the North Sea coast at the cost of those in South Wales. It is possible that the most significant result of the agreement was in its inter-regional consequences.

The treaty of the BISF with the IREG produced fixed export shares for the British steel industry and prevented loss-making competition. By raising export prices – a declared objective of the IREG – the steel cartel contributed to the improvement of export proceeds and the sales position of the companies. Export figures at the end of 1936 represented a doubling of the low point reached in 1932, while lying admittedly considerably under the level of 1929. From around December 1936 prices rose steeply and for a short time in 1937 exceeded the domestic prices of the steel exporting countries. Certainly in the literature the improvement in export figures is attributed less to market-regulating measures of the international selling associations than to world iron sales and other factors, chiefly of a political nature. However, without doubt, the International Steel Cartel contributed to the raising of export prices and the stabilisation of export profits, above all in the crisis of 1938.

The agreement ensured greater freedom of movement in price fixing in the domestic market for British industry through the regulation and control of imports from the Continent – they were distributed to consumers under the direction of the BISF. Whether and to what extent the agreement was responsible for the later increase in British steel prices cannot be determined with certainty. Clearly the agreement and involvement in the cartel made the price rises considerably easier. Through the connection of Continental steel sales in the British market to British domestic prices and on the basis of the importance of British quotations for the price structure in Empire markets, the cartel exercised pressure on the prices for steel products in the British domestic market.[19] On the other hand, one would have difficulty arguing that British iron and steel products would have done better on the eve of the Second World War if the industry had not been a member of an international steel cartel. The cartel of the 1930s was different from its predecessors in so far as it did not consider the domestic markets of the participants when fixing quotas and left their regulation up to the parties involved. Older existing associations for individual steel products such as the International Wire Rod Association, in which the domestic sales were taken into consideration in fixing quotas, were converted to pure export cartels in the course of the 1930s, according to the pattern of the other associations. The boom in British iron production and not the operation of the International Steel Cartel was responsible for the output level.

The BISF has been accused of directing its main attention during negotiations with the Continental groups to the security and control of the home market and neglecting exports. Without doubt, that accurately describes the priorities of the British negotiators: the main interest was command of the domestic market, and certainly a different relationship of import and export shares would have been more favourable. Soon after the signing of the treaty, supply bottle-necks appeared in the British market and showed that imports, especially of semi-finished products, had been reduced all too drastically. Whether the British steel exports would have been higher with better quotas is uncertain and would have to be investigated from case to case. The 'apathy' that the government repeatedly complained of in the export industries was particularly marked in iron and steel. Indeed, it was emphasised by industrialists that higher exports were worthwhile; they responded to the exhortations of government representatives not to neglect export connections as an insurance against the future, despite strong internal demand and the rearmament programme that was viewed by them as a temporary phenomenon. In view of the turbulent domestic demand for steel, however, there remained temporarily little surplus for export. In the financial year 1936–7 British industry was not in a position to use its quota fully in the marketing associations of the International Steel Cartel. During the period from July 1937 to 30 June 1938, however, it exceeded its quota. The International Tinplate Cartel (in which the British possessed by far the highest quota) directly limited British exports in 1935–6.

The agreement with the IREG shifted power within the industry to the steelmaking branch, at the cost of the consumer. It was an expression of the strong position possessed by the steel industry in the country's political-industrial system since the foreign trade upheavals of 1931–2, built up further in the succeeding period and internationally safeguarded by entry into the steel cartel. The steel industry's 'reverse of fortune' in comparison with the 1920s, already observed by contemporaries, occurred thanks to the state – not, or only to a small degree, to entrepreneurial initiative.

The example of the cotton industry and the unsuccessful British–Japanese textile conference makes it clear that negotiations over markets and prices had to march in step with the economic conditions of the moment and the interests of all involved (Lancashire's proposals were unrealistic; Japanese industrialists did not want to bind themselves). Political deals can only work under certain circumstances (as they did especially in the steel industry) and only within the limits of conditions for successful private economic negotiations and agreements.

Nevertheless, this case shows that it was inadmissable to leave the state – even the British – out of the analysis of international cartels. Its functions may have varied from branch to branch and its intervention may have been less noticeable with the 'new' industries, where it was less necessary since conditions were different. Still, even Sir Alfred Mond of ICI got backing from his country's political leadership for his position in the negotiations with IG Farbenindustrie AG. And also in the chemical industry the international cartel structure of the 1920s stood in close connection with the political constellation and power structures, as they arose out of the consequences of the First World War.[20]

NOTES

This article was translated from the German by Peter J. Lyth.
1 H. Nussbaum, 'International cartels and multinational enterprises', in A. Teichova, M. Lévy-Leboyer, and H. Nussbaum (eds.) *Multinational enterprise in historical perspective* (Cambridge, 1986), p. 131–44.
2 Alice Teichova, *An economic background to Munich. International business and Czechoslovakia 1918–1938* (Cambridge, 1974).
3 R. Liefmann, *Kartelle, Konzerne und Trusts*, 8th, extended edition, (Stuttgart, 1930), p. 187.
4 P. T. Fischer and H. Wagenfuehr, *Kartelle in Europa (ohne Deutschland)* (Nürnberg, 1929), p. 152.

5 G. von Haberler, *The theory of international trade, with its applications to commercial policy* (London, 1936), p. 329 (German edition, 1933).
6 Committee of Civil Research, Meeting of 17.7.1925; CAB 58/1.
7 C. A. Wurm, *Industrielle Interessenpolitik und Staat. Internationale Kartelle in der britischen Aussen- und Wirtschaftspolitik während der Zwischenkriegszeit* (Berlin and New York, 1987) (Evidence for the following is found here, where not otherwise stated). An English version is in preparation for publication by Cambridge University Press.
8 J. Craig to Lord Kylsant, 27 July 1928; British Steel Corporation Glasgow, File: 'Lord Kylsant 1928–1929' (David Colville & Sons Papers).
9 Board of Trade (eds.), *Survey of international and internal cartels*, vol. 2, (London 1944, 1946), p. 23 (author, J. D. Gribbin).
10 G. Jones, 'The expansion of British multinational manufacturing 1890–1939, in A. Okochi and T. Inoue [eds.], *Overseas business activities. Proceedings of the Fuji Conference* (Tokyo, 1984), p. 148.
11 *Ibid.*, pp. 146f.
12 Cmd 5436; cited in H. Hutchinson, *Tariff making and industrial reconstruction. An account of the work of the Import Duties Advisory Committee 1932–1939* (London, 1965), p. 69.
13 P. Salmon, 'Polish-British competition in the coal markets of Northern Europe 1927–1934,' in *Studia Historiae Oeconomicae*, 16 (1981), pp. 217–43; H. G. Schroeter, *Aussenpolitik und Wirtschaftsinteresse. Skandinavien im aussenwirtschaftlichen Kalkül Deutschlands und Grossbritanniens 1918–1939* (Frankfurt-am-Main 1983), p. 239.
14 Special Committee on Japanese Competition [Manchester Chamber of Commerce], meeting of 3.8.1933; M8/5/18.
15 Memorandum of the Mines Department of the Board of Trade 12 December 1932: 'The movement towards international agreement in the coal industry'; FO 371/16422 – W 11623/9819/50.
16 Special Committee on Japanese Competition (Manchester Chamber of Commerce), meeting of 25 january 1933; M8/5/18.
17 For the efforts towards international agreement in the coal industry, see J. R. Gillingham, *Industry and politics in the Third Reich, Ruhr coal, Hitler and Europe* (Stuttgart, 1985) pp. 95 ff. At the time of the negotiations of the British steel industry with the IREG (Spring, 1935), Sir F. Leith-Ross pressed for the conclusion of a 'coal convention between Germany and Britain for the whole world'; Record of A. Dufour-Feronce of his discussion with Leith-Ross, 11 March 1935; PA AA, Special Department 'W', Raw Materials and Goods, Coal, vol. 10; on the question of Leith-Ross's role, see also his letter to E. Poensgen 3 November 1936; HA/GHH 400101320/88. Also the Governor of the Bank of England, M. Norman, was active as a mediator between German and British pit owners. In the case of the steel industry he pressed the BISF to conclude an agreement with the IREG.
18 Compare the different estimates of Salmon, *Competition*; W. R. Garside, 'The north-eastern coalfield and the export trade 1919–1939' in *Durham University Journal*, 62 (1969), 9; T. J. T. Rooth, 'Limits of leverage: the Anglo-Danish trade agreement of 1933', in *Economic History Review*, 37 (1984) 225f. The literature concerns itself mainly with the general British trade policy on northern Europe and Poland, not especially with the coal treaty of the pit owners. Coal is thereby used as an example for the positive, negative or insignificant effects of British trade policy in general.

19 See Wurm, *Industrielle Interessenpolitik* (note 7).
20 A. Teichova, 'Changing political constellations and the Anglo-American-German cartel relations in the chemical industry in the first decade of the interwar period', in G. Schmidt (ed.), *Konstellationen Internationaler Politik 1924–1932. Politische und wirtschaftliche Faktoren in den Beziehungen zwischen Westeuropa und den Vereinigten Staaten* (Bochum, 1983), pp. 221–36.

THE ECONOMIC JOURNAL

JUNE 1954

IMPERIAL PREFERENCE: A QUANTITATIVE ANALYSIS [1]

INTRODUCTION

The Need for Quantitative Analysis

MUCH has been written, and perhaps even more spoken aloud, on the subject of Imperial Preference. But the discussion has been to a large extent theoretical and political rather than quantitative. There have, it is true, been analyses of the changing pattern of Commonwealth trade after Ottawa. But the figures are not easy to interpret, since the changes recorded are by no means wholly the result of Imperial Preference. There has been little attempt to analyse in a systematic way the proportion of trade enjoying preference and the size of the preferential margins. Information on such matters would seem to be essential in any attempt to assess the changing importance of Imperial Preference in Commonwealth trade over the past twenty-five years, and the main object of the present study is to provide some of the relevant orders of magnitude. Some of the more detailed results obtained are also given in the hope that they may be of value in the study of particular problems, but these are in general subject to a wider margin of error. No attempt has been made here to relate the results obtained to changes in Commonwealth trade; that would require much further research.

The Choice of Years

The statistical work involved in a study of this sort is very considerable; detailed analyses have to be made of the trade returns and tariff lists of a large number of countries. Only a few years could therefore be studied, and those selected were: 1929, to represent the position before Ottawa; 1937, as a typical

[1] We are indebted to the Oxford University Institute of Statistics for technical assistance and to government officials and others in many countries for valuable help and advice.

year after Ottawa but before the process of extending preferences went into reverse; 1948, as a post-war year.

1937 was chosen partly because work had already been done on this year in connection with an earlier article,[1] but it is probably as good a year as could be found for the purpose. The Ottawa Agreements of 1932 involved the overhaul of Dominion tariffs, and this was a lengthy task; nor was the extension of preference by the Colonies completed for several years after Ottawa. It would thus have been unwise to select a year before, say, 1936; and the U.S./U.K. Trade Agreement of 1938 is sometimes regarded as an important landmark in the " retreat " from Imperial Preference.

1929 was the latest pre-Ottawa year which it was thought fit to compare with the relatively prosperous 1937; 1930 and 1931 were years of depression.

1948 was the latest post-war year for which reasonably complete information was available when the calculations were made. But it is a useful year to take. By then a large part of the reduction in Imperial Preference that has occurred since 1937 had taken place. The tariff lists we have used in calculating the figures for 1948 incorporate most of the reduced preferences resulting from the negotiations at Geneva under G.A.T.T. in 1947; subsequent reductions have been less important. And by 1948 a large part of the rise in prices that has greatly reduced the *ad valorem* incidence of specific preferences since 1937 had already taken place. In a later section some broad indications are given of what is likely to be the present position (1953).

Scope and Definitions

The study covers U.K. exports to and imports from the Commonwealth, but not trade between Commonwealth countries other than the U.K.[2] The " Commonwealth " is defined to cover all countries classified as " British " in the U.K. trade returns for the three years, but to include Burma in 1948 as preference continued to be given; under this definition Eire is included throughout.

The analysis of U.K. exports does not include our trade with some of the least important Colonies, but covers countries that took some 95% of our total exports to the Commonwealth.

---

[1] ECONOMIC JOURNAL, September 1952.

[2] Trade of the latter type comprised about one-sixth of total intra-Commonwealth trade in 1929, one-fifth in 1937 and one-quarter in 1948.

Only tariff preferences are considered, and no account is taken of the preferential effects of other trade and financial measures.

For Commonwealth imports from the U.K., the margin of preference *on any item* is defined as the difference between the percentage duty paid on it when imported from the U.K. and the percentage it would have paid had it come from the U.S., specific duties being reduced to their *ad valorem* equivalents. The margin is reckoned as a percentage of the import value excluding duty; had it been based on the value including duty, which is more relevant when assessing competitive power, the figures would have been lower. The comparison was made with the U.S., since the practice in some Dominions of charging different rates of duty on goods from different foreign countries made some such clear-cut definition necessary; and the U.S., as our largest competitor in the world market for manufactures to-day, seemed the most interesting country to choose. Where statistical difficulties necessitated departure from the strict definition this has been mentioned in the notes to the tables concerned.

The margin of preference *on a country's total imports from the U.K.* is the average of the margins on all the items weighted by the value of imports of each from the U.K. The average margin of preference *on the U.K.'s exports to the Commonwealth as a whole* is likewise the average of the margins granted by the various countries weighted by the value of U.K. exports to each.

The method of calculation used may, incidentally, tend to overstate the average margins of preference, since the existence of preference tends to increase the proportion of U.K. exports enjoying higher preferences and to reduce the proportion enjoying lower preferences or none at all.[1]

For each country the average margin of preference is in fact the difference between the total duty paid on imports from Britain and the total duty that would have been paid had the goods been American, expressed as a percentage of the total value of imports from Britain. This is, of course, not at all the same as the difference between the average rates of duty actually paid on imports from the U.K. and from the U.S. in any year. For example, between 1900 and 1932, although Canada granted preference to Britain, the average rate of duty paid on Canadian imports from the U.S. was consistently below that paid on imports from the U.K.; Canada took large imports of heavily taxed alcoholic beverages from the U.K. and large imports of raw

---

[1] See ECONOMIC JOURNAL, September 1952, p. 519.

materials and semi-manufactures from the U.S., which paid low duties or none at all.

For U.K. imports from the Commonwealth the margins of preference are defined in a similar way.

The Tables

Table I shows, for each year, for each country and for all countries taken together : (a) the proportion of imports from the U.K. enjoying preference; (b) the average margin of preference on such " preferred goods "; and (c) the average margin on all imports from the U.K., including those enjoying no preference. (Outside limits are sometimes given instead of precise figures; this is usually where it has been impossible to reconcile the tariff lists with the trade returns for particular items.) Table II gives a fuller picture of the amounts of trade passing at different rates, and the chart a summary for U.K. exports to the Commonwealth as a whole. The main results in these tables are brought together in Summary Table A, which also gives similar figures for U.K. imports from the Commonwealth not included in Table I.

Summary Table B attempts to show how far the changes that occurred between 1929 and 1937 and between 1937 and 1948 in the proportion of trade enjoying preference and in the average rates of preference were the result of : (a) changes in the pattern of trade, both commodity-wise and country-wise; (b) changes in prices [1] which altered the *ad valorem* incidence of specific duties; and (c) changes by governments in tariff rates. To save space, no table is given of the figures for each country obtained in the course of this calculation; but some interesting cases where changes in the pattern of trade or in prices were important are mentioned in the footnotes to Table I.

Finally, Table III and Summary Table C give some details which help us to discover how far the intensification of Imperial Preference between 1929 and 1937 was brought about by reducing tariff rates on trade between Commonwealth countries and how far by increasing rates on foreign goods. Some similar figures are given for 1937–48.

The order of countries in the tables corresponds to the value of U.K. exports to them in 1937.

The rest of the article describes the main findings.

[1] Strictly speaking, " average values "; but, for the sake of brevity, we refer to changes in " prices " throughout this paper.

The Results
The Position in 1929
(a) *Preferences Accorded U.K. Goods in British Countries in* 1929

In 1929 preferences enjoyed by U.K. exports were already fairly widespread. Canada had introduced preference in 1898, New Zealand and South Africa in 1903, Australia in 1908 and India in 1927, while U.K. exports to the Irish Free State enjoyed

SUMMARY TABLE A

Proportion of Trade Enjoying Preference and Margins of Preference

	U.K. exports to Commonwealth.			U.K. imports from Commonwealth.		
	1929.	1937.	1948.	1929.	1937.	1948.
Percentage enjoying preference	35–36	55–57	49–51	7	60–61	54–56
Of which enjoying preferential margins of:						
10% or less	9	18	19	2	27	39
Over 10%, not over 20%	24	18	22	1	24	12
Over 20%	3	20	9	4	9	4
Average percentage margin of preference:						
On goods enjoying preference	13	19–20	14–15	29–49	17–20	11–13
On all goods	5	10–11	7	2–3	10–12	6–7

Notes: 1. See Tables I and II for further details and explanations.

2. To obtain the figures showing percentage of trade enjoying various rates of preference, the more detailed information contained in Table II has been adjusted:

    (a) to allow so far as possible for extra information contained in footnotes to Table II;

    (b) to be consistent with figures in first line of above table, which are based on fuller information.

3. The figures for U.K. imports cover 98% of imports from the Commonwealth in 1929 and 1937, and 100% in 1948, except the figures showing percentage of trade enjoying various rates of preference, which are based on less complete information (see Table II).

preferences from the inception of a separate Customs administration in the latter part of 1923. By 1929 Britain was thus receiving preferences in all the most important trading countries of the Commonwealth. They applied to over 80% of our trade to Australia and New Zealand, over 60% of our trade to Canada, but under 30% of our exports to South Africa and less than 10% of our exports to India and Eire. Among the smaller countries, we had preferences covering a substantial part of our exports to the West Indies and British Guiana and to the Rhodesias, but, partly as a result of treaty obligations, partly for other reasons, few preferences of much importance in the rest of Africa or elsewhere.[1]

All told, rather more than one-third of U.K. exports to British countries enjoyed preferences. The great bulk of these were of

SUMMARY TABLE B

Analysis of Changes Shown in Summary Table A

	U.K. exports to Commonwealth.			U.K. imports from Commonwealth.		
	Percentage enjoying preference.	Average percentage margin of preference.		Percentage enjoying preference.	Average percentage margin of preference.	
		On goods enjoying preference.	On all goods.		On goods enjoying preference.	On all goods.
1. 1929 actual .	35–36	13	5	7	29–49 [1]	2–3
2. 1937 if there had been no change in individual *percentage* margins of preference since 1929.	39–41	12–14	5	7	38–66 [1]	3–4
3. 1937 if there had been no change in *tariff rates* since 1929	39–41	12–14	5	7	47–80 [1]	3–5
4. 1937 actual .	55–57	19–20	10–11	60–61	17–20	10–12
5. 1948 if there had been no change in individual *percentage* margins of preference since 1937.	52–55	21–23	11–12	63–65	21–27	14–18
6. 1948 if there had been no change in *tariff rates* since 1937	52–55	17–18	9–10	63–65	14–17	9–11
7. 1948 actual .	49–51	14–15	7	54–56	11–13	6–7

[1] These figures have no great significance as so few goods are involved.

GENERAL NOTES TO SUMMARY TABLE B

Change from 1 to 2 and from 4 to 5 reflects change in trade pattern (commodity-wise and country-wise).
Change from 2 to 3 and from 5 to 6 reflects change in prices (which affect *ad valorem* incidence of specific duties).
Change from 3 to 4 and from 6 to 7 reflects change in tariff rates.
Lines 1, 4 and 7. As in Summary Table A.
Line 2. Figures obtained by weighting 1929 *percentage* margins of preference on each item by value of trade in each item in 1937.
Similarly *Line 5.*
Line 3. Figures obtained by applying 1929 *tariff rates* to the 1937 trade. This would give the same result as in line 2 if all duties were *ad valorem.* But in fact the percentage margins of preference are now different for all items subject to specific duties where prices have changed between 1929 and 1937.
Similarly *Line 6.*
This particular method of separating the effects of changes in trade patterns, prices and tariff rates was chosen largely for its statistical convenience. Other, equally plausible, methods might give different results. In particular, it will be noted that the method used in Summary Table C and in Table III differs from that used in Summary Table B, and does not always refer to the same categories of goods.

not more than 20%—under 3% of our trade to the Commonwealth did better than this—and the average preferential margin on goods enjoying preference worked out at 13%. As, however, this applied to little more than one-third of the total trade, the average margin of preference received by all our exports to the Commonwealth was only 5%.

[1] The only other countries covered by our calculations that granted preferences in 1929 were Gibraltar (on drink and tobacco) and the Channel Islands, but preferences were also granted by a number of smaller trading countries such as North Borneo, Fiji, Mauritius and Somaliland.

Summary Table C
Changes in Tariff Levels

A. U.K. Exports to Commonwealth
1. 1929–37

	%
Goods first granted a preference between 1929 and 1937	
Total value of exports of such goods in 1937	100
Of which goods subjected to:	
(i) Reduction in U.K. rate; no change in U.S. rate	5 [1]
(ii) Reduction in U.K. rate; increase in U.S. rate	5 [1]
(iii) No change in U.K. rate; increase in U.S. rate	30 [1]
(iv) Increase in U.K. rate; increase in U.S. rate	60 [1]

Goods already enjoying preference in 1929 (1929 *pattern of trade*)	Average percentage rate of duty.	
	Goods from the U.K. (U.K. rate).	Had goods been from the U.S. (U.S. rate).
(a) 1929 tariff rates, 1929 prices	13–16	25–30
(b) 1937 tariff rates, 1929 prices	14–16	33–36
(c) 1937 tariff rates, 1937 prices	17–19	37–41

2. 1937–48

Goods still enjoying preference in 1948 (1948 *pattern of trade*)		
(a) 1937 tariff rates, 1937 prices	17–20	38–43
(b) 1948 tariff rates, 1937 prices	24–26	42–47
(c) 1948 tariff rates, 1948 prices	14	27–29

B. U.K. Imports from Commonwealth
1937–48

Goods still enjoying preference in 1948 (1948 *pattern of trade*)	Average percentage rate of duty.	
	Goods from Commonwealth.	Had goods been from the U.S.
Including excise duties (a) 1937 tariff rates, 1937 prices	45–58	63–81
Including excise duties (b) 1948 tariff rates, 1937 prices	206–216	226–239
Including excise duties (c) 1948 tariff rates, 1948 prices	75–79	86–92
Excluding excise duties (a) 1937 tariff rates, 1937 prices	6–10	24–33
Excluding excise duties (b) 1948 tariff rates, 1937 prices	7–11	27–34
Excluding excise duties (c) 1948 tariff rates, 1948 prices	2–4	13–16

[1] Based on five countries only, but includes 85%, by value, of goods concerned; round figures.

General Notes to Summary Table C

1. No analysis is given of:
   (i) U.K. imports first granted a preference between 1929 and 1937. Such preferences were granted largely by imposing duties on non-Commonwealth goods.
   (ii) U.K. imports already enjoying a preference in 1929, U.K. imports and U.K. exports that lost preference between 1937 and 1948. Such goods were relatively unimportant.

2. Changes from (a) to (b) reflect changes in tariff rates.
   Changes from (b) to (c) reflect changes in prices.

3. In calculating lines (a), (b) and (c), the 1929 or 1948 values of imports have been used throughout. The reference in some of the lines to 1937 prices means only that these have been used in calculating the *ad valorem* incidence of specific duties.

4. Only the figures in lines A1(a), A2(c) and B(c) (both) are comparable with any of the figures in Summary Table B.

Table I
Proportion of Trade Enjoying Preference

	A. Percentage of total U.K. exports to British[1] countries.			B. Percentage of total imports from the U.K. covered in calculation.		
	1929.	1937.	1948.	1929.	1937.	1948.
Union of South Africa	10·0	16·5	14·2	100·0	98·8	100·0
Australia[4]	16·7	14·9	17·1	99·2	92·8	99·0
India	22·2	14·2	13·4[17]	99·4	99·1	100·0
Canada	10·8	10·9	8·3	100·0	99·7	99·6
Eire	11·1	8·6	8·9	99·7	99·3	98·8
New Zealand	6·6	8·0	6·2	99·3	100·0	79·1[23]
Straits Settlements[28]	3·8	3·4	2·4[16]	100·0	100·0	100·0[16]
Channel Islands[5]	1·1	2·2	1·8	100·0	61·0	80·5
Ceylon	1·8	1·6	1·5	100·0	97·2	97·1
Hong Kong[28]	1·9	1·3	2·4	100·0	100·0	100·0
Burma[29]	1·9	1·3	1·7	—	98·6	95·0
Southern Rhodesia	0·6	1·2	1·8	99·8	99·5	99·6
Federated Malay States	1·0	1·2	1·9[12]	100·0	97·9	99·9[12]
Trinidad and Tobago	0·5	1·0	1·0	98·6	99·4	—
Jamaica	0·5	0·8	0·8	99·7	99·9	—
Malta	0·4	0·5	0·8	100·0	100·0	100·0
British Guiana	0·3	0·5	0·4	97·9	99·8	—
Gibraltar[26]	0·2	0·4	0·4	100·0	100·0	—
Northern Rhodesia	0·1	0·4	0·4	99·9	99·8	97·1
Territories granting no preference in 1948[20]	6·1	8·2	10·4	100·0	100·0	100·0
Total of above	97·6	97·1	95·8			
Weighted average						

[1] Includes Burma after it left the Commonwealth, as preference continued to be granted. Otherwise "British" is defined as in the U.K. Trade Returns.

[2] Includes results of Geneva tariff negotiations under G.A.T.T. in 1947 (cf. footnote 11 and footnote 2 to p. 252).

[3] Allows for surtax on U.S. goods of $\frac{9}{20}$ or $\frac{1}{20}$ of duty. Also allows for provisions relating to exchange depreciation. About half of the fall in the percentage margins of preference between 1937 and 1948 is due to changes in the pattern of trade.

[4] In 1929 and 1937 margins are expressed as a percentage of the f.o.b. value of imports in terms of Australian currency in order to achieve comparability with 1948. This involved reducing 1937 margins of preference and tariff rates as shown in the tariff list in the ratio of 125 : 110 and increasing 1929 margins and rates in the ratio 100 : 110. In 1937 and 1948 allowance was made for primage duty and also for the Exchange Adjustment Act in 1937.

[5] Preference granted by charging same duties as the U.K. on U.S. goods and admitting U.K. goods free of duty.

[6] High because spirits and tobacco formed so large a proportion of dutiable imports.

[7] Allows for surtax of 30% of duty on most goods from the U.K. and the U.S.

[8] Allows for discount of 10% of duties of over 15% on U.K. goods. The change in the pattern of trade between 1937 and 1948 tended to increase the average margin of preference on all imports from the U.K., and the true fall was thus larger, say 24% to 10–11%. Of this fall nearly one-half was due to price changes. See also footnote 2 to page 252.

[9] Allows for discount of 10% of duties of over 15% on U.K. goods and for

and Average Margins of Preference

C. Percentage of imports from the U.K. enjoying preference.[22]			D. Percentage average margin of preference on goods enjoying preference.			E. Percentage average margin of preference on all imports from the U.K.		
1929.	1937.	1948.[2]	1929.	1937.	1948.[2]	1929.	1937.	1948.[2]
28–29	40–43 [25]	32–34 [25]	5	7	4–5	1	3 [19]	1–2
90–93	88–91	88–91	14–16	22	15–16	13–14	19–20	13–14
6–8	50	24–25 [18]	7–8	12	11–12 [18]	0–1	6	3 [18]
62–63 [8]	88 [9]	85–87 [8]	11 [8]	23 [9]	12–13 [8]	7 [8]	20 [9]	10–11 [8]
8	10–12 [13]	29–31 [14]	9–10	13–31 [13]	16–17 [14]	1	1–2 [15]	5 [14]
83–86	88–90	90–91	18–19	26 [3]	18 [3]	16	23–25 [3]	16–17 [3]
0	24	23 [16]	—	13	16 [16]	0	3	4 [16]
8	74–87	86–93	92–99 [6]	34–44	33–38	7	26–39	29–35
0	70–86	65–68 [11]	—	9–10	8–9 [11]	0	7–8	5–6 [11]
0	5	7	—	15	16–24	0	1	1–2
— [29]	62–92	61	— [29]	14	17	— [29]	9–13	11
93–94	96	97 [27]	6–7	19–20	15 [27]	6	19	14–15 [27]
0	44–58	36 [12]	—	14–15	13–14 [12]	0	6–8	5 [12]
90	64 [24]		11–16	19 [10]		10–14	12 [10]	
84	83		9	15		7	12–13	
0	70	76		12	13	0	8	10
90	93		17	18 [7]		15	17 [7]	
5	5–7		13	34–39		1	2	
42	93–97	98 [27]	10–11	9–10	10 [27]	4	9–10	10 [27]
0	0	0	—	—	—	0	0	0
35–36	55–57	49–51 [21]	13	19–20	14–15 [21]	5	10–11	7 [21]

excise duty of 3% on U.S. goods. Of the large rise between 1929 and 1937 in the percentage of imports from the U.K. given preference, 6 points are due to the change in the pattern of trade.

[10] Allows for surtax of 15% of duty on certain goods from the U.K. and the U.S.
[11] Does not include results of Geneva tariff negotiations in 1947.
[12] Malayan Union.
[13] Takes no account of additional 10% duty on certain U.K. goods.
[14] 1948 rates weighted by 1947 values (latest available when calculations made).
[15] Allows for additional 10% duty on certain U.K. goods.
[16] Singapore only.
[17] Includes Pakistan.
[18] 1948 rates weighted by 1947–48 values (latest available when calculations made). Includes Pakistan up to August 14, 1947, only. Weighted average thus assumes that Pakistan granted preference to same proportion of U.K. imports and granted same average margin of preference in the period August 15, 1947–March 31, 1948, as India. Of the fall in the percentage of imports from the U.K. given preference between 1937 and 1948, 10 points are due to the change in the pattern of trade.
[19] *Official Year Book* figure is 3·8, compared with 3·4 obtained by this calculation.
[20] Nigeria (including British Cameroons), Gold Coast (including Togoland), Kenya, Uganda, Tanganyika, Zanzibar, Nyasaland, Anglo-Egyptian Sudan, Palestine, Aden, New Guinea and Papua.

Notes continued on page 243.

General Notes to Table I

In calculating the margins of preference it was sometimes necessary to give upper and lower limits for a small percentage of items for which it was impossible to reconcile the classifications in the trade returns with those in the tariff lists. This kind of difficulty accounts for the outside limits in columns C, D and E, which take the place of precise figures. It also, together with rounding, accounts for the apparent slight inconsistencies between columns C, D and E and for the fact that the figures in column B are sometimes less than 100%.

Calculations for Australia and South Africa to replace the figures taken from *Official Year Books*, and slight revisions elsewhere account for the discrepancies between the figures for 1937 given here and those in the table published in the ECONOMIC JOURNAL for September 1952 (G. D. A. MacDougall, " British and American Exports : A Study Suggested by the Theory of Comparative Costs." Part II, Appendix E.).

Column A : Calculated from *Annual Statement of Trade of the U.K.*

Columns B–D : Financial years beginning July 1 for Australia and April 1 for India and for Canada 1929–30 and 1937–38. Calendar years for Canada 1948 and for all other countries.

Weighting : The margin of preference on each country's total imports from the U.K. is the mean of the margins of preference on each item weighted as follows :

(a) New Zealand, Australia, Northern and Southern Rhodesia, South Africa and Malta for all years; British Guiana, Eire and Hong Kong for 1937; Eire and Ceylon for 1948 : value of imports originating in the U.K.

(b) Channel Islands, Federated Malay States, Gibraltar and Straits Settlements for all years; Burma and Ceylon for 1937; Hong Kong and Burma for 1948 : U.K. exports of " U.K. produce and manufactures."

(c) India for all years; Eire for 1929; Canada for 1948 : value of imports consigned from the U.K.

(d) Canada, Jamaica, Trinidad and Tobago for 1929 and 1937; British Guiana for 1929 : margins of preference on each item were weighted by the value of imports from the U.K. actually admitted at preferential rates and then to obtain the average margin of preference on all imports from the U.K. the total of the margins so weighted was expressed as a percentage of the total value of imports consigned from the U.K. (for Canada, British Guiana and Trinidad 1929 and Canada 1937) or of the total value of imports originating in the U.K. (for the others). For these countries therefore some of the figures in columns C and E have a slight downward bias relatively to the others, since the weight given to items having no preference includes goods which did not qualify for preferential treatment because an insufficient percentage of their value was the result of British labour. This is not sufficient to affect the general picture.

To obtain average figures for all British countries covered, the figures for each country were weighted according to the value of exports of U.K. produce and manufactures to it (column A), except column D, which was weighted according to the value of exports of U.K. produce granted preference by each country.

The comparability of margins of preference for different countries is slightly reduced by differences in methods of valuing imports (c.i.f., f.o.b., etc.); but this does not affect the general picture.

Trinidad, Jamaica, British Guiana, Gibraltar: No calculations made for 1948; no sufficiently recent trade returns available when work was done.

Even where U.K. goods enjoyed a preference, they often had to pay substantial-duties, the average rate on such goods being 13–16%; had the goods been American they would have paid, on average, 25–30%. Many of these duties were, of course, imposed primarily to raise revenue rather than to protect domestic producers.

(b) *Preferences Accorded by the U.K. on imports from British Countries in* 1929

Preferences were introduced into the McKenna duties in 1919 and into the Key Industry duties in 1921, but with few exceptions the goods concerned were not important in Commonwealth trade. In 1929 preferences were granted on only 7% of U.K. imports from British countries, among the most important being those on sugar, cocoa, coffee, preserved fruits, spirits, wines, tobacco and road vehicles.

Many of the preferences granted were high, and averaged between about 30% and 50% (owing to statistical difficulties the margin of error is here unusually great), but as so few goods were involved, the average margin of preference on all U.K. imports from British countries was only 2–3%, well below the average preference enjoyed by British exports to the Commonwealth as a whole, and very much less than the preferences accorded by countries such as Australia and New Zealand, which, even in 1929, averaged 13–14% and 16% respectively. It would, however, be unwise to make too much of these comparisons, since, among other things, the conditions governing markets for primary products and for manufactures are very different.

---

[21] Figures for countries for which 1948 material was not available assumed to have changed since 1937 in same proportion as average of rest.
[22] Refers to imports from the U.K. that were covered in this calculation.
[23] This figure is relatively low because *Report on Trade and Shipping of the Dominion of New Zealand 1948* was not available when the calculations were made. See footnote 1 to Table II.
[24] Fall from 1929 due wholly to change in pattern of trade.
[25] Large part of rise 1929–37 and fall 1937–48 due to changes in pattern of trade (see also footnote 1 to p. 252).
[26] Duties are levied only on intoxicating liquors and tobacco.
[27] In 1948 some of the duties listed in the printed Customs tariffs were wholly or partially suspended. Allowing for these suspensions the figures in columns C–E would be approximately:

	C.	D.	E.
Southern Rhodesia	92	13	12
Northern Rhodesia	59	8	5

[28] In Singapore the only Customs duties levied are on intoxicating liquors, tobacco and petroleum. In Singapore and Hong Kong there is also a " first registration fee " of 15% on motor vehicles not of British Commonwealth origin. This was treated as a preference of 15%.
[29] Included in India for 1929 in respect of C, D and E.

The goods that enjoyed preference often had to pay a high rate of duty, usually of a revenue nature. The average worked out at about 100%, so that the margin of preference reckoned as a percentage of price *including* duty on Commonwealth goods was much lower than the figure of 30–50% given in the last paragraph.

The Position in 1937

(a) *Preferences Accorded U.K. goods in British Countries in 1937*

Between 1932 and 1935 many British countries introduced preferences on U.K. goods for the first time. These included the Straits Settlements, the Federated Malay States, Hong Kong, Ceylon and Malta among the countries included in our calculations, and other small trading countries such as Gambia, Sierra Leone, St. Helena, Seychelles, Gilbert and Ellice Islands, Solomons and Tonga. In addition, many countries that had already been granting preference in 1929 widened the range of their imports from Britain on which preference was given.

By 1937 the proportion of U.K. exports to the Commonwealth enjoying preference had, according to our calculations, risen to about 56%, compared with about 36% in 1929. This increase is due in part to a change in the pattern of trade, which would have raised the 1929 figure of 36% to about 40% in 1937, even if there had been no extension of preference;[1] but the great bulk of the rise to 56% is the result of new preferences. Those granted by India and Canada were of major importance.

Alongside the rise in the proportion of U.K. goods enjoying preference, there were substantial increases in the margins of preference on preferred goods. The proportion of U.K. exports to the Commonwealth enjoying preferences of over 20% jumped from one-fortieth in 1929 to one-fifth in 1937. The average preference on goods receiving preference rose from 13% to 19–20%.

As a result of these two developments—new preferences and increases in the margins—the average rate of preference on all U.K. exports to the Commonwealth rose from 5% in 1929 to 10–11% in 1937. Not much of this rise can be accounted for by changes in the pattern of trade or by changes in prices that altered

---

[1] In particular, a large part of the rise in the proportion of South African imports from the U.K. granted preference from about 28% in 1929 to 40% or more in 1937 can be accounted for by the change in the pattern of trade, while the surprising fall in the percentage for Trinidad and Tobago is entirely due to the change in the trade pattern.

the *ad valorem* incidence of specific duties. It was mainly the result of changes in rates of duty.

How far were these results accomplished by reducing rates of duty on U.K. goods, and how far by increasing the rates on goods from other countries (represented by the United States according

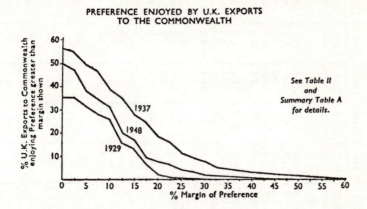

PREFERENCE ENJOYED BY U.K. EXPORTS TO THE COMMONWEALTH

See Table II and Summary Table A for details.

to our definition)? It is convenient to consider separately the manner in which : (i) margins of preference were widened on goods already enjoying preference in 1929; (ii) preferences were accorded to new goods.

(i) *Goods already enjoying preference in* 1929. We have worked out for 1929 the average rate of duty on U.K. goods (the U.K. rate) and the rate they would have paid had they been American (the U.S. rate). We have also worked out for comparison what the U.K. and U.S. rates would have been if the 1937 tariff lists had been operative in 1929, *i.e.*, we have applied the 1937 tariff rates to the 1929 trade. In this way we can eliminate the effects of changes in the pattern of trade and in prices, and are left with the effects of changes in tariff lists on the U.S. and U.K. rates.

In most countries the U.S. rate for 1937 is higher than that for 1929, and for all countries taken together it rises from 25–30% in 1929 to 33–36% in 1937. The average U.K. rate remained at around 15% in each year. However, the fall in prices between 1929 and 1937 raised the percentage rate on U.K. goods to 17–19%, and that on U.S. goods was raised further to 37–41%.

TABLE II

% Distribution of British Countries' Imports from the U.K. According to Margin of Preference Granted

Coverage, %:	South Africa.			Australia.[16]			India.			Canada.			Eire.		
	1929.	1937.	1948.	1929.[6]	1937.[7]	1948.	1929.	1937.	1948.	1929.	1937.	1948.	1929.	1937.[10]	1948.
	99·5	95·8	96·6	85·3	86·3	93·1	97·0	99·1	98·7	100·0	99·2	96·9	98·9	89·0	96·8
Percentage margin.															
0	71·9	59·4	68·3	7·5	12·7	10·7	94·3	49·8	76·0	37·8	12·6	12·9	92·3	84·8	72·3
Up to 2·5	0·1	0·2	2·7	0·2	0·0	6·9	—	2·6	1·7	2·1	—	6·4	0·1	0·1	0·3
2·6– 5·0	25·5	27·9	27·9	0·4	0·4	8·1	—	0·4	—	5·2	0·2	6·2	2·2	1·0	0·5
5·1– 7·5	1·3	1·4	0·1	5·7	0·1	3·5	5·4	4·3	5·3	3·0	0·9	18·7	0·0	0·0	3·3
7·6–10·0	1·2	1·6	0·9	0·5	1·3	3·9	—	30·2	1·2	8·7	4·4	10·6	0·1	0·6	2·9
10·1–12·5	—	0·0	0·0	30·3	2·9	26·9	—	2·0	13·5	30·6	7·4	4·7	5·2	0·8	11·1
12·6–15·0	—	9·2	—	3·2	18·1	6·0	0·3	1·0	—	8·1	9·4	4·7	—	0·5	0·7
15·1–17·5	—	0·2	—	37·8	10·5	12·2	—	—	—	3·9	8·9	20·6	—	2·1	2·3
17·6–20·0	0·0	0·0	—	3·4	14·0	0·5	—	0·2	—	0·5	13·8	4·1	—	0·4	1·0
20·1–22·5	—	—	—	3·3	11·5	4·1	—	—	—	0·1	2·6	4·2	0·0	0·9	0·1
22·6–25·0	—	0·1	0·0	0·0	1·0	5·6	—	9·5	0·0	0·0	12·6	6·0	0·1	0·6	2·9
25·1–27·5	—	—	0·1	3·2	9·3	3·9	—	—	0·8	—	2·6	0·8	0·0	—	0·0
27·6–30·0	—	—	—	0·1	3·4	2·8	—	—	0·0	—	4·3	0·1	—	—	0·1
30·1–32·5	—	—	—	2·5	6·2	2·1	—	—	—	—	8·4	—	—	0·0	0·0
32·6–35·0	—	—	0·0	0·3	1·6	0·3	—	—	—	—	1·2	0·0	—	0·0	0·6
35·1–37·5	—	0·0	0·1	0·4	0·6	0·2	—	—	0·3	—	0·9	0·0	0·0	—	0·0
37·6–40·0	—	—	—	0·2	1·1	0·4	—	—	—	—	3·9	—	—	—	—
40·1–42·5	—	—	—	0·4	0·7	0·0	—	—	1·2	—	0·5	0·0	0·0	0·0	0·1
42·6–45·0	—	—	—	0·6	0·2	0·3	—	—	—	—	0·8	0·0	—	—	0·6
45·1–47·5	—	—	—	0·0	0·1	0·0	—	—	—	—	0·2	0·0	—	—	0·0
47·6–50·0	—	—	—	—	0·1	0·1	—	—	—	—	—	—	—	—	—
50·1–52·5	—	—	—	0·0	3·0	0·6	—	—	—	0·0	0·1	—	—	—	0·1
52·6–55·0	—	—	—	0·0	0·1	0·5	—	—	—	—	0·8	—	—	—	0·6
55·1–57·5	—	—	—	—	0·3	0·1	—	—	—	—	0·1	—	—	—	0·2
57·6–60·0	—	—	—	—	0·1	—	—	—	—	—	0·0	—	—	—	—
60·1 and over	—	—	—	0·0	0·7	0·0	—	—	—	0·0	3·4	—	—	—	0·3
	100·0	100·0	100·0	100·0	100·0	100·0	100·0	100·0	100·0	100·0	100·0	100·0	100·0	91·8[8]	100·0

1954] IMPERIAL PREFERENCE : A QUANTITATIVE ANALYSIS 247

Percentage margin	New Zealand			Straits Settlements			Ceylon			Hong Kong			Southern Rhodesia		
	1929.	1937.	1948.	1929.	1937.	1948.	1929.	1937.	1948.	1929.	1937.	1948.	1929.	1937.	1948.
Coverage, % :	96·3	94·8	67·4[1]	100·0	100·0	99·6	100·0	81·8[3]	96·6	100·0	100·0	100·0	95·7	97·5	97·6
0	14·4	10·8	10·4	100·0	76·5	77·1	100·0	17·1	35·4	100·0	95·2	92·8	5·3	4·1	2·7
Up to 2·5	0·0	0·1	0·0	—	—	—	—	0·1	0·2	—	—	—	1·1	0·4	0·9
2·6– 5·0	0·1	0·3	0·1	—	—	—	—	19·4	12·8	—	—	—	48·2	30·2	33·4
5·1– 7·5	0·9	6·7	3·0	—	—	0·3	—	10·8	13·1	—	—	—	18·7	1·6	0·8
7·6–10·0	7·1	3·1	9·0	—	14·9	—	—	47·9	38·4	—	0·2	0·3	0·1	20·4	8·7
10·1–12·5	0·4	8·7	12·2	—	—	8·1	—	—	0·0	—	—	—	21·2	5·2	3·8
12·6–15·0	10·9	0·7	1·9	—	—	14·5	—	0·5	0·0	—	3·1	6·3	0·4	9·6	17·4
15·1–17·5	0·3	2·6	31·4	—	—	—	—	3·8	—	—	1·5	—	2·6	0·0	0·4
17·6–20·0	58·0	9·5	0·0	—	—	—	—	—	0·1	—	—	—	0·3	6·7	23·8
20·1–22·5	0·0	4·5	2·8	—	—	—	—	—	—	—	—	—	1·8	0·0	0·0
22·6–25·0	4·5	10·8	7·4	—	—	—	—	—	—	—	—	—	—	2·0	2·8
25·1–27·5	—	0·7	0·0	—	—	—	—	0·4	—	—	—	—	0·1	—	—
27·6–30·0	3·0	18·4	11·8	—	—	—	—	—	—	—	—	—	—	1·9	1·2
30·1–32·5	—	1·5	3·7	—	—	—	—	—	—	—	—	—	0·1	0·1	—
32·6–35·0	—	7·7	2·2	—	—	—	—	—	—	—	—	—	—	0·7	—
35·1–37·5	—	0·4	0·0	—	—	—	—	—	—	—	—	—	—	—	—
37·6–40·0	—	0·3	0·0	—	—	—	—	—	—	—	—	0·6	—	0·2	—
40·1–42·5	—	0·1	0·7	—	—	—	—	—	—	—	—	—	0·0	0·0	—
42·6–45·0	0·3	—	2·7	—	—	—	—	—	—	—	—	—	—	—	—
45·1–47·5	—	13·1	0·0	—	—	—	—	—	—	—	—	—	0·1	0·1	—
47·6–50·0	0·1	0·0	0·7	—	—	—	—	—	—	—	—	—	—	—	—
50·1–52·5	—	—	—	—	—	—	—	—	—	—	—	—	—	12·7	—
52·6–55·0	—	—	—	—	—	—	—	—	—	—	—	—	—	—	—
55·1–57·5	—	—	—	—	—	—	—	—	—	—	—	—	—	0·1	—
57·6–60·0	—	—	—	—	—	—	—	—	—	—	—	—	—	—	—
60·1 and over	0·0	0·0	—	—	—	—	—	—	—	—	—	—	0·1	4·0	2·9
	100·0	100·0	100·0	100·0	100·0	100·0	100·0	100·0	100·0	100·0	100·0	100·0	100·0	100·0	100·0

Notes to Table on p. 250.

Continued overleaf

TABLE II—(continued)

Coverage, % :	Federated Malay States.			Trinidad and Tobago.			Jamaica.			Malta.			British Guiana.		
	1929.	1937.[a]	1948.	1929.	1937.	1948.[2]	1929.	1937.	1948.[2]	1929.	1937.	1948.	1929.	1937.	1948.[2]
	100·0	85·3[a]	99·1	93·8	99·4	—	99·7	93·9	—	100·0	100·0	96·4	97·9	98·6	—
Percentage margin.															
0	100·0	48·8	64·0	10·7	36·3		16·5	18·4		100·0	29·9	24·7	10·1	7·5	
Up to 2·5	—	0·6	—	2·1	0·3		0·2	0·2		—	0·1	0·1	0·2	0·0	
2·6– 5·0	—	—	7·3	4·2	0·4		56·9	36·7		—	2·7	8·5	10·3	8·8	
5·1– 7·5	—	6·4	0·1	10·4	1·5		0·1	0·1		—	0·8	0·9	18·5	20·2	
7·6–10·0	—	28·0	9·4	21·2	8·9		19·4	26·6		—	52·3	6·9	3·9	8·7	
10·1–12·5	—	—	0·0	38·4	39·2		1·5	4·5		—	1·1	4·7	2·1	3·3	
12·6–15·0	—	—	1·3	0·3	0·5		0·2	1·6		—	1·2	51·4	2·8	12·9	
15·1–17·5	—	—	1·1	0·3	1·9		0·0	1·7		—	3·5	0·4	29·9	24·9	
17·6–20·0	—	8·2	16·2	3·3	1·6		0·1	4·1		—	5·0	1·2	6·8	2·7	
20·1–22·5	—	—	—	7·3	2·9		0·0	0·1		—	—	1·2	4·2	0·1	
22·6–25·0	—	—	0·6	0·7	2·3		0·1	0·2		—	3·3	—	4·2	0·2	
25·1–27·5	—	—	—	0·8	0·6		0·2	0·2		—	—	—	0·1	0·8	
27·6–30·0	—	6·9	—	0·2	0·1		—	1·7		—	—	—	0·7	0·6	
30·1–32·5	—	—	—	0·1	0·0		—	—		—	—	0·0	0·1	0·0	
32·6–35·0	—	—	—	—	—		0·0	2·0		—	0·0	—	0·8	0·0	
35·1–37·5	—	—	—	0·0	0·1		0·0	0·0		—	—	—	0·0	2·0	
37·6–40·0	—	—	—	0·0	0·0		2·0	0·6		—	—	—	0·0	0·0	
40·1–42·5	—	—	—	0·9	0·9		—	0·2		—	—	0·0	0·0	0·0	
42·6–45·0	—	—	—	—	0·0		—	0·5		—	—	—	0·0	0·1	
45·1–47·5	—	—	—	0·0	—		—	—		—	—	—	—	—	
47·6–50·0	—	—	—	—	—		—	0·1		—	—	—	—	—	
50·1–52·5	—	—	—	—	0·0		—	—		—	—	—	0·0	0·0	
52·6–55·0	—	—	—	0·0	0·0		—	—		—	—	—	—	0·2	
55·1–57·5	—	—	—	—	0·2		—	—		—	—	—	0·4	0·5	
57·6–60·0	—	—	—	—	0·0		—	—		—	—	—	0·2	—	
60·1 and over	—	1·1	—	0·0	2·3		2·8	0·5		—	0·1	0·0	4·7	6·5	
	100·0	100·0	100·0	100·0	100·0		100·0	100·0		100·0	100·0	100·0	100·0	100·0	

Coverage, %:	Gibraltar.			Northern Rhodesia.			All British countries covered.[11]			Percentage distribution of U.K. imports from British countries according to margin of preference granted.		
	1929.	1937.	1948.[2]	1929.	1937.	1948.	1929.	1937.	1948.	1929.[13]	1937.[14]	1948.[15]
	100·0	100·0	—	99·3	84·0[4]	88·3[5]				96·3	91·0	90·4
Percentage margin.												
0	95·3	95·0		58·2	4·2	2·4	64·8	46·3[12]	51·7	96·5	41·4	49·7
Up to 2·5	—	—		1·8	1·4	0·3	0·3	0·5	2·6	0·4	—	3·0
2·6– 5·0	—	—		2·1	40·4	22·0	3·9	6·2	7·8	1·1	10·6	0·2
5·1– 7·5	—	—		7·2	0·1	0·2	3·0	1·9	3·2	0·1	—	13·7
7·6–10·0	—	—		2·7	16·9	63·5	1·7	8·5	4·8	0·0	19·4	22·7
10·1–12·5	1·6	1·7		20·4	13·7	0·1	9·7	2·7	9·9	0·5	0·2	1·0
12·6–15·0	3·1	—		0·0	20·2	6·5	2·3	6·3	2·9	—	17·5	4·3
15·1–17·5	—	—		7·0	0·4	—	7·1	3·3	7·2	0·7	1·9	0·2
17·6–20·0	—	—		0·6	0·3	0·7	4·7	5·5	1·4	—	4·7	4·3
20·1–22·5	—	—		—	—	—	0·6	2·7	1·4	0·0	0·0	0·7
22·6–25·0	—	—		—	—	—	0·3	4·2	2·6	—	0·1	0·0
25·1–27·5	—	—		—	0·1	—	0·6	1·9	0·8	—	0·1	—
27·6–30·0	—	—		0·0	2·3	—	0·2	2·8	1·4	—	0·4	0·1
30·1–32·5	—	—		—	—	—	0·4	2·2	0·7	0·1	0·2	0·0
32·6–35·0	—	—		—	—	4·3	0·1	1·1	0·2	—	1·2	0·1
35·1–37·5	—	—		—	—	—	0·1	0·2	0·1	0·1	0·5	—
37·6–40·0	—	—		—	—	—	0·0	0·7	0·2	—	—	—
40·1–42·5	—	—		—	—	—	0·1	0·2	0·3	—	0·2	0·0
42·6–45·0	—	—		—	—	—	0·1	0·1	0·3	0·1	—	0·0
45·1–47·5	—	3·3		—	—	—	—	1·2	—	—	—	—
47·6–50·0	—	—		—	—	—	0·0	0·0	0·1	—	—	0·0
50·1–52·5	—	—		—	—	—	—	0·5	0·1	—	1·6	—
52·6–55·0	—	—		—	—	—	—	0·3	0·1	—		—
55·1–57·5	—	—		—	—	—	—	0·1	0·1	0·1		—
57·6–60·0	—	—		—	—	—	—	0·0	0·0	—		—
60·1 and over	—	—		—	—	—	0·0	0·6	0·1	0·5		—
	100·0	100·0	100·0	100·0	100·0	100·0	100·0	100·0	100·0	100·0	100·0	100·0

Notes to Table on p. 250.

(ii) *Goods First Granted a Preference between* 1929 *and* 1937. On only one-tenth of these goods, by value, was the rate payable on U.K. goods reduced. On 95% the rate on U.S. goods was increased and on no less than 60% the rate on U.K. goods was increased as well.

The increase in preference accorded to U.K. goods in British countries during this period was thus achieved very largely by increasing the rates on foreign goods, and only in minor degree by reducing the rates on U.K. goods; on the contrary, these tended to be increased as well.

GENERAL NOTES TO TABLE II

In Table I outside limits were given instead of precise figures where it was impossible to reconcile the tariff list with the trade return for particular items. These imprecise items have been omitted from the frequency distributions in Table II so as to obtain a clearer presentation of the data, and the coverage for the frequency distributions is therefore less good than for the calculations whose results are shown in Table I. The coverage is, however, given for each distribution, and it will be seen that it is generally sufficient to give a fairly complete picture of amounts of preference granted. Where coverage is definitely insufficient (Channel Islands and Burma) distributions have not been constructed.

For reasons of presentation, figures are given to one decimal point, but this degree of precision should not be taken as an indication of the margin of error involved.

See also notes to Table I.

FOOTNOTES TO TABLE II

[1] Calculation made from *External Trade 1948* (Census and Statistics Department, Wellington, N.Z., 1951), as *Report on Trade and Shipping of the Dominion of New Zealand 1948* was not available when the calculations were made. Of trade omitted at least 12% (of imports from U.K.), probably much more, granted preferences of 7·6–17·5%.

[2] Sufficiently recent trade figures not available when calculation was made.

[3] Additional duty of 10% on 8·2% of goods imported from the U.K.

[4] Over half trade omitted granted preference of 5% or 10%. The rest was granted none or preferences of up to 25%.

[5] Trade omitted was mostly granted 5% or 10% preference.

[6] Of trade omitted 7% (of imports from U.K.) was granted preference of 11–15%. Rest was granted none or preferences of up to 85%.

[7] Of trade omitted 4% (of imports from the U.K.) was granted preference of 13–22%. Rest was granted none or preferences of up to and over 100%.

[8] Most of trade omitted was either granted no preference or a preference of 10%.

[9] Most of trade omitted was either granted no preference or preferences of up to 15%.

[10] Preference on trade omitted varied between −10% (see note 3) and over 100%.

[11] Excluding British Guiana, Jamaica, Trinidad and Tobago and Gibraltar. Including territories granting no preference in 1948.

[12] Including 0·8 exports to Eire, on which additional duty of 10%.

[13] Of trade omitted 2·7% was granted preference of between 27% and 61%, 0·4% was granted preference of between 2% and 10%. The preference granted on the rest varied up to over 200%.

[14] Of trade omitted, at least 4·1% was granted preference at rates well above 30%, and at least a further 1·4% at rates above 15%. The rest was granted either no preference or preferences varying up to 25%.

[15] Of trade omitted, at least 3% was granted preference of 20% or less. A further 1·5% was granted either no preference or various rates up to 33·3%. A further 3% was granted preference of between 9% and 28%, and nearly a further 2% was granted preference of 47–53%.

[16] See footnote 4 to Table I.

(b) *Preferences accorded by U.K. on Imports from British countries in 1937.*

The Import Duties Act and the Ottawa Agreements greatly widened the scope of preference on U.K. imports from the Commonwealth. By 1937 over 60% of such imports enjoyed preference, compared with only 7% in 1929.

The average margin on goods accorded preference fell greatly, but this has no signficance, since the high level in 1929 reflected exceptional margins on a very few items, and the great bulk of the new preferences were of not more than 20%.

The average margin on all U.K. imports from British countries was raised from 2–3% to 10–12%, *i.e.*, to roughly the same average level as that enjoyed by U.K. exports to the Commonwealth as a whole.

A large part of this increase was, of course, achieved by imposing a tariff on foreign goods while retaining duty-free entry for goods from British countries. Taken in conjunction with the results obtained for U.K. exports to the Commonwealth, this means that the intensification of Imperial Preference during the thirties was achieved largely by increasing tariffs against the outside world, rather than by reducing tariffs between Commonwealth countries.

The Position in 1948

Between 1937 and 1948 there were important reductions in Imperial Preference. The average percentage margins of preference fell at least half-way back to the pre-Ottawa level. This was the result partly of the large rise in prices which reduced the *ad valorem* incidence of specific duties and partly of alterations in rates of duty made at the Geneva Tariff Negotiations under G.A.T.T. in 1947 and, for example, in the Trade Agreements between the U.K. and the U.S. (1938), the U.S. and Canada (1938) [1] and the U.K. and India (1939). (On the other hand, increased preferences were obtained under the U.K./Eire Agreement of 1938.) But while the average rate of preference was markedly reduced, the general structure of preference was not seriously modified; the proportion of intra-Commonwealth trade enjoying preference did not fall greatly.

[1] This Agreement made various changes which reduced the preference accorded to U.K. over U.S. goods, including the removal of a special excise tax on a long list of goods imported from non-British countries.

(a) *Preferences Accorded U.K. goods in British Countries in* 1948

The proportion of U.K. exports to British countries enjoying preference fell from about 56% in 1937 to about 50% in 1948, and a significant part of this fall can be explained by changes in the pattern of trade. The elimination of preferences was thus relatively unimportant. The proportion of trade enjoying preference fell quite markedly in South Africa, but this was largely the result of changes in the trade pattern.[1] India is the only important country where the elimination of preferences was of major significance (partly as a result of the 1939 Trade Agreement with the U.K.); the proportion of trade accorded preference fell from 50% in 1937 to about 25% in 1948, but even here some 10 points of the fall was the result of changes in the pattern of trade.[2]

But while comparatively few preferences were eliminated between 1937 and 1948, there were large falls in many percentage rates of preference. The average rate on goods receiving preference fell from 19–20% to 14–15%; and as changes in the trade pattern tended to increase the average rate, the true fall on a comparable basis was larger, and probably about one-third (roughly from 22% to 14%). High preferences became much less important; the proportion of Britain's exports to the Commonwealth enjoying preferences of over 20% fell from one-fifth in 1937 to under one-tenth in 1948.

The average margin of preference on *all* U.K. exports to the Commonwealth fell from 10–11% to 7% and by rather more assuming a constant pattern of trade. Of this fall about half seems to have been due to the rise in prices and about half to tariff changes.

The fall in margins of preference was on balance, but not in all countries, associated with reductions in *percentage* rates of duty both on U.K. and on U.S. goods. There were, it is true, steep increases in the *tariff rates* charged by some of the Colonies, partly no doubt to maintain the real value of revenue from specific duties in the face of rising prices; and for all countries taken together we find some increase in the average U.K. and U.S. rates on goods enjoying preference in 1948 when the effects of changes in prices

---

[1] We are advised that these changes were temporary and resulted from Britain's inability to supply South Africa with many goods on which preferences were granted.

[2] The Geneva Agreement of 1947 scheduled the elimination of preferences on 8% of Canada's imports from the U.K. (1937 trade), but 7% of this consisted of items on which the duty on the U.K. product was to be raised. This required specific legislation which was not completed until 1949. Its effect does not therefore appear in the 1948 figures given here.

and in the pattern of trade have been eliminated. But the rise in prices more than offset these increases in tariff rates. The net result was that, for all countries taken together, the U.K. rate fell from 17–20% in 1937 to 14% in 1948 and the U.S. rate from 38–43% to 27–29% (based on the 1948 pattern of trade throughout).

(b) *Preferences Accorded by the U.K. on Imports from British Countries in* 1948

Between 1937 and 1948 there was some fall in the proportion of U.K. imports from the Commonwealth enjoying preference— roughly from 60% to 55%. Since the change in the pattern of trade tended to increase this proportion, the true fall was larger.

There was a large fall in the average margin of preference on goods receiving preference, from 17–20% to 11–13%; and, as the change in the trade pattern tended to increase the average margin, the true fall was greater, and probably about one-half. The proportion of trade enjoying preferences of over 10% fell from one-third to one-sixth.

The average rate on all imports fell from 10–12% to 6–7%. Using the 1948 pattern of trade throughout, the fall is greater, from 14–18% to 6–7%. Of this fall well under one-half seems to have been due to tariff changes, and well over one-half to the rise in prices which reduced the *ad valorem* incidence of specific duties; U.K. import prices in general nearly trebled between 1937 and 1948, and specific duties were of importance for many imports from British countries.

The fall in preferential margins was accompanied by large increases in rates of Customs duty, which were not wholly offset by the effects of higher prices, on imports from both Commonwealth and non-Commonwealth countries. But many of these increases were imposed for revenue purposes, and were largely matched by increases in excise duty. The average rate of Customs duty less excise duty on goods enjoying preference in 1948 fell from 6–10% to 2–4% for imports from Commonwealth countries and from 24–33% to 13–16% for imports from other sources (based on the 1948 pattern of trade throughout). These falls reflect wholly the effect of the rise in prices on the *ad valorem* incidence of specific duties.

Thus, for trade in each direction between Britain and the Commonwealth, the reduction in Imperial Preference between 1937 and 1948 was accompanied by a general fall in percentage rates of duty (net of excise duty for U.K. imports), just as the

TABLE III
Average Rates of Duty on

	1929 tariff rates. 1929 prices.		1937 tariff rates.			
	(1)		Goods already enjoying preference in 1929 (1929 pattern of trade).			
			1929 prices.		1937 prices.	
			(2)		(3)	
	U.K. rate.	U.S. rate.	U.K. rate.	U.S. rate.	U.K. rate.	U.S. rate.
Union of South Africa	3	7	6–7	12–15	6–7	12–15
Australia (c)	14–23	29–39	17–20	37–43	18–21	39–45
India	11–17	18–26	7–8	11–13	9–10	14–16
Canada	17	28	18	42–43	18	42–43
Eire	31–37	40–45	77–90	106–126	92–108	127–150
New Zealand	10–11	29–30	9	32–33	9	33
Straits Settlements	(b)	(b)	(b)	(b)	(b)	(b)
Channel Islands	0	92–99	0	82–94	0	105–121
Ceylon	(b)	(b)	(b)	(b)	(b)	(b)
Hong Kong	(b)	(b)	(b)	(b)	(b)	(b)
Burma			Included in India			
Southern Rhodesia	5	12	4–5	18–19	5	19–20
Federated Malay States	(b)	(b)	(b)	(b)	(b)	(b)
Trinidad and Tobago	9–12	20–27	12–13	30–31	14	34–35
Jamaica	23	31	19–20	32–34	20–21	34–36
Malta	(b)	(b)	(b)	(b)	(b)	(b)
British Guiana	16	32	23–24	44–47	27–29	53–56
Gibraltar	40	53	40	53	51	68
Northern Rhodesia	9–10	19	9–10	20–22	9–11	21–23
Weighted average	13–16	25–30	14–16	33–36	17–19	37–41

U.K. rate: average percentage rate of duty on goods from the U.K.
U.S. rate: average percentage rate of duty had goods been from the U.S.
Change from (1) to (2) and from (4) to (5) reflects change in tariff rates.
Change from (2) to (3) and from (5) to (6) reflects change in prices (which affects *ad valorem* incidence of specific duties).
The high average rates of duty shown for some countries (such as Straits Settlements, Hong Kong, Federated Malay States and Gibraltar) are attributable in large part to the limited range of goods that enjoy tariff preferences and to the high level of duties on intoxicating liquors and tobacco (which are preferential).

increase in preference in the thirties had been accompanied by a general rise.

The Present Position (mid-1953)

Five years have elapsed since 1948, the latest year for which calculations have been made. Since then there have been further reductions in Imperial Preference, although the general picture given for 1948 cannot have been radically modified.

Probably the most important change has been the reduction

Goods Enjoying Preference

	1937 tariff rates. 1937 prices.		Goods still enjoying preference in 1948 (1948 pattern of trade).			
			1948 tariff rates.			
			1937 prices.		1948 prices.	
	(4)		(5)		(6)	
	U.K. rate.	U.S. rate.	U.K. rate.	U.S. rate.	U.K. rate.	U.S. rate.
Union of South Africa	3	8–11	3	8–9	2–3	7
Australia (c)	18–20	42–46	15–16	37–41	9	23–25
India	22	32	26–27	38–39	25–26	38–39
Canada	15	41	18	36	10	22
Eire	68–103	95–145	72–79	96–107	35–38	50–55
New Zealand	7–8	30–32	7–8	25–26	6–8	24–26
Straits Settlements	60	72	296	331	108	124
Channel Islands	0	36–45	0	62–65	0	33–38
Ceylon	14–15	22–24	26–27	35–36	23–24	31–32
Hong Kong	30–34	45–48	96–109	136–137	59–68	83–84
Burma	20–26	32–40	24–25	42–43	24	41
Southern Rhodesia	5	25	5	20	5	20
Federated Malay States	32	44	284–286	317–319	96	109–110
Trinidad and Tobago	(a)	(a)	(a)	(a)	(a)	(a)
Jamaica	(a)	(a)	(a)	(a)	(a)	(a)
Malta	12–13	24	27–29	41–42	19–20	33
British Guiana	(a)	(a)	(a)	(a)	(a)	(a)
Gibraltar	(a)	(a)	(a)	(a)	(a)	(a)
Northern Rhodesia	6–7	17–19	14–15	30–39	7–8	17–18
Weighted average	17–20	38–43	24–26	42–47	14	27–29

The figures for India, Burma and the Channel Islands are subject to particularly wide margins of error, possibly wider than those shown in the table.

See also notes to Summary Table C and to Table I.

(a) Not calculated; no sufficiently recent trade returns available when work was done.

(b) No preference in 1929.

(c) In all years amounts of duty paid were expressed as a percentage of the f.o.b. value of imports in terms of Australian currency in order to achieve comparability between the years (see footnote 4 to Table I).

in the *ad valorem* incidence of specific margins caused by a further rise in prices—British import and export prices in general have risen by around 25–30%. The results of the Annecy and Torquay tariff negotiations under G.A.T.T. in 1949 and 1951 scarcely affect our average figures, and it is unlikely that the reduction of preferences brought about in other ways has been much more important. The pattern of trade has also altered. We have not calculated the effect, beyond establishing that the shift in U.K. exports between Commonweath countries granting different average margins of preference has on balance been of no importance.

It is impossible to give any precise details of the present position, but what rough calculations we have been able to make suggest that the following broad picture is unlikely to be very wide of the mark.

Something like one-half of both British exports to and imports from the Commonwealth enjoy preference, but in some Commonwealth markets for U.K. exports the proportion is much higher. Well under one-tenth of the trade in either direction enjoys preferences of over 20%, although there are still a few very high preferences of 50% or more. The average percentage margin of preference on all U.K. trade with the Commonwealth has been greatly reduced since the late thirties, and is now probably in the neighbourhood of 6% in either direction. The margin is still smaller—probably around 5% on U.K. exports to the Commonwealth—if it is reckoned as a percentage of the value of trade *including* duty on British goods, which is more relevant when assessing competitive power.

A figure of 5% may seem surprisingly low to those with experience of very high preferential margins; but such margins, as we have seen, are few and far between. There is no doubt that preferences are of very considerable importance in certain trades, where the rate is relatively high or the market highly competitive and sensitive to price differentials. For many years tariff preferences were overshadowed by direct trade and exchange controls and by the existence of sellers' markets. They will regain importance to the extent that these conditions change. But the effect of preferences on our total export trade cannot be more than marginal. Following a rough method of calculation used in an earlier article,[1] it seems unlikely that an average preference of around 5% on our exports to the Commonwealth can make a difference of more than, say, 5% in our total exports to the world as a whole—although even marginal exports of this size can, of course, be of crucial importance while the balance of payments remains precarious. It is certain that the effect of Imperial Preference on the total sales of U.S. manufacturers is entirely negligible.

Summary of Main Results

Even before Ottawa, Britain was enjoying an average preference of 13% on over one-third of her exports to British coun-

[1] ECONOMIC JOURNAL, September 1952, p. 509.

tries, giving an average preference of 5% on all her exports to the Commonwealth. In return she gave preferences (admittedly high ones) on only 7% of her imports from the Commonwealth, making an average rate of preference of 2–3% on all her imports from British countries.

By 1937, mainly as a result of the Ottawa Agreements, the proportion of trade enjoying preference had risen to well over one-half in each direction, and many old preferences had been increased. This intensification of Imperial Preference, which was considerably more important for Britain's imports than for her exports, raised the average margin of preference to 10–12% on all trade in each direction. It was achieved largely by raising tariff rates on foreign goods and not by reducing rates on intra-Commonwealth trade; the latter, on the contrary, tended to rise as well.

Since 1937 there has been a large reduction in Imperial Preference. The proportion of trade enjoying preference has not fallen greatly, and is still about one-half in each direction. But the average rate has fallen to about 6% on both imports and exports. (The rate is, of course, about twice as high on goods enjoying preference, and higher still on many items.) The reduction in Imperial Preference since 1937 has been the result, first, of tariff changes, including those negotiated under G.A.T.T. and in other Trade Agreements, and secondly—probably more important—of the very large rise in prices which has reduced the *ad valorem* incidence of specific margins. The rise in prices has also brought about a substantial fall in percentage rates of protective duty, both on intra-Commonwealth trade and on similar goods imported from outside the Commonwealth.

Nuffield College,
  Oxford.   DONALD MACDOUGALL
University of Leeds.   ROSEMARY HUTT

[15]

The World Economic Conference 1933: The Failure of British Internationalism

Patricia Clavin*
King's College, London and Keele University

The World Monetary and Economic Conference convened in London's newly opened Geological Museum, for the first time on Monday, 12 June 1933. Gathered together under the chairmanship of the British Prime Minister, Ramsay MacDonald, delegates from 66 countries met "not to discuss mere economic theories and generalities, but to make practical proposals to meet urgent necessities."[1] The Conference was unprecedented in both its size and ambition. Yet it crashed to the ground in undignified recrimination amongst the major powers barely two weeks later, marking the end of interwar attempts at broad-ranging international economic co-operation.

The events in London that year had an important impact both on Anglo-American bilateral relations and on the context of economic diplomacy amongst the major powers for the remainder of the interwar period. Many scholars have blamed United States policy for the failure of the Conference and see American policy towards the Conference as the first incidence of Roosevelt's 'isolationism'. This interpretation centres on Roosevelt's famous bombshell message sent from his yacht

---

* I should like to thank Dr. Richard Overy and Professor Harold James for their comments on earlier drafts of this paper. Financial assistance was provided by the British Academy and the Central Research Fund of London University.
[1] *Journal of the Monetary and Economic Conference*, No. 3 (London, 1933), p. 6.

Patricia Clavin

Amberjack, three weeks after the Conference first convened, which scuppered any hopes for joint currency stabilisation between the floating pound, the dollar and the remaining gold currencies[2]. This article will attempt to show that much of the responsibility for the collapse of economic co-operation must, in fact, be borne by the British government. The nature of British tariff policy and the determination of the National Government to cancel its war debt payments to the United States soured the climate for international co-operation long before the arrival of the 'bombshell message'.

I

Following months of division over unemployment strategies and the question of protectionism, compounded by Britain's humiliating departure from the gold standard, the British domestic economic and political scene began to strengthen and stabilise in the summer of 1932. General economic indicators began to point to a gradual recovery, developments which were all the more significant when placed in an international context.[3] Germany and the United States were still in the troughs of depression whilst France began to show increased signs of a downward slide. Britain's relations with her Empire were also a source of some satisfaction after the successful conclusion of the Imperial Economic Conference at Ottawa which broadened

---

[2] C.P. KINDLEBERGER, *The World In Depression, 1929-1939*, (London, 1987); D.C. WATT, *Succeeding John Bull: America in Britain's Place, 1900-1975*, (Cambridge, 1984); A. SCHLESINGER, *The Age of Roosevelt: the Coming of the New Deal*, Vol. 2, (Boston, 1961). For further examples see H.V. HOBSON, *Slump and Recovery: a Survey of World Economic Affairs, 1929-1937*, (London, 1938), pp. 204-205; S.V.O. CLARKE, "The Reconstruction of the International Monetary System: The attempts of 1922 and 1933", *Princeton Studies in International Finance*, No. 33, 1973; JAMES R. MOORE, "Sources of New Deal Economic Policy: The International Dimension", *The Journal of American History*, No. 41, 1974, pp. 728-44.

[3] D.H. ALDCROFT, *The British Economy: the Years of Turmoil, 1920-51*, Vol. 1, (Brighton, 1986).

tariff arrangements between the United Kingdom and her Dominions. This flush of achievement was by no means enjoyed by all, but for the Conservative-dominated National Government it had the effect of consolidating Britain's move toward protectionism. The abandonment of Free Trade was a development warmly welcomed by the Conservatives.

The Prime Minister, Ramsay MacDonald, remained uneasy about the changes made to British economic policy and derived greater satisfaction from his success in Europe. German reparation payments had, in effect, been ended by a gathering of European statesmen under MacDonald's chairmanship at Lausanne in July 1932. And it was here that international agreement for a World Economic Conference was established to examine interrelated economic and monetary issues. Enshrined in Article Five of the Lausanne agreement, the Conference was intended to build upon the 'armistice' of Lausanne and the protection of this settlement in Europe became the foundation of British policy for the Conference. But these developments — Britain's tentative economic recovery, the consolidation of her transition to a protectionist trading policy and the determination to uphold the reparation settlement of Lausanne — also set up contradictions in Britain's claim to leadership of the World Economic Conference which she failed to resolve. Although the National Government sponsored the idea for a Conference, promoted it at Lausanne and assumed the responsibility for organising it (with MacDonald crowned Chairman), formulating an effective policy proved a greater challenge.

The Great Depression was awash with calls for co-ordinated action by international conference on questions of silver, gold, tariffs, currency restrictions, debts and reparations, to be tackled either together or separately[4]. But Britain's policies for promoting international economic recovery increasingly turned on a

[4] Lord Reading suggested a conference to Laval during a trip to Paris, 27 Jan. 31. An even earlier proposal for a World Economic Conference was made by Hoover through Sackett, his Ambassador in Berlin to Chancellor Brüning.

successful resolution of the sticky problem of reparations and war debts. The National Government considered that it had made a significant contribution not only to German, but also European economic recovery at Lausanne[5]. The next stage was to revise war debt payments due to the United States. Mindful of America's insistence that reparation payments and war debts were not connected, the British sought to present the United States with a *'fait accompli':* Britain would resolve the political debt issue in Europe and then use this achievement to persuade the United States to drastically revise their collection of war debts. Britain, in fact, hoped America would abandon war debts altogether[6].

MacDonald had been encouraged by France's increasingly "conciliatory state of mind" and friendliness after the Lausanne Conference which, in his view, seemed "unrivalled since the war"[7]. This was in marked contrast to the frustration and bitterness the Prime Minister had felt in early reparation discussions with the French and the problems which had marred disarmament negotiations. He also considered that his relations with President Hoover and Secretary of State, Henry Stimson, were sufficiently strong to make war debt re-negotiation possible. In correspondence with Stimson, the Prime Minister was confident that Britain could lead the rest of Europe into discussion with the United States to improve the economic climate. Hoover confirmed that he, too, laid great store in such co-operation: "Tell MacDonald that the civilisation which he speaks of can only be saved by the co-operation of Anglo-Saxons, we cannot count on other races"[8].

---

[5] B. KENT, *The Spoils of War: the Politics, Economics and Diplomacy of Reparations, 1918-1932,* (Oxford, 1989), pp. 371-2.
[6] MacDonald Papers, Public Record Office, London. (Hereafter P.R.O. PRO 30/69), PRO 30/69/678, Stimson to MacDonald, 18 Jan. 32; Baldwin Papers, University Library, Cambridge, (Hereafter Baldwin), Baldwin vol. 119, Runciman to Baldwin, 24.6.32.
[7] *Ibid.,* MacDonald to Baldwin, 24 June 32; *ibid.,* Hankey to Baldwin, 1 July 32.
[8] P.R.O. PRO 30/69/678, Stimson to MacDonald, 27 Jan. 33.

The World Economic Conference 1933: The Failure of British Internationalism

The National Government turned its attention to tackling the 12 December 1932 debt payment due to the United States and to preparations for the World Economic Conference almost simultaneously. The Conference appeared to offer an alternative, potentially less abrasive, avenue to debt negotiations than direct diplomatic negotiations. After all, Britain and France appeared to be demanding debt cancellation without offering the United States anything in return. Lausanne had set out the basic structure of the Conference. It was divided into monetary and economic sub-sections. Under financial questions fell monetary and credit policy, exchange difficulties, price levels and the movement of capital. Beneath the heading of economic questions, the need for improved conditions of production and trade was highlighted, urging that particular attention be paid to the issues of tariff policy, prohibitions, restrictions and quotas, and producers' agreements. Initially, the British cherished hopes that the United States would incorporate debt negotiations within the body of the conference but these ambitions were later dashed[9].

Detailed memoranda for the Conference outlining Britain's position on economic and monetary matters were prepared by the Treasury and the Board of Trade under the watchful eye of Frederick Leith-Ross, the government's Chief Economic Adviser. Lausanne had given the World Economic Conference a challenging brief: the world's economic problems were to be tackled by political co-operation. This was a distinction which did not pass unnoticed in the Foreign Office. Sir V. Wellesley, nervous of the import of economic foreign policy being made by the increasingly powerful Treasury, wrote: "If it is not clear at the start that we consider that these financial and economic questions cannot be divorced from foreign policy ... then I am grave-

---

[9] For the Treasury discussion of this issue see correspondence in the Frederick Leith-Ross Papers, P.R.O. (Hereafter T 188), P.R.O. T 188/43, Memoranda by Leith-Ross, July to December 1932.

ly apprehensive lest the whole control of foreign affairs will slip out of the hands of the Secretary of State and he will find that each question will be approached from its economic and financial side to the exclusion of wider political considerations"[10].

This tension between economic and diplomatic priorities grew more pronounced as the 1930s progressed. When the British briefed their experts for the preparatory discussions to be held in Geneva, economic interests invariably dominated diplomatic considerations. These meetings of experts nominated by the main powers, including British, French, American, German, Italian and Japanese economists and financiers, were held in Geneva in November 1932 and January 1933. Here political considerations dominated the choice of British representatives. The National Government was cautious in its choice of experts. It dismissed Hawtrey and Keynes as "too extreme", and preferred instead to send Sir Frederick Phillips, Under-Secretary of the Treasury, to sit on the Monetary Sub-Committee and Sir Frederick Leith-Ross on the Economic Sub-Committee[11].

The main issue to emerge at the November meetings was international hostility to Britain's sterling policy since her departure from the gold standard in September 1931. The National Government's policy on the floating pound remained unchanged from its announcement at the Imperial Economic Conference at Ottawa three months earlier. The Bank of England's observer at the preparatory meetings, Francis Rodd, reluctantly acknowledged that "there can be no question of our return to gold until we are satisfied that economic conditions at home and abroad permit the adoption of that course"[12]. In a pessimistic memorandum, Leith-Ross sketched out the conditions for Bri-

[10] Foreign Office, General Correspondence, P.R.O. (Hereafter FO 371) FO 371/16418, W8747/8034/50, Memorandum by Wellesley, 25 July 32.

[11] P.R.O. T 188/34, Leith-Ross to Fisher, 14 July 32; P.R.O. T 188/68, Memoranda on the Preparatory Committees by Leith-Ross and Phillips, November 1932 and January 1933.

[12] Committee of Treasury Papers, Bank of England, (Hereafter B/E), B/E OV4 PN72, Rodd to Hopkins, 3 Nov. 32.

tain's return to gold: a settlement of war debts on a basis that would enable the Lausanne Agreement to be ratified; an agreement on monetary policy involving legislation to give central banks in France and the United States wider powers coupled with assurances that these powers would secure a rise in the price level; some form of settlement which would produce a redistribution of gold; substantial modifications of the present protectionist policies, particularly those pursued by the United States and France[13].

All in all, it was a fairly substantial list and one which clearly exasperated the delegations of France, Germany and the United States. The German expert Julius Moritz Bonn reported to his government: "things are not the same as they used to be, in that England would to a certain extent lead at world economic conferences; now it is the reverse, she must be led"[14]. The German delegation were not alone it their disappointment. The American and French delegates, too, had looked to Britain to provide the diplomatic lead in Geneva and found the National Government wanting[15]. Deliberations at Geneva proved unfruitful, with little agreement on economic or monetary issues, and British hopes were dampened after the November meetings. Stressing the urgency of the task ahead and the primacy of effective political action, Sir John Simon, the Secretary of State for Foreign Affairs, through the Organising Committee, urged that the Preparatory Committees confine themselves to producing a Draft Annotated Agenda rather than a list of specific proposals. Thus, the government managed neatly to side-step the difficulty of forging any agreement in Geneva.

---

[13] P.R.O. T 188/43, Leith-Ross to Chamberlain, 21 Nov. 32.
[14] Julius Moritz Bonn Private Papers, Bundesarchiv, Koblenz. (Hereafter B.A. NL 82 Bonn), B.A. NL 82/18 Bonn, Memorandum by Bonn, 3 Nov. 32.
[15] *Documents Diplomatiqués Français, 1932-6,* Series 2, (Paris, 1966-), Vol. 2, No. 38, Herriot to Fleriau, 26 Nov. 32, pp. 77-8; General Correspondence of the United States State Department, National Archives, Washington D.C. (Hereafter N.A. SD), SD 550.S1/399, Report by Williams and Day, January 1933.

British policy, as it was unveiled at Geneva, remained largerly unchanged for the Conference proper. Her sensitivity to the question of the floating pound, plus her incomplete tariff legislation, meant that she found herself in the embarrassing position of "stone-walling" these first meetings[16]. The Treasury became increasingly fearful that the outgoing Republican government in the United States would make any settlement of war debt payments conditional on Britain's return to the gold standard or a reduction of British tariff levels. Leith-Ross counselled that the best course was to insist on the settlement of war debts before any progress could be made on monetary or economic questions. It was on this issue that Britain attempted to lead economic foreign policy[17].

It is a measure of Britain's influence that she managed to enshrine in the Draft Annotated Agenda that the "disturbing effects of such payments" would remain an "insuperable barrier" to financial and economic reconstruction[18]. Despite American protests that debts lay outside the Conference's terms of reference, this phrase was often repeated in communiqués sent during negotiations for the payments due on 12 December 1932 and 15 June 1933. The June payment was perilously close to the anticipated opening of the Conference and it was hoped that this would exert pressure on the recalcitrant United States Congress to grant release. The development of British policy towards the Conference increasingly focused on the economic damage caused by these debts, and with some justification. But in the following months there remained the menacing shadow of a question posed by Lord Lothian, and to which Britain failed to formulate a convincing answer: "what is the programme for World Recovery to which it is possible to secure both U.S. and

---

[16] *The Economist*, Supplement on the Agenda for the World Economic Conference, 28 Jan. 33, p. 4.

[17] Frederick Phillips Papers, P.R.O. (Hereafter T 177), P.R.O. T 177/12, Memorandum by Leith-Ross, 20 Dec. 32.

[18] P.R.O. T 188/58, Orme Sargent to Leith-Ross, 20 Dec. 32.

European co-operation - assuming that the Debt question is out of the way?"[19]

II

Amongst the European powers war debts and reparation payments were convenient and popular villains in the Great Depression[20]. The Treasury reasoned that not only were the reparations instrumental in causing Germany's economic collapse but the network of political debt was guilty of exacerbating the world's maldistribution of gold. From 1931 onwards, the Treasury had increasingly adopted the views of economists like Strakosch and Cassel. They argued that the slump had been caused by a profits squeeze compounded by an uneven placement of the world's gold reserves. On the political side, this movement of gold toward France and the United States had been assisted by war debts payments[21]. Britain felt this burden of debt particularly acutely because the nexus of world debt engendered by the Great War had also radically altered the economic balance of power between leading nations. The United States had displaced Britain in the centre as the largest creditor, with a net debt of over $11,315 million outstanding in November 1932 alone[22].

The main thrust of Britain's policy was to try to persuade the United States to accept a line of financial settlement similar to that made in July 1932 at Lausanne. The maximum possible

---

[19] P.R.O. T 188/58, minute from Leith-Ross to Waley enclosing a memorandum by Lothian, December 1932.

[20] C.P. KINDLEBERGER, *The World in Depression*, p. 24. The impact of War debts on the Great Depression is assessed to have played no role in starting it, but to have had some importance in aggravating it. Also see H. FLEISIG "War Debts and the Great Depression", in *American Economic Review*, Vol. 66, 1976, pp. 52-58.

[21] I.M. DRUMMOND, *The Floating Pound and the Sterling Area 1931-39*, (Cambridge, 1981), pp. 128-9.

[22] P.R.O. T 188/58, Table of Debt payments owed to the United States, compiled by the Treasury, November 1932.

German payment was calculated to amount to only $715 million. Thus European payment would have to be scaled down to recognise "this limitation upon the source from which Europe can draw"[23]. But the United States still adhered to the principle first laid down by President Wilson, refusing to recognise the connection between war debts and reparations no matter how loudly the European powers proclaimed it[24]. To try to circumvent this position, the British repeatedly emphasised the impact of political debt in the world's economic malaise during Conference preparations, while commencing direct negotiations with the United States for the payment due on 12 December 1932.

In the series of notes drafted by David Waley and Leith-Ross to the American Administration and published for American and domestic consumption, further arguments for non-payment, or at least a re-negotiated settlement, were advanced. The most significant note issued to Hoover's administration came on 1 December 1932. It stressed that the payments of war debts and reparations must be viewed in relation to the world economic crisis. War loans had not been issued against material assets and the payments made in the 1923-29 period were based largely on an illusory prosperity. The severity of the Depression with the collapse particularly of primary prices and international trade, coupled with currency depreciation, had enormously increased the burden and difficulty of debt transfer. The annuity paid by Britain in 1923 represented a value of six months' exports, whereas the payment due in 1932 equalled the value of four years' exports to the United States. The balance of payments was also seen as heavily weighted against Britain in favour of the United States and the burden was falling increasingly on a

---

[23] Cabinet Office, Cabinet Conclusions, P.R.O. (Hereafter Cab 23), P.R.O. Cab 23/75, minutes of conclusions, 8 Feb. 33.

[24] Stimson Diaries and Papers, (Microfilm at University Library, Cambridge. Originals held at Sterling Memorial Library, Yale University. Hereafter Stimson), Stimson reel 84, Hoover to Stimson, 27 Jan. 33.

tax-payer whose capacity and will to pay was seriously diminishing[25].

The National Government stressed that subsequent discussion on Britain's capacity to pay would be soured if she were forced to make the December payment and pointed to the practical difficulties in transferring such a sum to the United States. The British government maintained that, while its gold and foreign exchange reserves were adequate for the purpose of mitigating exchange fluctuations, they were insufficient to cover the payment of $95,500,000 due on 15 December, 1932. The only possible alternative would be a payment in gold. This would involve considerable sacrifice on the part of the Bank of England from gold reserves which were "widely regarded as no more than sufficient for the responsibilities of London as a financial centre". When it became apparent that the United States would not relent, Chamberlain decided to make the December payment in full and in gold. It was a decision which sprang from practical as well as moral considerations. The shipment of gold would have a less damaging effect on Britain's currency exchange and the complete payment was intended to give Britain a strong hand in the next round of negotiations[26]. Clearly unhappy, the final note accompanying Britain's December payment stressed that the procedure was "obviously exceptional and abnormal".

Such a solution to the 15 December payment question was politically impossible for France in view of the concessions granted to Germany at Lausanne. Despite the valiant efforts of Herriot, France defaulted. It was unthinkable for the French Chamber to cancel German reparation payments if France had to continue to meet American demands for war debts. Britain repeatedly argued it was the turn of the United States to live up to this same spirit of sacrifice. The United States, on the other

---

[25] *The Times*, 2 Dec. 32.
[26] A special supplement on War debts in *The Economist*, 5 Nov. 32, p. 817.

hand, felt that French policy was completely selfish. France had "withdrawn enough gold from the Federal Reserve Bank to repay its entire war-debt obligation" until 1942, and Britain was weakening her own case for war debt revision by siding with the French government[27]. Britain was caught on the horns of a familiar dilemma: making a straight choice, or so it seemed to the parties concerned, favouring either Europe or the United States. But Britain always attempted to examine such problems in a global context, tempered with domestic considerations. In the case of war debts, the solution favoured Europe. The same dilemma was to emerge again during the monetary deliberations at the Conference, with a rather different outcome.

Within Britain's coalition government, the war debts were also a useful means of bonding support for an international economic conference. Whatever their political colour, members of the Cabinet were solid in their desire to see war debts revised. Lord Hailsham, Secretary of State for War, expressed a view popular in Britain: debts owed to the United States were simply their share of the war effort. After all when "our cruisers brought US troops etc. over to Europe, (we) made no charge for the use of our navy"[28]. Although the Prime Minister and John Simon remained sensitive to the implications for British diplomacy which the debt issue held.

MacDonald was the chief promoter of the World Economic Conference in the Cabinet[29]. The Prime Minister hoped for a concerted international effort to promote economic recovery at the Conference which would also encompass a fair solution to

---

[27] P.R.O. T 188/47, Record of meeting to discuss war debts held in the Foreign Office, 21 Nov. 32. For the American view on France's capacity to pay see S.A. SCHUKER, American "Reparations" to Germany, 1919-1933", *Princeton Studies in International Finance*, No. 61, 1988; Stimson reel 83, Stimson to MacDonald, 12 Aug. 32.

[28] P.R.O. PRO 30/69/679, Hailsham to MacDonald, 17 May 33.

[29] Chamberlain feared that MacDonald's friendship with Stimson in particular, would weaken his commitment to cancellation: NC 18/1/786, Chamberlain to Hilda, 11 June 32.

the Debt problem[30]. However, apart from generally increasingly the prestige of the British government and stressing the importance of international economic co-operation, MacDonald had little notion of what the Conference could achieve in concrete agreements. If Neville Chamberlain's sentiments were anything to go by, the prospects were none too bright. The Chancellor complained to his sister: "I have a horrible time ahead of me with this awful World Conference coming on in June. The P.M. thinks it will be all over by Christmas! And it is difficult to see how anything valuable can come out of it"[31].

In November 1932, the Treasury had advocated a strategy which might have produced an early settlement to the wasteful and consuming problem of war debts and fostered a climate conducive to international economic co-operation: Britain should take a firm line and not pay her December instalment. In a conclusion reached primarily from examining the political rather than the economic climate, Leith-Ross argued that Congress was "completely irresponsible and not open to argument". Suspension was the only way to bring the Americans round. Moreover, the imminent change in Administration meant that Britain could begin with a clean slate once Roosevelt came into office and, if necessary, the new President could even blame Hoover for Britain's default. This would rid Britain and France of their debt payments and preserve the settlement in Europe achieved at Lausanne. Echoing Hoover's strategy that psychological improvement would lead to economic recovery, Leith-Ross urged that what the international economy most required was certainty[32].

The difficulty was to transform this aim into political reality. The National Government seems to have had little sympathy

---

[30] B.J. EICHENGREEN, "Sterling and the Tariff, 1929-1932", *Princeton Studies in International Finance*, No. 48, 1981, p. 1.
[31] NC 18/1/827, Chamberlain to Hilda, 14 May 33.
[32] P.R.O. T 188/49, Secret memorandum by Leith-Ross, 25 Nov. 32.

with the political realities of the economic crisis on the other side of the Atlantic. Both Republican and Democrat Administrations felt that the sums offered by the British would be insufficient to placate their own electorate without European concessions on other issues. The United States no longer wanted, or felt able, to play "fat boy" in Europe.[33] The American representatives at the Conference preparatory meetings in Geneva had focused on the Republican government's desire that Britain return to the gold standard and the introduction of the General Tariff. The departure of the United States from the gold standard in April 1933 removed this bone of contention, but the run on American banks which had precipitated it, coupled with the horrific collapse in primary prices, made America acutely aware of her own economic vulnerability. Large concessions on the part of the new Administration were impossible, regardless of any desire that Roosevelt may have had to give them. So American attention turned to the issues of disarmament and British tariff policy in attempts to broaden debt negotiation.

Facing a new American Administration on the other side of the Atlantic certainly made things more difficult for the British. But far more restricting were the conditions dictated by the primacy of domestic economic recovery. The dominant orthodox and nationalist economics of the Cabinet determined that Britain needed to keep her home and Empire market protected and a free hand in her monetary policy. Debt discussions could not be extended to encompass other questions. In an attempt to fudge the issue, Chamberlain urged that war debts owed to the United States be hidden amongst other economic questions like tariff reduction. "Roosevelt could then strengthen this argument by pointing out (to Congress) that these questions would have to be discussed by other nations, and that he did not want to have this great exploration upset by the default of one nation to

---

[33] R. MOLEY, *After Seven Years*, (London, 1943), p. 205.

another".³⁴ This amounted to stressing that war debts be settled before headway could be made at the World Economic Conference, but little else.

Britain's ambassador to the United States, Sir Ronald Lindsay, held conversations with members of the Senate and the President-elect in January and February 1933. He was armed with instructions to attempt a settlement of the problem on two conditions: it should not involve a reopening of the Lausanne settlement and future payments by the United Kingdom should be covered by British receipts from her debtors. Lindsay was not given any new proposals with which to bargain.³⁵

Following the December payment, the British government spent a considerable time watching developments in the United States, desperate for signs that the opinion of the American public and that of Congress was shifting. They found few crumbs of comfort. Typical of the suspicion and anxiety which dominated the issue was the report carried by the *Philadelphia Ledger*, which claimed that Britain had insisted on meeting her December debt payment in gold "in order to depress sterling, force down commodity prices, and increase unemployment in America".³⁶ Moreover, American suggestions that war debt reductions be traded against armament concessions found little favour in Britain or elsewhere in Europe.³⁷ The Foreign Office were adamant that moves to "bargain so many millions of war debts against the scrapping of so many British cruisers or so many more in millions of war debt in return for the extension to

---

³⁴ Records of Cabinet Office Cabinet Committee on the British war debt to the United States, P.R.O. (Hereafter Cab 27/548), P.R.O. Cab 27/548, record of meeting held 8 Feb. 33.

³⁵ The Cabinet was always nervous of the "wretched constitution" of the United States: NC 18/1/808, Chamberlain to Ida, 17 Dec. 32. They tried to console themselves with the notion that Congress was also capable of "hysterical generosities", P.R.O. T 188/47, Lindsay to Simon, 11 Jan. 33.

³⁶ P.R.O. T 188/58, Lindsay to Simon, 7 Dec. 32.

³⁷ *Ibid.*, Lindsay to Simon, March 1933.

such and such US exports of the Ottawa preference accorded to Canadian goods" must be resisted at all costs.[38]

The Cabinet did not dismiss a connection between an improved economic climate and disarmament out of hand.[39] It recognised that a less hostile economic climate would help soothe political tensions in Europe and pave the way for some progress in the disarmament talks which had reached a stalemate. But such ambitions lay at the end of a chain which began with the solution of war debts and reparations, through a revival of international trade and currency stabilization and culminated in a more secure political environment to aid disarmament negotiations.[40] The National Government rejected moves to introduce the question of disarmament any sooner. In a more immediate sense, it was hoped that Anglo-French co-operation over war debts could provide a potential avenue to resolving some of the hurdles in the disarmament conference. The World Economic Conference might provide a welcome distraction from the problems of disarmament in Geneva.[41]

From the American perspective, however, tariffs and a possible British return to the gold standard, could offer a means for solving the deadlock in debt negotiations. Fairly positive signals along these lines emanated from meetings between Ambassador Lindsay and President Roosevelt. The latter spoke of Britain and the United States working together to improve the economic climate through a "comprehensive programme. He wanted to figure before Congress as a man making a concerted attack on the economic difficulties of the economic situation, with the British government beside him. In that programme he was

---

[38] *Ibid.*, Orme Sargent to Leith-Ross, 20 Dec. 32.
[39] For a discussion of how this strand ties into the development of Appeasement see, *inter alia*, G. SCHMIDT, *The Politics and Economics of Appeasement*, (Leamington Spa, 1986), p. 57.
[40] K. JAITNER, "Aspekete britischer Deutschlandspolitik, 1930-32", in J. BECKER and K. HILDEBRAND (ed.), *International Beziehungen in der Weltwirtschaftskrise, 1929-33*, (Munich, 1978), p. 12.
[41] *Ibid.*

bound to include something about Debts. The gold standard was probably included in his programme. He knew that was a difficult subject for us, but it would be a great advantage if something could be done. Then he would probably include something about tariffs, on which he took a comparatively liberal view".[42] The sentiments Roosevelt expressed at these meetings were little different to the aspirations of his predecessor, Herbert Hoover, although the incoming President had dismissed the possibility of co-operating with Hoover on formulating a policy with which to face the British.[43] The British soon discovered that many leading Senators and Congressmen favoured trading one issue against another to scale down war debts.[44]

On the initiative of the United States, MacDonald was invited for discussions to Washington in the spring of 1933. This invitation to bilateral tallks was extended to numerous leading economic powers, and was indicative of the early internationalist phase of the New Deal. MacDonald arrived in April to discuss questions related to the World Economic Conference together with debts, an issue included at the insistence of the British. The United States, and especially Secretary of State, Cordell Hull, were far more interested in the possibility of tariff reductions. It was not difficult for the two governments to agree on monetary policy after the departure of the United States from the gold standard. At this stage the dangers of competitive dollar depreciation and a more nationalist New Deal remained hidden.[45]

Much more important, however, were the overtures which the Democrat Administration made seeking potential tariff reductions. As early as January 1933, Roosevelt toyed with the idea of negotiating tariff reductions for debts, especially in re-

---

[42] P.R.O. FO 371/17304, W1901/5/50, Lindsay to Simon, January 1933.
[43] Stimson reel 84, Hoover to Stimson, 27 Jan. 33.
[44] P.R.O. T 188/58, Memoranda by Lindsay of interviews with Senators and Congressmen, 6 Feb. 33-9 Feb. 33.
[45] P.R.O. FO 371/17305, W4442/5/50, Minute by Craigie, 25 April 33.

turn for concessions in agricultural products, but President Hoover had been correct in his suspicions that the British government, especially the Treasury, would veto such negotiations.[46] This approach was quite out of the question for the British. The agreements reached at Ottawa were still in their infancy and were seen as a purely domestic economic matter. The Board of Trade rejected as repugnant any notion of going "cap in hand" to the United States.[47] Not only were Britain's tariffs non-negotiable for debt settlement but her policy for the World Economic Conference made successful discussions to reduce the world's tariff barricades unlikely. Yet Britain wanted American co-operation on the revision of war-debts. In the spring of 1933 stalemate appeared inevitable.

As the June war debt instalment due to the United States loomed, the atmosphere of Anglo-American relations became increasingly sour. Once again, no solution seemed in sight. The constant flurry of telegrams across the Atlantic focused on whether this specific payment should be made, and if so by what means. Fearing a complete breakdown of Anglo-American relations prior to the opening of the Conference, Britain agreed to a "Token Payment". Apart from wrangling over whether it should be called a "token payment", as in America this meant "a small worthless object", British officials also began to bargain as to how much would be necessary to make a sufficient impact on American public opinion. Even good will in the Foreign Office towards the United States had run dry, as the Permanent Under-Secretary to the Foreign Office, Robert Vansittart reasoned, "If Paris were 'worth a mass', Anglo-American relations were worth $5 million". After all "we ought to think of the world at large before we bid them go hang".[48] Finally deciding on $10 million in silver, to sweeten the silver lobby in Con-

---

[46] R. MOLEY, *After Seven Years*, p. 202.
[47] P.R.O. T 188/49, Fisher to Chamberlain, 6 Dec. 32.
[48] P.R.O. T 188/74, Vansittart to Leith-Ross, 6 June 33.

gress, the matter was laid to rest for the duration of the Conference, or at least so the United States believed. It was certainly enough to purchase Roosevelt's declaration before Congress that he did not regard the United Kingdom to be in default of her debt payments.

Yet matters rested barely two days. Minutes into his opening address at the World Economic Conference, MacDonald announced that "the Conference is not constituted in such a way as to consider and settle war debts, but they must be dealt with before every obstacle to general recovery has been removed. The question must be taken up without delay".[49] This explicit reference to war debts, only days after the United States' eleventh hour proposal for a 'token' payment to settle the issue, excited much ill-will both amongst the American delegation in London and the Democrat Administration at home. The Americans charged the British with a breach of faith.[50] The United States' recently appointed ambassador to Britain, Robert Worth Bingham, complained that MacDonald's incursion into the question of war debts was "inexcusable and unwise". Bingham believed that the war debts reference antagonised matters for Roosevelt at home and he recorded "at the time I was convinced MacDonald had wrecked the Conference, unless the President should save it".[51] The American sense of betrayal was fuelled by the knowledge that no reference to war debts had been included in the advance copy of the Prime Minister's speech.[52] The World Economic Conference's first 'bombshell message' had come, not from the pen of Roosevelt, but the mouth of MacDonald. This was hardly an auspicious opening for the world gathering. The following year the debt issue grew even more

---

[49] N.A., S.D. 550.S1/1128, Atherton to Phillips, 19 June 33.
[50] Stimson reel 5, Diary of Visit to Britain, record of conversation with Atherton, 22 Sep. 33; Private Papers of Robert Worth Bingham, Library of Congress, (Hereafter L.C., Bingham), L.C., Bingham Diary, entry 14 June 33.
[51] L.C., Bingham Diary, entry 14 June 33.
[52] *Ibid.*; L.C., Bingham Diary, entry 10 Aug. 33.

acrimonious with the passage of the Johnson Act in the United States. Much to Britain's chagrin, the Act branded her as a defaulter in the same class as the French and the Act prohibited all further loans to defaulting nations.[53]

III

In all this haggling, the British firmly resisted overtures made by the United States for discussions which aimed at tariff reductions. As Cordell Hull had made clear to the representatives who converged on Washington in the spring and early summer 1933, the United States intended proposing a flat rate reduction of 10% on existing tariff rates, a corresponding enlargement of quotas, and bilateral negotiations with unconditional most-favoured-nation treatment.[54] This aroused some interest amongst the European powers,[55] but eyes were firmly fixed on Britain to see how she would react to such tariff reduction overtures from the Americans. German interest was firmly focused on the British response to such proposals. Germany believed a radical change had occurred in Anglo-German trading relations following Britain's departure from the gold standard, the Ottawa Agreements and her switch from free trade to an "exceptionally high protective tariff". The German Foreign Ministry was keen to see how Britain would now reconcile this economic nationalism with her alleged leadership of the World Economic Conference.[56]

The German government had long complained that its negative balance of trade with the United States had impeded its abil-

---

[53] Stimson reel 83, Diary of Trip to Britain, July 1933.
[54] Board of Trade, Commercial Department, General Correspondence, P.R.O. (Hereafter BT 11) BT 11/196, Lindsay to Simon, 10 April 33.
[55] Records of the German Foreign Ministry, Foreign Office and Commonwealth Library, London, P.R.O. (Hereafter GFM), P.R.O. GFM 9245/E 651361, Posse to Ritter, 9 Jan. 33.
[56] P.R.O. GFM 3177/D 68371, Memorandum by Ritter, 24 Jan. 33.

ity to make reparation payments. They were now anxious lest Britain's move to protectionism would further inhibit German exports. Germany was only too aware "that the British government had offered a very valuable service in 1932 on certain important political questions", and they were still likely to need such political assistance in 1933. The German government coolly calculated that Anglo-German relations could ill-afford to be compromised by conflict on questions of trading policy.[57] Germany was relieved, therefore, when American attempts to reduce tariffs were stymied by the British. Should Britain have promoted a policy to reduce protectionism at the World Economic Conference, Germany feared she would be forced to compromise her own protectionist trade policy for British political assistance on questions like the renegotiation of the Standstill agreements on her short-term loan obligations, or on questions of disarmament.

British tariff policy for the Conference had largely been formulated prior to the Preparatory meetings held in Geneva in November 1932. The rising tide of protectionist sentiment in postwar Britain became a flood during the Great Depression, and 1931 to 1932 witnessed one of the greatest changes in British commercial policy. The Abnormal Importations Act was passed in November 1931, swiftly followed by the Import Duties Act four months later.[58] These acts marked the end of British free trade and additional protection was secured by the pound's depreciation in September 1931.[59] Empire trade had always been intimately linked with protectionism in Britain. The Ottawa Conference 1932, added a further tier to the evolution of British tariff policy. MacDonald reluctantly agreed to it, as he remained anxious about the implications changes in British tariff

---

[57] *Ibid.*, p. 6.
[58] B.J. EICHENGREEN, "Sterling and the Tariff", p. 2.
[59] F. CAPIE, *Depression and Protectionism: Britain between the Wars*, (London, 1983), p. 41.

policy would have on diplomatic relations.[60] Neville Chamberlain was a far more enthusiastic promoter of Imperial economic ties, happy to continue his father's work. The quota agreements reached at Ottawa were not so much a systematic extension of British tariff policy, as a muddle of *ad hoc* concessions and desperate last minute bargaining.[61] Still, they were quickly incorporated into Britain's economic foreign policy and other nations were forced to reassess their trading relations with Britain. The United States, amongst others, felt themselves to be increasingly outside a "charmed circle" of agricultural producers.[62] This anxiety was magnified by a conviction shared by the Germans, that these agreements were not a conclusion but rather a beginning.

On tariffs, British policy for the Conference was rooted in what the Conservative-dominated National Government perceived to be the needs of the domestic economy. Any hopes for international agreements to reduce tariffs had already been weakened by the failure of the 1927 World Economic Conference, held in Geneva, which had been long on condemning tariffs and short on results. The Board of Trade discounted the possibility of any success coming from universal declarations on the tariff question. Both they and the Treasury had good reason for their misgivings. The practical difficulties in reducing tariffs were immense. They had been erected in a haphazard fashion with variable rates and structure, frequently pitched against depreciated currencies. The difference between nominal tariff rates and their effective level has long been hotly debated alongside their assessed contribution to economic recovery.[63] But whatev-

---

[60] Simon Papers, (Bodleian Library, Oxford. Hereafter Simon) Simon 70, MacDonald to Simon, 27 Dec. 31.

[61] M. DRUMMOND, *Imperial Economic Policy, 1917-1939: Studies in Expansion and Protection*, (Toronto, 1974), p. 31.

[62] M. TRACY, "Agriculture in the Great Depression" in ed. H. van der Wee, *The Great Depression Revisited*, (The Hague, 1972) p. 195.

[63] P.R.O. T 188/68, memorandum by Leith-Ross and Phillips 23 Jan. 33. For a contemporary summary see D.H. ALDCROFT, *The British Economy*, pp. 70-83.

er the variables, a firm, determined hand would be needed if any results were to be achieved in lessening obstacles to trade.

The United Kingdom decided "that the Conference should be led to stress the importance of effecting reductions of tariff barriers by means of bilateral negotiations in the light of any general principles that may be evolved at the Conference".[64] They remained suspicious of any multilateral tariff reductions, although a few exceptional cases, like the Danubian Basin, might be allowed to pass on historical grounds. Britain remained insistent that she would not follow the reasoning which had produced the Ouchy Convention, an agreement between the Netherlands, Belgium and Luxembourg for mutual tariff concessions of 5% a year for ten years, which clearly violated their most-favoured-nation (MFN) commitments.[65] The most-favoured-nation principle remained the basis of British tariff policy in her fairly extensive network of trading relations. It was seen as the most viable means of securing the best treatment for her goods in as many countries as possible as British trading interests were far too widespread and diversified to risk any discrimination which abandoning the principle might produce.[66]

Having championed the MFN clause against the call of Aristide Briand for some form of European economic organisation in 1929-1930, Britain again used the clause to avoid being drawn into specific tariffs negotiations at the World Economic Conference.[67] But this time international hostility to Britain's position on the clause was more pronounced because of the recently concluded Ottawa agreements. These imperial trade preferences were not to be passed onto countries with whom Britain had most-favoured-nation arrangements. The United States,

[64] P.R.O. BT 11/201, DPC Paper No. 24, Memorandum by the Board of Trade, May 1933.
[65] P.R.O. FO 371/17304, W 2992/5/50, Text of a speech by Runciman, 15 Mar. 33.
[66] P.R.O. BT 11/234, Memorandum by the Board of Trade, May 1933.
[67] R.W.D. BOYCE, "Britain's First 'No' to Europe: Britain and the Briand Plan, 1929-30", *European Studies Review*, Vol. 10, 1980, pp. 18-45.

Germany and France all saw these imperial agreements in direct conflict with the MFN principle and Britain could offer only a weak defence: the British government and its Empire enjoyed an "historic kinship" which could not be interpreted within traditional trading relations.[68] The Germans reported in frustration that it had obviously "not yet become clear to the English how they have damaged us in great measure by the direct and indirect contents of the Ottawa agreements".[69]

Germany correctly identified the inconsistency in Britain's trading policy.[70] The German government asked how London could on the one hand defend MFN and on the other, sign the Ottawa agreements, while declaring that nations send delegations to London to promote international economic recovery! Sir Walter Layton, editor of *The Economist* and a member of the Economic Advisory Council, urged the government to modify its attitude. Rather than piecemeal bilateral bargaining, he argued that the best way forward in tariff negotiations was by multilateral means. Certain countries could agree to use a flat-rate maximum tariff, like the Ouchy convention, which ought not to be higher than 10%. Layton gauged that international opinion was very favourable to such a plan. Calculating that Britain was the world's largest import market, buying 20% of goods exported by the rest of the world, few nations would dare to quarrel with her over such an initiative. She should take a "bold lead" in bringing about tariff reductions.[71] The Board of Trade remained unmoved and Layton felt compelled to resign his position as a British expert at the Preparatory meetings in Geneva.

Britain had also concluded a large number of bilateral treaties following the institution of the General Tariff in 1932. These agreements with Denmark, Argentina, Norway, Sweden,

[68] P.R.O. Cab 29/142, M.E.(B) 21, Memorandum by Board of Trade, 14 June 33.
[69] P.R.O. GFM 9245/E 651450, Posse to Berger, 12 Jan. 33.
[70] P.R.O. GFM 9245/E 651649, Rüter to von Neurath, 18 Mar. 33.
[71] P.R.O. T 188/68, Layton to MacDonald, 27 Sep. 32.

Finland and Iceland, as well as a preparatory exchange of notes with Germany, were confined to primary products like butter and beef. The British government's addiction to this "new" form of diplomacy was simply an attempt to catch up on tariff levels implemented by other nations. These agreements, like those reached at Ottawa, were defended as an incentive for other nations to enter into tariff negotiations with Britain because it would now give contracting parties something to bargain with.[72] Cordell Hull's view was less generous. He interpreted these agreements as a great threat to American trading interests and saw Britain's tariff rates as inflated, designed for use "as a club with which to beat down the trade barriers of other countries".[73]

But Britain was not prepared to do any clubbing at the Conference. She may have proclaimed the necessity that tariffs should be reduced at the Preparatory Commissions, but economic considerations determined that she should retain a free hand in her own tariff policy. In memoranda almost identical to those being composed by their counterparts in Germany, the Board of Trade argued that the percentage level of British tariffs were lower still than those of many of her competitors, particularly the United States. In his meeting with Georges Bonnet, held in March 1933, Chamberlain outlined why he was sceptical of any co-operation with the United States on the question of tariffs. "We were faced with the difficulty that the United States sells to us five or six times what she takes from us. We thought that it was for America first to lower her tariffs very substantially so

---

[72] J.P. NICHOLS, "Roosevelt's Monetary Policy in 1933", *American Historical Review*, No. 56, 1951, p. 295; H.V. HODSON, *The Slump and Recovery*, p. 165.

[73] Cordell Hull Private Papers, Microfilm, University Library, Cambridge. Originals held at the Library of Congress, Washington D.C. (Hereafter Hull), Hull reel 46, Memorandum by Hull, April 1933. He argues that the British had based their tariff policy on the misconception that because US tariffs were higher than their own, they were more damaging. This was not the case because US rates had been "in place for one or more decades", whereas British rates were new and therefore far more harmful.

that we could increase our trade with her".[74] Not only did Britain feel that the United States should make considerable reductions before Britain should need to make any, but possible tariff negotiations with France were also ruled out. The arch villain in using import quotas to strangle international trade, France's proclamations on the need for tariff reductions were treated with scepticism by the British.[75] They confidentially noted that French quotas primarily cut down on imports from Belgium, Czechoslovakia and Germany; their effect on Britain was "relatively unimportant".[76]

Britain's determination to promote bilateral trade negotiations at the World Economic Conference was also supported by her industrial advisers for the Conference.[77] The government asserted that, as tariffs had been constructed on the basis of "minimum protection", bilateral negotiations with countries who had a favourable balance of trade with Britain would make it possible for her to arrive at satisfactory agreements without making "any substantial concession upon her present level of tariffs".[78] This siege mentality on tariffs was by no means unique to the National Government, but Britain's strength as one of the world's leading trading nations did present an opportunity to initiate economic co-operation that was dismissed too easily.

This determination not to modify British tariff policy also

[74] P.R.O. T 188/63, W3292/5/50, Notes of the meeting held in the Treasury between Bonnet and Chamberlain, 17 Mar. 33.

[75] P.R.O. T 188/63, Memorandum by the Board of Trade on Anglo-French trade, March 1933.

[76] P.R.O. T 188/36, Memorandum by the Board of Trade, 31 Mar. 32.

[77] It has been argued that the government's sensitivity to business pressures reached a high water mark at the World Economic Conference, after which it declined, see R.F. HOLLAND, "The Federation of British Industries and the International Economy, 1929-1939", in *Economic History Review*, Vol. xxxiii, 1981, p. 293. This fails to take into account the government's desperation to keep business interests out of the Conference, for unlike Ottawa, the meeting in London was a political gathering.

[78] P.R.O. T 188/43, Memorandum by Industrial Advisers to the World Economic Conference, No. 7, 29 June 33.

applied to the Empire. Discussions between delegates from the Empire and Britain were limited to a reaffirmation of the agreements at Ottawa, but they were not extended. Indeed, there was very little attempt by the British government to collaborate with the Empire in preparations for the Conference. But until the Conference met in London, the sterility of British tariff policy was masked by her membership of the tariff truce established in Geneva.[79] The tariff truce had been created to preserve the status quo on tariff arrangements for the period prior to and during the World Economic Conference. Britain, like other participants, joined with the proviso that tariff arrangements currently passing into legislation could continue to do so. This condition was made with an eye on the agreements signed at Ottawa and British bilateral negotiations still in progress. At the talks held in Washington the following April, which the British had mainly seen as an opportunity to force a war debt settlement, the Americans had proposed a new formulation of the tariff truce. They also promised further proposals which would aim at broad tariff reductions.[80]

Britain was convinced that no good would come of the tariff truce.[81] Moreover, the Board of Trade quickly recognised that Norman Davis' new formulation of the truce was unconditional and threatened to restrict Britain's freedom to impose tariffs already in the pipeline. They suspected the United States of attempting to sabotage bilateral negotiations which were taking place between Britain and Argentina, and further implementation of Ottawa agreements pertaining to cod liver oil and frozen salmon.[82] Much to Britain's relief, American promises for further tariff reduction proposals made in April and May 1933, remained unfulfilled.

---

[79] P.R.O. BT 11/202, Memorandum by Board of Trade, May 1933.
[80] P.R.O. FO 371/17305, W5073/5/50, text of the new American resolution for a Tariff Truce, 29 April 33.
[81] P.R.O. FO 371/17305, W4450/5/50, Lindsay to Simon, 24 April 33.
[82] P.R.O. BT 11/196 134306, Minute by Leith-Ross, 8 June 33.

While the National Government had no difficulty in expressing their general agreement with the United States that tariff barriers should be reduced, this was a quite different matter from embarking upon specific proposals. Cordell Hull, in his innocence, was bitterly disappointed when President Roosevelt shelved the proposals for a reciprocal trade agreements bill which would authorise the administration to conclude tariff reduction agreements on a most — favoured — nation basis. He had hoped to show a draft of the bill to other nations to support his call for concrete action on tariffs. Roosevelt chose to postpone his authority for such a scheme for fear of compromising recovery measures being instituted by the National Recovery Administration and the Agricultural Adjustment Administration. The President confirmed his support for Hull's tariff action, "but the situation in these closing days of the session is so full of dynamite that immediate adjournment is necessary. Otherwise bonus legislation, paper money inflation, etc., may be forced... Therefore, tariff legislation seems not only highly inadvisable, but impossible of achievement".[83] Britain was spared the predicament of displaying how nationalist her tariff policy had become. Political events in the United States had drawn Roosevelt from making any specific initiatives towards reduction in London, although the nationalist tone of Britain's position was not lost on the United States.[84]

Ironically, the German government, unnerved by Britain's switch to bilateral trade negotiations, had harboured fears that the American and British governments would conclude some form of bilateral agreement at the London conference. Their apprehensions, of course, proved unfounded, and given Hull's later bitter denunciation of Britain's protectionism in the autumn of 1933, an Anglo-American trading agreement was now a

---

[83] L.C. GARDENER, *Economic Aspects of New Deal Diplomacy*, (New York, 1969), p. 20. Hull's disappointment on tariffs is clear in *The Memoirs of Cordell Hull*, (London, 1948), p. 267.

[84] Hull reel 46, Memorandum by Hull, April 1933.

remote possibility.⁸⁵ Hull continued to labour long and hard to sign a trading agreement with Britain for both economic and political reasons. It took him five more years to reach his goal,⁸⁶ and his interpretation of Britain's tariff policy at the Conference naturally had a profound impact on his attempts to negotiate tariff reductions with the British government in the ensuing period.

At the World Economic Conference, Hull remained authorised by Roosevelt to negotiate general reciprocal commercial treaties based on mutual tariff concessions.⁸⁷ Whilst the Conference began to crumble in disunity on monetary questions, he repeatedly attempted to push through some form of general statement about the desirability of all round tariff reductions, as he had first outlined in the spring. In his final speech at the Conference Hull reiterated his proposals and Neville Chamberlain countered them with his usual defence that British tariffs were still in a formative stage and were lower than elsewhere.⁸⁸ It was only Ashton-Gwatkin in the Foreign Office who took much notice of the proposals as a possible future basis for Anglo-American economic co-operation.⁸⁹

Neville Chamberlain remained adamant that the Conference adhere to specific initiatives and on economic issues all the British delegation could offer were plans to restrict the production of specific commodities. Encouraged by the limited adoption of this principle at Ottawa, Chamberlain saw it as an opportunity for lifting discussions on tariffs and other forms of protection from the level of mutual recrimination onto a more constructive plane. Agreements between producers were to be fostered and

---

[85] P.R.O. GFM 9245/E 651312, Memorandum by Ritter, 3 Jan. 33.

[86] For a detailed reappraisal of Hull's importance in Roosevelt's administration see T.K. McCULLOCH, "Anglo-American economic diplomacy and the European crisis, 1933-39", (Unpublished D. Phil, Oxford, 1978).

[87] C. HULL, *The Memoirs of Cordell Hull*, p. 251.

[88] *Journal of the Economic and Monetary Conference*, No. 39, 28.7.33, pp. 232-241.

[89] P.R.O. FO 371/17308, W 8178/5/50, Minute by Ashton-Gwatkin, 29 July 33.

specific commodities singled out for such action were wheat, cotton, wool, timber and for the benefit of the American domestic political scene, silver.[90] Even Leith-Ross recognised such measures were mere palliatives. But this line of action gave the conference its only concrete achievement: an agreement to restrict silver production and thus raise its price.[91] The American silver lobby under the leadership of Senator Key Pittman went home content.

IV

The notoriety of Roosevelt's 'bombshell message' is surprising given the twists and turns in international monetary relations since the summer of 1931. In the months before the London Conference matters again became complex. The departure of the United States from the gold standard whilst MacDonald and Leith-Ross were aboard the *Berengaria* en route to Washington was the first, but not totally unexpected blow. The second, and more unmanageable, came with fluctuating dollar exchange rates, and an increasingly evasive Roosevelt just as the Conference was convening in London.

As Herbert Feis, the economic adviser to the State Department, pointed out, it was the United States which lit the fuse by suggesting the temporary stabilization agreement at the first meeting of the Preparatory Committee for the Conference in Geneva, November 1932. The American delegates, Edwin Day and John Henry Williams, were representative of all nations still on gold who attended the Conference: Britain must stabilize before the ultimate aim of raising prices could be discussed. It was,

---

[90] Records of the Ministerial Committee for the World Economic Conference, P.R.O. (Hereafter, Cab 29/140-142), P.R.O. Cab 23/142, Memorandum by Board of Trade, May 1933.

[91] S.N. BROADBERRY, *The British Economy Between the Wars: a Macroeconomic Survey*, (Oxford, 1986), p. 132.

of course, "not foreseen that this demand for stabilisation would concentrate on the dollar".[92] By June 1933 events had altered radically, with Roosevelt's administration the focus of such demands and Britain seemingly anxious for the United States to acquiesce to Gold bloc pressures.

As far as Britain was concerned, the debate centred on a temporary agreement for stabilization for the duration of the Conference only. Her policy on currency stabilization remained constant from the time it was first coherently voiced at Ottawa. There could be no question of the government's return to gold until it was "satisfied that economic conditions at home and abroad permit the adoption of that course and the essential conditions are those concerned with freer trade and a higher price level".[93]

From being the outsider on stabilisation at the Geneva meetings, by June 1933 the British delegation found themselves urging the American President to concur with at least a limited statement of monetary policy co-ordination to calm dollar fluctuations. The details of the final drafts of the stabilisation agreement and Roosevelt's "bombshell message" have been ably chronicled elsewhere.[94] The drafts of the stabilisation agreements telegraphed to Roosevelt were simply designed to quell currency speculation and allow the Conference to turn its attention to other pressing issues. The language of Roosevelt's 'bombshell message' in denouncing the "old fetishes of so-called international bankers, was undeniably strong.[95] Roosevelt was indeed quite mistaken in his belief that the Conference was asking him to formally repeg the dollar and to restrict his free-

---

[92] H. FEIS, *1933: Characters in Crisis*, (Boston, 1966), p. 29.

[93] P.R.O. T 188/68, Memorandum by Leith-Ross and Phillips, 10 Nov. 32.

[94] For details of Moley's mercy dash to London see DRUMMOND, *The Floating Pound*, pp. 162-172; MOLEY, *After seven Years*, pp. 224-269.

[95] *Foreign Relations of the United States*, Washington D.C., 1950, Vol. 1, 1933, pp. 673-74. The original document was given by the President to FDR jnr., and is now retained at Hyde Park in FDR, OF:17.

dom of action in domestic policy. This would have been equally out of the question for the British. As Ian Drummond has pointed out, Neville Chamberlain would never have agreed to a policy which limited the scope of his domestic policies.[96]

But Roosevelt's message was also tempered with the claim that America's "broad purpose is the permanent stabilisation of every nation's currency". There was a sense of frustration in the President's plea that it "was a catastrophe amounting to a world tragedy, if the great Conference of Nations... should... allow itself to be diverted by the proposal of a purely artificial and temporary experiment affecting the monetary exchange of a few nations only".[97] For countries still on the gold standard, most notably France, Roosevelt's 'bombshell" did mark the end of any possible use the Conference may have had for their economic and monetary policies. In Europe the conclusion became almost uniform: the Conference had been sunk by Roosevelt's 'bombshell message'. This furore over the temporary stabilisation agreement and the almost universal condemnation of the United States, provoked a strong response from the other side of the Atlantic. Congressman Reynolds, a member of the American delegation to London and Chairman of the Congressional Committee on Foreign Affairs, vehemently protested "that stabilisation was made an excuse by some for wrecking the Conference, and for throwing the blame on us... (it) was no more than a pretext as they, judging from all the signs, did not intend to make any material agreements relative to quotas, tariffs and embargoes.[98] The American government felt it had been made a scapegoat for the Conference debacle.

America's deliberate decision to depreciate the dollar in the spring of 1933 had further complicated the already complex world of international economic co-operation. On the 19th

[96] DRUMMOND, *The Floating Pound*, p. 170.
[97] *Ibid.*
[98] Hull: reel 46, Memorandum by Reynolds, 5 Aug. 33.

April, the day MacDonald and Leith-Ross were due to arrive in New York, the United States left the gold standard in an attempt to raise wholesale prices.[99] The United States were not in the dire straits Britain had been when gold flooded out of her coffers in September 1931. The British Treasury began to signal Leith-Ross that other gold bloc countries could rapidly follow the United States off gold if the dollar were to depreciate heavily. "If (the) World Conference met during that period of confusion, its adjournment pending more settled conditions would prove inevitable".[100] It was a further twist to developments which had taken place since the first meeting of the Preparatory Committee in Geneva the preceding November.

At the meetings in Geneva, France and the United States had held common cause in urging Britain to return to the gold standard and it was the French delegates who saw themselves as providing a "nuance of moderation" in a "sort of duel between the United States and Great Britain".[101] The British kept their conditions for a return to a fixed standard of exchange relatively vague and preserved their freedom of action. The departure of the United States from the gold standard was certainly not unexpected and in the Washington talks with the Administration, British and American officials had no difficulty in establishing a common standpoint. The floating dollar seemed to remove one possible thorn from Anglo-American co-operation for the Conference and it moved France and the remaining nations on gold to the periphery of the arena for a few short weeks.

The Economic Advisory Council, reiterating the points made in a report drafted on this very possibility the preceding year, considered the impact of a floating dollar. Optimistic of the general effects of a devaluation of the dollar for American

---

[99] F.W. LEITH-ROSS, *Money Talks: Fifty Years of International Finance*, (London, 1968), pp. 160-161.

[100] P.R.O. Cab 29/142, Memorandum by Leith-Ross, 22 June 33.

[101] J. JACKSON, *The Politics of the Depression in France, 1932-6*, (Cambridge, 1985), p. 171.

economic recovery, it suggested the National Government should advocate a general *de facto* floatation of currencies on gold followed by a stabilization of the dollar-pound exchange rate.[102] The Treasury, on the other hand, decided that the Americans were not sufficiently organized to consider such a proposal and even if they were, Roosevelt would exact a price for participation. It was important that no concessions should be granted to the United States. The proposal was also dismissed because it was considered unlikely that France would abandon the gold standard voluntarily and, in any case, Britain was none too reluctant to cling to the economic advantage of a depreciated pound.[103] The British recognised that in time France would probably have to depreciate but rejected the possibility of exploring a co-ordinated currency devaluation in 1933.

At the World Economic and Monetary Conference, Britain found herself with one foot on either side of the crevasse as the French and American monetary strategies diverged. France was increasingly adamant that she would not participate in the Conference deliberations unless at least a temporary stabilisation agreement was made. The American Administration was increasingly unwilling to do so. Chamberlain was especially anxious to preserve the measure of agreement he had achieved in discussion with the French Minister of Finance, Georges Bonnet, in London that April. The talks seemed a continuum to the progress he felt he had made with the French at Lausanne.[104] Little disagreement was voiced on war debts, tariffs and public works and he reiterated the conditions necessary before Britain would return to gold. Chamberlain then stressed the desirability of central bank co-operation to alleviate the Depression,[105] and

---

[102] P.R.O. Cab 29/140, Memorandum by the Economic Advisory Council, No. 7, 12.6.33.
[103] DRUMMOND, *The Floating Pound*, p. 155.
[104] NC 18/1/820, Chamberlain to Hilda, 18 Mar. 33.
[105] P.R.O. T 188/63, W3292/5/50, Notes of meeting with Bonnet in the Treasury, 17 Mar. 33.

outlined what would have been one of Britain's main policies formulated for the full monetary debate had the Conference not collapsed so hastily: greater co-operation between central banks especially with regard to reserve ratios and credit structure.[106]

As on the question of war debts, a conflict existed between Chamberlain's anxiety to promote Anglo-French understanding, with Prime Ministerial and Foreign Office concern as to how these talks would be received in Washington.[107] It had little practical impact on policy. It was orthodox economic considerations which fuelled Britain and France's growing animosity to the United States' economic recovery policy in the summer of 1933. The Treasury believed that conditions for Britain's exports had been improved by sterling's floatation. But it also feared that too much downward pressure from sterling, compounded by the dollar depreciation, might provoke a round of speculative currency flotation by other currencies. This would be harmful to any hopes for international economic stability. According to Frederick Phillips, Permanent Under-Secretary to the Treasury, "currency depreciation is a game at which more than one can play - we may be forcing others to play".[108] Although other economists questioned the basis of Phillips' fears, the latter stressed that sterling policy must remain constant and internationally responsible by encouraging other nationas to adhere to stabile monetary exchanges.[109]

The stabilization crisis at the Conference came against a backdrop of mounting anxiety amongst gold bloc countries. The American delegation proved ineffective in explaining to the Brit-

---

[106] P.R.O. T 188/63, Joint memorandum by Board of Trade and Treasury, May 1933.
[107] P.R.O. FO 371/17304, W 267/5/50, Orme Sargent to vansittart, 27 Feb. 33.
[108] P.R.O. T 188/48, Memorandum by Phillips, November 1932.
[109] For good example of a critical examination on the views of Phillips, see Ralph G. Hawtrey Private Papers, (Churchill College, Cambridge. Hereafter HTRY), HTRY 1/15, Memorandum by Hawtrey, 18 May 33; P.R.O. Cab 29/142, M.E. (UK), Minutes of meeting held 24 July 33.

ish what the United States' position on this issue actually was. Even Raymond Moley was at a loss.[110] In June 1933, British disquiet mounted as the dollar continued to depreciate. Concern was also voiced about the implications for British trade and the trading advantage which Britain had enjoyed since her departure from gold.[111] The Federation of British Industries urged that the government announce, as soon as possible, measures intended to safeguard British commercial interests. Dollar depreciation had fostered the "belief that it is a matter of time before depreciations will lead to the displacement of British exports in markets of the world".[112] The Board of Trade produced a memorandum which concluded that it was not serious so long as other countries were not forced off gold too. They concurred with the Economic Advisory Council's view that the initial impact of a depreciated dollar might "be helpful to world trade" by reviving prices and demand.[113]

Here too, Britain was determined to retain her independence. She resisted pressure to ally herself with either the gold bloc or with a sterling bloc in a declaration of currency policy.[114] Independence in monetary policy remained a cherished objective. A policy dictated by domestic economic politics, it was seen as symptomatic by the gold countries of Britain's inability to decide whether to favour the United States or Europe in her economic relations.[115] France and the United States left London exasperated.

---

[110] MOLEY, *After Seven Years*, p. 241.
[111] CAPIE, *Depression and Protectionism*, p. 36.
[112] P.R.O. Cab 29/142, Locock to Colville, 7 July 33.
[113] P.R.O. Cab 29/142, Memorandum by Runciman, 12 July 33.
[114] P.R.O. Cab 29/142, Record of conversation between Hull and MacDonald, 12 June 33. For the failure of Dominion pressure see DRUMMOND, *The Floating Pound*, pp. 177-180.
[115] P.R.O. FO 371/17306, W6858/5/50, Tyrell to Simon, 10 June 33.

V

Ramsay MacDonald had been keen to use the Conference in London as a means of promoting Britain's prestige abroad; instead the events in London had deflated it further. The discords struck at the World Economic Conference were to reverberate on into the following years. In monetary policy, it was to be another three years before France, the United States and Britain were ready to co-operate in the Tripartite Stabilization agreement. The formation and history of this agreement shows monetary co-operation was still tense, but the political will of the participants to work together had become stronger. In the economic field, Britain and the United States finally signed a long overdue reciprocal trade agreement in 1938 along the lines first mooted by Hull in Washington five years earlier.[116]

The failure of the Conference was the failure of British leadership, a leadership which other nations had looked to her to provide. Britain's tariff policies were rooted in the National Government's interpretation of domestic economic needs and so set them beyond discussion and possible reduction at the London Conference. British monetary policy was conceived on the same basis but appeared less nationalist at the Conference because of the radical swing in Roosevelt's financial policy.

The National Government had certainly not abandoned internationalism altogether. It had chosen the war debt question to take centre stage as an issue with broad domestic and European support. In so doing, the British government hoped it could avoid the likely tensions of conflicting trade relations be-

---

[116] DRUMMOND, *The Floating Pound*, pp. 181-200; I.M. DRUMMOND, "London, Washington, and the Management of the Franc", *Princeton Studies in International Finance*, No. 45, 1979; S.V.O. Clarke's "Exchange Rate Stabilization in the Mid-1930's: Negotiationg the Tripartite Agreement", No. 41, *Princeton Studies in International Finance*, 1977; A.W. SCHATZ, "The Anglo-American Trade Agreement and Cordell Hull's Search for Peace, 1936-1938", *Journal of American History*, No. 57, 1970-71, pp. 83-103.

tween Britain and three important groups: Europe, the Dominions and the United States. But both Hoover and Roosevelt were unable to grant Britain the desired concessions on war debts. The ability of the United States to ease debts was hindered, partly by Congressional opposition, and partly by Britain's apparent unwillingness to co-operate on economic issues, notably trade policy.

Certainly, the diplomatic and economic backdrop to diplomacy in 1933 was not conducive to coherent policy making. Not only had the United States adopted a radical, national recovery strategy, but governments in Europe, notably in Germany and France, had continued to fall. Typical of this complex policy environment was Vansittart's response to Treasury's proposals to encourage Conference to make credit more freely available to countries in need. This suggestion fell foul of the Foreign Office line which urged that Britain should discourage any policy likely to support Germany's new National Socialist government. Perhaps Britain's economic nationalism at the Conference is understandable given the severity of the Depression, but it is surely less so given the menacing diplomatic climate. The German government drew great comfort from the obvious discord in Anglo-American relations. The Lord Major of Hamburg, von Krogmann, told Hitler that Britain appeared to be aligning herself far more closely with her Empire, and that Germany should rather engage herself with the United States who "are apparently looking about for friends".[117] Germany's Foreign Ministry and Cabinet were delighted that the acrimonious collapse of the World Economic Conference was "not our fault". Developments in London had been to Germany's advantage. All they now needed to do was "wait to heap the odium

---

[117] *Documents on German Foreign Policy*, London, 1966-, Series C, 1933, No. 386, Krogmann to Hitler, (copy to von Neurath), 1 Aug. 33.

for the failure onto others, while enduring that Germany reaped the benefits".[118] An ominous pattern for economic and diplomatic relations in the 1930s had been set.

---

[118] P.R.O. GFM 33:1231, 3177/D 684405, Neurath to Krogmann, 9 Aug. 33; Records of the Minutes of the Reichskanzlei, Bundesarchiv, Koblenz, (Hereafter R 43II), B.A. R 43II/365a. Lorenz to Lammers, 17 June 33.

[16]

Tariffs and Trade Bargaining: Anglo-Scandinavian Economic Relations in the 1930s*

by

T.J.T. ROOTH**

The British trade agreements programme of the 1930s was a striking example of the power which a major importer can exert over suppliers. After the introduction of full-scale protection in the winter of 1931-2, the UK made a series of treaties with its main suppliers of primary produce, pacts aimed principally at obtaining privileges for British exports. The countries selected for trade negotiations were exclusively exporters of primary products and in no case included a major industrial power.[1] All were unequal partners in the sense that they were far more dependent on the British market than Britain on theirs, and most also ran trade surpluses with the UK. Both these factors, it may be argued, gave the larger power a strong bargaining hand, and this may have been enhanced by relative factor immobility in smaller countries with less diversified economic structures.[2]

In this paper a comparison is made of the UK trade agreements with Denmark, Finland, Norway and Sweden. These countries provide contrasts both in production structure and in the degree of dependence on and vulnerability to Britain. It is argued that the outcome of the agreements with Denmark and Finland, the more dependent economies, was far more favourable to the UK than those with Norway and Sweden.

---

* The Author is grateful to Dr. Cliff Gulvin for helpful comments on an earlier draft of this paper. The research was supported by grants from the Economic and Social Research Committee (Great Britain) and the Nuffield Foundation.

** Dr. Tim Rooth is a senior lecturer in economic history at Portsmouth Polytechnic, England.

1. The major treaties were those signed with Australia, Canada, India, New Zealand and South Africa at Ottawa in 1932, and, between 1933 and 1935, with Argentina, Denmark, Norway, Sweden, Finland, Estonia, Latvia, Lithuania and Poland. The trade treaties with Germany (1933) and France (1934) were much more limited in scope, while that with the USA (1938) involved concessions by Britain on imports of agricultural commodities and reductions of imperial preferences. A study of the Ottawa Agreements has been made by I.M. Drummond, *Imperial Economic Policy, 1917-1939*, London, 1974. On the foreign agreements, see R. Gravil and T. Rooth, 'A Time of Acute Dependence: Argentina in the 1930s', *Journal of European Economic History*, 7, 1978, pp. 337-78; E.F. Early, 'The Roca-Runciman Treaty and Its Significance for Argentina, 1933-41', unpublished Ph.D. thesis, University of London, 1981; T. Rooth, 'Limits of Leverage: The Anglo-Danish Trade Agreement of 1933', *Economic History Review*, 2nd ser. XXXVII, 1984, pp. 211-28.

2. A.O. Hirschman, *National Power and the Structure of Foreign Trade*, Berkley and Los Angeles, 1945, p. 28.

TARIFFS AND TRADE BARGAINING:
ANGLO-SCANDINAVIAN ECONOMIC RELATIONS IN THE 1930s

I

The trade agreements between Britain and Denmark, Norway and Sweden came into force in June and July 1933. That with Finland, negotiated shortly afterwards, became operational in November 1933. The Scandinavian objectives had been to secure their exports to the UK in the face of the twin threat posed by British protectionism and by imperial preference. Essentially the Scandinavians were negotiating to limit a retreat in the British market. In contrast the UK was keen to capitalise on her new found bargaining leverage to expand markets for her exports. The fundamental aims of British tariffs in 1931-2 had been to protect the home market and, by limiting imports, to correct a current account deficit in the balance of payments and thus stabilise sterling.[3] But two of the prime movers in the adoption of protection, Neville Chamberlain, Chancellor of the Exchequer, and Walter Runciman, as President of the Board of Trade the Minister responsible for trade treaties, were well aware of the negotiating advantage that tariffs gave Britain. Chamberlain had argued in Cabinet that the tariff was a way of obtaining a 'private entrance for ourselves' into other markets.[4] The structure of the tariff, incorporating a sur-tax on selected products, had been influenced by Runciman's interest in trade bargaining.[5] Later, Runciman was to argue of the fruitless visit of the D'Abernon trade mission to Argentina in 1929 that 'one reason why nothing came of it was that we had no means of exercising any pressure. [With the tariff] we are now in a position to do that'.[6]

Britain's negotiating power with a number of her principal suppliers was greatly enhanced during the slump. Even in 1929 she had been the world's greatest importer. This predominance was accentuated as the depression deepened. The buoyancy of the UK market was one reason for this — the volume of food imports continued to rise between 1929 and 1931 — but the proliferation of trade restrictions in other countries was another important cause. The UK bought an astonishing proportion of world imports of livestock products. For example, Britain accounted for more than three-quarters of world pig-meat imports during the mid 1920s, but while other European countries began to restrict imports after 1927, UK purchases continued to rise so that by 1934 they represented 88 per cent of world trade in this commodity. The proportion of world exports of butter taken by the UK rose from just over 60 per cent in 1928-30 to more than 84 per cent in 1934.[7] While UK imports expanded during the slump, Germany, the second largest importer of butter, implemented higher duties in 1931, quotas in

---

3. S.H. Beer, *Modern British Politics*, London, 1965, pp. 279-92. B.J. Eichengreen, *Sterling and the Tariff, 1929-32*, Princeton Studies in International Finance, No. 48, 1981. F. Capie, *Depression and Protectionism: Britain Between the Wars*, London, 1983, Chs. 4 and 5.

4. Public Record Office (PRO), CAB 23/70, CAB 5, 32, 21 Jan. 1932.

5. Memorandum by Neville Chamberlain, 30 Jan. 1932, NC 8/18/1, N. Chamberlain Papers, University of Birmingham.

6. *Hansard* Commons, Vol. 277, No. 83, 10 May 1933, Col. 1546. In the same speech, Runciman reported that the Danes had been told to buy more British products, and had been reminded of the power that the new tariff gave London to regulate imports.

7. International Institute of Agriculture, *World Trade in Agricultural Products, Its Growth, Its Crisis and the New Trade Policies*, Rome 1940, p. 195 and Imperial Economic Committee, *Dairy Produce Supplies 1937*, London, 1938, p. 82.

1932, and then further tightened the noose in 1933. Other European importers, having increased their purchases in 1931, also imposed a battery of quotas and higher duties between 1931 and 1933. The obvious corollary of this was that a number of countries came to depend more heavily on the UK market. Denmark sold 55.5 per cent of her exports to Britain in 1928, and 64.5 per cent in 1933, while Finnish export dependence rose from 35.3 per cent to 45.8 per cent. Sweden and Norway, both sending approximately one quarter of their exports to the UK, were conspicious exceptions to this pattern. But in all cases there was strong resentment of the measures taken by Germany to cut imports in 1932 and especially in 1933. Germany, after announcing in July 1932 that her trade agreement with Sweden would not be renewed when it expired in the following February, became increasingly unpopular and stimulated a 'growing inclination in Sweden to turn to Great Britain'.[8] Norway, although not having a trade treaty with Germany, nonetheless benefited from most-favoured-nation (m.f.n.) rights and stood to lose from the termination of German treaties with Sweden and Yugoslavia; new duties threatened a range of Norwegian exports.[9] Denmark was especially hard hit by the German 'Fats Plan' initiated by Hugenberg, the Reich Agriculture Minister, in February 1933. A senior British Foreign Office official minuted, 'the Germans are presenting us with unparalleled opportunities in Scandinavia'.[10]

German autarky was creating a vacuum for British trade and influence, and from a British perspective was doing so at a peculiarly opportune moment. The desire in London to capitalise on the situation was fuelled by resentment that while Britain was the major customer of the north Europeans, she was, except in Norway, a long way behind Germany as a supplier of their imports. This was reflected in heavy trade imbalances. The precise amounts tended to be a matter of dispute, hinging on whose trade statistics were being used, and in turn depending whether country of production, consignment or payment was used. On British figures, both Denmark and Finland had exported in 1930 more than five times as much as they had imported from the UK, and Sweden about twice as much. Only in the case of Norway was there a rough equipose.[11]

By the time the international depression reached its trough in 1932-3, Britain's negotiating position with Scandinavia was an extremely strong one. Not only was this true of Norway and Sweden, but what is also important to this analysis is that Denmark and Finland were even more at the mercy of Britain, being critically and increasingly dependent on the British market as an export outlet, and running heavy trade surpluses with the UK.

It might be argued that the full exploitation of this leverage would be prevented by UK treatment of her trade partners' imports. In 1932 Britain had imposed duties on butter, eggs and a variety of forest products. Some of these duties had been increased as a result of the Ottawa

---

8. PRO, FO 381/16347, Sir Charles Clark Kerr, British Minister in Stockholm, to Sir John Simon, 15 Oct. 1932.

9. PRO, FO 381/17724, Sir Charles Wingfield, British Minister in Oslo, to Department of Overseas Trade, 20 Jan. and 11 Feb. 1933, and Wingfield to Simon, 14 Feb. 1933.

10. PRO, FO 381/17279, minute by L. Collier, 10 Feb. 1933.

11. In 1930 Britain had a surplus with Norway, but this was an exceptional year because of unusually large Norwegian purchases of British built ships. In both 1931 and 1932 the UK ran a deficit.

Conference where free entry for the Dominions, often fierce competitors with Scandinavia, had also been confirmed. The implications of the new tariffs for Scandinavian exports are indicated in Table 1 below. Denmark, having escaped relatively lightly in the first round of duty increases, but facing higher rates on butter and eggs, was the worst sufferer from Ottawa. Clearly London, having given first pickings in the UK market to the Dominions, had less enticing offers to make in the subsequent round of negotiations with the non-imperial suppliers. Denmark also looked likely to bear the brunt of any attempts made by Whitehall to restore British agriculture. Bacon featured prominently in the Ministry of Agriculture's schemes, which included proposals to cut total supplies, and within the reduced total to allow for a major expansion of home output and for a substantial increase in imports from Canada. But while prospects for Denmark looked particularly bleak, it is unlikely that they seriously hampered Britain's ability to secure a favourable treaty. As the *Economist* accurately predicted of trade discussions with Denmark, the British line of approach 'seems likely to resemble blackmail rather than bribery'.[12]

The greater problem for Whitehall lay not in the unattractive offers that might be made to the Scandinavians — although the precise nature of these was to be the subject of inter-departmental dispute and compromise — but in formulating a set of requests that would enable British industry to increase its exports. Tariffs in Scandinavia were generally low, and industry often well-established and competitive. Finnish mills, in 1929, produced three-quarters or more of the country's cotton requirements.[13] According to the Sheffield Chamber of Commerce the Swedes produced all classes of steel and tools and were efficient.[14] They were also highly competitive manufacturers of electrical machinery. This limited the possibilities of trade creation. Nor were the prospects of trade diversion good. The crucial constraint here was the British decision to maintain the most-favoured-nation (m.f.n.) clause as a central element in her trade relations.[15] In the context of the Nordic trade bargaining, this meant that any tariff concession Britain was able to secure would be open automatically to her competitors as well. Whitehall feared that Germany, well entrenched in Scandinavian markets, might end up as the major beneficiary from the trade pacts!

---

12. *Economist*, Vol. 116, 21 Jan. 1933, p. 109.

13. PRO, BT 11/199, memorandum from Manchester Chamber of Commerce, Feb. 1933.

14. PRO, BT 11/124.

15. The minutes and memoranda dealing with the decision are contained in PRO, BT 11/87 and BT 11/234. UK industrial organisations, including the Federation of British Industries, had pressed for abandonment of the m.f.n. clause. Britain was engaged in preferential trade with the Empire, and in the Board of Trade it was recognised that she was enjoying the best of both worlds with Empire preferences and m.f.n. treatment for her exports elsewhere.

Table 1. The Impact of the Import Duties Act and Ottawa Agreements on Tariff Incidence on Scandinavian Imports into the UK (1930 imports)

	Denmark	Sweden	Norway	Finland
% of imports taxed in 1930	0.1	2.2	0.6	0.7
% of imports subject to *new* duties, 1932, before Ottawa	48.2	64.0	67.3	69.8
% subject to 10% duties	46.7	36.7	47.2	59.2
% subject to 11% duties or above	1.5	27.3	20.1	10.6
% of imports subject to *new* duties, 1932, after Ottawa	48.2	64.0	67.3	69.8
% subject to 10% duties	5.9	26.4	46.4	46.5
% subject to 11% duties or above	42.3	37.6	20.9	23.3

Source: *Economist*, 'Ottawa Supplement', 22 Oct. 1932, p. 6.

The dangers could be limited partly by tariff manipulation geared closely to Britain's trade strengths. Hence textiles featured prominently in Britain's demands. Even there, however, requests had to be carefully gauged. Tariff reductions might be concentrated on cloths of 36 inches as opposed to 27 inches; dyed and printed cloths to Sweden were favoured above bleached and coloured woven cottons.[16] One demand that proved surprisingly effective was for a 20 or 30 per cent 'stop' on woollen textiles — the incidence of specific duties on low value cloths was often prohibitively high.[17] Whitehall, conscious of Britain's reputation as a producer of high quality cloths, was understandably dubious about the benefits, but in the event they were to prove substantial. Tariff manipulation was also thought likely to help the motor industry if duty reductions could be concentrated on the smaller-engined cars typically produced by UK manufacturers rather than the larger-engined models in which the USA dominated the markets of northern Europe. The British motor cycle industry was competitive, and lower duties were sought on parts and complete cycles. The Finnish negotiations included some novel features, British demands including lower duties on herring and wheat flour. But what is striking about demands for lower duties is how extraordinarily modest they generally

---

16. PRO, BT 11/124, memoranda from Manchester Chamber of Commerce, 2 and 14 Dec. 1932.

17. For example, up to 100 per cent on categories of lower quality woollen cloth to Finland. PRO, BT 11/200, note by J.J. Wills on UK textile proposals, 29 April 1933.

were. For example, they covered only 10.6 and 9.7 per cent respectively of Swedish and Norwegian 1930 imports from the UK, although slightly higher proportions of those into Denmark and Finland. In an attempt to block any further growth in protection the overriding emphasis was placed on the stabilisation of duties and on the maintenance of free entry.

It was evident then that tariff requests alone were likely neither to yield spectacular advances for British exports nor to make major inroads into the trade deficits. If the agreements were to be worthwhile for British trade, and were to escape the derision of free trade critics in Parliament, tariff demands had to be buttressed by further and more effective measures. Whitehall's efforts were concentrated on the coal industry. Britain had virtually monopolised the coal markets of northern Europe up until the middle of the 1920s. As late as 1925 UK coalfields had supplied 78 per cent of Swedish imports, 89 per cent of Denmark's, over 90 per cent of Finland's and practically the entire Norwegian import. But German embargoes on Polish coal in 1925 drove the Poles to seek outlets elsewhere, and they were able to take advantage of the long 1926 coal strike in Britain to penetrate Scandinavian markets. By 1931 British coal accounted for less than a quarter of Sweden's imports, 30 per cent of Finnish and 39 and 44 per cent respectively of Norwegian and Danish purchases abroad. London aimed at a restoration of Britain's pre-1925 position. Despite the depreciation of sterling from September 1931, which in the face of Poland's refusal to devalue the zloty gave British supplies an improved competitive edge, it was clear that if London's wishes were to be met, m.f.n. clauses would have to be ignored. Increased coal exports were to be secured by purchasing agreements in which the Scandinavians undertook to buy a specified proportion of their imports from the UK.

Apart from minor issues such as reduced licence fees for commercial travellers, Britain felt unable to ask more of Norway and Sweden. But demands on the more dependent Danes and Finns went further. Whitehall wanted special purchase arrangements whereby the inputs of products sold in Britain were also bought there. This included jute wrappers for bacon and salt used in the production of bacon and butter. Britain wanted undertakings from the Finns that supplies for the forestry and wood processing industries, including vehicles, machinery, sulphate of alumina and creosote would also be bought in the UK. More importantly, London demanded additional orders for iron and steel.

While the UK looked for an expansion of exports, the most the Scandinavians could achieve was some limitation to the damage being inflicted on their sales of primary products in Britain. The Danes, with more than 90 per cent of their exports to Britain consisting of bacon, butter and eggs, were acutely vulnerable. There was little prospect of reducing tariffs on food exports because preference margins on many products had been fixed at Ottawa. But from Whitehall's perspective, and in particular that of the Ministry of Agriculture, there were also the interests of British farmers to be considered. Walter Elliot, the Minister of Agriculture, was opposed to any type of guarantee that might limit his freedom of action in raising duties or applying import quotas, and he even attempted to have the negotiations postponed until British agricultural policy was more settled.[18] There was a battle in Whitehall between the Ministry

---

18. PRO, CAB 27/489 CFC 32 2, memorandum, 21 Oct. 1932.

of Agriculture and the Board of Trade, the latter supported by the Foreign Office.[19] While Elliot had to agree to the negotiations going ahead, he attempted to block any concessions on tariffs and quotas. In the view of the Board of Trade and the Foreign Office, refusals on these issues would have made successful negotiations with the Scandinavians and Argentina virtually impossible.[20] Elliot eventually relented on duties but managed to retain the right to introduce quotas provided they were combined with UK marketing schemes. The binding of existing duties on butter, cheese, eggs and fish together with free entry for bacon was therefore conceded by the UK. In contrast, of course, the Scandinavians achieved far less satisfactory assurances about quotas. Admittedly Denmark received a guarantee that if quotas on butter were introduced they would be allowed to ship at least 2.3 million cwts. But Denmark had to be content with an allocation of 62 per cent of UK imports of *foreign* bacon and failed to obtain any assurance about minimum quantities. Nor could the Nordic countries wring worthwhile undertakings from London about egg quotas. Yet these failures do not mean the agreements were valueless, even for Denmark. Free entry for bacon and stabilisation of existing duties on dairy products were later to save the Scandinavians from attempts by British Agriculture Ministers to impose more draconian restrictions on their imports.[21]

The North Scandinavian export structure, based heavily on forestry products, was far more favourable than that of Denmark. Duties of 10 per cent on foreign sawn wood gave Canada, and particularly British Columbia, little enough margin to offset higher freight charges, and the Scandinavians were content to see these stabilised. Duties on selected types of semimanufactured timber were reduced from 20 and 15 to 10 per cent. Perhaps more useful was continuance of free entry for newsprint (a not unimportant concession because the UK newsprint industry was applying for duties), and for wood pulp and pit props. More contentious were duty reductions on various types of paper. The British industry had applied for new duties on the heavier grades of paper and board: Whitehall hurriedly agreed to reduce the tariff from 25 to 16 2/3 per cent on specified categories of kraft and greaseproof paper, as well as setting a maximum duty of 20 per cent on millboard and wallboard.[22] Sweden, in the face of opposition from the British industry, also obtained duty reductions on a range of specialised steel products.[23] All these concessions applied automatically to other countries, including Finland. Essentially all that the Finnish delegation achieved was confirmation of what had already been granted earlier to Denmark, Norway and Sweden. But to satisfy Finnish *amour propre*, something extra had to be offered: duties on wooden thread reels were

---

19. PRO, CAB 27/489 CFC 32, contains memoranda and minutes of meetings. See also BT 11/162 for correspondence and interdepartmental meetings.

20. PRO, FO 381/17212, minute by F. Ashton Gwatkin, 6 Feb. 1933 on meetings of 1 and 2 Feb. 1933.

21. T. Rooth, 'Trade Agreements and the Evolution of British Agricultural Policy in the 1930s', *Agricultural History Review*, 33, 1985, pp. 173-90.

22. PRO, BT 11/129, meeting 30 March 1933.

23. PRO, BT 11/132, meetings, 21 Nov. 1932, 11 Jan. 1933, 1 and 10 March 1933, and PRO, BT 11/88, minute, 25 March 1933. Duty reductions on steel and paper, etc. were estimated to result in the loss of about 2,000 jobs in the UK. PRO, CAB 24/240 CP 104 33, 11 April 1933.

lowered from 20 to 15 per cent, and the 10 per cent duty on birchwood and plywood was conventionalised.[24]

How successful was London in securing its demands? The precise percentages of coal to be imported from Britain by each country formed a central part of the negotiations, and there were some interesting differences in the outcome. The extent of the final undertakings reflected variations in negotiating strength as well as the strategy of each Scandinavian state. Eventually the Danes agreed to take 80 per cent of coal imports from the UK, the Finns 75 per cent (they could have got away with 70 per cent),[25] the Norwegians 65 per cent while the Swedes, who had been pressed for 60 per cent, conceded only 47 per cent. Sweden was able to escape with a relatively light coal obligation because the delegation had been much more generous in its treatment of UK demands for tariff reductions than the Norwegians.[26] The Swedish negotiations, in which most British requests for tariff reductions had been met in full, had been cordial, and the Board of Trade, 'in sight of an admirable bargain', overrode the objections of the Mines Department to the small coal quota.[27] By contrast, the Norwegians were considered 'unaccomodating', probably strengthening the determination of Whitehall to secure a greater proportion of coal imports.[28] The higher percentages conceded by Denmark and Finland might reflect their greater vulnerability, but it is worth noting that the Danes were already importing a larger ratio of their coal from Britain than were the other Scandinavian countries.

It was primarily in the purchasing agreements that the weaker position of Denmark and Finland was revealed. The Danes were persuaded to take 80,000 tons of steel from the UK, perhaps double the amount that would have been bought if market forces had prevailed. These concessions, incorporating a price preference of 10 per cent on government purchases of selected iron and steel products, formed a secret part of the agreement, but were sweetened by permission to raise a one million pound loan in London to help finance construction of the Storstrøm Bridge.[29] The Finns were also induced to take a higher proportion of steel imports from Britain, and, as did the Danes, agreed to increase their purchases of a range of other

---

24. PRO, BT 11/199, meeting 20 July 1933.

25. PRO, CAB 24/242 CP 188 33, Anglo-Finnish Negotiations, note prepared in the Board of Trade, 21 July 1933.

26. The Swedish delegation was described as having met about 90% of British tariff requests. Textiles duties were reduced on 1931 trade worth £720,000, and reductions refused on only £40,000 of imports, most of it considered of more value to Germany than Britain; duties were stabilised on trade valued at £1 million. For wool textiles the British negotiators could write that they had got 'most of what we asked for and considerably more than we hoped for', PRO, BT 11/88, minute by A. Kilroy, 25 March 1933. Duties were reduced from 20 to 15% on small cars, reduced on men's shoes by one-quarter, and UK demands met in full on gramophones and records (duty halved), oil cloth (duty reduced by one-sixth), cycle tyres (duty reduced by 25%), and confectionary (duty reduced by 37%).

27. PRO, BT 11/88, minute by Sir Henry Fountain, 26 March 1933, and PRO, BT 11/174, meeting, 5 April 1933.

28. The Norwegians rejected British demands for lower duties on film, gramophones, vehicles, rubber footwear, liquid glue and door fittings. Stabilisation of duties on several categories of cotton textiles were refused. When duties were lowered, the concessions were often nominal: London asked for the duty on cotton prints to be reduced from 1.80 krone to 1 krone; the Norwegian delegation agreed only to 1.53 krone.

29. Rooth, 'Limits of Leverage', p. 217. This was on condition the money was used to purchase British steel.

products.³⁰ London conducted the Finnish negotiations in a somewhat high-handed manner, and despite the paucity of British concessions and the relative generosity of the Finns, twice threatened to terminate the talks.³¹

II

In the wake of the trade agreements the export performance of Denmark, Finland, Norway and Sweden varied widely, as Table 2 indicates. Denmark was unquestionably the worst sufferer. UK imports of Danish bacon fell in quantity and value as well. Not only did the Danish share of the British import market fall from 5.8 per cent in 1932 to a low point of 3.6 per cent in 1937, but the value of imports continued to decline until as late as 1935.

The Northern Scandinavians, on the other hand, did much better. Much more interested in timber and ores than bacon and butter, and therefore relatively immune from protection or preference, they also had the chance of benefiting from the buoyancy of the British market in the 1930s, stimulated by the house-building boom, and, later in the decade, by rearmament. Aided by their export structure, as a group they increased their share of the UK import market, imperial preference notwithstanding. The trade agreements minimised the obstacles in the way of timber and wood product imports. Supplies from Sweden began to recover as early as 1933 and by 1937 were above their pre-depression values. The contrasting experience of Norway and Finland demonstrates, however, the importance of competitiveness as a determinant of market performance. Unlike Sweden and Finland, Norway failed to increase its total share of British imports. Having accounted for 3.9 per cent of UK wood and timber imports in 1929, the Norwegians shipped only 1.3 per cent by 1936-8. They also lost ground in the market for paper and cardboard. The Finns made strenuous efforts to reduce costs in logging and wood processing operations.³² They overtook the Norwegians to become the second greatest supplier of paper and cardboard. Imports of Finnish timber rose from £6.8 million in 1928-30 to £9.3 million by 1936-8. Total imports from Finland, having troughed in 1931, then recovered so rapidly that in the years between 1929 and 1937 they rose by fifty per cent in value and the Finnish share of the UK import market nearly doubled.

One of the most conspicuous features of British export performance in Scandinavia during the 1930s is that sales to the more dependent economies, Denmark and Finland, increased substantially more than to Norway and Sweden. The overall expansion of 20.7 per cent is all the more remarkable when seen in the context of a decline in Britain's total domestic exports of 29.2 per cent between 1928-30 and 1936-38.

The trade agreements, of course, were only one of several influences on British exports to her trade partners. Generally, income levels and foreign exchange earnings determined the import capacity of countries. In turn, Britain's share of these imports was affected by changes

---

30. PRO, BT 11/199, meeting, 24 July 1933. The understanding was that the UK would supply 30,000 tons of an assumed import of 100,000 tons. Previously the UK had furnished about 10% of Finnish steel imports.

31. *Ibid.*, meetings 30 May and 20 June 1933.

32. J. Ahvenainen, 'The Competitive Position of the Finnish Paper Industry in the Inter-War Years', *Scandinavian Economic History Review*, XXII, 1974, pp. 1-21.

Table 2.   Imports into UK from Scandinavia, 1929-1938 £ millions and percentages.

	1929		1930		1931		1932		1933	
	£m	%	£m	%	£m	%	£m	%	£m	%
Denmark	56.2	4.6	54.1	5.2	46.7	5.4	40.6	5.8	35.4	5.3
Finland	14.9	1.2	12.6	1.2	11.6	1.4	11.7	1.7	12.8	1.9
Norway	14.1	1.2	12.0	1.2	8.6	1.0	8.3	1.2	7.0	1.0
Sweden	25.7	2.1	22.6	2.2	17.3	2.0	13.4	1.9	15.9	2.4
Total UK imports	1,220.8		1,044.0		861.3		701.7		675.0	

	1934		1935		1936		1937		1938	
	£m	%	£m	%	£m	%	£m	%	£m	%
Denmark	32.9	4.5	32.0	4.2	33.2	3.9	36.6	3.6	37.9	4.1
Finland	15.2	2.1	14.9	2.0	18.1	2.1	22.4	2.2	19.3	2.1
Norway	8.4	1.1	8.2	1.1	8.9	1.1	11.6	1.1	11.0	1.2
Sweden	17.9	2.5	17.0	2.3	20.6	2.4	26.2	2.6	24.5	2.7
Total UK imports	731.4		756.0		847.8		1,027.8		919.5	

Source: UK *Annual Statement of Trade* (various years).

Table 3.   UK Exports of Domestic Produce to Scandinavia, 1928-30, 1931, and 1936-8 (averages) £'000s (current)

	1928-30	1931	1936-8
Denmark	10,226	9,213	15,875
Finland	3,126	1,773	5,213
Norway	10,239	7,860	7,883
Sweden	10,109	9,213	11,709
	33,700	28,059	40,680

Source: UK *Annual Statement of Trade* (various years).

in the commodity composition of purchases, by the sterling exchange rate and general levels of competitiveness, as well as by the specific benefits accruing from the trade agreements.

Assessed from an international perspective, the four Scandinavian states recovered well from the depression and all experienced a growth in income during the 1930s. Estimates of gross national product suggest that Denmark's 18 per cent expansion between 1929 and 1938 was the most sluggish, while Sweden's g.n.p. rose 26 per cent, Norway's 31 per cent and that of Finland by 65 per cent.[33] In a decade notable for accelerated import substitution, it is surprising how much of this additional income was spent on imports. Although League of Nation's figures, expressed in pre-1933 gold dollars, show a marked decrease in imports for each country, when presented in their own (depreciated currencies), a different picture emerges, as shown in Table 4 below.

Except for Denmark, all countries experienced some growth of imports, even when measured in current values. This makes for a fair comparison with British exports to these markets, also quoted in current values. UK domestic exports increased slightly faster than Swedish imports (15.8 per cent against 13.3 per cent) and considerably faster than Finnish imports (66.7 per cent against 20 per cent). The UK appears to have faired dismally in Norwegian trade, but the picture is distorted by the exceptionally high export of ships early in the decade, especially in 1930, when British trade statistics record sales of £6.3 million.[34] If new ships are excluded from the figures, British exports were actually higher in 1936-8 than they had been in 1928-30, albeit by a modest eight per cent. Sales of UK produce to Denmark rose by 55 per cent, an astonishing performance in view of the overall decline of Denmark's imports.

Table 4. Total Imports into Denmark, Finland, Norway and Sweden, 1928-30 and 1936-8 (averages) millions, (current values)

	1928-30	1936-8
Denmark (kroner)	1,753	1,604
Finland (markkoissa)	6,754	8,094
Norway (kroner)	1,054	1,137
Sweden (kronor)	1,718	1,946

Sources: Denmark: Statistiske Departement, *Danmark's Handel* (Copenhagen, various years).
Finland: Suomen Tilastollinen Päätoimisto, *Suomen Tilastollinen Vuosikirja* (Helsinki, various years).
Norway: Statistisk Sentralbyrå, *Norges Handel* (Oslo, various years).
Sweden: Statistiska Centralbyrån, *Statistisk årsbok,* (Stockholm, various years).

---

33. P. Bairoch, 'Europe's Gross National Product: 1800-1975', *Journal of European Economic History,* 5, 1976, p. 295.
34. This was 31% of total British ship exports in 1930.

There is a measure of confirmation for this in the British share of imports into the different countries. In all four Britain appears to have improved her relative position, most notably in Denmark and Finland. These figures need to be interpreted cautiously. All are based on country of payment as opposed to origin, and greatly exaggerate the volume of British business. When from 1935 in Finland and Norway, and 1937 in Sweden, alternative data using country of origin become available, Britain is revealed as a much less important supplier.[35] Danish statistics were notoriously misleading. Nonetheless it seems probable that the figures provide a tolerably accurate guide to the main trends even if they are unreliable as an indicator of the real level of trade share. The UK position began to improve after 1931. Clearly therefore the trade agreements were not alone responsible for Britain's export performance. The depreciation of sterling from September 1931 gave the UK a competitive advantage against the USA and the gold bloc countries. But the Scandinavians, aware of their precarious position, had also taken measures to switch trade to the UK even before the negotitaions began in late 1932. The UK's share of imports continued to increase until 1934 in Sweden and 1935 in Finland. In Norway and Denmark the expansion appears to have been sustained until as late as 1937. In 1938, as is discussed below, Britain's position deteriorated in all four countries.

One of the objectives of the British negotiators had been to bind protectionism and to discourage the expansion of local output where it was likely to harm British exports. Hence the wide-ranging stabilisation of duties. This certainly did not prevent all the Nordic countries experiencing substantial industrial growth during the 1930s. Swedish industrial production rose by 46 per cent between 1929 and 1938, well ahead of g.n.p., that of Norway by 27 per cent, Finland by 56 per cent and Denmark by 36 per cent. Some import replacement occurred. Alfred Maizels calculated that the import content of supplies of manufactured goods into Sweden fell from 18 per cent in 1929 to 14 per cent by 1938.[36] The British Commercial Secretary in Stockholm reported in 1935 that the Swedish government was raising duties on a list of more than 25 articles of interest to British exporters.[37] Even when duties had been lowered or frozen, as for many textiles, the industry had been rationalised to meet foreign competition, and in the mid 1930s at least was experiencing high levels of production and employment.[38] Much the same was happening in Finland. New flour mills and the development of the Finnish herring industry after 1930 (the livelihood of fishermen had been threatened by a fall in demand for stromling and by the ending of prohibition in 1932 which had killed a useful income from smuggling)[39] led to a serious fall in imports. Local production of cement virtually extinguished imports, the State Railways began to use Finnish steel rails, and the British Commercial Secretary reported 'steady progress towards independence

---

35. In 1938, for example, the UK accounted for 18.2% of Sweden's imports based on country of payment, but only 12.2% by country of origin.

36. A. Maizels, *Growth and Trade*, Cambridge, 1970, p. 136.

37. Department of Overseas Trade, *Economic Conditions in Sweden, 1935*, p. 84.

38. *Ibid.*, p. 25.

39. PRO, BT 11/199, meeting, 29 May 1933.

of foreign supplies' was being made in textiles, rubber goods and hardware.[40] Renewal and modernisation of plant was reported as providing the cotton textile industry with a strong competitive base.[41] All this, however, meant openings for other lines of trade. Finnish production of consumer goods increased 78 per cent between 1929 and 1938, while investment goods production rose by only 22 per cent;[42] meanwhile imports of machinery more than doubled in value between 1930 and the late 1930s.[43]

Table 5. UK Share of Imports into Scandinavian Countries, 1929-1938 (By country of payment)

	1929	1930	1931	1932	1933	1934	1935	1936	1937	1938
Denmark	14.7	14.5	14.9	22.3	28.1	30.1	36.0	36.6	38.1	34.6
Finland	13.0	13.6	12.6	18.3	20.6	22.8	24.2	23.6	22.2	21.7
Norway	21.2	25.8	20.4	21.6	22.9	23.0	23.4	23.9	24.6	23.1
Sweden	17.3	15.8	14.1	16.8	17.9	19.5	19.3	19.0	19.0	18.2

Source: League of Nations: *International Trade Statistics* (Geneva, various years).
*Except for Sweden, the figures include imports from the Irish Free State.

There is also evidence that the trade agreements did limit protection. Since most duties in Scandinavia were levied on a specific basis, the real level of protection declined as prices began to recover after 1933. By binding existing rates, as well as reducing tariffs, the treaties served British industry well. The Finns had only agreed to lower textile duties under considerable duress. In subsequent treaties some of the advantages conceded to Britain, notably the textile duties, were specifically withheld from Germany, Poland and Czechoslovakia.[44] From 1934 the incidence of Finnish tariffs began to fall.[45] From 1935 industrialists were complaining of inadequate protection against foreign competitors and there is some suggestion that local production was being restrained: between 1935-7 raw cotton imports increased by 26 per cent while imported cotton tissues more than doubled in value.[46]

---

40. Department of Overseas Trade, *Economic Conditions in Finland, 1938,* p. 21.

41. *Ibid.*, 1935, p. 37.

42. League of Nations, *Statistical Year Book,* 1938/9, Geneva, 1939, p. 182.

43. Tilastollisen Päätoimiston, *Suomen Tilastollisen Vuosikirja,* Helsinki, various years.

44. Department of Overseas Trade, *Economic Condition in Finland,* 1935, p. 33.

45. *Ibid.*, p. 34 and *ibid.*, 1938, pp. 43-44.

46. *Ibid.*, 1938, p. 52.

By the later 1930s Swedish industry too was experiencing the growing severity of foreign competition. German export prices were so low that even Swedish machinery manufacturers were seriously threatened, woollen manufacturers feared Italian and German dumping, and worsted spinners were suffering because of European competition.[47] Norway made relatively little headway in import replacement, and it is significant that industrial production probably lagged behind g.n.p. during the decade.[48] In Denmark the tariff guarantees were potentially valueless because of the import licensing system employed by the authorities. But although a wide range of new industries emerged, the Danes were careful to minimise the damage to British trade.[49]

Curbing protection where it affected British exports had been one objective of the negotiations. The other principal aim had been to secure trade diversion in Britain's favour; the main methods had been tariff manipulation and the purchase agreements. The coal schemes were successful in raising exports to all four countries, particularly if compared with 1931. Despite the continued development of hydroelectric power in Scandinavia, the consumption of coal remained high, resulting in a growth of shipments far exceeding the estimates originally made in Whitehall. 1931 exports had been 3.7 million tons: by 1936-8 they averaged 8.8 million tons.[50]

Purchase agreements for steel had been made only with Denmark and Finland. World trade in steel was dominated by international cartel arrangements during the 1930s however, 85 per cent of British exports being affected in 1938, and for some steel products Scandinavia was allocated to Germany as a 'domestic' market.[51] This probably explains why much less British steel was shipped to Norway and Sweden in 1936-38 than in 1928-30. But despite the steel agreement with Finland not being observed, the UK share of the market remained comfortably beyond pre-depression levels and exports were worth 42 per cent more in 1936-8 than in 1928-30. Curiously, sales to Denmark rose by precisely the same proportion, but these increases only just offset the losses elsewhere in Scandinavia.

Where tariffs had been concerned, Whitehall had concentrated on improving conditions for the textile industries. Total exports certainly increased, even measured by value, and the volume record was better still. The quantity of cotton yarn exports more than doubled between 1928-30 and 1936-8, and piece goods exports rose by more than half. Yarn exports did well in all markets, especially Sweden, although by the late 'thirties British suppliers were tending to lose ground to Finnish and Swedish exporters and to Czechoslovakian producers.[52] Piece

---

47. Department of Overseas Trade, *Economic Conditions in Sweden, 1939*, pp. 44, 48.

48. Maizels, 'Trade and Growth', p. 136, calculated that the import content of manufactured supplies fell only from 38 to 36 per cent between 1929-38.

49. Rooth, 'Limits of Leverage', pp. 221-2.

50. Average exports between 1928-30 had totalled 5.5 million tons.

51. Board of Trade, *Survey of International Cartels, 1944*, Vol. I and E. Hexner, *The International Steel Cartel*, Chapel Hill, 1943.

52. Department of Overseas Trade, *Economic Conditions in Norway, 1936*, p. 37 and *ibid.*, *Economic Conditions in Finland, 1938*, p. 26.

goods exporters had a more varied experience. In Sweden, British supplies tended to lag behind total imports, and in Norway too Britain continued to lose her share of imports, especially to Japan. In Finland, duty reductions in medium weight cottons were a major factor in the growth of British sales, although here again Japanese competition was intense and the UK share of imports fell after 1935. Denmark provided the best market, volume doubling and earnings rising substantially. Wool and worsted yarn exporters achieved little. Belgian, French and Czechoslovakian competition was severe in the later 1930s in most of northern Europe. The clearest beneficiaries from tariff manipulation were the manufacturers of woollen and worsted fabrics. Since Britain had an established reputation as a supplier of quality woollens, there had been scepticism about her ability to capitalise on the *ad valorem* 'stops' when they had been negotiated in 1933. Subsequently the duty reductions and the 'stops' were singled out as major factors in the growth of exports to Norway and Finland.[53] The total export rose from 4.5 million square yards to 10.5 million square yards per year (1928-30 to 1936-8), with sales to both Finland and Denmark more than tripling. But even woollens were not immune to the tougher conditions prevailing in the latter part of the decade: subsidised German and Italian competition was rife, and Belgian and Czechoslovakian woollens and worsteds were also making inroads into north European markets. Serious losses were experienced throughout Scandinavia between 1936 and 1938.

Tariff manipulation for road vehicles, another prominent element in the negotiations, achieved much less. The Norwegians had refused to concede it at all, and UK vehicle exports remained unimportant, averaging only £126,000 at their peak in 1936-8. British vehicles also remained a rare sight on Finnish roads, and although sales to Sweden increased in the later 'thirties, the United States re-asserted its predominance as a supplier, with UK sales slipping. Only in Denmark was substantial progress made, and that was probably more a result of the allocation of import licences than of tariff adjustments.

By contrast, machinery exports to northern Europe increased sharply. It is unlikely that the gains in Norway or Sweden had much to do with the trade agreements. Both markets were thriving in the later 1930s, but in Norway Germany remained the chief supplier with Sweden also well ahead of Britain.[54] The main reason for the virtual doubling of sales to Sweden was the expansion of the market, although there was a modest increase in share. Only in the Finnish trade pact had there been much for Britain's engineering industry; the purchasing arrangements offered potential advantages for the suppliers of woodworking and paper-making machinery. A major increase in trade share accounted for a surge in exports to 1935. Early in the decade Britain supplied a tiny proportion of Finland's imports of machinery,[55] but by 1935 had passed Sweden to become second only to Germany. Textile and paper machinery imports were both at high levels. From 1935 relative losses were experienced, this partly reflecting a diversion of orders to Germany for paper and textile making machinery, but also the growing demand for electrical and metalworking equipment, little of which came

53. D.O.T., 'Norway, 1936', and PRO, FO 381/19437, Economic Report on Finland, 1935.
54. D.O.T., 'Norway, 1938', p. 51. Only in the supply of belts and packings did Britain take first place.
55. In 1931, for example, only 6%.

from the UK.[56] The dynamism of the market provided compensation however, and total British machinery exports continued to increase. Sales to Denmark, the license system notwithstanding, made only a small advance. Overall, however, sales of UK machinery to Scandinavia increased from £1.4 million per year at the end of the 1920s to £2.4 million by the late 1930s.

From a British perspective the trade agreements with Norway and Sweden were far less productive than those with Denmark and Finland. Nonetheless, coal exports to Norway and Sweden were given a substantial lift, and the concessions on textiles, especially the tariff 'stop' on woollen textiles, were useful. Other factors supplemented the trade agreements in increasing Britain's share of imports, notably the devaluation of sterling in late 1931, and possibly the linking of the Scandinavian currencies to the pound as the sterling area developed. A high volume of Swedish purchases of machinery helped the overall level of UK exports towards the end of the decade.

With the other two Scandinavian states, Denmark and Finland, Britain's bargaining leverage was substantially greater and the trade agreements were correspondingly advantageous for the UK. British exports were aided by the extraordinary recovery of the Finnish economy from the depression. But assisted by tariff reductions and by the purchase agreements, Britain also benefited from trade diversion. Up until 1936 the UK increased its import share of nearly every major commodity group. The agreement with Denmark was also valuable. The major instrument in securing a diversion of purchase to British exporters was the import licensing system introduced by the Danes in 1932. Ironically the trade pact contained not a single guarantee about the allocation of licences, and yet they were to be a key factor in trade relations. The trade performance to Denmark is all the more astonishing in view of the serious losses experienced by the Danes in Britain. Ultimately, however, lower British purchases restricted Danish foreign exchange earnings and were a crucial constraint on the overall allocation of licences. Increased sales to Denmark were entirely the result of trade diversion and had to be sustained in the face of the decline in total Danish imports.

III

The trade agreements enabled Britain to stake out a greater share for her exports in the markets of northern Europe. While it has been asserted that this diverted competition, causing losses for British trade in other markets, the author has argued elsewhere that this effect was probably minimal, certainly so far as German and Polish competitors were concerned.[57] But the trade agreements were not particularly effective instruments for withstanding the intensification of competition later in the decade, when the competitive edge of Belgian and French exports was sharpened by currency devaluation, and the US, Japan, Czechoslovakia, the Scandinavian

---

56. D.O.T., 'Finland, 1938', pp. 29-30. By 1937, lengthening delivery dates were adding to the price difficulties of British machinery salesmen. PRO, BT 11/911, memorandum on exports to Finland, n.d.

57. F. Benham, *Great Britain under Protection*, New York, 1941, pp. 146-7; Political and Economic Planning, *Report on International Trade*, London, 1937, p. 286 and J.H. Richardson, *British Economic Foreign Policy*, 1936, p. 102. Rooth, 'Limits of Leverage', pp. 225-6, for evidence that Britain suffered little in other markets through diversion of competition.

states, as well as Germany and Italy in isolated instances, were all making inroads into north European trade. Conditions became particularly acute during the recession of 1937-8. In northern Scandinavia British losses were experienced at the hands of most of these countries. But in Denmark the operation of import licensing allowed Britain to maintain her share of imports despite the resurgence of Germany. Facilitated by a clearing arrangement between the two countries, Germany regained her former position in Denmark, but did so at the expense of the USA, Belgium, France and Sweden rather than that of Britain.

London failed to make the correct diagnosis and therefore took the wrong measures to cure the problem. The main response in Whitehall to fierce competition was to seek market-sharing agreements with Germany.[58] These proved unattainable. Yet even if British and German industrialists had been able to reach an accord, it would only have dealt with part of the problem because competition came from many sources, not merely from Germany. Another possible course of action was to introduce clearing powers, thus establishing a direct link between imports and exports. London abjured these,[59] partly because of an awareness that Britain's bargaining position was weaker by the late 1930s than it had been earlier in the decade — with the recovery of international trade, northern Europe was no longer so acutely dependent on Britain as it had been in the trough of the depression, and there is some evidence of a decline in British prestige in Scandinavia. Rejection of clearing powers also reflected a lingering attachment to the principles of multi-lateralism among senior Treasury and Board of Trade officials, and reluctance to encourage further bilateralism. Denmark again was an exception, pressure being applied to the Danes in 1936 to increase licence allocations for British trade. But the rejection of clearing powers (other than as a debt recovering device) meant that the UK lacked equipment to stem an erosion of her position. In a period of re-expansion, the trade pacts were not capable of counteracting the economic forces that now loosened Britain's grip on her suppliers of primary produce.

The disparity in economic power between Britain and the countries of northern Europe enabled her to make a series of treaties that boosted exports. This was achieved despite the unfavourable conditions Britain imposed on the imports of her trade partners. The UK obtained privileged entry for its products in exchange for merely limiting the scale of restriction on and discrimination against Scandinavian exports. Of the countries discussed here, Britain treated Denmark the worst, yet secured the greatest absolute export expansion in return. Perhaps the most serious constraint on British exports to Denmark was that country's reduced foreign exchange earnings, in large measure a result of lower sales to the UK. The opportunities created by high vulnerability were also demonstrated in the Anglo-Finnish

---

58. PRO, BT 59/22/540 and 540 A contain the records of the departmental discussions. The issue is explored more fully in C.A. MacDonald, 'Economic Appeasement and the German 'Moderates' 1937-1939', *Past and Present*, 56, 1972, pp. 105-35; D.E. Kaiser, *Economic Diplomacy and the Origins of the Second World War: Germany, Britain, France and Eastern Europe, 1930-1939*, Princeton, 1980; R.F. Holland, 'The Federation of British Industries and the International Economy, 1929-39', *Economic History Review*, 2nd ser. XXXIV, 1981, pp. 287-300; J.S. Eyers, 'Government Direction of Britain's Overseas Trade Policy, 1932-37', unpublished D. Phil. thesis, University of Oxford, 1977, Chs. 5 and 6 and Rooth, thesis, Ch. 9.

59. The various minutes are in PRO, FO 371/20460, 6 June to 7 Sept. 1936. See also PRO, BT 11/753, W.B. Brown to Ashton Gwatkin, 2 Feb. 1937 for a summary of the Board of Trade view.

agreement. Sweden and Norway, less critically dependent on the British market, could, apart from coal, eschew purchase arrangements and substantial trade diversion. The agreements were particularly fruitful in their early years when the stimulus they gave was crucial for Britain. They helped offset retaliation against the Import Duties Act, and the expansion in sales to Scandinavia mitigated a decline in British exports that might otherwise have aggravated the current account deficit in the balance of payments and have encouraged the authorities to pursue more restrictive fiscal and monetary policies. So although the trade agreements proved too weak an instrument for securing enduring trade diversion, they were especially important to Britain in the early years of their operation.

[17]

Alan S. Milward

The Reichsmark Bloc and the International Economy

I

German international economic policy in the 1930s has almost invariably been interpreted as an integral aspect of an aggressive foreign policy designed to satisfy the major international political ambitions of the National Socialist government. The changes which occurred after 1933 in Germany's economic relationships with other countries are always presented as deliberate, positive, choices of policy. There has been considerably more doubt expressed about the precise purpose of these policies but the overwhelming majority of opinion has ascribed to them a nefarious purpose. Historical and economic discussion has focussed mainly on the pattern of bilateral trading agreements with central and south-eastern European countries and the creation of a central clearing system in Berlin to support the ever-increasing trade which these agreements produced. In effect six European countries forming a contiguous block of territory in central and south-eastern Europe, all of them relatively low per capita income economies and primary exporters, saw their trade with Germany under these conditions grow steadily as a proportion of their total foreign trade after 1933. They were Bulgaria, Greece, Hungary, Romania, Turkey and Yugoslavia. This phenomenon has already been much analysed and the statistical outline is presented briefly in the Statistical Appendix. This trading area was often thought of in the 1930s as forming a small German counterpart to the nascent sterling area and for convenience I shall refer to it as the Reichsmark bloc.

This growing commerce has been most frequently discussed as the 'exploitation' by Nazi Germany of the less-developed European economies, an 'exploitation' which was allied to the Nazi government's territorial and diplomatic ambitions, an economic domination which served in some sense as a preliminary to subsequent political or military domination. The Reichsmark bloc thus appears as an economic *Drang nach Osten*, a sinister foreshadowing of things to come [1]. The tone was set by the first scholarly analysis of European payments

---

[1] Probably the most-read work on the inter-war international economy, *William A. Lewis,* Economic Survey 1919—1939, London 1949, is a rare exception. Lewis was saved from this interpretation by the general bias of his work which was to exaggerate the extent to which the stagnation of the inter-war period was a consequence of the inadequacy of markets and prices for exports from the les-developed economies. He was thus as much influenced, rightly, by the benefits accruing to the lower income

patterns in the 1930s, that of Howard Ellis, whose work has had a great influence on most subsequent scholars in the area [2]. Ellis's argument was that the Nazi government, although it may have suffered initial losses from bilateral trade in the Reichsmark bloc, was deliberately using its monopsonistic powers against the less-developed economies to turn the terms of trade in its own favour. In this case the monopsony arose from the great disproportion between the high relative importance of the German market to the total foreign trade of each of the less-developed economies and the low relative importance as a proportion of total German imports of the imports which they despatched to Germany. That these disproportions were indeed very large can be seen from the Statistical Appendix (Tables 1 and 4). The total share of the Reichsmark bloc in German imports rose from 5.6 per cent in 1933 to 18.5 per cent in 1939, its share in German exports from 3.8 per cent to 18.3 per cent. However even from Greece, the Reichsmark bloc country with the lowest share of its total trade with Germany, exports to Germany represented 27.5 per cent of all exports in 1939, while 67.8 per cent of Bulgarian exports in the same year went to Germany. Germany's share in the total imports of each Reichsmark bloc country was in the same proportion, from which other scholars deduced that Germany could equally well turn the terms of trade in its own favour by overpricing its exports [3]. Accepting overpriced exports under the terms of annual bilateral trading treaties with a much stronger power was, it was argued, the only way to clear the accumulation of blocked mark *(Sperrmark)* balances. The idea that the clearing accounts were used in Berlin as a weapon to manipulate foreign trade prices and the corollary idea that the much greater overall size of the German economy compared to those of the other trading partners necessarily gave the opportunity for monopsonistic exploitation still deeply imbue most general accounts of the German and the international economies in this period [4].

Another strand is added to this argument by historians who explain the economic 'exploitation' of the 1930s as the first steps in attaining the foreign policy objectives of the Nazi regime. The increasing trade with central and south-eastern Europe is presented as the first stage in the creation of an autarkic *Großraumwirtschaft*, relatively isolated from exogenous economic forces, to be eventually realised in its entirety by invasion and occupation. Thus Volkmann, arguing that "In the Third Reich foreign trade was the expression of the political and economic struggle for power", has presented the formation of the

countries in the Reichsmark bloc as by the natural desire to condemn all policies of Nazi Germany.

[2] *Howard S. Ellis*, Exchange Control in Central Europe, Cambridge/Mass. 1941.

[3] *Claude W. Guillebaud*, The Economic Recovery of Germany, London 1958, p. 158.

[4] *Gustav Stolper, Karl Hauser, Knut Borchardt*, The German Economy 1870 to the Present, New York 1967, p. 143; *A. G. Kenwood and A. L. Loughheed*, The Growth of the International Economy, London 1971, p. 213.

Reichsmark bloc as an attempt to further Germany's rearmament, a device to permit greater strategic safety in the event of a further war and the formation of a *Großraumwirtschaft,* three policies which were economically and politically interdependent [5]. Using the Marxian concepts of 'unequal exchange' and Galtung's theories of the 'core' and the 'periphery' Doering explained the Reichsmark bloc within a general theory of imperialism. The National Socialist (fascist) government has frequently been portrayed as an example of an especially vicious stage of late imperialism, in which the role of the National Socialist party was to preserve an archaic capitalist structure in Germany by economic and political imperialism outside Germany. In a Galtungian framework the less-developed European economies become a periphery 'penetrated' by the core country, Germany, to its own benefit, the mechanism of 'penetration' being the theory of 'unequal exchange' of which bilateral trading treaties and exchange controls manipulated by the imperialist power are merely one expression. The interest in Doering's work is that she dates this deliberate policy on Germany's part from the depression itself, 1930, rather than from the Nazi take-over. The failed attempt at a customs union with Austria in fact presaged the Reichsmark bloc and was intended to serve the same exploitative purposes [6]. This is an interpretation, of course, which in a more traditional analytical framework is habitual in the German Democratic Republic and Berndt has sought to show that in this respect there was no inherent difference between the Nazi regime and the Weimar Republic [7]. An aggressive external economic policy thus becomes a test for classifying the stage and nature of the capitalist system.

Recently the problem has come to be seen rather more from the standpoint of the less-developed economies themselves as empirical research has shown more accurately the central importance of the fall in foodstuff prices after 1928 for their development [8]. Seen from their standpoint the main objective of

---

[5] *Hans-Erich Volkmann,* Außenhandel und Aufrüstung in Deutschland 1933 bis 1939, in: *Friedrich Forstmeier and Hans-Erich Volkmann* (eds.), Wirtschaft und Rüstung am Vorabend des Zweiten Weltkriegs, Düsseldorf 1975, p. 110; *id.,* NS-Außenhandel im geschlossenen Kriegswirtschaftsraum (1939—1941), in: *Friedrich Forstmeier and Hans-Erich Volkmann,* Kriegswirtschaft und Rüstung 1939—1945, Düsseldorf 1977.

[6] *Dörte Doering,* Deutsch-österreichische Außenhandelsverflechtung während der Weltwirtschaftskrise, in: *Hans Mommsen, Dietmar Petzina, Bernd Weisbrod* (eds.), Industrielles System und politische Entwicklung in der Weimarer Republik, Düsseldorf 1974; *id.,* Deutsche Außenwirtschaftspolitik 1933—1935. Die Gleichschaltung der Außenwirtschaft in der Frühphase des nationalsozialistischen Regimes, Thesis, F. U. Berlin 1969.

[7] *Roswitha Berndt,* Wirtschaftliche Mitteleuropapläne des deutschen Imperialismus 1926—1931, in: Wissenschaftliche Zeitschrift der Universität Halle, 14 (1965), 4.

[8] See, for example, *V. Bozga,* Criza agrară în România dintre cele două războaie mondiale, Bucharest 1975 and *R. Schönfeld,* Die Balkanländer in der Weltwirtschaftskrise, in: VSWG 62 (1975).

external economic policy became to secure markets which had some guarantee of continuity, at least in the medium term. This policy objective opened considerable political possibilities to the greater European powers who could expect important advantages in return for the extension of trade preferences or guarantees. The failure of the German-Austrian customs union plans and the growing political and economic interest of the Weimar Republic in central and south-eastern Europe during the depression have to be seen against a complex background of political manoeuvring tied to the possibility that France or, more remotely, Britain might offer better guarantees of markets to underdeveloped Europe [9]. After the *Machtübernahme* one foreign policy choice for Britain, a choice on occasions deliberately adopted, was to withdraw from this competition and in doing so to hope to 'satisfy' in a safe direction the aspirations of the Reich to a more influential status in Europe [10]. It might have been thought that empirical research in these directions would have examined the question whether for the less-developed European economies it did not in some ways prove fortunate to have found such firm markets in a major European economy where, although the distribution of power and income was shifted drastically away from lower income groups, disposable incomes were nonetheless rising throughout the 1930s. Indeed, it was surely implicit in the British policy of 'economic appeasement' that the Reich could only satisfy its ambitions in an easterly direction by sustaining the development and perhaps guaranteeing the 'stability' of the large tract of underdeveloped Europe lying between itself and the Soviet Union. Both in Germany and south-eastern Europe, however, the Reichsmark bloc, although it may be seen in these empirical studies as having a more complicated motivation, is still depicted as the result of a German economic offensive in which the weaker parties had to give ground.

How far is this view correct? Were the international economic relations between Germany and the Reichsmark bloc those between the strong and the weak, between exploiter and exploited? Did they presage the attempt to achieve *Lebensraum* in the east by military methods? Were they but the first step in this more drastic 'solution'? It is necessary at this stage to enter three warnings. Firstly, were the economic relations within the Reichsmark bloc not of this kind this, of course, would not mean that no such drastic military 'solution' was ultimately intended. If less-developed Europe benefitted from its close attachment to the German market after the depression this would in no way weaken

---

[9] H. Sundhausen, Politisches und wirtschaftliches Kalkül in den Auseinandersetzungen über die deutsch-rumänischen Präferenzvereinbarungen von 1931, in: Revue des Etudes Sud-Est Européenes, 14 (1976), 3; *Bernd-Jürgen Wendt*, England und der deutsche „Drang nach Südosten". Kapitalverflechtungen und Warenverkehr in Südosteuropa zwischen den Weltkriegen, in: *Imanuel Geiss and Bernd-Jürgen Wendt* (eds.), Deutschland in der Weltpolitik des 19. und 20. Jahrhunderts, Hamburg 1973.

[10] The diplomatic aspects of the question are discussed in *Bernd-Jürgen Wendt*, Economic Appeasement, Hamburg 1971.

the fearful threat to the whole area which the economic revival of National Socialist Germany implied nor diminish the very strong likelihood that Hitler would indeed seek to reshape the countries, with little regard for governments or peoples, as part of an intended war against the Soviet Union. Secondly, it was of great importance to Nazi propaganda to suggest that Germany drew great benefits from the Reichsmark bloc and that those benefits were consonant with the general economic *Weltanschauung* of National Socialism. Thus increased trade with the countries of the Reichsmark bloc had to be portrayed as a step towards independence from the 'plutocratic' international capitalist framework which was itself exploiting Germany. It had also to be portrayed as a triumph of consciously-planned, thrustful, self-confident economic and diplomatic action. There is therefore no shortage of statements at all levels of the Nazi power structure which could easily lead us to accept the propaganda picture and the economic ideology at face value and accept the Reichsmark bloc for what Nazi ideologists and propagandists wanted it to be, a device to further the economic policies of the new Germany by fashioning a new Europe. What it was really like is therefore much more accurately judged from the economic facts than from the written word. Thirdly, if the Reichsmark bloc was not, on the evidence of those facts, the exploitation of the less-developed economies by a stronger Germany, that would not necessarily mean that it was not intended to be so. That the aspirations and intentions of policy can be very different from reality is illustrated so frequently in the history of Nazi Germany that the point need hardly be emphasised. All that said, what do the economic facts indicate about the economic relations between Germany and less-developed Europe?

If an economic argument is to be made in favour of Germany's 'exploitation' of the Reichsmark bloc the precise element of 'exploitation' has to be identified. Two scholars have recently challenged the almost universally-held assumption that such an element did exist. Neal has convincingly shown the lack of empirical proof of the argument that Germany could use monopoly power to turn the terms of trade in her own favour and Marguérat has rejected the idea that Germany's economic relationship with Romania between 1933 and 1938 showed a growing subjection of Romanian to German economic interests over the period [11]. Both rely almost entirely on statistical and economic evidence. The wider and vaguer political arguments may therefore be set for the moment on one side for in general, until their work, the discussion has greatly suffered through arguing from political assumptions rather than from the data. However, to these political questions we shall return for they are fundamental and unavoidable.

---

[11] *Larry Neal*, The Economics and Finance of Bilateral Clearing Agreements: Germany, 1934—1938, in: Economic History Review 32 (1979) 3; *Philippe Marguérat*, Le IIIe Reich et le pétrole roumain 1938—1940, Leiden 1977.

Neal's evidence can be joined to the other empirical studies of terms of trade in the 1930s which indicate that they may not have moved in Germany's favour and indeed were more likely to have moved against her. Benham's calculations of the terms of trade of Hungary, Bulgaria, Romania and Turkey with Germany in this period show that in the case of Hungary, Bulgaria and Turkey export prices either rose more than or fell less steeply than import prices [12]. Neal in his recent article examines the unit values of the import and export trade of Romania and Hungary with the Reich and concludes that,

> In general, unit values increased for the exports of both Hungary and Romania to Germany after 1932, although they never reached the 1928 level. Unit values of imports of the two countries from Germany dropped considerably after 1928 and showed no tendency to rise after 1934 [13].

It might be impossible ever to offer by such methods a definitive proof that Germany did not succeed in turning the terms of trade within the Reichsmark bloc in her own favour. The structure of German trade was very complex. She exported raw materials in large quantities as well as the expected high proportion of manufactured goods. In such circumstances the variety of weightings which might be attributed to the various commodities in any such calculation is large. What is more the movement of prices, itself very erratic over the period, is further disguised by the utter artificiality of Reichsmark prices. Neal's calculations are all in the same currency, blocked marks *(Sperrmark)*. But the denominated price in *Sperrmark* of any commodity in a bilateral trade agreement was only one aspect of a complicated bargain and to that extent it might not be possible to get nearer to the heart of the argument other than by a painstaking and minute examination of the economic realities of each separate bilateral agreement and perhaps not even then. That caution entered, it must be firmly stated that both Benham and Neal tested the conventional historical and economic hypotheses about German 'exploitation' in a much more searching way than other historians and, to say the least, have found them wanting [14].

It was never a legitimate critique of German policy in the Reichsmark bloc to argue that *Sperrmark* prices were exploitative because they were in *Sperrmark*. As Neal shows, *Sperrmark* balances could function as reserves in the

---

[12] *Royal Institute of International Affairs*, Southeastern Europe, a Political and Economic Survey, London 1939, p. 197.

[13] *Neal*, p. 403.

[14] As Neal points out Benham's conclusions were in part suppressed. They appeared in 1939 and he was publicly attacked for giving comfort to the enemy. Both sets of calculations are in accord with the more long-term calculations of Kindleberger who found that over the period 1870—1952 the terms of trade of the United Kingdom and Belgium with ‚non-industrial Europe' improved more than those of Germany *(Charles P. Kindleberger*, The Terms of Trade. A European Case Study, New York 1956).

sense that they could be used as backing by the central bank for an increase in currency and credit. Where a country chose to pursue this policy, as Hungary, in contrast to Romania, did, it was accepting one way, possibly the only way, out of the severe deflation provoked by the drying up of capital inflows after 1928. Certainly payment in blocked marks through the mechanism of the central clearing in Berlin could enable Germany to postpone the date on which a Reichsmark credit would be transformed into actual commodities or services [15]. But that, after all, was one useful advantage of bilateral trade which was in theory equally available to any other member of the bloc, for their currencies were no less strictly controlled than that of Germany. In general the large balances were in marks and Germany the debtor. This, however, was by no means always so and no one has yet produced evidence to show that before 1939 countries in the Reichsmark bloc were forced to accumulate such debts. The movement of the German-Turkish clearing balances is instructive in this respect. When German debts accumulated beyond what the Turkish government considered desirable the strict application of import and export controls in Turkey reversed the situation in little longer than a year. Only with the increase in military imports from Germany in 1938 did the *Sperrmark* balance again build up [16]. Since it can be generally observed in the trade negotiations of that decade that Germany was always reluctant to commit a significant proportion of her armaments output to the export market it must be assumed that this swing back to Germany as the overall debtor was a deliberate act of choice on the part of the Turkish government.

This particular part of the argument badly needs to be seen in the common sense perspective of economic relations between less-developed and developed economies in the inter-war period and away from the lurid light thrown on it by the eventual outcome of German foreign policy. The six less-developed members of the Reichsmark bloc were, together with Denmark, the only European countries whose share of international trade increased in the 'thirties, an experience shared by only a small number of extra-European less-developed countries. When foodstuffs were at times destroyed elsewhere in the world because no worthwhile market could be found, there is a lack of proportion in suggesting that the European less-developed economies were particularly penalised through having to accumulate blocked balances in return for rising

---

[15] There is really no more to Einzig's criticisms of Benham's work than this, one more example of how the argument was always conducted in terms of the differences between the National Socialist and other capitalist economies rather than those between developed and less-developed economies. See *Paul Einzig*, Hitler's „New Order" in Europe, London 1941 and *id.*, Why Defend Nazi Trade Methods?, in: The Banker 58 (1941).

[16] *Osman Torgay*, Der deutsch-türkische Handel. Organisation und Technik, Hamburg 1939.

exports [17]. The balances were in any case far smaller than those which other less-developed economies were to accumulate in London in the immediately ensuing period. Their first cause was the collapse of international food markets and prices in the depression and the priority which thenceforward had to be attributed to continuity of markets over prices. In fact the disjointed information on prices suggests that the price of food imports into Germany was higher than the 'international' prices in Britain and the Netherlands, thus giving the European less-developed economies the best of both worlds.

This does not meet the criticism that trade under such conditions imposed severe restrictions on the freedom of choice of the less-developed importer. That their choice of capital goods imports was limited by the need to clear the mark balances is obvious. Whether the contrast with the 'free' choice of imports supposedly permitted in previous decades by capital imports is as strong as many authors seem to suggest may, however, be doubted. Ellis argued that German exports were initially priced low in order to acquire markets which the importer was subsequently forced to provide by the need to clear the balances even when import prices had become high. But as we have seen the evidence suggests that the relative rice of German imports compared to exports from the less-developed economies did not increase, so the penalties on the less-developed economies were no more than a restriction on the choice of supplier. Given the urgent priority which they had to attribute to their exports this penalty was not so severe.

There remains the classical criticism that trade under conditions of bilateralism, although is might initially benefit the less-developed economy if GNP was growing rapidly in the more developed partner (as in this case it was), would nevertheless ultimately result in costly misallocations of resources from which the weaker economy was more likely to suffer harm. Suppose that German import policy kept food prices so high in central and south-eastern Europe as to prevent exports from that area finding any alternative outlet. Those inefficiencies might then create political pressure groups and vested interests in the less-developed economies which would seek to perpetuate the established export trade to Germany and to prevent development beyond the stage of primary exporting [18]. The historian might well regard the theory of international trade under perfect competition as having so little to do with the realities of the 'thirties as to be no use even as an intellectual yardstick. What alternative

---

[17] There are certain inherent aspects of the international trade in foodstuffs which predispose the exporter towards the idea of accumulating credit balances, especially the fact that certain foodstuffs come on the market in very variable quantities over the year, which is not so with manufactures.

[18] This argument is briefly touched on by *Nikola Momtchiloff,* Ten Years of Controlled Trade in South-East Europe, in: N. I. E. S. R. Occasional Papers VI, Cambridge 1941.

markets did exist for the foodstuff exports within the Reichsmark bloc? Some evidence is provided to answer this question by Tables 12/17. Britain was the only other major food importing country to show in the 'thirties a comparable rise in food consumption to that in Germany. In these circumstances alternative markets for the less-developed economies, if they wanted them, could only have been obtained through a deliberate act of political choice by the British government and, as Wendt has shown, the choice was usually being strongly influenced in the opposite direction [19]. Even had Britain chosen to provide alternative markets it would have been at much lower prices.

It would be impossible here to deal satisfactorily with the suggestion that the primary export trades within the Reichsmark bloc introduced a damaging bias into the political structures of the less-developed economies. It can be readily agreed that political developments in those countries after 1933 offered no comfort to those of a progressive cast of mind. To attribute the gradual abolition of democratic forms of politics to the influence of the vested interests of primary exporters is, nonetheless, somewhat far-fetched when there were so many other political and economic forces making in the same direction. And in any case the political and economic bases of authoritarian rule in these countries in the 'thirties showed great differences from country to country, as did the choice of economic policy. Where Romanian governments pursued the same determined policies of industrialisation as their liberal precursors the Bulgarian royal dictatorship was, for example, more consciously 'agrarian' and conservative in its choice of development policy. There is certainly no apparent correspondence between the various unpleasant groups which exercised power in any of these countries and any vested interests created by the strength and persistence of the German export market. Nor, of course, did these governments have much in common with the government in Berlin apart from their authoritarian nature. If the Hungarian government was perfectly willing, as Neal shows, to use its *Sperrmark* balances as a basis for reflation, that was not out of political sympathy with the NSDAP but simply because Hungary had nothing to lose and probably very much to gain from tying herself more closely to German economic and political expansion. Romania could only lose from any revision of the Versailles settlement and that must have greatly influenced the decision in Bucharest to maintain a strict differentiation between reserves and blocked balances and in no way to regard the latter as backing for the money supply. In that way the internal economic shock of clearing the balances, which it was necessary to consider might have to be done at any time, would be less.

It must be acknowledged that where a country had 52 per cent of her import trade and 59 per cent of her export trade with Germany, as was the case with Bulgaria in 1938, the German bargaining position in bilateral negotiations was a strong one, especially as imports from Bulgaria accounted for only one and a

[19] *Wendt*, Economic Appeasement.

half per cent of all German imports in the same year. It would be absurd to suppose that Germany did not seek to obtain every advantage she could from this disproportion. This, also, however, has to be seen in context. No other Reichsmark bloc country had the same high proportion of its foreign trade with Germany and there were other economies outside the Reichsmark bloc in an equivalent degree of trade-dependence on one developed economy to Bulgaria. The dependence of Ireland and New Zealand on Britain was greater, but even larger and more complex economies could find themselves approaching the same state in the 'thirties. Of South Africa's exports 33 per cent went to Britain and 43.4 per cent of her imports came from the same source in 1938. For Australia the equivalent proportions were 55.7 per cent and 41.4 per cent and for India 33.7 and 31.4 per cent [20]. It should also, however, be pointed out that although the sterling area would provide most such examples of trade-dependence in the 'thirties its internal trade and payments arrangements were effectively multilateral whereas mark balances in the Reichsmark bloc were not transferable.

Marguérat's work brings another strand into the argument by illustrating the difficulties for Germany which arose from the entrenched positions which British and French capital had previously acquired in underdeveloped Europe [21]. It has most frequently been assumed that there was a close harmony between German foreign policy and the pattern of German foreign investment. Proportionately to the quantity of British and French investment in the underdeveloped Reichsmark bloc countries German investment was still very low in 1938 although it showed a marked upward trend. Marguérat traces German interest in Romanian oil supplies and the attempt to secure a greater proportion of them. Although it might have been thought that Romanian oil would have been of particular interest to Germany's rearmament plans from 1934 it was not so until summer 1938. Before that date German mobilisation plans envisaged an increase of oil consumption over peace-time levels of no more than about 20 per cent and much of this increase was intended to be met out of synthetic production. It was only Hitler's realisation that he might, after all, be at war with France and Britain simultaneously and at an earlier date than originally foreseen, together with the forced downward revision of synthetic fuel production targets in July 1938, the so-called *Wehrwirtschaftlicher Neuer Erzeugungsplan*, that caused Germany for the first time to bring severe economic pressure to bear on Romania. A comparison of the statistical evidence does, indeed, show that to classify Romania before that date with the other Reichsmark bloc countries is to a certain extent misleading. The increase in her trade with Germany as compared to the period 1925—28 is much

---

[20] Calculated from national trade statistics.
[21] *Marguérat*, see n. 11.

less marked after 1933 than in the case of the other countries although the increase as compared to the depression years is very high. It would be reasonable to argue from the evidence that the increase in German-Romanian trade in the 1930s represented no more than a recovery from the disastrous years 1928—32. However after 1938 when Germany sought to change this situation Marguérat argues that it proved very difficult for her to bring any effective economic pressure to bear on Romania because of the dominating position of British and French capital there. In 1939 Anglo-Dutch capital accounted for 39.8 per cent of all capital participation in the Romanian oil industry, by that time Germany's chief interest, French capital 16.6 per cent and American capital 12.5 per cent [22]. The international oil companies not only withstood German pressures but actually reduced the flow of Romanian oil to Germany until the annexation of Bohemia and the sponsorship of the annexation by Hungary of the Carpatho-Ukraine in March 1939. After that Germany forced the new trade agreement of 23 March 1939 [23].

Outside the sphere of international trade, therefore, at least in the case of Romania, evidence of 'exploitation' is lacking until the final collapse of Czechoslovakia. That this collapse was of major importance to the countries of the Reichsmark bloc can scarcely be doubted. Czechoslovakia was an important market for them and there were extensive Czech capital investments there. Basch berated the British and French for having made an economic surrender at Munich and for having thrown away an economic position in central and south-eastern Europe acquired over many decades [24]. Until the Munich agreements it would be impossible to claim that, setting aside foreign trade, German economic 'penetration' was a matter of any significance. History indeed records no greater disproportion between foreign trade and investment than that shown in the economic relationship between Nazi Germany and central and south-eastern Europe in the 1930s. It might be just as logical to ask the question, "Why, when the proportion of foreign trade with Germany was so very high for these countries, was the level of German investment there so low?" Part of the answer would obviously be the loss of German investments there in the aftermath of the First World War. The recovery of German investment after 1933 appears nevertheless on the scant evidence available to have been remarkably feeble compared to the recovery of German trade. In Bulgaria the proportion of German capital in total foreign capital in the one estimate that

---

[22] There are different estimates. These are the estimates of the British government given in *William N. Medlicott*, The Economic Blockade, vol. 1, London 1952.

[23] The oil companies were still frequently forced to act directly contrary to the wishes of the Antonescu government by the British and French governments.

[24] *Antonin Basch*, The Danube Basin and the German Economic Sphere, London 1944.

is usually cited is put at 16 per cent in 1939 [25]. Since the proportion of German foreign investment to total foreign investment was smaller in the other economies and the increase in foreign trade with them less, it seems unlikely that the increase in German foreign investment there would have been more striking. Lamer's calculations suggest that total German foreign investment in Yugoslavia in 1936 was statistically insignificant by the side of that of west European countries [26]. Even after the *Anschluß* German capital in Romania was probably no higher than eight per cent of total foreign capital [27].

The proportions of capital investment may be less revealing than the actions and plans of German companies. By 1940 at least some major German companies had far-reaching plans for central and south-eastern Europe, which could not unfairly be labelled as economic 'penetration' [28]. The military defeat of France offered large possibilities to a multinational like I. G. Farben. What is not known is how far German firms were able to pursue such policies before 1938 nor how far firms with much less intimate connections with the government than I. G. Farben harboured similar ambitions to control important sections of manufacturing in the less-developed economies. Teichova's study of foreign investment in Czechoslovakia argues that there was a close association between the political aims of the Nazi government to expand their power into central and south-eastern Europe and the investment policy of German firms. The mechanism by which these aims were to be realised was not, she argues, investment *per se* but the integration of firms in the smaller economies into German-controlled cartels [29]. Although Teichova's work contains an immense quantity of data on the intricate patterns of international ownership and agreement affecting Czech (and therefore in many cases Reichsmark bloc) firms the

---

[25] L. Berov, The Withdrawing of Foreign Capital from Bulgaria on the Eve of the Second World War, in: Studia Balcanica 4 (1971).

[26] Mirko Lamer, Die Wandlungen der ausländischen Kapitalanlagen auf dem Balkan, in: Weltwirtschaftliches Archiv 1938.

[27] Marguérat, pp. 34.

[28] Their plans are published in Dietrich Eichholtz, Geschichte der deutschen Kriegswirtschaft 1939—1945, vol. 1: 1939—1941, Berlin 1969, pp. 248; *Dietrich Eichholtz and Wolfgang Schumann* (eds.), Anatomie des Kriegs. Neue Dokumente über die Rolle des deutschen Monopolkapitals bei der Vorbereitung und Durchführung des Zweiten Weltkrieges, Berlin 1969; *Wolfgang Schumann*, Das Kriegsprogramm des Zeiss-Konzerns, in: Zeitschrift für Geschichtswissenschaft 11 (1963/4).

[29] „After Hitler came to power the well-known conscious long-term objective of German heavy industry, to penetrate into Czechoslovak industrial and banking combines in order to attain a basis for further advances into southeast Europe, was openly and aggressively pursued by German political and economic representatives" (*Alice Teichova*, An Economic Background to Munich, Cambridge 1971, p. 91).

precise data which would establish her argument seem lacking [30]. To establish them it would be necessary, no doubt, to trace the relationships of a large selection of firms with the National Socialist regime and to try to establish how far their economic interests coincided, or were made to coincide with, the external ambitions of the Nazi regime. Even were it to be shown that in a large number of cases they did do so it would still be necessary to show that in the period before Munich government and firm were able to implement their ambitions. It may not, indeed, as several studies including that of Teichova herself imply, have been all that easy even after Munich. And, lastly, the intimate embrace of German companies may not have been necessarily a bad thing on all occasions. That, too, might depend, even if it is accepted that the intentions of the Nazi government towards the Reichsmark bloc countries were ultimately aggressive, on the extent of the agreement between the Nazi government and German companies on the desired nature of political and economic society inside and outside Germany. That this is a richly-complicated subject on which scholars are far from agreement no student of the period nor reader of this volume will need reminding. As things stand, therefore, there is no more evidence of German economic exploitation of the Reichsmark bloc countries outside the field of foreign trade than there is inside it.

II

Those who argue that German trading policy was exploitative would surely be unhappy with any refutation of their argument which did not consider the longer run aims of German foreign policy. Most, like Ellis, appear to consider Germany's external policy as a set of predetermined goals wherein the political objectives were reinforced by the economic. The Reichsmark bloc thus becomes a stage in National Socialist foreign policy and there is little point in demonstrating that in its early stages the less-developed economies benefitted from it and may even have done so more than Germany since the ultimate disadvantages to them, seen from a political standpoint, were frightening. This view

---

[30] The large number of German-Czech cartel agreements is well-established by Teichova's work. But their rate of increase declined under the Nazi government while that of British-Czech cartels increased. *Ibid.*, table 1, p. 56, for example, gives a total of 243 German-Czech agreements over the period 1926—32 and only 170 over the period 1933—38. The comparable figures for British-Czech agreements are 21 and, in the Nazi period, 47. Given the very much greater volume of British and French direct and portfolio investment in Czechoslovakia compared to that of Germany their need for cartel agreements might well have been correspondingly less. German direct capital investment there at the end of 1937 was slightly more than one quarter of that of Britain (*ibid.*, Table IV, p. 48).

simplifies beyond acceptability the problem of Nazi foreign policy. The furious debate among diplomatic historians about Hitler's ultimate objectives and about the consistency with which they were pursued is far from a satisfactory conclusion. Even those scholars most committed to the argument that the firmly consistent intentions of the German government were to create by armed force a 'Greater Germany' beyond the eastern frontiers of the Weimar Republic [31] would now accept, however, that this goal involved many important, albeit temporary, shifts of policy along the way. Few would be so bold now as to maintain that the area of any future 'Greater Germany' did not depend on shifting diplomatic and economic eventualities in the thirties. Among these eventualities the shifting positions of the smaller central and south-eastern countries played an important role. It is wrong to attribute a consistent economic motive to Germany's relations with them on the grounds that it was part and parcel of a consistent political motive, for even if, which is not certain, in the long-run the political motive was consistent, in the short- and medium-run the fate which the Nazi government had in store for these smaller countries certainly varied as Germany's relationships with the greater powers changed.

One argument which seems to have been generally accepted throughout, although Marguérat's work refutes it in the case of Romania, is that one purpose of the Reichsmark bloc was to promote rearmament and permit a 'war economy' in Germany in pursuit of these political aims. Faced with the virtual certainty in any future war of another blockade of her overseas trade and this time with a much smaller domestic raw material base to fall back on Germany is claimed to have used the device of bilateral trading treaties to force exports of strategic materials from the Reichsmark bloc which were, so the argument normally runs, equipping the German armed forces for a future attack on her trading partners. For this it might well be worth paying over the odds for foodstuff imports.

This argument exaggerates the strategic economic importance of the Reichsmark bloc to the German economy. Setting aside for a moment the question of food supply there were only three strategic raw materials which the area could provide in such quantities that they were statistically significant as a part of total German supply, chromite, bauxite and oil. Although chromite was traded in only small quantities it was an almost irreplaceable component of armaments steel. Turkey was the world's second largest producer and chromite represented three per cent of the annual value of her exports [32]. Both Greece and Yugoslavia were also each larger producers than the United States and the

---

[31] Lest there be misunderstanding I should point out that my intention here is in no way to support Taylor's ‚revisionist' view of Hitler's foreign policy. Indeed there is nothing in this article that could logically do so.

[32] National trade statistics.

combined output of the region amounted to over a quarter of average annual world output. Similarly, Hungary, Yugoslavia and Greece produced between them about one quarter of the world's output of bauxite, effectively the sole ore from which aluminium could be manufactured on a large scale. The importance of aluminium was that it was the basic constructional material for most aircraft. Germany was devoid of significant reserves of either raw material. Chromite, of course, can be stockpiled much more effectively than bauxite which is consumed in far greater quantities and accumulation of a sufficient stockpile to meet the demands of the war of only limited duration and output at which German strategy aimed would mean that the level of demand from Germany, once this aim had been met, might be less high and less sustained than for bauxite. At the end of 1939 stockpiles of chromite were sufficient to meet presumed future demand for two years without further imports [33]. Nevertheless, it can also be presumed that Germany would not import chromite from hard currency areas if it could be obtained through bilateral agreements with the Reichsmark bloc countries. The strategic importance of oil needs no elaboration and Romania was the second largest European producer.

The exact figures for output and exports of bauxite and chromite remain in some doubt, a doubt which may well linger given their sensitive nature. Yet there is a clear difference in the two cases in the response of the Reichsmark bloc countries to German demand. Over the period 1935—38 Germany probably obtained no more than 30 per cent of the total output of Greek, Turkish and Yugoslav chromite (Table 5). The imprecision arises not so much from the lack of any Yugoslav export figures for 1935 as from the possibility that some of the relatively high exports to Austria could have found their way as ore or in semi-manufactures to Germany. Until 1938, however, the main market for Turkish chromite exports was the United States. The aftermath of the Turkish rearmament loan in 1938 was that the proportion of Turkish chromite exports going to Germany increased steeply but it was still only 49.6 per cent. Conversely the proportion of Yugoslav exports going to Germany (including Austria) fell to 12.6 per cent from its previous year's level of 30.1 per cent and of Greek exports the proportion dropped over the same two years from 42.8 per cent to 40.5 per cent. Italy was throughout the period a more important market than Germany for Greek chromite and Britain of almost equal importance. Chromite was one primary product which could still be sold for hard currency at competitive prices on world markets and with the growth of rearmament outside Germany this became still more the case. The Reichsmark bloc countries could in fact resist German pressure to include greater quantities of chromite in the

---

[33] United States Strategic Bombing Survey. The Effects of Strategic Bombing on the German War Economy, Appendix Table 83.

bilateral agreements and did so successfully until the outbreak of war. German supply from South Africa purchased in sterling between 1933 and 1938 was almost as large as from Turkey.

With bauxite the opposite applied because Allied demand was lower for a long time and could easily be satisfied elsewhere. Bauxite, unlike chromite, is a common raw material. British, American and Canadian aluminium companies obtained their raw material from the Caribbean and France. France was a major world producer with a large export surplus after meeting the demand from her own industry. Production of bauxite tended to be in exact measure to demand from predetermined markets and it was seldom offered freely for hard currency on open markets. The growth of bauxite mining in the Reichsmark bloc was thus a direct response to the surge of demand emanating from Germany, the world's biggest aluminium producer throughout the period. The rapidly rising output of bauxite in Hungary and Yugoslavia was almost entirely for the German market and only relatively small quantities of Greek output went elsewhere. These combined resources were supplying about three-quarters of total German consumption. Even though the main final consumer of these exports was the German aircraft industry, their immediate value to the exporting country must also of course be taken into account. In Hungary they were the origin of an important new industry.

The relative lack of importance of Romanian oil in Germany's total oil imports is explained by German strategy and mobilisation plans before 1938. Before 1939 exports of Romanian oil products to Germany never exceeded 15.7 per cent of total annual exports of these products. Imports of oil products from the Soviet Union were in fact marginally more important in the pre-war period than those from Romania. The largest part of imports remained vulnerable to blockade. The Anglo-Dutch refineries on Curaçao were the chief suppliers and in addition there was a high level of imports from the United States and Iran which, on the eve of war, was supplemented by increasing imports from Mexico. About 60 per cent of oil product imports still came from outside Europe. Oil, like chromite, could be sold on hard currency markets and there was every reason why the Romanian government and the oil companies alike should not allow any more than a small proportion to be sold for blocked marks and probably no way in which Germany could have acquired more of it through bilateral clearing other than by, as in 1939, extreme menaces.

There remains the question of food supply, for in the context of German military strategy in Europe and the intended Allied response of blockade, food was also a strategic good of the highest importance. It might well be worth paying more than the depressed world prices in order to establish direct links between producers and the German market, which governments would be reluctant to disrupt even when Germany was involved in hostilities and which Allied powers could not interrupt by naval blockade. In fact the biggest single component of the increase of Reichsmark bloc exports to Germany is exports of foodstuffs. The proportion of total German foodstuff imports coming from the area rose from 11.1 per cent in 1930 to 28.2 per cent in 1939 (Table 11). The actual volume and value of foodstuff imports as a proportion of total foodstuff consumption fell under the Nazi government's import-saving policies so that in real constant prices foodstuff imports from the Reichsmark bloc did not surpass their level of the previous period of rising German incomes, 1925—28. Nonetheless Germany was breaching its high trade barriers to let in increasing quantities of foodstuffs at prices well above prevailing averages. It was the shift in the origins of German foodstuff imports in the 1930s which constituted the biggest part of the altered pattern of European trade in that decade and it was the exchange of food against manufactured goods which held together the Reichsmark bloc as a trading area.

Yet even the statistical evidence on the development of these various foodstuff trades does not provide a convincing picture of trade-dependence. Here it is necessary to tread carefully. The statistical information is by no means all available, most usually because the particular commodities in question were not satisfactorily disaggregated in trade statistics. Nor would it be wise to draw too sweeping conclusions from the evidence presented here in Tables 12/17. Nonetheless these Tables are strongly suggestive of certain interpretations. No calculations have been made for Bulgaria on the grounds that if half its exports were to Germany and its exports largely consisted of foodstuffs it would be axiomatic that something like that proportion of its main foodstuff exports (those making the biggest contribution to the total value of all food exports) would also have gone to Germany throughout the period. For the other Reichsmark bloc countries the distribution of the most prominent foodstuff exports has been calculated, although the data for Yugoslavia are not such as to enable any satisfactory conclusions to be drawn. The conclusions which could be drawn from these Tables are the following.

Firstly, where a staple export of the underdeveloped economy became more heavily concentrated on the German market than it had been in 1928 that shift often took place most decisively before 1933. There are noticeable exceptions to this in the case of livestock exports from Romania and grain exports from Turkey. Secondly, the only non-German market which diminished in importance for these staple export trades in the 'thirties was Italy. That perhaps is explained by the movement towards import-substitution in the Italian economy. As that movement weakened after 1936 it is noticeable that Italy again re-enters these trades as an active purchaser. British purchasing in these trades in particular did not decline (the average level of food consumption was also increasing in Britain in the 'thirties) and there are certain striking examples of great increases of British purchases in Romania and Turkey after Munich, presumably as a political response. Lastly, and most importantly, the differences between the separate economies and also between separate trades in one economy dominate the picture. This might well suggest that the pattern of the foodstuffs trade in

393

the Reichsmark bloc was dominated by the particular commodity structure of each underdeveloped country's trade. Few of these trades were so dependent on the sole German market as to leave no hope at all of adjustment should there be a threat to withdraw that market [34]. In fact the increase in the proportion of these staple trades going to Germany does not seem adequately to account for the increase in the proportion of all foodstuff exports from the bloc to Germany and it may be that some part of that increase is accounted for by new foodstuff exports developed especially for the German market rather than by these staples. A certain amount of German capital did go into projects for cultivating oil seeds and other crops for export to Germany. The quantity was probably small and the schemes, still unstudied, do not seem on present evidence to have been very impressive. They would, nevertheless, have been beneficial to the underdeveloped economy rather than exploitative.

The increase in the proportion of any staple trade going to Germany seems on present evidence to be no more than a rational response to the higher prices prevailing on the German market. There is no attempt here to make a comprehensive comparison of the relative prices obtaining on different markets in these trades for, again, the evidence is not sufficiently comprehensive to justify such an effort. But such evidence as there is strongly bears out the conclusions of both Neal and Benham on the relative terms of trade. There is an especially striking example in 1939 of the price differentials that existed. In that year Germany and Britain took an exactly equal proportion by weight of Turkish nut exports (Table 16). Their sale price to Germany was 2.2 million Turkish pounds; to Britain 0.9 million Turkish pounds. France took a much larger share than Germany but at a price considerably lower, 1.4 million Turkish pounds, than the price paid by Germany for her smaller quantity [35].

"The exchange of grain for manufactured products", wrote Herbert Backe, Minister of Food in the National Socialist government, "is the sound and natural basis of trade with the east and south-east" [36]. From the perspective of the less-developed economies the advantage of the Reichsmark bloc was that with the decline in capital inflows exports had come to have a greater importance for development. For them exportable food surpluses were but a stage towards another goal, industrialisation. Whether this goal would be acceptable in Berlin or whether it would overturn the 'sound and natural basis' of trade

---

[34] One that clearly was was the export of hazel nuts from Turkey (Table 16). But it was almost matched in that respect by the Greek export trade of currants, etc. to Britain (Table 12).

[35] Turkey, Ministère des Finances, Statistiques Annuelles du Commerce Extérieur de la Turquie.

[36] *Herbert Backe*, Um die Nahrungsfreiheit Europas. Weltwirtschaft oder Großraum, Leipzig 1942, p. 225.

are questions which, once again, can only be answered by reference to Germany's political aims in Europe. If the interest in trade with the Reichsmark bloc stemmed from a static analysis of the European economy in which southeastern Europe remained perpetually underdeveloped it may also have stemmed from a similarly static analysis of Germany's economic future. Measured over the period 1926—1974 the proportion of German exports, including after 1953 the trade of the German Democratic Republic, going to the higher per capita income countries of Europe, has shown a slow but persistent increase with the striking exception of the period 1934—1939 when this trend was sharply reversed [37]. Exports to low per capita income European economies [38] showed a decisive upward trend from 1934 to 1939 which is also clearly distinguished from the long-term pattern of German trade, although the fluctuations of this trade between 1925 and 1933, it might reasonably be argued, are fluctuations around a much more slowly rising trend. Obviously this striking deviation from the long-run pattern of German trade was not reflected in lower rates of growth of GNP, they were higher in the Nazi period than at any time other than the boom of the 1950s. Nevertheless, foreign trade was not in the long run a force for growth in the German economy after 1933 for the constant increase in the proportion of German exports directed towards underdeveloped Europe between 1933 and 1939 was also a constant increase in the constraints which external economic policy imposed on growth and a constant increase in the pressures to sustain the growth of incomes through internal economic policy.

It would be foolish to assert that strategic considerations were not involved in this deviation from trend and impossible to extricate them from its foreign exchange saving component. Yet the origin of the growth of this trade, and indeed the origins of the Reichsmark bloc itself, date from before the Nazi take-over and were a response to the loss of foreign exchange in 1930, the difficulties created for Germany by the rapid burgeoning of exchange controls from Hungary to Greece and the British devaluation against gold in 1931. All the main principles of bilateral trading agreements with underdeveloped Europe were worked out in the Republic before 1933. Schacht's *Neuer Plan* in 1934 merely systematised into deliberate policy a set of trading devices which were already widespread and also extended into deliberate policy a geographical pattern of trade which had in any case begun to emerge as a response to Germany's

---

[37] The calculations to 1955 are represented in *Alan S. Milward*, Der deutsche Handel und der Welthandel 1925—1939, in: *Mommsen, Petzina, Weisbrod* (eds.), p. 477. No one is likely to require evidence of the extrapolation beyond that date in view of the more systematic and generalised evidence in *Alfred Maizels*, Industrial Growth and World Trade, Cambridge 1963.

[38] Bulgaria, Esthonia, Finland, Greece, Hungary, Latvia, Lithuania, Poland, Romania, Spain, Turkey and Yugoslavia.

alarming external situation in the depression. The main difference in 1934 was that as a result of National Socialist domestic economic policy the predicted foreign exchange deficit threatened briefly to acquire the proportions of 1928. In effect 1934 was the first year since 1928 when Germany recorded a deficit on the balance of commodity trade. It became necessary to classify as plans and policy what had over the last four years been only desperate expedients.

There is, lastly, little geographical congruence between the Reichsmark trading bloc and any future *Großraumwirtschaft* or *Lebensraum* which Hitler or the Nazi party may have intended. Two countries in particular stood immediately in the way of German expansion and the overwhelming weight of the historical evidence is that both, Czechoslovakia and Poland, were destined for 'reconstruction'. Those who maintain that Hitler's foreign policy was consistently aimed at obtaining *Lebensraum* in the east all accept that it was to be obtained at the expense of the Soviet Union also. These were the three countries most likely to be the victims of German territorial aggression. Czechoslovakia remained firmly outside the Reichsmark bloc and German trade with both Poland and the Soviet Union diminished to insignificance after 1933. In the period 1925—34 Poland provided an annual average of 2.15 per cent of all German imports and took 2.12 per cent of all German exports. In the period 1934—38 she provided only 1.4 per cent of German imports and took only 1.25 per cent of German exports. The example of the Soviet Union is even more striking. The Soviet Union had been a major trading partner of the Weimar Republic, so important indeed in 1932 as to have been responsible, by one of history's great ironies, for sustaining even the low level of German manufactured exports of that year and providing an invaluable prop to the international capitalist economy. Over the period 1925—1933 the USSR took an annual average of 4.71 per cent of German exports and provided 3.68 per cent of imports. Over the period 1934—38 the comparable figures were only 1.54 per cent of exports and 2.84 per cent of imports [39]. It remains only to add that once the *Großraumwirtschaft* of Nazi propaganda became a reality in 1940 the statistical contribution of the Reichsmark bloc countries to German supply dwindled into relative insignificance, not just when compared to the great increase of manufactured imports from western Europe, but even when the comparison is restricted to foodstuff imports. From 1940 onwards foodstuff imports from occupied western Europe far eclipsed imports from central and south-eastern Europe [40].

---

[39] Statistische Jahrbücher.

[40] See the calculations in *Alan S. Milward*, The New Order and the French Economy, Oxford 1970, pp. 257—8.

III

The grounds, therefore, for arguing that the Reichsmark bloc was a positive step in German foreign economic policy seem as unsure as those for continuing to argue that it was an instrument of 'exploitation' of the less-developed European economies. There is very little evidence for either and a certain amount of evidence to the contrary. Both arguments in fact are based on the assumption that the National Socialist government was able to choose a positive and aggressive external economic policy. But was it? Was not the economic reality more one in which in deeply discouraging economic circumstances the Nazi government gave overwhelming priority to its own domestic economic and social policies and in so doing made Germany's already weak external economic situation even weaker, untenable, indeed, without assuming permanent trade and exchange controls and a very wide and possibly permanent discrepancy between German prices and those of the other major traders? From the moment Hitler became Chancellor any chance of reintegrating Germany into an internationally-agreed payments system disappeared. The Reichsmark bloc, far from being a positive policy, was a desperately unsatisfactory attempt to maintain, at high international costs to the German economy, the absolute primacy of domestic economic policy.

The evidence that the terms of trade in the 1930s may have moved against Germany is in fact exactly what we should expect to find. It was part of the price paid for defending other priorities. As Romanian prices increased Germany was unable to maintain the Reichsmark/leu exchange rate at the level she would have wished. To put up the price of German exports would have made competition on the Romanian market in textiles and metal products against Britain and France impossible. Nor was Germany able to raise the Reichsmark's value in the annual bilateral trade negotiations, partly because Romania was still able to sell oil against sterling and hard currency and, later, because British imports of Romanian cereals showed a steep increase. Romanian *Sperrmark* balances in Berlin represented not a cunning exploitation by Germany, but genuine difficulties in footing the bill for cereal and oil imports, difficulties which threatened repeatedly to disrupt German-Romanian trade [41].

Exchange control began under the Brüning government in order to staunch the outflow of reserves. Germany had in fact only been able to meet her international obligations in 1930 because the collapse of primary product prices drastically reduced the cost of her imports. The fall in exports and the run on the reserves in 1931 left little choice but a system of exchange controls which

---

[41] *Pierre Marguérat*, Le protectionisme financier allemand et le bassin danubien à la veille de la seconde guerre mondiale. L'exemple de la Roumanie, in: Relations internationales 16 (1978).

was thought of as temporary, introduced by a series of administrative decrees in July and August. Immediately afterwards the Wiggin Committee sat to find a basis on which German trade could continue so that creditors (including recipients of reparations) could continue to be paid in spite of the cessation of capital inflows. Its deliberations took place against the background of a restless search by a powerful, if disunited, political opposition for a new basis of economic policy. In this search the National Socialist Party emerged triumphant, not least by combining all the various recipes of the other opposition groups. Like the parties of the left it espoused the cause of employment-creation programmes, like those of the right it demanded the removal of all international restrictions on German tariffs. It cut the ground from under the agrarian parties in rural areas by proclaiming the necessity of self-sufficiency in food production and high levels of agricultural protection. Even if this were ill-understood at the time by the leaders of the NSDAP it was still true that even half this programme would have meant perseverance with trade and exchange controls for a much longer time. Because the NSDAP started from the assumption that the existing state of affairs was intolerable and *must* be changed in order to offer any hope of a reasonable national existence it was not likely to be deterred by these international obstacles. As the Party approached electoral victory Germany's international situation became even more precarious by virtue of the relative fall in the price of British finished export goods compared to those of Germany.

In November 1931 a set of principles for foreign exchange allocation was determined whose intention was expressly nondiscriminatory. There were, however, finite limits over which any foreign exchange allocation scheme which was based, as this one was, on an average need for exchange in the pre-control period, could last while still making economic sense. In any case it was unthinkable that a party like the NSDAP would not manipulate such a scheme, if in power, for its own political purposes. The use of blocked mark balances began in February 1932 when German creditors were allowed to use up to 50 per cent of their loans to purchase German securities at the low prevailing prices providing the securities remained 'blocked' for five years. In the next two months the first bilateral trading agreements were signed and the agreement between the Reemstma cigarette company and the Greek government linked bilateral trade to the clearing of blocked balances in each currency [42]. In summer 1932 the Reichsbank allowed exporters, who were able to demonstrate that their trade would otherwise have been impossible, to buy German bonds at their low foreign values and re-sell them at the higher prices on the German market to subsidise losses sustained in exporting goods to markets where the price level was now below that in Germany. Every principle of trade and exchange control

---

[42] *Basch*, p. 167.

and export subsidisation used during the Nazi regime was already in place
before the seizure of power. The von Papen government's very restricted
expenditures on public works in September 1932 were left well behind by von
Schleicher and the Gereke Plan, which created the same methods of financing
job creation which the Nazi government would also employ under the Reinhardt
plan, far outdistanced any previous or other contemporary programme of public
works expenditure. Between 1932 and the seizure of power about 500 to 600 million marks were spent on purely 'civil' public works. The Nazi government was
to spend 2,450 million Reichsmark for the same purpose in 1934 alone and 4,000
million in the years 1933 and 1934 together [43]. Expenditure on armaments
reached roughly the same amount [44]. To this was added expenditure on the subsidisation of the agricultural sector. The foreign exchange deficit in autumn
1934 reached 700 million Reichsmarks. The purpose of the *Neuer Plan* was no
more than to permit domestic economic policy to continue in spite of this
deficit and the effect it would otherwise have had in any attempt to bring
exchange rates and prices back into line with those of western Europe. It used all
the earlier methods and in addition gave power to the exchange control boards,
whose number was increased, to discriminate against a wide range of finished
and semi-finished imports. In effect trade controls now had the positive purpose
of backing up the job-creation schemes rather than the merely negative one of
restricting the outflow of reserves.

Rearmament was still at low levels. The difficulties of distinguishing between
public expenditure on civil and on military purposes are insuperable and the
distinction does not in any case make much sense in the case of the Nazi government. Schweitzer estimates that expenditure on the second category had already
added 243 million Reichsmarks to the import bill in 1934 as compared to 1933 [45].
Be that as it may the lowest set of calculations of rearmament expenditure
(Klein) show expenditure for this purpose at 4,000 million Reichsmarks in 1935
and 6,000 million in 1936, increases of more than 50 per cent a year [46]. A
substantial part of these increases came, however, out of the decrease in expenditure on public works. In fact the deficit of government expenditure over
receipts fell slightly in 1935 but in spite of the great increase in revenue which
came with full employment and fuller utilisation of resources in 1936 the
budget deficit doubled in that year. If there had ever been a chance that full
employment and recovery would provide the occasion for re-establishing an
equilibrium rate for the mark it ended in 1936. The Four Year Plan with its

---

[43] *Kenyon E. Poole*, German Financial Policies 1932—1939, New York 1939, p. 94.
[44] *Burton A. Klein*, Germany's Economic Preparations for War, Cambridge/Mass. 1959, p. 16.
[45] *Arthur Schweitzer*, Big Business in the Third Reich, Bloomington 1964, p. 428.
[46] *Klein*, Statistical Appendix: Table 60, p. 254.

massive commitment of investment to synthetic production and import substitution pushed expenditure to new heights and led initially to a further demand for imports for which there was no means of payment. Total gold and foreign exchange reserves were about two and a half per cent their level of 1930 and in the second half of 1936 there was a foreign exchange deficit of 637.7 million Reichsmarks [47]. Yet this was the moment at which rearmament expenditure was to show a marked upward movement and also the starting point of the 5,300 million Reichsmarks extra expenditure between summer 1936 and the end of 1939 on the Four Year Plan itself [48].

In relation to the size of GNP the volume of German imports fell throughout the 1930s. Foreign exchange shortages and the desire for strategic safety from blockade alike combined to push economic policy towards import substitution and towards a shift in the source of imports. The high price of German goods reduced the choice of export markets. From this forced shift in German trade the Reichsmark bloc countries were the major beneficiaries supplying 18.5 per cent of all German imports in 1939 compared to the 3.9 per cent they had supplied in 1928. By contrast German trade with the gold bloc countries inevitably encountered severe difficulties. Imports from France, which had accounted for 5.3 per cent of all imports in 1928 were but 2.6 per cent of a lower total in 1938 even when Austrian imports from France in that year are included. The decline in German-United States trade is the most dramatic. The United States had been by a long way Germany's most important supplier in the twenties'. The drying-up of capital flows from America led to a fall in importance of United States imports from 14.4 per cent of all imports in 1928 to 7.4 per cent in 1938. This last figure was in fact exceptionally high because of the increase in wheat imports from America in that year; for 1937 the proportion was only 5.2 per cent. The increase in imports from America in 1938 was further testimony to the inadequacy of the Reichsmark bloc to sustain Germany's strategic needs [49]. Its inadequacy to cater for her longer-term economic needs has already been noted.

Even within the bloc the position of the Reichsmark was often a weak one. Turkey was not the only member to put Germany in difficulties by altering the balance of trade in order to mop up its accumulated *Sperrmark*. Romania similarly forced a reduction of the *Sperrmark* balances from September 1935 by allowing the Reichsmark effectively to float against the leu and from Sep-

---

[47] Dietmar Petzina, Autarkiepolitik im Dritten Reich, Stuttgart 1968, p. 30.

[48] Ibid., p. 183. Rearmament expenditures were about 8,000 million Reichmarks in 1937.

[49] Imports of wheat from the United States rose from 17,000 tons in 1937 to 243,900 tons in 1938, the highest annual quantity since 1928 (Sondernachweis des Außenhandels Deutschlands).

tember 1936 by placing stricter limitations on the permissible precentage of oil products in total exports to Germany. The flow of interest payments and profits on British investments in Romania was met by increased oil exports to Britain. Because the pound rose against the leu as the Reichsmark fell, Romanian exporters marked up prices to Germany to try to reach the equivalent rate of return on exports to Britain so that in bilateral negotiations the sterling/leu exchange rate was often dictating the negotiated Reichsmark/leu rate [50].

The long- and short-run weaknesses of Germany's position are unmistakable. That the formation of the Reichsmark bloc should be seen as Nazi 'exploitation' or 'penetration' of south-eastern Europe is a remarkable tribute to the ability of National Socialism to explain all events, however unwelcome, as being in accord with the new *Weltanschauung*. It is true that the Reichsmark bloc did save gold and foreign exchange and that it was an essential part of the trade and exchange controls which preserved the absolute primacy of domestic economic priorities. It may well be that had it not been for the determined attention paid to the mechanisms of Reichsmark bloc trade Germany's terms of trade would have been less favourable and in that sense, which is by no means the sense in which the word has so far been used, there would be a certain element of 'exploitation' of the less-developed economies. Otherwise, on present evidence, the word is entirely unjustified. National Socialist domestic economic policy meant that Germany's international economic bargaining power was distinctly weak before 1939. From this weakness the less-developed European economies were able to extract great advantages for themselves in what would otherwise have been a desperate situation. They, almost alone amongst the world's primary exporters in the 1930's, were able to show an increase in export earnings and an increase in the growth of national income. The concentration of economic policy on achieving the immediate internal aims of the Nazi regime opened up possibilities of development to underdeveloped Europe when the depression seemed otherwise to have foreclosed all such possibilities. Historians should turn their attention to the successful exploitation of Germany's economic weakness before 1939 by the small economies of central and south-eastern Europe.

---

[50] *Marguérat*, Le protectionnisme.

Statistical Appendix [1]

Table 1: *The percentage share of the Reichsmark bloc countries in total German imports*

	Bulgaria	Greece	Hungary	Romania	Turkey	Yugoslavia
1925	0.4	0.6	0.7	0.8	0.6	0.7
1926	0.4	0.5	0.9	1.5	0.5	0.8
1927	0.4	0.5	0.6	1.7	0.4	0.5
1928	0.4	0.7	0.5	1.3	0.5	0.5
1929	0.4	0.8	0.7	1.6	0.6	0.4
1930	0.6	1.0	0.8	2.3	0.7	0.7
1931	0.7	1.1	0.8	1.5	0.8	0.6
1932	0.7	1.3	0.8	1.6	0.9	0.6
1933	0.7	1.3	0.8	1.1	0.9	0.8
1934	0.8	1.3	1.4	1.3	1.5	0.8
1935	1.0	1.4	1.9	1.9	2.2	1.5
1936	1.4	1.6	2.2	2.2	2.8	1.8
1937	1.3	1.4	2.1	3.3	1.8	2.4
1938 [2]	1.5	1.7	2.0	2.6	2.1	2.0
	1.6	1.7	3.1	2.9	2.1	2.8
1939	2.3	1.9	4.6	4.4	2.6	2.7

Sources: Compiled from: Statistische Jahrbücher and Sondernachweis des Außenhandels Deutschlands.

---

[1] The author would like to thank the Social Research Council for the grant in 1968/9 which enabled him to collect the information from which these and subsequent figures were calculated and Mr. Kim Sweeney for his help in preparing them.

[2] The upper line for 1938 is for the Altreich, that is to say without Austria or the Sudetenland. The lower line includes the Sudetenland from October 1938 and shows the percentage figure with Austrian-German trade not counted as foreign trade from April. For 1939, trade with the Protectorate is not counted as foreign trade from April and the figures include Austrian imports as German imports.

Table 2: *The Percentage Share of Total German Exports Going to the More Important High Per Capita Income Markets*[1], *to Poland and the USSR, and to the Reichsmark bloc*[2].

	1925—34	1935—39
High Income Markets	54.99	46.59
Poland and USSR	6.51	2.79
Reichsmark Bloc	5.99	17.62

Source: Sondernachweis des Außenhandels Deutschlands.

[1] Countries taking less than 3.0 per cent of German exports in the period 1925—34 are excluded. Included are Belgium-Luxembourg, Czechoslovakia, France, Italy, Netherlands, Sweden, Switzerland, The United Kingdom and The United States. 'Germany' is henceforward defined in all tables as in Table 1 except that the definition in the lower line for 1938 in that table is now used exclusively.

[2] Annual averages for each country.

Table 3: *The Value of German Imports and Exports as a Proportion (%) of National Income (Current Prices)*

	Imports	Exports
1929	17.02	17.06
1933	7.37	8.55
1938 [1]	5.56	5.36

Sources: Walther G. Hoffmann, Das Wachstum der Deutschen Wirtschaft seit der Mitte des 19. Jahrhunderts, Berlin 1965; Statistische Jahrbücher.

[1] 'Altreich', excluding Austria and Bohemia-Moravia.

Table 4: *The Percentage of Imports (I) from and Exports (E) to Germany in the Trade of Reichsmark Bloc Countries*

Year	Bulgaria [1]		Greece [2]		Hungary [2]		Yugoslavia [2]		Romania [1]		Turkey [2]	
	I	E	I	E	I	E	I	E	I	E	I	E
1925	19.6	20.0	8.1	18.5	15.0	9.9	9.9	7.2	n.a.	n.a.	11.3	14.4
1926	21.9	19.5	7.6	21.9	16.6	12.9	12.0	9.3	n.a.	n.a.	13.8	12.6
1927	21.0	23.1	7.5	21.4	18.2	13.3	12.3	10.6	22.3	18.6	14.2	9.3
1928	21.2	27.9	8.6	26.9	19.5	11.8	13.6	12.1	n.a.	n.a.	14.2	12.8
1929	22.2	29.9	9.4	23.2	20.0	11.7	15.6	8.5	24.1	27.6	15.3	13.3
1930	23.2	26.2	10.4	23.3	21.3	10.3	17.6	11.7	25.2	18.8	18.6	13.1
1931	23.3	29.5	12.2	14.1	24.4	12.7	19.3	11.3	29.6	11.5	21.4	10.7
1932	25.9	26.0	9.7	15.1	22.5	15.1	17.9	11.3	24.5	12.4	23.2	13.5
1933	38.2	36.0	10.2	17.9	19.7	11.2	13.4	13.9	18.6	10.6	25.6	19.0
1934	40.1	42.7	14.7	22.5	18.3	22.2	14.2	15.5	15.5	16.6	33.9	37.3
1935	53.4	48.0	18.7	29.7	22.7	23.9	16.0	18.7	23.8	16.7	40.3	40.9
1936	61.6	47.9	22.4	36.4	26.0	22.8	26.8	23.7	36.1	17.8	45.1	51.0
1937	58.6	43.1	27.2	31.0	25.9	24.0	32.7	21.7	28.7	18.9	42.1	36.5
1938	52.0	58.9	28.8	38.5	30.1	27.4	32.6	35.9	36.6	26.5	47.0	42.9
1939	65.5	67.8	29.9	27.5	48.4	50.4	47.6	31.8	39.2	32.3	51.0	37.3

Sources: Annuaire Statistique de la Grèce; Annuaire Statistique Hongrois; Statistique Annuelle du Commerce Exterieur de la Turquie; Directinnea Statisticei Generale a Finanţelor si Comerţului Exterior, Comerţul Exterior; Statistiques du Commerce de la Bulgarie; Annuaire du commerce turque.

[1] Includes Austria 1938—1940
[2] Includes Austria 1939—1940

Table 5: *Chromite Exports from Greece, Turkey and Yugoslavia (000 tonnes), 1935—1939*

		Total	Germany	Italy	U.K.	U.S.A.
Greece	1935	32.0	4.3	15.3	6.9	0.1
	1936	48.0	5.3	25.9	12.2	0.8
	1937	55.9	11.2	23.3	9.6	5.6
	1938	35.7	18.2 [1]	5.6	1.9	1.0
	1939	n. a.	22.3 [2]	n. a.	n. a.	n. a.
Turkey	1935	145.7	40.4	9.4	5.9	21.0
	1936	149.6	64.5	1.0	1.0	13.9
	1937	198.4	58.4	4.8	1.0	45.6
	1938	208.1	68.5	32.2	3.7	13.4
	1939	192.8	104.8	15.7	n. a.	19.4
Yugoslavia	1935	n. a.	n. a.	n. a.	n. a.	n. a.
	1936	23.8	0.3 [3]	n. a.	n. a.	2.0
	1937	24.7	0.4 [4]	n. a.	n. a.	0.3
	1938	23.2	13.3 [5]	0.3	n. a.	3.3
	1939	18.3	5.6	0.1	n. a.	3.0

Sources: Annuaire Statistique de la Grèce; Annuaire Statistique du Royaume de Yougoslavie; Statistique Annuelle du Commerce Exterieur de la Turquie.

[1] Excludes Austria.
[2] N. E. Momtchiloff, Statistical appendix.
[3] 8.4 to Austria.
[4] 10.0 to Austria.
[5] 1.6 to Austria.

Table 6: *Chromite Imports into Germany* (ooo tonnes)

	Reichsmark bloc [1]	South Africa & Rhodesia	Australasia	India
1933	13.9	20.6	5.1	1.6
1934	30.2	27.4	10.9	2.1
1935	48.3	41.4	2.5	1.8
1936	75.0	36.8	10.3	1.2
1937	78.4	52.2	0	1.3
1938	81.2	73.4	7.3	4.3
1939	147.3	33.4	0	0

Source: Sondernachweis des Außenhandels Deutschlands.

[1] There are considerable variations for 1938 between the official German import figures and the Reichsmark bloc national export statistics. To a certain extent they can be resolved from the stockpile fluctuations in *Jörg-J. Jäger,* Die wirtschaftliche Abhängigkeit des Dritten Reiches vom Ausland dargestellt am Beispiel der Stahlindustrie, Berlin 1969, pp. 244; 267, but by no means entirely. The annual export statistics of the Reichsmark bloc countries, however, do not distinguish between the boundary changes in Germany for that year as do the monthly German trade figures.

Table 7: *Bauxite Exports from Greece, Hungary and Yugoslavia (000 tonnes)*

		Total	to Germany
Greece	1935	n. a.	n. a.
	1936	n. a.	n. a.
	1937	122.3	71.5
	1938	139.2	68.0
	1939	n. a.	n. a.
Hungary	1935	227.6	218.3
	1936	341.6	328.4
	1937	479.7	472.3
	1938	362.4	363.3
	1939	574.1	571.4
Yugoslavia	1935	n. a.	n. a.
	1936	253.1	232.2
	1937	388.4	384.6
	1938	379.7	379.6
	1939	266.5	257.5

Sources: Annuaire Statistique de la Grèce; Annuaire Statistique Hongrois; T. I. Berend and G. Ránki, Magyarország Gyáripara a Máśodik Világháború Elött es a háború Idöszakában (1933—1944), Budapest 1958, p. 163; Statistique Annuelle du Commerce Extérieur de la Turquie.

Table 8: *German Imports of Bauxite and Cryolite (000 tonnes)*

	Reichsmark bloc	France	Italy	Netherlands East Indies
1933	92.0	114.1	29.7	0
1934	187.2	120.5	16.3	0
1935	370.6	75.1	56.4	0
1936	587.5	95.6	164.1	127.6
1937	958.8	95.0	111.3	138.8
1938	796.2	92.3	96.6	192.7
1939	928.6	48.4	69.6	67.3

Source: Sondernachweis des Außenhandels Deutschlands.

Table 9: *Romanian Exports of Mineral Fuels, Oil and Oil Products (000 tonnes)*

	Total	Germany	U.K.	France	Czecho-slovakia	Italy	Egypt
1933	5885.6	200.6	986.0	738.6	129.4	904.0	588.9
1934	6547.4	434.2	793.9	708.7	148.9	975.5	557.3
1935	6613.1	863.1	738.9	336.4	217.9	1649.9	420.5
1936	6885.1	1072.4	846.3	866.3	29.8	655.1	300.9
1937	5668.9	435.4	580.2	603.9	354.2	582.8	279.3
1938	4496.5	704.5	540.5	289.3	295.0	556.5	283.3
1939	4178.1	848.6	618.9	238.1	436.6	635.0	85.9

Source: Directinnea Statisticei Generale a Finanţelor si Comerţului Exterior, Comerţul Exterior.

Table 10: *German Imports of Fuel Oils, Lubricating Oils and Paraffin (000 tonnes)*

	Total	Romania	Netherlands Antilles	Iran	USSR	USA
1933	2175.6	180.4	768.4	158.2	421.7	455.7
1934	2556.4	240.7	998.3	233.1	394.9	418.6
1935	2965.4	652.3	1022.9	52.7	407.1	485.8
1936	3243.1	852.6	1047.2	80.4	319.9	672.0
1937	3127.0	520.7	1021.4	148.2	302.7	760.5
1938	3650.1	425.4	1358.4	188.1	79.3	985.4
1939	3817.1	810.7	976.7	75.3	6.9	976.8

Source: Sondernachweis des Außenhandels Deutschlands.

Table 11: *The Value of Reichsmark bloc Food Imports into Germany and their Percentage share in German Food Imports* [1] (current prices)

	Reichsmark Bloc Food Imports	Percentage of Total Food Imports
1928	309.4	5.31
1929	389.7	7.19
1930	467.7	11.09
1931	259.5	9.32
1932	209.1	9.76
1933	167.6	10.28
1934	212.7	13.87
1935	251.8	17.80
1936	288.5	19.24
1937	440.1	21.52
1938 [2]	453.1	21.47
	624.5	26.09
1939	602.5	28.23

Source: Sondernachweis des Außenhandels Deutschlands.

[1] Food is defined from 1936 as the entry ‚Ernährungswirtschaft' in the German trade classification scheme. This includes also fodder, livestock and tobacco. Prior to 1936 the items have been selected from the earlier classification scheme to make them as comparable as possible with the later. If the earlier classification is used before 1936 the largest difference would be 2.1 per cent in 1935.

[2] The upper line is the Altreich, the lower is Großdeutschland (Germany + Austria + Sudetenland after October).

Table 12: *Destination of Exports of Tobacco and Fruit from Greece*
(% of total quantity)

	Tobacco			Raisins, Currants and Sultanas			
	Germany	U.S.A.	Italy	Germany	U.K.	Netherlands	Italy
1928	44.59	17.04	18.04	12.51	61.84	8.28	9.41
1933	42.00	17.63	5.32	8.74	55.17	17.59	10.80
1934	41.03	21.09	2.81	12.14	57.04	13.47	7.45
1935	44.05	19.87	2.80	13.92	51.43	12.44	5.03
1936	56.65	16.40	0.02	19.05	54.86	9.13	1.79
1937	44.22	22.23	3.51	23.48	43.51	7.59	11.83
1938	52.81	14.21	2.88	34.42	43.14	8.63	0.29
1939	48.67	21.78	0	9.16	66.10	11.64	n. a.

Source: Annuaires Statistiques de la Grèce.

Table 13: *Distribution of Hungarian Exports of Poultry (Living and Dead) and Draught and Meat Animals* (% share by value)

	Poultry			Animals		
	Germany	Austria	U.K.	Germany	Austria	Italy
1928	28.86	44.78	18.66	0	58.48	9.92
1933	21.77	35.79	35.42	7.96	53.15	25.93
1934	41.55	28.17	24.30	13.55	49.51	25.86
1935	44.94	25.47	22.10	15.01	48.03	22.14
1936	38.12	26.46	22.42	21.25	38.62	24.45
1937	27.24	29.57	33.07	19.08	29.99	39.31
1938	32.95	29.17	32.58	18.51	58.48	13.84
1939	62.20		31.71	84.54		9.49

Source: Annuaires Statistiques Hongrois.

Table 14: *Distribution of Romanian Exports of Grain and Grain Products (% share by quantity)*

	Germany	U.K.	Belgium-Lux.	Czecho-slovakia	France	Greece	Italy	Nether-lands	Switzer-land
1928	24.90	5.91	4.54	3.34	1.20	0.79	12.88	3.58	0.03
1933	13.59	15.81	11.28	5.11	8.40	2.28	7.49	19.08	1.14
1934	21.05	11.15	4.57	9.79	6.69	1.60	2.59	10.68	3.79
1935	2.74	11.85	1.33	4.15	2.32	3.68	12.09	0.47	10.71
1936	10.89	20.93	9.38	4.73	6.20	3.90	8.06	4.91	5.99
1937	29.56	6.65	11.12	6.29	1.66	9.73	7.16	5.54	4.45
1938	29.65	20.50	5.88	9.86	3.29	11.62	1.01	4.66	4.81
1939	30.00	24.19	6.86	4.03	2.47	5.78	15.19	4.55	3.11

Source: Romania, Comerţul Exterior.

Table 15: *Distribution of Exports of Livestock from Romania (% share by value)*

	Germany	Austria	Czecho-slovakia	Greece	Italy
1928	3.86	65.02	29.10	0.69	...
1933	14.35	49.34	14.45	...	17.82
1934	22.10	27.40	11.87	11.30	18.66
1935	11.30	29.13	24.25	13.10	7.46
1936	10.64	0	37.32	3.45	...
1937	11.81	0	33.65	5.42	10.00
1938	46.15	0	25.91	11.34	4.15
1939	46.43		39.06	9.18	0.02

Source: Romania, Comerţul Exterior.

Table 16: *The Distribution of Turkish Exports of Grain, Tobacco, Raisins and Nuts* (% share by quantity)

	Grain				Tobacco			Raisins				Nuts		
	Germany	U.K.	Belgium-Lux.	Italy	Germany	U.S.A.	Italy	Germany	U.K.	Netherlands	Germany	U.K.	France
1928	7.50	18.00	26.00	0.50	14.57	18.34	29.15	41.91	25.90	11.69	24.07	11.11	5.55
1933	0.13	5.10	10.34	19.50	40.92	19.30	5.40	47.81	20.61	12.72	42.49	5.70	8.81
1934	30.59	5.40	5.73	14.27	42.54	29.83	4.97	56.35	14.36	9.76	54.10	4.92	2.73
1935	6.33	1.45	0.77	37.81	41.55	31.05	0.91	56.81	16.36	10.60	65.75	3.94	3.54
1936	16.49	2.43	2.60	18.40	39.48	39.06	...	59.15	18.00	0.53	68.75	9.58	6.67
1937	18.83	1.40	9.44	9.85	40.05	32.75	3.02	46.18	17.71	5.55	45.49	5.74	6.97
1938	27.11	4.17	5.72	10.69	37.29	30.17	8.31	80.12	2.05	3.37	64.29	7.98	0.71
1939	50.11	0.33	10.04	...	44.11	25.17	7.62	24.61	40.00	9.49	13.99	13.99	17.62

Source: Turkey, Ministère des Finances, Statistiques Annuelles du Commerce Extérieur de la Turquie.

Table 17: *Distribution of Exports of Poultry, Eggs and Livestock from Yugoslavia* (% share by value)

	Poultry and Eggs					Livestock		
	Germany	U.K.	Czechoslovakia	Italy	Switzerland	Germany	Austria	Czechoslovakia	Greece
1936	51.38	6.86	10.96	2.35	19.84	7.74	41.85	28.55	13.68
1937	39.92	7.77	8.25	24.02	17.10	8.31	36.11	20.16	10.42
1938	49.70	15.87	3.10	13.16	16.47	52.43	19.98	14.52	6.23
1939	33.93	8.06	24.12*	17.53	12.74		45.87	32.84*	6.78

* Protectorate of Bohemia-Moravia.
Source: Annuaires Statistiques du Royaume de Yougoslavie.

[18]

The Economics and Finance of Bilateral Clearing Agreements: Germany, 1934–8[1]

By LARRY NEAL

EXCHANGE controls, both formal and informal, were put into operation by most countries during the international financial crisis of the early 1930s. By the beginning of 1934, when recovery was beginning in most European economies, the future of both domestic and foreign expansion lay in pawn to the political decisions to be made concerning the future extent of exchange controls and special trade agreements. In September 1934, Germany's course became clear. Dr Hjalmar Schacht, President of the Reichsbank and Minister of Finance under Adolf Hitler, announced his "New Plan" which continued and centralized Germany's foreign-exchange controls. Twenty-five supervisory centres allocated available foreign exchange for import transactions approved by the state. To facilitate trade under this regime of direct controls, bilateral clearing agreements were concluded with a number of countries, especially in central Europe and South America, in which German purchases were credited against offset purchases by foreigners in German markets. By spring 1938, some 25 countries had agreed to such arrangements and more than half Germany's foreign trade was carried on with them.[2]

The decisions about mundane matters of trade and finance were made, of course, in a much broader political and strategic context which eventually ended in World War II. The political nature and motivation of Germany's bilateral clearing agreements may or may not have contributed to the outbreak of war; before that question can be treated fully the economic effects of these agreements must be understood clearly. To date, the economic analysis of the bilateral clearing agreements of the 1930s has been cast in terms of the monopoly–monopsony theory which was being perfected at the same time.[3] This certainly appears to be the appropriate tool of analysis: the German economy was so much larger than that of any trading partner that the German authorities had an obvious bargaining advantage in the negotiations setting up the terms of each clearing, or barter, agreement. The final demise of each central European country to Nazi military power was a predictable, if extreme, outcome of monopolistic exploita-

---

[1] Grateful acknowledgement must be made of the careful reading and helpful comments made on previous drafts of this article by Profs. R. Alltmont, D. L. Kemmerer, C. P. Kindleberger, and L. Weiser. This is not to inculpate them for errors in fact and interpretation which may remain.

[2] Hjalmar Horace Greeley Schacht, *Confessions of the "Old Wizard"* (Boston, 1956), pp. 302–3.

[3] See, for example, Gustav Stolper, *The German Economy: 1870 to the Present* (New York, 1967), p. 143; Frank Child, *The Theory and Practice of Exchange Control in Germany: A Study of Monopolistic Exploitation in International Markets* (The Hague, 1958); A. G. Kenwood and A. L. Lougheed, *The Growth of the International Economy* (1971), p. 213; C. W. Guillebaud, *The Economic Recovery of Germany* (1939), p. 157; and Albert O. Hirschman, *National Power and the Structure of Foreign Trade* (Berkeley, California, 1945).

tion. Between the necessary conditions and the predictable outcome, however, there occurred four years of operation of the bilateral clearing agreements. During these years, according to monopoly theory, the terms of trade for Germany should have risen. Instead, in most cases, they fell.

Various explanations have been offered for this obvious inconsistency of the facts with the predictions of monopoly theory.[1] The explanation offered in this article is that the theory of monopoly is not the appropriate tool of analysis. First, that theory will be contrasted with an alternative theory of general equilibrium of trade under conditions of economic recovery; second, the evidence pertaining to terms of trade will be examined; finally, evidence bearing on the general equilibrium theory will be presented. The conclusion is that under the conditions of rapid economic recovery which characterized Germany in the mid-1930s it was relatively costless, and often politically rewarding, for Germany to forgo the advantages of monopoly exploitation. On the other side of the trading relationships, the various partner countries found political opposition to Germany economically costly and acquiescence rewarding. Unlike the monopoly theory of Germany's trade relationship, which assumes economic motivation for all Germany's trade policies, the alternative theory presented here allows a variety of outcomes in response to different policies whose primary motivation is political, or military, rather than economic. Since, however, the broader, and possibly more interesting, political and military implications cannot be treated both accurately and briefly, they are ignored in this article.

I

The two theories differ sharply in the way they characterize the background conditions for changes in the terms of trade between Germany and any one of her trading partners in south-eastern Europe. The monopoly–monopsony theory presumes that under conditions of autarky a given amount of tradeable goods will be produced in the two countries. If the internal price ratios of tradeable goods differ in the two countries, however, this opens up the possibility of both countries becoming better off in terms of final consumption by exchanging part of their domestic production, say German guns for Romanian grain. Under conditions of perfect competition, it is possible for both countries to settle upon a common price ratio for any pair of traded goods. If both countries are open economies, moreover, the common price ratio will reflect the effects of competition from other external sources of supply for each of the traded goods. The

---

[1] Child, for example, argues that the official value of the mark was so much higher than its market value by 1934 that optimum monopoly exploitation required that its nominal value in the clearing agreements be reduced in 1934. Why this should continue to be the case for the next five years is not explained. Other authors have noted the limitations placed on German monopoly practices by the broader economic context of the 1930s. H. C. Hillman, 'Analysis of Germany's Foreign Trade and the War', *Economica*, n.s. VII (1940), 66–88, points out the increased trade of France, Britain, and Japan with their respective colonial possessions from 1929 to 1938 and comments that to some extent "Germany was forced to intensify her trade drive in other regions." Charles Kindleberger, *The World in Depression, 1929–39* (Berkeley, 1973), notes that the bilateral agreements of Germany were expansionary in the dismal environment for international trade caused jointly by the United States and Great Britain—the United States is blamed for not assuming leadership; Great Britain for not relinquishing it. Philip Friedman, *The Impact of Trade Destruction on National Incomes* (Gainsville, Florida, 1974), argues that Britain's abandonment of the gold standard in 1931 was the primary action causing the collapse of international trade.

exercise of monopoly–monopsony power by Germany in this context changes the common price ratio so that either fewer guns from Germany purchase the same amount of Romanian grain or the same number of guns command more bushels of grain—i.e. the German terms of trade improve. Both countries can still be better off with this trade than without it, but Germany's increase in final consumption is greater, while Romania's is less, than in the case of open competition from other sources.

None of the measures ever made of the gross commodity terms of trade (to be presented below) shows such improvement in the German terms of trade with any of its trading partners in south-eastern Europe. It might seem that this empirical evidence settles the case. It does not, proponents of the textbook approach have argued, because there are serious theoretical problems in measuring terms of trade under the conditions of a bilateral clearing agreement. The unit of measurement is one national currency or the other, but each is kept in blocked accounts within the country issuing the currency. These accounts cannot be tapped except under the conditions of the clearing agreement; i.e. the calculated terms of trade under bilateralism are the product of "funny-money" prices quite different from those determined under more competitive conditions of multilateral trade. Appropriate adjustments can only be made with the aid of information on the open market value of the "funny-money"—the black-market rate of exchange of the blocked currencies. For obvious reasons, these are not available, although there is evidence on the extent to which various central banks supported or did not support the official exchange rate of the blocked currencies as determined in the clearing agreements.

There is a more serious objection than the "funny-money" argument to the terms of trade evidence, however. This stems from the rapid expansion of the German economy in the period 1934–8 when gross domestic product rose at an annual rate of 11 per cent. When trade is carried out under conditions of rapid growth, falling terms of trade indicate that a country is increasing its productivity more rapidly than its trading partners. It may become better off relative to its trading partners just as surely as if it had exercised monopoly-monopsony power in a static production situation. Empirical tests of this possibility usually require adjusting the barter terms of trade for different rates of increase in factor productivity. Under bilateral trade agreements, however, the barter terms of trade are suspect for reasons already explained, while domestic wage and price controls exercised by Germany and some nations in south-eastern Europe make it difficult to compare productivity. In this study, an alternative empirical test is used which bypasses the problems of terms-of-trade evidence, although it loses in the process the precision theoretically possible by the terms-of-trade approach.

The alternative approach is to note that all the trading partners of Germany in south-eastern Europe were depressed in 1933 as well and could generate rapid productivity gains if they could find some means of reflating their economies. The relative advantage Germany gained in trade with them was therefore less if they reflated as well. The novel hypothesis offered here is that the bilateral clearing agreements offered them the best means available for financing economic recovery. To use them effectively, however, the trading partner had to run an export surplus with Germany and then have its central bank purchase the blocked *Sperrmarks* from its exporters. The larger the export surplus and the higher the exchange rate of the *Sperrmarks*, the greater became the expansionary efforts of the central bank. The contrasting central-bank policies and economic results in Hungary and Romania are then examined to show that in these two cases, at least, central-bank policy with respect to the clearing agreements was associated with the pace of economic recovery.

II

If the German goal in negotiations of clearing agreements with smaller countries was to attain economic advantages, there were basically only two ways to attain it: either the exercise of *monopsony power*, which forced the small trading partner to accept lower than competitive prices on its products imported by Germany, or the use of *monopoly power*, which forced the small country to pay higher than competitive prices on the German exports it purchased.[1] The first technique appears to be what one textbook suggests was used when it states, "as Germany soon discovered, a lack of balance in its trade with other exchange control countries provided a means whereby it could take advantage of its buyer's position to exploit countries largely dependent on Germany for their support market."[2]

The difficulty with this suggestion is that the prices offered by Germany to its trading partners for its imported commodities were consistently above both the world price and the internal price within the partner country. Thus, the foreign foodstuffs it purchased from south-eastern European countries were acquired at prices from 20 to 40 per cent above the world market price.[3] Basch cites the case of Germany paying prices for Romania's soybeans that were several times those charged overseas.[4] Further, Germany on average paid more for the same commodity when it was imported from a clearing-agreement country than when it was imported from a non-clearing country. Of course, it may be argued, with Guillebaud, that these high prices were used merely for the sake of entrapment, and that renewal of the clearing agreements would bring a substantial reduction in them.[5] Indeed, it is true that German officials were dissatisfied with the low value of the mark in free exchange markets and attempted to raise it in order to lower the cost of imports when revising clearing agreements. This was not accomplished with any success, however, until 1942—after Germany had absorbed nearly all of central Europe into the Third Reich.[6]

Granting the failure of Germany to act in a manner befitting a monopsonist, the argument can still be made that the high prices it paid for imports were not

---

[1] This argument is valid only on the assumption of both economies being fully employed. Since Germany and south-eastern Europe were the areas hardest hit by the great depression (other than the United States), one should immediately doubt the applicability of this kind of argument. Such doubts did not occur in the analysis of this problem in the late 1930s, when it seemed that here was a perfect place to apply the recently developed tools of analysis of imperfect competition. Since monopolies were evil, the results of the analysis appeared quite plausible. It is the residue of this misapplied analysis which remains in the textbooks today.

[2] Kenwood and Lougheed, op. cit. p. 213.   [3] Guillebaud, op. cit. p. 157.
[4] Antonin Basch, *The Danubian Basin and the German Economic Sphere* (New York, 1943), p. 218.
[5] Guillebaud, op. cit. p. 151.   [6] Basch, op. cit. p. 219.

high compared with German domestic prices while the prices of German exports were high compared with world prices. That is to say, if Germany did not exploit its relative size by exercising power as a monopsonist, it did this to exercise all the more power as a monopolist on the export side. Thus, Guillebaud argued that "in large compensation transactions, Germany is often able to secure a price for her exports which is well above the ordinary competition price. Since Germany maintained an overvalued mark (for the official rate) throughout the period of exchange control, the exercise of monopoly power on the pricing of exports was necessary to avoid either a deficit on trade or a significant reduction in the volume of trade."[1]

This argument was explicitly rejected by Howard Ellis, who examined in particular the German export drive to the south-east after 1934. His description of the prototype case of Yugoslavia is especially revealing:

> In order to give the German buying drive momentum, German export goods had been offered at low prices during the first year or two. But when German purchases had raised even the level of domestic prices in Yugoslavia, and when the limit of full employment began to be felt in Germany, the prices of export goods began to rise, not only overtly but also covertly in the deterioration of quality and in long delays in delivery. *To offset these effects* [my italics], German purchasing agencies offered to sell at incredibly generous "terms" with almost negligible down payments.[2]

The Yugoslav example helps explain why the terms of trade continued to move against Germany throughout the operation of the New Plan from 1934 to 1938. From 1935 to 1936 import prices rose by 3·8 per cent while export prices fell by 2·9 per cent. From 1936 to 1937 import prices rose by 10·2 per cent while export prices rose only 3·6 per cent.[3] The situation became even worse when the war broke out.

Repeated studies of Germany's terms of trade with south-eastern Europe have found that, contrary to the predictions of either the monopsonist or the monopolist hypothesis, the prices of Germany's exports declined relative to the prices of its imports from partner countries. The earliest authoritative study of the empirical data was by Frederic Benham.[4]

His results for Hungary and Romania are reproduced in Table 1. They show that after falling rapidly in the early stages of the world depression, the terms of trade for these two countries did not improve until Germany's trade drive began. Benham's figures are for all foreign trade conducted by Hungary and Romania. Germany's terms of trade with each country show a marked fall after 1934. The two independent calculations are consistent in showing that Germany's increased share of trade was not accompanied by monopolist-monopsonist behaviour.

Benham's findings were roundly condemned by Paul Einzig on three grounds: first, individuals dealing with the Germans in south-eastern Europe had reported cases of bad faith and sharp dealings by German exporters, which cast doubt on

---

[1] Guillebaud, op. cit. p. 158.
[2] Howard S. Ellis, *Exchange Control in Central Europe* (Cambridge, Mass. 1941), p. 264.
[3] Guillebaud, op. cit. pp. 100, 149.
[4] Royal Institute of International Affairs, *South-East Europe: A Political and Economic Survey* (1939), pt. II.

Table 1. *Terms of Trade*

A. GERMANY'S TERMS OF TRADE, 1928-38

With Hungary

1928	1932	1934	1935	1936	1937	1938
100	70	70	73	51	54	55

With Romania

1928	1932	1934	1935	1936	1937	1938
100	28	33	45	50	43	19

B. SOUTH-EASTERN EUROPE'S TERMS OF TRADE WITH GERMANY, 1929-37

Hungary

1929	1930	1931	1932	1933	1934	1935	1936	1937
100	98	93	93	90	102	111	108	102

Romania

1929	1930	1931	1932	1933	1934	1935	1936	1937
100	69	49	56	56	54	63	63	77

Sources:
A. Tables 5 and 6.
B. Royal Institute of International Affairs, *South-eastern Europe. A Political and Economic Survey* (1939), p. 197.

the validity of reported prices; second, German marks paid by German importers should be discounted heavily, since they were paid into blocked accounts; and third, anything that could be used by German propagandists should not be published when war was imminent. In reply, Benham defended his empirical findings as based on official records rather than businessmen's gossip, and noted that if marks earned should be devalued, marks paid for German exports should be equally devalued, but agreed that he would publish nothing further on the subject for the duration of the war.[1] Kindleberger re-examined the Benham–Einzig debate in the light of his empirical study of the terms of trade for all Europe from 1870 to 1952. He found that Germany's terms of trade with non-industrial Europe increased less than they did with any other trading region. The terms of trade of the United Kingdom and Belgium with non-industrial Europe rose higher than Germany's. Kindleberger concluded that his evidence broadly supported Benham, rather than Einzig.[2]

The counter-arguments in favour of the hypothesis are stated most forcefully by Ellis. He argues first that the exploitation by Germany of the bilateral clearing agreements took the form of establishing a monopoly "in significant segments of her partner's market" rather than exacting the price concessions possible from the existing degree of monopoly power. Greater future gains were purchased at the expense of present gains. Alternatively, he argues that Germany's unprofitable pricing policies were designed for political purposes, but that Germany's growing political power "could scarcely fail to menace the economic status of Southeastern Europe generally".[3] In either case, it appears from the evidence that Germany made a considerable investment over a number of years (at least five) to achieve a monopoly position that it never exploited.

[1] Paul Einzig, 'Why Defend Nazi Trade Methods?', *Banker*, LVIII (1941), 108-13; Frederic Benham, 'A Reply to Dr Einzig', *Banker*, LVIII (1941), 182-6.
[2] C. P. Kindleberger, *The Terms of Trade: A European Case Study* (New York, 1956), pp. 120-2.
[3] Ellis, op. cit. pp. 264-5.

BILATERAL AGREEMENTS

Even the percentage rise in Germany's share of trade with these countries overstates the extent to which the bilateral agreements were used to establish a monopoly position for Germany. During the depression this share fell in general, so that the rising shares under the New Plan represent to a large extent the effects of restoring prosperity to the economies concerned. Table 2 shows the percentage share of both imports and exports that Germany enjoyed in south-eastern Europe both before and after the New Plan. It is clear that Germany did increase its share of the trade in that area but it is also clear that its trade was already substantial before the depression. Indeed, since Germany had carried on a substantial part of its foreign trade with eastern and south-eastern Europe before World War I, the provisions of the various peace treaties of 1918, which divided these areas into a large number of small countries, actually set the stage for the exercise of economic power by Germany.[1] Further, the revival of international trade during the "five good years" of 1924–8[2] saw a substantial increase in Germany's share of the foreign trade of the new cessionary and succession states.

Table 2. *Germany's Percentage Share in the Foreign Trade of South-Eastern Europe*
(I = imports of Germany's partner; E = exports of Germany's partner)

Year	Bulgaria		Greece		Hungary		Romania		Turkey		Yugoslavia	
	I	E	I	E	I	E	I	E	I	E	I	E
1913	20	18	7	10	—	—	40	8	—	—	29*	22*
1922	—	—	6	21	17	9	20	6	—	—	7	8
1923	20	8	25	19	14	6	23	7	—	—	9	4
1924	20	18	6	26	13	8	19	6	—	—	8	4
1925	20	20	8	19	15	10	17	9	—	—	10	7
1926	22	19	8	22	17	13	—	—	14	13	12	9
1927	21	23	7	21	18	13	23	19	14	9	12	11
1928	21	28	9	26	20	12	—	—	14	13	14	12
1929	22	30	9	23	20	12	24	28	15	13	16	9
1930	23	26	10	23	21	10	25	19	19	13	18	12
1931	23	29	12	14	24	13	29	11	21	11	19	11
1932	26	26	10	15	22	15	24	12	23	13	18	11
1933	38	36	10	18	20	11	19	11	26	19	13	14
1934	40	43	15	23	18	22	16	17	34	37	14	15
1935	54	58	19	30	23	24	24	17	40	41	16	19
1936	61†	48†	22	36	26	23	36	18	45	51	27	24
1937	55†	43†	27	31	26	24	29	19	42	36	32	22

Source: League of Nations, *International Trade Statistics, 1930, 1934, 1936, and 1937* (Geneva, 1932, 1935, 1936, 1937, and 1938).

* The Yugoslavian figures are for 1912.

† The Bulgarian official publication, *Glavna direcktsiia na statistikata*, gives different percentages for 1936 and 1937: 1936 58 80; 1937 43 51. I have no explanation for this discrepancy.

While Ellis agrees that the economic effects of the clearing agreements cannot be separated from the effects of domestic recovery, he does argue on theoretical grounds that they created economic losses for both Germany and the partner nations. The economic losses were not from the exercise of monopoly power by Germany, but from the resource misallocation which was the result of Germany's drive to build up a monopoly position. This process is epitomized, in Ellis's view, by the diversion of Germany's cotton imports from the United States to Brazil, which previously had produced very little cotton and almost none for export. This meant that Germany was receiving cotton from a high-cost producer while

[1] Hirschman, op. cit. p. 94. [2] The phrase is from W. A. Lewis, *Economic Survey, 1919–39* (1949).

Brazil was losing the export proceeds which could be obtained from other export crops.[1] This argument is valid, but only if the implicit economic assumptions of the argument were validated by the economic conditions of the 1930s. These are, at a minimum, that the partner nation be at full employment (otherwise, the resources Brazil put into cotton production would have zero opportunity cost) and that the previous allocation of resources was optimal. Given the dangers of monoculture for an underdeveloped nation and the frequent use of Brazil's reliance upon coffee as an example of these dangers, the latter assumption may be questioned.[2] Certainly, all countries relying upon the export of primary products for earning foreign exchange had large amounts of unutilized capacity after the depression in 1933. Even as late as 1938, League of Nations studies found that Latin America was making substantial increases in the production of cocoa, tobacco, cotton, wheat, meat-packing, wood products, fuels and power, metals, and non-metallic minerals. Only for coffee was the level of production falling from 1936 to 1938.[3] On the German side, reviving trade with "lowest-cost" producers (in the U.S. case, low cost had been achieved by a major devaluation) would have required giving up the advantage of the moratorium on transfer of foreign exchange to service the huge foreign debt of Germany—the largest of any nation before the depression. Ellis therefore overstates the real costs to both Germany and its partner countries of the clearing agreements. Indeed, the only basis he suggests for using the resource misallocation argument is that the total volume of Germany's foreign trade with these countries recovered to pre-depression levels—which is a tribute to the efficacy of the New Plan rather than a criticism of its efficiency.

III

If Germany did not actually exploit the potential economic advantages of a monopsonist or monopolist position, and if the economic advantages of competitive pricing were forgone with little real cost to either Germany or Germany's partners, innovative financial arrangements were required. The key arrangements were but a few of the welter of innovations and regulatory interventions made by the German officials responsible for administering the New Plan. The effectiveness of the financial arrangements is registered by the fact that so many of the other regulations seemed designed to oppose their effective operation.

The government administrators of the New Plan probably did not know what it was that they were doing which was working so well in the field of foreign trade. There are reports that German officials tried to reduce the prices paid on imports and made constant efforts to improve the terms of trade. If so, they were doomed to failure by the maintenance of an officially overvalued mark which meant that deficits would be incurred with respect to trade with countries where trading agreements were not in effect. To carry out trade without running a deficit, it was necessary for German exporters and importers to make *private compensation agree-*

[1] Ellis, op. cit. p. 252.
[2] Brazil became one of the world's leading cotton producers during the American Civil War, long before the crisis of the 1930s. It continues to be the fifth leading producer of raw cotton in the world.— Food and Agricultural Organization, *Production Yearbook, 1975* (Rome, 1976), p. 222. Further, the bulk of Brazilian production is long-staple cotton and superior to the short-staple cotton of the United States. There can be little doubt that Brazil's natural resource endowment, rather than artificial demand from Hitler's Germany, accounted for its export of cotton.
[3] League of Nations, *Europe's Trade* (Geneva, 1941), pp. 172–81.

ments. German importers needed to find exporters who could provide them with foreign-exchange claims so they could get permission to import. The exporter's price, due to the overvalued mark, was *x* per cent over the world price. The importer would pay him this premium of *x* per cent in marks, the exporter would make the foreign sale, but sell the foreign exchange gained to the importer. The import would be made, the domestic price increased by *x* per cent to recover the premium, and all private parties to the transactions in Germany and abroad were content without a capital outflow from Germany.

This process was greatly facilitated by the development of ASKI marks (acronym for *Ausländer Sonderkonten für Inlandszahlung*) which would be received in the first instance by an exporter of goods to Germany (who charged more than he would have for payment in regular marks). He could sell these, at a discount, to the importer of goods from Germany who then used them to pay the German price.[1] The mark remained overvalued, but the ASKI mark effectively floated. This was in effect a two-tier exchange rate, so highly favoured by France and Belgium today, since Germany made payments on its huge foreign indebtedness in gold marks,[2] but made payments on merchandise accounts in ASKI marks.

More important for the states of south-eastern Europe were the *clearing agreements*. Since German exports to these states were limited to the non-essential goods that were allowed out of the country, while German imports from them were substantial and priced about 30 per cent above the world price, export surpluses were built up in the partner nations. In south-eastern Europe, Germany was accumulating large debts amounting to RM 450 million in 1934 and to RM 367 million in March 1935.[3] The exporters in the countries of south-eastern Europe who had accumulated these claims tried to sell them in their own countries. In each case it was necessary for the central bank to intervene if the blocked marks (*Sperrmarks*) were not to depreciate relative to the gold mark or relative to the exchange rate fixed upon in the original clearing agreement with Germany. Much of the literature apparently assumes that such intervention always took place as a matter of course in each country. In fact, however, the responses varied widely.

The actions of the central banks in response to accumulating clearing balances could fall anywhere between two extremes: one based on the financing principle, the other based on the waiting principle.[4] If the central bank employed the financing principle, it would pay out domestic currency at a fixed rate in exchange for the claims on blocked marks earned from Germany by its exporters. In one sense, this operation is correctly viewed as an extension of credit to Germany by its small trading partner—a case of "capital flowing uphill".[5] In another sense, however, it is best seen as a support operation on the exchange rate for the mark agreed upon in the bilateral clearing agreement under which trade was being conducted. The effect was to keep the domestic currency from rising relative to the mark and thereby decreasing the competitiveness of domestic

---

[1] Guillebaud, op. cit. pp. 68–70.
[2] A provision put in the Dawes Plan by E. W. Kemmerer, the American monetary expert from Princeton.
[3] Basch, op. cit. p. 175.
[4] This is the terminology used by Poul Nyboe Andersen, *Bilateral Exchange Clearing Policy* (Copenhagen, 1946).
[5] League of Nations, *World Economic Survey, 1931–2* (Geneva, 1932), p. 177.

goods exported to the German market. For if the bank operated on the waiting principle, it would refuse to buy blocked marks from its exporters until it had received requests for the marks from domestic importers of German goods. With exporters earning more blocked marks than were being demanded by importers the value of their marks would necessarily fall below the agreed rate by *at least* the interest charges paid while waiting for importers to work their way through the backlog of available marks. This amounts to a devaluation of the mark, or a revaluation of the domestic currency. Bulgaria was the only country in which the rate remained unchanged from the original parity; in Hungary a premium was added to the mark for trade in certain commodities by agreement between the national banks; in Romania the national bank's initial refusal to support the price of clearing banks in the open market was overcome by German pressure in future commercial negotiations; Yugoslavia exercised considerable independence, letting the clearing marks fall to 12·5 dinars when the official rate was 17·5; the Bank of Greece maintained the official rate by steady intervention.[1] Export surpluses by the partner countries were being sustained by capital exports to Germany in the blocked accounts. On the basis of foreign credits held by the central bank in the partner country, domestic note issues could be made. The effects of domestic monetary expansion under the depressed conditions prevailing were upon employment rather than prices.

The expansionary effects of central-bank activities in the partner nations were strongest when the bank supported the German *Sperrmarks* which were earned by its exporters; weakest when the *Sperrmarks* were allowed to depreciate. So Hungary and Bulgaria benefited most in economic terms from the clearing agreements, while politically these two countries were most favourable to German influence. Romania and Yugoslavia, on the other hand, refused to accept the economic benefits possible from increased German trade, motivated by their lingering hopes for the success of the *Petite Entente* or some regional economic bloc in the Danubian basin which would exclude Germany.[2]

To show more clearly the economic results which could be generated by the two different central-bank policies, it is useful to compare the experiences of Hungary and Romania. Hungary is chosen as the country which came closest to operating on a full financing principle; Romania is selected as a country with roughly the same export mix to offer Germany but which clung to the waiting principle until complete capitulation in the German-Romanian trade agreement of 1939. Table 3 shows the pattern of trade balances of the two countries with Germany from 1928 to 1938. The exports and imports of three other countries in south-eastern Europe are also shown for the sake of comparison. The data for all countries clearly demonstrate the collapse of trade flows in the period 1931 to 1933 with a dramatic resumption of trade in the years of the New Plan, 1934–8. In the case of Romania, exports to Germany in 1934–8 never reached the levels of 1928–30, while for Hungary, exports to Germany reached pre-crisis levels in 1935 and 1936 and rose well above them in 1937 and 1938. The trade balances show strikingly different developments as well. Before the crisis, Romania consistently enjoyed a substantial export surplus with Germany; in the 1934–8 period small export surpluses alternated with deficits. Hungary, on the other hand, transformed a consistently large balance-of-trade deficit to a modest, but

[1] Basch, op. cit. pp. 176–7. [2] Ibid. chs. 9, 17.

BILATERAL AGREEMENTS

Table 3. *Trade Balances of South-Eastern Europe with Germany, 1928–38*
(millions of RM)

	1928	1929	1930	1931	1932	1933	1934	1935	1936	1937	1938
Romania											
Exports	188·1	211·0	236·9	102·4	74·4	46·1	59·0	79·9	92·3	179·5	140·4
Imports	173·0	164·1	137·3	92·5	64·2	46·0	50·9	63·8	103·6	129·5	148·8
Balance	+15·1	+46·9	+99·6	+9·9	+10·2	+0·1	+8·1	+16·1	−11·3	+50·0	−8·4
Hungary											
Exports	71·9	89·3	82·1	55·2	36·4	34·2	63·9	77·9	93·4	114·1	109·8
Imports	154·0	146·8	118·3	84·4	47·4	38·1	39·6	62·9	83·0	110·5	110·0
Balance	−82·1	−57·5	−36·2	−29·2	−11·0	−3·9	+24·3	+15·0	+10·4	+3·6	+9·8
Bulgaria											
Exports	51·0	51·2	58·9	48·3	34·5	31·3	33·7	41·4	57·6	71·8	95·7
Imports	36·0	44·7	22·9	25·3	20·8	17·7	19·3	39·9	47·6	68·2	61·6
Greece											
Exports	94·0	103·7	108·1	70·3	58·9	53·4	55·3	58·5	68·4	76·4	101·0
Imports	60·2	76·8	56·3	56·6	23·5	18·7	29·3	49·1	63·5	113·1	121·2
Yugoslavia											
Exports	66·6	60·9	74·8	40·1	29·5	33·5	36·3	61·4	75·2	132·2	172·1
Imports	117·6	152·6	172·1	95·1	43·3	33·8	31·5	36·9	77·2	134·4	144·6

Source: Various issues of *Statistisches Jahrbuch für das Deutsche Reich*.

persistent, export surplus with Germany. The diversity in trade patterns of the two countries with Germany reflects faithfully what we expect from differences in behaviour of the central banks.

Table 4 compares the holdings of blocked foreign exchange by the two central banks. In the case of Hungary, these are included under the heading "Other Assets" and not published separately after 1935. If they continued to account

Table 4. *Foreign-Exchange Holdings of the National Banks of Hungary and Romania, 1929–37*

Hungary (millions of pengő)	1929	1930	1931	1932	1933	1934	1935	1936	1937
Gold reserve	163	163	102	97	79	79	79	84	84
Foreign exchange	80	68	23	20	33	34	71	42	59
(a) Cover	39	34	16	14	12	20	33	42	59
(b) Other	41	34	7	6	21	14	38	*	*
Other assets	21	15	15	11	8	8	50	154†	268†

Source: League of Nations, *Money and Banking, 1937–8*, II, *Commercial and Central Banks* (Geneva, 1938), 109.
* This item had been published separately until 1935. In 1936 and 1937 it was not. For those two years only, it is included in "Other assets".
† Includes "Other foreign exchange".

Romania (millions of lei)	1929	1930	1931	1932	1933	1934	1935	1936	1937
Gold reserve	9,185	9,275	9,675	9,527	9,895	10,285	10,802	15,568	16,458
Foreign exchange	6,791	1,823	323	560	270	1,226	1,953	3,585	2,338
(a) Cover	6,745	1,746	278	495	257	91	92	—	—
(b) For payment of imports	—	—	—	—	—	366	139	1,738	703
(c) Available for clearing	—	—	—	—	—	732	1,709	1,836	1,615
(d) Other	46	77	45	64	13	36	14	12	20
"Special exchange provisions"	—	—	—	1,247	2,186	2,236	2,819	894	3,314

Sources: Ibid. p. 159; Virgile Madgearu, *Mémoire sur le Contrôle des changes en Roumanie* (Paris, 1939), Annexe 1.4.

for the same share of the increase in total "Other Assets" in 1936 and 1937 as in 1935, they would have amounted to 60 million pengö in 1936 and 100 million in 1937. Large and continued increases in blocked foreign currencies held by the National Bank of Hungary correspond to the continued balance-of-trade surplus maintained with Germany. The Romanian figures are more difficult to interpret. The variety of accounts kept for foreign exchange by the National Bank of Romania and the large, often offsetting, fluctuations in them make it impossible to relate any one account, or the total foreign-exchange holdings, to the course of the Romanian trade balance with Germany. If the "Exchange available on various clearing accounts" was primarily from Germany, it appears that the trade deficit with Germany in 1936 merely halted and did not reverse the growth of blocked marks held in Romania while the small surplus in 1937 was accompanied by a fall in credits to Germany. Given the constant renegotiation of the terms of the clearing agreement which was being conducted, a clear-cut correspondence of trade balances and clearing account totals cannot be expected. It is clear, however, that Romania was not willing to let any of the various accounts rise steadily.

The new patterns of trade with Germany which developed for the two countries are shown in Tables 5 and 6. Taken from German sources, the tables show only

Table 5. *German Imports from and Exports to Hungary, 1928–38*
(unit value: RM per ton)

Imports	1928	1932	1934	1935	1936	1937	1938
Cattle	—	—	327	396	437	511	484
Wheat	224	96	—	—	—	—	135
Corn	—	—	—	—	—	104	104
Fruit	335	194	192	270	236	239	308
Meats	1,704	944	807	901	909	922	891
Butter	3,704	1,599	1,092	1,798	1,737	1,770	1,320
Lard and tallow	—	—	597	674	810	760	613
Feathers and bristles	5,088	3,341	3,046	2,891	3,243	4,832	4,456
Wool, flax, hemp	1,707	984	—	—	185	—	—
Non-oil seeds	1,652	873	910	795	842	726	754
Bauxite, cryolite	—	—	—	—	19	18	18
Electrical equipment	12,162	13,131	13,502	14,798	16,522	18,261	15,185
Poultry, eggs	1,532	996	1,058	853	332	871	807
Exports							
Wool and fibres	3,306	928	—	—	—	—	—
Textiles	16,868	10,572	—	—	10,000	10,000	10,000
Leather goods	21,296	14,814	—	—	15,714	20,000	12,500
Furs	93,220	54,054	40,678	40,000	25,714	50,909	49,166
Paper	853	728	—	—	197	263	265
Chemicals	—	1,320	1,216	1,253	1,468	1,573	1,696
of which:							
Paints etc.	1,980	2,851	—	—	—	—	—
Dyestuffs	—	—	—	—	4,835	—	—
Rayon	12,686	4,285	3,960	2,961	2,913	3,187	3,600
Machine parts	2,302	2,222	—	—	—	—	—
Iron goods	—	—	2,019	864	3,716	6,468	4,211
Machinery	—	2,122	2,353	1,861	2,093	2,060	2,485
Electrical equipment	7,477	9,722	9,804	10,145	3,000	4,200	2,689
Motor vehicles	4,060	—	2,214	2,203	2,594	2,685	2,076

Source: Various issues of *Statistisches Jahrbuch für das Deutsche Reich*.

BILATERAL AGREEMENTS

Table 6. *German Imports from and Exports to Romania, 1928–38*
(unit value: RM per ton)

Imports	1928	1932	1934	1935	1936	1937	1938
Wheat	237	—	—	—	—	153	152
Rye	208	—	—	—	—	136	—
Barley	194	88	58	93	—	123	121
Corn	186	74	66	73	—	107	110
Fruit	432	368	557	539	335	408	466
Meat	1,752	870	866	936	941	966	880
Poultry, eggs	1,715	839	859	986	1,136	984	—
Vegetable oils	361	122	132	109	111	111	186
Oilcake	175	74	—	—	—	124	—
Hides and skins	27,272	22,826	—	—	—	59,231	—
Timber	105	79	81	79	91	114	112
Oil	158	63	56	55	62	76	80
Exports							
Thread	9,824	5,541	6,646	5,340	4,643	6,971	6,848
Textiles	14,499	7,950	—	—	6,757	6,286	7,895
Furs	96,591	36,471	—	—	53,333	57,500	62,500
Chemicals	—	1,501	1,820	1,370	1,349	1,749	1,622
of which:							
Paints etc.	2,926	2,235	2,372	1,749	—	—	—
Dyestuffs	—	—	—	—	5,287	6,140	6,071
Machine parts	1,769	1,604	1,891	1,733	—	—	—
Sheet iron and tubing	301	—	—	—	212	285	369
Ironware	1,672	1,563	—	—	1,466	1,534	971
Copper goods	3,685	3,662	2,457	1,584	5,238	5,862	4,565
Non-electrical machinery	—	1,661	1,710	1,703	1,607	1,756	1,710
Electrical equipment	3,868	3,683	1,873	1,507	1,544	1,904	2,166
Pharmaceutical	—	—	—	—	21,818	26,842	28,000
Motor vehicles and aircraft	3,918	—	—	—	2,390	2,184	2,176

Source: Various issues of *Statistisches Jahrbuch für das Deutsch Reich.*

the most important commodities entering the bilateral trade. Since both values (in Reichsmarks) and volumes (in tons) are given it is possible to calculate *ersatz* unit values for each commodity group. It is these unit values which underlie the terms of trade calculated for Table 1. They have the advantage of all being calculated in the same currency (the *Sperrmarks* used in the respective clearing agreements) so comparisons can be made directly of unit values for imports and exports. They have the disadvantage, however, that values per ton of a commodity group may not reflect or respond to movements in the value per item of that commodity group. The further difficulties of relating unit values to actual price movements still remain. These deficiencies may vary greatly, depending on the characteristics of each commodity. Table 1 weights each commodity group by its share of the total recorded value of trade, but the total includes only those commodities common to each of the two years which are compared successively. The reader may wish to calculate terms of trade with other subsets of commodities and weighting schemes. However, whichever subset is selected, and whatever weighting scheme is employed, it will be difficult to find support for the monopolist–monopsonist thesis. In general, unit values increased for the exports of both Hungary and Romania to Germany after 1932, although they never reached the 1928 level. Unit values of imports of the two countries from Germany dropped considerably after 1928 and showed no tendency to rise after 1934.

The overall impression is that German trade policy, in terms of setting relative prices of imports and exports, did not differ greatly between Hungary and Romania. Central-bank policy in the two countries towards the implementation of the respective clearing agreements did differ, however, and markedly so. The financing principle, pursued by the Hungarians, should have had a more reflationary effect upon the depressed economy than the waiting principle, persisted in by the Romanians. Whether it did, in fact, is an empirical question worthy of more detailed study and involving the consideration of many more factors influencing the relative recovery rates of the various national economies of south-eastern Europe.

IV

Hungary's response to the New Plan, combined with a transfer moratorium, had the felicitous result of isolating capital-account from current-account transactions at least long enough for domestic economic recovery to occur. In effect, Hungary obtained the economic benefits of a *de facto* receivership, while suffering the loss of independence in policy direction that receivership implies. Romania's attempts to avoid German receivership, which had much more ominous implications for a cessionary state, were ultimately unsuccessful owing in part to the economic losses such attempts incurred.[1]

On the German side, a continued trade deficit with Hungary on balance meant a small economic loss in terms of promoting domestic expansion, while the small deficits and occasional surpluses with Romania did not hinder in any way the rapid recovery of the German economy. By the end of 1938, however, Germany's economic recovery, attributable to rearmament and highway building,[2] had achieved nearly full employment, Hungarian real output had increased substantially above pre-crisis levels and some kind of change in the economic and political relationship of the two countries was indicated. As Germany approached full employment the economic costs of a trade deficit became less, while the necessity of "receivership" for Hungary was much less pressing. The advantage in renegotiation of terms clearly lay with Germany, but the outcome which actually occurred was determined more by political events[3] than by diabolical elements in the economics of Dr Schacht and his bilateral clearing agreements. The relationship of Germany with Romania was complicated by the increasing military need of Germany for petroleum and the continued dependence upon foreign oil companies by Romania. Strategic concerns may have been the overriding consideration in determining Romania's economic policy of pursuing the waiting principle, but the adverse outcome of this policy only weakened Romania further for renegotiation of the trade agreement with Germany in 1939.

University of Illinois

[1] Virgile Madgearu, *Le Contrôle des Changes en Roumanie* (Paris: International Institute of Intellectual Co-operation, 1939), p. 10. Madgearu comments, one supposes ironically, that the measure was "originale en son genre".

[2] See R. J. Overy, 'Cars, Roads, and Economic Recovery in Germany, 1932–8', *Economic History Review*, 2nd ser. XXVIII (1975), 466–83.

[3] On 25 November 1937, Hitler accepted Schacht's resignation as Minister of Economics. After a year of continuing conflict between the two men over economic policy, Hitler dismissed Schacht from the Reichsbank on 20 Jan. 1939. For a reassessment of Schacht as something other than Hitler's willing financial wizard, see Amos Simpson, *Hjalmar Schacht in Perspective* (The Hague, 1969).

[19]
Indicators of Real Effective Exchange Rates of Major Trading Nations from 1922 to 1937

Volker Hentschel

In grateful memory of Werner Conze

I.

From the beginning of the First World War to the beginning of the Second World War trade was affected by frequent, varied and unusually extensive shifts in international price relations and exchange rate parities. The First World War and the varying degrees of inflation caused by the war economy in every country gave rise to the first wave of extensive change. The situation was further distorted by the success in combatting inflation in some countries and the progressive deterioration in the currency in others during the immediate postwar years. The violent fluctuations took place during a period when exchange rates were free to move. In the midtwenties relative calm was restored when most of the major international currencies returned to the gold standard and the price trends steadied somewhat. But, of course, the inherent deviations from the price and exchange rate relations of the 'halcyon' prewar days in world trade continued to have an effect. Moreover, the calm was of short duration, and the world slump set off a second wave of hectic fluctuations in price and exchange rates, which only gradually ebbed after 1934. This was a period of arbitrary changes in exchange rates that were on principle fixed[1], and it corrected or accentuated the results of the first wave.

The literature on the economic history of that period contains a large number of more or less fixed assumptions, ideas and statements on the effects of these many and varied changes in price and exchange rate relations on international trade in goods and services, and hence on the prosperity of nations. It is, for instance, largely assumed that the successive, uncoordinated return of the major currencies to the gold standard during the twenties led to considerable distortions in exchange rate relations which were ill adjusted to the changes in price relations, and brought the United States and France very considerable international competitive advantages, while Great Britain certainly and Germany with some probability suffered no less remarkable disadvantages. That is why Britain and Germany encountered hitherto unknown obstacles to exports, which hampered growth in their economies, while the United States accumulated extensive trade balance surpluses, although its newly acquired position as international creditor would really have required deficits to help keep the world economy functioning. It is also assumed that the controversial devaluation of the pound in September 1931 brought about a decisive and lasting improvement in British price competitiveness but burdened the world markets,

---

[1] To be more precise, these were arbitrary devaluations stretched over time, the extent of which the monetary authorities *on principle* left to the market. *De facto*, admittedly, they intervened on the markets to bring rates where they desired.

already shaken by crisis, with a very difficult adjustment requirement. That is why it is generally regarded as a key event in the world economic crisis.[2]

These are only a few rough indications. They could be multiplied, and, naturally, should be formulated with more differentiation to give a comprehensive survey of the comments in the relevant literature on our problem. But that is not our concern here. Whatever such comments may tell us, they have one thing in common: they are all at most analytical or intuitive conclusions drawn from fragmentary data. Such conclusions may be correct. They frequently are. But they are not based on very strong empirical statistical evidence, for there has not so far been any attempt to work out systematically the actual extent of the changes that are assumed, or said to have happened, in international price competitive positions in the period between the wars, and *that* is what we are concerned with here. It is the purpose of this article to quantify the changes in international price competitive positions of 15 of the most important world trading nations between 1913 and 1937[3], and give a brief comment on the results for the seven countries with the biggest shares of world trade.

The article makes no claim to give a full 'explanation' of the development in foreign trade and its effects on growth and prosperity during that period. There are factual, methodological and statistical reasons for not attempting to do this. Firstly, the direction and size of the international trade flows depended on more than price relations and price movements. But where they did depend on these, the degree of dependency was a question of price elasticities, and very little is known about these.[4] Secondly, the values that are presented and reflected are only 'correct' within the framework of the conditions of the arithmetical concept with the help of which they

---

[2] On these two areas see z.B. Gerd *Hardach* Weltmarktorientierung und relative Stagnation. Währungspolitik in Deutschland 1924–1931, Berlin ;]76, p. 70ff., 149, 161, Knut Borchardt, Wirtschaftliche Ursachen des Scheiterns der Weimater Republik, in: K.D. *Erdmann* u. H. *Schulze*. Weimar. Selbstptreisgabe einer Demokratic, Düsseldorf 1980, p. 228 (against the view that the RM was overvalued right from the start A.J. *Youngyon*. Britain's Economic Growth 1920–1931. The Normann Conquest of Dollar 4,86. Cambridge 1972, p. 100ff., D.H. *Aldcroft* Britische Währungspolitik und Wirtschaftstätigkeit in den zwanziger Jahren, in: H. *Winkel*, ed. Finanz- und wirtschaftspolitische Fragen der Zwischenkriegszeit, Berlin 1973, p. 100, S. *Howson*, Domestic Monetary Management in Britain 1919–1938, Cambridge 1975, S. 47ff., H. v.B. *Clereland*, The International Monetary System in the Interwar Period, in: B.M. *Rowland*, Hrsg., Balance of Power versus Hegemony: The Interwar Monetary System, New York 1976, p. 32f., J. L. *Kooker*, French Financial Diplomacy. The Interwar Years, in: ibid, p. 96ff., Melchior *Palyi*, The Twilight of Gold 1914–1936. Myths and Realities, Chicago 1972, p. 185f. against the view that Poincaré had undervalued the franc in the twenties M. *Falkus*. US Economic Policy and the "Dollar Gap" of the 1920's in: EHR 24, 1971, p. 599–623, S. *Glynn* u. A.L. *Lougheed*. A Comment on US Economic Policy and the "Dollar Gap" of the 1920's, in: EHR 26, 1973, p. 693. A summary Ch. P. *Kindleberger*, Die Weltwirtschaftskrise. Geschichte der Weltwirtschaft im 20. Jh. Bd. 4, München 1973, p. 42ff. J.B. *Condliffe*. The Reconstruction of World Trade. A Survey of International Economic Relations, London 1941, p. 71ff., W.A. *Lewis*, Economic Survey, 1919–1939, London 1949, p. 82ff., S. *Howson*, Sterlings Managed Float. The Operation of the Exchange Accounts 1932–1939, Princeton 1980. D.H. *Aldcroft*, The Interwar Economy: Britain 1919–1939, London 1970, p. 281.

[3] 1913 is the base and reference year. The first year used for comparison is 1922, for that is the first year for which enough of the necessary data is available.

[4] Instead of a number of individual studies see the review by Hang Sheng Cheng: Statistical Estimates of Elasticities and Propensities in International Trade. A Survey of Published Studies, in: IMF Staff Papers, Vol. 7, 1959/60, pp. 107–158.

were produced. The concept is not beyond all doubt or criticism. Thirdly, and finally, the base data for the calculations are burdened with the uncertainties of historical economic statistics in general and the problems of indexes in particular.

So these extensive calculations and brief comments are presented in the more modest hope that they may help to widen what has been the rather narrow basis for assessment, and perhaps make it more informative as well.
Section II contains a brief discussion of the analytical concept and the reliability of the data. Sections III to V comment on the results of the calculations, which are contained in the tables and graphs in the Appendix.

II.

As an instrument of analysis we have used the concept of *real effective exchange rates*. The development of the real effective exchange rate shows whether the price competitive position of a country on international markets improved or deteriorated over time, and it consists of changes in the relations of the country's own prices to those of other countries[5], and of movements in exchange rates (changes in the price of the country's own currency, expressed in units of other currencies). The price and exchange rate relations of one country against those of many other countries are grouped into *one* indicator, and this requires weighting the many bilateral relations.

So the concept of real effective exchange rates contains four analytical problems, some of which are interrelated. Since the real effective exchange rate only tells us something as a flow over time, the first problem lies in selecting a suitable reference year. The second is to work out a meaningful price index. Thirdly, the question arises what countries should be included in the price and exchange rate comparison, and fourthly, it is difficult to decide how to weight the price and exchange rate relations with the countries included.

Admittedly, the four problems are of differing degrees. The first two are ultimately a matter of analytical intent and the interpretation of the results, and they can be solved on a pragmatic, case-to-case basis.

It is best to choose as reference year one which seems 'normal' taking a long view, or one in which a development began which is interesting scientifically or practically. In our case 1913 is the obvious choice.

It is less easy to find the most suitable price index than base year. The aim to show changes in international price competitiveness would at first seem to point very definitely to the index of the average value of exports, and, in fact, the calculations are based on this. But it has its analytical weaknesses. Exports compete in the countries to which they are imported both against the domestic prices in those countries and against the prices of third countries' exports. Competition from the

---

[5] Changes in *cost* relations would be analytically more desirable, because they would tell us more. Changes in price relations can reflect the greater or less earnings power of exports, as well as better or worse price competitiveness, and it would be helpful if this double significance could be excluded in assessing the trend over time of real effective exchange rates. But there is no adequate data for the calculation of real effective exchange rates on a cost basis. Even in calculating figures that apply to the present one has to use one element of costs, wage costs, for which adequate statistics are available, and for older periods not even sufficient data on wages is available.

domestic prices of import countries is not covered by the index of average export values, and that *can* lead to distortions, if a country's exports are concentrated on a few countries, and the movements in their domestic prices differ greatly from those in its export prices. Moreover, similarities and differences in the export ranges cause some problems. But since calculating a more suitable combined index gives rise to more uncertainties than it promises advantage of knowledge, we can only hope that the apparent presumed distortions will be slight. The hope is not unfounded, at least in the context of the broad spread of trade of the major industrial states.

The third and fourth analytical problems are of a more fundamental nature, and ultimately they cannot be solved, either pragmatically or in any other way. They are also closely related.

The question of what countries should be included in the comparison of prices and exchange rates can be answered in two ways. Firstly, all the countries with which the economy, with whose competitive position we are concerned, is competing. The second is: all the countries with which it trades. For the advanced industrial economies the two groups are usually largely identical, and that was true even between the wars. The intensity of the competition and trade with certain countries, however, differed from one economy to another, and that leads us to the problem of weighting, which ultimately cannot be solved.

Out of a range of alternatives two are particularly appropriate.[6] In one case the bilateral price and exchange rate relations are weighted with the shares of the buyer countries in the exports of the country with whose competitive position we are concerned, and in the other with the shares of the competitors in world trade. The first variant stresses the intensity of trade relations between certain countries and regions. This is the method used by the Deutsche Bundesbank and the German Council of Experts (Sachverständigenrat).[7] The second method puts more weight on the density and adjustment elasticity of the world trade network, and this is the method used, for instance, by the American Federal Reserve Board.

In both alternatives the question also arises whether one should weight with "current" shares, that is, changing from year to year, or with constant shares. Weighting with current shares could show, in the development of the real effective exchange rate, not only changes in price and/or exchange rate relations, but also shifts in shares that might have been caused by changes in relative prices and effective exchange rates. The use of constant weights excludes from the calculation such intercorrelation of changes in prices, exchange rates and shares, together with their repercussions on the course of the real effective exchange rate. There are sound, objective reasons for both methods. Control calculations with current shares from 1922 to 1937 on the one hand, and with constant shares from 1929 and 1936 on the other, helped the decision in this case between the two possibilities. The deviations proved to be slight. They are at most two, but usually less than one percent. In view of the general uncertainty of the data the choice between current and constant weighting is therefore virtually of no account.

---

[6] On effective exchange rates see Rudolf R. Rhomberg: Indices of Effective Exchange Rates, in: IMF Staff Papers XXIII, 1976, pp. 89ff.
[7] See Annual Report by the Council of Experts for 1976/77, p. 80f.

That does not apply to the decision between using export shares or world trade shares as weights. The regional composition of exports of all countries shows more or less high degrees of concentration and so differs notably from the regional composition of world trade. So if the calculations using the two sets of weights produced virtually identical results, this could only be by chance. Deciding between such clearly different figures is always tricky, and averaging the two sets of figures, which is sometimes proposed, is not basically different from using a third indicator, which can be closer to reality but can also deviate further from it than the two others.[8] It is therefore advisable not to decide for one or the other or to "average out", but to use both sets of figures. That is the method used here, with justifiable reservations. To prevent excessive arithmetic only real effective exchange rates were worked out on the basis of export shares for every year and 15 countries. The calculation of real effective exchange rates on the basis of world trade shares, on the other hand, is limited to five "key years" – more are only used when need required – and the seven countries with the highest shares in world trade, the United Kingdom, the United States, Germany, France, Canada, Japan and India.[9]

The key years were 1925, 1929, 1932, 1934 and 1937. In the spring of 1925 the pound returned to the gold standard, and the world economy seemed to have found its way back to normality. The semblance of normality lasted until 1929. Then the world slump broke out, throwing international competition and trade relations into total confusion. First came dramatic price shifts. Then in 1931 the devaluation of the pound, the Yen and a number of other currencies set new accents, which were reflected in the figures for 1932. In 1934 the violent fluctuations in prices returned to relative calm. In addition, at the beginning of the year, the exchange rate for the dollar was de facto re-stabilised at a lower level. 1937 is the last year before the Second World War for which sufficient data is available.

The calculation with export shares did not include all the exports of the countries concerned, nor did the calculation with world market shares include total world trade. That was not necessary for the analysis, nor was it statistically possible. In the calculation with – current – export shares all the trade partners were usually considered which had a share of at least one percent in the exports of the country whose real effective exchange rate was being considered[10], and this generally meant that between 65 and 90 percent of exports was covered. The degree to which this was representative dropped noticeably in the later 1930s.[11] Analogous to this, the

---

[8] Very much more complex procedures are possible and are practised. See especially Jaques R. Artus and Rudolf R. Rhomberg: A Multilateral Exchange Rate Model, in: IMF Staff Papers, Vol. 20, 1973, pp. 591–611. However, the IMF's MERM requires a knowledge of data that is not available for older periods.

[9] India was only one of the seven largest trading nations in the twenties, being replaced by Belgium in the thirties. Whether it is methodologically justifiable and meaningful to treat India the same as the four industrial countries and the two "threshold contries", Canada and Japan, in the analysis and interpretation, is very questionable. The data and notes are given with considerable reserve. Similar reservations apply to the unannotated data on China and Argentina. On the fundamental problem see Gérard Bélanger: An Indicator of Effective Exchange Rates for Primary Producing Countries, in: IMF Staff Papers XXIII, 1976, pp. 113ff.

[10] Minor exceptions had to be made to this owing to lack of data.

[11] It fell to under two thirds for Japan, Italy and China.

calculation using constant world trade shares (from 1929) covered the countries with at least one percent of world trade[12], which was rather more than three quarters of total world trade.

With these conditions and reservations the indices of relative prices, effective exchange rates and real effective exchange rates (price competitive positions) given in the Appendix were worked out as follows[13]:

1. Indices of relative prices =

$$\frac{P_{i(1922-1937)}}{(P_{j1(1922-1937)})^{g_{j1}} \times (P_{j2(1922-1937)})^{g_{j2}} \times \ldots (P_{jn(1922-1937)})^{g_{jn}}} \cdot 100$$

P_i = Index of average export values in the country whose competetive position is being calculated, from 1922 to 1937 using 1913 as the base year (= 100).

$P_{j1\ldots n}$ = Indices of average export values of the trade partners included in the calculation, or world trading countries in the appropriate years, also 1913 as the base year

$G_{j1\ldots n}$ = Export shares or world trade shares of countries j_1 to j_n

$\sum_{j=1-n} g_j = 1$ = The export or world trade shares not included were distributet proportionally between the shares that we included

An index figure over 100 indicates that the price relations have changed to the *dis*advantage of country i in comparison with conditions in 1913. Export from country i had become relatively more expensive, even if they were cheaper in absolute terms. A figure under 100 indicates the opposite. Accordingly, the increase (or reduction) in the index figure from one year to a later year shows that the relative export prices of i had risen (or fallen) in the meantime.

2. Indices of effective exchange rates =

$$(R_{ij1(1922-1937)})^{g_{j1}} \times (R_{ij2(1922-1937)})^{g_{j2}} \times \ldots (R_{ijn(1922-1937)})^{g_{jn}}$$

Rij = Index of the value of one unit of a currency of the country whose competitive position is being calculated, expressed in units of the currency of country j from 1922 to 1937, with 1913 as base year (= 100).

An index figure over 100 indicates that the currency of the country i had become more expensive on a weighted average of foreign currencies since 1913.[14] It had

---

[12] Spain, Brazil and British Malaya are exceptions, owing to lack of data.
[13] On the reason why the geometric link between weighted prices (and exchange rates) is preferable to the arithmetical link used at the beginning see the Monthly Report of the Deutsche Bundesbank, 1979, pp. 22–25.
[14] The development in relations between two currencies will show this:
1913: 1 US $ – 5.18 Ffrs. = 100; 1925: 1 US $ – 20.96 Ffrs. = 405; 1934: 1 US $ – 15.22 Ffrs. = 294
So the dollar quadrupled in value against the French franc from 1913 to 1925, and then lost a good quarter of this again by 1934.

upvalued. A figure under 100 indicates the opposite. Accordingly, the increase (reduction) in the index figure from one year to a later year shows that the currency of i had been upvalued (devalued) in the meantime.

3. Index of real effective exchange rates =

$$\frac{\text{Index of relative prices} \times \text{index of effective exchange rates.}}{100}$$

An index figure over 100 indicates that the price competitive position of the country for which the real effective exchange rate applies had deteriorated since 1913. The deterioration could be for the following reasons: an increase in relative prices *and* an upvaluation in the currency; an increase in relative prices, which was only partly compensated by a devaluation in the currency; an upvaluation in the currency which went beyond the fall in relative prices.

A figure under 100, on the other hand, indicates an improvement in the price competitive position since 1913. This could result from a reduction in relative prices *and* a devaluation of the currency; a fall in prices only partly compensated by an upvaluation of the currency, or a devaluation of the currency beyond the rise in relative prices.

Accordingly, the increase (or reduction) in the index figure from one year to a later year shows that the price competitive position of the country had deteriorated (or improved) in the interim.

Once more: changes in the price competitive positions say nothing definite on whether and to what extent the export chances of the country affected had improved or deteriorated. That depended on the price-export elasticities and many other influences on international trade flows. But noticeable and lasting fluctuations in real effective exchange rates will certainly have had an effect on a country's international competitiveness and foreign sales.

Before finally coming to our calculations, a few sentences on the source and quality of the basic data. The figures are taken from the League of Nations international economic statistics, and the data is available in the desired quantity for the years 1922 to 1937. The original data for the individual countries was not collected absolutely identically. The usual doubts must be entertained on comparability, but this is not fundamentally in question. The annual data is composed of partly weighted, partly unweighted monthly figures, and the time flows were constructed by the League of Nations using a uniform procedure.[15]

The average export figures are of course arithmetical fictions and have the familiar problems of such usual fictions.

The exchange rates are usually shown as the rate for the dollar in New York, in exceptional cases in London, and for our purposes they were converted using the dollar rates for the currency whose real effective exchange rate we are concerned

---

[15] The question arose whether this should be supplemented or replaced by contemporary, estimated or calculated, "national" figures. In some cases that was unavoidable (see sources given on p. 62), but otherwise it was deliberately avoided to preserve the uniformity of the procedure and, as far as possible, the consistency of the data base.

with: $R_{sj} / R_{si} = R_{ij}$.[16] That corresponds to the procedure now used by international monetary authorities. Control calculations of the effective rate for the pound using London quotations for the pound, and the effective rate for the Reichsmark using Berlin quotations for that currency yielded results which agreed with the figures worked out using the dollar rates.

It is, however, doubtful whether the official rates in the later thirties still accorded with the actual trade conditions in every case. In Nazi Germany they certainly did *not*, at the latest after the New Plan was passed in the summer of 1934.[17] It was a question whether there would be more distortion of the results by nevertheless including Germany in the calculations for the period after 1932, or by leaving it out. It was included after 1932, because the distortion *this* would cause seemed to be controllable. Since the official rate for the Reichsmark was higher than the actual value of the currency in the labyrinth of barter and offset agreements being made by German suppliers, the price competitive positions of the countries that were engaged in intensive trade with Germany, and competing with it, was slightly worse in the later 1930s than the results of the calculations show. So the German competitive position must have been somewhat better. But conventionally calculated real effective exchange rates make very little sense in any case for the Reichsmark at this period.

III.

The tables and illustrations 1 to 7 show the developments in relative prices, effective exchange rates and real effective exchange rates for the United States, the United Kingdom[18], Germany, France, Canada, Japan and India, and the following commentary is limited to this.[19] The tables contain both the figures calculated on the basis of export shares and those calculated using world trade shares. The illustrations only show the curves obtained using export shares. The commentary always refers first to the results obtained using export shares. Then, where necessary, reference is made

---

[16] In words: the price of the dollar expressed in units of the currency j divided by the price of the dollar in units of the currency i shows the price of the currency i in units of j. For example: if 1 $ = 4.20 RM = L0.205, then L 1 = (4.20 : 0.205) = 20.40 RM.

[17] On the foreign exchange regulations in Germany and the "split" exchange rate see Howard Ellis: Exchange Control in Central Europe, Cambridge 1941, pp. 191–289, Frank C. Child: The Theory and Practices of Exchange Control in Germany, The Hague 1958, Knut Borchardt: Ein neues Urteil über die deutsche Währungs- und Handelspolitik von 1931 bis 1938, in: VSWG 1959, pp. 526–546.

[18] See John Redmond: An Indicator of the Effective Exchange Rate of the Pound in the Nineteen-Thirties, in: EHR 1980, pp. 83–91. The appropriate figures in Table 2 are lower than Redmond's, and this is mainly the systematic expression of a different method of calculation. Redmond links the bilateral exchange rates arithmetically, while here they are geometrically linked.

[19] The word "commentary" should be taken as simply as it is meant. The following remarks are in the main a verbal paraphrase of the results of the calculations, with occasional reference to possible historical causes and consequences. They are not intended to be a thorough-going interpretation, and I have deliberately refrained from references to the very extensive literature on the history of international trade between the wars. I regard it as appropriate to present the method of calculating and the results for *discussion* first, and not just assume that the data is viable by making extensive interpretations.

to deviations resulting from weighting with world trade shares. This method is facilitated (and at the same time justified in many respects) in that the different weightings usually only affect the extent of improvements or deteriorations in international competitive positions, but do not distort the flows.

Tables 8 to 15 and illustrations 8 to 10 give reduced data, on which no further comment is given, for Belgium and the Netherlands, Sweden, Italy and Switzerland, as well as for China, Argentina and Australia. The tables are limited to show the figures calculated from export shares, and the illustrations only show the curves of real effective exchange rates.

The subject itself, and the need for clarity, made it appropriate to subdivide the period considered when commenting on the results into three shorter phases. The first covers the restabilisation and relatively calm development in the twenties, the second the extremely violent fluctuations from 1930 to 1934 and the third the repercussions of the crises up to 1937.

In the twenties the seven countries with the largest world trade shares fell into two groups. The first includes the United Kingdom and Japan. The price competitive positions of these two countries had deteriorated notably during the course of the First World War and the transition from the war economy to a peacetime economy, and until the great slump they remained in a worse position than they had been in 1913. The second group includes the USA, Germany, France and Canada. The price competitive positions of these countries were better, at least for most of the twenties, than before the war. India moved between the two groups, taking a less clear course.

But apart from such immediate similarities there were singular characteristics in the development in all the countries:

For the *United Kingdom* we must say first that the competitive disadvantage fixed up to 1929 by retying the pound to gold was very much greater, according to evidence from the real effective exchange rate, than is generally supposed. Keynes had warned against returning to the old gold parity in 1924/25, because British prices were still about 10% above US prices. And many economic historians have become accustomed to seeing this price differential as an indication of the continued loss of competitiveness which Churchill imposed on British exports when he disregarded Keynes' warning, albeit with a heavy heart. It is possible that the economic historians have become used to what is in fact an error. For it was not only the price and exchange rate relation to the USA that mattered. Our calculations show that Britain's relative prices had returned to their prewar level, and actually fallen slightly below it, by the time of the stabilisation of the pound, while the effective exchange rate at the old gold parity moved to nearly 20% above its prewar level. Necessarily, therefore, the real effective exchange rate was between 15 and 20% higher. This more marked deterioration in the price competitive position was conserved by Britain's return to the gold standard. A calculation using world trade shares shows the deterioration to be actually even more marked.

In *Japan* the situation was just the reverse. Here the war and a powerful postwar inflation had driven prices up far beyond the average price level on international markets. Unlike the British and American governments the Japanese government prevented a thorough-going deflationary correction to the upward drive in the early twenties. That widened the gap further, and between 1922 and 1925 Japan's relative export prices were around half as high again as their prewar level. Nevertheless, the

Bank of Japan and the Finance Ministry were trying to return to the old gold parity of the Yen as soon as possible. The currency was supported with all means to keep it near the prewar level. After the catastrophic earthquake of 1923 strength failed for a time, but as soon as possible the support actions were resumed. Although at the same time prices for Japan's main export commodity, silk, began to fall drastically, continuously and with extremely difficult economic, social and finally political consequences as well, the competitiveness of Japanese exports remained severely affected throughout the whole of the nineteen-twenties.[20]

The developments in the four countries whose competitive positions improved also differed in many ways. American and French exports only gained noticeable advantages of price competitiveness at the time of the stabilisation of the pound and the Mark[21], while German and Canadian exports enjoyed such advantages before that. But the French and the Americans were able to increase, or at least maintain, their advantages in the next few years, while the improvement in the German competitive position was continuously eroded.

The *United States* could afford a powerful increase in the rate for the dollar, because its export prices were falling far below the average price level of their trade partners and competitors, thanks to the superior productivity of US labour. The contrary movements are even more evident in a calculation with world market shares, but the result is the same using real effective exchange rates.[22]

France, on the other hand, balanced the rise in its relative prices, which was hardly checked until Poincare's de facto stabilisation in 1926, with a fall in the effective rate for the franc, and made sure that none of the competitive advantages thus gained was lost when the franc was officially tied to gold in 1928. The improvement in the real effective exchange rate in the second half of the twenties

---

[20] If the calculations were weighted with world trade shares the effect would be the same. The developments in relative prices and the effective rate for the Yen would, however, be different. Since with this alternative way of calculating trade with the United States and China, which together took about two thirds of Japanese exports, would be playing an inappropriately low part, the method would not appear to be so advisable.

[21] It is of course very tempting to conclude that they gaind those advantages *as a result of* the stabilisation. Nor would it presumably be entirely wrong, but it cannot be definitely proved, and for that reason caution is advised.

[22] The United States has frequently been accused of burdening the world economy with a problem that was heavy, could not be resolved over the longer term and so was ultimately disastrous, through the improvement of its international price competitiveness (usually branded as the 'undervaluation' of the dollar) in connection with its newly acquired position as creditor to the world economy. This certainly brought America high trade balance surpluses, even if other factors than the better real effective exchange rate made a major contribution to this. It was also argued that the continued trade balance surpluses prevented America's debtors from earning the dollars they needed for the interest and redemption payments on their loans. That is also largely true. But it is highly questionable and probably not correct to conclude that an upvaluation of the dollar would have been a way out of the dilemma. There is much to suggest that the price-demand elasticities of American foreign trade in the twenties were extremely low. Under that condition an upvaluation of the dollar would hardly have reduced American exports, but would have made the goods more expensive in other currencies, nor could it hardly have improved American imports, but would have made them cheaper in dollars. America's trade balance surplus might well have increased and the dilemma been greater for the debtors.

was between 15 and 25%. When calculated with world trade shares – though this is the less illuminating method[23] – it is larger than when calculated with export shares.

Germany's return to the prewar gold parity for the Mark was clearly justified by international price relations. It maintained for German exports at least some of the price competitive advantage they had enjoyed during the period of inflation, according to contemporary accusations and more recent calculations.[24] However, this advantage dwindled rapidly in the ensuing years, and after 1927 it had gone altogether. The reasons for this differ according to the weighting used. In weighting with export shares the rise in the real effective exchange rate is mainly due to a noticeable upvaluation of the Reichsmark, but in calculating with world trade shares it is mainly due to a marked rise in relative prices. Weighting with world trade shares gives the USA and Britain a larger role, with their falling prices and fixed rates, while France and Belgium play a smaller part, with their rising prices and falling rates, than when weighting with export shares. In view of the intensive international competition between German, American and British industries weighting with world trade shares should, no doubt, be seen as more realistic, and the loss of the German price advantage as due mainly to the rise in relative prices. But however one calculates, the result certainly contradicts the widespread view that the Reichsmark was "overvalued" at the time and Germany's exports simply too expensive. Germany's price competitive position in the twenties was generally better and never worse than before the First World War. That German goods nevertheless had a much more difficult time on international markets must be mainly due to other reasons.

In *India* finally the development was on principle similar, though it differed in time, moved in different dimensions and was very much less even. But there too relative prices had fallen clearly below their prewar level in 1922, while the Rupee was slightly upvalued. The result was a noticeable improvement in the Indian competitive position. The fall in prices and upvaluation went on until 1926. The upvaluation, however, was the result of political decisions, and it moved faster than the fall in prices. That destroyed the price competitive advantage within a short space of time. After 1924 the real effective exchange rate oscillated around its prewar level.

IV.

The world slump came almost like a severe shock, completely confusing the price and exchange rate relations that had been readjusted in a so lengthy and difficult process, and were hardly consolidated. From the autumn of 1929 to the autumn of

---

[23] The difference results mainly from the fact that in the calculation with world trade shares America plays a very much bigger part and Belgium a similarly smaller part. In relation to the dollar the franc was strongly devalued, but it was noticeably upvalued in relation to the Belgian franc or the Belga, apart from 1925/26. So the effective exchange rate, and with it the real effective exchange rate, is lower right through when calculating with world trade shares. But virtually everything suggests that Belgium should be given greater weight as a trading partner *and* competitor of France than the United States, and for that reason the higher real effective exchange rates seem more realistic.

[24] Carl-Ludwig Holtfrerich: Die deutsche Inflation 1914–1923, Berlin 1980, pp. 22f.

1931 dramatic price shifts predominated, after which often described and much decried changes in exchange rates set the signals, namely the devaluation in the pound, the Yen and the dollar between September 1931 and January 1934.[25] The Rupee followed the devaluation of the pound. The Canadian dollar followed it only partly, but later it followed the devaluation in the dollar far enough to restore the old relation between the two currencies. Germany and France kept to the gold parities for the Reichsmark and the franc fixed in 1924 and 1928 respectively.

The price and exchange rate changes turned the price competitive disadvantages Japan and India were suffering – still measured by the 1913 level – into considerable advantages. The upwards movement in the real effective exchange rate for the Reichsmark accelerated above the critical borderline. The competitive advantages enjoyed by France and the United States shrank and at times disappeared altogether. The competitive disadvantages to the United Kingdom increased remarkably. The real effective exchange rate for the Canadian dollar remained fixed, with the exception of a brief improvement in 1931.

The great improvement in the *Indian* competitive position was due to a successive fall of about ten percent in relative prices in 1930, and an effective devaluation of just on 15% the following year. Together these resulted in a plunge in the real effective exchange rate by a good 20%.

Japan, on the other hand, did not derive any competitive advantages from the even deeper fall in its export prices in 1930. In January the Yen was at last brought back to its old gold parity and then upvalued by 20% in the two following years. That neutralised the downward plunge in prices. Contrary to an opinion still widely held, the ill-timed stabilisation did not worsen Japan's competitiveness, but it did prevent the urgently needed improvement in it. In December Finance Minister Takahashi drew the long overdue conclusions, in extremely unfavourable political conditions, and uncoupled the currency from gold. The effective rate for the Yen dropped, with the help of the Japanese monetary authorities, down to half of its gold standard level within two years. The fall created scope for considerable price increases, which helped the (silk) farmers back on to at least a subsistence level income and increased the chances of profit for commercial firms. But by far the main effect of the unique devaluation was to improve Japan's international position in trade. Since 1932 the real effective exchange rate for the Yen had been 30 to 40% lower than in the crisis years from 1928 to 1931, and the admittedly more questionable method of calculating with world trade shares actually accentuated the fall further.

The deterioration in the *German* price competitive position in the two first crisis years was mainly due to an increase of about 10% in relative prices. Brüning's deflationary policy was to force German prices down below the world market level, but this was foiled by the actual development, and it was not until 1932 that relative prices began to move downwards, hesitantly at first, and then forced down by the National Socialists' price policy, until they went into a downslide that continued until the outbreak of the war. Admittedly, from the same year onwards the effects of first the devaluation in the pound and then that in the dollar were felt. The Mark moved upwards effectively in 1932 and 1933 more than relative prices fell. The real

---

[25] To prevent misunderstanding: in January 1934 the dollar was restabilised and its downward slide *ended*.

effective exchange rate for the Reichsmark rose by 20 to 30% from 1929 to 1933, and remained unchanged in the following year. The higher figure results from calculating with world trade shares, and it is the more likely, for the reasons already explained. The disastrous effects on German exports, which were further accentuated by worldwide protectionism, are well known.

The *United States* were able to maintain their international competitive position, more or less, up to the devaluation of the pound, the Yen and the Canadian dollar, as relative prices fell slightly on the whole and the effective exchange rate rose slightly. A noticeably sharper fall in prices then had no further effect against the devaluation in the three countries – which after all took 40% of American exports. The real effective rate for the dollar rose by 10% in 1932, but the loss in position was corrected in the following year by a powerful devaluation of the dollar, although this was not the primary aim. Roosevelt's main concern was to raise the level of prices, since he believed that too low prices were the main cause of the American crisis, and that a politically arbitrary increase in the gold price would necessarily pull commodities prices, that are regulated by the market, up in turn. At first sight it does look as if events confirmed the President's strange theory, but a closer examination will show that the powerful increase in prices in 1933 and 1934 was due to other causes.[26] The devaluation simply ensured that the marked rise in prices did not damage the competitiveness of American exports further. Whether conversely the price increases prevented the competitive advantages accumulated up to the outbreak of the crisis from being regained through the devaluation is uncertain. If calculating with export shares is more realistic, they did; but if calculating with world trade shares is more realistic, then they did not. But however one sees it, at the end of the period of violent fluctuations in prices and exchange rates America was certainly in the best position compared with the three major European industrial states, but only as far as its international price competitiveness was concerned, and not in its recovery from the crisis as well. For in the United States there was remarkably little interrelation between the two.

France's competitive position deteriorated steadily and strongly, especially after 1931. Although the effective upvaluation of the franc by 25 to 45% was partly compensated by an extraordinarily drastic policy of deflation, the real effective exchange rate in 1934 was 20 to 30% above its prewar level, depending on the method of calculation used. In many respects France acted in the early thirties completely contrary to its action in the midtwenties. Then an inflationary price upward movement had been compensated by a deliberately over-proportional devaluation, and now a price deflation, mainly induced for political reasons, softened the effects of a strong upvaluation, which the monetary authorities, for mistaken ideological reasons, did not want to change, and which at first they probably could hardly have changed for more tangible political reasons.

The real effective exchange rate for the pound took what was presumably the most surprising development during this period. It is generally assumed that the devaluation of the pound brought a basic improvement in the *British* competitive position, at least for a time, but according to our calculations that was not the case.

---

[26] Volker Hentschel: Wege aus der Arbeitslosigkeit – USA, Frankreich, Japan, in: Vierteljahrshefte des Deutschen Instituts für Wirtschaftsforschung 1, 1984, pp. 70ff.

As is well known, Britain was relatively mildly affected by the slump, and mainly in its foreign markets. The two were related. Since the domestic economic situation suffered less in Britain than elsewhere prices did not fall so far. Britain's relative export prices rose from 1929 to 1932 by 25%. Moreover, by the autumn of 1931 the pound had moved upwards by around 10%. The two together caused a deterioration in the price competitiveness of British exports, which was in any case weakening, to a hitherto unknown degree, and together with the reduced purchasing power of buyers this led to a collapse in exports by 30% in two years, which brought about a crisis. In 1931 the real effective exchange rate was about 20% higher than in 1929. The effective devaluation of the pound by a good 15% – not by the oft-named third, which results from measuring the rate for the pound only against the dollar – was just enough, as the rise in relative prices continued for a time, to reverse part of the unwelcome upward movements. On a calculation with export shares this was the smaller part, and on a calculation with world trade shares it was the larger part. But however one looks at it, the British competitive position was even worse in the thirties, despite the devaluation, than it had been in the twenties. At most the devaluation helped to ensure that the deterioration was less than in Germany and France. But taking 1913 as the standard, Britain was still the industrial country with the most price competitive disadvantages.

Canada's international competitiveness was not lastingly changed by the fluctuations in prices and exchange rates. The fall in relative prices which began in 1926 continued until 1932, and up to 1931 the real effective exchange rate continued to fall, while the currency remained stable. In the two following years the Canadian dollar first moved up by a good 10%, and then down by rather less. The upvaluation concealed the continued decline in relative prices and took the real effective exchange rate back to the level of 1929. As in America and Japan the devaluation was used to achieve a powerful increase in prices. So relative prices rose to the same extent as the effective exchange rate fell, leaving the competitive position unchanged.

V.

After 1934 the fluctuations in prices and exchange rates moderated somewhat. Prices moved upward again worldwide. The only important exception were German prices. Exchange rates remained for the most part firm, and the most important exception to *this* was the French franc.

The real effective exchange rates for the US dollar, the pound, the Yen and the rupee reflected the fluctuations, which in any case had moderated, only in a more weakened form. Relative price reductions compensated for the moderate rise in effective exchange rates which resulted from the successive devaluations of the gold block currencies, with minor deviations in the extent and time patterns of the movements. There were no more significant changes in competitive positions up to 1937.

But the exception countries, Germany and France, and Canada, which had played a rather modest role up to then, showed greater fluctuations. Germany and France experienced a noticeable improvement in their price competitive positions for very different reasons, while Canada lost competitive advantages.

As the National Socialist price and foreign trade policy depressed German export prices beyond 1934/35, while prices elsewhere started moving upwards again more or less strongly, Germany's relative prices fell by a further 20 to 25%. Admittedly, on the other hand the Reichsmark moved up further, but not so much as prices fell, so a considerable part of the cumulative loss of international competitiveness between 1929 and 1934 was reversed. The calculation with world trade shares shows this as less remarkable than the calculation with export shares. For the rest, it should be pointed out again that all this is on the arithmetical basis of the "official" prices and exchange rates, which were not de facto prices or rates.

France's competitiveness continued to fall at first, because the other gold block currencies began to devalue *before* the franc.

After a short interruption continued relative price reductions did neutralise the resultant upvaluation of the franc, but at the same time they caused a major deterioration in the domestic situation and the social climate, which was in any case wretched. Finally, in September 1936 the Popular Front government could no longer resist the pressure to devalue, and the result was a deep fall in the effective exchange rate. However, some of the hoped-for effect failed to materialize, because other components of the "Blum experiment", which was largely motivated by the desire for social reform, drove prices steeply up again. And so the effective exchange rate moved back to its pre-crisis level in 1937, while at the same time relative prices shot up far beyond this. So French exports remained less competitive than they had been in the later twenties.

After 1932 *Canada* experienced a rise in prices that was both powerful and continued, and this drove its relative export prices up by about 15% from 1934 to 1937. Since the exchange rate remained firm, Canadian price competitiveness fell to the same extent. On the eve of the Second World War the real effective exchange rate for the Canadian dollar was back on the same level as on the eve of the First World War, and so higher than at any time in the intervening years.

We can now move away from the subdivision into periods and trace these movements in a way that is less awkward and confusing, if at the same time less differentiated and more immediate:

Britain's international competitive position was worse right through the interwar period than it had been before the First World War. The deterioration was worsened by the slump, despite the devaluation of the pound.

North American exports generally enjoyed a better competitive position than before the war, thanks to a clear change to their favour in international price relations and despite higher rates for their currencies. Their price competitive advantage increased during the twenties and shrank or disappeared again in the thirties. This was first due to temporary effective upvaluations, and then continued relative price rises.

Germany emerged from the postwar inflation with visibly better price competitiveness, but soon lost these advantages again, mainly through relative cost and price increases, and also through a moderate upvaluation. From the beginning of the world slump a lasting deterioration in Germany's international competitive position, which varied only in its – admittedly uncertain – size, replaced the now eroded improvement.

Exactly the reverse happened in *Japan*, which found itself in a very much worse price competitive position at the beginning of the twenties than before the war, with excessively high relative prices. The disadvantage was largely eliminated by 1930 but not completely neutralised. From 1932 onwards an effective devaluation of hitherto unknown proportions turned the shrunken disadvantage into a definite advantage.

Similar movements took place in *India*, with a time differential, in a more even movement and on a rather smaller scale.

France, finally, created for itself a notable price advantage in the mid-twenties with a deliberately excessive devaluation of the franc. It retained this until the beginning of the slump and then gradually lost it again through clinging too long to the gold value of the franc as established by Poincare.

Appendix

Tables 1–7; diagrams 1–7; tables 8–15; diagrams 8–10

Sources: The figures were calculated using base data from the following works:

Price indices: League of Nations: Review of World Trade 1930, Geneva 1931, pp. 63–65

Société des Nations: Memorandum sur le Commerce et sur les Balances de Paiements 1938, Vol. 1: Apercu General du Commerce Mondial 1938, Geneva 1939, pp. 84–87

Charles P. Kindleberger: Industrial Europe's Terms of Trade on Current Account 1870–1953, in: E.M. Carus-Wilson, Essays in Economic History, Vol. 3, London 1966, p. 304 (Belgium and Netherlands)

Kazushi Ohkawa et al.: Patterns of Japanese Economic Development, A Quantitative Appraisal, New Haven 1979, pp. 331 (Japan)

Exchange Rates: League of Nations, Memorandum on International Trade and Balances of Payments, 1927–1929, Vol. I, Geneva 1930, pp. 110–119

Société des Nations: Memorandum sur le Commerce et sur les Balances de Paiements 1938, Vol. 1: Apercu General du Commerce Mondial 1938, Geneva 1939, pp. 84–87

Charles P. Kindleberger: Industrial Europe's Terms of Trade on Current Account 1870–1953, in: E.M. Carus-Wilson, Essays in Economic History, Vol. 3, London 1966, p. 304 (Belgium and Netherlands)

Kazushi Ohkawa et al.: Patterns of Japanese Economic Development, A Quantitative Appraisal, New Haven 1979, pp. 331 (Japan)

Exchange Rates: League of Nations, Memorandum on International Trade and Balances of Payments, 1927–1929, Vol. I, Geneva 1930, pp. 110–119

Société des Nations, Memorandum sur le Commerce et les Balances de Paiements 1934 Vol. 1: apercu General du Commerce Mondial 1934, pp. 90f., ibid 1938, pp. 88f.

World Trade Shares: League of Nations, Review of World trade 1930, Geneva 1931, pp. 19

Export shares: League of Nations, Memorandum on the Balances of Payments and Foreign Trade Balances 1911–1925, Vol. 1, Geneva 1926, pp. 218–235

League of Nations, Memorandum on International Trade and Balances of Payments 1927–1929, Vol. III, Geneva 1931, pp. 328–345

Société des Naitons, Memorandum sur le Commerce et sur les Balances de Paiements 1933, Vol. 3, Statistiques du Commerce International 1933, pp. 323–245, ibid 1935, pp. 324–241, ibid 1937, pp. 396–414

Indicators of Real Effective Exchange Rates of Major Trading Nations from 1922 to 1937   63

Tables 1–7. Relative prices, effective exchange rates, real effective exchange rates 1922–1937 – Indices 1913 = 100

1. United States

Year	Relative prices	effective ex. rates	real effective ex rates	Rel. prices	eff. ex rates	real eff. ex rates
	on the basis of current export shares			on the basis of world trade shares in 1929		
1922	83.42	125.07	104.33			
1923	79.66	127.92	101.90			
1924	74.41	132.53	98.62			
1925	72.98	128.59	93.84	68.28	138.47	94.54
1926	71.06	128.86	91.57			
1927	72.17	123.12	88.86			
1928	70.86	124.03	87.88			
1929	74.30	126.00	93.61	65.76	141.96	93.36
1930	75.14	129.16	97.05			
1931	69.89	135.45	94.67			
1932	62.59	166.32	104.11	58.66	171.80	100.77
1933	63.15	146.41	92.46			
1934	76.91	121.95	93.80	74.64	116.64	87.06
1935	79.54	124.20	98.77	82.20	117.69	96.74
1936	76.88	128.18	98.55			
1937	73.32	132.90	97.44	72.16	134.78	97.26

2. United Kingdom

Year	Relative prices	effective ex. rates	real effective ex rates	Rel. prices	eff. ex rates	real eff. ex rates
	on the basis of current export shares			on the basis of world trade shares in 1929		
1922	126.05	112.91	142.30			
1923	108.49	120.59	130.80			
1924	102.34	116.85	119.59			
1925	98.34	118.17	116.20	92.07	136.20	125.40
1926	104.82	116.47	122.09			
1927	101.12	116.92	118.23			
1928	99.56	118.23	117.71			
1929	97.84	112.26	119.62	88.25	141.22	124.63
1930	107.60	126.95	136.60	95.68	143.32	137.13
1931	116.05	129.89	150.74	105.13	139.88	147.09
1932	124.93	111.94	139.86	111.98	114.94	128.71
1933	124.01	115.60	143.35			
1934	120.59	116.19	140.12	110.54	120.64	133.39
1935	125.03	113.26	141.61			
1936	117.81	116.30	137.02			
1937	114.74	121.10	138.95	101.61	135.88	138.08

3. Germany

Year	Relative prices	effective ex. rates	real effective ex rates	Rel. prices	eff. ex rates	real eff. ex rates
	on the basis of current export shares			on the basis of world trade shares in 1929		
1923	55.54	142.64	79.22			
1924	57.94	151.85	87.97			
1925	59.76	152.47	91.11	64.01	135.28	86.59
1926	58.60	162.15	95.02			
1927	63.01	156.45	98.58			
1928	60.75	163.16	99.12			
1929	60.83	165.69	100.70	72.03	138.53	99.79
1930	63.54	172.21	109.42			
1931	67.93	168.75	114.63			
1932	66.46	182.45	121.20	77.91	165.67	129.08
1933	62.86	194.96	122.55			
1934	55.59	217.88	121.10	62.47	206.09	128.74
1935	51.12	222.73	113.86			
1936	48.23	242.90	117.15			
1937	42.14	253.79	106.90	48.83	240.73	117.54

4. France

Year	Relative prices	effective ex. rates	real effective ex rates	Rel. prices	eff. ex rates	real eff. ex rates
	on the basis of current export shares			on the basis of world trade shares in 1929		
1922	152.16	64.21	97.71			
1923	182.04	54.55	99.31			
1924	209.33	47.40	99.21			
1925	212.95	42.42	90.30	276.10	29.21	80.64
1926	239.30	32.51	77.79			
1927	221.36	37.03	81.96			
1928	208.25	39.47	82.19			
1929	204.60	39.78	81.39	299.60	24.19	72.47
1930	217.83	39.12	85.21			
1931	208.51	40.56	84.56			
1932	188.20	46.90	88.29	312.42	28.71	89.69
1933	181.61	49.29	89.51			
1934	194.78	50.26	97.89	273.57	35.65	97.51
1935	187.53	56.00	105.02	267.82	36.28	97.17
1936	173.12	53.95	93.41			
1937	222.25	39.91	88.66	346.43	23.51	81.69

Indicators of Real Effective Exchange Rates of Major Trading Nations from 1922 to 1937   65

5. Canada

Year	Relative prices	effective ex. rates	real effective ex rates	Rel. prices	eff. ex rates	real eff. ex rates
	on the basis of current export shares			on the basis of world trade shares in 1929		
1922	79.46	108.60	86.28			
1923	73.34	108.51	79.58			
1924	80.55	110.43	88.95			
1925	84.25	107.24	90.35	77.49	132.12	95.77
1926	87.26	109.37	95.44			
1927	85.73	107.84	92.45			
1928	82.98	110.41	91.62			
1929	78.94	108.35	85.53	72.63	133.67	97.09
1930	76.94	110.70	85.17			
1931	72.64	109.93	79.85			
1932	68.83	122.71	84.46	64.11	138.95	89.09
1933	81.55	101.82	83.04			
1934	81.75	105.19	85.99	79.13	114.17	90.34
1935	86.57	105.14	91.02			
1936	89.96	106.52	95.82			
1937	93.64	105.90	99.16	83.96	129.31	108.57

6. Japan

Year	Relative prices	effective ex. rates	real effective ex rates	Rel. prices	eff. ex rates	real eff. ex rates
	on the basis of current export shares			on the basis of world trade shares in 1929		
1922	149.18	100.51	149.94			
1923	149.33	99.47	148.54			
1924	140.12	88.58	124.12			
1925	147.63	82.66	122.03	116.45	108.10	125.88
1926	134.50	97.61	131.29			
1927	121.57	101.44	123.32			
1928	114.97	99.20	114.05			
1929	117.86	98.74	116.37	92.25	125.47	115.75
1930	95.62	114.20	109.20			
1931	96.99	120.14	116.53			
1932	116.57	68.50	79.86	82.05	83.60	71.11
1933	138.30	59.39	82.14			
1934	123.69	60.04	74.26	93.73	66.82	62.63
1935	114.64	59.15	67.81			
1936	110.25	62.45	68.85			
1937	118.24	63.88	75.53	95.09	73.79	70.17

7. India

Year	Relative prices	effective ex. rates	real effective ex rates	Rel. prices	eff. ex rates	real eff. ex rates
	on the basis of current export shares			on the basis of world trade shares in 1929		
1922	79.99	107.36	85.88			
1923	71.20	123.14	87.68			
1924	72.24	138.58	100.11			
1925	70.05	152.16	106.59	76.33	147.22	112.37
1926	64.18	153.81	98.72			
1927	67.99	151.12	102.75			
1928	68.42	148.08	101.31			
1929	65.08	148.09	96.37	65.86	150.43	99.08
1930	57.60	149.86	86.32			
1931	56.45	130.99	73.94			
1932	57.43	134.38	77.17	61.68	124.76	76.95
1933	56.82	135.14	76.79			
1934	57.78	136.36	78.79	59.66	130.16	77.65
1935	61.24	141.20	86.48			
1936	59.41	140.49	83.46			
1937	55.35	147.43	81.60	57.20	147.36	84.29

Diagrams 1–7. Relative prices, effective exchange rates, real effective exchange rates 1922–1937 on the basis of current export shares (1913 – 100)

relative prices   effective exchage rates   real effective exchage rates

1. United States

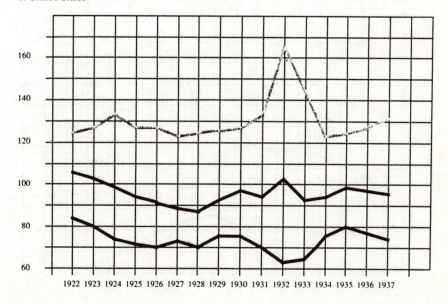

Indicators of Real Effective Exchange Rates of Major Trading Nations from 1922 to 1937

2. United Kingdom

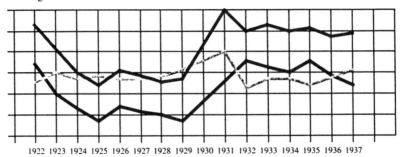

3. Germany

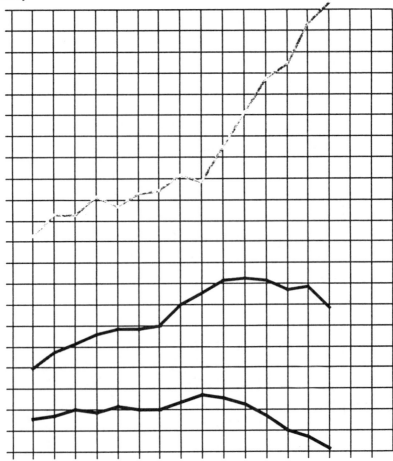

4. France

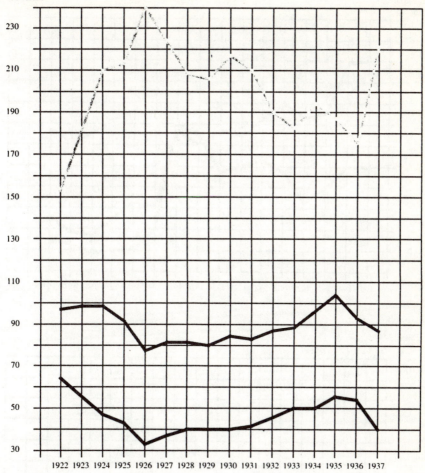

5. Canada

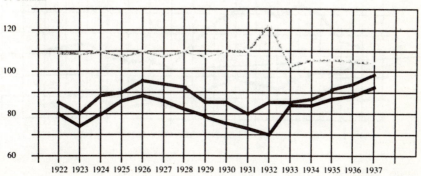

Indicators of Real Effective Exchange Rates of Major Trading Nations from 1922 to 1937

6. Japan

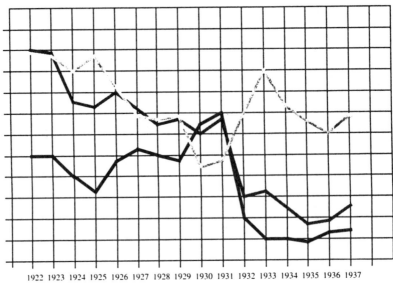

7. India

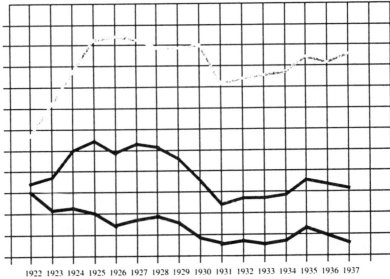

Source: Tables 1–7

Tables 8–15. Relative prices, effective exchange rates, real effective exchange rates on the basis of current export shares 1922–1937 – Indices 1913 = 100

8. Italy

Year	rel. Pr	eff. ER	r. e. ER
1922	291.10	37.71	92.31
1923	255.30	33.86	86.42
1924	243.47	32.65	79.49
1925	271.20	28.38	76.97
1926	311.40	29.87	93.01
1927	280.54	35.57	99.78
1928	247.28	37.34	92.34
1929	238.50	36.84	87.85
1930	207.41	38.71	80.29
1931	207.14	39.55	81.93
1932	206.07	37.88	78.05
1933	182.06	42.91	78.12
1934	168.58	43.39	73.15
1935	177.94	41.79	74.35
1936	221.11	31.42	69.46
1937	227.42	28.45	64.70

9. Sweden

Year	rel. Pr.	eff. ER	r. e. ER
1922	99.63	126.81	126.34
1923	88.35	132.40	116.97
1924	80.39	138.43	111.29
1925	82.48	130.65	107.77
1926	89.22	133.05	118.71
1927	96.65	124.79	120.60
1928	91.17	131.67	120.05
1929	91.49	130.43	119.33
1930	93.47	129.51	121.05
1931	98.78	125.85	124.31
1932	104.29	111.34	116.11
1933	98.62	112.98	111.42
1934	102.42	109.25	111.88
1935	100.29	110.23	110.55
1936	100.99	112.46	113.57
1937	101.01	120.23	121.45

10. Switzerland

Year	rel. Pr	eff. ER	r. e. ER
1922	98.34	136.40	134.13
1923	79.07	137.37	108.61
1924	80.32	136.42	109.57
1925	77.54	140.19	108.69
1926	72.34	151.00	109.23
1927	76.96	140.10	107.82
1928	76.45	146.94	112.33
1929	74.49	154.89	115.37
1930	75.13	160.90	120.88
1931	75.75	173.09	131.12
1932	69.68	212.68	148.19
1933	68.89	216.41	149.08
1934	70.27	213.95	150.33
1935	69.56	223.74	155.64
1936	70.17	209.93	147.30
1937	74.36	182.24	135.52

11. Netherlands

Year	rel. Pr.	eff. ER	r. e. ER
1922	83.98	131.96	110.82
1923	72.53	143.36	103.98
1924	80.35	135.50	108.88
1925	81.16	125.83	102.12
1926	72.68	136.28	99.05
1927	72.01	139.15	100.21
1928	71.06	140.68	99.97
1929	68.74	145.95	100.33
1930	65.37	153.30	100.21
1931	59.25	165.21	97.98
1932	51.52	190.19	97.99
1933	49.25	151.67	95.76
1934	51.89	113.01	97.73
1935	51.44	118.47	103.29
1936	52.87	126.44	107.82
1937	60.40	133.26	110.26

12. Belgium

Year	rel. Pr	eff. ER	r. e. ER
1922	179.97	54.96	98.92
1923	201.19	38.70	77.90
1924	240.39	33.46	80.43
1925	267.26	33.24	88.83

13. China

Year	rel. Pr.	eff. ER	r. e. ER
1922	73.79	128.96	95.16
1923	71.73	125.54	90.05
1924	71.11	139.60	99.27
1925	72.15	149.06	107.55

Indicators of Real Effective Exchange Rates of Major Trading Nations from 1922 to 1937   71

Year	rel. Pr	eff. ER	r. e. ER	Year	rel. Pr.	eff. ER	r. e. ER
1926	363.67	23.86	86.77	1926	80.08	133.82	107.14
1927	414.95	19.21	79.71	1927	95.68	117.57	112.49
1928	431.35	19.20	82.81	1928	96.84	120.84	117.02
1929	450.07	19.43	87.44	1929	102.47	107.17	109.82
1930	444.91	20.42	90.83	1930	131.10	72.73	95.34
1931	439.37	21.93	96.37	1931	165.53	50.88	84.22
1932	417.99	24.40	102.00	1932	147.96	67.33	99.62
1933	389.29	26.84	104.50	1933	127.93	76.65	98.06
1934	383.76	27.53	105.66	1934	112.15	83.30	93.42
1935	403.89	21.82	88.13	1935	119.93	89.54	107.38
1936	438.86	20.27	88.95	1936	146.84	73.94	108.58
1937	424.02	23.18	98.30	1937	156.00	71.62	111.73

14. Argentina

Year	rel. Pr	eff. ER	r. e. ER
1922	65.28	112.42	73.38
1923	61.66	113.57	69.41
1924	62.71	120.32	75.09
1925	67.34	137.86	92.83
1926	51.38	147.60	75.83
1927	55.14	150.01	82.71
1928	62.76	150.34	94.36
1929	57.80	151.31	87.45
1930	57.21	125.48	71.79
1931	49.26	105.96	52.19
1932	51.98	110.37	57.37
1933	55.09	104.93	57.81
1934	67.94	78.42	53.28
1935	71.12	81.36	57.87
1936	82.03	89.96	74.70
1937	83.88	101.18	84.87

15. Australia

Year	rel. Pr.	eff. ER	r. e. ER
1922	65.30	119.93	78.32
1923	72.25	129.05	93.24
1924	82.03	142.02	116.50
1925	102.66	105.44	154.44
1926	71.59	157.34	112.66
1927	74.87	151.38	113.34
1928	82.11	149.22	122.52
1929	78.05	148.24	115.70
1930	68.79	124.81	85.86
1931	55.80	97.77	54.55
1932	62.92	95.91	60.35
1933	61.45	97.92	60.17
1934	81.11	82.91	67.24
1935	65.13	100.13	65.22
1936	82.60	103.44	85.44
1937	87.16	106.93	93.20

Diagrams 8–10. Real effective exchange rate 1922–1937 on the basis of current export shares

8. Italy, Sweden, Switzerland

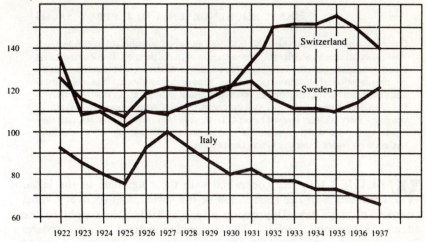

9. Belgium, Netherlands

10. China, Argentina, Australia

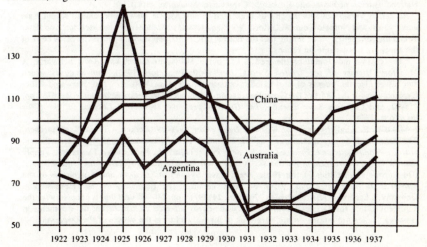

[20]
Exchange Rates and Economic Recovery in the 1930s

BARRY EICHENGREEN AND JEFFREY SACHS

> Currency depreciation in the 1930s is almost universally dismissed or condemned. This paper advances a different interpretation of these policies. It documents first that depreciation benefited the initiating countries. It shows next that there can be no presumption that depreciation was beggar-thy-neighbor. While empirical analysis indicates that the foreign repercussions of individual devaluations were in fact negative, it does not imply that competitive devaluations taken by a group of countries were without mutual benefit. To the contrary, similar policies, had they been even more widely adopted and coordinated internationally, would have hastened recovery from the Great Depression.

WHETHER they are concerned with the magnitude of the initial contraction or the retardation of the subsequent recovery, most analyses of the Great Depression attach considerable weight to the effects of economic policy. The misguided actions of the Federal Reserve and the unfortunate commercial initiatives of the executive and legislative branches are blamed for transforming the American recession into an unprecedented depression.[1] Perverse monetary and fiscal responses in such countries as Germany and France are blamed for reinforcing the deflationary pressures transmitted from the United States to the rest of the industrial world.[2] In desperate attempts to promote recovery, or at least to provide insulation from destabilizing

---

Journal of Economic History, Vol. XLV, No. 4 (Dec. 1985). © The Economic History Association. All rights reserved. ISSN 0022-0507.

Both authors are affiliated with the Department of Economics at Harvard University and the National Bureau of Economic Research, Cambridge, Massachusetts 02138.

An earlier version of this paper was presented to seminars at New York, Queen's, and Yale universities, and Nuffield College, Oxford. We thank Charles Kindleberger, Ian McLean, and Peter Temin for comments, while noting that the normal disclaimer applies with special force. A copy of the appendix is available on request.

[1] The classic indictment of the Fed is of course Milton Friedman and Anna Schwartz, *A Monetary History of the United States, 1867–1960* (Princeton, 1963). For analyses which emphasize also the effects of protectionist initiatives, see Alan Meltzer, "Monetary and Other Explanations for the Start of the Great Depression," *Journal of Monetary Economics*, 2 (1976), pp. 455–72; and Christian Saint-Etienne, *The Great Depression, 1929–1938: Lessons for the 1980s* (Stanford, 1984).

[2] Charles P. Kindleberger, *The World in Depression, 1929–39* (Berkeley, 1973); Karl Hardach, *The Political Economy of Germany in the Twentieth Century* (Berkeley, 1976); and A. Sauvy, *Histoire économique de la France entre les deux guerres* (2nd ed., Paris, 1984). This is not to imply that the Great Depression in Europe was solely a reflection of the downturn in the United States. (On Europe's difficulties in the 1920s, see Ingmar Svennilson, *Growth and Stagnation of the European Economy* (Geneva, 1954); or Peter Temin, "The Beginning of the Depression in Germany," *Economic History Review*, 2nd ser., 24 (1971), pp. 240–48.) All that is necessary for the argument is that the Depression in Europe was heavily affected by concurrent developments in America. Space limitations do not permit us to formally address the causes of the Depression.

925

foreign shocks, national authorities had recourse to currency devaluation and tariff escalation. Such initiatives are typically characterized as beggar-thy-neighbor policies. Individually they are seen as attempts to better a country's position at the expense of its neighbors; together, it is argued, they disrupted international economic relations and, by impeding foreign trade, destroyed one of the only remaining sources of autonomous demand.[3]

With notable exceptions, such as "cheap money" in Britain after 1931, fiscal expansion in Sweden, and industrial policy giving way to central control in Germany, public policy receives little credit for helping the economies of Europe find their way out of the Great Depression.[4] One can conceive of various policies these nations might have pursued: devaluation, protection, monetary expansion, and fiscal stimulus. In practice, however, there was little scope for significant policy initiative within the institutional and intellectual framework inherited from the 1920s. Fiscal policy, except in Sweden, would continue to be guided by the principle of balanced budgets until the adoption of Keynesian approaches to taxation and spending.[5] Even had there existed a belief in the efficacy of countercyclical fiscal policy, it might have been of little practical consequence on the national level so long as the fixed parities of the gold-exchange standard served as an external constraint. The potential of monetary initiatives, although more widely recognized and acknowledged, was equally inhibited by the gold standard constraint.

The critical decision for national economic authorities therefore concerned the stance of external policy. Not only might currency devaluation, exchange control, tariff protection, and quantitative trade restrictions have macroeconomic effects of their own, but by changing the external constraints they could open the way for initiatives on other fronts. Some have argued, however, that such policies provided a country relief from the Depression only at the expense of its neighbors, and that by eliciting retaliation they only exacerbated the global crisis.

---

[3] For a statement of this view, see Ragnar Nurkse, *International Currency Experience* (Geneva, 1944).

[4] Even these cases have been disputed. Lars Jonung, "The Depression in Sweden and the United States: A Comparison of Causes and Policies," in Karl Brunner, ed., *The Great Depression Revisited* (Boston, 1981), pp. 286–315, has questioned the role of fiscal policy in Swedish growth. M. Beenstock, F. Capie, and B. Griffiths, "Economic Recovery in the United Kingdom in the 1930s," Bank of England Panel of Academic Consultants, *Discussion Paper* (London, 1984), have attempted to show that policy had little role in Britain's recovery. The German situation is in many ways special and will be given relatively little attention here.

[5] An extensive literature analyzes the extent to which public officials, especially in Britain, were or were not converted to Keynesian views in the 1930s. See for example Susan Howson and Donald Winch, *The Economic Advisory Council, 1930–1939* (Cambridge, 1977); G. C. Peden, "Keynes, the Treasury and Unemployment in the Later Nineteen-thirties," *Oxford Economic Papers*, n.s., 32 (1980), pp. 1–18; and Alan Booth, "The 'Keynesian Revolution' in Economic Policy-Making," *Economic History Review*, 2nd ser., 26 (1983), pp. 103–23.

Thus, many studies of the Depression which do not dismiss the effects of policy as negligible condemn them as positively harmful.

A proper understanding of the role of external economic policy must begin with a sharp analytical distinction between protectionist measures (such as tariffs and quotas) and exchange rate management. Tariffs and devaluation are often spoken of as two sides of the same coin, both being policies designed to shift demand from foreign countries to the domestic economy. But in fact the general equilibrium implications of the two sets of policies are very different. Tariff changes inevitably create output price distortions, while a series of devaluations in many countries can leave relative output prices unchanged.[6] A tariff increase in one country is likely to reduce economic welfare in other countries and provoke retaliation; and a global round of tariff escalation is likely to reduce welfare in all countries.[7] The implications of exchange rate management are far more complex. One country's devaluation need not beggar the remaining countries, and a series of devaluations can easily leave all countries better off.

This paper offers a new interpretation of the effects of currency depreciation in the 1930s. We will argue that depreciation was clearly beneficial for the initiating countries.[8] We then establish that there is in fact no theoretical presumption that depreciation in the 1930s was a beggar-thy-neighbor policy. While there is evidence that the foreign repercussions of individual devaluations were negative—that policy had beggar-thy-neighbor effects—the finding does not support the conclusion that competitive devaluations taken by a group of countries were without benefit for the system as a whole. Although it is difficult to determine whether the devaluations which actually took place had on

---

[6] Exchange control is effectively a combination of tariff and devaluation policy, in the sense that it both changes the relative prices of national currencies and causes distortions in output prices.

[7] See Harry G. Johnson, "Optimum Tariffs and Retaliation," *Review of Economic Studies*, 21, no. 2 (1953/54), no. 55, for one of the original game-theoretic analyses of tariff wars. Johnson shows that all countries suffer from a tariff war with retaliation if their economies are symmetric, while some countries may be better off, relative to free trade, in an asymmetric environment.

[8] In this respect, our work supports the findings of E. Choudri and L. Kochin, "The Exchange Rate and the International Transmission of Business Cycle Disturbances," *Journal of Money, Credit and Banking*, 12, no. 4 (1980), pp. 565-74. Choudri and Kochin document the relationship between exchange depreciation and relative national price levels and outputs for several European countries. An analysis almost identical to theirs appears in George F. Warren and Frank A. Pearson, *Prices* (New York, 1933). Neither set of authors, however, works with a formal macroeconomic model, as in this paper, and thus they do not attempt to describe the structural mechanisms linking exchange rates with other aggregate variables. Neither do they discuss the foreign repercussions of exchange rate changes. The conclusion that the currency depreciation in the 1930s benefited the initiating country is itself controversial, since it has recently been argued, in the spirit of the new classical macroeconomics, that the effects of depreciation were in some instances negligible. Beenstock, Capie and Griffiths, "Economic Recovery," passim. The new classical macroeconomics insists that purely monetary changes, such as changes in the price of gold, can have no real effects since other nominal values will adjust proportionately to the monetary change. We argue that the experience of the 1930s is clearly inconsistent with this doctrine.

TABLE 1
PRINCIPAL MEASURES AFFECTING EXCHANGE RATES AS OF 1937
(month and year of introduction)

Country	Official Suspension of Gold Standard	Exchange Control	Depreciation or Devaluation
Belgium	3.35	3.35	3.35
Denmark	11.31	11.31	11.31
Finland	12.31	–	10.31
France	–	–	9.36
Germany	–	7.31	–
Italy	–	5.34	3.34
Netherlands	9.36	–	9.36
Norway	9.31	–	9.31
Sweden	9.31	–	9.31
United Kingdom	9.31	–	9.31

Source: League of Nations Economic Intelligence Service, *Monetary Review* (Geneva, 1937), appendix table 1.

balance an expansionary or contractionary impact on the world economy, there is little doubt that similar policies, had they been adopted even more widely and coordinated internationally, would have hastened economic recovery from the Great Depression.

I. CURRENCY DEPRECIATION IN THE 1930S

Table 1 sets out the basic chronology of departures from the gold standard in the ten European countries whose macroeconomic experience is considered here.

Britain's departure from the gold standard in 1931 is often taken to signal the beginning of the "devaluation cycle" of the 1930s.[9] It is important to recognize therefore that the start of the cycle preceded Britain's departure from gold by nearly two years. Argentina and Uruguay suspended gold payments in December 1929, while Hungary, Paraguay, and Brazil found themselves unable to maintain their currencies at par.[10] In 1930 the exchanges of Chile, Venezuela, Peru, Australia, and New Zealand fell and remained below the gold export point. Most of these countries were both primary producers and international debtors. The reasons for their difficulties will have a familiar ring to modern observers: first, the decline in foreign lending by the United States starting in 1928; second, the fall in primary commodity prices which accelerated dramatically in 1929; and third, the

---

[9] The phrase is from Nurkse, *International Currency Experience*. We elaborate on its meaning below.

[10] In addition, at the end of 1929, Canada, which like the United States until 1914 adhered to the gold standard without the benefit of a central bank, introduced new restrictions on the operation of the gold standard in response to its deteriorating economic position.

imposition of protective tariffs by industrial countries, notably on their imports of food.[11]

The international system, then, had already shown signs of weakness when financial difficulties surfaced in Europe and America in 1930. Banking crises in the United States at the end of 1930 and in Austria and Germany the following summer led to the introduction of exchange control by Germany, in July 1931. By undermining the credibility of the gold standard the controls helped to set the stage for Britain's departure from gold, in September.[12] Britain was forced to devalue, but many of the countries that followed sterling off the gold standard were not. Their reasons for depreciation varied, but the fear that export market share would otherwise be lost to countries with depreciated currencies surely bulked large. In this sense their actions have been viewed as competitive depreciations. By the end of October 1931 all of the British Dominions (except South Africa), the rest of the British Empire, the four Scandinavian countries, and Portugal, Egypt, Bolivia, and Latvia had turned to depreciation.[13] They were followed within six months by Japan, Greece, Siam, and Peru.[14]

The next round of depreciation commenced with the fall of the U.S. dollar in 1933. In March of that year President Roosevelt unexpectedly restricted foreign exchange dealings and gold and currency movements, and the following month he issued an executive order requiring individuals to deliver their gold coin, bullion, and certificates to Federal

[11] U.S. foreign lending began to contract in 1928 as the New York stock exchange boom drove up interest rates and diverted funds from foreign lending to domestic financial markets, and this contraction accelerated as the Federal Reserve failed to accommodate the rising demand for credit. The decline in primary commodity prices following the downturn in the United States was not an entirely new development, as commodity prices had been trending downwards for much of the decade owing to the vast expansion in non-European productive capacity that had taken place during World War I. See Svennilson, *Growth*. The same can be said of the move toward protection, which was well underway before the onset of the Depression. See for example H. Liepman, *Tariff Levels and the Economic Unity of Europe* (London, 1938); or J. B. Condliffe, *The Reconstruction of World Trade* (New York, 1940).

[12] The Austrians followed the Germans with a lag, imposing exchange control in October 1931. Britain's devaluation has been examined recently by Alec Cairncross and Barry Eichengreen, *Sterling in Decline: The Devaluations of 1931, 1949 and 1967* (Oxford, 1983). There is some dispute over the importance of financial difficulties such as the Continental bank failures relative to the development of Britain's balance of payments position. See also Donald Moggridge, "The 1931 Financial Crisis—A New View," *The Banker* (1970), pp. 832–39.

[13] South Africa's decision must be understood in terms of its unusually strong external position and exceptional attachment to a stable gold price, attributable to its position as a gold producer.

[14] By December 1931, when sterling reached a trough, it had depreciated by 40 percent relative to the currencies which remained on gold. This raises the question of how countries which did not engage in depreciation could ignore such a large relative price effect. The answer is that they concluded almost universally that the costs of a loss of competitiveness were more than outweighed by the benefits of avoiding the inflation that devaluation might provoke. This was clearly the basis for the French decision: see Marguerite Perrot, *La Monnaie et l'opinion publique en France et en Angleterre, 1924–1936* (Paris, 1955). Despite the popularity of competing explanations, Kindleberger, *World in Depression*, pp. 163–64, concludes that this was the basis for the German decision as well.

Reserve Banks. From this point the dollar began to float. By setting a series of progressively higher dollar prices of gold the Administration engineered a substantial devaluation. When the dollar was finally stabilized in January 1934 at $35 an ounce it retained but 59 percent of its former gold content.[15] The U.S. action is typically viewed as a clear instance of beggar-thy-neighbor policy, since on the eve of decision the American balance of payments was already strong; depreciation represented a further shift of demand away from the products of the rest of the world.

The dollar's depreciation set off another wave of retaliatory devaluations. South Africa joined the emerging Sterling Area, and the South American currencies, many of which established links with the floating dollar, fell at accelerating rates. The Japanese yen, which had remained relatively stable in terms of sterling, now moved lower, rupturing its de facto link with the Sterling Area. The only major currencies that remained freely convertible were those of the Gold Bloc countries: France, Belgium, Holland, Italy, Poland, and Switzerland.

The international financial history of the subsequent two years was dominated by the battles fought by the Gold Bloc countries against the forces threatening to undermine their parities. The devaluation of the dollar weakened their international competitive positions and induced a reflux of capital to the United States.[16] The need for increased public expenditure on rearmament compromised the fiscal position of even the countries most committed to a deflationary policy in defense of the gold standard. The financial positions of the Gold Bloc countries deteriorated seriously beginning in 1934, culminating in May 1935 in a marked loss of confidence in the sustainability of their parities and flight of international capital. Belgium, which suffered exceptionally because of unusual dependence on foreign trade, and which had experts studying the devaluation option as early as 1933, was the first Gold Bloc country to leave the fold, in March 1935.[17] Similar difficulties were experienced in all of the other Gold Bloc countries except Poland. In each of these

---

[15] There is considerable dispute over the extent to which the U.S. administration understood the relationship of its gold-buying program to the exchange rate and the price level. See John Morton Blum, *From the Morganthau Diaries, vol. I: Years of Crisis, 1928–1938* (Boston, 1959), p. 73; or Kindleberger, *World in Depression*, pp. 226–27.

[16] These difficulties were reinforced by the downward movement of sterling and its allied currencies, the tightening of exchange control by countries that used this device to reconcile expansionary initiatives with the balance-of-payments constraint, and by growing social resistance to further reductions in wages and nominal incomes.

[17] In addition, the deterioration of economic conditions in its colonial possessions further undermined Belgium's budgetary position. Moreover, late in the summer of 1934, the government turned to a reflationary program, lowering the central bank discount rate and expanding credit in an effort to revitalize the economy. These efforts were sufficient to undermine confidence in the currency but inadequate to stimulate recovery. See H. van der Wee and K. Tavernier, *La Banque Nationale de Belgique et l'histoire monétaire entre les deux guerres mondiales* (Brussels, 1975).

countries, as the burden of deflation mounted, working-class resistance grew, and devaluation was increasingly discussed.[18]

By the second quarter of 1936 the external situation in the Gold Bloc countries had reached a crisis. Poland in April 1936 imposed exchange control for the first time. France, Holland, and Switzerland resisted exchange control, and suffered heavy gold losses. In France, the Popular Front, which came to power in April 1936, committed itself to a vigorous reflationary policy and to defense of the gold standard. Within months of its accession, the incompatibility of the two goals was recognized. Currency depreciation was postponed to September, with considerable difficulty, while the French negotiated with the British and Americans to prevent competitive depreciations.[19] But once the franc was allowed to begin its descent the other Gold Bloc currencies followed without delay. Devaluation had come full circle.

II. FORMS OF CURRENCY DEPRECIATION

Currency depreciation in the 1930s took a number of forms, with differing implications for domestic and foreign economies. The precise character of the devaluations hinged on the domestic and international financial policies that accompanied the change, including the allocation of profits on revalued central bank reserves, the restrictions on dealings in foreign exchange, and the mechanisms to control fluctuations in the exchange rate.

Not all countries wrote up the book value of foreign reserves to reflect the higher domestic-currency price at which gold would now be traded. The United Kingdom and many members of the Sterling Area, for example, continued to value gold reserves at par. Revaluation profits were put to various uses. One option was to use them to support an expansion in the money supply, without reducing the proportionate backing of the currency by international reserves. Revaluation profits were transferred directly to the fiscal authorities (the method used in

---

[18] These difficulties were least pronounced in Holland, whose trade was heavily concentrated in its seven colonies and hence immune to the effects of foreign tariffs, and whose coal, electricity, and cement industries actually continued to expand between 1929 and 1933. See Fernand Baudhuin, "Europe and the Great Crisis," in Herman van der Wee, ed., *The Great Depression Revisited* (The Hague, 1972). The French case bears a remarkable resemblance to that of Belgium. In September 1935, the French government, which had previously remained firm in its commitment to deflation, demanded new constitutional powers to enable it to carry through its program, which were ultimately denied. This government fell and was replaced by another which included a policy of domestic credit expansion as part of its program. See Sauvy, *Histoire*.

[19] These negotiations culminated in the Tripartite Agreement of September 1936. See S.V.O. Clarke, "Exchange-Rate Stabilization in the Mid-1930s: Negotiating the Tripartite Agreement," *Princeton Studies in International Finance*, no. 41 (Princeton, 1980); and Barry Eichengreen, "International Policy Coordination in Historical Perspective: A View from the Interwar Years," in Willem Buiter and Richard Marston, eds., *The International Coordination of Economic Policies* (Cambridge, 1985) for details.

Argentina, Italy, and to a limited extent in Romania), or else were allocated to special funds designated for purchases of government securities (the method used in Belgium starting in April 1935 and in France starting in July 1937). The alternative of using revaluation profits to extinguish government debt held by the central bank—adopted wholly or in part by France in October 1936, Czechoslovakia, Romania, and Japan—had no direct effect on the money supply.[20]

Another alternative was to allocate the revaluation profits to newly established exchange stabilization funds, as was done in the United States, Belgium, Switzerland, and France in 1936. In these cases, the profits on revalued gold reserves were reflected neither in the book value of the central bank's reserves nor in its reserve ratio. But to the extent that a fund was entitled to use the currency it got to purchase securities held by the public, through the intervention of the fund the revaluation profits might ultimately support an expansion in the money supply.

The ostensible purpose of these funds was to smooth short-term fluctuations in the exchange rate. If they restricted their intervention to damping temporary fluctuations, their operations would have no lasting impact on the money supply. Yet in practice many such funds intervened to defend the competitive advantage conferred by devaluation, preventing any subsequent appreciation of the exchanges. The actions of the British Exchange Equalisation Account, for example, among the most active funds, have recently been interpreted in this light.[21] The American Exchange Stabilization Fund, in contrast, bought and sold dollars only occasionally, as required to maintain the $35 gold price.[22]

The other way in which exchange rates were regulated following devaluation was through the imposition of exchange control. In many cases exchange control had first been adopted during the 1931 financial crisis as a way of stemming capital flight. In nearly every instance the restrictions adopted then were retained after the immediate convertibility crisis subsided (for details, see Table 1). Restrictions on capital exports ranged from attempts to impose a complete prohibition on capital exports, as in Austria and Estonia, to relatively moderate disincentives such as the 4 percent tax imposed by Mexico on all remittances not of commercial origin. In order to prevent disguised capital transfers, countries imposing tight exchange control adopted new regulations on commercial transactions.[23] In many countries the authorities nonetheless proved incapable of preventing the development

---

[20] In France, some 35 percent of the profits were so applied.

[21] For qualitative evidence see Susan Howson, "Sterling's Managed Float: The Operations of the Exchange Equilisation Account," *Princeton Studies in International Finance*, no. 46 (Princeton, 1980); and for econometric support see Cairncross and Eichengreen, *Sterling in Decline*.

[22] The Fund instituted in Belgium was abolished once the exchange rate was stabilized. Similar funds were also created by Canada and China.

[23] In many cases this need to increase oversight of commercial transactions reinforced the tendency toward increased trade restrictions.

of black markets in foreign exchange.[24] Potential international borrowers attempted to discriminate in the treatment of new and old loans in such a way as to encourage further capital imports. Thus, provisions were included in several exchange control laws to guarantee the free transfer of service on new foreign investments.[25]

III. SINGLE-COUNTRY EFFECTS OF DEPRECIATION

There are four principal channels through which the currency depreciations of the 1930s could have affected domestic and foreign economies: real wages, profitability, international competitiveness, and the level of world interest rates. Our analysis makes use of a simple two-country model, drawing on the work of Mundell and Fleming, but extended to encompass the determinants of aggregate supply and the gold-standard constraints. The model, whose elements appear in the note to Table 2, incorporates Keynes's characterization of labor and output markets: in each country nominal wages adjust only slowly, but prices adjust with sufficient speed to clear commodity markets. Aggregate supply in each country depends on profitability, as measured by the ratio of product prices to wages. Aggregate demand in each country depends on competitiveness (or the ratio of domestic to foreign prices) and on interest rates (which determine the division of spending between present and future). Money demand depends on output and interest rates, where interest rates are linked internationally by the open interest parity condition. Expectations of exchange rate changes are neglected; domestic and foreign interest rates can therefore be taken as equal, and no distinction need be made between real and nominal interest rates.

The effects of depreciation depend on its form, and in particular on the accompanying monetary measures. In "sterilized devaluation" the depreciating country expands the domestic component of its money supply sufficiently to leave gold reserves unchanged. In "unsterilized devaluation" the depreciating country adjusts domestic credit only enough to keep unchanged the ratio of gold backing to money in circulation. Gold reserves may rise or fall. Two other cases useful for analyzing competitive depreciation are simultaneous unsterilized devaluation, when both countries leave the ratio of gold backing unchanged but allow the total base to fall; and simultaneous devaluation in which both countries leave their monetary base, and money supply, unchanged. Following the notation in Table 2, sterilized devaluation is when $dg < 0$ but gold backing is adjusted to permit reserves to remain unchanged ($dr = 0$). Unsterilized devaluation is when $dg < 0$ and the gold backing remains unchanged ($d\psi = 0$).

[24] See Bank for International Settlements, *Annual Report* (Basle, 1934), for examples.

[25] For example, a regulation was adopted in Poland in November 1937, under which the transfer of principal and interest on new foreign loans was exempted from exchange control. Similar measures were adopted in Italy and elsewhere.

TABLE 2
IMPACT OF EXCHANGE-RATE DEPRECIATION ON ENDOGENOUS VARIABLES

	Variable				
Case	Domestic Output	Foreign Output	Domestic Reserves	Foreign Reserves	Interest Rate
I. Sterilized devaluation	+	−	0	0	−
II. Unsterilized devaluation	+	+/−	+/−	+/−	+/−
III. Simultaneous devaluation, unchanged gold backing	+	+	0	0	−
IV. Simultaneous devaluation, unchanged monetary base	0	0	0	0	0

Note: A plus or minus indicates the sign of the comparative statics result. +/− indicates that the direction of the effect cannot be signed.

These results are derived from a model of two symmetrical countries, in which each country is characterized by relationships of the following form. (Lower-case letters denote logs of variables, and asterisks denote foreign values.)

Aggregate supply is a negative function of the real product wage:

$$q = -\alpha(w - p)$$

where q is the log of GDP, w is the log wage (taken as fixed), and p the log price of domestic goods. Under a gold standard, each country fixes the domestic price of gold, where G is ounces of gold per unit of domestic currency. The foreign price of domestic currency is G/G^* and the log exchange rate $g - g^*$. Aggregate demand is a decreasing function of the relative price of domestic goods and of the nominal interest rate:

$$q = -\delta(p + g - g^* - p^*) - \sigma i$$

where the domestic interest rate i equals the foreign rate by open interest parity. The demand for money takes the form:

$$m - p = \phi q - \beta i$$

where m is the log of nominal money balances. Money supply is defined as the value of gold reserves R/G (where R is the volume of reserves) times the reciprocal of the gold-backing ratio $\psi = (R/G)/M$.

$$m = r - g - \psi$$

Since the (fixed) world gold stock is divided between the two central banks:

$$\gamma dr + (1 - \gamma)dr^* = 0$$

where γ is the domestic bank's initial share of the world total.

The effects of depreciation are summarized in Table 2. In all cases of unilateral devaluation, currency depreciation increases output and employment in the devaluing country. By raising the price of imports relative to domestic goods, depreciation switches expenditure toward domestic goods. The increased pressure of demand will tend to drive up domestic commodity prices, moderating the stimulus to aggregate demand and (by reducing real wages) stimulating aggregate supply, until the domestic commodity market clears. The same effect switches demand, of course, away from foreign goods, exerting deflationary pressure on the foreign economy. But the extent of the change in domestic production and the beggar-thy-neighbor outcome depend not only on adjustments in commodity markets; they depend also on conditions in asset markets. Devaluation, if accompanied by sufficient monetary expansion to cause gold to flow abroad, will tend to reduce *world* interest rates and thereby stimulate demand in *both* countries. The stimulus from lower interest rates can exceed or fall short of the contractionary shift of demand away from foreign goods and towards the devaluing country. Thus foreign output may rise or fall after the devaluation. Necessary though not sufficient conditions for foreign output to increase are that the foreign country gain gold reserves after devaluation in the home country, or that the foreign country allow its own ratio of gold backing to decline.

The change in foreign output and employment depends, therefore, on the home-country measures that accompany depreciation. For example, the devaluing country could expand the domestic credit component of its monetary base sufficiently to prevent any international movement of reserves, the case of sterilized devaluation. Output rises at home and falls abroad, while world interest rates decline. Alternatively, the devaluing country might refuse to initiate any change in domestic credit. Since the volume of gold remains linked to the quantity of money at the initial ratio, the impact on the foreign country will be more contractionary than with sterilized devaluation. Domestic output rises, foreign output falls and, in the case of symmetrical countries, world interest rates are unchanged.

A third possibility is that the devaluing country recognizes the existence of capital gains on its gold reserves and expands the monetary base by the percentage devaluation, leaving the gold backing of the base unchanged (with gold valued at the new parity).[26] This is the case of unsterilized devalution. The gold reserves of the devaluing country can either rise or fall. The decline in world interest rates may swamp the expenditure-switching effect, causing foreign output to rise.

This analysis is premised on a framework in which monetary variables are non-neutral. One may ask whether this is an appropriate premise. Figure 1 provides an example of the relationships which led to it. The figure shows the percentage change in the exchange rate between 1929 and 1935 and the percentage change in industrial production. The terminal date of 1935 is chosen to permit depreciations as much time as possible to work their effects.[27] We include all the economies of western Europe for which comparable data could be obtained.[28] A depreciation,

---

[26] To keep the percentage of gold backing unchanged, open market operations are required not just to inject into circulation currency in the amount of the capital gains on gold reserves but also to increase the domestic credit component of the monetary base by the proportion of devaluation. Compare Gottfried Haberler, *Prosperity and Depression* (Geneva, 1937).

[27] Still later dates are undesirable because by 1936 all countries had devalued and there hence remain no gold standard countries with which to compare, but also because the course of recovery becomes increasingly dominated by rearmament expenditure.

[28] We purposely excluded the United States on the grounds that the Depression to a large extent originated there rather than being imported from abroad and therefore would have had very

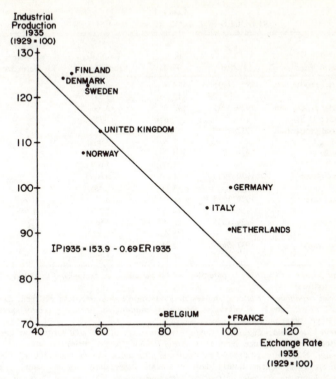

FIGURE 1
CHANGES IN EXCHANGE RATES AND INDUSTRIAL PRODUCTION, 1929–1935

plotted along the horizontal axis, is expressed as the gold price of domestic currency in 1935 as a percentage of the 1929 parity; a value of 100 for France indicates no depreciation, while a value of 59 for the United Kingdom indicates a 41 percent depreciation. The change in industrial production, plotted along the vertical axis, is the ratio of production in 1935 to 1929 multiplied by 100.

There is a clear negative relationship between the height of the exchange rate and the extent of recovery from the Depression. The countries of the Gold Bloc, represented here by France, the Netherlands, and Belgium, had by 1935 failed to recover to 1929 levels of industrial production. Countries which devalued at an early date (the United Kingdom, Denmark, and the Scandinavian countries) grew much more rapidly; and there appears to be a positive relationship between the magnitude of depreciation and the rate of growth. Germany

---

different implications for the characteristics of both the downturn and the recovery. We did no experimentation with different samples of countries but intend to increase the size of the sample in future work.

Exchange Rates

TABLE 3
REDUCED FORM REGRESSION RESULTS

Dependent Variable	Period	Constant Term	Exchange Rate Term	Dummy Variable for Germany	R^2
1. Industrial production	1929–1935	153.9 (10.06)	−0.69 (3.51)		.56
2. Industrial production (including U.S.)	1929–1935	142.9 (7.61)	−0.59 (2.32)		.32
3. Industrial production (including U.S.)	1932–1935	2.04 (7.40)	−0.97 (2.96)	0.58 (4.10)	.62
4. Real wage	1929–1935	0.73 (3.00)	−0.0065 (2.07)		.27
5. Export volume	1929–1935	1.39 (8.30)	−0.0075 (3.46)		.55
6. Discount rate	1929–1935	−4.29 (4.26)	0.031 (2.25)	−1.861 (1.95)	.47
7. Tobin's q	1929–1935	136.8 (5.62)	−0.933 (2.96)		.46
8. Gold reserves	1931–1935	2.40 (4.84)	−0.018 (2.79)		.43

Notes and Sources: *t*-statistics in parentheses. All variables are normalized to 100 in 1929 and defined as follows:

1. *Industrial production*: National indices of industrial production, from Mitchell, *European Historical Statistics*; and H. W. Methorst, *Recueil international de statistiques economiques 1931–1936* (La Haye, 1938).
2. *Exchange rate*: Gold value of currencies as a percentage of 1929 gold parity, from League of Nations Economic Intelligence Service, *Monetary Review* (Geneva, 1938).
3. *Real wage*: Nominal wage deflated by wholesale price index. Wages, from Mitchell, *European Historical Statistics*, measure hourly, daily, or weekly wages, depending on country. Note that wages for Belgium are for males in transport and industry only, that wages in France are for men only. Wholesale price indices are from Mitchell, *European Historical Statistics*.
4. *Export volume*: Special trade, merchandise only, measured in metric tons, from League of Nations, *Monthly Bulletin of Statistics* (Geneva, July 1936); League of Nations, *Review of World Trade, 1936* (Geneva, 1937).
5. *Discount rate*: From League of Nations, *Review of World Trade, 1936*.
6. *Gold reserve*: Gold stock valued in constant dollars of 1929 gold content, as of December of the year. From C. D. Hardy, *Is There Enough Gold?* (Washington, D.C., 1936); and Federal Reserve Bulletin (various issues).
7. *Security prices*: Indices of industrial share prices. From League of Nations, *Monthly Bulletin of Statistics*; and Methorst, *Recueil*.

and Belgium are outliers, Belgium presumably because she devalued only at the end of the period, leaving relatively little time for exchange rate changes to influence growth, and Germany presumably because of the influence of capital controls whose effects were analogous to an explicit depreciation.[29]

The first regression in Table 3 shows the reduced-form relationship between changes in industrial production and the exchange rate. As explained above, the United States was excluded from the sample on

[29] Belgium's participation in the Gold Bloc and her decision to leave in 1935 are discussed in detail by van der Wee and Tavernier, *La Banque*. A detailed description of German exchange control is provided by Howard S. Ellis, *Exchange Control in Central Europe* (Cambridge, 1941).

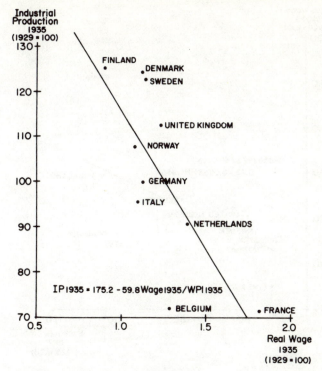

FIGURE 2
CHANGES IN REAL WAGES AND INDUSTRIAL PRODUCTION, 1929–1935

the grounds that the Great Depression to a large extent originated there, rendering the downturn unusually severe and differentiating the course of the subsequent recovery. In fact, including the United States weakens the relationship only slightly, as shown in the second line of Table 3. Moreover, if the distinguishing characteristics of the Depression in the United States had their greatest impact on the depth of the initial decline rather than on the effects of subsequent exchange-rate changes, then the relationship should be stronger when growth between 1932 and 1935 is compared with the extent of depreciation. Since the German economy becomes tightly regulated after 1931, it is necessary to add a dummy variable for Germany. The regression appears in the third line of Table 3.

It can be objected that both the exchange rate and industrial production are endogenous variables, so that we should not attribute variations in economic growth to movements in exchange rates rather than vice versa. We prefer our interpretation for several reasons. First is a matter of timing. In all cases, devaluation preceded the beginning of recovery, judged on the basis of annual data. Second is a matter of logic. It is hard to make a case for reverse causation, that faster growing countries were

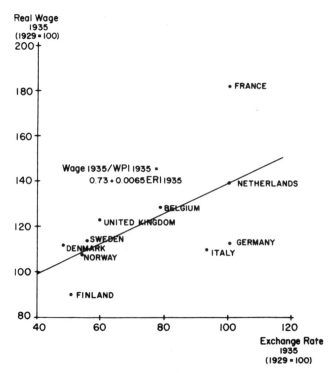

FIGURE 3
CHANGES IN EXCHANGE RATES AND REAL WAGES, 1929–1935

pushed into devaluation. Indeed, we will demonstrate that the faster growing countries were absorbing, not losing, gold, so that it would be tricky indeed to make the case that fast growth forced countries off their gold parities. Third is a matter of history. Exchange rates in the 1930s depended not merely on economic pressures but on national attitudes toward the monetary standard, where the attitudes towards the standards were predetermined relative to the events of the early 1930s. The allegiance of nations to their gold standard parities appears to have been largely dependent on their stabilization experiences in the early 1920s. Ironically, those nations which made the most concerted efforts to restore prewar gold standard parities in the early 1920s showed the least hesitation to devalue in the early 1930s. The obvious contrast is between Britain and France, although the point applies generally. French opinion was so traumatized by the successive "battles of the franc" that took place between 1922 and 1926 that it was hesitant even to contemplate the option of devaluation before 1936.[30] In Britain, where the decision

---

[30] French opinion on monetary and financial questions, along with British comparisons, is reviewed by Perrot, *La Monnaie*. Political aspects of the French debate are summarized by Sauvy, *Histoire économique*.

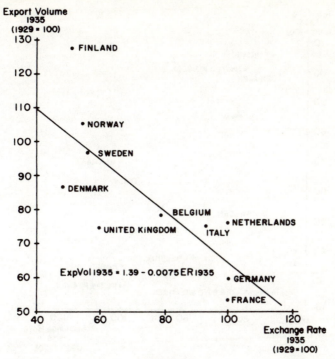

FIGURE 4
CHANGES IN EXCHANGE RATES AND EXPORT VOLUME, 1929–1935

to return to the prewar parity was little questioned in 1925, there was nearly no mention of a return to the gold standard once convertibility was suspended.[31] The important point is that the decision of whether to devalue in the 1930s was heavily influenced by considerations exogenous to our macroeconomic model, namely, the historical experience of the 1920s.

Figures 2 through 5 show various aspects of the mechanism linking exchange rates to economic activity. In Figure 2 the change in real wages (on the horizontal axis) is plotted along with the change in industrial production (on the vertical axis). The clear negative relationship indicates that supply considerations strongly influenced the rate of economic recovery.[32] Countries which succeeded in reducing real wages enhanced profitability and boosted aggregate supply. Again, Belgium appears as something of an outlier, perhaps because the late

---

[31] The definitive analysis of the decision to return to par in 1925, which highlights the role of the few dissenters such as Keynes, is Donald E. Moggridge, *The Return to Gold, 1925* (Cambridge, 1969). An account which emphasizes the implications of the 1925 decision for attitudes toward depreciation in 1931 is Cairncross and Eichengreen, *Sterling in Decline*.

[32] Although both industrial production and the real wage are endogenous variables, we report the regression for completeness.

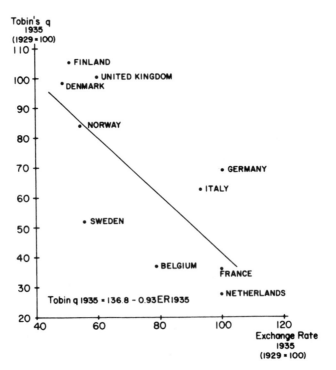

FIGURE 5
CHANGES IN EXCHANGE RATES AND TOBIN'S q, 1929–1935

date of devaluation there left little time for its effects. Figure 3 and Table 3 show the relationship between the change in the exchange rate and the change in the real wage, suggesting that depreciation, by putting upward pressure on prices, contributed to the reduction in the real wage which stimulated supply in devaluing countries. Of course, other factors in addition to exchange-rate policy influenced the evolution of real wages. These other factors appear to have played relatively large roles in Germany, Italy, Finland, and France. In Italy and especially in Germany the labor market came under increasingly strict government regulation as the 1930s progressed; it is not surprising that the change in real wages only moderately reflects the market forces considered.[33]

$IP1935 = 175.2 - 59.8 \, (WAGE1935/WPI1935)$
    (7.39)   (3.14) $\bar{R}^2 = .50$

Similar relationships are reported by Sheila Bonnell, "Real Wages and Employment in the Great Depression," *Economic Record* (1981), pp. 277–81.

[33] Control of the German labor market has been analyzed by Otto Nathan, *The Nazi Economic System* (Durham, 1944); and, more recently, by Frank Kim, "The German Economy during the Interwar Period: Preparation for War?" (thesis, Harvard College, 1983).

The impact of depreciations on demand is apparent in Figure 4, where they are plotted against the change in export volume. The fifth regression in Table 3 documents the statistical relationship: countries which depreciated succeeded in promoting the recovery of export volume compared with countries that remained on gold.[34] The result may or may not be consistent with the beggar-thy-neighbor characterization of exchange-rate policy, but it indicates that a single depreciation, taken in isolation, did increase demand in the depreciating country. In Figure 4, France and Finland are the noticeable outliers, presumably reflecting the impact of the same supply-side factors causing these countries to be outliers (in Figure 3) in terms of wage performance.

A second major channel through which depreciations could have influenced demand is through the world level of interest rates. Countries that devalued could have taken advantage of the relaxation of gold-standard constraints and engineered a reduction in interest rates through the adoption of accommodative money and credit policies. In the formal model, depreciation and accompanying monetary initiatives affect only the overall level of world interest rates. In a more general model, depreciation might give rise to interest-rate differentials among countries, creating not only the expenditure-increasing effect but also an expenditure-switching effect. In practice it is difficult to marshall evidence concerning the impact of exchange-rate policy on interest rates. Interest rate on assets with even approximately comparable maturities and risk characteristics are available for only a subset of European countries. In the sixth line of Table 3 we therefore report a regression of the change in the exchange rate against the change in the central bank discount rate. The discount rate is an administered price rather than a direct measure of market conditions. Yet in market economies the discount rate could not diverge markedly from freely determined rates, since central banks which discounted the eligible paper of the private sector could not afford to do so at rates far out of line from market levels. The regression indicates a positive relationship between the height of the exchange rate and the discount rate once account is taken of the extent of capital controls in Germany.[35] When currencies were devalued, central banks were able to capitalize on the increased strength of the external position by reducing interest rates.

A third major channel through which exchange-rate changes could have stimulated demand was by promoting domestic investment. In-

---

[34] The same picture would emerge were we to construct measures of the real exchange rate and plot them against export volume, since each country's real exchange rate is dominated by the movement of its nominal exchange rate.

[35] The relationship is strengthened when a further dummy variable is added for Italy, the other country with stringent capital and exchange market controls.

$$\Delta CBDR = -4.77 + 0.040 \, \Delta ER - 2.31 \, GERMANY - 1.55 \, ITALY$$
$$(5.37) \quad (4.19) \qquad (2.73) \qquad\qquad (1.92) \qquad \bar{R}^2 = .51$$

creased competitiveness, by raising current sales, could have enhanced profitability and provided an incentive to invest. To the extent that central banks were able to utilize the leeway provided by depreciation to reduce the level of interest rates, the present value of expected future profits also would have been raised, further increasing perceived profitability, while the reduction in interest rates at the same time lowered the cost of investment. Adequate data on the volume of domestic investment is available only for a few European countries. We therefore examine the behavior not of investment itself but of a measure of the incentive to invest: Tobin's q. In theory, q—the ratio of security prices to output prices—incapsulates all the information relevant to the investment decision.[36] Figure 5 plots the change in the exchange rate along with the change in the ratio of security prices to wholesale prices. Again, a negative relationship is evident: countries which depreciated their currencies in the 1930s succeeded in raising Tobin's q and increasing the incentive to invest. The result is consistent with the view that both domestic investment demand and foreign export demand promoted their economic recovery.

IV. INTERNATIONAL REPERCUSSIONS OF DEPRECIATION

Together this evidence on the structural relationships linking exchange rates to economic recovery suggests that the cross-section pattern depicted in Figure 1 is not a spurious correlation. Exchange-rate policy promoted growth not through one but through each one of the major channels: by reducing real wages, enhancing competitiveness, promoting exports, and permitting a reduction of interest rates. Whether the gain to devaluing countries had as its counterpart a loss to those which remained on gold—in other words, whether this policy was beggar-thy-neighbor—depends on the precise form of the devaluations. If the devaluing country increases its money supply sufficiently to induce an outflow of gold, the stimulus to demand of lower interest rates abroad may be sufficient to expand the foreign economy. As mentioned earlier, gold outflow is a necessary but not sufficient condition for the foreign expansion. Thus, the direction of gold flows provides an indicator of whether devaluation was necessarily beggar-thy-neighbor. The final equation in Table 3, therefore, regresses the exchange rate against the change in gold reserves. The negative relationship is apparent: depreciating countries gained rather than lost gold reserves. Further evidence to this effect appears in Table 4. Currency depreciation, beneficial from the individual country's point of view, was in fact beggar-thy-neighbor.

[36] See James Tobin, "A General Equilibrium Approach to Monetary Theory," *Journal of Money, Credit and Banking*, 1 (1969), pp. 15–29.

TABLE 4
GOLD RESERVES AND GOLD COVER RATIOS OF CENTRAL BANKS

Country	Ratio of Gold Reserves to Notes and Other Sight Liabilities (%)		Amount Held (in millions of 1929 U.S. dollars)	
	1929	1936[a]	1929	1936
Belgium	38.1	67.8	163	373
Denmark	39.6	50.8	46	32
Finland	19.0	61.3	8	21
France	47.4	59.1	1,631	1,769
Germany	36.1	1.0	560	16
Italy	27.5	22.0	273	123
Netherlands	49.9	81.4	180	289
Norway	36.0	74.2	39	58
Sweden	29.0	63.8	66	142
United Kingdom	27.4	78.3	711	1,529

[a] With gold at market prices.
Source: League of Nations Economic Intelligence Service, *Monetary Review* (Geneva, 1937), table 6.

Whether the gain to the devaluing countries outweighed the loss to their neighbors is an extremely difficult question. It remains true, however, that had such policies been adopted even more widely and in a coordinated fashion, they could have been beneficial for all the countries involved. In our model, a simultaneous devaluation taken by all countries may have no immediate effects; simply raising the domestic-currency price of gold in each country affects none of the equilibrium conditions in goods or asset markets.[37] But if money supplies are expanded to reflect the capital gains on gold reserves (thus holding the gold cover ratio constant), then the reduction in interest rates stimulates activity both at home and abroad.

The cogent criticism of exchange-rate depreciation in the 1930s, therefore, is not that it was used unfairly but that the policy was pursued sporadically, and was avoided altogether by some major countries. Often, exchange rates were adjusted in the wake of a crisis, although this was not uniformly the case.[38] Financial crises shifted from one country to another, because each time a country known to be in a delicate position devalued a new country was elevated to the position of being the next one expected to fall. Nurkse labels this sequential pattern the "devaluation cycle." The resulting uncertainty about exchange

---

[37] This experiment is analyzed as Case IV in the appendix, available on request. We stress *immediate* effects. By raising the price of gold in terms of commodities, an increased flow supply of new gold could be elicited in the long run. For contemporary discussion of this mechanism, see Gold Delegation of the League of Nations, *Report* (Geneva, 1932).

[38] An obvious contrast is between the successive financial crises in Austria, Germany, and Britain in the summer of 1931, which gave rise to either devaluation or the imposition of exchange control, and the voluntary decisions of many of the countries which decided to follow Britain off gold in the course of subsequent months.

rates may have had the depressing impact on trade so emphasized by contemporaries but also may have led international investors (including central banks) to liquidate a portion of their foreign exchange holdings and replace them with gold. In our model the effects of such actions are captured by a rise in the gold cover ratio.[39] The same world stock of gold can then support only a smaller money supply, raising interest rates and exerting deflationary pressure. To the extent that demands for gold were increased by the "sequential" or "successive" nature of the devaluations of the 1930s, the benefits of an "all-round" devaluation were reduced.[40]

Protection, like devaluation, also is capable of exerting expansionary effects at home. But the adoption of tariffs by all countries (reducing producer prices and lowering output and employment) leaves everyone worse off; coordinated devaluation both at home and abroad together with accommodative monetary measures is likely to leave everyone better off.[41] Too often competitive devaluation and tariff protection have been viewed as interchangable. They are not.

V. CONCLUSIONS

Given the number of unanswered questions posed along the way, our paper has been as much an agenda for research as a statement of results. The main limitation of the present analysis is the subset of policies on which it focuses. Currency depreciation was only one of several instruments of external economic policy, along with exchange controls and trade restrictions. Moreover, internal economic measures—notably fiscal policy—can and should be incorporated into the model, although their empirical analysis awaits construction of adequate measures of fiscal stance.[42] Above all, we have taken the formulation of policy as exogenous to our analytical framework. A full understanding of the role

---

[39] This experiment is analyzed as Case V in the appendix, available on request.

[40] It is conceivable that this could yield the outcome suggested by Kindleberger, namely that devaluation could lower prices abroad while leaving home-country prices unchanged. Note, however, that the mechanism is very different from his argument concerning a ratchet effect in commodity markets. Kindleberger, *World in Depression*, chap. 4.

[41] For a formal analysis of the effects of commercial policy, see Barry Eichengreen, "A Dynamic Model of Tariffs, Output and Employment Under Flexible Exchange Rates," *Journal of International Economics*, 11 (1981), pp. 341–59; Barry Eichengreen, "The Smoot-Hawley Tariff and the Start of the Great Depression" (unpublished manuscript, 1984).

[42] To date, constant employment measures of the government budget have been constructed only for the United States and Britain. See E. Cary Brown, "Fiscal Policy in the Thirties: A Reappraisal," *American Economic Review*, 46 (1956), pp. 857–79; and Roger Middleton, "The Constant Employment Budget Balance and British Budgetary Policy, 1929–39," *Economic History Review*, 2nd ser., 34 (1981), pp. 266–86. For an extension to the analysis of commercial policy, see Barry Eichengreen, "The Australian Recovery of the 1930s in International Comparative Perspective" (unpublished paper presented to the conference on the Australian Economy in the 1930s, Canberra, August 1985, and forthcoming in the conference volume).

of policy in the economic recovery of the 1930s requires an integrated analysis of both policy's formulation and effects.

This much, however, is clear. We do not present a blanket endorsement of the competitive devaluations of the 1930s. Though it is indisputable that currency depreciation conferred macroeconomic benefits on the initiating country, because of accompanying policies the depreciations of the 1930s had beggar-thy-neighbor effects. Though it is likely that currency depreciation (had it been even more widely adopted) would have worked to the benefit of the world as a whole, the sporadic and uncoordinated approach taken to exchange-rate policy in the 1930s tended, other things being equal, to reduce the magnitude of the benefits.

Part III
Trade Policy, Global Depression and the Developing World

[21]
The effects of the depression on primary producing countries

C. H. Lee

By the end of the 1920s most of the countries of the world were still primary producers.[1] In 1930 about 65 per cent of the world's population was engaged in some form of agricultural pursuit. It must be borne in mind, therefore, that while for the purpose of this essay primary producers must be treated as a generally homogeneous group, they differ greatly in structure and degree of advancement. A number of the countries classified as primary producers by one definition are by other criteria industrial nations, such as Australia, New Zealand, and Argentina, all of which had less than a third of their labour force employed in agriculture in the 1930s, and less than Japan, Italy, or France, which are usually grouped amongst the most advanced economies. At the other extreme Mexico, Brazil, and Bulgaria had over two-thirds of their labour force employed in agriculture and fishing. In this essay we shall examine the situation of the primary producers in the 1920s, then the main effects of the depression upon trade, production, prices, and investment, and how they influenced national income, employment, and consumption, and finally the response of the primary producers to their situation in the 1930s.

It is important to look first at the situation of primary producers in the decade before the depression, and to see that the depression was not sudden and cataclysmic, although it was of unprecedented severity, and that the drama of the Wall Street crash did not, for primary producers at least, turn buoyant prosperity into despair and ruin. In fact the economic position of primary pro-

[1] Only seven countries had fewer people employed in fishing and agriculture than in manufacturing and extracting industry. One of these was Australia, whose prosperity still depended heavily on the production and export of primary products.

ducers was extremely weak and insecure during the 1920s. Most of them were heavily dependent on exports for their prosperity, as indicated by the fact that on average between 1927 and 1930 the share of world production exported was 73 per cent coffee, 50 per cent wool, 49 per cent cotton, and 43 per cent sugar.[2] During the 1920s, however, both prices and demand for primary commodities were falling, and the disparity between these prices and those of manufactured goods in world trade was growing wider.[3]

Even though the earning power of primary produce in international trade was thus declining in the 1920s, both productivity, through increased mechanization, and production increased. Since this was attended by both falling prices and the accumulation of stocks, it would seem that demand was not keeping pace with production. There was a noticeable growth of stocks in the late 1920s, and by 1929 the general world index stood 24 per cent above the average of the previous four years, while wheat and coffee stocks had risen 50 per cent above the average, and sugar and rubber 29 per cent.[4] While it is generally true that temporary over-production in primary production exists in the form of stocks, the accumulation of the late 1920s was unusually large, as well as being accompanied by other symptoms of over-production.

In an attempt to counter the trend of falling prices and rising stocks, numerous price-fixing schemes for the marketing of primary produce were put into operation. The Brazilian coffee valorization scheme marketed the country's output through a central agency, and restricted the amount available on the market in order to keep up the price, thus creating excess capacity in the coffee trade. Between 1925 and 1929 Brazil's coffee production increased by about 100 per cent, but demand remained steady even though it was a period of rising prosperity. Since about two thirds of the production was exported, and since in 1929 the value of coffee inventories was equivalent to 10 per cent of Brazil's gross national product, the situation was extremely insecure and hazardous,

[2] Royal Institute of International Affairs, *World Agriculture* (London, 1932), 6.
[3] United Nations, *Relative Prices of Exports and Imports of Underdeveloped Countries* (New York, 1949), 22.
[4] League of Nations, *World Economic Survey 1932–3* (Geneva, 1933), 93. These reports, published annually throughout the 1930s, provide one of the best sources for statistical material on the international economy and have been used extensively in the preparation of this essay.

EFFECT OF DEPRESSION ON PRIMARY PRODUCERS

particularly as coffee production was increasing in Haiti and Colombia.

Falling prices and rising stocks were not the only problems. In the trade boom of 1925–9 the volume of world trade in primary products increased by 15 per cent, but the volume of trade in manufactured goods increased by 32 per cent. Equally significant was the fact that by 1925 Europe had recovered sufficiently from the effects of the war to reach its pre-war production level and exceed its 1913 volume of world trade. This meant intensified competition in the sale of some primary products, and between 1928 and 1930 Europe's share of world wheat exports increased from 4 to 25 per cent.

Given the insecurity of their position in the late 1920s, the primary producers were one of the sectors of the world economy least able to resist the effects of a severe trade depression. Agricultural production is often a highly localized pursuit carried out on a small scale, and thus very vulnerable to fluctuations in demand or price. Furthermore, production does not respond quickly to short-term fluctuations. Rubber trees cannot be tapped until they are five years old and reach maturity only in seven years. Plantation crops like cotton and coffee also require several months between planting and harvesting; in other cases, like the wheat prairies of Canada, it is difficult to turn to alternative kinds of production. Similar limitations apply to the production of most agricultural primary products, indicating a very low elasticity of supply and consequently a dependence upon the maintenance of prices and demand. The annual growth rate of 4·7 per cent in raw material production between 1913 and 1925 was based upon such an expectation. Since the supply of primary products was inelastic, a fall in price due to declining demand would not lead to an immediate reduction in supply. Consequently in a prolonged depression primary products would suffer a severe fall in prices.

Thus by the end of the 1920s the position of primary producers was extremely insecure. Production and stocks were increasing within a framework of inelastic supply, while competition was becoming more intense and prices and demand were falling. Even without the depression it is difficult to see how the position of primary producers could have been less than desperate in the 1930s.

CONTEMPORARY HISTORY

The onset of the depression accentuated all the weaknesses of the situation. Its most obvious and immediate manifestation was the fall in the volume and value of international trade. By 1937, at the peak of the business cycle, both food and raw material trade was less than 50 per cent of the 1929 value. By the same date the volume of foodstuffs in international trade had not recovered its 1929 level, although the volume of raw materials had risen by 11·5 per cent.[5] Certainly the depression in trade was more severe by far than any previously recorded; in 1929–30 the value of trade fell by 19 per cent, compared with 7 per cent in 1907–8 and 5 per cent in 1873–4, the worst records till then. Between 1929 and 1932 the volume of trade fell by one quarter while stocks of staple commodities rose by 50 per cent, and the value of trade fell by two thirds. The primary producers, however, seem to have kept and slightly increased their share of world trade between 1929 and 1935 as compared to the decline in their share in the 1925–9 boom.[6] The decline in trade together with the insensitivity of production to reduced demand, accelerated the growth of stocks. By 1930–1 wheat stocks stood at 20 per cent of the annual crop, sugar stocks were one third of the annual supply, and coffee stocks were equivalent to fifteen months consumption at current rates. By 1932 stocks were almost double the 1925–9 average, with particularly large accumulations in sugar, coffee, and rubber. The production of foodstuffs did not diminish during the depression, since short run demand and supply are inelastic, and although production of raw materials fell between 1929 and 1932, the pre-depression level of world production was almost reached by 1935. Nearly all primary producers had recovered or passed the 1929 level of output by 1935 in almost every category of food and raw material production. The failure of world production to recover completely was due to the fall in European and North American output between 1929 and 1935. Commodities to recover quickly were coffee and wheat, both of which exceeded 1929 production in 1933, with considerable expansion in the middle 1930s in cotton, rubber, and petroleum.

While primary producers were affected temporarily by the fall in the volume of trade, the main problem they faced in the 1930s was the failure of primary product prices to recover, and the closely related deterioration in their terms of trade. The problem

[5] League of Nations, *World Economic Survey 1937–8* (Geneva, 1938), 119.
[6] Op. cit., *1936–7* (Geneva, 1937), 124.

EFFECT OF DEPRESSION ON PRIMARY PRODUCERS
was obviously most acute for those countries which were heavily dependent on the export of primary products. Australia exported a third of her agricultural produce; in 1928–9 wool and wheat together accounted for 60 per cent of all Australian exports. On the basis of the 1924–5 trade in terms of average value per unit of export, Australian export prices fell by 67 per cent in the depression while import prices fell by only 34 per cent. Thus Australia had to export three times as much in 1930–1 as in 1924–5 to meet the service charges on her foreign debt, and twice as much to buy her imports. Equally difficult was the situation of the Latin American countries, several of which were committed to the export of a single raw material or foodstuff. In 1929 coffee provided 71 per cent of Brazilian exports, while copper and nitrates accounted for 84 per cent of Chilean exports; oil was 76 per cent for Venezuela and tin 73 per cent for Bolivia.

The severe reduction in export earnings, accentuating the trend of the 1920s, sharply reduced the purchasing power of primary producers for imported goods and particularly for manufactured commodities. Thus over the main years of the depression 1929–32, while the fall in dollar values of Chile's exports was 84 per cent, the fall in her import values was 87 per cent. The same was true of a large number of primary producing nations, including Denmark, New Zealand, Greece, and Argentina. As a result many primary producers showed a better current trade balance position in 1932 than in 1929, either by turning a net deficit into a credit, as in Hungary, Egypt, and Uruguay, or by reducing the size of the deficit. Those whose position deteriorated most appear to have been the countries with a large net credit in 1929 which was subsequently reduced, in particular the United States, India, Mexico, and Chile.[7] Obviously this improvement in current trade balances was mainly if not exclusively achieved by the reduction of imports, not by an expansion of exports. In Latin America this was certainly the case. Compared with the annual average for 1925–9, the capacity to import or earning power of exports fell by 31·3 per cent between 1930 and 1934, and by 12·9 per cent between 1933 and 1939.[8] In Argentina the share of imports in the total supply of

[7] League of Nations, *World Economic Survey 1932–3* (Geneva, 1933), 214; ibid., *1934–5* (Geneva, 1935), 203–4.
[8] United Nations, *Economic Survey of Latin America 1949* (New York, 1951), 19.

CONTEMPORARY HISTORY

goods fell from 52·9 per cent in 1929 to 34·9 per cent in 1938, while the earning power of Brazilian exports over the same period was reduced by 36 per cent. In most cases the gap left by this reduction of imports was filled by home produced goods. In Argentina production, at constant prices, increased by 9 per cent between 1929 and 1938 but exports fell by 37 per cent. In many countries this reorientation of production towards the home market was spontaneous and undoubtedly occasioned by the necessity to produce commodities which it was no longer possible to import. Elsewhere it was the result of government policy. Australia turned a trade deficit of £22 million in 1929 into a credit of over £27 million by 1931 by import restrictions and domestic deflation in the form of higher import duties, cuts in government expenditure, increased taxation, compulsory conversion of the internal debt, exchange depreciation, and the voluntary conversion of a large part of the government's external sterling debt. As a result, imports were reduced by over two thirds between 1929 and 1931. Canada was another country which improved its trade balance by heavy duties on imports, government control of wheat exporting, and the negotiation of new trade agreements.

Not all primary producers were able to negotiate favourable trade treaties in the 1930s, since the depression weakened their position more than that of exporters of manufactured goods. In 1931 Denmark sold to Britain five times as much as she bought in return; by the first half of 1935 this had fallen to less than one and a half times her purchases. In a wider context one observer noted in 1935 that 'bounties, barter agreements and clearing discriminations have been costly and on the whole unsuccessful. They represent efforts to buttress agriculture at the expense of other elements in the national economy . . . they have not in fact brought a better adjustment of supply and demand, but on the contrary have further increased production and diminished consumption.'[9] Such schemes could be self-defeating. The Brazilian coffee valorization scheme kept her export prices so high that Brazil was losing markets to competitors selling more cheaply. Her share of world coffee exports fell from 59·4 to 47 per cent between 1929

---

[9] J.B. Condliffe in League of Nations, *World Economic Survey 1934–5* (Geneva, 1935), 96.

144

EFFECT OF DEPRESSION ON PRIMARY PRODUCERS

and 1937, a situation which led to a modification of the scheme in 1937 to allow more competitive pricing of exports.

While primary producers were thus inhibited and circumscribed in the ways in which they could improve their trading position in the depression, either by treaty, legislation, or other forms of government action, they were not able to prevent importers of primary produce discriminating against them by tariffs. Between 1928 and 1934 wheat production rose by 20 per cent in the wheat-importing countries of Europe, while it fell by a third in the Danube region and by 18 per cent in the four main non-European exporting countries. Manufacturing countries helped their own balance of payments by protecting domestic agricultural production and thus further limited the exports of the primary producers.

The fall in the value of international trade and the disruption in trading activity severely depressed incomes everywhere. Worst affected was the United States, which suffered a 53 per cent fall in income between 1929 and 1932, and Germany with a 39 per cent fall. Amongst the primary producers, the percentage fall in national income was 48 for Hungary, 34 for Australia and New Zealand, and 8 for Denmark. There is no clear difference of experience between any closely related or similar countries, and primary producers as a whole did not fare especially well or badly. The heaviest falls were sustained by those countries most exposed to the international financial situation and the sharp fall in export prices.

Within each national economy, too, the worst hit sectors were those dependent upon the international price and market mechanism. In New Zealand between 1929 and 1932 incomes from pastoral farming fell by 55 per cent, incomes from dairying by 25 per cent, from agriculture as a whole by 19 per cent, and from manufacturing by 22 per cent. In Canada the relative percentage decline in income groups was 62 in agriculture, 36 in manufacturing, and 31 in mining. The same sector of production fared differently in each country, farm incomes falling by over 50 per cent in Canada between 1929 and 1934, while in the United States they fell by 40 per cent and in Argentina by only 33 per cent in the same period. In this as in so many other aspects of the depression it is difficult to find common experience between groups of countries or sectors of production.

As the volume of international trade recovered from the worst

CONTEMPORARY HISTORY

years of the depression, national incomes began to rise. Amongst primary producers, the Scandinavian countries and Australasia had regained the 1929 level of national income by 1936–7. Amongst the countries which failed to recover, there appears no clear distinction between primary producers and industrial nations. It may well be, however, that those countries which were worst affected lacked the records and statistical evidence to show it. Unfortunately there are no regional or sector income figures to indicate the relative recovery of agriculture and industry from the depression within various primary producing countries.

The same difficulty arises with the data on employment and unemployment, and again trends have to be discerned from aggregate national statistics. Figures for unemployment show that while several primary producers were above the world average in 1929, notably the Scandinavian countries, by 1937 no clear distinction appeared between unemployment levels in primary producing and industrial nations. The heaviest unemployment rates in 1937 were recorded in the Netherlands, Norway, Denmark, and the United States in descending order, but the limited scope of the statistics precludes any firm conclusion.[10] Data covering a wider range of countries show the trend in unemployment in absolute figures. Here the main increase during the period 1929–37 is found in the more advanced economies like Belgium, France, Czechoslovakia, Canada, and the Australasian countries.[11] Thus while primary producers were severely affected by the fall in trade and prices, and while their position within the international economy was greatly weakened, in terms of national income and unemployment they did not fare worse than the industrial nations of Europe and North America.

Besides the decline in the value and volume of international trade, the main problem for primary producers posed by the depression concerned foreign investment, upon which many of them were heavily dependent for economic development. In 1930 external debts accounted for almost the whole public debt of countries like Poland, Rumania, Hungary, and Chile, and was over half the total debt of Australia, Brazil, China, Denmark, and Peru. A large share of the world's overseas investment came from Britain and the

[10] League of Nations, *World Economic Survey 1938–9* (Geneva, 1939), 128.
[11] Ibid. *1936–7* (Geneva, 1937), 109.

146

EFFECT OF DEPRESSION ON PRIMARY PRODUCERS

United States, and upon them depended the ability of many primary producers to pay their international debts. Any contraction of this source of capital put immediate and severe pressure on the balance of payments of debtor nations, as was indicated by the initial fall of American investment abroad in 1928–9. The depression had a severe effect on foreign investment from both private and government sources. There was a sharp fall in the number of new capital issues for foreign account, a decline which showed little recovery by the end of the 1930s. New issues from the United States fell from $1251 million to 2·4 million between 1929 and 1937; for the United Kingdom the fall was from $720 million to 96·4 million. After the depression, British investment abroad was heavily oriented towards the Dominions and colonies, albeit on a smaller scale than before, but other foreign investment fell from nearly £40 million in 1929 to less than £3 million in 1935. Not only did the volume of foreign investment decline enormously in the slump; there was a complementary repatriation of funds. Between 1928 and 1929 a net outflow of short term capital from the United States was reduced from $348 million to four million, and a net outflow of long term capital from $847 to 278 million. By 1932 the latter had become a net inflow of $225 million. On a rather more modest scale funds returned to the United Kingdom, a capital outflow of $574 million in 1929 becoming an inflow of $340 million by 1931.

This rapid contraction in investment funds made a severe impact on recipient nations who were principally primary producers. They were affected in two ways: in the loss of investment capital for the further development of trade and production, and in the pressure exerted on their balance of payments by their diminished power to meet foreign debts as a result of the trade slump. British and American issues on foreign account by region indicate the extent of this fall.

Investment in Canada by the two major creditor nations fell from $283 to $38 million between 1928 and 1932; in Latin America from $427 million in 1928 to nil, and in Asia and Oceania from $369 to $40 million. The fact that exchange depreciation of the dollar and sterling relieved the external debt of these countries in the slump was a compensating factor, but hardly one which offset the loss of investment.

CONTEMPORARY HISTORY

Investment issues on foreign account
(million dollars)[12]

		Asia & Oceania	Latin America	Africa	Canada
USA	1928	137	331	—	185
	1932	—	—	—	29
UK	1928	232	96	80	98
	1932	40	—	46	9

Thus the depression put the primary producers in a position in which their earning power was reduced by the fall in prices and business activity, while their costs in the form of fixed payments on loans and the price of necessary imports declined less: they were caught in what has been called a scissors effect. In Argentina in 1931, compared to the pre-war situation, the average price of agricultural products had fallen slightly, while farm rents and rail transport had risen by over 60 per cent, and the cost of agricultural machinery, food, and clothing had doubled. The loss of new investment funds removed one of the brightest hopes for recovery after the depression both for international trade and for the primary producers who had been so dependent on it. The debtor countries were able to improve their balance of payments by the reduction of imports, and their position was eased somewhat in the mid 1930s by the recovery of business activity in the creditor countries which stimulated demand for primary products. Even so, their economic development was hampered to an extent which it is impossible to calculate by the cessation of the flow of investment capital from Britain and the United States.

Nevertheless, the record of the primary producing countries in the 1930s was not one of unrelieved gloom, nor were all the effects of the depression bad. One of the most notable and hopeful trends in the 1930s was the growth of industrialization in many primary producing countries and a redistribution of resources away from agricultural pursuits into industry. An index of industrial activity for a varied group of primary producers, Chile,

[12] League of Nations, *World Economic Survey 1932–3* (Geneva, 1933), 294.

148

EFFECT OF DEPRESSION ON PRIMARY PRODUCERS

Denmark, Finland, Estonia, Rumania, Greece, and Hungary, shows that production increased by 21 per cent between 1929 and 1935, particularly the production of textiles, which rose by 60 per cent. In the mid 1930s countries as different as Australia, China, Yugoslavia, and Argentina all showed a considerable increase in their imports of machinery and tools for the development of domestic capital goods industry essential to economic growth. In addition to the USSR and Japan, where growth was particularly rapid, between 1929 and 1937 primary producers showed some of the highest rates of growth of industrial production (from a low starting point, it is true). Nine nations, among them Hungary, Denmark, and Chile, actually recorded an increase in industrial production of over 30 per cent; some primary producers also showed a marked expansion in their exports of manufactured goods, notably the Scandinavian and Baltic countries.

Given the diversity of their experience, it is impossible to assess the impact of industrialization on all or even a representative selection of primary producers, or to evaluate in general terms their response to the problems of the depression. It can be done for a limited number of countries, and here the experience of Chile, Brazil, Denmark, and Egypt will be analysed, the choice having been determined primarily by the availability of suitable data.

At the time of the depression both Chile and Brazil were amongst the least industrialized primary producers. Both were also heavily dependent on the export of a small range of commodities, namely coffee and to a much less extent cotton in the case of Brazil, and copper and nitrates in the case of Chile. Both lost heavily in the depression in terms of export earnings, and both needed the foreign investment which was no longer available in the 1930s. Economic growth, however, appears to have been stimulated rather than retarded by the depression. In Brazil there was a fall in agricultural employment as a share of total employment from 72·6 to 67·5 per cent between 1920 and 1940. Increased productivity made it possible to release this manpower, since over the same period agricultural output increased by 62 per cent while the labour force increased by only 18 per cent. As has already been seen, the reduced export earnings of primary producers during and after the slump obliged them to produce commodities at home or do without them in order to restore some measure of equilibrium to their balance of payments. In Brazil this gave a marked stimulus to home production of goods which had hitherto been largely imported.

Index of production (1929=100)[13]

		1925	1932	1937
Brazil:	Agriculture	79	103	128
	Industry	67	95	137
	Steel	30	126	282
	Cement	—	155	595
Chile:	Total production	80	70	107
	Industry	88	85	126
	Cotton fabrics	139	118	579
	Mining	70	26	86

In both Brazil and Chile industrial production rose more rapidly than production in the traditional export staple commodities. Brazil showed rapid growth in the capital goods industries like steel and cement, which supplied an increasing share of the domestic market. In 1925 domestically produced steel supplied only 2 per cent of home consumption, its share increased to 5·5 per cent in 1929 and 15 per cent in 1937. Even more striking was the performance of the cement industry, which increased its share of the home market from 15 to 88 per cent between 1929 and 1937. Even during the worst depression years domestic production of steel and cement continued to expand. In Chile import substitution was particularly important in the iron and steel industry and in the production of building materials. Domestic production of iron, which according to the statistical records was non-existent before 1935, was supplying 11 per cent of the country's consumption by 1937. The most spectacular increase in output was recorded for cotton fabrics, which increased its share of the home market from 9 per cent in 1929 to 50 per cent by 1937, while imported cottons fell by 40 per cent. This is a very impressive record of industrial growth, particularly since industrial production in Chile lagged behind the growth rate of total production between 1925 and 1929, and far behind mining, which was so badly hit in the slump.

[13] United Nations, *Economic Survey of Latin America 1949* (New York, 1951), 206, 250, 287, 367.

EFFECT OF DEPRESSION ON PRIMARY PRODUCERS

Coffee, for so long the predominant element in the Brazilian economy and the staple export crop, was ironically an important element in Brazil's recovery, for although its export earning power was greatly reduced in the depression, and added to the stocks which had been accumulating in the years before 1929, the government policy of buying up and destroying coffee crops which could not find a market helped to maintain output. This in turn maintained employment and boosted national income by creating purchasing power. After the depression coffee production declined, falling by 61 per cent between 1933 and 1944. This led to a more widely based export composition: in 1925 coffee provided over 72 per cent of the country's exports by value; by 1938 its share had fallen to 45 per cent, leaving Brazil much less exposed to the vagaries of the world market for a single commodity. Reduced export earning power also promoted industrialization by breaking the vicious circle in which an export-led boom in production in a primary producing country generated increased income which stimulated import consumption. Such a situation, as in the heyday of the coffee export boom, encouraged the production of those commodities upon which exports depended, and discouraged the domestic production of the commodities imported. This might make possible a consumption boom lasting as long as the buoyancy of the international market, but inhibited the diversification of production and the development of capital goods industry requisite for economic growth. There is no doubt that much of the industrial growth in Brazil in the 1930s can be attributed to the enforced reduction in imports. Their share in total supplies available fell between 1929 and 1937 from 44 to 31·3 per cent, and even by the latter date Brazil had not regained her pre-depression capacity to import.

Another primary producer severely affected by the depression was Denmark. In 1929 export earnings accounted for 44 per cent of Denmark's national income, most of it from the sale of primary commodities. In the 1930s Denmark showed a rapid growth of industrialization and a considerable redeployment of labour from agriculture into industrial occupations. Between 1931 and 1934 the country's butter production fell by 6 per cent, between 1931 and 1935 the number of pigs slaughtered fell by 40 per cent, but industrial output rose by 21 per cent. Much of this was undoubtedly due to greater productivity in agriculture which enabled it to reduce its labour force. A comparison of the decades 1921–9 and 1930–9 at constant prices shows a very high rate of growth in net domestic product in agriculture compared to other decades since 1870.[14] It also showed a productivity increase more than twice as great as in any other similar period, together with a fall of 5·5 per cent in the labour force. At the same time the labour force employed in other industries increased by 25 per cent, indicating the extent of occupational redistribution.

The loss of foreign earnings from agricultural exports undoubtedly played a major role in bringing this about. As in the case of Chile and Brazil, in the 1930s industrial production in Denmark expanded more rapidly than agriculture or the net domestic product. This no doubt accounts for the rapid recovery of investment, which had almost reached its pre-depression level by 1937. Manufacturing growth was also aided by the generally rapid recovery from the depression of the Scandinavian countries, which provided Danish industry with the additional stimulus of an export market for industrial goods; between 1926–9 and 1936–8 her output of manufactures increased by 47 per cent compared with a world increase of 33 per cent. While world trade in manufactures fell by 12 per cent over the same period, Danish imports rose by 12 per cent and her exports by 32 per cent.[15]

Perhaps Egypt offers the most spectacular example of industrial expansion in a primary producing country in the 1930s. Until 1929 Egypt was heavily dependent on the export of cotton which accounted for 92 per cent of total exports. The drop in the price of raw cotton in international trade in the 1930s, sharply affecting Egypt's balance of trade, led to a drastic fall in imports of all kinds, including footwear, furniture, cement, flour, yarns, and processed foods. Between 1928 and 1935 the main change in the composition of Egyptian imports was the fall in the share of foodstuffs from 18 to 11 per cent and a rise in the share of raw materials from 22 to 30 per cent. As in the case of other primary producers, loss of importing capacity and export earnings stimulated domestic production. In fact industrial expansion in Egypt in the 1930s has

---

[14] S. Kuznets (ed.), *Income and Wealth, Series V* (London, 1955), 125.
[15] League of Nations, *Industrialisation and Foreign Trade* (New York, 1945), 26–7.

EFFECT OF DEPRESSION ON PRIMARY PRODUCERS

been called 'a textbook example of development through import substitution'.[16] Its extent is illustrated by the following table.[17]

Percentage increase in employment in manufacturing in Egypt 1927–37		Percentage increase in production 1930–40	
Total	66	Cement	95
Food processing	127	Refined sugar	106
Chemicals	121	Petroleum	227
Clothing and footwear	104	Raw cotton consumed	390
Textiles	90	Mechanically woven cloth	695
		Yarn and thread	733

Many of these enterprises were new or in the early stages of development in the 1930s. A census taken in 1937 showed that two thirds of the industrial enterprises in Lower Egypt had been founded within the last ten years. Particularly significant is the growth of output in cotton manufacturing. Before the depression raw cotton had been almost exclusively for export; once it was diverted from export to home production, it exerted an important multiplier effect within the Egyptian economy through the provision of work, stimulating the demand for cotton machinery and generating income and consumption.

Industrial growth was aided by tariff protection made possible by the lapse of international agreements in 1930 which freed the country from customs restrictions. The slump was also responsible for diverting investment funds from export-oriented agriculture towards industry. The developments of the 1930s also brought a fall in the share of cotton in agricultural production from 50 to 30 per cent, accompanied by a decline in the share of cotton in Egyptian exports from 92 to 72 per cent between 1930 and 1939. Undoubtedly the effects of the depression on Egypt were beneficial and brought a decade of unprecedented economic growth.

To say that the depression was an important factor in accelerating industrial growth in some primary producing countries is not, of

---

[16] P. O'Brien, *The Revolution in Egypt's Economic System* (London, 1966), 14.
[17] C. Issawi, *Egyptian Economic and Social Analysis* (London, 1947), 51; P. O'Brien, *op. cit.*, 15.

course, to dismiss its impact on employment and the standard of living, which in many places was very severe. In Denmark, despite industrial growth and the reallocation of manpower, unemployment stood at 21·9 per cent in 1937; in Chile the food consumed per inhabitant fell between 1925–9 and 1935–9 by 5·8 per cent, for while domestic production increased by 0·4 per cent, population grew more rapidly and supplies of imported food fell by 38 per cent. Similarly, the consumption of cotton fabrics in Chile declined after 1929 and did not regain the level of that year until 1936. Statistics for the consumption of commodities such as tobacco, coffee, sugar, meat, and cereals in Egypt show a fall after 1929 from a level which was not reached again before the end of the 1930s. In terms of consumption and standards of living, primary producing countries probably fared worse than the more advanced economies, where the demand for foodstuffs at least seems to have remained steady. Indices for meat consumption per head in fifteen countries show that by 1934 only Canada and Italy had not regained their 1929 level, while the greatest increases were found in Denmark, Switzerland, and New Zealand.[18]

It is impossible in a study of this length to draw any but the most general conclusions about the effects of the depression on primary producers. Since the sharpest and most prolonged aspect of the depression was the fall in the activity and prices of international trade and the attendant decline in the terms of trade of primary producers, the experience of countries or regions was largely dependent on their commitment in the international market and their reliance on its continued prosperity. Similarly, the cessation of foreign lending impinged most severely on those who were most dependent on that source of capital. In so complex a situation, it is impossible to establish a clear demarcation between the experience of primary producers and of industrial nations. It is equally impossible to treat primary producers as a homogeneous group; in their structure and growth they varied from each other as much as from industrial countries.

But two points emerge clearly. First, that many of the problems and weaknesses of the primary producers were present in the 1920s before the depression; whatever the plight of primary producers during or after the slump, it arose not from the depression itself but from the essential instability of the international economy

[18] League of Nations, *World Economic Survey 1935-6* (Geneva, 1936), 115.

EFFECT OF DEPRESSION ON PRIMARY PRODUCERS

between the wars of which the depression was the most dramatic manifestation. Second, the effects of the depression were not completely disastrous. Some primary producers like Brazil and Egypt were obliged and enabled to develop domestic industry because the depression reduced their export earnings and thus their capacity to import manufactures. This stimulated internal economic growth, led to the diversification of production, and reduced their dependence on the export of a single primary product. Both Brazil and Egypt were economically more advanced and well balanced at the end of the 1930s than they had been a decade earlier. It may be therefore that the great depression, generally regarded as one of the main economic disasters of modern times, was in fact a major catalyst stimulating economic development in some underdeveloped countries by forcibly diverting their resources to more productive purposes.

Excerpt from Vladimir P. Timoshenko (1933), 'World Agriculture and the Depression', *Michigan Business Studies,* V (5), 66–100.

THE COLLAPSE OF 1929-30

> The economic situation of the leading agricultural countries was endangered as early as 1928. The year 1929-30 was a poor agricultural year for many countries outside of Europe while it was favorable for European countries. Exports from the leading non-European agricultural countries declined sharply in 1929-30, both in value and in quantity. This unbalanced their trade and created financial difficulties for them which were magnified by the strain on the international capital market. The flow of capital into agricultural countries was checked because of loss of confidence in their financial stability. Those countries which were affected by the poor crops of 1929-30 first went off the gold standard. The financial collapse of the agricultural countries accelerated the price decline which was already under way. But previous to 1929 there was no serious financial strain in the agricultural countries which could have caused prices to fall.

The foregoing study of the development of agricultural production, stocks, and prices, together with the analysis of world trade and the movements of capital, has shown that the situation of the leading agricultural countries had become endangered as early as 1928. Production of the principal exported agricultural commodities was overexpanded; consequently stocks were accumulated above the normal level and their prices tended to fall. If some prices were sustained that was because stocks were kept away from the market and financed with capital borrowed mostly abroad. Exports of agricultural products were increasing but slowly—both in value and in volume—for the world market for agricultural products from surplus countries was narrowed by the stimulation of domestic agricultural production in industrial countries. At the same time, imports into agricultural countries were increasing, and consequently their balance of merchandise trade was becoming less and less favorable, while the financial obligations abroad to be covered with this balance were growing heavier and heavier. The actual purchasing power of agricultural countries for manufactured goods was not growing, and the increase which occurred in the purchases of these countries was made possible only by new borrowings. Any decline in agricultural exports or any strain on the international capital market was bound to

AGRICULTURE AND THE DEPRESSION

put the whole system of international trade out of gear and to upset the equilibrium. Such a condition arose during 1929-30, and this precipitated the world economic crisis. The foundation for this crisis was prepared much earlier, however, by the developments during the years preceding 1929.

Unfavorable Agricultural Conditions in 1929-30

The year 1929-30 was a poor agricultural year for many countries outside of Europe, particularly in the production of cereals and other food crops, as may be seen from Table 17, in which are given indexes of production prepared by the League of Nations.

TABLE 17—INDEXES OF PRODUCTION OF PRIMARY COMMODITIES, 1925-31*
(1925-29 = 100)

Continents and Commodities	1925	1926	1927	1928	1929	1930	1931
North America							
Cereals	96	97	103	111	93	91	92
Cereals and other food	96	97	103	111	93	91	92
Latin America							
Cereals	94	98	105	114	89	106	97
Cereals and other food	96	97	100	111	96	98	93
Oceania							
Cereals	84	116	91	116	94	150	124
Cereals and other food	88	106	95	112	99	137	121
Europe (ex. Russia)							
Cereals	102	94	93	100	111	102	101
Cereals and other food	102	92	85	100	111	106	102
All continents							
Cereals	98	99	99	104	101	102	99
Cereals and other food	98	98	99	104	102	104	100

NOTE: The 1925 values are used as weights.

* See *Review of World Production 1925-1931*, Appendix, Table III, pp. 118-121. Commodities included in cereals are: wheat, rye, barley, oats, maize; other food crops included are: rice, potatoes, beet sugar, cane sugar.

The crops of cereals and other food were especially poor in North and South America and in Oceania; their cereal crops in 1929 were the poorest in several years. This was particularly true of wheat, which is of great importance in world trade. The four largest exporters of wheat—the United States, Canada,

Argentina, and Australia—had poor wheat crops in 1929, particularly Canada and Argentina. For the principal exporters of wheat the year 1929 was especially unfavorable because their poor crops were coincident with very good crops in Europe, both in the wheat-importing countries and in the exporting European countries which compete with the principal exporters on the European markets. As a result there was the worst possible combination for exporting countries outside of Europe: small volumes of crops which they were obliged to sell at low prices, because the total world production was only a little lower than in the exceptionally good year of 1928, from which, moreover, heavy stocks were carried over into 1929. So in 1929-30 the leading agricultural countries outside of Europe, particularly Canada, Argentina, and Australia (as well as the agricultural regions of the United States), were affected not only by declining agricultural prices, as they had been in previous years, but also by a small volume of production. This reduced their exports greatly.

It has already been mentioned that the value and the volume of exports from agricultural and raw-material-producing countries were smaller in 1929 than in 1928. But the decline in the value of exports for all agricultural countries of the world (excluding Russia) from $13,202,000,000 to $12,912,000,000 in 1929 does not present the full decline in the value of exports from agricultural countries outside of Europe, because the value of exports from European agricultural countries increased in 1929 as compared with 1928. If we exclude European agricultural countries from the total, then the value of exports from agricultural countries outside of Europe shows a decline from $10,840,000,000 in 1928 to $10,372,000,000 in 1929. The decline took place in countries of all continents except Europe, as may be seen from Table 18.

Yet even the decline from 1928 to 1929 of about half a billion dollars in the value of exports from non-industrial countries outside of Europe does not show the total decline in the value of agricultural exports following the crop of 1929. Analysis of the statistics of international trade by individual countries shows that the value of exports from several countries

AGRICULTURE AND THE DEPRESSION

outside of Europe the exports of which consist mainly of mining products (such, for instance, as Chile, Peru, Bolivia, Venezuela, Mexico, and the Union of South Africa) did not decline in 1929; on the contrary, they increased substantially in most

TABLE 18—EXPORTS FROM AGRICULTURAL COUNTRIES, 1928 AND 1929*
(In millions of dollars)

Continent	1928	1929
North America (excluding U. S.)†	1,433	1,236
South and Central America	3,001	2,934
Oceania	939	915
Asia (excluding Japan)	4,152	3,990
Africa	1,313	1,296
Total	10,840	10,372
Europe	2,364	2,541
World total	13,202	12,912

* Compiled from the statistics of world trade in terms of dollars published in the *Statistical Yearbook* of the League of Nations for 1931-32. Special trade, merchandise only.

† The United States is classified with the industrial countries of the world and hence its exports are not included in the exports from North America. The value of the total exports from the United States increased in 1929 as compared with 1928. However, agricultural exports from the United States, taken separately by agricultural years, show a great decline for 1929-30 as compared with 1928-29. This decline was not only in the value of exports but also in their volume. The differences in the trends of agricultural and other exports from the United States may be seen from the following statistics:

VALUE OF EXPORTS FROM THE UNITED STATES
(In millions of dollars)

Years Beginning July	Total Exports	Agricultural Exports	Per Cent of Agricultural to Total Exports
1924-25	4,778	2,280	47.7
1925-26	4,653	1,892	40.7
1926-27	4,867	1,908	39.2
1927-28	4,773	1,815	38.0
1928-29	5,283	1,847	35.0
1929-30	4,617	1,495	32.4
1930-31	3,031	1,038	34.2

The relative decline in agricultural exports is well illustrated by the percentage of agricultural to total exports, which fell from 47.7 in 1924-25 to 35.0 in 1928-29 (a good agricultural year). During the next agricultural year, 1929-30, which was unfavorable for several crops, particularly wheat, the value of agricultural exports declined more than did that of other exports, and it constituted only 32.4 per cent of the total value of exports. That the decline in the value of agricultural exports in 1929-30 was caused not only by the price decline but also by a decrease in the volume of exports may be seen from the following indexes of the volume of agricultural exports from the United States:

INDEXES OF AGRICULTURAL EXPORTS FROM THE UNITED STATES
(1910-14 = 100)

Year	All Commodities	Grain and Grain Products	All Commodities Excluding Cotton	Cotton Fiber
1924-25	126	225	167	95
1925-26	106	117	123	93
1926-27	136	188	143	131
1927-28	112	188	138	92
1928-29	117	174	141	99
1929-30	97	130	117	82
1930-31	90	104	101	81

The total volume of agricultural exports (excluding as well as including cotton) dropped in 1929-30 by 17 per cent, taking 1928-29 as 100, while the volume of the exports of grains and grain products dropped by 25 per cent.

It thus appears that the United States, considered as an agricultural country, showed the same tendencies as did other agricultural countries outside of Europe. These tendencies were concealed by different tendencies for the industrial production and trade of the United States.

The statistics for agricultural exports are taken from the U. S. Department of Agriculture *Yearbook* for 1932, pp. 858, 860.

cases. Furthermore, the statistics of exports for the calendar year 1929 do not reflect the crop of 1929 only but also the previous year's crop, which was exceptionally good for some products. This applies particularly to the southern hemisphere; there the crop of 1929 was the crop at the end of 1929 and the beginning of 1930, and hence the exports for 1929 reflected for the southern hemisphere the good crop of 1928 and not the poor crop of 1929, which was exported during 1930. The decline in exports from the countries of the southern hemisphere in 1929 was due not to poor crops and small volumes but to the tendency of prices to decline. In 1929 the decline in the prices of wool and hides affected particularly exports from agricultural countries of the southern hemisphere. The decline in the prices of sugar, coffee, and cotton, as well as of some other commodities also affected the value of exports from countries in tropical regions such as Brazil, Cuba, the Dutch East Indies, Egypt, and some others. The poor crop of cereals in 1929 was reflected in the exports of 1929 only for countries of the northern hemi-

AGRICULTURE AND THE DEPRESSION

sphere such as Canada,[1] the exports of which dropped severely in 1929 both in value and in quantity. If, instead of exports for the calendar year 1929, exports for the agricultural year 1929-30 were taken, the effect of the poor crop of 1929 upon exports from agricultural countries outside of Europe would be shown much better and would appear to be of much greater importance than is shown by the statistics of exports for the calendar year 1929.

The great drop in exports from Australia and Argentina in 1930, or during the agricultural year 1929-30, not only in value but also in quantity, shows this quite clearly. The quantity indexes of exports for the three leading wheat-exporting countries are given in Table 19. There was no decline in the

TABLE 19—QUANTITY INDEXES OF EXPORTS FOR ARGENTINA, AUSTRALIA, AND CANADA, 1927-31*

Country	1927	1928	1929	1930	1931
Argentina	100.0	91.9	90.2	65.1	89.9
Australia†	100.0	98.1	107.4	96.2	117.8
Canada‡	100.0	118.9	96.4	84.3	73.6

* *Review of World Trade 1931 and 1932*, Annex I, pp. 71 ff.
† Years ending June 30.
‡ Years beginning April 1.

physical volume of exports from Argentina and Australia until 1930, while in Canada the decline was marked even in 1929. The further decline in the volume of exports from Canada in 1930 wa snot caused by poor crops. Exports of wheat from Canada in 1930 were larger in volume than in 1929. Other (non-agricultural) exports were responsible for the further decline in 1930 and 1931. Argentina and Australia, which are more pronouncedly agricultural countries than Canada, recovered the volume of their exports in the following year (1931), when their crops were more favorable.

[1] The poor crop of 1929 was also reflected in the exports of the United States. See footnote † to Table 18.

Financial Difficulties in Agricultural Countries, 1929-30

Thus, the decline in 1929-30 in the value of exports from agricultural countries outside of Europe reflected two factors: (1) the downward tendency of prices, which had existed for several years, and (2) the decline in the volume of exports because of poor crops in 1929-30, particularly for the leading countries producing and exporting cereals, especially wheat. The combined effect of these two factors was that the exports of agricultural countries outside of Europe declined greatly in 1929-30. This decline in exports for some of the leading agricultural countries outside of Europe was so great and so sudden that it was bound to cause them difficulty in balancing their international payments, because of the very heavy fixed charges connected with their interest and dividend payments abroad. For the principal indebted agricultural countries these payments, even in 1927-28 and 1928-29, were only half covered by export surpluses, and to meet the other half it was necessary to continue borrowing (see the previous section, pp. 60-61).

For the six agricultural countries whose balance of payments was analyzed in the previous section,[1] the balance of merchandise trade (corrected for wrong valuation and contraband) dropped from a credit of $261,000,000 in 1928-29 to a debit of $482,000,000 in 1929-30; that is, it decreased by $743,000,000 in one year. And in 1929-30 the net fixed charges (interest payments) of these countries were $772,000,000. (See Appendix Table 7 and Chart 11.) This means that in 1929-30 a double financial burden was imposed on these countries: In addition to paying their fixed charges—which were normally covered in part by their credit balance of merchandise trade—they were obliged to find means to cover their negative trade balance. If to the above-mentioned six countries is added one other heavily indebted agricultural country—the Dutch East Indies—for which data on the balance of payments are published, then the change in the balance of merchandise trade

---
[1] Canada, Australia, India, Argentina, the Union of South Africa, and New Zealand.

AGRICULTURE AND THE DEPRESSION

for these seven countries from 1928-29 to 1929-30 was from a credit of $491,000,000 to a debit of $347,000,000—a drop of $838,000,000 in one year. (See Appendix Table 7.) Even the countries which are financially strongest could not suffer such a change in their balance of merchandise trade in one year without strain, and the financial position of the above-mentioned countries had already been greatly weakened by the developments of the preceding three years. Moreover, this sudden change in the balance of trade of agricultural countries occurred at a time when the international capital market was already strained by developments in the leading industrial countries of the world, particularly in the United States.

In order to show that the sudden change which took place in 1929-30 in the balance of trade of agricultural countries outside of Europe was caused not only by the tendency of agricultural prices to decline, which affected the values of agricultural exports, but also by the poor crops of 1929, we give below (Table 20) the changes in the balance of trade for three agricultural countries outside of Europe which were particularly affected by the poor crops of 1929.

TABLE 20—BALANCE OF MERCHANDISE TRADE FOR ARGENTINA, AUSTRALIA, AND CANADA, 1927-29
(In millions of dollars)

Country	1927	1928	1929
Argentina *	+199	+115	−103
Australia †	− 32	− 7	−147
Canada	+ 20	+ 16	−234
Total	+187	+124	−484

NOTE: Excess of exports +; excess of imports −.
* Years beginning September 1.
† Years beginning July 1.

The balance of trade for these three countries together changed from a credit of $124,000,000 to a debit of $484,000,000. This means a drop of $608,000,000. Inasmuch as it has been shown that for all of the seven agricultural countries studied the decrease in the balance of trade was only $838,000,000, this means that for the four other countries (India, the Dutch East Indies, the Union of South Africa, and New Zealand) which were not affected by the poor crop of cereals (wheat), the balance of trade changed by only $230,000,000 during this year. It was less favorable in 1929-30 than in 1928-29, but it was still on the credit side. (From +$367,000,000 it dropped to +$137,000,000—see Appendix Table 7.) The drop in the credit balance of these countries was caused by increases in their imports as well as by decreases in the value of their exports due to the falling prices of those agricultural products which were important in their export trade, but their balance of trade was not affected in such a catastrophic way as was that of the three countries which experienced simultaneously poor crops and low prices.

The financial difficulties of agricultural countries resulting from unfavorable developments in their balance of trade and payments coincided with strained conditions in the world capital market caused by the development of economic conditions in industrial countries—by speculation on the New York Stock Exchange and by industrial booms in the leading industrial countries. The generally accepted opinion is that the financial difficulties of agricultural countries were created by the sudden cessation of the flow of foreign loans to them caused by the capital stringency in industrial countries. But, as was shown above, agricultural countries were approaching a critical situation from a much earlier date, and, moreover, the sudden strain in their balance of payments in 1929-30 was due at least as much to the unfavorable crop conditions in that year and the consequent decline in their exports as to difficulties in obtaining new loans in the international capital market because of the capital stringency in industrial countries. The difficulties of agricultural countries were caused not only by the fact that it was not easy in 1929 to obtain new foreign loans in the amounts obtained in previous years but also by the fact that agricultural countries needed greater borrowings to cover their less favorable balance of trade. Moreover, the curtailment of loans to agricultural countries (to some—Argentina, for instance—in the second half of 1928, to others during 1929) was caused not mainly by the

[74]

AGRICULTURE AND THE DEPRESSION

shortage of capital on the international capital market but to a considerable degree also by economic and financial conditions in the agricultural countries themselves. An official analysis of the American market for foreign securities at that time gives the following explanation: "Economic conditions in Latin America were partly responsible for the decline in Latin American security offerings. The exports of corn and the production of wheat by Argentina, two of the most important items in the national economy of that country, declined seriously in 1929. Low coffee and sugar prices seriously affected business in Brazil and Cuba and to some extent in Colombia and Central American Republics. In addition, the appearance of an unfavorable fiscal situation furnished other deterrents to new Latin American issues. As these economic and fiscal developments became more widely known, the prices of Latin American securities already outstanding in the United States declined, diminishing the probabilities for the success of new issues."[1] Similarly, economic and fiscal conditions in Australia affected the confidence of British investors, and consequently Australia had difficulty in floating long-term loans and was obliged to increase its short-term indebtedness from June 30, 1929, to June 30, 1930, by £33,000,000 (about $160,000,000).[2]

Thus, economic and fiscal developments in the agricultural countries themselves made difficult their further borrowing abroad. But, as we know, these "economic and fiscal developments" took place during the several years previous to 1929, while foreign capital was still flowing abundantly. Perhaps just this abundance of capital and credit (during 1927 and 1928) was responsible for magnifying the difficulties of these countries later (in 1929-30). Easy credit from abroad was used by Brazil to carry over large stocks of coffee and thus to support high prices for coffee even when its overproduction was already felt (as early as 1927). Abundance of capital permitted Canada to finance the large carry-over of wheat and so to peg

---

[1] *Handbook of American Underwriting of Foreign Securities*, U. S. Department of Commerce, Trade Promotion Series, No. 104 (Washington, 1930), p. 38.

[2] See *The Crisis in Australian Finance, 1929-31, Documents on Budgetary and Economic Policy*, with introduction by E. O. G. Shann and D. B. Copland (1931), pp. 151 and 159 ff.

wheat prices, which had been tending to fall since 1924-25. Cuba had enough capital to keep from the market its surplus stocks of sugar. Stocks of other commodities (such as cotton and rubber) also were carried with borrowed money. With the development of a relative shortage of capital beginning in the second half of 1928, such financing evidently became more difficult, and it is possible to say that the curtailment of loans was responsible for the drastic decline of prices in 1929-30. But this explains only the last link in a long chain of events. The collapse of 1929-30 was prepared by the more distant and at the same time more fundamental causes discussed above.

Abandonment of the Gold Standard

Even the immediate precipitation of the collapse was caused not only by the financial stringency on the international market in industrial countries but also by special conditions in specific agricultural countries. The great importance for the explanation of the economic collapse in 1929-30 of poor crops in several agricultural countries outside of Europe may be seen from the fact that just those countries which were affected by poor crops experienced financial difficulties the first, and their monetary systems were disorganized earlier than those of other countries. These countries first began to lose their gold reserves. From the previous section we know that during the years preceding 1928 agricultural countries were importing large quantities of gold. Argentina imported $147,000,000 as late as 1927. But, beginning in the second half of 1928, gold began to flow from Argentina. Slight at first, this outward flow became strong after March, 1929. (See Appendix Table 7.) The peso was at a discount even in 1928, but the discount was moderate (below 1 per cent). After the middle of 1929 the peso exchange rate fell rapidly, and by the middle of 1930 the peso had declined to a level 15 per cent below parity with the United States dollar. The conversion office was closed in December, 1929, and gold exports were discontinued.

Australia, because of credit inflation, began to lose gold earlier. From 1925 on, its exports of gold were larger on the average than was its gold extraction, and consequently

AGRICULTURE AND THE DEPRESSION 617

Australia's gold reserves and total stocks of monetary gold declined. But before 1929 these exports were on a moderate scale. After August, 1929, the outward flow of Australian gold became rapid. During the year 1929-30 (July to June) Australia lost $126,000,000 of gold. (See Appendix Table 7.) The Australian pound was discounted as early as 1927-28, but the discount was below 1 per cent. During the second half of 1929 the depreciation of the Australian pound proceeded further, and early in 1930 Australia departed from the gold exchange standard.

Canada, as a gold-producing country, normally exported gold, but with 1928 its gold exports began to exceed its gold extraction, and its reserves declined. This situation continued in 1929, and in some months of the second half of 1929 the Canadian dollar was discounted by more than 1 per cent in terms of United States dollars. Canada was financially stronger than the two above-mentioned countries, and its dollar returned to par in 1930, but the country has not been exactly on the gold standard since 1929.

Thus we see that the three countries most affected by poor crops in 1929 departed first from the gold standard.

Of the larger agricultural countries Brazil was the next to lose its gold reserves because of financial difficulties created by an unfavorable balance of payments. Brazilian currency was not on a real gold basis because there was always an embargo on gold. During the second half of 1929 the milreis was depreciated, and in 1930 Brazil was obliged to lose its gold reserve in order to balance its payments. Brazil was not affected by a shortage of crops in 1929. On the contrary, it had a second record crop of coffee in this year, there having been a huge crop in 1927. But just this second huge crop of coffee resulted in a further increase in the already heavy stocks and caused the collapse of the valorization scheme for Brazilian coffee. Brazil perhaps more than any other agricultural country used its foreign borrowings to carry over excessive stocks of commodities (coffee) and to sustain prices on a level which did not correspond to the relationship between supply and demand. This policy caused strong inflation of all Brazilian economy after

1927 and Brazil was very vulnerable to the changes on the international capital market. The stringency on the capital market made it impossible to finance the new bumper crop of coffee and to keep away from the market the excessively heavy stocks from the two bumper crops. Finally, the price of coffee declined drastically and the balance of payments was upset.[1] (See Chart 5.)

Thus, the financial systems of those countries outside of Europe whose agricultural situation was particularly unfavorable were the first to collapse in 1929-30. The foregoing analysis has shown that it was not financial difficulties which caused the decline of prices preceding the middle of 1929, but rather that the declining agricultural prices caused by the development of the world market for agricultural products created financial strain in these countries which, coupled with unfavorable crops in 1929, brought about the collapse in 1929-30. There is no doubt that once the financial collapse occurred it caused a further decline of prices and that this decline was accelerated after the end of 1929, but the earlier decline of prices had little to do with financial stringency in these countries for they did not experience such a stringency. Credit inflation, not only in the form of an expansion of domestic credit but also in the form of a rapid inflow of foreign capital, was characteristic of these countries during 1927 and 1928 and even during the first half of 1929. Perhaps only the indebted European countries, Germany and the European agricultural countries, experienced financial strain as early as the second half of 1928. Of course, financial stringency in these European countries affected the agricultural countries outside of Europe: the German market for exports of food and raw materials was curtailed with the check on German borrowings, and the efforts of European agricultural countries to improve their balance of payments heightened their competition on the market for agricultural products.

---

[1] The Dutch East Indies did not suffer a drastic collapse in their monetary system, because of the unfavorable development of the world market for their principal agricultural exports (sugar, rubber, etc.). However, they also have been losing their gold reserves since 1927.

AGRICULTURE AND THE DEPRESSION 619

Financial Situation of Agricultural Countries
before 1929

There was no extraordinary financial stringency in countries outside of Europe before the middle of 1929. This may be seen from an analysis of monetary conditions in the leading non-European agricultural countries.

Statistics of commercial banking for these countries[1] show that between 1924 and 1929 the credits extended by commercial banks increased greatly, as may be seen from Table 21.

TABLE 21—DEFLATED INDEXES OF CREDITS (DISCOUNTS, LOANS, AND ADVANCES) EXTENDED BY COMMERCIAL BANKS, 1929*
(As of the end of the year)

Country	1924	1929	
Canada	100	162	
Argentina	100	134	
Brazil	100	151	(1928)
Australia	100	146	
New Zealand	100	122	
Union of South Africa	100	181	

* From data in *Commercial Banks 1913-1929*, pp. 32-35. The indexes are deflated by the national wholesale price indexes for December. For Brazil the gold value of credits is taken for the computation of the index.

In most cases, the credits extended by commercial banks increased by about 50 per cent or more during the five years. Such a rapid growth in the volume of credit suggests that credit inflation rather than a deflationary process took place in practically all the leading agricultural countries outside of Europe. If, in spite of the rapid expansion of credit, the prices of the principal agricultural commodities exported from these countries had a tendency to fall, then the causes of their decline must have been other than monetary factors.

The rapid expansion of credit was reflected in a rapid growth of deposits also, as may be seen from Table 22. The growth of deposits was somewhat slower than the expansion

[1] See *Commercial Banks 1913-1929* published by the League of Nations (Geneva, 1931). In this publication statistics of commercial banking are given for the following important agricultural countries outside of Europe: Canada, Argentina, Brazil, Australia, New Zealand, and the Union of South Africa.

of credit. This was particularly true of sight deposits, the increase in which was substantially less than the increase in credit. In this respect the tendency in agricultural countries was similar to that in all countries of the world during the post-war period. In practically all countries during the post-war period, time or savings deposits increased more rapidly than did demand deposits. At the same time loans and advances increased more rapidly than discounts. Discounts represent chiefly short-

TABLE 22—DEFLATED INDEXES OF DEPOSITS IN COMMERCIAL BANKS AT THE END OF 1929*
(1924 = 100)

Country	Current Accounts and Sight Deposits	Savings and Time Deposits	Total Deposits
Canada	135	128	130
Argentina	115 (in 1928, 124)	149	135
Brazil	142 (1928)	194 (1928)	157 (1928)
Australia	108 (in 1928, 110)	151	132
New Zealand	106	159	130
Union of South Africa	148	174	161

* For the method of deflation see footnote to Table 21.

term credit, while loans and advances as a rule are not self-liquidating in the same sense as are discounts and are generally granted for longer periods. In all countries there was a decisive shift of commercial bank credit from shorter-term to longer-term accounts and a similar, even more marked, shift in deposits. After the war banks devoted less attention than formerly to discount credit and to an increasing extent financed industry by direct advances.

The drop in demand deposits relative to time deposits is generally considered a deflationary factor, but the data presented above on the rapid expansion of credit hardly permit us to conclude that there was monetary deflation in the agricultural countries outside of Europe. Demand deposits were increasing, although more slowly than all forms of credit together, until the end of 1929, when they were on the highest level since 1924.[1]

---
[1] With the exception of Australia and Argentina, where demand deposits at the end of 1929 were lower than at the end of 1928.

AGRICULTURE AND THE DEPRESSION

Neither do the changes in the cash ratios of commercial banks (cash as a percentage of demand deposits or cash as a percentage of total deposits) indicate the development of financial stringency in the agricultural countries under consideration during this period. These ratios are presented in Table 23. In

TABLE 23—CASH RATIOS OF COMMERCIAL BANKS*
(As of the end of the year)

Country	1924	1926	1928	1929
Canada				
Cash as per cent of demand deposits	40.7	37.7	32.7	28.9
Cash as per cent of total deposits	14.1	12.3	11.1	10.1
Argentina				
Cash as per cent of demand deposits	----	----	----	----
Cash as per cent of total deposits	17.7	19.3	22.6	----
Brazil				
Cash as per cent of demand deposits	29.7	31.7	37.8	----
Cash as per cent of total deposits	20.7	21.8	23.7	----
Australia				
Cash as per cent of demand deposits	39.4	43.1	46.1	42.6
Cash as per cent of total deposits	17.7	18.4	18.1	15.9
New Zealand				
Cash as per cent of demand deposits	23.0	23.3	24.0	21.7
Cash as per cent of total deposits	13.8	13.6	12.5	10.9
Union of South Africa				
Cash as per cent of demand deposits	25.5	23.8	20.0	21.6
Cash as per cent of total deposits	14.1	13.6	11.0	11.1

* From *Commercial Banks 1913-1929*, pp. 51-52.

the two most pronouncedly agricultural countries—Argentina and Brazil—the cash ratios even increased during this period. This was in contrast to other countries, for in practically all countries of the world the ratio of cash reserves to total deposits showed a more or less marked tendency to decline during the period.[1] But Argentina and Brazil reinforced their gold reserves during the years 1924-28 by importing large amounts of gold. For Australia and New Zealand the cash ratios were more or less stable until 1929. The cash ratios as of the end of 1929 reflect the difficulties which developed in these countries during the second half of that year. In Canada and the Union

[1] See *Commercial Banks 1913-1929*, p. 55.

of South Africa the ratios of cash reserves declined substantially during these years but not much more than did the cash ratios of most industrial countries during the same period.

Thus, financial conditions in the leading agricultural countries previous to 1929 were not such as would cause prices to fall. There was credit inflation in these countries rather than a deflationary process. But the rapidly increasing inflow of foreign capital and the expansion of domestic credit made the financial situation of these countries very unstable in 1928-29. Their balance of foreign payments was especially endangered by the overexpansion of imports without a corresponding increase of exports. Only a small part of the heavy fixed charges to be paid abroad were covered by the credit balance of merchandise trade even in good years, and when the unfavorable agricultural situation in 1929-30 shifted the balance of trade from the credit to the debit side, the financial systems of the leading agricultural countries collapsed. They were obliged to abandon the gold standard, and, finally, their credit was ruined. After that time financial difficulties created by previous developments became an important factor in the further decline of prices and in an acceleration of the shrinkage of the purchasing power of these countries for goods exported from industrial countries.

THE SPREAD OF DEPRESSION

The balance of trade of the agricultural countries outside of Europe continued to be on the debit side in 1930. Their borrowing abroad recovered early in 1930 but was checked later by the loss of confidence by investors in their solvency. Industrial countries increased greatly their protection of agriculture and thus narrowed the market for agricultural exports. Under the necessity of balancing their trade, the agricultural countries forced large quantities of food and raw materials on this narrowed market. Prices consequently declined greatly and the total value of exports and the purchasing power of agricultural countries shrank in proportion. As a result, the volume of exports of manufactured goods was bound to fall, although prices of manufactured goods were maintained to some extent by control of production. Especially strict control of imports was introduced by the heavily indebted countries (the agricultural countries and some of the industrial countries), and consequently it was the creditor countries whose exports declined most. The entire world trade, especially the trade between agricultural and industrial countries, was strangled. Agricultural production was not curtailed, and agricultural prices fell greatly. Industry maintained better prices, but the volume of production shrank seriously.

Financial Situation of Agricultural Countries in 1930-31

We have seen that there was no indication of the existence before the middle of 1929 of a financial stringency in the agricultural countries outside of Europe which could explain the downward trend of agricultural prices preceding that date. Rather a strong and increasing flow of foreign capital contributed to the maintenance of prices above the level which corresponded to the relationship between supply and demand. The fact that the imports of agricultural countries were increasing more rapidly than their exports indicates that the general level of prices in these countries was sustained at a higher figure than abroad. For some agricultural countries—for instance, Australia—this fact is indisputable.[1] But during the second half of

---

[1] "The Basic Wage Inquiry," Award of the Commonwealth Court of Arbitration, January 22, 1930, from *The Crisis in Australian Finance 1929 to 1931*, p. 109. In this judgment delivered by the court the following statement may be read: "It cannot be disputed that the Australian level (of prices) was sustained

1929 and in 1930, under the combined influence of poor crops in several agricultural countries and the tightening of the international capital market, some of the agricultural countries experienced great financial difficulties, particularly in connection with the balancing of their international payments. These difficulties reflected themselves in prices, and the fall of agricultural prices proceeded at an accelerated rate.

Agricultural countries outside of Europe could not improve their balance of payments in 1930. As was mentioned above, the exports of some agricultural countries, particularly those in the southern hemisphere, declined further in 1930, not only in value but also in volume, because the exports of 1930 reflected the poor crops of 1929. On the other hand, the imports of these countries had been permitted to increase so much up to 1929 that even the drastic curtailment of imports which took place in 1930 could not effect a balancing of the merchandise trade. The balance of merchandise trade for agricultural countries outside of Europe continued to be on the debit side in 1930 and the deficit from this source increased in that year. Consequently, in 1930 these countries had no sources for covering the enormous fixed charges connected with their interest payments abroad. As has been mentioned above, they let their gold reserves flow out, and they borrowed on short-term notice as much as they could. These were only emergency measures, however, and the definite balancing of payments, if further long-term borrowings were checked, could be effected only by swinging the balance of merchandise trade from the debit to the credit side. But this could be done only by pushing exports of agricultural products (food and raw materials) upon the world market, or by curtailing imports (mostly manufactured goods), or by both means. Agricultural countries which were heavily indebted were obliged to follow these lines.

---

at a high figure whilst overseas prices were falling, or had reached a fixed lower level. Our policy to maintain this higher level was largely contributed to by the maintenance of credits in London through borrowed money." The general level of prices reflects all prices, including not only the prices of staple export commodities but also prices in those manufacturing industries which were protected by tariffs.

AGRICULTURE AND THE DEPRESSION 625

The question now arises, why further borrowing of long-term capital by agricultural countries was impossible. Was it because of the shortage of capital on the international capital market, or for some other reasons? We know that during 1929—particularly in the second half of the year—capital stringency on the international capital market in industrial countries was serious indeed, but from the time of the liquidation at the beginning of 1930 of the collapse on the New York Stock Exchange money in the capital markets became much less tight and it was easier to contract new long-term loans and to issue fixed-interest foreign securities. The fact that there was a sufficient supply of capital for foreign loans may be seen from a comparison of the statistics of foreign issues on four principal security markets (the United States, United Kingdom, Netherlands, and Switzerland) during 1930 with the statistics of issues in 1928 and 1929.

TABLE 24—FOREIGN ISSUES ON FOUR PRINCIPAL SECURITY MARKETS, 1928-31*
(In millions of dollars)

Period	1928	1929	1930	1931
First quarter	636.3	584.8	491.7	277.0
Second quarter	754.9	373.5	727.3	169.6
Third quarter	324.7	132.0	184.4	68.1
Fourth quarter	386.4	194.9	304.0	0.5
Total year	2,102.3	1,285.2	1,707.4	515.2

* Data from *Vierteljahrshefte zur Konjunkturforschung*, 6 Jahrgang, Heft 3, Theil A, p. 25. The data for the fourth quarter of 1931 are from the article by F. Sternberg, "Die Weltwirtschaftskrisis," *Weltwirtschaftliches Archiv*, Vol. 36, Heft 1 (July, 1932), p. 131. The figures for 1928 and for the first half of 1929 differ a little from the figures in Table 12 for these respective years. This is evidently the result of a further verification of the currently published statistics of foreign issues, since the source is the same as that on which our previous table is based.

During the first half of 1930 on these four principal markets $1,219,000,000 in foreign securities were issued. This amount was not only 27 per cent above the amount issued during the first half of 1929, when the capital stringency still was not extremely great, but it was practically the same as the amount issued during the first half of 1928, when the foreign securities

[85]

boom was at its peak. For the countries outside of Europe, the issue of securities during the first half of 1930 was even larger than that during the corresponding period of 1928, for the issues for European countries were much smaller in 1930 than in 1928. Thus it appears that at the beginning of 1930 foreign capital was about to resume its large flow into the agricultural countries outside of Europe, and if this flow was checked during the second half of 1930 the reason was not so much the shortage of capital for investment as the economic, fiscal, and political conditions in the agricultural countries themselves. Their departure from the gold standard, their inability to recover their balance of payments by improving their merchandise balances, their fiscal difficulties, and the ensuing political disorders which occurred in several of them (particularly in the Latin American countries) all caused loss of confidence by investors in the solvency of these already heavily indebted agricultural countries, and this stopped the further flow of loans to them. It became evident that it was impossible to continue indefinitely the balancing of the interest payments on previous debts by new borrowings. The impossibility of continuing such a policy became evident in the case of Germany as early as 1928-29. For the agricultural countries outside of Europe, it became clear in 1929-30. The difficulties of agricultural and raw-material-producing countries in paying their fixed charges abroad were augmented because during the boom of foreign securities many loans had been extended for unproductive purposes and it was difficult not only to transfer the interest on them abroad but even to collect the interest in the respective countries. Careless lendings and careless borrowings in 1927 and 1928 were responsible for this. As a result, foreign investors reacted in a convulsive way. The issues of foreign securities during the second half of 1930 were only 40 per cent of those during the first half. They were somewhat larger than the issues had been during the period of severe capital stringency in the second half of 1929, but they were one-third smaller than during the second half of 1928, when foreign issues had already been checked after the boom of the last months of 1927 and the first months of 1928. Consequently, from the second half of 1930, the finan-

AGRICULTURE AND THE DEPRESSION

cial situation of agricultural and raw-material-producing countries, already strained by the unfavorable development of world markets during the year 1929-30, became intolerable. With heavy fixed charges abroad, with exhausted gold reserves, and with accumulated floating debts which they had incurred during 1929-30 to balance their payments, they had no choice but to push to the limit their exports of food and raw materials and to cut to the bone their imports of manufactured goods. But they met extreme difficulty in expanding their exports.

Advance of Agricultural Protection in Industrial Countries

As investors in creditor countries reacted convulsively upon disclosure of the financial weaknesses of the heavily indebted agricultural countries by suddenly curtailing their loans to them, so all industrial countries importing food and raw materials—debtor countries more than creditor ones—reacted convulsively to the efforts of agricultural countries to force upon them their exports of food and raw materials in order to restore their balance of trade. The demand for raw materials naturally declined with the depression in business in industrial countries, but the demand for imported food was artificially strangled by such measures as protective tariffs, restrictions on imports, quotas, and other methods of controlling imports developed since 1929. Agricultural protectionism, re-established by continental European countries about 1925, had been increasing under the pressure of declining prices upon the world market and even by 1928 had been carried further than before the war. But after 1928, agricultural tariff rates in Europe (as also in the United States by the Hawley-Smoot tariff) rose with such kaleidoscopic rapidity that it was impossible for agricultural surplus countries outside of Europe to get their products over these barriers, which were raised each time an attempt was made to surmount them. We shall not try to analyze in detail the changes in agricultural tariff rates and other measures of protection during recent years. They are sufficiently known, and they are too changing to make it worth while to present their detailed history. Merely for the purpose of illustration, we give here a comparison of tariff rates on the major agricultural commodities as they were in Germany during pre-war years, in 1928, and in 1931. The agricultural protection policy of Germany presents perhaps the extreme in this development, because Germany under the pressure of reparations and foreign debts was obliged to curtail its imports of agricultural commodities the most, but other industrial countries of the European continent (such as France, Italy, Czechoslovakia, and others) followed Germany rather closely. An international comparison of tariff rates on the principal agricultural commodities would show this.[1]

Table 25 compares German tariff rates in the years preceding the war, in 1928, and in 1931. Whereas in 1928 the tariff

TABLE 25—GERMAN TARIFF RATES ON IMPORTANT AGRICULTURAL COMMODITIES*
(In RM per quintal)

Commodities	1906-14	1928	May 15, 1931
Wheat	5.50	5.00	25.00
Rye	5.00	5.00	20.00
Fodder, barley	1.30	2.00	18.00
Barley for brewing	4.00	5.00	20.00
Corn (maize)	3.00	2.50	Monopoly
Beef cattle	8.00	16.00	27.50
Pigs	9.00	16.00	40.00
Beef	27.00	37.50	55.00
Pork	27.00	32.00	55.00
Butter	20.00	27.50	50.00
Eggs	2.00	5.00	5.00
Cheese	15.00	20.00	20.00

* From the data in *Die deutsche Landwirtschaft* by Max Sering and others (Berlin, 1932), pp. 832, 840.

rates on grains were about on the pre-war level, by the spring of 1931 they had increased from four to nine times. The tariff rates on live stock and animal products, on the other hand, were much higher in 1928 than before the war. Protectionism for

---

[1] See for instance "Die wichtigsten landwirtschaftlichen Zolle des Auslandes," Zusammengestellt von Dr. Walter and Dr. Engel. *Berichte uber Landwirtschaft.* Neue Folge. 42 Sonderheft (Berlin, 1931). Also, *Handbook of Foreign Tariffs and Import Regulations on Agricultural Products*, Part V, U. S. Department of Commerce, Trade Promotion Series, No. 131, pp. 4-5.

AGRICULTURE AND THE DEPRESSION 629

animal husbandry was much more pronounced in the post-war than in the pre-war period. By 1931 this protectionism had developed further, and tariff rates on animals and animal products were in 1931 two, three, and four times as high as the pre-war rates. And it should not be overlooked that tariff protection of agriculture was not the only means used to curtail imports at that time nor even the strongest one. The whole arsenal of various means of protection was used in addition, such as quota systems, limitations on the use of imported cereals by flour mills, misused veterinary control on frontiers, regulation and rationing of foreign exchange, and monopoly of imports. These drastic measures suddenly applied by industrial countries to curtail their imports of food and other agricultural products stimulated their domestic agricultural production and caused further replacement of imported food by domestically produced food. The overproduction of the principal agricultural commodities, which existed even before 1929, was thus increased, and agricultural surplus countries outside of Europe, in attempting to push their exports, met narrower and narrower markets for their products. This was evidently bound to affect the prices of these products.

Foreign Trade during the Depression

The situation of agricultural countries outside of Europe was exceptionally unfavorable in 1930, as it had been in 1929, because European agricultural countries, acting under the same pressure, were throwing upon the markets of industrial countries their surpluses, which, because of favorable crops, were as large in 1930 as they had been in 1929. As may be seen from the tabulations given below, the physical volume of exports from European agricultural countries was substantially larger in 1930 than in 1929, though the value of their exports was smaller because of the drastic price decline. (See also Chart 12.) The U. S. S. R. had in 1930 an exceptionally favorable crop year, and was able to increase its exports, particularly of wheat, in 1930 and 1931, dumping its surpluses at low prices and spoiling once more the market for agricultural products from the non-European countries. Under such conditions, the efforts of

[89]

these countries to expand their exports were bound to be unsuccessful, at least so far as the value of their exports was concerned. Some of the over-sea countries (particularly those in the southern hemisphere) succeeded in increasing the physical volume of their exports in 1931 but at such low prices that the value of their exports was much smaller. There remained nothing

TABLE 26—DOLLAR VALUE OF EXPORTS AND IMPORTS FROM AGRICULTURAL AND INDUSTRIAL COUNTRIES, 1929-31*
(In millions of dollars)

Group of Countries	1929	1930	1931	1931 when 1929 = 100
European industrial				
Exports	13,011	10,911	8,058	61.9
Imports	16,166	13,710	10,313	63.8
All industrial				
Exports	19,137	15,400	10,983	57.4
Imports	21,505	17,654	12,994	60.4
European agricultural (ex. Russia)				
Exports	2,541	2,375	1,619	63.7
Imports	3,067	2,646	1,835	59.8
All agricultural (ex. Russia)				
Exports	12,912	10,129	7,093	54.9
Imports	12,946	10,227	6,893	53.2
Seven industrial creditor countries				
Exports	13,241	10,412	7,050	53.3
Imports	15,113	12,679	9,540	63.1

* From the statistics of world trade (recorded values, special trade, merchandise only) by countries published in the *Review of World Trade 1931 and 1932* (*First Half*), pp. 24-25. See Appendix Tables 1 and 2.

for the over-sea agricultural countries to do but control their imports of manufactured goods, using the same means which European industrial countries had applied in curtailing their imports of agricultural goods. And this they did after 1930. In this they were preceded by the European agricultural countries, which had experienced financial difficulties earlier—in 1928-29. Thus, the international trade of the whole world was strangled. Table 26 presents quantitatively the development of world trade during the depression, subdividing it between the groups of countries which have been used in the analysis of the

AGRICULTURE AND THE DEPRESSION

development of international trade during prosperity. As the flow of international capital ceased to rise and began rapidly to fall, it is not surprising that the development in the exports and imports of agricultural and of industrial countries shows characteristics just opposite to those observed during the period of prosperity.

The value of foreign trade declined greatly during the two years of depression for agricultural countries and for industrial countries as well. However, the foreign trade of agricultural and raw-material-producing countries suffered the more. Generally speaking, the trade of countries outside of Europe—agricultural as well as industrial—suffered more than did that of European countries. Of especial interest is the fact that there was a difference in the relative intensity of the decline of exports and of imports between industrial and agricultural countries. For agricultural countries the value of imports declined more than did that of exports and so these countries recovered somewhat their balance of trade during the depression. For industrial countries, on the other hand, the value of exports declined more than did the value of imports, and their balances of merchandise trade became less favorable. These

TABLE 27—RATIOS OF EXPORTS TO IMPORTS (IN DOLLAR VALUES), 1929-31*

Group of Countries	1929	1930	1931
European industrial	80.5	79.6	78.1
All industrial	89.0	87.2	84.5
Industrial creditor countries	87.6	82.1	73.9
European agricultural	82.9	89.8	88.2
All agricultural	99.7	98.6	102.9

* See also Appendix Table 5.

tendencies were just opposite to those which characterized the development of exports and imports for agricultural and for industrial countries during the period of prosperity, 1925-29. Table 27 shows the changes which occurred in the ratio of exports to imports for different groups of countries.

During the years 1925-29 the ratio of exports to imports for agricultural countries declined substantially and finally the balance of merchandise trade became unfavorable—in 1929.

During the years of depression it recovered, and in 1931 it became favorable once more. For European agricultural countries the balance of trade recovered earlier—in 1930—for countries outside of Europe, only in 1931. Being debtor nations, agricultural and raw-material-producing countries were obliged to achieve this balancing of their trade at the same time that the flow of foreign capital to them was decreasing. This flow had helped them to balance their payments during the period of prosperity but now they had to balance their payments without such help. However, despite all the efforts of the agricultural countries, the improvement in the balance of merchandise trade was not sufficiently great. The ratio of exports to imports for all agricultural and raw-material-producing countries in 1931 was only 102.9, as compared with 113.0 in 1925. The credit balance of merchandise trade for these countries was only $200,000,000 in 1931, whereas in 1925 it had been about $1,500,000,000. It is not surprising that, having no other source out of which to pay the interest on the foreign debts which they had incurred earlier, many agricultural countries defaulted in 1931 and in 1932, that their credit was completely ruined, and that the flow of foreign capital to them definitely ceased. Indeed, an outward movement or flight of capital took place whenever possible, and many agricultural countries were obliged to check this movement, introducing one kind or another of moratorium or "standstill" agreement.

The fact that among the industrial countries also there were several heavily indebted countries—notably Germany—conceals to some degree the opposite tendency in the development of the exports and imports of industrial countries. Generally speaking, their balance of merchandise trade became less favorable, and the ratio of exports to imports for all industrial countries of the world declined from 89.0 in 1929 to 84.5 in 1931. But the ratio for Germany increased during this period from 94.2 (excluding reparations in kind) to 136.8, and for Italy from 70.3 to 86.2. Taking only creditor industrial countries (six countries in Europe and the United States), we find that the decline in the value of their exports was much greater than that of their imports. The value of the exports of industrial

AGRICULTURE AND THE DEPRESSION 633

creditor countries declined even more than the value of the exports of agricultural and raw-material-producing countries. Their debit balance of merchandise trade was $2,500,000,000 in 1931. But even with such a negative balance of merchandise trade, gold was flowing to the creditor countries, because, after the world credit crisis in the middle of 1931, all foreign investment of capital (short-term as well as long-term) practically stopped, as may be seen from Table 24, and all creditors tried to bring home what they could from their short-term investments abroad.

During the depression it was not primarily the agricultural or industrial character of a country, but its creditor or debtor status that determined the development of exports relative to imports. The pressure of debts obliged countries to push exports and curtail imports. Indebted industrial countries such as Germany acted in the same way as indebted agricultural countries. During the period of prosperity the situation was different: In the years 1925-29 exports were increasing more rapidly than imports not only for creditor industrial countries financing their exports through foreign loans, but also for industrial debtor countries such as Germany. All industrial countries (with the exception, perhaps, of Great Britain, whose position was special) were rapidly developing their exports of manufactured goods, more rapidly than they were increasing their imports of agricultural goods (food and raw materials). During the depression the indebted industrial countries were forced to continue pressing their exports upon the world market and, at the same time, to curtail their imports. Creditor countries were less pressed to do this and their imports declined less than their exports.

But if during the depression there was a similarity in the position of all debtor countries—agricultural as well as industrial—there were important differences between the two last groups which are concealed in the statistics of the value of foreign trade, because these statistics reflect changes both in the volume of trade and in the prices of commodities.

The fact that agricultural prices (of both food and raw materials) declined during the depression much more than did

[93]

prices of manufactured goods affected in different ways the exports and imports of industrial and agricultural countries. Food and raw materials are exported by agricultural countries, and a decline in their prices diminishes the value of the exports of these countries, while in the case of industrial countries food and raw materials are primarily imported and their low prices make for a smaller value of imports. A quantitative measure of the importance of this fact may be derived from the following data on the changes in the gold prices of exports and imports for agricultural and for industrial countries (Table 28).

TABLE 28—GOLD PRICE INDEXES OF EXPORTS AND IMPORTS, 1927-31*
(1927 = 100)

Group of Countries	1927	1928	1929	1930	1931
European industrial countries					
Exports	100.0	99.3	96.3	90.0	75.0
Imports	100.0	100.4	97.8	85.0	65.8
European agricultural countries (including Russia)					
Exports	100.0	99.9	98.4	83.6	63.4
Imports	100.0	99.3	98.8	86.0	71.5
Agricultural countries outside of Europe					
Exports	100.0	99.7	94.0	75.3	54.8
Imports	100.0	95.5	92.7	82.9	67.0

* Computed as weighted averages from the gold price indexes of exports and imports for individual countries as they were published in Annex II to the *Review of World Trade 1931 and 1932* (*First Half*). As weights were taken the values of the exports and the imports (respectively) for each country for the period 1926-29. European industrial countries include: France, Germany, the United Kingdom, Italy, Switzerland, Sweden, and Czechoslovakia; European agricultural countries include: Denmark, Estonia, Finland, Hungary, the Irish Free State, Latvia, Russia, and Yugoslavia; agricultural countries outside of Europe: Canada, Argentina, Uruguay, Australia, New Zealand, India, the Dutch East Indies, China, French Indo-China, British Malaya, the Union of South Africa, and Algeria. See also Appendix Table 9.

For industrial countries the prices of imports declined much more than did the prices of exports; for agricultural countries, on the other hand, the prices of exported goods declined more than did those of imported goods. For this reason, statistics of the value of foreign trade do not represent fully the contraction of the exports of industrial countries relative to their

AGRICULTURE AND THE DEPRESSION 635

imports nor the curtailment of imports into agricultural countries as compared with their exports. The quantity indexes of exports and imports present more clearly the true relationship between exports and imports for agricultural and for industrial countries. It was possible to compute such indexes for representative groups of industrial countries and for agricultural countries outside of Europe. The sample from agricultural European countries is perhaps less representative but it is also of interest, because it shows some differences between the position of European agricultural countries and that of the countries outside of Europe.

The quantity indexes of exports and of imports illustrate first of all that the volume of world trade during the depression generally declined much less than the statistics of value may suggest. This relates particularly to the volume of foreign trade in food and raw materials, which are exported mostly by agricultural and raw-material-producing countries and are imported by industrial countries. The quantity indexes show a rather surprising stability of foreign trade as represented by the exports from agricultural countries and the imports of industrial countries. The volume of exports from industrial countries, consisting mostly of manufactured goods, declined greatly, however, and this decline was reflected also in the imports of agricultural countries. Table 29 illustrates these facts. (See also Chart 12.)

The volume of trade in agricultural commodities (food and raw materials), as indicated by the imports of industrial and the exports of agricultural countries, did not increase much during the period of prosperity, but neither did it decline extremely during the depression. On the other hand, the volume of foreign trade in manufactured goods—as represented by the exports from industrial countries and the imports of agricultural countries—developed rapidly during the period of prosperity and fell off greatly during the depression (by one-fourth or one-third in two years).

The statistics of foreign trade in terms of value show only slight differences in the decline of exports and of imports for either agricultural or industrial countries. The quantity indexes demonstrate that the imports of agricultural countries declined greatly while their volume of exports remained more or less stable and that, on the other hand, exports from industrial countries shrank greatly in volume although these countries continued to import in about the same quantities as before. In other words, agricultural and industrial countries reacted quite differently to the changed business conditions. Agricultural

TABLE 29—QUANTITY INDEXES OF EXPORTS AND IMPORTS BY GROUPS OF COUNTRIES, 1927-31*
(1927 = 100)

Group of Countries	1927	1928	1929	1930	1931	
					1927 =100	1929 =100
European industrial countries (7)						
Exports	100.0	105.2	111.2	96.6	85.7	77.1
Imports	100.0	101.2	105.5	102.9	98.9	93.7
United States						
Exports	100.0	104.9	107.5	87.2	69.6	64.7
Imports	100.0	100.9	114.8	98.0	87.8	76.5
Agricultural countries outside of Europe (12)						
Exports	100.0	104.9	102.1	93.8	91.5	87.2
Imports	100.0	109.5	113.0	97.7	77.4	68.5
European agricultural countries (excluding Russia)						
Exports	100.0	102.5	113.6	116.3	108.9	95.9
Imports	100.0	108.0	108.6	109.7	98.5	90.7
European agricultural countries (including Russia)						
Exports	100.0	103.0	116.5	136.9	137.5	118.0
Imports	100.0	114.5	110.4	—	—	—

* For the method of computation of the quantity indexes of exports and imports and the countries included, see the footnotes to Appendix Table 3.

countries, pressed by the necessity of meeting the fixed charges on their heavy obligations abroad, exported as much as they could from their surpluses of food and raw materials, the supply of which was inelastic, and in this way spoiled their markets. To get their exports upon the markets of industrial countries, they were obliged to accept low prices in order to surmount the rapidly rising tariff barriers. Accordingly, even though the volume of exports from agricultural countries remained more or less stable, there was a great decline in the value of their

[96]

AGRICULTURE AND THE DEPRESSION

CHART 12—QUANTITY INDEXES OF THE FOREIGN TRADE
OF INDUSTRIAL AND AGRICULTURAL COUNTRIES
(1927 = 100)

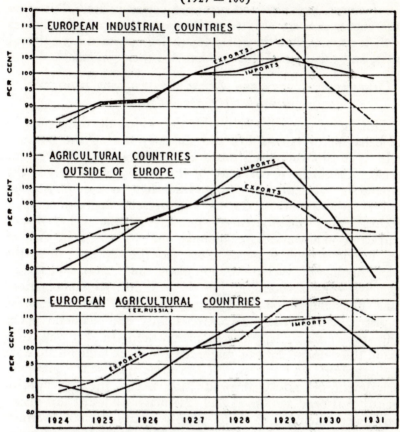

SOURCE OF DATA: Appendix Table 3.

exports. It was impossible for these countries, through their exports, to improve their balance of trade, and they were forced to curtail the volume of their imports, consisting mostly of manufactured goods. Industrial countries, meeting narrowed markets for their exports of manufactured goods, adjusted their supply to the demand by contracting their production and exporting smaller volumes of their products but at more stable prices. Only those industrial countries which had exceptionally heavy financial burdens abroad, such as Germany, forced on the world market consistently large volumes of their exports of manufactured products and accepted lower prices.[1] But even these countries were able to maintain relatively higher prices for their exports than they paid for their imports of agricultural goods, and this helped them to balance their payments.

Differences between Agriculture and Industry during the Depression

During the present world-wide depression the differences in the behavior of agriculture and industry during the business cycle have probably been more evident than in any previous period. The inelastic character of the supply of, as well as the demand for agricultural commodities has been demonstrated with especial plainness during the present depression. The production of manufactured goods, on the other hand, contracted in a convulsive manner not witnessed in any of the previous depressions. Perhaps the spread and the strengthening of various monopolistic combinations in industry have been responsible for this. Industrial combinations think of stabilization of business in terms of stabilization of prices, and in order to control supply and maintain prices they stop at no curtailment of production. In this way, they curtail the demand for raw materials and cause wide fluctuations in the volume of business. At the same time such convulsive curtailment of industrial production makes the demand for agricultural products (food and raw materials) still less elastic and lowers their prices. The supply of agricultural products during the present depression has been particularly inelastic, perhaps because just before the collapse there were several unsuccessful experiments with the "control" of the supply of agricultural products. Agricultural producers tried to apply in

---

[1] When we say exports were "forced" on the world market because of heavy financial burdens abroad, we understand a complex mechanism of private economic relations which cause such a pressure. Private enterprises indebted abroad are affected directly; under obligation to pay interest abroad, they are forced to export in order to get exchange. Public institutions which are unable to balance their budgets by new foreign borrowing are obliged to secure new taxes and in this way shift their burden upon private enterprises.

AGRICULTURE AND THE DEPRESSION

agriculture the methods of controlling the market used in industry, but in most cases they were unsuccessful. It is much more difficult to achieve such monopoly control in agriculture, with the biological character of its production and its multitude of small independent enterprises, than in a highly centralized industry. So the attempt at monopolization in agriculture succeeded merely in keeping surplus stocks away from the market without effecting any control of production, but rather stimulating it. When finally all these schemes of valorization collapsed, agricultural producers were faced with markets still more disorganized than they had been before these attempts were made at "controlling" supply.

Competition between agriculture in the Old World—in Europe—and in the new countries outside of Europe also may have been responsible for the extremely severe crisis in agriculture. Table 29 shows that the volume of exports from European agricultural countries in 1930 and in 1931 was on a much higher level than during the period of prosperity. These statistics do not reflect the increase of agricultural production in European industrial countries importing agricultural products, but we know that, under the influence of extreme agricultural protectionism, these countries increased their domestic agricultural production substantially and continued to increase it during the years of depression and heavy agricultural overproduction.

Agricultural countries outside of Europe have been in a particularly unfavorable situation during the present depression. The unfavorable crops of 1929-30 outside of Europe, coincident with good crops in European countries, have already been mentioned. But other conditions also were unfavorable for the countries outside of Europe. They are much more dependent upon the world market than are the European agricultural countries and, since the depression was caused and greatly magnified by the crisis in world trade, the surplus countries outside of Europe were chiefly affected. They cannot help themselves by adopting a policy of isolation, using tariff barriers and other means, as some of the European countries are trying to do, and the only solution for their difficulties lies in re-establishing the world economy and the flow of capital and goods which stopped so suddenly after the collapse of 1929. Those industrial countries, such as the United States and Great Britain, which depend, in their exports of manufactured goods, chiefly upon the agricultural and raw-material-producing countries outside of Europe, have experienced the greatest difficulties with their exports, because of the extreme decline in the purchasing power of these countries. The re-establishment of their exports of manufactured goods is largely dependent on the recovery of the agricultural countries outside of Europe.

DEBT AND DEFAULT IN THE 1930s

Causes and Consequences*

Barry EICHENGREEN
Harvard University, Cambridge, MA 02138, USA

Richard PORTES
University of London, London, WC1E 7HX, UK

This paper studies interwar experience with external debt and default. It begins with a description of the contours of international borrowing and lending in the 1920s. We then use some empirical models from recent literature on the 1970s to describe the interwar data. Macroeconomic variables for over 20 countries are related to cross-section variations in borrowing and debt during the period from the end of the 1920s to 1938. The paper then considers the incidence and correlates of sovereign default for 1934–1938, using regression to determine the association between standard measures of economic structure and performance and subsequent interruptions to debt service. Such variables as the magnitude of the debt burden, the deterioration of the terms of trade during the Great Depression, and the stance of monetary and fiscal policies provide a remarkably accurate explanation of the incidence of default. We go on to provide a long-run perspective on default and on the remedies available to creditors. The provisions of loan contracts are reviewed with an eye toward analyzing the scope for renegotiation. The discussion emphasizes the contrast between the regime of bond finance that prevalied in the interwar years and the current regime of bank lending. We analyze the roles of governments, banks and bondholders' protective committees in the negotiation process. We then present new estimates of the ex post realized rates of return on British and American foreign lending in the 1920s. This empirical analysis uncovers a striking contrast in the returns realized on loans floated in the two countries: while the (nominal) internal rate of return on dollar loans was less than 1% per annum, the comparable return on sterling loans was in excess of 5%. The paper concludes with a discussion of factors which help to account for this dramatic difference.

1. Introduction

Observers familiar with the history of international lending approach the 'debt crisis' of the 1980s with a sense of deja vu. The debt-servicing difficulties experienced in recent years by many Latin American and Eastern

---

*Prepared for the International Seminar on Macroeconomics, 23–25 June 1985. We are grateful for advice from Stephen Yeo and for the research assistance of Steve Martin and Chris Martin in London and of Hugh Aller, Susie Kim and Kathy Vigna in Cambridge. Our discussants at ISOM offered helpful comments, some of which we have been able to implement in revising the paper. Carlos Diaz-Alejandro was to be one of the discussants; we can only imagine how much he would have improved the paper had he been able to attend.

European nations represent only the latest in a series of similar episodes stretching back over a period of centuries. Not infrequently did the problems encountered by sovereign borrowers culminate in default, the widespread defaults of the 1930s being merely the most dramatic and generalized instance of a repeated phenomenon. Quite often, defaulting debtors were able to re-enter the international capital market only to default again, occasioning criticism of creditors for engaging in reckless lending ascribed to myopia or excessive competition.

The widespread defaults of the 1930s offer the most suggestive precedent for recent difficulties. In the 1930s as in the 1980s, illiquidity was not confined to any one country or region. In neither instance can the problems experienced by external debtors be attributed exclusively to domestic economic and political developments; rather, they must be linked to disturbances to the world economy including, in each instance, real interest rate shocks, commodity price fluctuations and exceptionally severe recessions in industrialized regions. The extent of the parallels has tempted many observers to see in recent developments the potential for a replay of the collapse of international capital markets witnessed in the 1930s.

Skeptics object that institutional arrangements governing international lending have changed so fundamentally that interwar experience contains few meaningful lessons for the 1980s. Perhaps the most prominent institutional innovation is the switch from bond to bank finance, a development which, by changing the provisions of loan contracts and reducing the number of creditors party to negotiations, is said to facilitate rescheduling of debt as an alternative to outright default. The International Monetary Fund now provides illiquid borrowers an external lender of last resort which at the same time serves the capital market in a signalling capacity, providing information on domestic adjustment programs. Analogous to the foundation of an international lender of last resort, the establishment of domestic lenders of last resort, the spread of deposit insurance and the implementation of macroeconomic stabilization policies are said to have diminished significantly the likelihood of a business cycle downturn on the scale of the Great Depression, thereby reducing the danger that borrowing countries will again be so severely affected by vicissitudes in the industrialized world.

In the absence of a systematic analysis of the interwar record with which recent developments might be compared, it is difficult to determine the relevance of this historical experience to recent difficulties in international capital markets. To provide a basis for comparison, this paper sets out to analyze the pattern of borrowing, the incidence of default and the returns realized by foreign lenders. Its first part describes the contours of international lending in the 1920s and 1930s. Drawing on work by Eaton and Gersovitz (1981) and other investigators of the experience of the 1970s, we use regression analysis to summarize cross-section variations in the pattern and magnitude of sovereign indebtedness. The next part of the paper considers the incidence and correlates of default, estimating variants of modern models of debt capacity to explore the extent of association between standard measures of economic structure and performance and subsequent interruptions to debt service. In the final part of the paper we provide a long-run perspective on default and on the remedies available to creditors. The provisions of loan contracts are reviewed with an eye toward analyzing the scope for renegotiation. We then present new estimates of the rate of return on foreign loans floated in the 1920s, disaggregating these estimates between loans in default and loans in good standing as a way of constructing a measure of the costs of default as incurred by lenders, and comparing realized rates of return on loans made in different years, to different countries and to different classes of borrowers.

We are conscious that this paper only skims the surface of a topic with many additional dimensions deserving exploration. Our defence is that establishing the quantitative dimensions of international borrowing and lending in the 1920s is a necessary precondition for analyzing other quantitative and qualitative aspects of the problem certain to be of interest. In the concluding section to this paper, we therefore indicate the most promising directions for research.

2. Who were the lenders?

Between the wars, international lending remained the almost exclusive preserve of the United States and a few countries of Northwest Europe. Of the long-term foreign investments outstanding in 1938, the vast majority were assets of the United States, United Kingdom, The Netherlands, France, Switzerland and Belgium. The U.S. and U.K. alone accounted for nearly 2/3 of the gross value of long-term foreign investments (inclusive of foreign loans, corporate securities and direct investments but excluding war debts and reparations).[1] Hence interwar trends and fluctuations in foreign investment are largely trends and fluctuations in American and British lending.

No country had as illustrious if controversial a history of foreign lending as the United Kingdom. The traditional figures suggest that more than 55%

---

[1] 65.1% to be exact. These figures are from Lewis (1945, pp. 48–50). Note that foreign investment in the U.S. and U.K. has not been netted out from the totals. Since the ratio of long-term liabilities to assets was 61% for the U.S. but only 5% for the U.K., netting out inward investment would change the picture somewhat for the U.S. but not the U.K. While these statistics are the best available, they are not without their limitations. The most serious is the omission of short-term lending, on which adequate information is not available. Although Lewis (1945, p. 7) warns that some direct investments may simply have been missed in compiling the totals, a more serious source of bias is likely to be the fact that bonds were valued at par. This is problematic for bonds in default which traded at a considerable discount. On the other hand, the market value of many direct investments was considerably above book value in 1938. For Britain at least, Lewis suggests, the two sources of error roughly cancel out.

of total British investment in the period 1871–1913 was directed overseas.[2] World War I occasioned a considerable liquidation of Britain's external assets, and in the second half of the 1920s the share of new capital issues for overseas borrowers declined from its prewar range in excess of 50% to 37–44% before slumping to very much lower levels in the 1930s. Nonetheless, in 1938 Britain's gross-external-asset-to-gross-national-product ratio remained an impressive 79%.[3] Of these investments, half were placed in Empire countries and 15% in each of North and South America, with the remainder split evenly between Europe and Asia–Oceania. Fifty-eight percent of total overseas new issues floated between 1920 and 1934 was comprised of public borrowing and 7% of railway bonds, with the remainder allocated to sundry industrial and commercial ventures. British imperial lending was disproportionately concentrated in government bonds, foreign lending in other assets.[4]

Tight credit conditions in London and official restrictions on the export of capital combined to encourage foreign borrowers who had traditionally floated new issues in Britain to turn increasingly to the United States. Except for British Dominions and colonies upon whose borrowing the Colonial Stock Act of 1900 conferred preferential treatment or who continued to borrow in London for political as much as economic reasons, for much of the 1920s London and New York were in very real competition in the floatation of overseas loans.[5] For the United States, large-scale foreign lending was a recent development. The long-term-foreign-asset/national-income ratio of the United States was still less than 9% on the eve of World War I.[6] In contrast to Britain, America's foreign assets doubled over the course of the war and, after fluctuating in the immediate postwar years,

---

[2] These traditional figures have been criticized by Platt (1984) for making unduly conservative assumptions about the repatriation of foreign funds and hence for overestimating the value of outstanding stocks. But if the required adjustments would moderate the apparent dominance of overseas assets in British portfolios, they would still fail to alter the picture of Britain's prewar dominance in international capital markets.

[3] Long-term assets only, from Lewis (1945), are included in the numerator, while Feinstein's (1972) estimate of GNP at market prices comprises the denominator.

[4] In the case of non-governmental lending, just over half the total took the form of bonds and slightly under half the form of shares. These figures from Royal Institute (1937) are based on calculations by Robert Kindersley, published annually in the *Economic Journal*.

[5] The Colonial Stock Act enabled certain trusts to invest in the bonds of colonial but not foreign governments. If a trust was not governed by specific instructions about assets in which to invest, statute limited foreign investments to East India stock, English corporations with direct foreign investments, guaranteed Indian railways, and registered and inscribed stocks of colonial governments. The importance of these restrictions has been questioned on the grounds that the vast majority of trusts were in fact governed by specific instructions and defended on the grounds that in the 1920s foreign governments and municipalities which attempted to borrow in London were forced to pay at least $1\frac{1}{2}$% and up to $2\frac{1}{2}$% more than comparable entities within the Empire. See Edelstein (1981, p. 83).

[6] Foreign asset estimates are those of Lewis (1945), while GNP is from U.S. Department of Commerce (1976). If Dunn's (1926, p. 3) estimates of foreign assets are preferred, the ratio is still lower.

soared in the mid-'twenties. Compared to their British counterparts, American investors exhibited a stronger preference for direct over portfolio investments. Still, some 40% of American long-term foreign assets took the form of portfolio investment, of which 2/3 were government securities.[7] In contrast to Britain, where considerations of empire dominated, the geographical distribution of American investment seems to have been influenced if not governed by considerations of proximity. Nearly 40% of total American foreign investment was in Canada, 30% in Latin America and the West Indies and 20% in Europe, with the residual scattered across Africa, Asia and Oceania.[8]

Fig. 1 depicts the pattern of American foreign lending in the interwar years. In the 1920s it is dominated by the steady increase in new lending,

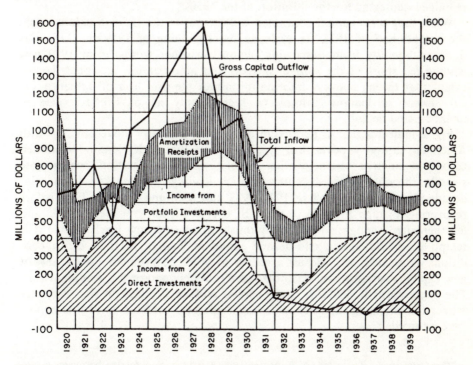

Fig. 1. Income and amortization receipts from United States long-term foreign investments and gross capital outflow, 1920–40. (*Source*: Foreign Investment Experience of the United States, 1920–1940, Bureau of Foreign and Domestic Commerce, 19 March 1945, Mimeo.)

[7] For information on the composition of U.S. portfolio investment circa 1930, see Royal Institute (1937, p. 189).
[8] Considerations other than proximity also influenced the international distribution of American loans. Before the War, for example, investment in the West Indies and northern portions of Latin America was actively promoted by the State Department as a way of minimizing European financial influence in the region. See Angell (1933).

which was maintained in each year between 1920 and 1927 with the exception of 1923, when France's occupation of the Ruhr and attendant political uncertainties increased the perceived riskiness of foreign investment. Conclusion of the Locarno Pact and successful placement of the Dawes Loan in 1924 signalled full recovery of the international capital market, which continued to expand until 1928 when its growth was stifled by the portfolio shift toward domestic assets associated with the Wall Street boom. By 1929 new foreign lending had fallen back to 1924 levels, before recovering slightly in 1930 following the collapse of the stock market. In 1931, with the further deterioration of economic conditions and the first defaults abroad, lending slumped to near-negligible levels, with Canada the only remaining major foreign borrower. By 1932 even Canadian loans had dried up, and lending remained depressed for the duration of the 1930s.

While long-term capital continued to flow out of the U.S. on balance until the second half of 1931, as early as the beginning of 1929 the U.S. was draining liquidity from borrowing regions; in other words, from 1929 new lending fell short of the sum of interest and amortization receipts.[9] To the extent that timing conveys information about the direction of influence, the curtailment of lending cannot be seen simply as passive response to unanticipated default.

Fig. 2 indicates that U.K. foreign investment generally moved in step with American capital exports, but it also shows that U.K. lending exhibited certain distinctive characteristics. Unlike American lending, which rose steadily throughout the 'twenties, British lending was marked by a mid-decade slump, levelling off in 1922–1923 and declining through 1925 before recovering through 1927. As in the U.S., overseas lending peaked in 1928 and fell thereafter, though not as precipitously or to such low levels. While it is tempting to ascribe the mid-decade slump in lending to tight credit conditions associated with Britain's return to gold, government policy toward new capital issues for overseas borrowers probably played the dominant role. The fluctuations in Britain's gross capital outflow depicted in Fig. 2 closely mirror the changing intensity with which informal controls on capital export were inforced.[10]

---

[9]This 'cross-over point', after which the debt-service obligations of foreign borrowers exceed the value of new lending, is given considerable emphasis in recent accounts of sovereign borrowing in the 1980s. According to Kaletsky (1985, Table 2.1), the recent cross-over point was 1982–1983. Note that the reason the gross outflow in table 1 appears to turn negative in 1937 and 1940 is that American direct foreign investment is included on a net basis, since these are the only estimates available.

[10]Of course, the two explanations for the stagnation of British capital exports are not incompatible, since restrictions on capital exports were imposed largely to strengthen the exchange rate and ease the transition back to the prewar parity. See Moggridge (1971). Short descriptions of these regulations and their changing nature are provided by Richardson (1936) and Cairncross and Eichengreen (1983).

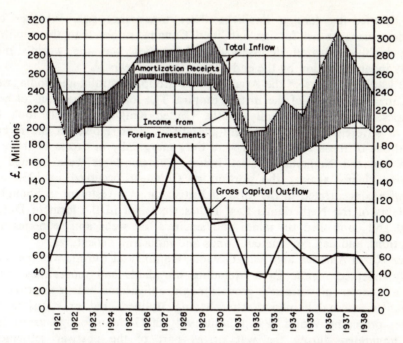

Fig. 2. Income and amortization receipts from United Kingdom foreign investments and gross capital outflow, 1920–38. [*Source*: Sayers (1976, vol. III, pp. 312–313).]

Together, the two figures suggest that the U.K. contributed less than the U.S. both to the rise in the gross indebtedness of borrowing regions and to the pronounced cyclical movements in their liquidity position. In fact, the U.K. contributed nothing at all to the former during the interwar years. While the gap between the total capital inflow and outflow of the U.S. swings from large positive numbers in the late 1920s to large negative numbers in the 1930s, British interest and amortization receipts exceed the value of the new lending throughout the interwar years, albeit by a smaller margin in the 1920s than in the 1930s.

3. Who were the borrowers?

In contrast to foreign lending, which remained the preserve of a small number of industrialized economies, a wide range of countries engaged in foreign borrowing between the wars. According to C. Lewis' (1945) estimates of total long-term foreign indebtedness, the regions with the largest gross international obligations in 1938 were North America and Asia. North American debts were almost entirely offset by foreign assets, since the U.S. was by this time a net creditor, but Canada's foreign assets of U.S.$2 billion were dwarfed by foreign liabilities three times that size. Whether one considers gross or net foreign liabilities, Canada, rather than the countries facing highly-publicized debt-servicing difficulties, was the world's most heavily indebted nation by the end of the interwar years.[11]

The leading debtors of the Asia–Oceania group, Australia and India, were like Canada members of the British Empire. The foreign obligations of both countries, owed predominantly to the United Kingdom, largely took the form of sovereign and government-guaranteed debt. However, the foreign obligations of these two debtors were only marginally in excess of those of China and the Netherlands East Indies. Chinese debts were inflated by Japanese claims against the portion of China it occupied in 1938 and otherwise concentrated in the form of British direct investment in Shanghai. The debts of the Netherlands East Indies were half in the form of Dutch-owned and controlled tin mines and smelters, oil wells and refineries and plantations, and half government bonds and industrial debentures.

After North America and Asia–Oceania, Continental Europe was the most heavily indebted region. Even excluding war debts and reparations, more than a quarter of Europe's gross foreign obligations was comprised of Germany's external liabilities. After having attained creditor status in the decades preceding World War I, some 90% of German foreign assets had been liquidated during the war or as part of the postwar settlement. Germany then received extensive capital inflows between the time of the Dawes Loan in 1924 and the imposition of exchange control in 1931. The countries of Eastern Europe were also external debtors; the bulk of their external obligations took the form of sovereign debt, although western investment in extractive industries such as Romanian oil, Polish zinc and Yugoslav copper and bauxite achieved significant levels.

Given the attention devoted to Latin American debt, it is interesting to note that the value of Latin America's gross external obligations was smaller than the obligations of these other continents. Concern may have been heightened by the fact that Latin American debt was heavily concentrated in certain countries. Thus, Argentina ranked behind only Canada and Australia in terms of the value of gross external debt. However, only 1/6 of this total was public debt; the rest took the form of direct foreign investment, of which British investment in Argentine railways and private enterprise comprised the majority. Brazil, the second largest Latin American debtor, contrasts sharply with Argentina. Nearly 2/3 of Brazil's gross external debt represented the obligations of federal, state and local governments. The finance of railway construction is indicative of the two national strategies: where Argentine railways were largely British owned and controlled, Brazilian railways were owned by the state but financed by foreign borrowing.

[11]Her liabilities were split approximately 60–40 between the U.S. and U.K. and between portfolio and direct investment. See Lewis (1945).

4. Cross-section analysis of international borrowing

To summarize the pattern of international indebtedness between the wars in a fashion which facilitates comparisons with studies of recent decades, we estimate variants of the borrowing models advanced by such recent investigators as Eaton and Gersovitz (1981), Edwards (1984) and Riedel (1983). While these authors each provide a theoretical rationale for their favored specification, we do not justify or defend their estimating equations. The results of estimating their equations are reported here only as a way of providing a basis for comparison between the 1930s and 1970s.

With the exception of consumption and investment, reliable estimates of which are simply unavailable, we have assembled information on the major variables used in recent empirical analyses.[12] Table 1 reports estimates of the equation proposed by Eaton and Gersovitz to explain the stock of debt held by borrowing countries. Total external central government debt is related to GDP, population, openness, a measure of export variability and the rate of growth of GDP. Eaton and Gersovitz use export variability to proxy for income variability and argue that it should be positively related to desired borrowing. They use openness to proxy for the magnitude of the penalty incurred with retaliation against default, which they argue should be positively related to desired lending. The sign of the coefficient on income growth is theoretically ambiguous. Eaton and Gersovitz suggest that the rate of income growth should be positively related to the demand for borrowing, since some consumption out of future income is desired now, but that it may be negatively related to the willingeness to lend, since 'rapidly growing countries may have less to fear from the future effects of a credit embargo...'[13] If borrowers are on their demand-for-debt schedules, this variable's coefficient should therefore have a positive sign; but if they are credit-rationed, as it is reasonable to assume was the case after 1930, the sign should be negative.

Ordinary least squares estimates like those reported in table 1 should be interpreted cautiously for a number of reasons, not the least of which is potential simultaneity bias. The general impression conveyed by these estimates is that the Eaton–Gersovitz model provides a less adequate account of international indebtedness in the 1930s than in the 1970s. While the results are consistent with the notion that the level of debt is positively associated with export instability and degree of openness, the coefficients are not statistically well determined. The only coefficient which differs from zero at standard confidence levels in every year considered is that on the log of GDP; in no case can we reject the hypothesis that this coefficient equals unity. However, there is some tendency for the coefficient of GDP to shrink

---

[12]These data are described in the appendix.
[13]Eaton and Gersovitz (1981, p. 302).

Table 1
Determinants of stock of debt, annual cross sections, 1930–1938 (dependent variable is LDEBT).[a]

Years	n	Constant	SDX	MD	LGDP	LPOP	GRP	R^2
1930	20	−3.71 (2.10)	−0.43 (11.04)	2.25 (2.14)	1.03 (0.15)	0.22 (0.28)	−0.22 (2.12)	0.89
1931	21	−3.55 (1.59)	0.80 (2.40)	3.10 (1.66)	1.10 (0.11)	1.14 (0.21)	0.001 (0.001)	0.94
1932	21	−1.23 (1.81)	0.80 (1.92)	−0.75 (3.22)	1.04 (0.12)	0.03 (0.24)	−0.06 (0.48)	0.92
1933	18	−1.31 (2.01)	0.13 (1.94)	−1.20 (2.72)	0.97 (0.12)	0.12 (0.25)	0.38 (0.77)	0.93
1934	23	−2.17 (1.84)	4.41 (4.74)	1.57 (1.65)	1.02 (0.10)	0.11 (0.21)	0.29 (0.48)	0.92
1935	23	−2.25 (1.77)	4.06 (17.35)	1.44 (1.76)	0.94 (0.12)	0.24 (0.24)	−2.58 (1.26)	0.93
1936	22	−0.26 (2.07)	21.50 (15.68)	0.77 (2.24)	0.85 (0.11)	0.16 (0.22)	−6.15 (0.85)	0.94
1937	19	−3.24 (4.33)	13.37 (15.30)	3.23 (3.94)	0.74 (0.38)	0.48 (0.45)	−2.26 (1.53)	0.67
1938	16	−1.64 (2.27)	28.52 (21.35)	3.78 (2.85)	0.77 (0.20)	0.18 (0.29)	2.14 (4.16)	0.81
1930–1938	184	−3.36 (0.70)	1.85 (1.33)	1.72 (0.71)	1.01 (0.05)	0.24 (0.09)	−0.001 (0.001)	0.84
1931–1938	163	−3.36 (0.79)	1.83 (1.38)	1.78 (0.86)	1.01 (0.05)	0.24 (0.10)	−0.001 (0.001)	0.83

[a] Equations estimated by ordinary least squares. Standard errors in parentheses. n denotes the number of observations. Variable definitions include:

LDEBT: log of total external central government debt,
SDX: standard deviation of exports (over years $T-2$, $T-1$, T), scaled ($\times 10^{-4}$)
MD: import/GDP ratio,
LGDP: log of GDP,
LPOP: log of population,
GRP: growth rate of GDP (over years $T-2$, $T-1$, T).

in size as the 1930s progress, indicating that relatively high-income countries had the greatest tendency to repay previously-acquired debts. By the end of the decade relatively low-*GDP* countries were left most heavily indebted. The predominantly negative coefficient on *GDP* growth can be taken as indicative of credit rationing.

The results from pooling the time-series and cross-section data give a clearer picture, with positive coefficients on all regressors except the growth rate of *GDP*, all significant at the 5% level except that on export instability. The coefficient on the log of *GDP* is so close to unity and so well determined that it seemed sensible to try debt per unit output as the left-hand variable. The consequence of deflating the stock of debt in this way is to give predominantly better determined coefficients on the remaining regressors, with no qualitative changes. The results from the pooled equation for 1930–38 are characteristic:

$$LDG = -3.37 + 1.86\,SDX + 1.74\,MD + 0.24\,LPOP - 0.001\,GRP,$$
$$\quad\;\;(0.69)\;\;(1.32)\qquad\;(0.71)\qquad(0.07)\qquad\;\;(0.0007)$$

$$n = 163,\quad R^2 = 0.10,\quad F = 5.02,$$

[$LDG = \log(\text{debt}/GDP)$. Other variables defined as in table 1. Standard errors in parentheses.]

All this uses Eaton and Gersovitz's explanatory variables for the purposes of comparative description of the data. We have not sought at this stage to use on our data the disequilibrium modelling approach which they employ. This is not because we think it inappropriate – quite the contrary, as our verbal discussion above suggests. We believe, however, that it requires a tighter theoretical specification and perhaps better data than we have developed so far. Although from a quantity-rationing modeller's standpoint we might criticize the 'quasi reduced form' underlying table 1 [see Portes and Winter (1980)], it still provides interesting information about the data we do have.

Edwards (1984) has suggested that the stock demand for debt is better viewed in terms of the government's problem of selecting its optimal portfolio of assets and liabilities. Hence stocks of international reserves and foreign debt should be simultaneously determined, and the latter will depend in general not only on the variables suggested by Eaton and Gersovitz but also on the value of reserves. We have estimated a variant of Edwards's reserve demand function, using gold reserves as our dependent variable, and obtained results remarkably similar to his, as reported in appendix table A.1. We then added reserves to the equation reported in table 1, but neither OLS nor instrumental variables estimates indicated that reserves had any impact on the level of debt.[14]

Another attempt to permit balance-of-payments developments as reflected in reserves to influence the accumulation of external debt is provided by Riedel (1983), who analyzes flow supplies and demands for new borrowing rather than stocks of debt. Riedel relates the flow of borrowing to the following ratios: reserves to imports, debt service to exports, the government budget deficit to GDP, investment to national income, and income per capita.

---

[14]Before dismissing Edwards's hypothesis, one should note the possibility that gold stocks are an inadequate measure of reserves.

Results of estimating this equation are reported in table 2, where we have added dummy variables for Latin America and British Empire countries (where the latter include only Australia in our sample) to flag any differences in their experiences and have dropped the investment ratio due to absence of data. The overwhelming impression is, as anticipated, one of pronounced shifts in the relationship of net lending to its determinants between 1928 and 1935. The coefficients on per capita income suggest that high income countries had the greatest tendency to borrow before 1932 and, consistent with table 1, to repay thereafter. Although the regional dummy variables are unstable across periods, they suggest on balance that both Australia and the Latin American countries had unusually high propensities to borrow until the total collapse of international capital markets after 1931.

Whether countries experiencing the inital effects of the Great Depression were able to use foreign funds to help finance the shock is sensitive to whether or not 1931 is included in the sample. The positive coefficient on the reserve ratio for the period prior to 1931 suggests that even at this early date countries experiencing balance-of-payments difficulties found it relatively difficult to borrow abroad. This coefficient becomes negligible, however, when the period is extended through 1931. Similarly, when 1931 is included in the sample, the positive coefficient on the fiscal deficit suggests that countries which chose to run deficits in response to the impact of the Great Depression initially had some ability to finance them through foreign borrowing. This evidence dissipates when 1931 is excluded from the sample. Whether the sensitivity of the results to inclusion of 1931 is due to the appearance that year of the first defaults, to the increasing inadequacy of our reserve measure given pronounced shifts between gold and foreign exchange, or to some other peculiar feature of 1931 remains to be determined.

5. Factors in default

Part of the explanation for the incidence of default lies in special national circumstances, including particular primary commodity endowments, domestic economic policies and the uses to which borrowed funds were put. Yet in the 1930s as in the 1980s, developing countries were subjected to common external shocks which affected both the costs and benefits of interruptions to debt service. The list of common external disturbances – recession in the industrialized world, declining relative prices of primary products, rising real interest rates and resurgent protectionism – will have a familiar ring to those who follow the current situation. It is important therefore that observers struck by the resemblance of the 1930s to the 1980s should not lose sight of the greater severity of the earlier shocks.

A severe business-cycle downturn in the United States could not but exercise a powerful influence over the liquidity and solvency of sovereign

Table 2

Flow of borrowing, cross-sections for three-year and four-year averages 1928–1935 (dependent variable in BOR/GDP).[a]

Years	n	Constant	RES/IMP	SRV/XP	DEF/GDP	GDP/POP	LA	AUS	R^2
1928–30	20	−0.01 (0.02)	0.11 (0.07)	−0.06 (0.09)	0.19 (0.42)	0.51 (0.61)	0.02 (0.02)	0.84 (0.06)	0.93
1928–31	21	−0.03 (0.02)	0.01 (0.01)	0.06 (0.06)	1.06 (0.37)	0.70 (0.48)	0.07 (0.03)	0.89 (0.05)	0.96
1932–35	22	0.23 (0.15)	−0.48 (0.12)	0.33 (0.11)	−0.14 (2.00)	−6.80 (3.39)	−0.02 (0.20)	−0.26 (0.35)	0.46

[a] Equations estimated by ordinary least squares. Standard errors in parentheses. n is number of observations.
Variable definitions include:
BOR/GDP: Flow of external central government borrowing as a share of GDP,
RES/IMP: reserves/imports*,
SRV/XP: total debt service/exports*,
DEF/GDP: central government budget deficit/GDP*,
GDP/POP: GDP/population*,
LA: dummy variable for Latin American countries,
AUS: dummy variable for Australia,
where * denotes an average for the period.

debtors. The obvious indicator of this influence is size: in 1929 the U.S. accounted for more than half of the industrial output and nearly 40% of the primary product consumption of the 15 leading industrial economies.[15] Another indicator is the magnitude of the contraction: one need only note that the Harvard Economic Society index of the volume of manufacturing fell by 25% between October 1929 and October 1930 and that real *GDP* fell at twice the rate typical for the first year of a recession.[16]

One of the principal channels through which these deflationary pressures were transmitted to developing regions was via primary commodity prices. In 1929, the most important agricultural goods in world trade were, in declining order of importance, cotton, wheat, sugar, coffee, silk and rubber.[17] Countries were variously affected by their luck in the 'commodity lottery', to use Diaz-Alejandro's (1983) term. Between 1929 and 1930 the fall in average annual dollar prices ranged from nearly 20% for wheat and tin to 30% for cotton, sugar and silk and 40% for rubber.[18] In many cases the fall in export prices understates the impact on primary commodity exports. Export volumes declined with export prices as foreign demand curves shifted inwards and domestic producers moved back down their supply curves. The decline in foreign demand attributable to the depression was reinforced by protectionist initiatives which heavily affected foreign food producers. Ironically, the measures which created special difficulty for foreign debtors – tariff and non-tariff barriers to imports of foodstuffs – were adopted by industrial countries to bail out another class of debtors, namely farmers hit by falling agricultural prices. Together, recession and protection depressed the export revenues of 41 primary product exporting countries by some 50% between 1928–1929 and 1932–1933, an unprecedented shock by recent standards.

Another way of gauging the shock to indebted regions is in terms of the change in real interest rates. The fall in U.S. prices that got underway in the final quarter of 1929 raised ex post short-term real interest rates to more than 15%.[19] While the real interest rate shocks of recent years are by no means to be dismissed, they pale in comparison with the shocks experienced after 1929.

---

[15]This 40% figure refers to consumption of nine major commodities. See Lewis (1949, p. 57). While the share of imports in GNP was not high by modern standards, the sheer size of the American economy still permitted changes in an import share which was low on average to affect world markets powerfully on the margin. See the discussion in Dornbusch and Fischer (1984).

[16]Industrial production figures are from Tinbergen (1934), while *GDP* estimates are those reported in U.S. Department of Commerce (1976).

[17]Taylor and Taylor (1943, pp. 10–12).

[18]These figures overstate the change in the terms of trade, since U.S. wholsesale prices were falling as well [by 9% on average between 1929 and 1930, according to Tinbergen (1934, p. 212)].

[19]These are the calculations of Summers and De Long (1984, p. 53).

6. Cross-section analysis of the incidence of default

Existing accounts tend to portary decisions in the 1930s of whether to default on sovereign debt in one of three ways: (i) as the result of idiosyncratic national circumstances about which it is difficult to generalize, (ii) as a function of 'bandwagon effects' that proved irresistible even to basically solvent debtors once the initial defaults occurred, and (iii) as the only feasible alternative available to developing countries given the magnitude of the shock to the world economy. Yet the incidence and extent of sovereign default varied enormously across countries. None of these approaches provides much help in understanding that incidence or that extent. This is in contrast to modern models of debt capacity, in which the incidence of rescheduling is assumed to be systematically related to a vector of national characteristics proxying for its costs and benefits, such as the ratio of debt to *GNP* and various measures of trade performance.[20] In this section, we adapt these debt-capacity models to the circumstances of the 1930s to examine the extent to which country-specific variables associated with the costs and benefits of default help to explain its incidence. If these variables possess explanatory power, then it will be necessary to supplement if not replace existing characterizations with an analysis of the incidence of sovereign default in the 1930s couched in terms of its differential costs and benefits across countries.

As in modern studies of rescheduling, empirical analysis is complicated by the fact that the variable of interest – in this case sovereign default – can take on a number of forms of varying severity. Least serious was to be in default on sinking fund payments only. The Dominican Republic, for example, while continuing to faithfully service its dollar debt, temporarily fell into default on sinking fund early in the 1930s, before making a proposal in 1934 concerning readjustment of amortization which received the endorsement of the Foreign Bondholders Protective Council.[21] More serious was to be in default on all or a portion of interest payments. Most serious of all was repudiation, a rare event in the interwar years.[22] The best available indicator would appear to be the share of dollar- and sterling-denominated government and government-guaranteed debt in default as to interest or sinking fund.[23]

[20]See for example the well-known studies of Feder and Just (1977), and Feder, Just and Ross (1981). The debt-capacity literature is surveyed by McDonald (1982). A recent discussion of the costs and benefits of default from the policymaker's perspective is provided by Diaz-Alejandro (1984).

[21]For details, see the Foreign Bondholders Protective Council's *Annual Report* for 1934.

[22]The two notable instances of repudiation in this period are a partial repudiation by the Mexican government in 1914 and the Soviet government's repudiation of debt contracted by the Czarist and Kerensky regimes.

[23]These two denominations of debt comprise the very great majority of the total. Only dollar- and sterling-denominated debt are considered because, while the Foreign Bondholders Protective Council provides information on the former and the British Corporation of Foreign Bondholders on the latter, information on the status of debt denominated in other currencies is much more difficult to obtain. Details on these data can be found in the data appendix.

Our measure of default is constructed from data covering national, state and provincial, municipal and government-guaranteed debt. The share of dollar- and sterling-denominated debt in default as to interest or sinking fund is calculated for the period from 1934, the first year for which the newly-established Foreign Bondholders Protective Council published information on arrears, through 1938. The explanatory variables include proxies for the burden of the debt, the degree of openness, the severity of the external shock and the stance of domestic economic policy. Given their significance in table 2 above, dummy variables for Latin America and Australia are added to test whether political or economic factors not otherwise accounted for help to explain the incidence of default. The external-government-debt-to-national-income ratio is used as a measure of debt-servicing requirements – in other words, the burden of the debt. We proxy openness by the ratio of exports to *GDP* and the severity of the external shock by the percentage deterioration in the terms of trade after 1929. It is likely that simultaneity will affect any attempt to estimate the impact of the current export share on the incidence of default, since countries which defaulted may have run policies or experienced sanctions which subsequently influenced their reliance on trade. Therefore, we use the lagged export share as a proxy for openness, employing two alternative formulations: the 1928 export share and the export share six years prior to the year for which the dependent variable is defined. It is similarly possible that simultaneity may contaminate the coefficient on the change in the terms of trade after 1929, since countries which defaulted may have run policies or experienced sanctions which influenced the evolution of relative prices. As an alternative to the change in the terms of trade between 1929 and the year under consideration, we employ the change in the terms of trade between 1929 and 1931.

The next two variables are indicators of the stance of fiscal and monetary policies. To avoid problems of simultaneity, both variables are measured as percentage changes between 1929 and 1931, since countries which defaulted thereafter subsequently had available different policy options than countries that continued to service their external debt. The fiscal policy variable is defined as the percentage change in the central government budget deficit. Data on other levels of government, while desirable, are not available on a consistent basis. The monetary policy variable is defined as the percentage change in the ratio of gold reserves to note circulation. Almost all the countries in the sample remained on the gold standard into 1931; in the long run, therefore, their money supplies were endogenously determined. In the short run, however, governments could attempt to influence money supply and any domestic economic conditions it affected through domestic credit creation which would have as its eventual consequence a loss of international reserves. Therefore, the greater the rise in the ratio of reserves to money supply, the more restrictive was monetary policy. While it would be desirable to include other foreign assets in addition to gold and to use a broader measure of money supply than notes and coin in circulation, adequate data are not available for the range of countries included here.

Two-limit probit analysis is used to analyze the incidence and extent of default in light of the fact that the observed dependent variable is obtained as zero for countries which did not default, as unity for countries in default on all their obligations, and as a range of intermediate values for countries partially in default.[24]

Pooled time-series cross-section results are reported in table 3.[25] The results are striking for their conformance with basic economic intuition. First, the most heavily indebted countries, as measured by the debt/income ratio, appear to have had the greatest tendency to default. Second, countries which experienced relatively severe deteriorations in their terms of trade also had a tendency toward default. This is true regardless of the terms-of trade measure used. Thus, the commodity lottery looms as important not only for explaining the impact of the Depression on primary-producing countries but also in explaining their response.

These results seem quite inconsistent with the notion that all developing countries experiencing the Great Depression had no alternative but simply to opt for default. Rather, they suggest that the magnitude of the debt burden and severity of the external shock influenced the extent to which countries fell into arrears. At the same time, they are inconsistent with the view that non-economic factors, such as political ties to the principal creditor countries, provide the entire explanation for the incidence of default. This is not to say that the regional dummy variables can be dismissed. That for Australia has a negative sign which differs significantly from zero at any reasonable confidence level, indicating that the extent of default was significantly less than predicted by the economic variables included in the equation, a result tempting to interpret in terms of Australia's political and cultural ties to the United Kingdom. In contrast, the incidence of default among Latin American countries is sufficiently well predicted by the economic variables in the equation that the coefficient on the Latin American dummy retains no residual explanatory power.

The coefficient on the change in the budget deficit is positive and differs significantly from zero at the 90% confidence level or better when the dummy variables for region are included. In other words, governments which ran austere budgetary policies in response to the Great Depression were best able to avoid debt-servicing difficulties. Those which engaged in what were

---

[24]The two-limit probit model is a generalization of the Tobit model to the case where the data are censored at both tails. Rosett and Nelson (1975) provide a description of the estimator.

[25]Estimates based on data for individual years are consistent with the pooled time-series cross-section results discussed in the text, although statistically less well defined, due presumably to limited degrees of freedom.

Table 3
Two-limit probit regressions of covariates of default: Pooled time-series cross-section results, 1934–1938 (dependent variable is percentage of dollar and sterling debt in default as to interest and/or amortization).[a]

Variable	(i)	(ii)	(iii)	(iv)
Constant	0.519 (0.054)	0.521 (0.047)	0.003 (0.190)	0.026 (0.136)
Debt/income ratio	0.328 (0.164)	0.345 (0.182)	0.659 (0.298)	0.931 (0.258)
Percent deterioration, terms of trade, 1929–1931	0.223 (0.083)		0.567 (0.266)	
Percent deterioration, terms of trade, 1929–current year		0.271 (0.089)		0.822 (0.260)
Lagged export/GDP ratio		0.062 (0.044)		−0.326 (0.480)
1928 export/GDP ratio	0.071 (0.207)		0.159 (0.770)	
Percent increase in budget deficit, 1929–1931	0.005 (0.002)	0.005 (0.003)	0.005 (0.005)	0.004 (0.003)
Percent increase in reserve ratio, 1929–1931	0.169 (0.049)	0.185 (0.047)	0.305 (0.195)	0.386 (0.186)
Latin America	−0.001 (0.033)	−0.006 (0.052)		
Australia	−1.253 (0.251)	−1.289 (0.223)		
Log-likelihood	−139.67	−143.06	−84.23	−81.23

[a]Coefficient estimates are accompanied by standard errors in parentheses. Number of observations = 95. Variable definitions include: *Debt/income ratio*: total external government debt/GDP, *Percent increase in budget deficit*: central government deficit only, *Percent increase in reserve ratio*: ratio of gold reserves to notes and coin in circulation. For further details, see the text and data appendix.

by the standards of 1929–1931 relatively heterodox fiscal policies had the greatest tendency to default. The obvious interpretation of this result is in terms of the absorption approach to the balance of payments – that, ceteris paribus, deficit spending raised domestic absorption of imports and exportable goods, reducing the foreign-exchange receipts available for servicing external debt.

The coefficient on the monetary policy variable indicates that countries experiencing relatively large increases in the ratio of gold reserves to currency circulation had the greatest tendency to default. This result is inconsistent with the notion that countries engaging in expansionary monetary policies were driven to default by any balance of payments difficulties that resulted. Similar results have been found when estimating debt capacity models for the

1970s and interpreted to indicate that sovereign debtors anticipating eventual default hoarded reserves to finance subsequent import purchases whose expense could no longer be defrayed by additional foreign borrowing.

An alternative explanation for this result would appear to be the inadequacy of gold as a proxy for international reserves and of note circulation as a proxy for money supply. Consider for example the first of these problems. Countries in our sample held gold and convertible foreign exchange in various proportions. The use of gold reserves as a proxy for the total would not be a problem if those proportions remained constant. However, Nurkse (1944, p. 41) notes that the share of foreign exchange in the gold and exchange reserves of 18 debtor countries for which he has information fell from 33 to 15% between 1929 and 1931. Yet certain countries swam against this tide; Australia, for example, liquidated a major share of its gold reserves and replaced them with foreign exchange. Hence eliminating the dummy variable for Australia, as in columns (iii) and (iv) of table 3, alters the coefficient on the monetary variable, which no longer differs uniformly from zero at the 95% confidence level.[26]

The mystery of the monetary variable should not be permitted to detract from the other conclusions. Overall, the results suggest that basic economic intuition and simple economic variables go a long way toward explaining the incidence and extent of sovereign default in the 1930s.

7. The scope for renegotiation

To understand the scope for renegotiation, it is necessary to consider the mechanics of foreign borrowing. Procedures in London and New York were quite similar. The first step for a sovereign borrower wishing to obtain funds on the London market was to issue a prospectus. Typically, the terms of the offer and solvency of the debtor had already been examined by a reputable issuing house, which endorsed the loan by attaching its name to the prospectus.[27] In New York, specialized marketing houses played an analogous role. The revenues accruing to the managing houses took the form of the spread between the bonds' purchase price (the price received by the foreign borrower) and the sales price (the price paid by the ultimate bondholder).

---

[26]For further discussion of Australian policy toward gold reserves in this period, see Eichengreen (1985). Another possible explanation for the sign of the monetary variable is simultaneity bias – that countries which defaulted then capitalized on the opportunity to promote recovery via monetary expansion. However, most of the movement in this variable takes place before the second half of 1931, when the serious defaults began. Moreover, replacing this variable with the gold/currency ratio over the period 1928–1930 does not alter the result.

[27]To maintain their good reputations, the issuing houses supposedly had an interest in insuring the prospectus contained accurate information. Committe on Finance and Industry (1931, para. 387).

Flotation might be undertaken by a syndicate of issuing houses and banks. Since different institutions might have a comparative advantage either in negotiating an acceptable loan contract with the borrower or in marketing the bonds, it was not uncommon for one syndicate to resell a loan to another before making the bonds available to the public. Short-term advances were often extended to the foreign borrower in anticipation of successful placement of the loan. To market the securities, issuing houses based primarily in New York and Chicago employed itinerant bond salesmen and established branch offices across the United States and Canada. Some New York banks established special security affiliates which could directly serve in this capacity without violating American branch banking laws. If at first observers hailed the verve with which these travelling salesmen trumpeted the virtues of foreign bonds, after the first defaults they accused these same promoters of a variety of excesses.[28] The facility with which these securities were marketed is evidenced by the extent of sales to persons of relatively moderate means. Although the available statistics are incomplete, they suggest that in the 1920s the mean value of lots of foreign bonds was less than $5,000. Since this figure is inflated by a small number of very large purchases, the typical lot would appear smaller still had we an estimate of the median. For example, the face value of the average holding of Chilean bonds in the 1930s appears to have been no more than $800 when the 4% of largest holdings is eliminated.[29] The small size of holdings and large number of bondholders is often credited with creating a severe free-rider problem in the event of default and negotiation.

There was little scope for litigation as an avenue for obtaining satisfaction from defaulting debtors. American and British courts had no jurisdiction over foreign sovereigns, who could be sued in their own courts only with their consent.[30] One way in which lenders attempted to protect themselves

---

[28]'These agents for the first time taught the small investor in a hundred small provincial towns, and in the countryside of the Middle and Far West, to link their fortunes with those of the Governments and enterprises of distant lands whose very names he often scarcely knew. It was an astonishing achievement of modern organisation, and for its first purpose of inducing the investor to lend his money, and making this money available in the continents which most needed capital, it was extremely successful. But, as we shall see, at the other end of the operation, namely the examination of the character and purposes of the loan, the capacity of the borrower and the likelihood of his using the money productively, the methods adopted were less satisfactory. There was too much competition and too little caution.' Salter (1933, pp. 99–100). Compare the anecdotal accounts of lending in the 1980s reported in Darity (1985).

[29]Similarly, 80 to 90% of dollar bond purchasers in the 1920s took no more than $5,000, with 45 to 65% of the total value of an issue typically taken by this category of buyer. These amounts need to be multiplied by six to express them in mid-1980s prices. The figures reported are based mainly on a survey of 24 representative American bond houses conducted in 1924–1926. See Morrow (1927) for details. Estimates of the average value of holdings of Chilean bonds are from the *Annual Report* for 1935 of the Council of Foreign Bondholders, p. 99.

[30]In the 1970s, this situation was altered. The U.S. Foreign Sovereign Immunities Act of 1976 and the U.K. State Immunity Act of 1978 distinguished a nation's commercial activities from its acts as a sovereign power. This legislation established the legal liability of foreign governments

was by writing into loan contracts provisions which earmarked certain revenues for debt service. Unfortunately, nothing prevented a foreign government from also breaching these provisions if it fell into default on interest or amortization. Bondholders therefore tried to enlist the aid of their governments. Government involvement could range from informal negotiations through diplomatic representations and economic sanctions to armed force. The U.S. State Department maintained a policy of official non-interposition in negotiations between American bondholders and foreign governments, although diplomats and officials did not hesitate to express their interest in a settlement. The British, in contrast, permitted the bondholders to delegate a British minister to the foreign country, or his consul-general, as their local agent, a practice certain to raise questions in the debtor's mind about the capacity in which the minister was negotiating.[31] The use of armed force, however nostalgically viewed by bondholders, was basically a thing of the past. The U.S. Securities and Exchange Commission advised bondholders to eliminate from their consideration the use of force as a means of debt collection.[32]

This left economic sanctions. The threat of sanctions in response to Germany's 1933–1934 default illustrates the use of this instrument. In the summer of 1933 the German government declared a moratorium on the overseas transfer of interest payments.[33] Negotiations between the head of the Reichsbank and foreign creditors ensued, yielding a compromise under which Germany agreed to meet a portion of its obligations. The Dutch and Swiss rejected the pact, however, and threatened to impose sanctions. The credibility of their threat was enhanced by the fact that both countries ran

---

for purely commercial acts and permitted such governments to waive their immunities from litigation. The effect of these acts has, however, been questioned. See Kaletsky (1985, ch. 4). Even in the 1930s, the situation was different for loans to non-governmental entities. Loan contracts for private foreign bond issues were nominally subject to the laws of place of performance, not those of foreign debtor. Disputes over private loans floated in New York or London were therefore heard in American or British courts. Thus, when in 1934 two German shipping companies contended that they were precluded from complying with the terms of their loan contracts by German exchange control, the U.S. District Court in New York ruled that '... As the contracts were made here and were to be performed here, the German law relative to performance is of no legal significance in the courts of this country'. Madden et al. (1937, p. 282). However, such jurisdiction as American or British courts claimed over foreign private debtors was usually of little significance. In practice, creditors could use a legal decision to obtain satisfaction only if the defendant had attachable assets abroad. Not surprisingly, the notable instances where arrears were paid in full or an acceptable readjustment plan was offered involved shipping companies, like those cited above, with attachable assets anchored in American ports.

[31] See Securities and Exchange Commission (1936, vol. IV, pp. 28–29).
[32] Securities and Exchange Commission (1936, vol. IV, p. 25). This new restraint was ascribed to the adoption of a more balanced attitude by the major powers. Royal Institute (1937, p. 99). A more pragmatic interpretation is that, however effective against an isolated debtor, gunboat diplomacy was an impractical response to (geographically) widespread default.
[33] See Harris (1935).

trade deficits against Germany, implying that the costs of German retaliation were likely to exceed the benefits. The Germans settled separately with both countries, with Dutch and Swiss nationals ultimately receiving full interest on their Dawes and Young plan bonds and cash payments of $3\frac{1}{2}$ to $4\frac{1}{2}\%$ on most other German bonds.

Similar threats were then issued by and agreements reached with Sweden, France and Belgium. The mere opening of debate over sanctions in the British Parliament was sufficient to prod Germany into action. Before the measure could be passed into law, a German delegation arrived in London, and within a month an agreement was reached providing for full interest payments to British nationals on Dawes and Young plan bonds.[34] In contrast, the nationals of countries whose governments maintained their policy of official non-interposition received less favorable treatment. The U.S. State Department protested such discrimination against American bondholders, but to little effect.[35]

Bond finance and the associated free-rider problem are blamed for the difficulty of negotiating settlements when debt-servicing difficulties arose. Under bank finance, illiquid debtors can turn to their creditors, who are relatively few in number, for bridging loans, while insolvent debtors can negotiate a mutually-acceptable sharing of losses. Under bond finance, creditors were allegedly too many and bond covenants too inflexible for illiquidity to result in anything but default or for insolvent debtors and their creditors to achieve a mutually-acceptable sharing of losses. In fact, there existed a number of mechanisms for internalizing the externalities that gave rise to free riding. The major difference between the interwar and postwar periods lies not in the prevalence of negotiations designed to achieve an equitable sharing of losses, since negotiations were commonplace in both eras. Rather, the difference is the extent to which some form of default was a necessary prerequisite for getting negotiations started.[36]

The fact that bond issues were floated by issuing houses and banks meant that there existed agents sufficiently few in number and large in size to have

---

[34]Madden et al. (1937, pp. 267–268).

[35]The treatment of these bondholders is described in the *Fifth Annual Report* of the Bank for International Settlements. On State Department protests, see Securities and Exchange Commission (1936, vol. IV, p. 24). Whether American restraint is attributable to principle or to the fact that the U.S. ran trade deficits against few of the defaulting nations (Brazil, Colombia and Cuba being the notable exceptions), U.S. policy of delinking the trade and debt issues clearly influenced the course of negotiations. In its negotiations with Colombia, for example, the bondholders' representatives threatened that failure to settle would cause the adoption of increased tariffs on Colombia coffee. (See the 1934 Annual Report of the Foreign Bondholders Protective Council, p. 95.) Knowing U.S. policy, the Colombians appear to have discounted the threat. As Colombian President Lopez put it, 'this threat does not modify in any way the intent of the Colombian Government to study quietly the best plan to meet the external obligations of the Republic....'. Securities and Exchange Commission (1936, vol. IV, pp. 378–379).

[36]See also Sachs (1983).

in principle provided bridging loans. Such short-term loans and advances had been common in the 1920s [see De Cecco (1984)]. Moreover, it was in the banks' interest to tide over illiquid debtors, since they suffered embarrassment from default on bonds with whose issue they had been associated. It is troubling, therefore, that little such lending occurred after 1929. It could be that the debt crisis was quickly recognized as a problem of insolvency rather than illiquidity, and that money center banks rationally refused to throw good money after bad. This hypothesis imputes considerable foresight to the lending institutions. Moreover, it overlooks the possibility that their very unwillingness to provide short-term credit may have been directly responsible for transforming what remained a problem of illiquidity into one of insolvency. The banks' unwillingness to provide short-term loans preceded by a year the onset of default. For example, in 1930 Bolivian officials confronted with debt-servicing difficulties visited New York to 'treat with' American banks. Negotiations to obtain short-term loans were unavailing, and in 1931 Bolivia became the first Latin American debtor to default, setting off a chain reaction.[37] The alternative hypothesis is that, with only the goodwill of their customers rather than their own assets at stake, financial institutions had little incentive to bear the risk that what might appear to be illiquidity was really insolvency. If so, then a major difference between bank and bond finance is that under the latter a default was a necessary precondition to the successful restructuring of a loan. It does not follow, however, that under bond finance there was little scope for serious negotiation.

If default ensued, a readjustment program might be negotiated by the issuing house or by a committee it organized. Issuing houses characterized themselves as 'moral trustees' obliged to protect the bondholders' interests.[38] Bondholders recognized, however, that the issuing house was likely to be torn between the interests of two sets of customers: bondholders and foreign borrowers. Moreover, the indebted government was the issuing house's single largest customer, with whom the lender was likely to have established a valued long-term relationship. Given the potential for conflict of interest, most readjustments were therefore negotiated not by issuing houses but by independent committees. The legal status of these committees varied: some obtained the physical deposit of bonds which they were authorized to use at their discretion; others took a proxy or power of attorney from bondholders who retained possession of their certificates; and still others received no legal authorization from bondholders, who they could claim to represent only informally.

The British Corporation of Foreign Bondholders (known less formally as

---

[37]U.S. Senate (1932, vol. II, pp. 749–750).
[38]U.S. Senate (1932, vol. II, pp. 288–289).

the British Council and less favorably as the 'conscience of the loanmongers') was the oldest such organization, having been founded in 1868.[39] With six of its 21 members appointed by the British Bankers' Association, six by the London Chamber of Commerce and nine by the Council as a whole, it could claim to represent the interests of both the City of London and the bondholding community. Until the end of 1933 there existed no comparable organization in the United States.[40] American practice was to form ad hoc committees in response to individual defaults. The shortcomings of the method were notorious. Administrative expenses were inflated by the inability to exploit the scale economies offered by simultaneous negotiations with various debtors. Ad hoc committees could not bring the same pressure to bear as so august an institution as the British Council. Moreover, rivalry among competing committees undermined the credibility of each. Multiple committees might be formed for various reasons, including competition for profits, since the organizers typically received a commission paid out of debt service charges upon the conclusion of a settlement. More often, rival committees were formed when issuing houses established one and disenchanted bondholders another. The two then competed for support, employing newspaper publicity and agents who were paid on a commission basis to secure the deposit or registration of bonds. Not only did this encourage committees and their agents to make extravagant promises, but a debtor government was faced with the problem of determining which committee best represented its creditors. In 1933 the Foreign Bondholders Protective Council was finally established in the U.S. on a non-profit basis. It proved a popular vehicle for subsequent readjustment negotiations, although its critics continued to suggest that it was unduly influenced by the banks.

Readjustment plans were signalled by the publication of a decree or simply an announcement that bond covenants were henceforth modified. If the plan was a result of successful negotiations, its acceptance would be recommended by the bondholders' committee involved. A new coupon was specified and the principal might be adjusted. A new date by which the loan would be called was specified. Bondholders indicated their acceptance of the arrangement by cashing a coupon and, when requested, by exchanging an old certificate for a new one. If acceptance of the offer was recommended by a prominent agency such as the Foreign Bondholders Protective Council, few options remained for dissident bondholders. In theory, they could withhold their coupons and form another committee to negotiate a better settlement.

---

[39] Jenks (1927, pp. 288–289).
[40] There had been two notable attempts to form central protective agencies in the United States: the non-profit Latin American Bondholders Association incorporated in New York in 1931, which failed after managing to secure only $515 in membership fees, and the for-profit American Council of Foreign Bondholders, which was only slightly more successful in attracting subscribers.

In practice, foreign governments had little further interest in negotiations once their good standing had been restored by the seal of approval of the Foreign Bondholders Protective Council. Only the possibility of widespread dissatisfaction with the terms negotiated by the councils provided a check on the process.

How the bondholders fared under these arrangements is an empirical question, to which we now turn.

8. The impact of default and bondholders' ability to recover

Little is known about the realized rate of return on foreign bonds purchased during the 1920s. Madden et al. (1937) estimated the current rate of return on foreign bonds (excluding Canadian issues) on an accrual basis; as shown in table 4, they took interest as it accrued plus or minus gain or loss on redemption as a percentage of the amount of bonds valued at the original purchase price.[41] The figures reveal that over the decade of the 1920s the current rate of return on dollar bonds fluctuated in the range of 7–8%. The highest rates of return occurred at the beginning of the decade; then between 1923 and 1929 the rate of return exhibited no obvious trend. With the onset of the Depression, that rate declined to 6.90% in 1930, and in 1931 the first defaults combined with the repurchase of bonds for cancellation at prices below par reduced the yield further. Additional defaults continued to depress the yield until 1934, when the redemption of Netherlands East Indies, Swiss and French issues on a gold basis, in conjunction with the depreciation of the dollar, temporarily raised the return.[42]

The rate of return on a class of sterling assets, sterling bonds in Latin America, was calculated on a similar basis in 1940 by the *South American Journal*. These estimates appear in the second column of table 4. One is struck first of all by the fact that throughout the 1920s the required rate of

---

[41]Madden et al., speculate that inclusion of Canadian dollar bonds would reduce somewhat the average yields shown in the table. According to U.S. Department of Commerce (1932, p. 14), the average annual yield offered on new Canadian issues floated in the U.S. ranged from 7.03 in 1920 to 4.19 in 1931, and averaged 5.32% over the period.

[42]American loan contracts, both domestic and foreign, typically contained provisions which specified repayment in terms of 'gold dollars of the standard weight and fineness'. When Roosevelt issued an Executive Order in June 1933 abrogating the gold clause provisions of all U.S. government bonds, setting the stage for the devaluation of the dollar, questions arose about the treatment of analogous clauses in other bond contracts. In following months, many foreign debtors chose to continue to honor the gold clauses in their liabilities. Most, however, quickly followed the American government's lead, making payment in depreciated dollars. In this they were encouraged by the attitude of the American Executive itself. Creditors whose assets contained gold clauses were characterized by the U.S. Attorney General as 'a privileged class ... squatters in the public domain, and when the Government needs the territory they must move on.' (Cited in Feuerlein and Hannan, 1941, p. 23.) Various steps were taken to relieve domestic debtors, principally farmers, of the obligation to make repayment in gold. Most foreign debtors took this as justification for their decisions to make payment in current dollars.

Table 4
Previous estimates of the rate of return on overseas loans (rate of return is measured in percentage points).[a]

Year	Foreign dollar bonds	Sterling bonds in Latin America
1920	7.67	
1921	7.78	
1922	7.58	
1923	7.03	3.8
1924	7.30	3.9
1925	7.28	4.1
1926	7.24	4.5
1927	7.07	4.2
1928	7.25	4.4
1929	7.03	4.5
1930	6.90	4.3
1931	5.81	3.2
1932	4.47	2.0
1933	3.67	1.7
1934	6.17	1.6
1935	3.54	1.8
1936		1.9
1937		2.2
1938		1.7
1939		1.6

[a] Rate of return on foreign dollar bonds (exclusive of Canadian issues) is from Madden et al. (1937, p. 154). This is interest paid in cash as a percentage of the amount invested adjusted for principal repaid in cash. Rate of return on Latin American securities quoted on the London Stock Exchange at the end of each year is from the *South American Journal* (January 20, 1940, p. 44). This is dividends, interest, arrears of interest and bonus as a percentage of the book value of investment.

return on sterling bonds in Latin America was below the rate of return on foreign dollar bonds, perhaps reflecting the greater perceived riskiness of American loans. With the onset of default, the rate of return falls by roughly 50%, not unlike the percentage decline in the current return on dollar bonds. Yet it is not known whther the returns on Latin American bonds are representative of British investments abroad.

The inevitable limitation of estimates constructed in 1937 or 1940 is that they have no way of incorporating the impact on the rate of return of subsequent interruptions to debt service, notably those associated with World War II, or of subsequent settlements between creditors and defaulting debtors. Many Italian dollar bonds, for example, went into default in the autumn of 1940, and no additional interest was paid until 1947. Most German bonds which fell into default in 1933 or 1934 were only validated in 1955 as part of the London Agreement, after which service was resumed. Several early Latin American defaults, such as Bolivia's in 1931, were not settled until after World War II.

We have therefore constructed new estimates of the realized rate of return on bonds issued on behalf of overseas borrowers in the United States and United Kingdom during the 1920s. Tracking these bonds, sometimes for more than half a century, proves to be a daunting task. Rather than attempting to follow all overseas issues, we took random samples of 50 dollar bonds for foreign borrowers issued in the United States in the period 1924–1930 and 31 colonial and foreign government loans offered for subscription in London in the period 1923–1930.

Dominick and Dominick, in their annual reviews, provide a listing and brief report on all foreign dollar issues.[43] Out of approximately 300 bonds, we selected every sixth one listed by this publication to form our sample of 50. The source for information on sterling bonds was the publications of the London Stock Exchange.[44] Our procedure for selecting sterling bonds was the same as with dollar bonds except for the sampling factor and the treatment of Australian loans. Since Australian issues were so heavily represented in sterling loans offered on behalf of overseas governments, to ensure adequate geographical coverage we included one in five rather than one in six of the colonial and foreign government issues listed by the Stock Exchange and stratified the sample by including only half the Australian loans which would have otherwise been selected.[45]

We then collected information on interest and principal paid, as reported on dollar bonds by Dominick and Dominick through 1937 and by the Foreign Bondholders Protective Council thereafter. Comparable information on sterling loans was extracted from Stock Exchange Yearbooks and the Stock Exchange Daily Official List. Since amounts paid fluctuated by year, as our measure of the yield we calculated the internal rate of return.

Assumptions had to be adopted in order to estimate these rates of return. For example, in many cases no information was provided on the share of bondholders who accepted a plan offered by a foreign government in settlement of its default. Lacking evidence to the contrary, we assumed that bondholders accepted the plan. When two options were offered in settlement

---

[43] Dominick and Dominick (1924–1937).
[44] Issues of the *Stock Exchange Yearbook* were supplemented as necessary by the *Stock Exchange Daily Official List*.
[45] In the calculations to follow, the return on individual issues is weighted by the value of the loan. To adjust for stratification, we doubled the weight on each Australian issue included in the final sample of sterling loans.

of default, it was straightforward to construct the overall rate of return by weighting the rates under the alternative plans by the shares of bondholders which accepted each. When no such information was provided, we were forced to assume that half the bondholders accepted each alternative. Only interest paid in cash is included. Interest paid in scrip or blocked balances is not counted as a component of the rate of return until the year it actually accrued to the lender in sterling or dollars.

Our estimates of the internal rate of return on the two samples of bonds, weighted by the value of the initial issues, are 0.72% for the entire sample of dollar bonds and 5.41% for sterling loans. If we restrict the sample of dollar bonds to those issued by governments or with government guarantees (all the sterling loans in our sample are in this category), the IRR is 3.25%, much closer to the comparable sterling loan figure.

The first observation to be made is that these numbers are positive, a fact not previously known. A second observation is that investors in sterling and dollar bonds appear to have fared differently in the long term. While the internal rate of return on sterling issues is quite close to the statutory rate under the bond covenants, the return on the full sample of dollar issues is small relative to the statutory rate. The latter is only 10% of the average rate of return on foreign dollar bonds for the period 1924–1930 as it appears in table 4. Moreover, the 1924–1930 returns in table 4 underestimate the yield to maturity since they deflate interest payments by the initial sales price of the bond.[46] Similarly, our internal rate of return calculations may overstate the return received by typical American investors, some of whom may have resold their bonds to the defaulting government at deep discounts in transactions of which we have no record.

On the other hand, converting the time series of returns on each sterling loan into dollars at the applicable exchange rates and recalculating the IRR gives somewhat lower IRRs, reflecting the secular depreciation of sterling. The average IRR falls by 0.6% and therefore comes closer to the figure for dollar bonds. The pattern does not change much, however, nor would any of the results reported here.

By themselves, the adequacy of these yields is difficult to gauge. Comparisons with the yields on other bonds may be helpful; these are provided in table 5. Note that no correction for default has been made to the municipal, railroad and corporate bond yields in the table; doing so would require another extensive calculation. However, the yield on high grade municipals was not dissimilar from the yield on U.S. Treasury bonds, a default-free asset. In comparison, the realized rate of return on foreign dollar bonds is

[46]Most of the bonds in the sample sold at considerable discounts and were expected to yield capital gains when redeemed at par. The most dramatic case is the German United Industrial Corporation's Hydro-Electric First Mortgage, a 20 year bond which sold at 84.5% of par due to its relatively low 6% coupon.

Table 5
Rates of return on alternative dollar and sterling bonds (in percentage points).[a]

Dollar bonds		Sterling bonds	
Bond	Yield	Bond	Yield
High grade municipals	4.11	Treasury bills	3.84
10 railroad bonds	4.45	Short dated gilts	4.46
Aaa corporate bonds	4.71	Consol rate	4.48
Aa corporate bonds	4.97	31 Government and government-guaranteed overseas bonds	5.41
A corporate bonds	5.31		
Baa corporate bonds	5.97		
33 Government and government-guaranteed foreign bonds	3.25		
50 Foreign bonds (including corporate issues)	0.72		

[a] All figures except for foreign and overseas bonds are average yields to maturity over the periods 1924–1930 for dollar bonds and 1923–1930 for sterling bonds. For foreign and overseas bonds, the internal rate of return is reported. *Source*: For foreign and overseas bonds, see text. Railroad bond yields are from Tinbergen (1934, pp. 211–212). Other dollar–bond yields are from Federal Reserve Board (1935, p. 185). British consol rate is from Mitchell and Deane (1962). Other sterling–bond yields are from London and Cambridge Economic Service (1970).

disappointing. Note that the same cannot be said of sterling loans: their internal rate of return exceeds the average yield on consols over the period.

One way to gauge the impact of default on the realized yield is to regress the internal rate of return (IIR) on a constant and a dummy variable for default. Since all the sterling bonds in our sample are government-issued or government-guaranteed, for comparability we use here only the subsample of dollar bonds which are government or government-guaranteed (although in fact a regression for the full sample of 50 dollar bonds gives results almost identical to those for the subsample of 33). Weighted least squares (WLS) is used where the weights are the value of the bond issue relative to the mean value of issues in the sample. This yields:

$$\text{IRR (dollar bonds)} = 6.74 - 11.02 \text{ DEFAULT,}$$
$$(2.80) \quad (2.87)$$
$$n = 33, \quad \text{S.E.} = 12.17,$$

$$\text{IRR (sterling bonds)} = 5.82 - 1.68 \text{ DEFAULT,}$$
$$(0.06) \quad (0.48)$$
$$n = 31, \quad \text{S.E.} = 0.98$$

with standard errors in parentheses. The constant terms can be interpreted as the internal rate of return for issues on which there was no default. It is clear that differences in the return to bonds on which there was no default do not account for the very different experience of British and American investors; rather, the greater cost of default on American issues more than accounts for the difference. That differential in constant terms which exists is, however, consistent with the information on the rate at which interest accrued in the 1920s as summarized in table 4.

In each case, the internal rate of return on foreign bonds that fell into default was significantly less than the rate of return on bonds which continued to be serviced despite the best efforts of the bondholders' protective committees and the American and British governments. However, according to the point estimates of the dummy variables for all issues experiencing some form of default, an interruption to debt service on dollar bonds reduced the internal rate of return by, on average, 11%. On sterling bonds the cost of an interruption to debt service averaged in contrast less than 2%. That the return on continuously serviced sterling loans was lower than that on comparable dollar loans while the cost of the average default on dollar loans was higher reinforces the hypothesis that this differential default risk was recognized in the 1920s and incorporated into the required rate of return on the two categories of assets.

As an accounting exercise, the weighted rates of return can be regressed on vectors of dummy variables for year of issue, location, or type of borrower. In this way the returns realized by investors in different types of bonds can be compared. Table 6 reports WLS regressions of the internal rate of return against a constant term and a vector of dummy variables for year. The first year in the sample – 1923 for sterling loans and 1924 for dollar loans – is the omitted alternative, and its average rate of return is the constant term. It has been argued that the quality of loans deteriorated as the decade progressed and that this should have been reflected in the realized rate of return. There is weak evidence to this effect in the case of dollar bonds. Realized rates of return are lower for loans issued in most years after 1924, but not significantly at standard confidence levels. The variation in the internal rate of return on sterling bonds by year of issue is quite different. For reasons that are not obvious, that rate is significantly lower for loans issued in the period 1924–1926 than either before or after.

Table 7 shows regressions of the internal rate of return on a vector of geographical dummy variables. The omitted alternative is Germany, so the rate of return on German bonds is picked up by the constant term. The positive coefficients suggest that investors in non-German bonds did relatively well; the returns on Central American, South American, Western European, Eastern European and Japanese bonds are all significantly greater than the returns on German bonds at the 90% confidence level or better. It is

Table 6
Realized rates of return on overseas loans by year of issue (dependent variable is rate of return in percentage points).[a]

Variable	Dollar loans (i)	Sterling loans (ii)
Constant	4.815	6.408
	(4.76)	(0.39)
1924		−3.243
		(0.85)
1925	−0.330	−1.285
	(5.39)	(0.52)
1926	−0.776	−1.623
	(5.37)	(0.71)
1927	−14.980	−0.581
	(5.43)	(0.39)
1928	−5.139	−2.877
	(5.75)	(2.804)
1929	−0.201	0.962
	(16.54)	(15.90)
1930	0.138	−0.633
	(46.45)	(0.50)
S.E. of regression	13.151	0.923
R^2	0.34	0.99
Number of obs.	50.00	31.00

[a]Equations are estimated using weighted least squares. Standard errors in parentheses. In column (i), the omitted alternative is 1924; in column (ii) it is 1923. Note that the entire sample of 50 foreign dollar bonds is used in these estimates. *Source*: See text.

not surprising that the rate of return on German bonds proved particularly low, since most of them fell into default in 1933–1934 after which no interest was paid for two or even three decades. Nor is it surprising that the return on Western European bonds was significantly higher, since most of those in the sample were continuously serviced, the Italian bonds providing a notable exception. However, the difference between Germany on the one hand and Japan, Latin America and Eastern Europe on the other is intriguing since default occurred on all the Japanese and East European dollar bonds and most of the South American dollar bonds in the sample. However, while the German bonds remained in default for two or three decades, the Japanese bonds in the sample fell into default only in 1942 and service was resumed as early as 1952. Partial interest continued to be paid on many of the South American bonds, and readjustments, involving conversions to new principal and interest amounts, were offered on the South American bonds in our sample between 1936 and 1948.

Table 7

Realized rates of return on overseas loans by country or continental group (dependent variable is rate of return in percentage points).[a]

Variable	Dollar loans (i)	Sterling loans (ii)
Constant (Germany)	−14.451 (1.49)	3.021 (2.42)
Central America	19.087 (10.23)	
South America	19.231 (2.01)	−1.752 (3.11)
Australia	19.911 (13.31)	2.804 (2.42)
Japan	20.876 (4.16)	2.429 (2.50)
Western Europe	21.171 (2.01)	−0.053 (2.54)
Eastern Europe	13.491 (5.50)	1.483 (2.88)
S.E. of regression	7.644	0.928
R^2	0.76	0.99
number of obs.	50	31

[a] Equations are estimated using weighted least squares. Standard errors in parentheses. The constant term is a point estimate of the return on bonds floated for the omitted borrower, Germany. The point estimate of the return on bonds issued on behalf of borrowers in other regions is the sum of the constant and the relevant slope coefficient. The entire sample of 50 dollar bonds is used for these estimates. *Source*: See text.

In contrast, there is little statistically significant variation by borrowing country or continent in the rate of return on sterling bonds. It appears that British investors, perhaps due to their government's anticipated threat of trade sanctions, were able to secure a positive rate of return on their German investments which did not fall significantly short of the return on other overseas loans.

In a similar accounting exercise, tables 8 and 9 show regressions of the weighted internal rate of return on a vector of dummy variables for type of borrower, where national government is the omitted alternative. Despite the preoccupation of many commentators with sovereign default, it appears that investors who lent to national governments ultimately received respectable rates of return. According to table 8, concerned with dollar bonds, only returns on loans to corporations and to banks affiliated with national governments (which include in this sample the Mortgage Bank of the

Table 8
Realized rates of return on dollar loans by category of borrower (dependent variable is rate of return in percentage points).[a]

Variable	(i)	(ii)
Constant	5.706	5.706
	(1.09)	(1.08)
State	−3.129	
	(5.59)	
Provincial	−0.093	
	(29.19)	
State or provincial		−3.03
		(5.43)
Municipal	−0.951	−0.951
	(3.29)	(3.27)
Nationally affiliated bank	−23.54	−23.54
	(2.33)	(2.31)
Other bank	−5.004	−5.004
	(7.22)	(7.13)
Corporate	−10.93	−10.93
	(2.48)	(2.46)
S.E. of regression	8.208	8.110
R^2	0.72	0.72

[a] Equations estimated by weighted least squares. Standard error in parentheses. The constant term is the point estimate of the return on loans to the omitted borrowers, national governments. The point estimate of the return on loans to other types of borrowers is the sum of the constant and the relevant slope coefficient. The entire sample of 50 dollar bonds is used in these estimates. Source: See text.

Kingdom of Denmark, the German Central Bank for Agriculture, the National Bank of Panama, the Mortgage Bank of Chile, and the Mortgage and Agricultural Mortgage Banks of Colombia) fell significantly short of the returns on loans to national governments at the 95% confidence level. Table 9 shows for sterling bonds that the rate of return on loans to national governments was virtually indistinguishable from the return on loans to corporations and on British Funds. (British Funds was the name given to loans insured or guaranteed by the British government itself.) Contemporary preoccupation with defaults by national governments may have been justified insofar as sovereign default encouraged or provided a rationale for defaults by the country's other foreign borrowers. But the settlements provided by national governments which defaulted on their sterling obligations, such as Italy, Chile, and Colombia, appear to have been relatively favorable to the creditors, yielding internal rates of return in the range of 3 to 5%.

Table 9
Realized rates of return on sterling loans by category of borrower (dependent variable is rate of return in percentage points).[a]

Variable	(i)	(ii)
Constant	4.260	4.260
	(0.52)	(0.51)
British funds	0.650	0.650
	(2.45)	(2.40)
Dominion: Provincial or colonial government securities	1.559	1.559
	(0.524)	(0.51)
Dominion: Provincial or colonial corporation stocks	0.979	
	(12.79)	
Foreign corporation stocks	−0.470	
	(2.19)	
All corporation stocks		−0.431
		(2.13)
S.E. of regression	1.045	1.026
R^2	0.99	0.99

[a] Equations estimated by weighted least squares. Standard errors in parentheses. The constant term is the point estimate of the return on loans to the omitted borrower, national governments. The point estimate of the return on loans to other types of borrowers is the sum of the constant and the relevant slope coefficients. *Source:* See text.

9. Directions for research

In this paper we have focused exclusively on three aspects of interwar experience with external debt and default: the pattern of borrowing, the incidence of default, and the returns realized by the lenders. Despite conscious efforts to circumscribe the range of issues considered, important aspects of each question have been left untouched. Thus, we have not considered the role of the League of Nations in the League Loans of the 1920s and their relationship to the expansion of the international capital market. Nor have we considered the similarities and differences between the Kemmerer Missions to Latin America and IMF conditionality. A further omission especially relevant to our analysis of default is the treatment of war debts and reparations generally and the 1931 Hoover Moratorium in particular.

Another intriguing issue which we have not yet begun to address is the relationship of default to the subsequent economic performance of the borrowing countries. Whether default disrupted trade and capital flows in ways with serious implications for the subsequent growth of the capital-importing economies is a question with obvious implications for our assessment of the management of recent debt-servicing difficulties.

Appendix tables

Table A.1
Demand for international reserves, annual cross sections, 1930–1938 (dependent variable is LGOLD).[a]

Years	n	Constant	LGDP	LMD	LCVX	R^2
1930	22	−4.53 (0.91)	1.17 (0.10)	0.16 (0.29)	0.14 (0.18)	0.91
1931	21	−1.32 (2.20)	0.23 (0.18)	0.36 (0.71)	0.51 (0.13)	0.52
1932	21	−3.53 (1.32)	1.13 (0.10)	0.39 (0.44)	−0.06 (0.07)	0.85
1933	18	−3.90 (1.34)	1.17 (0.14)	0.42 (0.76)	−0.06 (0.08)	0.84
1934	23	−3.13 (1.35)	1.17 (0.16)	0.86 (0.34)	−0.09 (0.09)	0.73
1935	23	−3.04 (1.56)	1.14 (0.16)	0.79 (0.46)	−0.02 (0.10)	0.69
1936	22	−2.22 (1.73)	1.11 (0.19)	1.16 (0.62)	0.06 (0.12)	0.60
1937	19	−3.11 (3.27)	1.23 (0.29)	1.58 (0.68)	0.16 (0.15)	0.59
1938	16	−2.35 (3.92)	1.20 (0.36)	1.65 (0.81)	0.15 (0.19)	0.51
1930–1938	185	−2.87 (0.52)	1.16 (0.05)	0.76 (0.13)	0.26 (0.12)	0.75

[a] Equations estimated by ordinary least squares. Standard errors in parentheses. Variable definitions include:

LGOLD: log of gold reserves,
LGDP: log of GDP,
LMD: log of the import/GDP ratio,
LCVX: log of the coefficient of variation of exports for the three years $T-2$, $T-1$, T.

Table A.2
List of foreign dollar bonds used in rate of return calculation.[a]

(1) Alpine Montan Steel Corporation (Austria, 1926, $5m, 5.92%)
(2) Kingdom of Belgium Stabilization Loan (Belgium, 1926, $50m, 7.89%)
(3) Kingdom of Denmark (Denmark, 1925, $30m, 5.49%)
(4) Mortgage Bank of the Kingdom of Denmark (Denmark, 1927, $4.3m, 5.33%)
(5) Finnish Guaranteed Municipal Loan of 1924 (Finland, 1924, $7m, 8.66%)

Continued overleaf

Table A.2 (continued)

(6) International Power Securities Corp., Delaware Corp., Collateral Trust 'B' (France, 1924, $4m, 7.57%)
(7) Free State of Oldenburg (Germany, 1925, $3m, 4.99%)
(8) City of Berlin (Germany, 1928, $15m, 3.0%)
(9) City of Hanover Convertible Bond (Germany, 1929, $3.5m, 4.49%)
(10) German Central Bank for Agriculture (Germany, 1927, $50m, −19.41%)
(11) General Consolidated Municipal Loan of German Savings Banks and Clearing Associations (Germany, 1928, $17.5m, 3.67%)
(12) Saxon State Mortgage Institution (Germany, 1925, $5m, −8.58%)
(13) Brandenburg Electric Company (Germany, 1928, $5m, 2.49%)
(14) Gelsenkirchen Mining Corp. (Germany, 1928, $15m, 6.53%)
(15) Hamburg Electric Company (Germany, 1925, $4m, −8.95%)
(16) Leipzig Overland Power Companies (Germany, 1926, $3m, −3.52%)
(17) Oberpfalz Electric Power Corp. (Germany, 1926, $1.25m, −11.97%)
(18) Rhine-Westfalia Electric Power Corp. (Germany, 1925, $10m, −8.68%)
(19) Seimens and Halske A.G. Siemens Schuckertwerker G.m.b.H. (Germany, 1926, $24m, −14.20%)
(20) United Industrial Corp. Hydro-Electric First Mortgage (Germany, 1925, $6m, −9.49%)
(21) Westphalia United Electric Power Corp. (Germany, 1928, $20m, −24.12%)
(22) Hungarian Consolidated Municipal Loan (Secured) (Hungary, 1925, $10m, −6.36%)
(23) Hungarian–Italian Bank, Ltd. Mortgage Loan 'AC' (Hungary, 1928, $1m, −20.01%)
(24) Irish Free State (Ireland, 1927, $15m, 5.23%)
(25) Fiat (Italy, 1926, $10m, 7.73%)
(26) Italian Credit Consortium for Public Works (Secured 'B') (Italy, 1927, $7.5m, 4.82%)
(27) Terni First Mortgage for Hydro-Electric 'A' (Italy, 1928, $12m, 4.57%)
(28) City of Bergen (Norway, 1930, $1.9m, 5.71%)
(29) Norwegian Hydro-Electric Nitrogen Corp. (Refunding 'A') (Norway, 1927, $20m, 6.19%)
(30) Land Mortgage Bank of Warsaw Guaranteed First Mortgage (Poland, 1924, $15m, 0.76%)
(31) Swedish Government (Sweden, 1924, $30m, 5.57%)
(32) Republic of Cuba Public Works Certificate (Cuba, 1929, $9.75m, 4.63%)
(33) National Bank of Panama (Panama, 1926, $1m, 5.19%)
(34) Government of the Argentine Nation (Argentina, 1925, $45m, 6.57%)
(35) Province of Buenos Aires (Argentina, 1930, $3m, 4.65%)
(36) Province of Tucuman (Argentina, 1927, $2.1225m, 7.54%)
(37) Pan-American Independent Corp. First Lien Collateral Trust Loan (Argentina, 1927, $3m, −26.45%)
(38) State of Parana (Brazil, 1928, $4.86m, 1.93%)
(39) State of Sao Paulo Secured Loan (Brazil, 1925, 15m, 3.61%)
(40) Republic of Chile (Chile, 1925, $27.5m, 2.52%)
(41) Mortgage Bank of Chile Guaranteed Agricultural Notes (Chile, 1926, $10m, 2.37%)
(42) Republic of Colombia (Colombia, 1928, $35m, 3.92%)
(43) Department of Caldas Secured Loan (Colombia, 1926, $10m, 2.98%)
(44) City of Baranquilla Secured Loan 'C' (Colombia, 1926, $0.5m, 5.04%)
(45) Agricultural Morgage Bank Guaranteed Loan (Colombia, 1927, $3m, 3.50%)
(46) Mortgage Bank of Colombia (Colombia, 1927, $4m, 5.18%)
(47) Republic of Uruguay (Uruguay, 1926, $30m, 4.96%)
(48) City of Brisbane (Australia, 1927, $7.5, 5.46%)
(49) City of Tokio (sic) (Japan, 1927, $20.64m, 5.82%)
(50) Toho Electric Power Corp. Ltd. First Mortgage 'A' (Japan, 1927, $15m, 7.57%)

*Borrowing country, year of issue, face value of issue in millions (m) of dollars, and estimated internal rate of return appear in parentheses.

Table A.3
List of colonial and foreign government sterling bonds used in rate of return calculation

(1) 1923 Sudan Govt. 4½% Guaran. Stk [R 1/1/73]
3,763,400; IP 93; LT 1; IRR 4.91 (4.97)[a]

(2) 1923 Roumanian 4% External Loan of 1922
[R 1980] 2,500,000 IP 67; LT 5; IRR 4.68

(3) 1923 Rangoon (City of) 5½% Debentures [R 1/9/53]
300,000; IP 98½; LT 3; IRR 5.78

(4) 1923 Union of South African Govt. 5% Inscribed Stk
[R 15/1/34] 13,000,000; IP 99½; LT 2; IRR 8.14

(5) 1923 South Australia Govt. 5% Registered Stk
[C 15/3/34] 5,650,300; IP 99; LT 2; IRR 5.08

(6) 1924 Amsterdam (City of) 5½% Strlng Loan 1924
[R 1/10/35] 2,500,000; IP 96½; LT 4; IRR 6.13

(7) 1924 Czechoslovak 8% Strlng Loan of 1922 (series B)
[R 31/12/60] 2,050,000; IP 96½; LT 5; IRR 8.41 (8.49)[a]

(8) 1924 Greek Govt. 7% Refugee Loan of 1924
[Serviced] 10,000,000; IP 88; LT 5; IRR 2.76

(9) 1925 Danzig (Municipality) 7% Strlng Bonds of 1925
[R 1/8/76] 1,500,000; IP 90; LT 4; IRR 4.79 (6.32)[a]

(10) 1925 South Africa (Union of) 5% Inscribd Stk
[R 10/10/41] 23,000,000; IP 99½; LT 2; IRR 5.14

(11) 1925 Gold Coast Govt. 4½% Inscribd Stk
[R 1/1/56] 4,628,000; IP 94; LT 2; IRR 4.75

(12) 1926 Chilean Govt. 6% Loan 1926
[R 1/2/78] 2,809,000; IP 94; LT 5; IRR 1.03 (2.70)[a]

(13) 1926 New Zealand Govt. 5% Inscribed Stk 1946
[R 1/1/46] 12,893,925; IP 98½; LT 2; IRR 5.01

(14) 1926 Westphalia (Province) 7% Strlng loan of 1926
[R 15/7/71] 835,000; IP 98½; LT 5; IRR 4.08

(15) 1926 Hamburg (State of) 6% Strlng Bonds of 1926
[R 1/10/71] 2,000,000; IP 93¼; LT 5; IRR 2.89 (3.25)[a]

(16) 1926 Newfoundland Govt. 5% Bonds 1951
[C 19/11/34] 1,027,300; IP 99; LT 2; IRR 5.218

(17) 1927 Port Elizabeth Corp. 5% Redeemable Stk 1962
[R 30/6/62] 350,000; IP 99; LT 3; IRR 5.27

(18) 1927 State of Rio de Janeiro 7% Strlng Bonds
[Serviced] 1,891,000; IP 97; LT 5; IRR 1.14

(19) 1927 Free City of Danzig 6½% Twenty-Year Strlng
Bonds [R 1/8/76] 1,900,000; IP 91; LT 5; IRR 1.94 (4.05)[a]

(20) 1927 City of Santos (Brazil) 7% Consolidated Strlng loan
[Serviced] 2,260,000; IP 97; LT 4; IRR 1.73

(21) 1927 Govt. Commonwealth of Australia 5% Registered Stk
[C 1/5/45] 72,114,734; IP 97¼; LT 2; IRR 5.83

(22) 1928 City of Wellington 5% Debentures
[R 1/3/50] 63,000; IP 98; LT 3; IRR 5.29

(23) 1928 Govt. New Zealand 4½% Inscribed Stk
[R 1/11/47] 11,224,998; IP 94½; LT 2; IRR 4.91

(24) 1928 Govt. Newfoundland 5% Bonds 1953
[C 19/11/34] 2,055,400; IP 100; LT 2; IRR 5.0

(25) 1928 City of Cologne 6% 25-Year Strlng Bonds
[R 31/10/73] 1,150,000; IP 95½; LT 4; IRR 2.35 (3.10)[a]

(26) 1928 City of Munich 6% Strlng Bonds
[R 1/12/73] 1,625,000; IP 94; LT 4; IRR 1.77 (4.02)[a]

(27) 1929 City of Abo (Finland) 30-Year 6½% Strlng Bonds
[R 1/4/39] 500,000; IP 94½; LT 4; IRR 7.37

Continued overleaf

(28)	1930	City of Hobart 6% Debentures 1940
		[R 1/5/40] 85,000; IP 100; LT 3; IRR 6.19
(29)	1930	Japanese Govt. 5½% Conversion loan 1930
		[R 1/1/70] 12,500,000; IP 90; LT 5; IRR 5.45 (5.83)[a]
(30)	1930	Austrian Govt. International Loan 1930 7% String Bonds
		[R 1/7/79] 3,500,000; IP 95; LT 5; IRR 3.83 (4.05)[a]
(31)	1930	City of Bloemfontein 5% Inscribed Stk 1960
		[R 31/12/60] 500,000 IP 101; LT 3; IRR 4.92

Each loan is accompanied by the following information:
Date of issue
Title
Redemption date [R...] or date of conversion [C...] or still being serviced [Serviced]
Total face value of issue in pounds sterling
Issue price IP (par value always 100)
Loan Type (LT)
(1) British funds
(2) Dominion, provincial and colonial govt. securities
(3) Corporation stocks–dominion, Indian and colonial
(4) Corporation stocks–foreign
(5) Foreign stocks, bonds, etc.
Internal rate of return, in %

[a]Repayments of principal outstanding can be undertaken by purchases at or under par or by drawings at par. The figure within brackets assumes annual repayments of principle are made at par. The other assumes repayments at market price, if less than par, otherwise at par.

Data appendix

The macroeconomic data used in our cross-section analysis are drawn from a variety of sources. While problems of comparability between the statistics of different countries will be familiar to many readers, who are used to interpreting the results of international cross sections with special care, an additional cautionary word is in order. A number of the series used here, notably the national income accounts and price deflators, must be regarded as approximations. We have attempted therefore to maintain a provisional tone in interpreting the results. Major series are as follows.

National income. Gross domestic product is used wherever possible. For Europe estimates are drawn from Mitchell (1976). Data for South America can be found in CEPAL (1978) and for Central America in Thorp (1984). Constant price series for Latin America were adjusted to current prices using Wilkie (1974). The series for Japan is from Mitchell (1982) and for Australia from Butlin (1977).

Balance of trade. Special trade, which excludes gold and silver bullion and specie. The value of imports and exports for the majority of European countries is from Mitchell (1976). For Austria, Hungary, Czechoslovakia, Poland, Latin America, Australia and Japan, figures are from the League of

Nations publications on trade and payments listed at the end of this appendix.

Terms of trade. Import unit values divided by export unit values, normalized to 1929 = 100 and drawn from sources described above.

Population. From League of Nations *Statistical Yearbooks*.

Central government revenue and expenditure. For Europe, from Mitchell (1976). For other countries, from League of Nations *Statistical Yearbooks*.

Exchange rates. From League of Nations *Statistical Yearbooks*. Where both market rates and official rates were reported, market rates were used. For Spain, the Burgos rate was used because it exhibited more variability than the Madrid rate.

Prices. Few reliable consumer price indices are available for this period. The wholesale price index was used where available while composite price indices were used for certain Latin American countries. These indices are drawn from League of Nations *Statistical Yearbooks*, except for Central America, data for which is from Thorp (1984).

Money supply and gold. The only comparable monetary measure is total central bank note (and, where available, coin) circulation, from Mitchell (1976), except for Austria, Hungary, Czechoslovakia, Poland, Latin America, Australia and Japan, in which cases it is drawn from League of Nations *Statistical Yearbooks*. Gold reserves are drawn from these same sources.

Debt and debt service. Domestic and external debt, along with total and, where available, external debt service (interest plus amortization) were drawn from League of Nations *Statistical Yearbooks*. These are end-of-year figures. Where *Statistical Yearbooks* provide no information, data are drawn from the League's *Memoranda on Public Finance*.

Default and arrears. Data on these variables are found, for sterling bonds, in the *Reports* of the Council of the Corporation of Foreign Bondholders and, for dollar bonds, in the *Annual Reports* of the Foreign Bondholders Protective Council.

The following countries were included in the cross-section analysis of borrowing: Hungary, Czechoslovakia, Poland, Brazil, Colombia, Mexico, Australia, Japan, Honduras, Ecuador, Bulgaria, Denmark, Finland, Germany, Greece, Italy, The Netherlands, Norway, Spain, Sweden, Guatemala, and El Salvador.

The following countries were included in the cross-section analysis of default: Austria, Hungary, Czechoslovakia, Argentina, Brazil, Colombia, Mexico, Australia, Japan, Chile, Bulgaria, Denmark, Finland, Germany, Greece, Italy, The Netherlands, Norway, Spain, Sweden, Costa Rica, and El Salvador.

Sources and Documents cited in data appendix

Butlin, M.W., 1977, A preliminary annual database 1900/01 to 1973/74 (Reserve Bank of Australia, Sydney).
CEPAL, 1978, Series historicas del crecimiento de America Latina (CEPAL).
Council of the Corporation of Foreign Bondholders, various years, Report (Corporation of Foreign Bondholders, London).
Foreign Bondholders Protective Council, various years, Annual report (Foreign Bondholders Protective Council, New York).
League of Nations, various years, Statistical yearbook (League of Nations, Geneva).
League of Nations, various years, Memorandum on public finance (League of Nations, Geneva).
League of Nations, various years, Review of world trade (League of Nations, Geneva).
League of Nations, various years, Balance of payments and foreign trade balances (League of Nations, Geneva).
Mitchell, B.R., 1976, European historical statistics (Macmillan, London).
Mitchell, B.R., 1982, International historical statistics: Africa and Asia (Macmillan, London).
Thorp, Rosemary, ed., 1984, Latin America in the 1930s (Macmillan, London).
Wilkie, J., 1974, Statistics and national policy (UCLA, Los Angeles, CA).

References

Angell, J.M., 1933, Financial foreign policy of the United States (Council on Foreign Relations, New York).
Cairncross, Alec and Barry Eichengreen, 1983, Sterling in decline (Blackwell, Oxford).
Committee on Finance and Industry, 1931, Report (HMSO, London).
Darity, William A., Jr., 1985, Loan pushing: Doctrine and theory, Board of Governors of the Federal Reserve System, International Finance discussion paper no. 253.
De Cecco, Marcello, 1984, The international debt problem in the interwar period, European University working paper no. 84/103.
Diaz-Alejandro, Carlos, F., 1983, Stories of the 1930s for the 1980s, in: P. Aspe Armella, R. Dornbusch and M. Obstfeld, eds., Financial policies and the world capital market: The problem of Latin American countries (University of Chicago Press, Chicago, IL).
Diaz-Alejandro, Carlos F., 1984, Latin-American debt: I don't think we are in Kansas anymore, Brookings Papers on Economic Activity 2, 335–404.
Dominick and Dominick, 1924–1937, Dollar bonds issued in the United States (A. Iselin and Co., New York).
Dornbusch, Rudiger and Stanley Fischer, 1984, The open economy: Implications for monetary and fiscal policy, NBER working paper no. 1422.
Dunn, Robert W., 1926, American foreign investments (Viking Press, New York).
Eaton, Jonathon and Mark Gersovitz, 1981, Debt with potential repudiation: Theoretical and empirical analysis, Review of Economic Studies 48, 289–309.
Edelstein, Michael, 1981, Foreign investment and empire 1860–1914, in R. Floud and D. McCloskey, eds., The economic history of Britain since 1700 (Cambridge University Press, Cambridge), vol. 2, 70–98.

Edwards, Sebastian, 1984, The role of international reserves and foreign debt in the external adjustment process, in: J. Muns, ed., Adjustment, conditionality and international financing (IMF, Washington, DC).
Eichengreen, Barry, 1985, The Australian economic recovery of the 1930s in international comparative perspective, prepared for the conference on Australia in the great depression, Canberra, and forthcoming in the conference volume.
Feder, Gershon and Richard E. Just, 1977, A study of debt servicing capacity applying logit analysis, Journal of Development Economics 4, 25–38.
Feder, Gershon, Richard E. Just and Knud Ross, 1981, Projecting debt servicing capacity of developing countries, Journal of Financial and Quantitative Analysis 16, 651–669.
Federal Reserve Board, 1935, Annual report for 1934 (GPO, Washington, DC).
Feinstein, Charles, 1972, National income, expenditure and output of the United Kingdom, 1855–1965 (Cambridge University Press, Cambridge).
Feuerlein, Willy and Elizabeth Hannan, 1941, Dollars in Latin America (Council on Foreign Relations, New York).
Harris, C.R.S., 1935, Germany's foreign indebtedness (Oxford University Press, Oxford).
Jenks, Leland, 1927, The migration of British capital (Allen and Unwin, London).
Kaletsky, Anatole, 1985, The costs of default (Twentieth Century Fund, New York).
Lewis, Cleona, 1945, Debtor and creditor countries: 1938, 1944 (Brookings Institution, Washington, DC).
Lewis, W.A., 1949, Economic survey 1919–1939 (Allen and Unwin, London).
London and Cambridge Economic Service, 1970, The British economy: Key statistics, 1900–1970 (Times Newspapers, London).
London Stock Exchange, 1923–1983, Yearbook (T. Skinner, London).
London Stock Exchange, 1923–1983, Daily official list (T. Skinner, London).
McDonald, Donogh C., 1982, Debt capacity and developing country borrowing: A survey of the literature, Staff papers 29, 603–645.
Madden, J.T., M. Nadler and H.C. Sauvain, 1937, America's experiences as a creditor nation (Prentice-Hall, New York).
Mitchell, B.R. and P. Deane, 1962, Abstract of British historical statistics (Cambridge University Press, Cambridge).
Moggridge, Donald E., 1971, British controls on long term capital movements, 1924–31, in: D.N. McCloskey, ed., Essays on a mature economy (Princeton University Press, Princeton, NJ) 113–142.
Morrow, Dwight W., 1972, Who buys foreign bonds? Foreign Affairs 5, 219–232.
Nurkse, Ragnar, 1944, International currency experience (League of Nations, Geneva).
Platt, D.C.M., 1984, Foreign finance in Continental Europe and the U.S.A., 1815–1870 (Allen and Unwin, London).
Portes, Richard and David Winter, 1980, Disequilibrium estimates for consumption goods markets in centrally planned economies, Review of Economic Studies 47, 137–159.
Richardson, J.H., 1936, British economic foreign policy (Allen and Unwin, London).
Riedel, James, 1983, Determinants of LDC borrowing in international financial markets: Theory and empirical evidence, Mimeo.
Rosett, Richard N. and Forrest D. Nelson, 1975, Estimation of the two-limit probit regression model, Econometrica 43, 141–146.
Royal Institute of International Affairs, 1937, The problem of international investment (Oxford University Press, London).
Sachs, Jeffrey, 1983, LDC debt in the 1980s: Risks and reforms, in: Paul Wachtel, ed., Crises in economic and financial structure (Lexington Books, Lexington, MA).
Salter, Sir Arthur, 1933, Recovery: The second effort (G. Bell, London; revised edition).
Sayers, Richard S., 1976, The Bank of England, 1891–1944 (Cambridge University Press, Cambridge).
Securities and Exchange Commission, 1936, Report on the study and investigation of the work, activities, personnel and functions of protective and reorganization committees (GPO, Washington, DC).
Summers, Lawrence and J. B. De Long, 1984, The changing cyclical variability of economic activity in the United States, Harvard Institute of Economic Research discussion paper no. 1077.

Taylor, Henry C. and A.D. Taylor, 1943, World trade in agricultural products (Macmillan, New York).

Tinbergen, Jan, ed., 1934, International abstract of economic statistics, 1919–1930 (International Conference of Economic Services, London).

United States Department of Commerce, 1932, American underwriting of foreign securities in 1931 (GPO, Washington, DC).

United States Department of Commerce, 1976, Historical statistics of the United States: Colonial times to 1970 (GPO, Washington, DC).

[24]

INDUSTRIAL GROWTH AND TRADE POLICY IN PREWAR JAPAN

IPPEI YAMAZAWA

I. INTRODUCTION

JAPAN'S GROSS domestic product grew at an average 3.9 per cent per annum during half century prior to World War II, and it was the rapid expansion of manufacturing output (5.9 per cent per annum) that led aggregate economic growth. Industrialization was the proper choice for development of Japan which was endowed with few natural resources and a large labor force. A natural consequence of factor endowments is that Japan's industrialization was closely related to development of foreign trade. For the first two decades after beginning foreign trade in 1859, Japan traded raw silk and other specialty articles for manufactured consumer goods such as cotton and woolen textiles, but gradually shifted to a trade pattern in which raw materials were imported in exchange for processed exports.

Thus successful import substitution and export promotion were needed to accompany industrial growth. Figure 1 shows Japan's manufacturing production growth (including intermediate products) and imports and exports of manufactures (including trade between Japan and the prewar colonies of Taiwan and Korea). Imports of manufactured goods grew more rapidly than gross output of manufactures before 1900 but import growth rate slowed afterwards. Manufactured goods exports grew more rapidly than both imports and gross output throughout the whole period. The export growth rate was 7.6 per cent per year for the 1890–1940 period. Exports have exceeded imports since the mid-1920s and were ten times greater in 1965.

The output expansion that accompanied successful import substitution and export promotion was not made at the same time in all manufacturing industries. Production of cotton textiles, matches, and other miscellaneous labor-intensive articles was already taking place in the 1880s. By the turn of the century, after these articles were substituted for imports, they were exported. Production of iron and steel began in 1901. Domestic output has exceeded imports of iron and steel since 1923 and exports have been greater since 1932. Machinery and

---

The original research was carried out as a part of Professors Bhagwati and Krueger's NBER project on industrialization policies in less developed countries. The author is indebted to Professor Kazushi Ohkawa for encouraging him to take up this study. An analysis of Japan's trade policy in the post-World War II period will follow.

Fig. 1. Gross Output, Exports, and Imports of Manufactures
(Million yen at 1934–36 price)

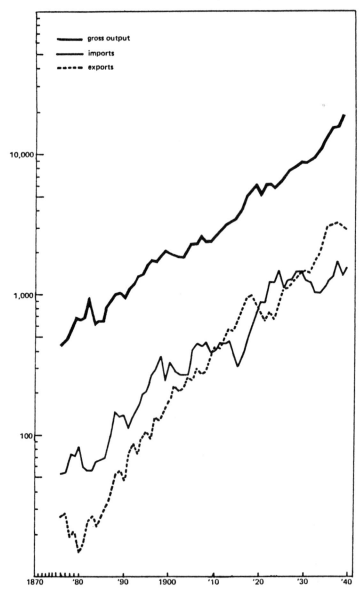

Note: Before World War II figures of output represent those of Japan proper and exports and imports in Figure 1 and trade balance in Figure 2 include trade between Japan proper on one hand and Taiwan and Korea on the other. For more details on figures and sources see [8].

chemical industries developed at about the same pace as the iron and steel industry. Full import substitution was almost completed by these industries before World War II. Exports of these commodities were confined primarily to Japan's sphere of influence (Taiwan, Korea, Manchuria, and Kwantung Province in China). Only after World War II were they exported to world markets at competitive prices.

The process of Japan's industrial growth was always under a balance of payment constraint. Figure 2 depicts the situation of Japan's balance of payments for the period before World War II. The dotted line shows the balance between exports of manufactures and imports of manufactures and raw materials, the balance of trade directly related to Japan's industrial growth. Balance of payment deficit continued for the first half of the period and, apart from the extraordinary export boom and set-back during and after World War I, made steady improvement in the late-1920s and 1930s. No doubt it was this balance of payment deficit in the early years of Japan's industrialization that made import substitution of manufactures one of the main aims of Japan's foreign trade policy.

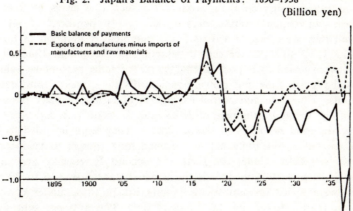

Fig. 2. Japan's Balance of Payments: 1890–1938
(Billion yen)

Source: See Figure 1.

The most important thing we have to examine is the role played by central government in industrial growth. What policies were taken to protect and promote industrial growth? Import duties were fixed at a less than 5 per cent ad valorem equivalent rate by 1899 and were raised afterwards. But what were the basic principles of government tariff policy and how did the tariff structure change? The main purpose here is to explain the institutional aspects of tariff policy and compiles quantitative data on the tariff structure during the period of 1890–1940.[1]

---

[1] Professor Lockwood appraised the role of tariff protection during this period. "On bal-

Non-tariff protection policies such as import quotas, production subsidies, government purchases, and export promotion cannot be neglected in our discussion but the lack of reliable data prevents us from giving more than a brief comment.

II. HISTORY OF TARIFF PROTECTION

The tariff treaty with foreign powers in 1866 established initial conditions for development of Japan's industry and trade. It limited Japanese import and export duties unilaterally to as a low rate as 5 per cent for specific duties (ad valorem equivalent) on most commodities. Except for foodstuffs, grains, and coal, most raw materials for industrial production were not exempted from those duties. The ad valorem equivalent rate of these duties declined to 2 or 2.5 per cent due to inflation in the first two decades of the Meiji era.

After continued efforts to revise the treaty, Japan resumed tariff autonomy in 1899. The Tariff Law was established in March 1897, and went into effect in January 1899. General revision of the Tariff Law was made in 1906, 1911, 1926, and 1932 but partial revision were made almost every year. On the other hand, the tariff treaty with the United Kingdom and other foreign powers in 1866 restricted tariffs on their products to such low levels as 5 to 15 per cent. These conventional tariffs were levied on 40 per cent of all dutiable imports and they were maintained until the complete resumption of tariff autonomy in 1911. With a 35 per cent devaluation of the yen in 1932 all specific duty items were levied as import surcharges of the same percentage value.

Besides the Tariff Law and conventional tariffs there was a third category—special tariffs. Complete and partial exemption of tariffs on daily necessities at the time of the Great Earthquake of 1923 and those on rice and wheat in bad crop years are good examples of this category. They were intended to be temporary at the outset, but quite a few remained long enough to be incorporated in the tariff schedule. Under the First and Second Emergency Special Tariffs enacted in 1904 and 1905 to finance the Russo-Japanese War, 5 to 20 per cent surcharges were levied on almost all imports except those under conventional tariffs. This tended to be maintained thereafter. The 100 per cent duties on luxury merchandise consisting of 147 items in 1924 were enforced primarily for balance of payment purposes but were incorporated into the tariff schedule of 1926 and continued in effect until World War II.

Figure 3 shows changes in the average rates of tariffs which are defined as the ratio of total tariff revenues to either the value of total imports or that of

---

ance there can be little doubt that protection in home and colonial markets helped to extend the range and diversity of Japanese manufacturing. The older industries—silk and cotton textiles, and small scale consumer trades in great variety—needed little shelter from foreign competition over and above that provided by cultural differences and transport costs. But many newer industries requiring radical departures from traditional techniques and a large market for economical operation certainly benefited from tariff assistance, at least for a period of years" [6, p. 544].

Fig. 3. Average Tariffs Collected: 1868–1945

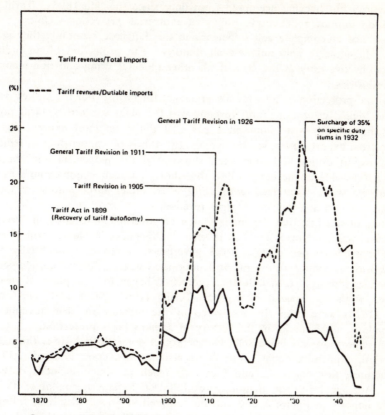

Source: Appendix Table I.

dutiable imports. Average tariff rates remained low until 1899, and then increased and, except for the fall during and after World War I, they continued their upward trend until the early 1930s. This tendency was not so clearly seen in changes of the average tariffs on total imports as in those on dutiable imports. The fall during the World War I period reflects the decrease in effective ad valorem equivalent rates of specific duties during inflation. Since the late 1930s average tariffs were pushed downward partly because of enlarged tariff exemptions for important heavy manufactures and partly because of the shrinkage of Japan's import trade from outside of the trade blocs.

The increase in average rate of tariffs was accompanied by an increasing degree of differentiation among commodities or commodity groups from 1900 to 1940. This is easily seen in the widening gap between average tariffs on total imports and on dutiable imports after 1899. The share of the value of dutiable imports as part of total imports declined rapidly from a high level of 95 per cent before 1890 to 30 per cent in 1940. This was partly due to the increasing share of raw material imports, which were subject at first to the same degree of tariffs as manufactures but became exempted from duty since the late 1890s. Tariff differentiation implies a deliberate policy of industrial protection. Unless policy makers aimed at complete self-sufficiency in the Japanese economy, they would not levy high tariffs uniformly on all imports. The protection of an industry becomes effective only at the cost of all other manufacturing and non-manufacturing industries.

Industrial protection is not the only argument for tariffs. For the earlier period after the Meiji Restoration, tariff revenue was the main concern of tariff policy. During that period Japan imposed 5 per cent duties on most exports and the revenue from export duties was on average two-thirds of import duties. Irrationality of export duties had long been shown and the movement for abolition spread nation-wide in the early 1890s, but duties on such major exports as raw silk and tea were maintained until 1899 when under tariff autonomy import duties were raised and yielded a larger revenue.

In spite of the fact that the main source of government revenue in Japan in this period was land taxes and, as is seen in Appendix Table I, tariff revenue was at most 5–10 per cent of total government revenue, undoubtedly tariff revenue was the main purpose of tariff imposition at least for the earlier period. However, as industry grew, industrial protection began to take place of revenue purpose. Both the Special Emergency Tariffs (1904–1905) and the Luxury Tariffs (1924) were originally motivated by the increase in tariff revenue but they made peculiar marks in the history of Japan's tariff protection.

Tariff imposition was made selective to protect domestic industries throughout this period. Appendix Table I also shows changes in average rates of tariffs on manufactures, raw materials, and foodstuffs (each of which includes duty-free items). Average tariffs on manufactures followed a pattern similar to that of dutiable imports in Figure 3 and will be analyzed in greater detail in following sections. Average tariffs on raw materials were at the same level as those of manufactures until the early 1890s but tended to lower as individual important raw materials were exempted from duty one by one: ginned cotton in 1896, iron ore in 1901, and so on. The number of duty-free raw material items was increased from forty-nine to eighty-nine by the general revision of 1906.

The abolition of import duties on raw cotton marked Japan's step toward import dependence on raw materials. At first the Meiji government encouraged home cultivation of cotton in its pursuit of import substitution of cotton textiles. But Japanese cotton was not fit for spinning fine thread and the growing domestic production of cotton textiles was accompanied by increasing imports of cotton yarn in the early 1980s. The abolition of cotton duties reflected the change in governmental policy into import substitution of cotton yarn depending on imported raw cotton of fine quality. At the same time export duty on cotton yarn was also abolished, although there was little export then. The abolition of both duties greatly encouraged domestic spinning of imported raw cotton and export of cotton yarn exceeded import in a few years, whereas domestic cultivation of raw cotton not only for market but also for home consumption decreased rapidly after 1896.

It is interesting to note the changes in tariffs on agricultural products from the protection point of view.[2] Tariffs on agricultural products were originally intended to balance emergency surcharges on the land tax during the Russo-Japanese War; rice had been exempted from duty until 1905 when a 15 per cent duty was levied; duties on wheat and barley were raised from 5 to 15 per cent. These agricultural tariffs remained after the Emergency Surcharges were abolished and they were incorporated into the tariff schedule in 1906.

These tariffs initiated agricultural protection in Japan. The duty on wheat was raised further to 20 per cent in 1911. The duty on rice, on the other hand, provoked a public controversy on agricultural protection between landowners and manufacturers. In 1913 the controversy was finally concluded in the Diet by compromising tariffs such as a specific duty of one yen per 60 kg (ad valorem equivalent was 23 per cent of average import prices in 1910–12) on imports of rice from outside the Empire coupled with exemption from duty for rice imports from Taiwan and Korea. Contrary to the British "Corn Laws" debate, the Japanese version resulted in the self-sufficiency of rice within the Japanese Empire as a whole.[3] After all agricultural protection resulted in the encouragement of colonial agriculture and, through cheaper rice and lower wages, added to industrial protection of Japan.[4]

The volatile movement of average tariffs on foodstuffs in the 1910s was largely affected by tariffs on sugar imports. Duties on refined sugar continued to be as low as 10 per cent under the treaty until 1911 when they were raised to a 50–60 per cent ad valorem equivalent. Under tariff protection, sugar production in Taiwan could be developed rapidly to take place of imported sugar from outside the Empire.

It should be emphasized that the time trend changes in Japan's tariff policy

---

[2] Readers should be careful in examining tariff figures on rice and sugar whose imports into Japan were largely supplied by Korean and Taiwanese producers in the 1920s and 1930s as shown below. Tariff figures for these commodities in Appendix Table II apply only to imports from outside the Japanese Empire.

RICE AND SUGAR IMPORTS OF JAPAN PROPER: 1898-1933   (%)

	1898	1903	1908	1913	1918	1924	1928	1933
Rice and paddy:								
from outside the Empire	97.7	91.4	69.1	63.3	52.4	25.1	16.9	5.0
from Korea				14.9	33.1	57.8	56.4	66.7
from Taiwan	2.3	8.6	30.9	21.8	14.5	17.1	26.7	28.3
Sugar:								
from outside the Empire	94.7	87.2	67.5	70.4	38.0	34.1	34.7	9.7
from Taiwan	5.3	12.8	32.5	29.6	62.0	65.9	65.3	90.3

Note: Imports of sugar from Korea were small, almost negligible.
Sources: Ministry of Finance, *Dainihon gaikoku bōeki nempyō, 1898–1933* [Annual return of the foreign trade of the empire of Japan: the customs]; Government of Taiwan, *Taiwan bōeki nempyō, 1898–1933* [Annual return of the trade of Taiwan]; Government General of Chōsen, *Chōsen bōeki nempyō, 1898–1933* [Chōsen: table of trade and shipping].

were not free from the world-wide waves of free trade movement and protectionism. Initially, free trade was forced on Japan in the midst of the free trade movement initiated by the 1860 Cobden-Chevalier Treaty between Great Britain and France. The trend reversed toward protectionism from the late 1870s to World War I during which time Japan resumed tariff autonomy and began to raise tariff barriers. When protection was strengthened further in the post–World War I years and escalated to autarky within each trade bloc in the world-wide tariff war of the 1930s Japan had the highest level of tariff protection.[5]

III. INDUSTRIAL PROTECTION BY TARIFFS: INSTITUTIONAL ANALYSIS

In the preceding section the hypothesis was suggested that Japan's tariff imposition became selective aiming mainly toward industrial protection. More evidence should be given for this hypothesis, and the structure of tariff protection for manufactures during the period 1890–1940 will be analyzed in detail in this and the next section. The main thing here is to examine the changes in tariff structure in response to the progress of industrialization. There are two approaches in analyzing this problem. One is to detail such institutional facts as the principle of tariff imposition and nominal structure of the tariff schedule. The other is to compile tariff data on individual principal commodities and analyze quantitatively the changes over time in tariff protection for manufactures. The two are complementary and the former will be examined in this section and the latter in the next section.

A. *Principles for Tariff Policy*

We can find good evidence for industrial protection by selective tariffs in the report of the committee for tariff study made at each general tariff revision. The tariff report at the general tariff revision in 1911 proposed the principle that tariffs should be levied principally for revenue purposes and industrial protection should be given secondary consideration in the establishment of tariffs. But this principle seems to show the fact that the government did not want to appear to be protectionistic and in effect industrial protection dominated the structure of the tariff schedule. Two special tariffs for Emergency Surcharges in 1904–1905 and Luxury Duties in 1924 were motivated by revenue purposes but the former began agricultural protection and the latter incorporated prohibitive tariffs on consumer goods imports of foreign origin into the general tariff schedule.

After World War I and during the early 1920s, special tariffs were effected for the protection of individual industries on various occasions. There were

---

[3] For more details on this debate, see [4].
[4] For the role of cheap supply of colonial rice in Japan's industrial development, see [7, Chap. 10].
[5] See [3].

tariff increases for iron and steel products, synthetic dyestuffs, and other chemical products. All of these industries started or developed rapidly during World War I and demanded tariff protection on being confronted with revived foreign competition. There was still strong enthusiasm for industrialization after World War I and extreme autarky prevailed to the extent that it was believed that all existing manufacturing industries should be maintained at any cost.

The report of the tariff committee (October 1921) established in preparation for general tariff revision of 1926 explicitly proposed that industrial protection be the principle of tariff policy. General criteria for tariff imposition were described in the report, which are as follows.

1. *Criteria from protective point of view*
  (1) Tariff protection should be confined to such industries as (a) important industries which have not started yet but have prospects for development, (b) important industries which have already started but not fully developed and have prospects for further development, and (c) important industries which have already fully developed but need to be maintained in the future.
  (2) Rates for protective tariffs should not exceed those under which domestic products can just meet fair competition with foreign products in the domestic market.
  (3) Natural products and industrial materials which are either not produced domestically or domestically produced but without any prospect for future increase should be, in principle, exempted from duties.
  (4) Higher tariffs should be levied on semi-manufactures than on raw materials, and even higher tariffs on finished than on semi-finished products.

2. *Criteria from revenue point of view*
  (1) Revenue tariffs should be limited to such imports which yield tariff revenue, and their rates should not be high enough to reduce the value of imports.
  (2) For revenue tariffs the highest rates should be levied on luxury consumption goods and lower rates on other goods according to their needs in the national welfare.

3. *Exceptions from the preceding rules*
  (1) Daily necessities, especially foodstuffs, should be either exempted from duty or given the lowest possible rates.
  (2) High protective tariffs should be levied on commodities for military use with future prospects for domestic development but should be abolished for those not having such prospect.
  (3) Free or lowest possible rates should be given to commodities for cultural, educational, and sanitary purposes.

These criteria are rational and could have been easily extended to all-round protection as was partly realized in the series of tariff revisions in the 1920s. Newly developed heavy manufactures were given higher tariff protection under this general tariff revision. This was followed by tariffs on sugar and starch in 1927, lumber in 1929, artificial silk in 1931, and increases for pig-iron and other heavy manufactures in 1932. Another general tariff revision was planned in 1936 to give additional protection to new industries but it resulted in an increase for several commodities including automobiles and petroleum in 1937.

There were strong objections raised by free traders to this increasing tendency towards protectionism. They argued against all-round protectionism and contended that protection should be confined to fewer promising industries and that those industries under protection should be surveyed for achievement. Abolition of tariff protection for fully developed industries was also demanded but the attempt failed in most cases as clearly evidenced in the case of the abolition movement for the duty on cotton yarn. There was no import of cotton yarn at the time but 5 per cent duties were continued. Cotton weavers and hosiers, typically small and medium sized firms, pleaded for the abolition of cotton yarn duty both publicly and in the Diet (1925) to increase the pressure from Chinese cotton yarn which became increasingly competitive as a result of the silver depreciation. But cotton spinners, several big firms, succeeded in maintaining it until 1930 when it was finally lowered to 3.3 per cent.

B. *Disaggregation in the General Tariff Schedule*

The degree of commodity classification in the general tariff schedule provides more evidence for tariff differentiation. The tariff schedule effected in 1899 included only 532 classes and was rearranged in the general tariff revision of 1906 into the standard commodity classification of nineteen categories, 538 classes, and 819 items, which lasted until the shift to the BTN system in 1961. The tariff schedule was disaggregated further into 1,599 items in 1911 and 1,699 items in 1926. The disaggregation of the commodity classification reflected the emergence of new industries and commodities in foreign trade but was also needed for deliberate protection of domestic industries.

C. *Escalated Tariff Structure*

The first tariff schedule of 1899 set up nine classes of tariff rates at 5 per cent intervals from zero to 40 per cent. Individual commodities were assigned one of these rates according to the rule of raising the rates for higher stages of processing. That is, 0–5 per cent was levied on raw materials, 10 per cent on semi-manfactures, 15–20 per cent on finished manufactures, and more than 25 per cent on luxury goods. The escalation in tariff structure became steeper in the schedule of 1906. Raw materials were assigned tariffs of 0–5 per cent, finished manufactures 30–40 per cent, and luxury goods 50–60 per cent. In the tariff schedule of 1911 and 1926 commodities were differentiated, within the same structure of escalation, by such factors as the need for protection for import-competing products, the future prospects for domestic production, the effects on export competitiveness (in case of materials used in export industries), and so on. The effective rates of protection produced by this escalated structure differed from the nominal structure of tariffs and we can conclude that this escalated structure of nominal tariffs gave higher effective protection to manufacturing than they appeared to.

D. *Ad Valorem vs. Specific Duties*

The Tariff Law of 1899 principally adopted ad valorem duties but for administrative convenience it set up specific duty rates using average import prices for the preceding six months. The Tariff Law of 1906 set up principal rates as either ad valorem rates or specific rates by commodities and afterwards an increased proportion of imports were made subject to specific duties. The ad valorem equivalent of specific duties declined during the period of increasing import prices before 1920, and were revised upward several times. Especially, during World War I the rapid rise of import prices lowered ad valorem equivalents to such low levels (a few per cent) that tariffs were raised back to old levels by changing many specific duties to ad valorem rates in 1921. (Most were returned to specific duties again in the general revision of 1926.)

The ad valorem equivalent of specific duties increased in the 1920s with decreasing import prices, but they were seldom revised downward. In June 1932, specific duties were raised uniformly by 35 per cent so as to adjust to the exchange depreciation. It was alleged that the adjustment was needed to maintain the ad valorem equivalent of specific duties against the increased yen prices of imports resulting from a 35 per cent increase in yen price of the dollar (in early 1932). However, since yen prices for many imports were raised by less than this percentage and exchange depreciation by itself has the combined effect of import tariff and export subsidy, this uniform adjustment of specific duties gave double protection to domestic producers.

E. *Other Aspects of Tariff Policy*

Besides the increased industrial protection seen in the tariff schedule, supplementary tariff policies were provided by the tariff laws in 1906. Export duties had already been abolished by 1899 as mentioned in Section II. On one hand, three specific purpose tariffs: countervailing tariffs, retaliatory tariffs, and anti-dumping tariffs were effected. They were established to safeguard domestic production against "unfair competition" by foreign exporters but were seldom enforced before the 1930s. In the world-wide trend toward industrial protection in the 1930s they were strengthened into the Trade Protection Law in 1934, under which a retaliatory levy of a 50 per cent surcharge on all imports from Canada and Australia was enforced in retaliation against the discriminatory tariff on Japanese merchandise by those two countries. Both were abolished in six months by new trade agreements with the two nations. On the other hand, exemption and payback rules were established for materials used in export industries.

Temporary Storage Yard Law was enacted in 1900 under which materials were exempted from import duties provided that they were simply processed for re-export in particular permitted areas called the "temporary storage yard." In order to promote processing re-exports further, domestically produced materials were permitted processing in 1912. In the early 1920s the free port argument was predominant in business circles and discussed in the Diet in 1925. The government responded in 1927 by enacting the Tariff Factory Law under which temporary storage yards were changed into tariff factories and improvement was made including simplification of procedures and extension of the storage period from six months to one year so that the number of tariff factories increased in the late 1920s.

IV. INDUSTRIAL PROTECTION BY TARIFF: QUANTITATIVE ANALYSIS

In Section II, the trend of tariffs was analyzed in terms of average tariffs on total imports or those on large commodity groups such as manufactures, foodstuffs, and raw materials. But in order to depict the pattern of industrial protection by tariffs we should look not so much at the average level of tariffs but rather at their upward or downward deviations from the average, that is, the structure of individual tariffs. For that purpose data is needed on individual tariffs throughout the period. Therefore tariff data has been compiled for sixty-one principal commodities at five-year intervals from 1893 to 1938. A quantitative study of the tariff structure can then be made on the basis of this data.

Let us begin with an explanation of the main features of this data. Its original source is the "Quantity and value of merchandise imported by each port," in *Dainihon gaikoku bōeki nempyō* [Annual foreign trade of the Japanese Empire], published by the Ministry of Fiance. In the original data the value was recorded for every individual commodity imported into each of Japan's main ports, from outside the Japanese Empire, coupled with tariff duties collected on the commodity at port. Both values of imports and tariffs collected on each commodity are summed up for all ports and the rate of tariff burden, that is, the ratio of tariffs to values of imports, is calculated. The rate of tariff burden is called the rate of tariff.

Each of the sixty-one commodities does not correspond to each category of commodity classification in the original statistics. The commodity classification was disaggregated further in later years and sums of the sixty-one commodities in terms of the share of import value in total imports is between 60 and 70 per cent. They are divided into six to eight groups by industry and by economic use (or stages of processing) and the tariffs on each groups are compared with each other in order to derive some facts in the structure of tariff protection.

A well-known fact is that the rate of tariff burden is liable to underestimate the import restricting effect of tariffs. That is, the rate of tariff burden calculated for an aggregated commodity group such as total commodity or manufactures in Section II reduces to an arithmetic mean of tariffs collected on individual commodities in the group weighted by value of imports. Higher tariffs on individual commodities tend to restrict import and lower the weighted arithmetic mean of tariffs. Our data for tariffs on individual commodities, however, is fairly free from this bias. Further, simple arithmetic means are calculated as average tariffs for groups classified by industry and economic use in order to evade this bias. Considering the following difficulties pertaining to nominal tariffs (tariffs listed in the tariff schedule), the rate of tariff burden is the only feasible figure for the rate of tariffs.

(1) Besides general tariff revision, nominal tariffs were changed partly almost every year (including special tariffs), and they were subject to conventional tariffs or complete or partial exemptions. It requires much time to find an effective rate of nominal tariffs on each of the sixty-one commodities through the period.

(2) Quite a few commodities were subject to specific duties and it is time consuming to find reliable levels of import prices to derive ad valorem equivalents.

Tariff rates are calculated for approximate ten year periods of 1893, 1898, 1903, 1908, 1913, 1918, 1924, 1928, 1933, and 1938 (see Figure 3). Original import data for 1922 and 1923 are not complete for the Port of Yokohama due to the Great Earthquake of 1923. Thus, 1924 was selected instead of 1923. It is also worthwhile to note that the import of daily necessities were exempted from duty in March 1924, which tends to lower the rates for 1924. On the other hand, the publication of import statistics of important commodities was stopped for security purposes in 1937 and coverage of our sample declined to 30 per cent in 1938. The rates of tariff burden of sixty-one individual commodities are shown in Appendix Table II. Tariff figures for group classified by industry and by economic use are summarized in Tables II–III.

One problem here is to give empirical support to the hypothesis of differentiated tariff structure and to depict the principle of tariff differentiation. Table I summarizes changes in average tariffs (both simple and weighted arithmetic means) of the sixty-one commodities. The simple mean increased after 1898 and, except for the fall in 1918 and 1924, continued to increase until World War II. The arithmetic mean weighted by import values of individual commodities, however, increased until 1913 and tended to decline in the 1920s

TABLE I
ARITHMETIC MEANS AND STANDARD DEVIATIONS OF 61 TARIFFS

(%)

	Simple Arithmetic Means	Weighted Arithmetic Means	Standard Deviations Around Simple Means
1893	3.9	3.4	1.7
1898	3.7	1.7	1.8
1903	9.9	3.3	7.0
1908	16.2	9.9	16.7
1913	19.8	9.7	15.8
1918	10.7	3.5	10.9
1924	10.9	3.1	12.5
1928	22.6	6.2	22.9
1933	23.8	5.7	22.8
1938	29.2	1.2	45.0

Source: Appendix Table II.

INDUSTRIAL GROWTH

TABLE II
SIMPLE AVERAGE TARIFFS ON INDIVIDUAL COMMODITY GROUPS
(Classified by Industry) (%)

No.	Year	1893	1898	1903	1908	1913	1918	1924	1928	1933	1938
A	Agricultural products	2.52	2.49	8.57	20.61	19.99	14.39	8.63	14.37	23.08	24.24
C	Raw materials	3.96	2.79	5.66	8.73	6.42	3.34	1.77	4.01	7.63	4.16
S	Primary Products (A+C)	3.43	2.68	6.63	12.69	10.94	7.02	4.06	7.46	12.78	12.19
B	Manufactured foodstuffs	3.22	3.36	12.61	35.89	42.67	24.44	19.02	47.37	50.55	58.31
D	Textile manufactures	3.20	2.84	12.43	14.86	20.68	9.55	11.85	26.31	25.54	39.17
E	Other light manufactures	4.71	4.62	11.86	16.21	21.11	11.71	10.33	20.97	19.15	18.00
Q	Light manufactures (B+D+E)	3.78	3.69	12.24	20.87	26.13	13.99	13.07	29.35	29.13	34.96
F	Chemical products	4.63	4.75	6.29	6.51	13.50	4.13	17.15	32.63	28.43	47.15
G	Metals and metal products	4.17	3.83	9.83	12.06	15.31	6.30	3.74	17.19	17.99	21.45
H	Machineries	4.20	4.24	12.59	24.33	25.45	18.25	17.34	22.38	26.94	19.46
R	Heavy manufactures (F+G+H)	4.32	4.24	9.32	13.33	17.66	9.06	12.34	23.47	23.89	31.75
T	Total	3.91	3.71	9.88	16.19	19.81	10.68	10.93	22.60	23.76	29.16

Source: Appendix Table II.
Note: Simple arithmetic means of individual tariffs belonging to each group. Commodities not imported are excluded from calculation.

TABLE III
SIMPLE AVERAGE TARIFFS ON INDIVIDUAL COMMODITY GROUPS
(Classified by Economic Use) (%)

No.	Year	1893	1898	1903	1908	1913	1918	1924	1928	1933	1938
A+B	Foodstuff	2.91	2.97	10.81	29.78	33.60	20.42	14.86	34.17	39.56	44.69
C	Raw materials	3.96	2.79	5.66	8.73	6.42	3.34	1.77	4.01	7.63	4.16
I	Intermediate goods 1−L	4.04	3.45	6.60	4.07	12.25	5.74	6.80	13.60	16.48	9.54
J	Intermediate goods 1−H	4.84	4.44	3.72	3.84	6.41	2.84	13.92	14.68	15.02	13.99
O	Intermediate goods 1 (I+J)	4.49	3.95	5.16	3.96	9.60	4.42	10.04	14.09	15.82	10.65
K	Intermediate goods 2−L	4.24	4.17	10.59	8.10	18.11	7.67	6.14	15.27	11.05	6.75
L	Intermediate goods 2−H	4.04	4.03	8.88	9.42	16.21	3.44	7.08	19.88	17.29	15.97
P	Intermediate goods 2 (K+L)	4.14	4.09	9.56	8.89	16.97	5.13	6.67	17.90	14.61	10.85
M	Capital goods	3.67	3.86	8.75	13.75	17.33	6.98	10.60	14.27	16.89	7.27
N	Consumer goods	4.04	4.12	17.31	31.21	30.12	20.55	20.43	41.43	41.59	63.10
T	Total	3.91	3.71	9.88	16.19	19.81	10.68	10.93	22.60	23.76	29.16

Source: See Appendix Table II.

and 1930s. This is partly because the imports of free-of-duty or low duty items (such as raw materials) increased their shares but it also reflects underestimation due to the restricting effect of higher tariffs. On the other hand, the standard deviation of tariffs of the sixty-one commodities increased from low levels before 1900 up to World War I and despite the drops in 1918 and 1924 continued to increase until World War II. This evidence is consistent with the hypothesis of selective structure of tariffs mentioned above.

In what way was the tariff structure differentiated throughout the period? The sample commodities are classified into several groups by industry and by economic use respectively and changes in average tariffs for each group can be examined (see Tables II and III). To begin with, let us have a look at changes in average tariffs for four broad groups, agricultural products, other raw materials, light manufactures, and heavy manufactures. The average tariffs of the four groups remained at almost the same level until 1898 but tended to diverge after 1903. The rates of both light and heavy manufactures followed a pattern similar to the total average in Table I but the rate for light manufactures exceed that for heavy manufactures throughout the period. On the other hand the rate for agricultural products increased, keeping pace with that of light manu-

Fig. 4. Average Tariffs on Commodity Groups Classified by Industry

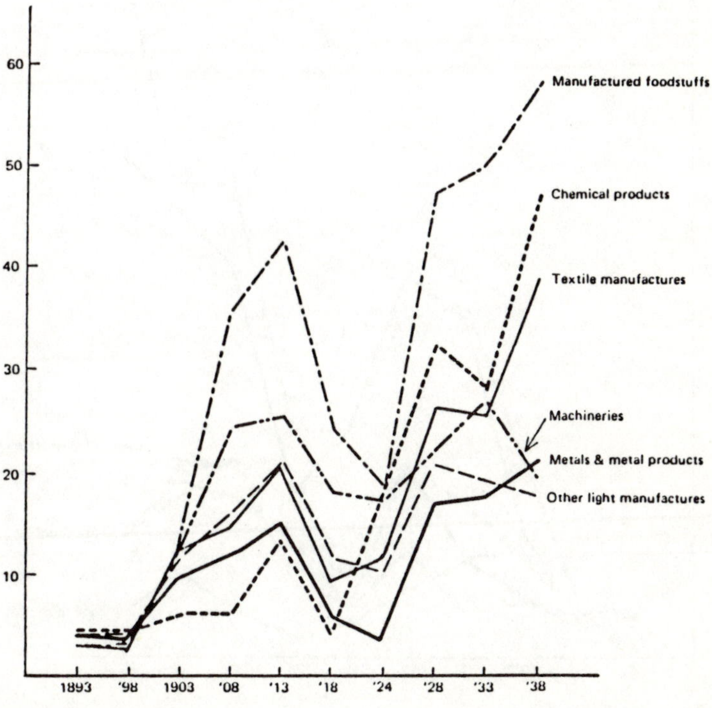

Source: Table II.

factures until 1913, but its rate of increase slowed down and fell short of that of heavy manufactures after the 1920s. The rate for raw materials fluctuated between 2 and 8 per cent. (This fluctuation of average rates of raw materials seems to be dominated by changes in tariffs on mineral oils.)

Let us disaggregate light and heavy manufactures (see Figure 4). The rates of tariff on manufactured foodstuffs increased earlier and remained at a higher level than of any other group. Textiles kept pace with other light manufactures until 1924 but exceeded the latter after 1928. On the other hand, the rates for heavy metals and chemicals in heavy manufactures lagged behind other groups but after 1924 the rate for heavy metals and chemicals increased so rapidly as to exceed that for textiles. Average tariffs on machinery were raised relatively earlier but remained at 20–25 per cent and were caught up by the rate for metals

Fig. 5. Average Tariffs on Commodity Groups Classified by Economic Use

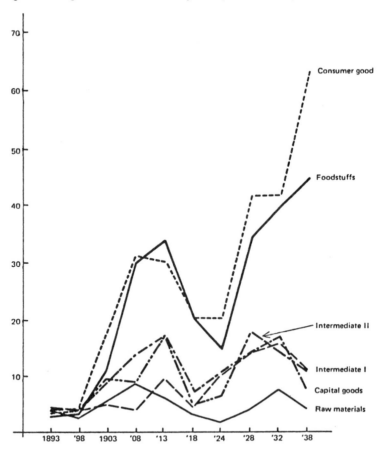

Source: Table III.

in the 1930s. In Figure 4, we cannot discern any clear principle for tariff differentiation.[6]

On th contrary the average tariffs of groups classified by economic use showed a clearer pattern of differentiated structure (see Figure 5). Both consumer goods (excluding foodstuffs) and foodstuffs increased earlier than any other groups and maintained the highest level throughout the period. Raw materials constituted the group with the lowest percentage of between two and eight points. Intermediate goods I and II and capital goods did not show any rapid increase and stayed at 17 per cent. This shows a structure of tariffs escalated and is clearer than tariff differentiation by industry.

The obscure relationship between light and heavy manufactures depicted in Table II and Figure 4 can be attributed to tariff differentiation by economic use that was incorporated into differentiation by industry. A large part of the rapid increase in average tariffs on chemicals and textiles after the late 1920s resulted from the increase of tariffs on individual commodities in the consumer goods category within the two groups. We may conclude that the basic structure of differentiation was the escalation of tariffs according to economic use (or stages of processing) of individual commodities.[7]

V. INDUSTRIAL PROTECTION POLICIES OTHER THAN TARIFF POLICY

Tariffs were a main policy instrument for industrial protection used by the Japanese government before World War II (especially after tariff independence). The preceding three sections were devoted to the analysis of tariffs. But the government had to resort to policies other than tariffs such as quantitative import restrictions, production subsidies, and other direct and indirect government aids to industrial development. It is difficult to quantify the magnitude of these policies but they cannot be neglected for our discussion of industrial protection. In this section we will give a brief comment on each.

A. *Quantitative Restriction on Imports*

The import approval system was first introduced for rice under the Rice Law (1921) empowering the government to adjust the supply of this grain in the market. It was also applied only temporarily for synthetic dyestuffs and ammonium sulfate in special occasions (the former in 1924 being confronted with German dumping and the latter in 1931 after the breakdown of the international cartel).

---

[6] Protective effects of tariffs on domestic manufacturing activities are properly measured not in terms of nominal rates but in terms of their effective protective rates, which are, however, not available for the prewar period because of the lack of systematic data for input-output relationships.

[7] In the first draft of this paper, I made an attempt to find the tendency of tariffs on heavy manufactures exceeding those on light manufactures in the process of heavy industrialization, but could not produce statistically significant evidence.

But it was not until 1937 that the Japanese government resorted to quantitative restrictions on general imports. Quantitative restrictions themselves had not been adopted as a permanent policy by any country until 1931, when France resorted to this measure in the world-wide increase of protectionism. The main European countries soon followed. Japan was far behind in the adoption of this policy.

In Japan, quantitative restrictions began with the exchange control system in January 1937, which was introduced for the purpose of stabilizing the exchange of yen and licenses were given to each importer according to his past performance. But in September of the same year the system was changed under the Trade Adjustment Law into a stricter import quota system. The system was devised in order to improve the persistent deficit in the balance of payments and to secure supplies of commodities for military purposes. But we can safely conclude that, except for a few industries such as automobile and metal working machinery, quantitative import restrictions had little effect on industrial development throughout the period before World War II.

B. *Production Subsidies*

The government used subsidies to promote the modernization of the Japanese economy. They were used especially in the 1880s and 1890s and the interwar period. This was reflected in the ratio of subsidies given to industry by government expenditure, 4–5 per cent for 1880–90, declining to 1–2 per cent between 1900 and World War I, and increasing again to 8 per cent in the interwar period. The distribution of subsidies changed over time. Subsidies were given mainly to construction in the 1880s, to transportation and communication between 1890 and 1910, and to agriculture after the late 1920s. Production subsidies for mining and manufacturing were relatively small (see the table below). The ratio of subsidies to manufacturing income was less than 1 per cent throughout the whole period. We should consider, however, not so much the quantitative magnitude as the qualitative aspect, for subsidies were directed at building infrastructure and at fostering "strategic" industries such as ship-building under Ship-Building Encouragement Law in 1896, steel production,[8] and automobiles.[9]

SUBSIDY SHARES TO SECONDARY INDUSTRY IN THE TOTAL VALUE OF SUBSIDY FOR SELECTED YEARS (%)

1890	1900	1910	1920	1925	1929	1938
17.3	19.4	10.9	25.3	3.6	2.3	5.4

Sources: [1].
Note: Including administrative subsidies.

[8] Since 1927, a subsidy of three to six yen per ton (10–20 per cent tariff equivalent) was provided for the use of domestically produced pig iron as a substitute for tariff increase.
[9] Under Military Truck Subsidy Law in 1918, for the production, maintenance, and purchase of motor trucks.

On the other hand the exemption from corporate tax and other taxes has the same effect as a production subsidy. For example, steel-producing firms with more than a certain production capacity were exempted from all domestic taxes under the Steel-Manufacturing Encouragement Act in 1917. The exemption was not included in the calculation of subsidies mentioned above.

C. Direct Aid by Government

We should not neglect direct aids by government given to initiate and develop new industries. One such direct example of aid was the government finance for risks accruing to the initiation of new industries. Experimental plants were established by government at the start of the silk, cotton, and woolen industries and were turned over to private firms after success was achieved. The early development of chemical, metal, and machinery benefited much from the activities of government-owned foundries, research institutes, and the national universities. These governmental institutions played an important part in introducing new techniques and in training and supplying engineers to private firms.

Stronger leadership was taken by government to develop steel production. After the failure of private firms for two decades, Yawata Iron Works was established by the government and it succeeded in the integrated production of iron and steel for the first time in Japan. It took Yawata nine years before it could operate at a profit, but the deficit over the period and the expansion of investment afterwards were financed by government expenditure. Yawata played a central role in the expansion of steel production in Japan throughout the period before World War II. (Its share in steel production was more than 90 per cent in the 1900s and remained at the level of 50 per cent during the 1920s.)

D. Government Purchase

The pace of development of an industry is principally determined by the scale and growth of the domestic market. In the process of import substitution, domestic producers have to compete for domestic market shares with imports. Import substitution was achieved basically by the improvement of domestic products both in cost and quality. If, however, part of domestic demand is preferentially reserved for domestic products irrespective of the remaining cost and quality differences between domestic product and import, the pace of import substitution will be accelerated considerably.

A buy-Japanese movement was started at the end of 1914 by Kokusan-shōreikai (Society to Encourage Domestic Manufacture). This was a semi-official movement working for the substitution of domestic products for such imports as drugs and chemicals, iron and steel, machinery, glass, paper, and woolen fabrics. They had been largely supplied by imports until 1914 when World War I broke out and the volume of those imports decreased and their prices increased rapidly. It is important to note the fact that domestic products in these commodities groups were widely considered inferior to imports at the time so that, only foreign products could do for example in some heavy electric machinery in government factory work [9]. The aim of the society was to encourage the manufacture of domestic products and to increase their use.

Led by Baron Eiichi Shibusawa, one of the most eminent business leaders in the Meiji and Taishō period (up to 1925), the society "pledged itself to conduct the following program; surveys of home industries; holding fairs and exhibitions to display domestic products; give public lectures; answer inquiries on home manufactures; collect and display samples and catalogues; publish a review, etc." [5, pp. 238–39]. The government made 3,000 yen appropriation for the society's maintenance in 1914, and 5,000 yen a year from 1915 on.

In the 1920s the buy-Japanese movement was given further impetus by such additional moves as protection of domestic industries against revived competition with foreign competitors and the need for improvement in balance of payments. The British consulate in Tokyo sent a report on this movement as follows.

> Though it is not strictly within the category of legislation mention should be made of an extremely strong official campaign to encourage the use of domestic products. This has ramifications in all quarters, such as, for example, the issue of instructions by the Railway department laying down what domestic good must be used and what imported goods may be used. It is understood that certain government departments when calling for tenders now specify in many cases articles of Japanese manufactures irrespective of quality. [2, p. 64]

But it is difficult to make a quantitative appraisal of the effect of this policy on import substitution. Before World War I, a large part of domestic demand for such manufactures as steel, ships, and automobiles came from the government for railroad construction, military use, and so on. Take steel products for an example. Two-thirds of the Yawata's sales were to the government in 1903. The ratio was 50 per cent in 1921 and as high as 20–25 per cent in the late 1920s. The ratio is much higher if we include indirect demand by private producers of machinery and metal manufactures induced by government demand. It cannot be doubted that the government pursued the policy of preferential purchasing for domestic products within the extent permissible by cost and quality differences between domestic products and imports.

At the same time efforts were made on the producer's side to catch up with imports both in quality and cost. In industries where there were great technological difference between domestic and foreign products as electric machineries, major Japanese manufactures rushed to introduce advanced technology from European and American manufacturers under license contracts in the mid-1920s [9].

E. *Export Promotion*

As European competition revived in the world market after World War I, Japan's exports staggered and export promotion became more important in her trade policy. Export promotion of various types was pursued in the 1920s and 1930s. One was to establish a quality control system for traditional Japanese exports as silk, cotton textiles, celluloid, and other miscellaneous commodities. Another was to encourage these exports to new markets such as Latin America, the Middle East, and Australia by giving government guarantees to the bank acceptance of export bills to these markets. These policies were enacted in the mid-1920s and strengthened in the early 1930s.

On the other hand, markets were provided by governments for the emerging exports of heavy manufactures (metals, chemicals, and machineries). Exports of these commodities expanded steadily to Manchuria and Kwantung Province in the 1930s but it should be noted that they were tied with growing national investment in these areas.

VI. CONCLUSION

After 1900, Japan adopted industrial protection, under which such industries as metals, machinery, and chemicals developed and succeeded in import substitution. Protection was also provided to developed industries such as cotton textiles and matches. This could easily be extended to all-round protection and was seldom removed once provided.

A major instrument of industrial protection was the tariff. From 1900 to the early 1930s Japanese tariffs were differentiated according to stage of process, thereby gradually developing the trade pattern of raw material imports and processing exports. More direct import restriction was seldom used until 1937 with minor exceptions for synthetic dyestuffs and ammonium sulfate.

A few strategic industries such as steel-making, ship-building, automobile, and airplanes were provided more direct, promotional aid such as production subsidies (including exemption of corporate income tax), and government ownership. There was no clear explanation provided for the provision of promotional policies for particular industries. It was explained that subsidies were provided as a substitute for tariff increase when tariffs could not be raised either because of a tariff agreement or because of the fear of tariff retaliation. Considering the fact that subsidies were not replaced by tariff increase after external constraints were removed, the subsidy seems to have been adopted with the following considerations; first, an increase of tariffs on such basic intermediate products as pig iron might have caused an upward pressure on general price level, and second, that subsidies were more effective than mere import restriction in promoting the development of strategic industries. Government-owned factories and firms were established to give a strong impetus to those areas of production related to defense. Many were small and medium size except for Yawata Iron Works.

While subsidies and government ownership were confined to a few strategic industries, government purchase policy and semi-official buy-Japanese movements affected import substitution of a wider range of manufactures. Due to the lack of documents and statistics on these policies, we cannot tell how widely they were applied or how effective they were in promoting import substitution, but it would be safe to say that they contributed at least to some extent to the development of heavy manufactures of domestic demand for which military and other official demands occupied a large share.

In spite of the fact that other forms of protection were adopted and more effective than tariff protection in a few strategic industries, tariffs were considered the orthodox measure for industrial protection in prewar Japan and were assigned a more important role relative to other protection measures than in the LDC's today.

How much protection contributed to Japan's industrial growth cannot be answered merely on the basis of the present study. But other studies of Japan's industrial growth and trade tell us that its industrial development was accompanied by successful import substitution and export promotion brought about by basic factors other than protection [8]. First, the domestic demand for manufactures was large enough even in initial stages and grew rapidly enough in subsequent years to induce rapid development of domestic manufacturing production. Second, output expansion induced by rapid growth of domestic demand was accompanied by cost reduction through scale economies, learning effects, and other forms of technical progress. These two factors combined, generated industrial growth with successful import substitution and export, while protection accelerated it. In the absence of these two generating factors, heavy protection would not have succeeded in aiding industrial development. Rather, too much protection, especially by means of import restriction, could mitigate competition in the domestic market and discourage the cost reducing efforts by domestic producers. Import substitution could be achieved but not export to outside markets.

In the process of Japan's industrial development, protection did not retard the two generating factors mentioned above. Subsidies and other promotional policies assisted the development of key industries and tariff protection was kept at low or medium levels for intermediate and capital goods so as not to retard all manufacturing activities, apart from prohibitive tariffs on consumption goods. It should be noted that Japan's tariff protection reached its highest level in the late 1920s and early 1930s, during which the most rapid cost reduction was realized in many production areas.

REFERENCES

1. Emi, K., and Shionoya, Y. *Zaisei shishutsu* [Government expenditure], Chōki keizai tōkei shirīzu [Estimates of long-term economic statistics of Japan since 1868], Series No. 7 (Tokyo: Tōyō-keizai-shimpōsha, 1966).
2. Great Britain, Department of Overseas Trade. *Economic Conditions in Japan* (London: His Majesty Stationary Office, 1930).
3. Haberler, G. "Integration and Growth of the World Economy in Historical Perspective," *American Economic Review*, March 1964.
4. Hayami, Y. "Rice Policy in Japan's Economic Development," *American Journal of Agricultural Economics*, February 1972.
5. Kobayashi, U. *The Basic Industries and Social History of Japan: 1914–1918* (New Haven, Conn.: Yale University Press, 1930).
6. Lockwood, W. W. *The Economic Development of Japan 1868–1938* (Princeton, N.J.: Princeton University Press, 1954).
7. Shinohara, M. *Growth and Cycles in the Japanese Economy* (Tokyo: Kinokuniya Bookstore, 1972).
8. Shionoya, Y., and Yamazawa, I. "Industrial Growth and Foreign Trade in Japan," in *Economic Growth, the Japanese Experience since the Meiji Era*, Vol. 2, ed. K. Ohkawa

and Y. Hayami (Tokyo: Japan Economic Research Center, 1973).
9. TAKEUCHI, H. "Denki kōgyō" [Development of Japan's electric machinery industry], in *Nihon bōeki no kōzō to hatten* [Structure and development of Japan's foreign trade], ed. K. Kojima (Tokyo: Shiseidō, 1972).

APPENDIX TABLE I

THE TARIFFS OF JAPAN: 1868–1945

Column 1: Average rate of tariffs on total imports.
Column 2: Average rate of tariffs on dutiable imports.
Column 3: Shares of dutiable imports in total import values.
Column 4: Shares of import tariff revenue in total sum of central government's revenue.
Column 5: Average rate of tariffs on foodstuff imports.
Column 6: Average rate of tariffs on manufactured imports.
Column 7: Average rate of tariffs on raw material imports.

(%)

Year	(1)	(2)	(3)	(4)	(5)	(6)	(7)
1868	3.5	3.7	93	1.1			
1869	2.2	3.0	72	1.3			
1870	1.8	3.6	52	3.0			
1871	3.0	3.4	91	3.0			
1872	3.5	3.6	98	1.9			
1873	3.5	3.8	93	1.2			
1874	3.8	4.1	94	1.2			
1875	3.6	4.3	86	1.3			
1876	4.4	4.5	97	1.5			
1877	4.1	4.2	97	2.2			
1878	4.4	4.6	97	2.4			
1879	4.6	4.8	95	2.5			
1880	4.6	4.8	95	2.7			
1881	4.7	4.8	97	2.1			
1882	4.7	4.8	97	1.9			
1883	4.7	4.8	98	1.6			
1884	4.5	5.9	92	1.8			
1885	4.6	5.0	93	2.2			
1886	4.8	5.0	97	1.8			
1887	4.7	5.0	95	2.4			
1888	4.1	4.3	97	2.9			
1889	4.3	4.5	96	3.0			
1890	3.5	4.4	81	2.8	0.2	5.2	4.2
1891	3.8	4.3	87	2.3	0.3	5.6	2.8
1892	3.8	4.2	90	2.7	0.3	4.9	4.4
1893	3.5	3.9	86	2.7	0.4	4.7	3.0
1894	2.9	3.4	88	3.6	0.3	4.7	1.4
1895	3.2	3.5	92	3.6	0.5	5.0	1.0
1896	2.8	3.7	76	2.6	0.5	4.3	1.0
1897	2.4	3.7	64	2.3	0.4	4.1	0.9
1898	2.2	3.7	60	2.9	0.4	4.4	0.9
1899	6.0	9.7	62	5.2	4.3	10.8	1.3

Continued overleaf

INDUSTRIAL GROWTH

APPENDIX TABLE I (Continued)

(%)

Year	(1)	(2)	(3)	(4)	(5)	(6)	(7)
1900	5.8	8.3	70	5.7	2.9	8.9	1.8
1901	5.6	8.7	65	5.3	2.1	10.4	1.8
1902	5.4	9.7	56	5.0	3.0	9.0	2.6
1903	5.1	9.7	53	6.3	2.3	10.3	2.3
1904	5.5	9.8	56	6.3	2.0	10.2	3.1
1905	7.0	11.6	60	6.4	5.3	9.7	4.2
1906	9.8	14.6	67	7.8	10.7	12.7	5.0
1907	9.5	15.2	62	5.5	11.1	13.2	4.2
1908	10.2	15.9	65	5.6	10.0	13.6	5.6
1909	8.9	15.9	56	5.2	11.3	13.0	4.2
1910	7.7	15.5	50	5.4	10.9	12.2	3.5
1911	8.1	15.0	54	6.4	12.3	12.1	3.3
1912	9.4	18.6	52	8.5	20.5	14.2	2.6
1913	10.0	19.9	50	10.2	26.2	13.6	1.9
1914	8.4	19.7	43	6.9	25.8	12.8	1.6
1915	5.6	17.2	33	4.3	25.9	8.7	1.6
1916	4.4	11.4	30	4.2	23.9	7.0	1.0
1917	3.6	8.4	43	3.5	19.3	5.8	0.7
1918	3.7	8.2	46	4.2	14.0	4.8	0.6
1919	3.1	8.5	38	3.8	5.7	5.7	0.6
1920	3.1	8.2	38	3.7	5.6	6.3	0.6
1921	5.5	11.7	47	4.3	18.3	8.7	0.9
1922	6.2	13.2	47	5.6	12.1	12.2	0.8
1923	4.8	12.8	38	4.7	7.2	10.0	0.9
1924	4.6	13.7	34	5.4	6.2	8.2	1.2
1925	4.2	12.5	34	5.2	6.8	9.8	0.9
1926	6.2	15.7	39	7.2	10.4	13.7	1.1
1927	6.6	17.4	38	7.0	10.7	16.2	1.4
1928	7.0	17.7	40	7.7	12.1	13.4	1.6
1929	7.6	17.2	39	8.1	10.2	13.4	1.7
1930	7.3	19.3	38	7.1	10.9	13.4	2.5
1931	9.0	24.0	38	7.3	18.7	14.9	3.1
1932	7.5	22.7	33	5.3	15.5	12.7	3.2
1933	6.0	21.0	29	5.0	10.0	11.4	2.8
1934	6.0	21.1	29	6.1	9.3	11.6	2.8
1935	6.1	20.0	31	6.9	7.8	11.9	2.9
1936	5.8	20.1	29	7.5	8.7	11.2	2.9
1937	5.2	18.7	28	6.5	6.4	7.3	3.4
1938	6.6	19.9	33	4.6	5.5	7.7	5.8
1939	5.2	17.3	30	3.0			
1940	4.3	14.3	30	2.2			
1941	3.9	13.7	28	1.0			
1942	3.2	14.0	23	0.6			
1943	2.7	14.3	19	0.3			
1944	0.8	4.5	19	0.1			
1945	0.9	6.0	13	0			

Sources: Data source for columns (1)–(4): Ministry of Finance, *Zaisei kinyū tōkei geppō* [Monthly report of financial statistics], No. 178.

Columns (1) and (2) are the percentage of import tariff revenue in total import values and in dutiable import values respectively. Figures of column (4) during 1935–45 represent values of each fiscal year but those before 1935 are derived by dividing tariff collected during the individual calendar year by government revenue [1].

The data source for columns (5)–(7) is Ministry of Finance, "Quantity and value of merchandise imported into all ports" in *Dainihon gaikoku bōeki nempyō*. (See the note to Appendix Table II for more details of these statistics.) Seventeen divisions of commodities are aggregated into three groups—foodstuffs, manufactures other than foodstuffs, and raw materials. The average rate of tariff for each group is calculated by dividing the value of tariffs collected by the c.i.f. value of imports of each group.

APPENDIX TABLE II
TARIFFS ON INDIVIDUAL COMMODITIES (%)

No. Year	1893	1898	1903	1908	1913	1918	1924	1928	1933	1938
1. Rice and paddy	0.00	0.00	0.00	13.67	18.72	9.92	0.72	13.98	41.24	28.20
2. Wheat	0.00	0.00	4.22	13.46	17.49	8.80	2.90	17.09	9.38	11.47
3. Coffee	5.05	4.94	25.68	44.81	32.72	32.51	27.44	25.23	40.21	55.62
4. Flours, meals, and starches	0.00	0.00	9.26	31.63	28.43	15.60	17.93	27.48	36.41	17.13
5. Sugar	3.38	3.00	5.05	33.32	44.35	34.56	14.50	13.27	1.91	6.64
6. Vegetable and fruits in tin	—	—	—	42.41	33.16	22.91	21.99	100.00	100.45	90.62
7. Meat and fish in tin	2.86	3.81	10.01	19.72	33.42	17.22	6.51	25.00	24.97	27.67
8. Condensed milk	4.99	5.00	5.44	4.68	20.80	12.48	4.74	18.48	39.55	24.74
9. Whisky	4.87	5.01	33.28	83.60	95.87	43.90	48.44	100.00	100.00	183.06
10. Cotton ginned	2.45	0.00	0.00	0.00	0.00	0.00	0.00	0.00	0.00	0.00
11. Wool	5.01	0.00	0.00	0.00	0.00	0.00	0.00	0.17	0.01	0.00
12. Cotton yarns	4.28	2.94	5.79	4.08	8.33	3.37	1.19	3.77	3.02	0.04
13. Woolen yarns	3.21	2.90	7.49	4.47	7.30	4.27	2.01	7.37	14.36	5.94
14. Artificial silk	—	—	—	—	35.16	12.82	21.55	53.85	60.85	32.62
15. Cotton fabric	5.26	4.12	7.12	5.98	10.87	3.59	3.18	14.23	0.81	—
16. Woolen fabric	3.01	2.53	9.39	9.16	16.43	6.78	4.90	12.68	12.95	12.48
17. Jute fabric	3.12	3.38	10.17	4.50	15.30	8.22	4.60	3.50	8.10	5.57
18. Undershirts	1.79	1.84	18.74	30.70	29.16	13.25	7.22	25.52	25.16	4.35
19. Hosiery	0.00	0.00	20.04	23.27	33.94	16.73	29.49	—	—	—
20. Carpets	4.94	4.99	20.72	36.69	29.62	16.92	32.48	89.57	79.02	213.21
21. Pine, fir, and ceder	4.96	4.99	5.00	7.13	6.50	2.81	0.17	2.06	15.52	4.71
22. Natural rubber	6.45	5.08	4.70	0.00	0.00	0.00	0.00	0.00	0.00	0.00
23. Sole leather	2.23	1.34	8.68	7.58	18.16	12.05	13.51	13.69	17.04	16.86
24. Pulp for paper making	—	5.01	6.35	4.24	4.59	1.91	2.55	2.92	3.60	1.76
25. Rubber manufactures	4.98	5.00	9.99	10.90	28.54	12.21	11.41	21.97	14.61	7.86

Continued overleaf

INDUSTRIAL GROWTH

APPENDIX TABLE II (Continued) (%)

No. \ Year	1893	1898	1903	1908	1913	1918	1924	1928	1933	1938
26. Paper	5.01	5.00	10.51	11.32	15.94	6.16	8.38	12.38	15.24	0.81
27. Glass (sheets and plate)	4.06	5.01	16.36	6.77	21.57	9.06	4.36	26.84	14.61	7.02
28. Shoes	4.84	5.10	19.95	40.00	36.67	27.41	7.52	48.87	50.00	75.00
29. Pencils	4.96	5.00	14.99	25.95	31.21	8.94	—	21.42	15.64	23.40
30. Films for photograph	—	—	—	—	19.62	16.61	19.66	30.77	23.55	17.55
31. Musical instruments	5.18	5.06	15.18	39.12	34.85	22.75	25.56	30.84	37.18	29.70
32. Oil seeds	5.01	5.00	4.37	10.49	11.03	6.30	3.48	1.17	1.48	1.70
33. Vegetable oil	5.05	4.53	10.68	8.33	2.14	2.56	5.43	12.00	10.56	11.80
34. Animal fats	5.22	5.00	8.44	8.47	4.68	2.88	0.01	5.02	8.66	8.44
35. Mineral oils	5.00	5.00	14.54	45.89	38.06	18.45	8.55	12.82	26.31	—
36. Coal	0.00	0.00	6.58	0.00	0.00	0.00	0.00	0.00	0.00	0.00
37. Paraffin wax	4.98	4.99	0.00	2.17	13.93	9.36	50.11	49.10	17.66	8.09
38. Caustic soda	4.99	4.99	9.36	9.15	10.81	2.65	14.86	17.88	21.07	19.88
39. Chlorate of potash	5.00	5.00	0.00	0.00	0.00	0.00	0.00	0.00	16.40	—
40. Ammonium sulfate	—	—	0.00	0.00	0.00	0.00	0.00	0.00	0.00	0.00
41. Synthetic dyestuff	5.01	5.00	10.00	7.06	13.95	1.21	31.33	44.98	32.79	26.46
42. Celluloid	—	4.99	10.66	17.09	33.83	0.00	—	—	—	—
43. Soaps	2.34	3.29	11.95	9.32	23.78	13.43	13.37	60.75	55.36	96.12
44. Perfumed water	5.45	4.97	8.34	7.32	11.67	6.39	10.37	55.70	55.76	132.33
45. Iron ore	—	—	0.00	0.00	0.00	0.00	0.00	0.00	0.00	—
46. Pig iron	4.17	3.61	4.20	3.87	3.53	0.54	2.63	3.77	15.23	—
47. Lead, ingot	.5.09	3.59	5.06	4.00	3.79	1.63	2.01	2.67	4.77	—
48. Iron and steel (bar, rod, shapes)	3.73	2.60	6.56	6.88	13.22	3.16	5.16	18.00	24.13	—
49. Iron and steel (plate, sheets)	3.33	2.68	6.63	6.43	9.62	1.78	1.27	16.87	23.51	—
50. Iron and steel (pipes, tubes)	4.96	5.00	10.00	10.04	13.56	4.63	5.46	17.23	11.34	—
51. Nails	2.19	1.96	11.40	9.14	20.28	6.33	2.69	16.64	12.34	8.01
52. Rails	5.01	5.00	4.65	3.14	19.82	6.00	4.34	29.02	24.34	—
53. Materials for construction	—	5.00	20.01	25.00	21.65	7.84	6.38	16.29	9.82	29.41
54. Cutlery	4.92	5.07	20.00	40.00	32.27	24.80	—	34.18	36.46	26.93
55. Ships	1.46	0.40	5.00	10.00	15.52	2.76	19.79	13.19	37.50	—
56. Working machines	4.55	5.00	10.00	15.00	14.31	7.49	7.42	13.09	12.73	1.61
57. Spinning machines	5.00	5.00	10.00	15.00	18.70	8.52	6.09	13.16	8.99	7.17
58. Dynamos and electric motor	—	5.03	10.00	15.00	20.78	9.14	9.07	17.64	8.36	13.02
59. Automobiles	—	—	—	—	30.60	31.06	14.03	29.06	34.45	—
60. Camera	5.00	5.01	15.03	50.00	48.55	49.79	51.05	42.31	60.71	45.27

APPENDIX TABLE II (Continued) (%)

No.	Year	1893	1898	1903	1908	1913	1918	1924	1928	1933	1938
61.	Watches		5.01	5.00	25.52	40.95	29.67	19.00	13.94	28.20	25.84	30.24
62.	Total imports		3.51	2.26	5.17	10.30	10.09	3.76	4.65	7.06	6.03	6.60

Note: Figures show over time changes in tariffs on sixty-one individual commodities during 1893–1938. The tariff rates are calculated by dividing tariff duties collected on individual commodity imports by import values.

Values (c.i.f.) of imports of individual commodities and tariff duties collected on each are taken from "Quantity and value of merchandise imported into each port," in *Dainihon gaikoku bōeki nempyō* [Annual return of the foreign trade of the empire of Japan] (Ministry of Finance). Imports are those of Japan proper from foreign countries so that imports from Taiwan since 1897 and those from Korea since 1912 are excluded but imports from Manchuria and Kwangtung Province are included. The commodity classification of these statistics has changed several times but corresponds to the classification used in the tariff tables.

Sixty-one commodities are selected in order to represent the tariff structure. Many correspond to individual commodity categories in statistics throughout the whole period but some are aggregated over several commodity categories in some years. Not all commodities continued to be imported over the whole period and such new products as artificial silk (No. 14) and photographic films (No. 30) were imported only in later years. The symbol of — in Appendix Table II indicates that the commodity concerned was not imported in that particular year.

The sixty-one commodities are classified into several groups both by industry and by economic use and simple average rates of tariffs are calculated for individual groups (Tables II and III in the text). Details of the classification are shown in Appendix Table III.

APPENDIX TABLE III

COMMODITY CLASSIFICATION BY INDUSTRY AND ECONOMIC USE

Industry Economic Use	Primary Products	Light Manufactures		Heavy Manufactures		
		Textiles	Other Light Manufactures	Chemical Products	Metals & Metal Products	Machinery
Foodstuffs	1 2 3 32		4 5 6 8 7 9			
Raw materials	10 11 21 33 34 35 36 45					
Intermediate goods I		12 13 14	22 23 24	37 38 39	46 47	
Intermediate goods II		15 16 17	25 26 27	40 41 42	48 49 50 51 52 53	
Capital goods						55 56 57 58
Consumer goods		18 19 20	28 29 30 31	43 44	54	59 60 61

Note: Numbers represent commodities listed in Appendix Table II.

[25]
Latin America in the 1930s

CARLOS F. DIAZ ALEJANDRO*

INTRODUCTION

Latin American development experienced a turning-point during the 1930s. The contrast between 'before and after 1929' may often be exaggerated, but there is little doubt that the decade witnessed a closing toward international trade and finance, and a relative upsurge of import-substituting activities, primarily but not exclusively in manufacturing. Other trends visible before 1929, such as urbanisation and a growing interest by the State in promoting economic development, continued into the 1930s and accelerated in some countries. Memories of the 1930s have profoundly influenced the region's attitude toward international trade and finance; per capita foreign trade indicators reached by the late 1920s were not surpassed in many nations until the 1960s.

At least some Latin American economies performed surprisingly

---

* This essay both expands and abstracts who earlier ones (Diaz Alejandro, 1980 and 1981). All tables have been omitted; interested or sceptical readers are referred to those papers, others in the references, and the Statistical Appendix to this volume for fuller, albeit still incomplete, documentation. Workshops organised by Rosemary Thorp at St Antony's College Oxford during September 1981 and in Manchester during September 1982 were very helpful for the preparation of this essay. I am grateful to her and to other participants in those workshops for many useful comments. Those of Victor Bulmer-Thomas, Enrique Cárdenas, José Antonio Ocampo, Arturo O'Connell and Gabriel Palma were especially influential in making me rethink a number of points. Virginia Casey edited and typed these pages in the cold from a sticky manuscript completed in the tropics. Sabbatical leave from Yale University and the joyful and stimulating hospitality of the Pontifical Catholic University of Rio de Janeiro are gratefully acknowledged. Two Rio colleagues, Edmar Bacha and Winston Fritsch, were particularly generous in sharing with me their reflections on the 1930s. The Ford Foundation kindly made possible both the trip to Oxford and the stay in Rio. The Social Science Research Council of the United States financed the Manchester trip. The usual caveats should apply.

well during the 1930s, relative to North America, and relative to what average opinion would have expected to happen in quite open, primary-product exporting nations. This essay will view the economic performance of each country as the result of the magnitude of the exogenous external shock received, of the policy measures undertaken by domestic authorities to speed adjustment to those shocks and to seek external and internal balance, and of the resilience of local private agents in responding to the new constellation of profit opportunities, including those opened up by new technologies and products. (This formulation owes much to the chapter by Bulmer-Thomas in this volume.) Shocks, policies and capacities to transform differed substantially from country to country.

Ability and willingness to manipulate policy instruments such as nominal exchange rates, tariffs and domestic credit were greatest in countries which were either relatively large, such as Brazil, or had relatively autonomous public sectors, such as Costa Rica and Uruguay. Smaller countries, e.g. Honduras, or those with highly dependent governments, e.g. Cuba, had less room for policy manoeuvre. Large domestic markets encouraged resource reallocation in the circumstances of the 1930s and had already induced substantial industrial capacity before then. Other structural features, such as the production characteristics of traditional exports, and the extent of foreign control of local banking and land, also played a role in determining the elasticity of response to the new relative prices. The generalisation that largeness and policy autonomy were favourable to performance covers only republics with nominal sovereignty. Paradoxically, some clear-cut colonies in the Caribbean appear to have performed better than Cuba or the Dominican Republic.

An era of export-led growth culminated in Latin America during the 1920s. In some countries, such as Chile, Cuba and Brazil, the limitations of external demand for the traditional staple had become clear by the late 1920s, while in others those years witnessed unprecedented export booms. Foreign capital, both portfolio and direct, flowed massively into both types of countries up until 1929, so balance-of-payments surplus or at least equilibrium was the rule. As in the rest of the world, there had been a return to the gold-exchange standard in Latin America, and price stability was also the rule, for the last time in this century. It is a moot point whether the terms of trade and the capital inflow of the late 1920s could have been expected to persist. In fact such external and internal balances were rudely and repeatedly shocked from the outside, starting in 1929 and throughout the 1930s.

The external shocks were at once reflected in balance-of-payments deficits, which by themselves triggered mechanisms of adjustment, some very clumsy and painful.

The rest of the chapter will chronicle how various Latin American countries coped with the crisis and the extent to which they were able to mobilise mechanisms of adjustment beyond deflation. The nature and magnitudes of the external shocks will first be narrated. Second, the various policy reactions to those shocks will be discussed, covering measures seeking to regain external and internal balance, as well as policies targeted toward longer-term goals. Then the global, sectoral and welfare performances will be explored, and the sense in which economies did or did not do reasonably well will be analysed. In evaluating performance, emphasis will be placed on quantitative indicators. An overall interpretation of events during the 1930s will close the paper.

EXTERNAL SHOCKS AND TRENDS

The breakdown during 1929–33 of the international economic order was transmitted to Latin America first of all by sharp changes in relative prices: dollar export prices collapsed more steeply than dollar import prices. Within four years the terms of trade fell by 21 to 45% in countries for which comparable data are available (Naciones Unidas, 1976). Latin American terms of trade had, of course, experienced steep declines before, as during 1920–1, but the magnitude of the collapse combined, for many countries, with the continuation of unfavourable terms of trade throughout the rest of the decade, in spite of some post-1933 recovery, was unprecedented at least during the era of export-led growth. The terms of trade deterioration may be regarded as primarily exogenous to Latin America; countries which could influence the international prices of their exports, such as Brazil, had been doing so since earlier in the century. During the early 1930s other Latin American countries began regulating their traditional exports so as not to worsen further their dollar prices.

For a country with a ratio of exports to Gross National Product (GNP) of one-third a deterioration of the terms of trade by 30% would represent a loss in real income of about one-tenth, assuming no change in physical output. The blow to GNP appears to have been softened in some countries by a more than proportional fall in the profits of exporting foreign enterprises; data on the fall of real returned value are unavailable for most countries. On the other hand, there are hints that out of the lower foreign profits a larger share may have sought to be remitted abroad, especially during the early years of the crisis, which may have brought further pressure on the balance of payments.

Except for the spectacular Chilean and Cuban cases, the contraction in the export quantum during 1929–33 was substantially less than the terms of trade deterioration, and by the late 1930s the export quantum of several countries had surpassed the 1928–9 level. Latin American exports were predominantly rural and mining products, the former showing a smaller price elasticity of supply than the latter. Some rural products, such as coffee and livestock, followed *sui generis* output cycles rooted in their productive characteristics, contributing to short-run price inelasticity of supply.

The commodity lottery brought relief to some countries even in the midst of gloomy external conditions. Gold prices were raised by US monetary policy; US support programmes for silver and agricultural commodities also improved a few Latin American export prices (although sometimes at the expense of market shares, as with Cuban sugar). Droughts in North America favoured exporters of temperate foodstuffs. Post-1933 German expansion allowed export diversification for several countries, as to products and markets. Brazilian cotton, Argentine corn, Peruvian and Colombian gold, Mexican silver and Venezuelan oil are examples of generally 'lucky' staples. Tropical colonies with preferential access to metropolitan markets for sugar and bananas gained at the expense of sovereign producers.

As noted earlier, during the late 1920s Latin American payments balances were bolstered by large capital inflows, with New York replacing London as the leading source of long-term portfolio funds. Already during 1929, well before Latin American countries showed signs of skipping scheduled servicing of the external debt or blocking profit remittances, gross capital inflows fell sharply. After mid-1930 little fresh capital came in. With the dollar price level falling unexpectedly by no less than one-quarter between 1920–9 and 1932–3, debt servicing rose dramatically in real terms, compressing the capacity to import beyond what data on the purchasing power of exports suggest. During the early stages of the crisis the import quantum fell even more than the purchasing power of exports in most countries, as they struggled to meet debt obligations in spite of the cessation of capital inflows. Defaults started in 1931 and by 1934 only Argentina, Haiti and the Dominican Republic maintained normal servicing of their external national debt. From then to the end of the decade import volumes as a rule recovered faster than the purchasing power of exports.

Direct foreign investment, in magnitudes more significant for specific branches of production than for the balance of payments, did not disappear during the 1930s, but shifted its marginal orientation away from traditional exports, export-oriented services and social overhead capital, and toward import substituting activities, with the important Venezuelan exception. This trend had been visible already during the 1920s, particularly in the more developed countries of the region. Exchange controls and multiple exchange rates discouraging profit remittances may have induced in the short run some reinvestment of profits in new local activities, especially after the early 1930s. The late 1930s also witnessed the inflow of refugee capital from Europe, and there were even proposals to make Buenos Aires an international money centre, replacing those threatened by European tensions.

The emergence of a protectionist and nationalistic Centre was the greatest shock to Latin American economies during the 1930s, going beyond its direct negative impact on the region's terms of trade. As late as 1931 it was still unclear whether the decline in economic activity in industrialised countries was another passing recession or something more serious. But by that date it seemed very likely that one was witnessing the end of *laissez-faire* and of the commitment of leading countries to relatively free trade. Already during the 1920s imperial preferences were advocated in Britain by influential groups, and the 1928 presidential election in the USA was accompanied by a protectionist wave. That ferment was followed by passage of the Smoot–Hawley tariff in 1930 and the British Abnormal Importations Act of 1931. Even if prosperity returned to the Centre, the outlook for Latin American exports competitive with production in industrial countries or in their colonies or commonwealths, ranging from sugar and copper to meat, corn and wool, looked grim. As the Depression deepened, protectionism gained ground: British Commonwealth preferences were adopted in Ottawa in 1932, while France, Germany and Japan also reinforced their protectionism and discriminatory trade arrangements for areas under their political hegemony.

It is true that in 1934 Cordell Hull, US Secretary of State, started a policy of reducing US tariffs, but such policy made slow progress, and had to whittle down a tariff wall raised not only by the Smoot–Hawley Act, but also by the deflation-induced increase in the incidence of specific duties. The brightest and best-informed observers of the international economy as it stood by 1934 probably had difficulty in forecasting the shape of the new international economic order for the next ten years, but it is unlikely that they would have urged Latin American countries to wait for export-led expansion. As it turned out, by that date circumstances had pushed many Latin American policy-makers into considerable experimentation, without the need of sage foreign advice, which had sharply depreciated during the crisis.

POLICIES

Under gold-exchange standard rules, a deficit in the balance of payments set off automatic mechanisms of adjustment without the need for discretionary actions by policy-makers. As the slowdown in the Centre economies already visible in 1929 and rampant protectionism were quickly translated into a decline of export values in the Periphery, a balance of payments already weakened by a decline in capital inflows turned negative, and gold and foreign exchange flowed out of Latin America. Nominal money supplies declined during the early stages of the crisis, while interest rates were kept no lower than those in the major international financial centres, all in accord with the then orthodox rules of the game. Falling price levels helped maintain real liquidity, also as textbooks predicted, although setting off less textbookish expectations and fears of bankruptcies.

As early as 1930 some Latin American policy-makers began to reconsider the wisdom of remaining faithful to the orthodox rules of the game. The reconsideration was not due to new theoretical insights, but to the pressure of circumstances. Maintaining gold parities when foreign-exchange reserves were disappearing and foreign capital markets were practically shut to new Latin American bond issues became foolhardy. Balancing the budget when customs revenues were collapsing and civil servants were rebelling became nearly impossible. Timidly at first and loudly promising a quick return to late 1920s parities and practices, policy-makers in countries where instruments were at hand or where sufficient autonomy allowed their creation began to replace gold-exchange standard rules with 'emergency' discretionary tinkering. Peripheral shame and self-doubts gradually gave way to self-confidence, especially after Britain abandoned the gold standard in 1931 and Germany and the USA embarked on their own experiments.

The following description of measures undertaken throughout the

1930s risks attributing to 'Autonomous Policy' a series of improvisations more or less forced by circumstances, and whose logic may be clearer *ex post* than at the time of their adoption. One would search in vain among public statements by economic authorities of those days for reasoned explanations for the switch from the old rules to the new discretion; only by the late 1930s *ex post* rationalisations of some intellectual weight began to appear. Yet, whatever their political and ideological motivations, the thrust of policies adopted by the more autonomous and reactive republics may be viewed as attempts to avoid the costs of the deflation called for by the classical mechanism of adjustment, and to speed up the achievement of a new constellation of relative prices and resource allocation consistent with the post-1929 realities of the international economy.

Exchange-rate Policies

Reactive countries by 1933 had nominal exchange rates relative to the dollar significantly above the late 1920s parities. The use of multiple exchange rates buttressed by exchange controls became widespread following the September 1931 devaluation of the pound sterling. Rates applicable to imports suffered the sharpest depreciations. Fears that devaluation would further worsen foreign prices for traditional exports motivated lower depreciations for rates applicable to them, but non-traditional exports received more favourable rates. Fiscal self-interest led to advantageous rates for servicing the public debt; the spread between major buying and selling rates also became a convenient source of public revenue. Memories of late nineteenth-century inflations under the 'inconvertible paper standard', such as those of Argentina and Brazil, made policy-makers anxious about exchange-rate depreciations, and some domestic and foreign advisors urged either an eventual or an immediate return to the parities of the late 1920s. Lip service was paid to an eventual restoration of the gold standard, but policy-makers in reactive countries went no further than checking 'excessive' depreciations.

Small or very dependent countries, such as Honduras, Haiti, Dominican Republic, Panama and Cuba, maintained their peg to the US dollar throughout the 1930s. The last two countries did not even have a central bank or a corresponding monetary authority, such as those of Brazil or pre-1935 Argentina. Exchange-control measures in the small or passive countries were on the whole less forceful than in reactive countries.

Data on price levels and money wages are scarce for the 1930s, especially for the smaller countries. Nevertheless, available information indicates that nominal devaluations in the reactive countries had weak inflationary consequences, contrary to the experience in later years. By 1930–4, therefore, *real* import-exchange rates with respect to the dollar, which take into account price-level changes domestically and abroad, had risen (depreciated) between 30 and 90% in Argentina, Brazil, Chile, Colombia, Mexico, Peru and Uruguay, relative to 1925–9 levels. Such real prices of dollars in terms of local currency remained at those depreciated levels also during 1935–9. As money wages in those countries appear to have followed price-level movements, when the decade is regarded as a whole the ratio of exchange rates to nominal wages also rose significantly.

For the smaller or passive countries one may conjecture that there was no such rapid and large real depreciation of exchange rates. In the Caribbean and Central America the sharpest Depression-induced devaluation occurred in Costa Rica, with a smaller one occurring in El Salvador; other small countries maintained their pegs to the dollar or underwent monetary changes due to domestic turmoil. Some countries having a steady peg to the dollar attempted to raise the ratio of the exchange rate to nominal wages by extraordinarily repressive labour policies; such was the case of Guatemala under General Ubico, at least until 1934 (see Chapter 11 by Bulmer-Thomas).

Regardless of the exchange-rate policy followed, a country subjected to an exogenous and permanent worsening of its international terms of trade should witness over the long run a decline in the price of its non-traded goods and services (or money wages) relative to the domestic price of importable goods, encouraging a movement of resources, including fresh investments, toward the import-competing sector, additional to that generated by the decline in exportable-goods prices. A permanent decline in net long-term capital inflows would also induce a decline in the prices of non-traded goods relative to all traded goods. Under a gold-exchange standard with fixed rates and with collapsing international nominal prices for both imports and exports, non-traded goods prices and domestic liquidity had a long way to fall to adjust to the 1929–33 decline in terms of trade and the cessation of capital inflows. It is the working hypothesis of this chapter that countries willing and able to devalue their exchange rate moved toward the new constellation of domestic relative prices more speedily and less painfully than those with fixed rates, limiting both price and monetary deflation, containing their negative impact on real output, or reducing pressures to depress money wages by extraordinary measures. It is worth emphasising that the depreciating trend in the reactive countries appears smooth only in *ex-post* five-year averages focusing on exchange rates with respect to the dollar. Besides confusing signals emanating from promises to return to earlier parities the early 1930s also witnessed changes in the rates between major currencies, particularly the dollar–pound sterling rate, which added to fluctuations in *effective* exchange rates of several countries, especially in South America, and complicated the formation of expectations about the future price of 'foreign exchange'.

Other Import-repressing and Import-diverting Policies

The domestic price of importable goods relative to non-traded goods prices, or to money wages, also received an upward push in many Latin American countries as tariffs rose and quantitative restrictions, via import or exchange controls, were introduced. Contrary to what would happen in the late 1940s and 1950s, exchange-rate and *de facto* protectionist policies reinforced each other as import-repressing mechanisms, especially in Brazil and the Southern Cone. Indeed, by the mid-1930s in some of the reactive countries there may have been redundancy in this formidable battery of measures; this has been argued for the Chilean case, for example.

The small or passive countries appear to have been, with some exceptions, as impotent regarding protection as with nominal exchange-rate management. Cuba actually lowered tariffs in 1934, undoing much of the protectionist effect of her anomalous Tariff Act of 1927. Even larger countries were pressured into reversing some of their early-1930s tariff increases; wielding the threat of Commonwealth preferences and meat import quotas, the UK obtained tariff concessions from Argentina under the controversial Roca–Runciman treaty of 1933. Argentina and Cuba shared awkward memberships in 'informal empires', although the autonomy of the former country was, of course, much larger than the latter.

Tariff rates appear to have undergone few changes in levels or structure in Mexico and Peru. These countries also behaved in a manner more like the smaller countries in regard to import and exchange controls; in contrast with Brazil and the Southern Cone they employed those instruments only sparingly. Colombia, as usual, had an intermediate set of policies: most of the change between 1927 and 1936 in the prices of her imported non-traditional manufactures has been attributed to devaluation rather than tariff increases, although increments in effective protection stimulated some industries, including cement, soap and rayon textiles. Colombia also exercised import and exchange controls with greater vigour than did Mexico and Peru.

Import and exchange controls, together with multiple rates, had the additional task of managing key bilateral balances, especially in Brazil and the Southern Cone; in countries with less diversified trading and financial patterns such management was less of a problem. Argentine controls were practically forced upon her by the UK pressure for bilateral clearings; to achieve that goal Argentina had to discriminate against US exports. Such 'buying from those that bought from her' generated hostility in the US against Argentina, and some North Americans viewed her controls as a sign of Nazi rather than British influence. Brazilian controls, in fact, received impetus from her expanded trade with Germany during the 1930s.

Other Balance-of-payments Policies

Toward the end of the 1920s the stock of British and US investments of all kinds in Latin America amounted, in per capita terms, to about one-sixth those in Canada. The heaviest concentration occurred, in descending order and still in per capita terms, in Cuba, Argentina, Chile, Mexico, Uruguay and Costa Rica. Both in Canada and Latin America the two major foreign investors had accumulated claims of all kinds of around four times the annual value of merchandise exports. Assuming a 5% rate of return, profits and interests of foreign capital must have accounted for about 20% of annual export earnings, and were punctually transferred abroad. With the exception of Mexico the 'investment climate' appeared reasonably good; the nineteenth-century defaults on bonds issued in London had been settled, and while numerous frictions were generated by direct investments they seemed negotiable.

The unexpected post-1929 fall in dollar and sterling prices sharply increased the real cost of external obligations denominated in those currencies. Servicing the Argentine public debt, for example, which had absorbed about 6% of merchandise exports during the late 1920s, by 1933 reached nearly 16% of exports. Chile in 1932 faced interest and amortisation charges, including those on short-term maturities, far exceeding export earnings. The ratio of the stock of long-term external public debt to yearly merchandise exports for all Latin America rose from 1.5 in 1929 to 2.3 in 1935. The drying up of foreign capital markets made roll-over operations for both long- and short-term debt very difficult. The collapse of import-duty revenues cut a traditional budgetary source for payments on the external debt.

Starting in 1931, authorities delayed granting exchange to importers for settling their short-term debt and to foreign companies for profit remittances. Also in 1931, many Latin American countries began to skip scheduled servicing of the external long-term public debt. Defaulting countries did not dramatically repudiate their obligations, but asked foreign creditors for conversations aimed at rescheduling and restructuring the debt. Different countries carried out those conversations with various degrees of enthusiasm: Cuba, for example, while servicing her debt irregularly during the 1930s maintained better relations with her creditors than Brazil, whose dealings with creditors during the late 1930s, especially with British ones, were acrimonious. For many countries those negotiations were to stretch out well into the 1940s, and into the 1950s in some cases. The contrast between Argentine and Brazilian policies toward debt service in the 1930s casts light on the nature of international economic relations during those years; see Chapter 6 for a discussion of those policies. One may emphasise that the relative abundance of exchange reserves in Argentina, whose gold holdings remained one of the highest in the world, gaining an important windfall by the increase in the international gold price during the 1930s, plus the fact that a substantial amount of the Argentine sterling- and dollar-denominated debt was held by Argentines (just as a share of 'domestic', peso-denominated debt was held by foreigners) also contributed to punctual servicing of even dollar-denominated bonds, presumably mostly held in the USA, in spite of British hints about the convenience for Anglo-Argentine trade of defaulting on that part of the debt. Furthermore, tampering with the normal servicing of the Argentine debt would have involved not only a bruising commercial clash with the UK, but probably also a major restructuring of the Argentine domestic political scene at the expense of groups linked with Anglo-Argentine trade.

There is little reason to doubt the consensus among those who have examined the Latin American defaults of the 1930s: if the Depression had been mild, and if the steady expansion of world trade and capital flows had been continued, defaults would have been infrequent and could have been settled without much difficulty. Once the Depression came and productive resources were allowed to go to waste in idleness, while countries everywhere restricted imports to protect jobs, it made no economic sense to insist on the transfer of real resources as debt servicing. No doubt the capital markets of the 1920s contained significant imperfections: during the 1930s many underwriters were accused not just of negligence in seeking information about borrowers and their projects, but also of deliberately misleading bond-buyers, motivating New Deal regulatory legislation. Latin American countries were encouraged to borrow excessively, and a good share of the funds went into projects of doubtful social productivity. But one may question whether these microeconomic factors were decisive. One may also note that the industrialised countries themselves led in the undermining of belief in the sanctity of contracts; examples include the British default on the war debt, Germany's failure to make payments on the greater part of her international obligations, the derogation of the gold clause in the USA, and domestic moratoria legislated in several countries.

By the late 1930s foreign-exchange availability had improved and indeed some debt servicing was paid by defaulting Latin American countries throughout the 1930s. Some countries purchased their own partially or wholly unserviced bonds selling at a discount in foreign markets; those bonds by the late 1930s were probably held mostly by speculators. Such 'repatriations' of the debt avoided a rigid settlement schedule at a time when the international economic outlook was very uncertain, and were carried out by central banks, whose financial positions were generally better than those of the Treasuries, which still suffered from the fall and change in composition of imports and the induced decline in duties.

In spite of exchange controls regulating profit remittances abroad by foreign enterprises, direct foreign investments occurred throughout the 1930s, although in amounts more significant for the expansion of specific branches of production than for balance-of-payments equilibrium. It has been argued that the local reinvestment of foreign-enterprise profits may have been encouraged by limitations on remittances abroad, an argument more plausible in the short run than in the long. In some countries exchange controls were also employed to ward off unwanted short-term capital inflows, as in Argentina during the late 1930s; such 'hot money' movements were perceived as destabilising macroeconmic balance. Capital accompanying European refugees was considered a more permanent and welcomed addition to local resources and these combinations of entrepreneurship and finance were important in the expansion of several economic (and cultural) activities in many Latin American countries.

Monetary and Fiscal Policies

The decline in exports and capital inflows signalling the beginning of the crisis was accompanied at once by balance-of-payments deficits which drained reserves and money supplies, according to gold-standard, fixed-exchange rates rules. The export fall had important multiplier effects. This section will examine responses to those deflationary pressures on aggregate demand. In countries without well-developed financial markets it is difficult to isolate purely fiscal from monetary policies. During the 1930s only Argentina had financial markets of some sophistication, so this section will discuss aggregate macroeconomic policies without establishing fine distinctions between monetary and fiscal ones.

Money-supply data indicate that reactive Latin American countries show briefer or shallower post-1929 declines in nominal money supplies than the USA. By 1932 the Brazilian nominal money supply exceeded that of 1929; the corresponding Colombian date is 1933. The end of convertibility into gold was helpful in stemming the loss of liquidity among reactive countries. In contrast the Cuban inability to break out of the then orthodox rules led to a monetary deflation even greater than that of the USA.

Domestic price levels for 1930–4 were below those of 1925–9 excepting Chile, although the decline appears smaller for most reactive countries than that in the USA. By 1935–9 price levels in those countries had mostly returned to about 1925–9 levels, with only Chile and Mexico cleary surpassing them. *Real* money supplies in 1930–4 in most reactive countries were above those for 1925–9; by 1935–9 real money supplies in Argentina, Brazil, Chile, Colombia, Mexico and Uruguay were substantially above 1925–9 levels. The Cuban real money supply in 1935–9 was below that for 1925–9 and this probably was the case in many of the Central American and Caribbean republics. This contrast suggests that the increase in real money supplies of reactive countries was not just the result of automatic mechanisms of adjustment triggered by the fall in the international price level, but also the result of domestic policies.

Maintenance of liquidity was not simply a matter of ending convertibility into gold or foreign exchange at the old parities. Even after the abandonment of the gold standard some countries, such as Argentina, shipped gold to service the external debt and sold some foreign exchange to stem currency depreciation. Both measures cut the monetary base if orthodox practices were followed. But as early as 1931 South American monetary authorities adopted measures which would have been regarded as unsound during the 1920s. Thus, the Argentine Caja de Conversión whose only classical duty was to exchange gold and foreign exchange for domestic currency at a fixed price, and vice versa, starting in 1931 began to issue domestic currency in exchange for private commercial paper, relying on obscure and nearly forgotten laws, and later on even issued domestic currency against Treasury paper, which was also accepted as payment for gold sent abroad for public debt servicing. Young technocrats in charge of Argentine monetary policy successfully resisted pressures from the orthodox to 'redeem' the Treasury paper, recall the new currency issues, and return to the old parity. The Colombian Central Bank in 1930 for the first time engaged in direct operations with the public, discounting notes and lending on the security of warehouse receipts; during 1931 ingenious subterfuges were found by the Bank to grant credit directly to the central government, involving as 'collateral' future public revenues from a salt mine (Ocampo, Chapter 5, below). Government bonds were purchased from private banks in large quantities by the Colombian Central Bank since 1932. In Colombia, as in other reactive countries, since the introduction of exchange controls in 1931 international reserves ceased to govern monetary issue, which from then on was predominantly influenced by internal considerations of economic policy or budgetary expediency.

The South American and Mexican monetary policies, started around 1932, were in some ways a relapse into past inflationary propensities, a past which was supposed to have been exorcised by the adoption during the 1920s of gold-standard rules and up-to-date budgetary and monetary mechanisms. These mechanisms became popular in the region during the second half of the 1920s, often following visits of foreign 'money doctors'. Memories of wild inflation under inconvertible paper during the late nineteenth century, memories still fresh during 1929–31, as well as episodes of financial disorder as recent as the early 1920s, hampered and slowed down the adoption of more self-assured and expansionist monetary policies. It should also be remembered that as late as the first half of 1931 there were optimistic reports of an upturn in the major industrialised economies.

In contrast with the USA there are no reports of widespread bank failures in reactive countries during the early 1930s. Also in contrast with the USA, monetary aggregates fail to reveal in flight into currency and away from bank deposits; if anything, during the early stages of the Depression the opposite appears to have occurred in Argentina, Brazil, Colombia and Uruguay. In reactive countries monetary authorities simply did not let many banks fail, casting fears of moral hazard to the winds. In many of those countries a substantial share of deposits were held in state-owned banks, which may have been decisive in avoiding financial panics. While moratoria on urban and rural domestic bank debts were decreed in many countries (earlier than in the USA), thus freezing banks' assets, commercial banks were supported in a number of *ad hoc* ways, not all of them conducive to maintaining actual liquidity. For example, in Brazil as early as October 1930 withdrawals of bank deposits were restricted by decree. Domestic moratoria, of course, had an expansionary influence on debtors. Rediscounting of commercial banks' loans was also vigorously carried out by Central Banks and institutions such as the Banco do Brasil and the Banco de la Nacion Argentina. Unorthodoxy was sometimes cloaked by gestures to the old financial hocus-pocus; Argentina claimed to have used profits from increases in the peso price of gold to create an institution which supported commercial banks.

The financial impotency of passive countries may be illustrated by the contrasting experiences of Cuba and Mexico in their tinkering with silver for monetary and fiscal purposes. Although Cuba was not a major silver producer while Mexico was, both countries hit upon the expedient of issuing silver coins, which added to liquidity and yielded seignorage profits to the Treasury, justifying expenditures. Depending on the acceptance by the public, both countries planned to issue paper notes backed by silver stocks, increasing seignorage. In Cuba modest issues were made during 1932–3, and in 1934 a revolutionary government appeared to herald a bold new monetary system independent of the dollar by planning new issues and by making silver pesos full legal tender for the discharge of old as well as new obligations contracted in dollars or in old Cuban gold pesos. Shortly thereafter a mild form of exchange control was decreed. Foreign banks on the island apparently threatened to export all dollars from Cuba; capital flight followed. The government caved in, lifting rather than expanding controls. Only the legal tender status of silver for all contracts in such currency remained of the 1934 reform. Even a Central Bank was to wait until 1948.

Mexico, after some deflationary measures in 1930 and 1931, adopted early in 1932 expansionary policies, relying mainly on issues of silver pesos. Central Bank control over commercial banks was extended and strengthened. Foreign banks threatened to leave Mexico, and as the Mexican authorities held firm, most of them left. Mexican-owned banks took their place. Campaigns were launched to convince the public to use 'silver' paper notes rather than coins; remarkably, the share of paper notes in the money supply jumped dramatically in a few years, for reasons still somewhat obscure (see Chapter 9, by Cárdenas). Public banks were created or expanded to finance housing, public works, foreign trade, industry and agriculture, and these instruments were used with increasingly self-conscious expansionist purposes. By the late 1930s the Mexican monetary and financial system was quite different from that of the late 1920s. In contrast with the disastrous Chinese experience, Mexican reliance on a silver standard did not generate unmanageable problems when the USA raised silver prices; Mexico simply prohibited the export of silver money in April 1935 and ordered all coins to be exchanged for paper currency. A year and a half later, after the world price of silver had fallen, silver coinage was restored, partly due to pressure from the US silver lobby. As a major exporter of silver Mexico, of course, benefited from higher international silver prices.

Even during the confusion of the early 1930s, fiscal policy in reactive countries appears to have contributed to the maintenance of aggregate demand, at least in the sense of *not* balancing the budget in the midst of the crisis, in spite of the protestations of policy-makers that they intended to do so. Although data are particularly shaky in this field, real government expenditures were not significantly cut during the early 1930s, while real tax revenues fell as imports collapsed, inducing an increase in fiscal deficits in spite of new taxes and higher tariffs. The financing of budget deficits even in reactive countries during the early 1930s was not all particularly expansionary; payment delays to civil servants and government suppliers increased the 'floating debt', a debt whose holders usually could only turn into cash at huge discounts, thus coming close to forced loans (but see Chapter 4, by Thorp and Londoño, who argue that such debt came closer to quasi-money). A fiscal policy, expansionary in the sense of increasing the full-capacity real budget deficit during the early 1930s, has been amply documented only for Brazil; the Chilean experience has some similarities to the Brazilian case, according to Palma, in this volume. The cases of Argentina and Brazil will illustrate the variety of fiscal policies in reactive countries.

Real expenditures of the Argentine central government rose in 1929 and again in 1930; the provisional regime of General Uriburu, which took power in September 1930, pledging to eliminate populist budgetary excesses, reduced 1931 real expenditures slightly below those for 1930, but left them above 1929 levels. The lowest real expenditure figures for the 1930s, which were registered in 1933, were still higher than those for 1929; for the rest of the decade real government expenditures expanded so that by 1938–9 they were around 50% above 1929. A major road-building programme was undertaken by the government of General Justo (1932–8), adding 30 000 kilometres of all-weather and improved roads by 1938 to a system that had only 2 100 kilometres of such roads in 1932. This programme had important effects not just on aggregate demand, but also on productivity and aggregate supply, both complementing and competing with the vast Argentine railroad network. The late 1930s also witnessed an expansion of military expenditures. The ratio of all government expenditures to merchandise exports, a useful index suggested by Rosemary Thorp, which in 1928 was less than 0.4 had risen to more than 0.9 by 1938–9.

The technocrats in charge of the economic policies of the Uriburu and Justo Administrations, including Federico Pinedo and Raúl Prebisch, took a dim view of the large deficits registered in 1930 and 1931; the fall in revenues from import duties aggravated a fiscal situation which already in 1928 and 1929 yielded taxes covering only 76–80% of all government expenditures. Tariff rates were increased, an income tax was introduced (in 1932), a gasoline tax was coupled with the road-building programme and use was made of multiple exchange rates to generate government revenues. As in other Latin American countries, fiscal heterodoxy was discredited in Argentina by dubious expenditures and lax budgets during the late 1920s.

The budget deficits of 1930 and 1931 were financed primarily by delays in payments to suppliers and civil servants, or payments in public debt instruments of low liquidity, contributing to the unpopularity of government deficits. Starting in 1932, however, such floating debt was sharply reduced and by the second half of the 1930s the government placed in an active local market both short- and long-term public securities at rates of interest much below those of 1929–32. Refunding operations were also carried out to reduce the cost and improve the structures of domestic and foreign debts.

The countercyclical potency of Argentine fiscal policy during the early 1930s was reduced by the increased share in total expenditures of debt-service payments, largely made to foreigners. All payments on the public debt reached 29% of expenditures in 1932; this may be contrasted with the meagre 5% devoted to public works. By 1938 the figures were 15% for debt service and 20% for public works. Other Latin American countries were to find the budgetary weight of debt service, exacerbated by exchange-rate depreciations, a strong inducement to suspend normal payments.

In short there is no evidence that during the early 1930s the Argentine government sought to increase the full-capacity budget deficit to compensate for the fall in aggregate demand. On the contrary, attempts were made to shift upward the tax schedule and to lower that for government expenditures. But even during the early 1930s efforts to reduce the deficit induced by the decline in foreign trade and output were tempered by either common sense or the sheer inability to cut expenditures and raise taxes fast enough. The relative size of public expenditures in the income stream thus grew by default already in the early 1930s, helping to sustain economic activity. Since 1933 public expenditures expanded in a deliberate way, and this expansion had at least a balanced-budget–multiplier effect on the rest of the economy. In addition, since 1935 the new Central Bank encouraged the expansion of a market for the domestic public debt, facilitating modest deficit financing. Finally, the structure of expenditures during the late 1930s on balance favoured domestic expansion, in spite of some increase in the import content of military expenditures.

Brazil provides an example of a compensatory increase in government expenditure in the early 1930s. Since 1906 the State of São Paulo and the federal government sustained coffee prices via buffer stocks; during the sharp recession of 1920–21 the countercyclical potency of the coffee valorisation scheme had already been demonstrated. As coffee prices fell during the early 1930s the government again purchased large quantities of that product. A good share of those purchases were financed either by a foreign loan or new taxes, but about one-third were financed essentially by money creation. It has also been argued that the new taxes levied on exports, and the exchange-rate appreciation generated by foreign loans, improved Brazilian terms of trade, relative to the relevant counterfactual situation. Argentina also started regulating the production and export of major traditional exports during the 1930s, notably wheat, but without the massive fiscal impact of the Brazilian coffee purchases, partly due to the recovery of their international prices. The exchange differential profits were the Argentine counterpart to the Brazilian export taxes, both attempting to raise government revenues as well as to protect the terms of trade. Brazil also expanded public expenditures during the late 1930s, and probably reduced the import content of those expenditures even more than Argentina, as beginning in September 1931 it met debt-service obligations only partially. In 1937 Brazil announced the suspension of all debt servicing, and none occurred during 1938 and 1939. In both Argentina and Brazil the 1930s witnessed diversification of public revenues, with a remarkable expansion in non-customs taxes, which by 1932 (Argentina) and 1933 (Brazil) had exceeded the 1929 levels, at current prices. A similar trend toward tax diversification has been reported for Colombia, where direct taxes were increased during 1935–6, and Mexico. In the Brazilian case state revenues, especially those of São Paulo, appear to have expanded by more than those of the federal government.

Calamities, civil disturbances and border wars during the early 1930s led to increased real public expenditures in several countries, apparently financed directly by monetary expansion. Examples include political turmoil in Chile during late 1931 and 1932 (when that country had a short-lived socialist government); the war between Peru and Colombia over Leticia in 1932 (partly financed on the Colombian side by voluntary donations); the second Gran Chaco War between Bolivia and Paraguay, also in 1932; and the São Paulo rebellion of 1932, plus a severe drought in the north-east, which added to coffee deficits in Brazil (the former more than the latter). In some countries weak central control over regional governments also contributed to the maintenance of public expenditures.

Whatever the hesitations and improvisations of the early 1930s, by the second half of the decade the reactive Latin American countries had developed a respectable array of both monetary and fiscal tools, as well as the will to use them to avoid deflation. Thus, the 1937–8 recession in the USA was felt in the foreign trade statistics more than those for industrial output. South American countries damaged by the loss of European markets and shipping shortages in 1939–40 mobilised to adopt emergency stabilisation measures, such as the remarkable Plan Pinedo in Argentina, which included proposals for closer regional economic ties, particularly between Argentina and Brazil. That Plan was never adopted, due to Congressional opposition and an improvement in the economic outlook.

Much of the new state activism discussed in this section may have been motivated by a desire to help influential rural exporters. One may note, however, that it is difficult to imagine macroeconomic policies in Latin American countries at that time which did not involve heavy emphasis on traditional export activities. This is due not just to the large weight of those sectors in national income, but also to the need to regulate their sales abroad, to avoid further declines in their international prices. Thus, apparently sectorial policies had a major impact on both aggregate demand and the balance of payments.

In passive countries an activist fiscal policy continued to be checked by exiguous foreign and domestic demand for public debt, and by convertibility into dollars at fixed rates that limited monetary expansion not backed by international reserves.

Other Policies

While nominal exchange-rate behaviour during the 1930s is well documented, much less is known regarding wages and how they were influenced by public policy, except for a few cases. In Guatemala, for example, where the exchange rate fixed during the 1920s was maintained throughout the 1930s, the regime of General Ubico enforced until 1934 draconian labour practices, some originating in the Spanish conquest, generating a cheap supply of quasi-forced labour for both landowners and public works. (But see Chapter 11 by Bulmer-Thomas for changes after 1934.) Flexibility and moderation regarding money wages was induced by more subtle means in other countries, particularly where non-traditional labour markets already existed. In some of those countries, like Argentina, soft economic conditions during the early 1930s, rural–urban migration and cheap foodstuffs kept increases in nominal wages substantially behind exchange-rate depreciations. In others, such as Colombia, Brazil and Mexico, those market trends were accompanied by public policies encouraging trade unions which often controlled from above rather than promoted wage gains, especially *vis-à-vis* nationally-owned firms. Mass deportation of Mexican workers from the USA during the 1930s also added to the pool of mobile labour available in that country.

Public policies went beyond those seeking short-term adjustment to outside shocks, and Latin American governments, whose attachment to *laissez-faire* was never particularly deep, became increasingly committed during the 1930s to promoting long-term growth and structural transformations. The Lazaro Cárdenas Administration (1934–40) accelerated the land reform programme of the Mexican Revolution, and in 1938 nationalised the petroleum industry. Government regulation of the pricing and marketing of rural products, and of public utility rates expanded in most countries. As noted earlier for Mexico, the 1930s witnessed in several other Latin American countries the strengthening and creation of public institutions granting medium- and long-term credits, which the unregulated financial markets of the 1920s had not provided in amounts regarded as sufficient, or whose supply had been left in foreign hands. Housing, public works, agriculture and, increasingly, industry benefited from such credit, which during the 1930s, when inflation was moderate at worst, was still priced not far below plausible estimates for the shadow cost of capital.

The public works undertaken in many countries had a long-lasting impact on productive capacity and urbanisation patterns. Vast road programmes accelerated the transition from the railroad age to that of motor vehicles. That transition stimulated many manufacturing activities including cement, rubber, petroleum refining and the assembly and eventual production of cars, trucks, and buses; generated public revenues via gasoline taxes; diversified and completed transport networks, lowering their costs and encouraging new activities, such as US tourism in Mexico, while opening up new lands for rural production; and even helped to change international economic relations, as motor-vehicle activities were dominated by the USA, while railroads had been dominated by the UK. (See Fodor and O'Connell, 1973.) Irrigation works, like those undertaken in Mexico, together with new roads and credit facilities, encouraged the transition from traditional to modern capitalist agriculture.

During the 1930s governments and public opinion showed a keener interest in increasing the national share in value added by foreign-owned activities and the control over the processing and marketing of exports. Foreign-owned enterprises came under closer scrutiny and supervision by host countries; several traditional export activities witnessed a rise in the share owned by domestic capitalists, as in the case of Cuban sugar. Finally, as the European and Asian political scenes continued to deteriorate, the Armed Forces, especially in South America, showed increased interest in promoting the expansion of certain types of infrastructure and the local manufacture of steel and armaments.

PERFORMANCE

Even in countries performing reasonably well during the 1930s, structural changes were more impressive than overall growth; during that decade some economic activities stagnated or collapsed while others surged ahead. The former were generally associated directly or indirectly with external markets, while the latter typically involved domestic sales. Reactive countries on average performed better than passive ones, and in both types of nations some regions did much better than others. Pockets of profitability within agriculture and industry coexisted with liquidations; textile mills worked three shifts even in 1932 while meat-packing plants and sugar mills were idle. The larger the pre-1929 share of exports (or their returned value) in total output the smaller the absolute size of the domestic market, and the greater the institutional barriers to domestic resource mobility, the more difficult it was for the growing sectors to dominate the shrinking ones to yield a reasonably good overall performance. These factors, plus luck with external commodity prices, trade partners and local leadership, generated a continuum of quantifiable economic performances, rather than clear-cut typologies. In these still heavily agricultural economies, weather and pests remained important influences even on ten-year growth rates. In what follows, aggregate performance will first be examined as far as data allow, turning later to sectoral and welfare performances.

Macroeconomic Performance

National accounts for the four largest Latin American countries (Argentina, Brazil, Colombia and Mexico) register growth rates for Gross Domestic Product (GDP) steadier and higher than those of Canada and the USA for 1929–39. Neither the absolute GDP growth nor its level relative to the growth achieved during the 1940s and early 1950s, however, are impressive, ranging from around 2% per annum for Argentina and Mexico, to about 4% per annum for the two major coffee countries. Argentine and Colombian GDPs grew during the 1920s at clearly faster rates than those of the 1930s; Brazilian GDP during 1919–29 also seems to have outperformed the 1929–39 expansion.

Measurements of GDP ignore losses of real income from deteriorating terms of trade. Taking these losses into account would reduce Brazilian annual growth for 1929–39 by about 1 percentage point (while increasing those for the 1920s and 1940s). Population growth in Latin America during the 1930s was higher than that in industrialised countries. Thus, measuring performance by growth in per capita real domestic income during 1929–39 would reduce the differential favouring reactive Latin American countries compared with industrialised countries. Correcting for the reduction in factor payments abroad which occurred during the 1930s, to obtain real *national* income, is unlikely to offset corrections for terms of trade and population in evaluating overall performance. Even for reactive countries data for these calculations are shaky, however, and for others they are generally unavailable.

In reactive countries GDP recovery apparently started in 1932, earlier than in the USA. Neither the 1929–32 decline nor the 1932–7 recovery were as dramatic as those in the USA.

Consumption and investment also show disparate behaviour in their component parts, making the use of those aggregates of only limited value. Investment shares in GDP seem to have declined relative to the late 1920s, yet some sectors expanded their productive capacity while others experienced net disinvestment. Imports of machinery and equipment for railroads and electricity waned, while those for some manufacturing activities rose. It would strain available data to discuss the evolution of national savings during the 1930s relative to the 1920s, but it is clear that they rose relative to external savings and it seems that changes in the domestic financial system and in government budgets encouraged their mobilisation. Private consumption must have also undergone significant structural changes after 1929, some reflecting ongoing long-term trends such as urbanisation and the adoption of new products, others induced in the short- and medium-term by the income and substitution effects of higher prices for imported goods.

SECTORAL PERFORMANCE

Economic performance during the 1930s for the reactive Latin American countries looks more impressive when attention is focused on manufacturing. While growth in this sector during the 1940s and early 1950s was to exceed that for the 1930s in most countries, manufacturing growth rates for 1929–39, ranging from more than 3% per annum in Argentina to more than 8% per annum in Colombia, far outstripped those of the USA and Canada, which hovered around zero. The relatively modest Argentine manufacturing expansion was higher than that of Australia, even though both countries experienced roughly similar GDP growth rates between 1928 and 1938. In the important Brazilian case, manufacturing growth during the 1930s, of more than 6% per annum, was significantly higher than during the 1920s; the pace of Colombian industrialisation during the 1930s could not have been much behind that of the 1920s, if at all. Another interesting comparison involves Chile and Uruguay, on one side, and Cuba, on the other; the former reactive countries experienced manufacturing expansion of 3 to 5% per annum, while the latter country saw its total industrial production shrink even more than in the USA. Chilean industry also grew during the 1930s faster than during the previous decade (Palma, Chapter 3 below).

Pre-1929 Latin American manufacturing tended to grow only slightly ahead of the rest of the export-led economy. Beyond moderate protectionism, public policy departed little from neutrality toward industry. Important segments of manufacturing exported (slightly) processed primary products; examples include meat-packing plants and flour mills in the River Plate and sugar mills in several countries, which also sold their products domestically. Growth of manufacturing during the recovery phase of the 1930s relied heavily on import substitution, defined in the usual accounting sense (decrease in the share of imported goods in total supply), which focuses on output rather than on installed capacity. Manufacturing during the 1930s grew in reactive countries much faster than GDP, in contrast with pre-1929 experience.

The uneven performance in various GDP components is echoed by heterogeneous growth within manufacturing. Activities tied to pre-1929 export-oriented prosperity shrank, while others (sometimes a handful) made dramatic output advances. Leading sectors typically included textiles, petroleum refining, tyres, pharmaceuticals, toiletries, food-processing for the home market (e.g. vegetable oils), chemicals, cement and other building materials. Cotton and wool textiles were the most important leading sectors, often providing more than 20% of the net expansion of value added in manufacturing, and growing at annual rates above 10%. Between the late 1920s and late 1930s cement production multiplied by more than 14 times in Colombia, by more than 6 times in Brazil and by almost 4 times in Argentina. Even in passive countries one finds some import-substituting industries growing very fast, such as milk-processing and cotton cloth in Cuba, but in the midst of depressed export-related manufacturing. The remarkable industrialisation of major coffee countries (Brazil and Colombia) was partly due to having pre-1929 manufacturing sectors with few direct links to exports, in contrast with Argentina and Cuba. Pre-1929 growth, and the industrialization it had induced, were the more helpful to the import-substituting drive of the 1930s the greater the extent to which social overhead capital, trained labour force, and other productive capacity which had been created were not rigidly tied to specialised needs of exporting activities and could be reallocated quickly to serve other productive purposes.

Output growth in the booming industrial sectors far outstripped the expansion of total domestic absorption of those manufactured goods, which either followed more closely the somewhat sluggish growth of GDP, or declined in some cases even in reactive countries. Apparent domestic cement consumption, for example, increased by far less than the spectacular output increases noted earlier; it rose by 26% in Colombia, 12% in Brazil, and 50% in Argentina (in the USA it *declined* by 36%, in Canada and Haiti by 50% and in Cuba by 63%). Exports explain little of the gap between high output and low domestic absorption expansion; the share of local production in domestic absorption of cement rose between the late 1920s and the late 1930s from 6 to 72% in Colombia, from 14 to 89% in Brazil, and from 35 to 94% in Argentina. In contrast, in Cuba, Haiti, the Dominican Republic and Central America the share of domestic output in national cement absorption changed very little during that decade (although the Cuban share had reached levels higher than those of South American countries in the late 1920s). A similar import-substitution tale applies to textiles. For other commodities, such as automobiles, the decline in imports could not be matched by expansion of local production; for those goods, primarily consumer durables and machinery and equipment, domestic absorption fell, not to recover in per capita terms until the 1960s in many cases. Such 'postponement' of expenditures with high import content would become a standard feature of the mechanism of adjustment in the balance of payments of many Latin American countries in later years.

Capacity in manufacturing and ancillary social overhead capital expanded by less than output during the 1930s; statistics do not show either an upsurge in imports of machinery and equipment or a compensating expansion of local production of those goods. Indeed, in some countries imports of certain types of machinery (e.g. textile machinery in Brazil) were banned based on allegations of excess capacity. The late 1920s left substantial slack or malleable capacity in industry, electricity and some transport facilities. There are frequent reports of textile mills increasing their number of shifts during the early 1930s, and of large investments made during the late 1920s coming to fruition during the 1930s, as in the Brazilian cement industry.

Electricity capacity oriented toward export-related production during the 1920s could fairly easily be switched to supplying booming import substituting activities. Nevertheless, output expansions such as those registered for cement in Argentina, Brazil and Colombia *must* have relied on some increases in capacity, and imports of machinery and equipment. One may conjecture that there were substantial changes in the composition and allocation of capital goods imports between the 1920s and 1930s, so even if their total fell, plenty of room was left for the investment needs of dynamic branches of manufacturing.

The industrialisation of the 1930s, at least in South America, was quite labour-intensive, and involved many small- and medium-sized firms. Between 1930 and 1937 industrial employment in São Paulo grew at nearly 11% per year. The output elasticity of employment was about 1 in both Argentina and Brazil; increases in average labour productivity for specific activities seem to have been rare, in spite of the entry of new firms. In Argentina, for example, the increase in the number of textile firms accounted during the 1930s for approximately 65% of the increase in spindles held by the industry.

There are other indications that import-substitution relied heavily on new national and foreign-born entrepreneurs, including fresh immigrants from the troubled Europe of the 1930s. The rise of Hitler and Franco led to significant gains of human and financial capital for Latin America. There was also direct foreign investment in import-substitution by tariff-jumping enterprises, whose home markets showed weak prospects. For sectors like tyres and cement these investments and the technology they supplied provided significant impetus. There is little systematic evidence on the overall financing of manufacturing investment during the 1930s. It may be conjectured that traditional sources, e.g. reinvestment of gross profits and short-term and informal-market borrowing supplied the bulk of finance for national entrepreneurs as the contribution of public credit institutions to manufacturing capital formation was still modest.

New import-substituting activities clustered, not surprisingly, mainly around major consuming centres, such as Buenos Aires, Mexico City and São Paulo. While industrialisation thus contributed to support ongoing urbanisation trends, the latter appear to have had a dynamism of their own, making one sceptical of any close short-term links between the two phenomena.

Import-substitution was the engine of growth during the 1930s, but not just in manufacturing. The rural sector also witnessed gains in the production of goods sold in the domestic market relative to those primarily sold abroad. Food-importing countries, such as those in the Caribbean and Central America, engaged in either modest import-replacement, as in Cuba, or more ambitious efforts as in Guatemala. Countries which during the 1920s imported beverages and cooking oils, like Argentina, turned to domestic substitutes during the 1930s. Cotton textiles imported during the 1920s were replaced partly by value added in expanding local production of cotton, which later led to exports. In contrast with import-replacement in industry, much of agricultural import-substitution was at the expense of intra-Latin American trade, e.g. Argentine production of *yerba maté* was at the expense of imports from Paraguay.

Agricultural import-substitution naturally had a greater weight in overall growth in the smaller, less-developed countries. Land was an apparently malleable and not fully utilised 'installed capacity' which could be turned from export cash-crops to production for either the local market or subsistence, and could also be expanded using little foreign exchange. The ease of land reallocation and expansion depended partly on tenure arrangements and agronomic characteristics of export crops. Thus, it appears that the presence of foreign-owned banana and sugar plantations in Cuba and Central America reduced, *ceteris paribus*, flexibility in land use, while lands planted with coffee were more receptive to sharing at least their idle capacity with other crops. (An identification problem exists as bananas and sugar were often produced in foreign-owned plantations and coffee by local farmers; see Chapter 11, by Bulmer-Thomas.) As noted earlier, all types of rural production were encouraged by new irrigation works, feeder roads, credit facilities and price support programmes. Publicly-sponsored agricultural research programme also had important payoffs during the 1930s, as in the case of Brazilian cotton.

Import-substitution extended to services; those of foreign labour and capital were to a large extent replaced with local inputs or dispensed with, while it is likely that many Argentines substituted visits to Bariloche and Mar del Plata for vacations in Paris. Among expanding sectors one can also find, especially in reactive countries, some producing non-traded goods and services using relatively few imported inputs, such as construction, housing and government.

The level of imports and exports reflected primarily exogenous shocks and trends, but their structures responded to the differing sectoral performances described above. The shares in total imports of consumer goods and intermediate products like cement and textiles fell, while those for metallurgical and other intermediate products rose. Machinery and equipment imports going to export-related manufacturing and to social overhead facilities which had expanded during the 1920s fell, while those going to import-substituting manufacturing rose. Export bills also underwent changes, partly because of the collapse of traditional exports, but also due to exportable surpluses generated by expanding activities, such as Argentine fruits and Brazilian cotton. Tourism also became an important non-traditional Mexican export during the 1930s. Export diversification extended to regional origin within the country (Rio Grande do Sul in Brazil and Rio Negro in Argentina emerging as exporting areas), and to their geographical destination, with Germany becoming an expanding market for many Latin American exports. New markets and higher exports for one Latin American country often meant a loss in traditional exports for another; thus, Colombia and Central America gained shares in the international coffee market at the expense of Brazil; Venezuelan oil advanced, replacing Mexican crude; bananas from Honduras took the place of Colombian ones; and a large number of countries nibbled at Cuban sugar hegemony.

Welfare Performance

Since colonial times it has been noted that a boom in Latin American land-intensive exports may not improve the welfare of lower-income groups, as during booms prices of locally produced foodstuffs rose sharply, and access to land became more difficult. Where coercive labour systems were applied, booms meant longer and more intense working hours. Busts frequently led to cheaper home-grown foodstuffs, a greater availability of land for subsistence crops, and slacker working regimes. One may conjecture that part of these ancient effects were still visible in the 1930s; for those employed in reasonably competitive labour markets it is likely that real wages in terms of foodstuffs rose, even as they fell in terms of importable goods. Access to rural land in many countries appears to have become easier and cheaper for lower- and middle-income groups, as the opportunity cost for land held by exporters declined and plantations were parcelled. These market trends were carried further in Mexico by a major land reform, while in Colombia and Cuba milder public measures also pointed in the same direction, increasing the tenure security of lower-income farmers.

Primarily coercive labour systems survived into the twentieth century in several Latin American localities where descendants of American Indians were concentrated, such as Bolivia, Peru and Central America, coexisting with freer labour arrangements. During the 1930s in Guatemala roads and public works were built using taxed Indian (and convict) labour, as had been the case during the 1920s under the Leguía dictatorship in Peru. Even in Guatemala, however, labour legislation was liberalised after 1934.

In the more urbanised countries where free labour systems predominated, at least in the cities, open unemployment seems to have been rare after the initial years of the crisis. A lack of strong institutional barriers to downward money wage flexibility and a rapid end to immigration contributed to the elimination of open unemployment; during the early 1930s many European immigrants returned to their old countries, and some recent arrivals to urban centres returned to their rural birthplaces. In Cuba the seasonal importation of Jamaican and other West Indian labour for the sugar harvest was eliminated. Nevertheless, the welfare consequences of the crisis appear worse in Cuba than in some Central American countries which had larger and more flexible subsistence sectors.

On the whole income and wealth distribution during the 1930s were buffeted by contradictory influences. Groups linked to traditional exports must have seen their relative and even absolute position decline, in spite of government actions aimed at ameliorating the external blows. Entrepreneurs in import-substituting agriculture and industry must have accumulated handsome profits, with their output fetching high domestic prices while labour and raw-material costs were unusually low. Entrepreneurs who had inherited excess capacity from the 1920s were especially fortunate, receiving unexpected capital gains. High- and middle-class families, with budgets having low shares for foodstuffs and high shares for imported consumer goods, faced unfavourable relative price trends. Beloved durable goods, such as automobiles, or European vacations, became very expensive, and their consumption often was to be postponed for many years. For lower-income groups, whether urban or rural, it is unlikely that real income gains in terms of foodstuffs could have been very substantial; the best guess is that even in reactive countries performing reasonably well by the late 1930s real wages for unskilled and semi-skilled labour, taking into account all components of their consumption basket, were no higher than a decade earlier. Gains in employment security arising from new labour legislation were limited to pockets in the labour force and of moot significance even for them. The tax reforms carried out in several countries were more important for public revenue raising and diversification than for significant changes in income distribution. Perhaps with the exception of Mexico, the 1930s did not witness a discontinuity in the inherited trends for public services in education and health. Secular improvements in literacy and health indicators appear to have continued without obvious leaps or retardations, seemingly following more the sluggish urbanisation trends than the vagaries of import substitution.

A CONCLUDING INTERPRETATION

Much of the evolution of Latin American economies during the 1930s, particularly the coexistence in reactive countries of vigorously growing branches of agriculture and manufacturing with declining or stagnant foreign trade, can be explained as a response to incentives created by policies aimed primarily at coping with balance-of-payments disequilibria generated by the unexpected worsening of the terms of trade and the abrupt cessation of capital inflows. As it became clear that the new constellation of external and domestic relative prices were not fleeting phenomena, and that the international economy was not to return to the pre-1929 rules of the game, both private and public agents reoriented their production and investment plans.

Admittedly incomplete evidence appears to support the view that countries willing and able to devalue their exchange rate forcefully early in the decade moved toward the new pattern of accumulation more speedily than those nations which kept their exchange rate fixed or devalued slightly. For the latter type of country the required deflationary process involved the marking down of a myriad of non-traded goods prices (and wages) without clear guidance from either markets or governments as to what the correct new level should be. The confusing circumstances of the 1930s, whose macroeconomics are debated even today in industrialised countries, made guessing about the new equilibrium non-traded goods prices singularly difficult. In contrast, devaluing the exchange rate involved a clear signal and a species of 'price guideline', reducing uncertainty for economic agents in reactive countries.

As devaluations typically occurred while exports of goods and services exceeded imports of goods and non-factor services (i.e. excluding immigrant remittances and those of profits and interest abroad) their expansionary effects were strengthened. Note also that purchasing-power parity should not be expected to hold in an economy subjected to real shocks, so it is not surprising that the nominal devaluations of the 1930s, in contrast with those occurring in Latin America since the Second World War, were offset only to a slight degree by movements in domestic price levels. Plentiful idle resources, of course, contributed to this outcome. One may also conjecture that in several reactive countries during the late 1920s an unusually large inflow of foreign capital financing domestic public works had resulted in what during the 1970s became known as *atraso cambiario*, i.e. a low price for dollars and sterling and a high price for non-traded goods and services, which made the real depreciations of the early 1930s the more dramatic. The late 1920s may have also left a legacy of plentiful liquidity in some countries, cushioning the impact of the crisis.

The abandonment of the old parities and of unlimited convertibility into foreign exchange allowed in several countries the maintenance and expansion of domestic liquidity, which combined with other policies led to the reasonably good economic performance in reactive countries. The balance-of-payments crisis and the threat of financial collapse were of greater significance in the adoption of those policies than whether the new governments which came to power during the 1930s represented a shift to the right, as in Argentina, or toward more reformist positions as in Colombia and Mexico. Purely domestic political factors may have accounted for whether or not a country engaged in land reform during the 1930s, but those factors had much less to do in reactive countries with the adoption of policies which induced import substitution. The latter depended on the magnitude of the foreign-exchange and financial crisis, and on country-specific characteristics of the external sector. Thus, revolutionary Mexico was more timid regarding exchange control than conservative Argentina, largely because of its open border with the USA. Policymakers who abandoned gold convertibility, allowed the exchange rate to depreciate, supported banks at the edge of bankruptcy, permitted budget deficits induced by economic and foreign trade decline, and financed them by monetary expansion, on the whole did so moved by survival instincts rather than inspired by the writings of economists, either defunct or live. But in reactive countries, including Chile and Uruguay, the institutional structure was compatible with actions involving a degree of policy autonomy, while in smaller or passive countries, such as Cuba, it was less so.

While the economic performance of reactive countries was reasonably good, per capita real incomes grew less during the 1930s than during the 1920s or 1940s. Had the industrialised countries maintained full employment, open markets for foreign goods and bonds, and a peaceful international environment, it is likely that the aggregate output performance in reactive countries (and of course in passive ones) would have been better. Sectoral patterns of growth would have been different, and it is likely that under such counterfactual circumstances some activities, like cement and textiles, would have grown less than they actually did during the 1930s. The diversification which took place in agriculture, manufacturing, exports and government revenues, as well as in the geographical sources and destination of exports, could very well have been less under the hypothesised counterfactual conditions. It is also conceivable that institutional reforms in banking, taxation and even land tenure would have been weaker. Under the counterfactual circumstances there might have been less structural change but more growth not just in aggregate output, but also in physical and technical capacity. Output growth during the 1930s wore out much of the capital stock accumulated during the 1920s and earlier and was accompanied by relatively little fresh investment and technical change. At the outbreak of the Second World War, a good share of the Latin American social overhead capital and industrial capacity was already stretched thin and at the verge of obsolescence; war shortages were to aggravate these conditions.

The crisis at the Centre did induce policy experimentation in the Periphery; as in the Centre, not all innovations were attractive. Bold foreign examples were plentiful: the New Deal in the USA; Fascism in Italy, and later in Germany and Spain; and radical Socialism in the Soviet Union. Examples of a successful maintenance of old-fashioned orthodoxy were fewer. The collapse of international financial markets encouraged attempts to mobilise domestic savings and the creation of new domestic financial institutions. The lamentable state of banks in the USA and other industrialised countries during the early 1930s made Latin Americans think twice about the wisdom of capital flight, increasing the potency of domestic monetary and tax policy. Rivalries among industrialised countries, exacerbated by the crisis, plus the Good Neighbour policy of Franklin Delano Roosevelt also encouraged, directly or indirectly, policy initiatives favouring the geographical diversification of foreign trade, greater national control over natural resources, and the rescheduling of external debt obligations. A poor profits outlook at the Centre encouraged some direct foreign investment into Latin America, and helped to concentrate the animal spirits of local entrepreneurs within the domestic market. Schemes for closer Latin American economic integration were proposed from the Southern Cone to Central America, although very little was done to carry them out. In short the disastrous news from the rest of the world reaching Latin America during the 1930s made policy-makers and informed opinion feel not only that local conditions were not so bad, after all, but also that no one knew, in Centre or Periphery, exactly what were the roots of the crisis nor how it could be overcome. After a terrible fright, this stimulated an almost exhilarated creativity. The old authorities and rules on economic policy were shattered. It was a time calling for reliance on one's discretion.

REFERENCES

C. F. Diaz Alejandro, 'A America Latina em Depressao 1929/39', *Pesquisa e Planejamento Económico 10* (1980) 351–82.
––––––– 'Stories of the 1930s for the 1980s', *NBER Conference Paper* no. 130 (November 1981).
J. Fodor and A. O'Connell, 'La Argentina y la economía atlántica en la primera mitad del siglo *XX*', *Desarrollo Económico*, vol. 13, no. 49 (April–June 1973) 3–66.
Naciones Unidas, *América Latina: Relación de Precios del Intercambio* (Santiago, 1976).

Exchange Rates and Economic Recovery in the 1930s: An Extension to Latin America

José Manuel Campa

In a study of ten European countries during the 1930s Barry Eichengreen and Jeffrey Sachs show that devaluation benefited the initiating countries and that there can be no presumption that depreciation was beggar-thy-neighbor.[1] I apply their methodology to ten Latin American countries.

Examining the behavior of the Latin American economies is important in several respects: these countries were hit first by and reacted earlier to the effects of the Depression; they were part of the "periphery" and their policies did not directly affect the behavior of the "center"; and their experience during the 1930s led them to select a subsequent inward-oriented path of development, based on import substitution.[2]

This model of development built upon a particular set of social and economic structures that were seen as shaping the world economic order, notably a center and a periphery with different structures of production. Unlike those of the periphery, the industrialized economies of the center are self-sustained; specifically, the periphery is constrained by an export sector confined to a very small range of goods and offering only limited backward and forward linkages with the rest of the economy.[3]

This note shows that Latin America reacted in the same way to depreciation as did Europe, and so offers evidence against the argument that Latin American economies were structurally constrained during this period.

I. LATIN AMERICAN DEPRECIATIONS IN THE 1930s

Latin American countries varied greatly in their ability to manage their economic policies independently. Countries which either were relatively large, such as Brazil, or

---

The Journal of Economic History, Vol. L, No. 3 (Sept. 1990). © The Economic History Association. All rights reserved. ISSN 0022-0507.

The author is a graduate student in the Department of Economics, Harvard University, Cambridge, MA 02138.

I am grateful to Paul Hohenberg, Eric Rice, Wendy Wisbaum, and the referee for their comments. I am specially indebted to Jeffrey Williamson for his encouragement and advice.

[1] Barry Eichengreen and Jeffrey Sachs, "Exchange Rates and Economic Recovery in the 1930s," this JOURNAL, 45 (Dec. 1985), pp. 925–46.

[2] The causes were a deterioration in the terms of trade due to the fall in primary commodity prices in 1929, a decline in foreign lending from the United States in 1928, and later the emergence of protective tariffs in industrial countries. The terms "center" and "periphery" were used in this context by Raúl Prebisch, *The Economic Development of Latin America and its Principal Problems* (New York, 1950), to refer to the industrialized countries and to the developing world, respectively.

[3] The "structuralists," as this school of thought came to be known, describe the structure of production in the periphery as poorly integrated and very specialized, characterized by exports of primary products and imports of manufactures. Because demand for imports in developing countries tends to grow faster than the demand for exports, the periphery terms of trade deteriorate, resulting in a structural external disequilibrium. The only long-term alternative is for the developing country to satisfy its highly income-elastic demand for manufactures through a process of industrialization and import substitution. For an explicit description of the structuralist framework, see Raúl Prebisch, "International Trade and Payments in an Era of Coexistence," *American Economic Review*, 49 (May 1959), pp. 251–73; and Raúl Prebisch, "The Economic Development of Latin America and its Principal Problems," *Economic Bulletin for Latin America*, 7 (Feb. 1962), pp. 1–22. Good economic critics of Prebisch's work are Robert E. Baldwin, "Secular Movements in the Terms of Trade," *American Economic Review, Papers and Proceedings*, 45 (May 1955), pp. 259–69; and G. Haberler, "Terms of Trade and Economic Development," in H. S. Ellis, ed., *Economic Development of Latin America* (New York, 1961), pp. 275–97.

TABLE 1
PRINCIPAL MEASURES AFFECTING EXCHANGE RATES
AND MONETARY GOLD RESERVES

Country	Suspension of Gold Standard	Exchange Controls	Depreciation Relative to Gold	Central Monetary Gold Reserves[a]
Argentina[b]	Dec. 1929	Oct. 1931	Nov. 1929	0.50
Bolivia	Sep. 1931	Oct. 1931	Mar. 1930	0.25
Brazil[b]		May 1931	Dec. 1929	0.09
Chile[b]	Apr. 1932	Jul. 1931	Apr. 1932	2.43
Colombia[b]	Sep. 1931	Sep. 1931	Jan. 1932	0.38
Costa Rica[b]		Jan. 1932	Jan. 1932	
Cuba	Nov. 1933	Jun. 1934	Apr. 1933	
Ecuador	Feb. 1932	May 1932–Jul. 1936	Jun. 1932	2.00
Guatemala[b]			Apr. 1933	
Honduras[b]		Mar. 1934	Apr. 1933	
Mexico[b]	Jul. 1931		Aug. 1931	2.14
Nicaragua[b]	Nov. 1931	Nov. 1931	Jan. 1932	
Panama			Apr. 1933	
Paraguay		Aug. 1932	Nov. 1929	
Peru	May 1932		May 1932	0.57
Salvador, El[b]	Oct. 1931	Aug. 1933	Oct. 1931	0.80
Uruguay	Dec. 1929	Sep. 1931	Apr. 1929	0.56
Venezuela		Dec. 1936	Sep. 1930	1.67

[a] Ratio of 1935 to 1929 gold reserves
[b] The country has been used below for my analysis.
Source: League of Nations Economic Intelligence Service, *Monetary Review* (Geneva, 1937), appendix tables I, VI.

had autonomous public sectors, such as Costa Rica and Uruguay, followed more active exchange rate policies. Carlos Díaz-Alejandro calls these "reactive" countries. Small countries, like Honduras, or those with highly dependent governments, such as Cuba, followed much more passive policies.[4]

Table 1 shows the timing of depreciations in Latin America. A decrease in foreign capital inflows, a small decrease in the quantity of exports, and a sharp decline in export prices were the precipitating forces. By December 1929 Argentina and Uruguay had suspended gold payments and both had suffered a depreciation. Paraguay and Brazil devalued their currencies shortly thereafter. In 1930 Bolivia and Venezuela had to devalue officially. All of these devaluations preceded Britain's departure from the gold standard in 1931. These precocious Latin American countries faced great pressure from the balance of payments.

The second round of depreciations started with the devaluation of the British pound in September 1931. Countries that had their currency tied to sterling and had already devalued, like Argentina and Bolivia, were forced to do it once more. Mexico, Costa Rica, Colombia, and Peru followed within six months. Most of these countries suspended their currency's parity with gold as well.

The fall of the U.S. dollar in 1933 provoked a new round of depreciations among the Latin American economies. All Central American currencies were pegged to the U.S. dollar, and some had not even developed their own monetary policies. Therefore their

[4] Carlos Díaz-Alejandro, "Latin America in the 1930s," in Rosemary Thorp, ed., *Latin America in the 1930s, The Role of the Periphery in World Crisis* (Oxford, 1984), chap. 2.

currency immediately depreciated with respect to gold.[5] Argentina, Colombia, Mexico, and Uruguay suffered new depreciations during that year.

Beginning in 1933 most countries implemented complex systems of exchange controls, with multiple and preferential exchange-rate regimes. These regimes were intended to promote import substitution and economic activity or to avoid currency speculation and capital outflows. The official rate was applied to certain "official" imports, and the lower free trade rate was used for all other commodities, as in Colombia and Argentina. In Uruguay the free rate was de facto a multiple exchange rate, with a different rate depending on the type of transaction. Most countries distinguished between import and export rates, and among the commodities being traded. Moreover, the exchange rates also differed depending on the partner country. Chile, for instance, in addition to the official exchange rate had three other exchange rates: the "export rate" for transactions with the United States and the United Kingdom, the "compensation rates" for transactions with other European countries, and the "free rates" for other transactions.[6]

II. COUNTRY-SPECIFIC EFFECTS OF DEPRECIATION

Eichengreen and Sachs use a simple two-country model based on the work of Robert Mundell and J. Marcus Fleming.[7] In each country wages adjust slowly, but prices move to clear the commodity markets. Eichengreen and Sachs show that devaluation in a country has either a positive effect or no effect on domestic output, and can have a positive or negative effect on foreign output, depending on the monetary measures that accompany the devaluation. In particular, whether the devaluation is unilateral or simultaneous and whether it is "sterilized" or not determines the kind of effect the devaluation will have.[8] Then they proceed to analyze the response of industrial production, real wages, export volume, discount rates, Tobin's q, and gold reserves for ten European countries.

I explore the same issues for ten Latin countries: Argentina, Brazil, Chile, Colombia, Costa Rica, Guatemala, Honduras, Mexico, Nicaragua, and El Salvador. Data constraints make it possible to examine only the effects of depreciation on industrial production and export volume. I assume that unilateral devaluations by Latin American countries had no effect on the rest of the world.[9] Therefore I focus only on the devaluating country's domestic economy.

A currency depreciation causes an increase in the price of imports relative to domestic goods, an aggregate-demand switch toward domestic goods, and a total increase in employment and output. Excess demand raises domestic commodity prices, stimulating aggregate supply and moderating the inflationary impact. Resources move

---

[5] One may conjecture that these were not important, real depreciations. It is fair to say that Central America followed a passive exchange-rate policy because even in the countries where the exchange rate was allowed to float, Costa Rica and El Salvador, it did not change very dramatically. See Victor Bulmer-Thomas, "Central America in the Inter-War Period," in Thorp, *Latin America in the 1930s*, p. 289.

[6] For a more detailed explanation of the different exchange-rate regimes applicable in each country, see League of Nations Economic Intelligence Service, *Monetary Review* (Geneva, 1937).

[7] See Robert Mundell, "Capital Mobility and Stabilization Policy under Fixed and Flexible Exchange Rates," *Canadian Journal of Economics and Political Science*, 29 (Nov. 1963), pp. 475–85; and J. Marcus Fleming, "Domestic Financial Policies under Fixed and under Floating Exchange Rates," *International Monetary Fund Staff Papers*, 9 (Nov. 1962), pp. 369–79.

[8] A devaluation is sterilized when the depreciating country adjusts its money supply in order to leave unchanged the ratio of gold backing to money in circulation.

[9] This small-country assumption seems realistic since all of these countries were part of the periphery.

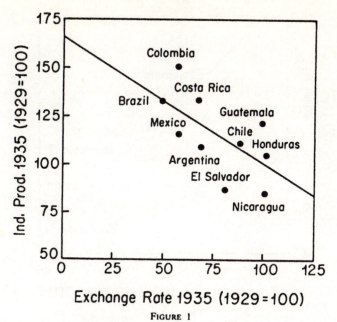

FIGURE 1
CHANGES IN INDUSTRIAL PRODUCTION, 1929–1935

from the nontraded sector toward the traded sector. Since manufactures constituted the main imports of most Latin American countries, this import-substitution effect served to reallocate resources from the primary sector to the industrial sector.[10]

Figure 1 shows the relationship between depreciation and the index of industrial production. The variables are defined the same way as in Eichengreen and Sachs.[11] A clear negative relationship exists. Reactive countries which devalued more performed better than passive countries. All countries except for El Salvador and Nicaragua experienced a relative increase in their industrial sector during this period, reflecting the shift in resources described above.[12]

[10] There is a general agreement that the import-substitution policies followed by the governments of the Latin American countries as an answer to the Depression were basically correct. These policies did not come from an existing theoretical framework but were the reaction to enormous macroeconomic imbalances. For a better description of the general policies, see Díaz-Alejandro, "Latin America in the 1930s." For a detailed description of individual countries' policies, see Angus Maddison, *Two Crises: Latin America and Asia, 1929–38 and 1973–83* (Washington, DC, 1985), pp. 23–32.

[11] A depreciation is expressed as the gold price of domestic currency in 1935 as a percentage of the 1929 parity. A value of 69 for Argentina indicates a 31 percent depreciation. Industrial production is the ratio of the production index in 1935 to that of 1929 multiplied by 100.

[12] El Salvador is a special case in the sense that it suffered a 17 percent reduction in industrial production in spite of an almost 20 percent depreciation. This was probably caused by the government's decision to keep promoting coffee production despite the drop in coffee prices. A more detailed exposition of the policies followed by the Salvadorian government in this period can be found in E. A. Wilson, "The Crisis of National Integration in El Salvador, 1919–35" (Ph.D. dissertation, Stanford University, 1970).

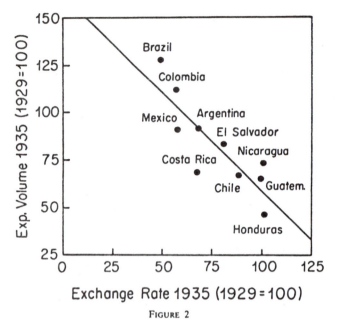

FIGURE 2

CHANGES IN EXPORT VOLUME, 1929–1935

Figure 2 shows the relationship between export performance and exchange rates. The vertical axis reflects the ratio of export volume of 1935 to the export volume of 1929, and the horizontal axis represents the same variable found in Figure 1. There is a clear negative relationship between the two variables, demonstrating that a higher currency depreciation served to improve that country's exports.

In order to analyze whether the Latin American countries reacted in a different manner to the depreciations than the European countries, I pooled my Latin American sample with the Eichengreen and Sachs European sample. Table 2 shows the results of simple OLS regressions. Regressions 1 and 2 reflect the results of the European sample used by Eichengreen and Sachs.[13] Regressions 3 and 4 correspond to the results using only the Latin American countries. Finally, regressions 5 and 6 correspond to the results of the pooled sample of European and Latin American countries, where the coefficients are restricted to be equal for both subsamples.

Taking as the null hypothesis that the structural coefficients are not different, the F-ratio test gives a value equal to 2.96 for the case of industrial production and 0.48 for export volume. In both cases the null hypothesis cannot be rejected at the 1 percent level of confidence. This implies that there is no statistical evidence of different behavior by the Latin American countries when compared to the European countries. One should realize, however, that even though there is no statistical difference in the behavior of both sets of countries, the underlying mechanism was somewhat dissimilar since the Latin nations traded less among themselves than the European countries.

Two straightforward conclusions emerge from these results. First, they show the robustness of the framework developed by Eichengreen and Sachs. This framework not

---

[13] These regressions reproduce equations 1 and 5 in table 3 of their paper.

TABLE 2
REGRESSION RESULTS, 1929–1935

Dependent Variable	Constant Term	Exchange-Rate Term	R^2	N	Sum Square Residuals
Ten European Countries					
(1) Industrial Production	153.55	−0.71	0.63	10	1349.285
	(14.59)	(−3.66)			
(2) Export Volume	140.87	−0.80	0.63	10	1714.387
	(8.56)	(−3.67)			
Ten Latin American Countries					
(3) Industrial Production	166.79	−0.66	0.40	10	2334.101
	(7.22)	(−2.29)			
(4) Export Volume	162.91	−1.04	0.71	10	1515.124
	(8.75)	(−4.45)			
The Twenty Countries Pooled					
(5) Industrial Production	156.40	−0.63	0.40	20	5048.950
	(10.84)	(−3.42)			
(6) Export Volume	149.44	−0.89	0.65	20	3424.112
	(12.56)	(−5.82)			

Note: *t*-statistics are in parentheses.
Sources: For European countries: Exchange Rate: League of Nations Economic Intelligence Service, *Monetary Review* (Geneva, 1937); Industrial Production: Brian Mitchell, *European Historical Statistics, 1750–1975* (2nd rev. edn., London, 1981); and H. W. Methorst, *Recueil international de statistiques économiques, 1931–1936* (The Hague, 1938); Export Volume: League of Nations, *Review of World Trade 1936* (Geneva, 1937). For Latin American countries: Exchange Rate: J. Wilkie, "Statistics and National Policy," in *Statistical Abstract of Latin America*, supplement 3 (Los Angeles, 1974); Industrial Production: Index value in Rosemary Thorp, ed., *Latin America in the 1930s, The Role of the Periphery in World Crisis*, appendix (Oxford, 1984); Export Volume: for Argentina, Brazil, Chile, and Mexico, index of export volume quantum in ECLA, *Economic Survey of Latin America 1949* (New York, 1950), for Colombia, export quantum index in M. Urrutia and M. Arrubla, eds., *Compendio de estadísticas históricas de Colombia* (Bogota, 1970), for the rest an export volume index was computed taking the ratio of real export values in 1935 over real export values in 1929 from Wilkie, "Statistics and National Policy."

only applies to a few European countries, but it can be generalized without altering the results. Second, although Latin American countries were hit first by and reacted earlier to the Depression, their response to exchange rate policies cannot be distinguished from that of European economies. Thus there is no evidence here to support the popular view that the Latin American economies were structurally constrained in the interwar period.

Part IV
Contemporaries Look Forward

THE ECONOMIC JOURNAL

MARCH 1938

THE FUTURE OF INTERNATIONAL TRADE [1]

1. THE question to which I am seeking an answer is—What is the future of international trade? Will it ever play again the same dominant part in the economic life of the world that it played in the nineteenth century?

Let me put the question another way. Consider two well-known sets of facts. Ever since the war, and expecially since 1931, the course of international trade has been throttled by an incredible maze of obstacles and restrictions, culminating in that startling bid for economic self-sufficiency, the German four-year plan. Yet in 1929 the volume of world trade was greater by more than a quarter than in 1913; even in the trough of 1932 it did not sink below three-quarters of its 1929 level: and it has now come near to regaining that level. Which of these two sets of facts represents the true mind of the world for the future —the apparent determination of Governments, egged on by their citizens (for it is no use pretending it is all the fault of the Governments), to strangle international trade, or the obstinate determination of trade not to be strangled? or are the two sets of facts reconcilable in terms of some intelligible trend, some fumbling purpose to which the nations will one day learn to give fruitful effect?

2. Forgive me if I go back to the beginning. The case for a large volume of international trade rests on the different endowment of nations in respect of natural resources, human quality and skill, and acquired equipment. Where these differences are great, it is to the immediate economic advantage of all parties that a large volume of trade should take place. The fact that Utopia *can* grow wheat, even the fact that she can grow more wheat per acre or more wheat per man than Ruritania, is not in itself an argument against her importing wheat from Ruritania if she can turn her resources to the production of other things in which her advantage over Ruritania is greater still. The volume

[1] A lecture delivered to the Liverpool Economic and Statistical Society on October 13, 1937, here printed with a few minor alterations.

of profitable trade depends on the width of these gaps in the *comparative* advantages of different countries for the production of different things.

Let us first put ourselves back in the first decade of this century, endow ourselves with ordinary economic foresight but not with prevision of the war and its consequences, and ask ourselves what the future then seemed to hold in store as regards these gaps in Comparative Advantage. It was, I think, fairly evident that they were tending to become narrower. The sharpness of the outline between the granaries and the workshops of the world, to put it briefly, was already becoming blurred. In the first place, it was becoming plain that proficiency in the arts of mechanised industry could not remain for ever the monopoly of the nation, or even of the group of nations, that had first learnt to use them. Secondly, electricity was already promising to release the factory from the pull of the coalfields and pointing both to a different, and to a less intense, localisation of manufacturing industry. Thirdly, to turn to the other side of the picture, the exploitation of virgin soils in the new countries appeared to be reaching its limit, and agriculture there too to be coming up against its old enemy, the law of diminishing returns. Thus the long-term prospect seemed to be that of a world in which the international exchange of goods would play a smaller part relatively to total production, and would be conducted on terms progressively more disadvantageous to the teeming industrial populations of western Europe.

3. Now let us demand of ourselves a great feat of the imagination, and picture ourselves living indeed in 1937, but in a world in which there has been no war. Have the forces which we described at work thirty years ago worked themselves out as we expected in reducing the advantages of international specialisation, or have they been modified in any way? Has any new force made its appearance?

As regards the first two forces, there is no doubt, I think, as to the answer. The diffusion of industrial capital and of industrial skill has proceeded even more rapidly than most people would have prophesied. In particular it has become evident that the simpler processes of textile manufacture can be carried on with approximately equal efficiency by almost any kind of population in almost any part of the world. The oil-engine and the hydro-electric plant have continued to press home their assault on the sovereignty of coal. From this side the narrowing of the gap of comparative advantage has proceeded apace.

4. When we turn to the other side, the conclusion is not so clear. There are three far-reaching factors to be taken into account, and it is by no means evident how their net effect is likely to work out. The first and most obvious is the astonishing achievements of science in the domain of agriculture. These achievements fall into two main groups, the mechanisation of agricultural operations and the improvement of the breeds of animals and plants; I have neither the time nor the knowledge to appraise them in any detail. Their most spectacular effect has been to cheapen the cost of the products of agriculture in terms of the products of industry, so that one of the tendencies which we thought we saw at work thirty years ago—the tendency of the terms of trade to turn against the manufacturing countries—has been dramatically reversed. To step for the moment into the real world (since for the hypothetical warless world which we have agreed to explore we dare not invent figures), the price of Britain's imports in terms of her exports was in 1931 some 30 per cent., and is even now some 20 per cent., lower than in 1913.[1] But for the purpose of our main problem what we want to know is not how much scientific progress has cheapened the products of the earth, but whether it has increased or diminished the economic advantages of international specialisation. And in spite of some confusing cross-currents, there seems at first sight to be no doubt about the answer. It is on the side of the large prairie wheat-factory, not of the fragmented country-side of the Old World, that the tractor and the combine weight the scales. It is in outlandish regions in the cold north or the drought-ridden desert rather than on the rich soils of temperate zones that the Mendelian plant expert confers his richest gifts. And it is not only in the field of the production of raw things but also of their transport that science, on the whole, still seems to fight on the side of regional specialisation and long-distance trade. Man has learnt to control temperature, and therefore the good fairies of ripening and the demons of decay; meat that is no worse than chilled can at last voyage safely from the Antipodes, and the most telegonous fruits appear in our shop-windows at the most unlikely seasons.

True, nothing in this world works only one way; and scientific invention, which can thus confer its blessing on the localised producer, can also suddenly turn round and smack him in the

[1] These figures, it is true, reflect not only the relative movement of *costs* in agriculture and industry, but also the relative change in ability to control production by monopolistic methods.

face. In the warless world in which we are still moving in thought, we can perhaps forget about Buna rubber; but we can hardly think away synthetic fertilisers and artificial silk. Air and wood are more widely diffused over the globe than nitrate deposits or fibrous annuals, as water is more widely diffused than coal; at the bid of science a Chile yesterday, a Texas or Bengal to-morrow, may wake up to find its occupation gone.

5. Furthermore—and this is the second of the far-reaching factors to which I alluded a few minutes ago—there hangs over the populations of the new countries, or some of them, a cloud of which they were scarcely aware thirty years ago. It is being increasingly borne in upon them that their vast specialisations of the late nineteenth century were to a certain extent bogus specialisations, founded on reckless mining of the soil, on natural but disastrous ignorance of the cyclical misbehaviour of sun and cloud, on improvident sacrifice of the leisurely tree to the crop which is here to-day and gone to-morrow. Behind the restriction schemes of Secretary Wallace and the financial junketings of Mr. Aberhart looms the enormous spectre of the Dust-Bowl. The same charge of living on capital lies, of course, ultimately against specialisations founded on the exploitation of mineral wealth, though the pigeon takes longer to come home to roost,— *how much* longer the South African in particular does well from time to time to ask himself. But whether it work slow or fast, we have here a factor tending, like the diffusion of manufacturing skill, and on the whole *unlike* the factor of agricultural improvement, to limit the advantage of international specialisation and the growth of international trade.

6. Thus even for the peaceful 1937 of our imaginings, the picture is already somewhat complex and confusing. But perhaps we can fairly sum the argument, so far as it has yet gone, by saying that on the balance the tendencies which we descried thirty years ago towards the curtailment of long-distance trade have received a moderate check. It is true that the oversea populations have become cleverer at twisting and hammering things; but they have also become cleverer at their old game of growing things: so that if the gap of Comparative Advantage has been encroached upon from one side, it has also been widening out on the other.

Is that, still barring war and the mentality begotten by war, a picture which, however sketchy, is complete as far as it goes, or have we left something vital out? Yes, I am afraid the answer is that, apart altogether from war and the rumour of war, we have left out something of great importance—the third of the far-reaching factors which I mentioned some minutes ago. When we try to introduce it, the picture becomes more complex still; and I think on the whole the balance of the argument changes.

The specialisations of the nineteenth century were not simply a device for using to the greatest effect the labours of a given number of human beings; they were above all an engine of *growth*. Their most spectacular effect was to hold at bay for a century the devil which Malthus had unchained, so that, just as the Red Queen was five times as rich as Alice *and* five times as clever, so the inhabitants of these islands in the pre-war decade managed, according to a commonly quoted though obviously not very reliable computation, to be four times as well off as their ancestors of a hundred years before *and* four times as numerous. And then, just as we were wondering whether the devil of population pressure could be kept at bay much longer, we looked over our shoulders, and lo and behold !—he was gone. But he has left a curious smell behind, and we are none of us quite sure whether it is brimstone or roses. So far as the future of international trade is concerned, there is at present a strong disposition among thoughtful persons to believe that the brimstone predominates.

It is important, though it is not always quite easy, to make out exactly what these thoughtful persons are saying. Let us try to give definiteness to the problem by supposing that the populations of the whole world, at any rate outside Soviet Russia and Eastern Asia, become stationary within the next few years, and continue practically stationary for, let us say, the next half-century. Naturally we shall not expect the aggregate either of world production or of world trade to grow as fast as they did while population was still increasing smartly; we should expect production to grow, for instance, by an annual average of say 2 per cent. instead of 3 per cent. But are there any reasons to expect that in such circumstances world *trade* will grow more slowly than world *production*, and indeed perhaps will cease growing at all?

Yes, say the thoughtful persons who smell brimstone, there are such reasons. As people become richer they spend a smaller proportion of their income on food of any kind, and a smaller proportion still on the simpler and cheaper kinds of food. Now, as long as the industrial populations were still increasing at a brisk rate, it was possible to rely on a constantly expanding market for the simpler foodstuffs. Anything which cheapened their cost of production in the overseas countries was an unequivocal blessing to their farming populations; even falling prices were compatible with rising profits and increasing employment on the land. But if the increase in aggregate world output has to be absorbed entirely in the form of increased consumption of goods per head, that is no longer true. The combine and the tractor and the researches which produced Marquis wheat and P.O.J. 2878 have come in a sense too late. For they bring with them now not only lowered costs, but glutted markets, and a formidable problem of occupational transfer for the farming populations of the overseas lands. And even if that problem could be solved quickly and without friction, which is not the case, it seems likely that it would be solved in ways that tend to close rather than to widen the gap of Comparative Advantage, and so to limit the scope for international exchange.

7. There is, say the thoughtful persons, one outstanding reason why this process of readjustment should lead to a relative decline in international trade. The Great Specialisation of the nineteenth century was not simply an exchange of industrial products for agricultural products. Following Mr. Hartley Withers, we may visualise it as in part an exchange of capital goods for pieces of paper called securities, followed at a later date by an exchange of other pieces of paper, called interest-coupons, for agricultural products. Thus the volume of trade was kept at a high level by two closely-connected facts—first, the fact that the new countries keenly desired a type of goods, which we may think of for short as steel rails and girders, which the older countries were peculiarly fitted to supply, and secondly, the fact that the old countries did not demand immediate payment for these goods, but were willing in effect to supply them on tick, so that the volume of trade was continuously larger than it would have been had it depended solely on the opportunities for simultaneous barter.

Now this process of foreign investment, so the argument runs, was bound up with the growth of population rather than of production. In whatever exact form a stationary population elects to take its rising standard of life, it is not likely to be a form which entails the same hectic construction of railways and harbours and bridges in distant lands as did the clamour for bread and shirts which rose in the last century from the growing millions in the factory towns. Thus three consequences will follow, all of them damaging to the volume of international trade. In the first place, the imports of overseas countries will tend to be confined to what they can pay for out of their current output. In the second place, their demand will shift away from those things in which the gap of Comparative Advantage between agriculture and manufacture is widest—for when all is said and done there is stronger reason why steel should be forged in Sheffield than why cotton should be spun in Oldham or saucers baked in Staffordshire. And thirdly, so far as the overseas countries still *do* desire to borrow and to import capital goods, they will tend to make their interest payments in subsequent years not by expanding their exports but by curtailing their imports—a method equally satisfactory, perhaps, to the foreign creditor, who is concerned only to receive his money, but by no means equally satisfactory to those whose livelihood is bound up with the processes of international trade.

Now I think myself that there is at present a little too much disposition to smell brimstone rather than roses in the wake of the vanished devil of population pressure. It would seem as though we ought to be able to make the roses predominate if we really wish. But as regards the problem immediately in hand, the probable behaviour of the volume of international trade in the next half-century, I think there is much force in the argument which I have just tried to set forth, and that it goes a long way to cancel the argument on which I laid stress earlier—the argument, namely, that the progress of agricultural improvement has lowered agricultural costs more in the new than in the old countries, and so on the face of it favoured a still higher degree of international specialisation.

8. Let us now enlarge the range of our enquiry by asking a further question. Granted that we must learn to accommodate ourselves permanently to a smaller relative volume of international trade, does it also follow that we must learn to accommodate ourselves permanently to a more restrictionist trade policy throughout the world ? Or is the tangle of restrictionism in the midst of which we live the result not of the deep-seated economic forces which we have so far been attempting to analyse, but of the factors which we have been deliberately trying to think out of the way—of the war and its unhappy aftermath ?

The logical connection between trade *shrinkage* and trade *restriction* is not, I think, immediately self-evident. The mere fact that the balance of advantage is on the side of having a smaller relative volume of international trade than in the past is not *in itself* an argument for taking steps to make that volume smaller still, for the benefit of particular groups of producers, any more than it is an argument for trying to keep the volume uneconomically large, for the benefit of the owners of ships or dockyards. It is good fun for the Protectionist to be able to catch the Free Trader out, as he sometimes can, adopting the posture of a defender of vested interests and the *status quo*—shedding over laid-up ships and closed bill-brokers' offices those tears which he would condemn as unmanly weakness if they were allowed to flow over derelict wheat-fields and idle cotton-mills. But to cry *Tu quoque* is not the same thing as to prove one's case. Why should the fact that the scope for advantageous exchange between nations is narrowing be an argument for putting increased obstacles in the way of such exchange as still remains advantageous? Is it not rather an argument for sweeping away those obstacles which exist?

Something like a rational answer to this question can perhaps be put forward on these lines. A narrowing of the gap of Comparative Advantage will not only diminish the volume of advantageous foreign trade, but will tend to produce a state of affairs in which there is a relatively large volume of foreign trade trembling, as it were, on the margin of advantageousness, and liable to be blown to one side or the other of that margin by small changes in the wind of circumstance. If, having been for some time just outside the range of profitableness, it is suddenly blown just within that range, great dislocation and distress will be caused to those who have laid their plans on the expectation of its remaining outside that range; and at the same time the benefit conferred on the community as a whole will be relatively small. To take an extreme example, the exchange of ice for coal between North Polia and Infernia not only yields a large measure of benefit to consumers, but is also likely to remain very stable, since a violent change in climatic conditions would be needed to disturb it. But the exchange of black shirts and red shirts between Fascia and Bolschevia is liable to ebb and flow in the most confusing fashion in accordance with minute technical changes; to eliminate it altogether would confer a great boon of security upon the shirt-makers of the two countries, at a cost to the shirt-wearers negligible compared with the sums of which they are already being mulcted for the benefit of their respective party funds.

It is very difficult to make up one's mind how much weight *ought to be* attached to this argument in any particular case. We must not overlook the fact that specialisation by different countries even in what look to the outsider like very similar branches of the same industry may bring great advantages, owing to the economics of production on a large scale, and may remain fairly stable over decades. But I think we can be certain that great weight *will* be attached to this argument from stability whenever it can be made to seem at all plausible to do so. And we can therefore affirm as a fact, so to speak, of natural history, that a relative shrinkage of world trade due to a narrowing of the gap of Comparative Advantage *is* likely to be associated with a further shrinkage due to policy, since it tends both to make more prominent the evils of instability and insecurity and to lower the real cost to the community of attempting to mitigate them.

9. So far as the prospective relative shrinkage of world trade is due to the agricultural revolution and the flight of the Malthusian devil, the connection with increased restrictionism appears to be of a somewhat different kind. For, as we have seen, the agricultural revolution has not diminished the relative advantage of the overseas countries in the production of food, but rather increased it. To the urban populations, therefore, the cost of agricultural protectionism, in the sense of the benefits now within their reach which it forces them to forgo, is not less but greater than it was. But since they have benefited absolutely from the agricultural revolution, they are not too acutely aware of this; and it proves politically feasible, in various countries in various degrees, to extract from them the sacrifices necessary to accord to the home agricultural populations some protection against that instability of livelihood which results from the recurrent tendency to world-wide agricultural glut. Indeed, it proves feasible in some countries to go further, and to hold in check, perhaps indefinitely, that migration from the soil which the agricultural revolution and the flight of the Malthusian devil prescribe. Thus it becomes possible to indulge in a certain measure those deep non-economic instincts—in part military, in part social, in part aesthetic,[1] in part apparently sheerly mystical—which instruct all of us, in greater or less degree, that a country whose agriculture is " too small " (whatever exactly that may mean) is a country not fit to live in.

10. Now once more the prime object of my enquiry is not how far these developments of policy are justifiable, but how far they were in any case to be expected as a bye-product of fundamental economic change, as distinct from being merely the spawn of war and the atmosphere of war. It is, I think, quite

---

[1] My own ideal agricultural policy would make the payment of a subsidy on the production of wheat conditional on the sowing of a handsome quota of poppies in among it.

extraordinarily difficult to determine. One cannot lay one's finger on this duty, that quota, that piece of exchange control and say that one is due to the check to the growth in population, the second to currency disturbance and the third to political ambition or military precaution. As our British tariff conspicuously illustrates, the arguments by which a measure is defended do not always bear much relation to the pressures which have led to its imposition; and the reasons for which it remains in force may differ widely both from the real and from the avowed reasons for its original introduction. But it may perhaps serve to throw some light on the prospects for the future if we attempt to distinguish three phases in the progressive orgy of restrictionism in which the world has in fact indulged since the end of the Great War. The first, taking principally the old-fashioned form of tariff protection, may be said to have arisen fairly directly out of the war itself: for its chief motive force was the desire of individual industries in numerous countries to perpetuate the natural protection which they had enjoyed, with the end of the submarine and the blockade, during war-time. Sir Arthur Salter has vividly described how the great difficulty in making head-way against the " cumbrous, complex and provocative " tariff system which thus grew up in the twenties lay not in any " real conflict between divergent national interests and national policies," but in the fact that " there were no genuine national policies conceived as a whole but only a series of national systems improvised under pressure."[1] It would be difficult, I think, to argue that this system, at any rate as it actually developed, represented any real or rational attempt on the part of the world to adjust itself to long-term changes in the underlying conditions of international economic relations.

The second wave of restrictionism, extending far beyond mere tariff protection into the jungles of quantitative regulation of imports and control of exchange dealings, was of course associated with the rush for cover from the depression of 1929 and the financial crisis of 1931. In the case of every country the primary and ostensible object of the intensified restrictionism was the protection of its balance of payments, endangered, as the case might be, by the collapse of the market for its exports, by a drying up of the long-term loans on whose continuance it had based its economic life, by a flooding of its market with dumped imports, by a withdrawal of short-term loans which had been incautiously woven into the fabric of its monetary system—or by

[1] *World Trade and its Future*, p. 30.

some combination of these various misfortunes. Now since in every country this wave of restrictionism had its immediate origin in a crisis of currency and exchange, there has been a tendency to hope that it would recede automatically as, by one expedient and another, the various countries got their currency and exchange position into some sort of order; and the Tripartite Monetary Mouse of October 1936 was loudly acclaimed as heralding a return towards what seems in retrospect the economic liberalism of 1929. This has turned out to be an over-optimistic view; for, apart from the special troubles of the French, and from that darkening of the political atmosphere to which I will come in a moment, the truth seems to me to be that, so far as one can now distinguish between them, the post-1929 restrictions, whether justifiable or not, were more in the nature of a genuine reaction to a long-period change in underlying conditions than was the hugger-mugger tariff-building of the nineteen-twenties. For it was in the crisis of 1929–33 that the world first woke up to the long-term problems created by the agricultural revolution and by the precariousness of the whole system of foreign lending. Whatever measure of recovery has been achieved since, these problems still remain unsolved; and the refusal of the post-1929 restrictions to disappear is therefore less surprising, if not less annoying, than is sometimes pretended.

In the third and latest era of restrictionist policy, we must, I think, detect a different strain. For though in a sense it dates from the fall of the dollar and the breakdown of the World Economic Conference in 1933, and thus represents an intensification of the crisis policies of 1929–31, in another and deeper sense it is, it has lately been suggested,[1] more instructive to connect it with two slightly earlier events, the Japanese seizure of Manchukuo and the inauguration of the Ottawa System of Empire trade. Each of these events, however different otherwise in character, represented the deliberate use of political power for the attainment of exclusive economic advantage, and in turn foreshadowed the sacrifice of economic well-being to the consolidation of political power. With the closure of Germany for rearmament and repair, with the breakdown of the world peace system in the face of aggression, with the exhibition of the inconvenience which even half-hearted economic sanctions could inflict, with the tardy re-arming of the British Empire, the Economics of Crisis have tended to pass insensibly into the Economics of War. And in the Economics of War the subtleties

[1] PEP *Report on International Trade*, p. 223.

of Comparative Advantage become a foolish irrelevance. *A* must grow, not what he is most fitted to grow, but what will save most shipping space. *B* must make, not what he is most fitted to make, but what can be made most easily out of local sawdust and mud.

Confusingly enough, this final efflorescence of economic nationalism has been accompanied by a striking expansion of world trade, and even by a slight tendency towards the relaxation of certain trade restrictions. But we must not, I think, be too much uplifted by these facts. For in the first place the rise in the price of raw materials on which the trade recovery has been largely based has increased the economic pressure on the hungry Powers, and reinforced their motives for achieving ultimate self-sufficiency. And secondly, a temporary Governmental thirst for deadly metals is not a very firm foundation on which to base our hopes of freer trade.

11. We have now, I think, at last, however summarily, taken all the elements of the confused story into account. What kind of picture emerges? It is, I am afraid, neither a very clear nor a very cheerful one. But it seems to be a picture of a world in which a volume of international trade, relatively diminished as compared with pre-war or even pre-crisis days, will continue to be conducted by mechanisms more cumbrous, in the face of hindrances more severe, than then prevailed. In some degree, whatever political appeasement may achieve, these restrictive policies will continue inevitably to be coloured by the Economics of War. But in some degree they will be based on conceptions of national advantage, expressed in terms like " stability " and " balance," which would not be unintelligible or unworthy even in a world where peace was assured. So vague, however, are these concepts, so difficult of measurement are the advantages claimed, that there will be constant danger of the whole system degenerating into a struggle of interested groups, and constant need for initiative and endeavour to prevent the volume of international trade from being constricted beyond what is necessary or reasonable.

What particular courses of action does it behove a wise man, who wishes to keep his feet upon the earth, to advocate in this situation? That is what I wish to learn. For my own part, I can only pass on, in my own grouping, the thoughts which I have picked up from better instructed persons than myself—I have in mind particularly Sir Arthur Salter, and the anonymous authors of that remarkable production, the PEP *Report on International Trade*, on which I have already freely drawn. I propose therefore to end by flinging down, without argument, six propositions to serve as bones of contention.

(1) We should do our best to widen and exploit such gaps in Comparative Advantage as remain. The broad dichotomy between agriculture and manufacture does not exhaust the truth; there is agriculture and agriculture, manufacture and manufacture. In agriculture, the deflecting menace of war obstructs, perhaps fatally, the full exploitation of the economically obvious specialisation—durable foods from the prairies, perishable foods from the home acres : but subject to its pressure, we must do what we can. In manufacture there is still room for specialisation between the simple and the complex, the low grade and the high, the goods for consumption and the machine that makes the goods. If, say the PEP experts, manufacturing industries abroad are assisted to grow on sound lines with active participation by United Kingdom manufacturers, the inevitable decline in the export of directly competitive goods should be accompanied by increasing exports of capital and other specialised goods. How much is there in this idea?

But I think the event may show that sooner or later we must go further, and reconsider in some measure that wholesale lopping off of manufactured imports from Europe which constituted, together with the depreciation of the pound, our main contribution to the international beggar-my-neighbour of 1931. For the wise-acres who sneer at three-cornered trade have not appreciated, I think, the full dimensions of the world agricultural problem. For reasons already emphasised, we are not in a position to make up to the primary producers overseas for the loss of those European sales which gave them pounds with which to buy from us—pounds which they can no longer obtain because the European manufacturer is hindered by our tariffs from earning them by the sale of his goods in our markets.

(2) National complexes about the balance of payments, while less acute than they were, still exist among creditors and debtors alike; they are not wholly irrational, and we must take account of them. Thus we must be prepared for a time to see foreign investment largely take the form of the export of machinery and the like, financed by credit of a few years' duration, rather than of the old long-term untied loan; though the opportunities for that may return some day. In a different field, here is another interesting suggestion of the fertile PEP. In the old days, they point out, the balancing of imports and exports was not left so wholly to chance as we are sometimes taught to believe. For the merchant who sold British goods abroad frequently did a two-way trade, providing a market for the wares of his customers. This the big manufacturing firm, who has learnt to dispense with

the merchant's services, fails to do; and the opportunities for trade are curtailed accordingly. There is room, suggests PEP, for a new type of trading company to fill the gap.

(3) We must be thankful for small mercies. Bilateral agreements are better than nothing to start with; so perhaps even are the despised exchange clearings with which the Continent of Europe is honeycombed. Groups for the mutual expansion of trade would be better still. Our rigid insistence on the maintenance of our most favoured nation rights hampers their formation; it is also, in view of the Ottawa system, something of an impertinence.

(4) In the light of what is now known about the nutrition of the people, it is not tolerable that we should chatter for ever, as I have been chattering, about there being too much food in the world, though too much of *some* foods there may from time to time be. The recent report of the League of Nations Committee on Nutrition has given some striking illustrations of how far, even in the richest countries in the most prosperous years, the diet of large sections of the people falls below what is reasonable. If increases in direct taxation are needed to implement a nutrition policy which shall reap the fruits of modern dietetic knowledge and at the same time go some way towards reconciling the conflicting claims of Wiltshire, New Zealand and the Argentine, sooner or later they will have to be forthcoming.

(5) A detached matter, but one of great importance. It is our bounden duty to contribute to political appeasement by the reversal of the policy of discrimination in favour of British goods in the Colonial Empire—a policy which has been indifferent economics, bad morals, and shocking diplomacy—though it may not be an economist's business to say so. The recent stirrings of Government policy in this direction are much to be welcomed, though it does not look as if Lancashire is going to allow them to go very far.[1]

(6) To relax import control in booms and tighten it in slumps is a bright thought as far as it goes: the trouble is that it is likely to occur to other people as well, and that spoils half the fun. The truth is, commercial policy is not enough. Unless we can work towards international control of the cyclical movement of trade, sooner or later we shall all be back in the gutter playing beggar-my-neighbour. But that is another story.

D. H. ROBERTSON

Cambridge.

[1] Since the lecture was delivered, the quota system in Malaya has been further extended.

[28]

PROBLEMS OF INTERNATIONAL ECONOMIC POLICY FOR THE UNITED STATES

(Three papers)

BASIC ISSUES IN POSTWAR INTERNATIONAL ECONOMIC RELATIONS

By ROBERT B. BRYCE
Ministry of Finance, Canada

This paper is concerned with those fundamental international economic issues which seem likely to persist for some years after the war, and not with immediate postwar questions, which are of a more specialized and interim character. It must obviously be an essay in speculation. It should be emphasized at the outset that the views either expressed or implied in it are purely personal and in no sense either official or intended to represent other Canadian opinion.

For the purpose of this paper it is assumed that the war will end several years hence with a victory for Britain, the United States, Russia, and their allies. It is taken for granted that this victory will involve a Western Europe, at least, under the influence of Britain and the United States, and some organization of Central and Eastern Europe that will give it more political and economic stability than it has enjoyed in the past, with an opportunity for an increase in its productivity. In addition to the European outcome, it is assumed that China is freed from the domination of Japan.

Of course other ends to the war are conceivable. However, a consideration of the issues that would arise in such cases would involve fewer economic questions and more political and military ones. Consequently the more optimistic and more probable outcome is also best suited to the purpose of this discussion.

I propose to confine what I say to about half a dozen issues which seem to me important and interesting, leaving other issues to other speakers. In this selection I shall consider only questions of policy and action, and not the organization or machinery needed to decide upon policies or carry them out. Obviously some of us must give hard thought to organization and machinery—they cannot be improvised when the need arises. But I think that experience between the wars has taught us that the most elaborate international machinery will avail us little, even in the economic field, unless nations, and particularly Great Powers, can reach some agreement on basic issues of policy and then be prepared to pay the price, and take the risks, of putting their policies into effect.

From the prewar period we have inherited two great economic problems: first, the need to achieve a much higher, as well as a more stable, level of employment; and, second, the need to make more effective use of our labor and other resources by taking advantage of the possibilities of international exchange of goods, services, and capital. Is is easy to distinguish these two problems in terms of generalities and on paper. It is important, I think, to realize that both of them relate not only to one another but to all the myriad particular economic issues that plague so many nations. We must bear both of them in mind in viewing probable postwar issues. The first of them—the need to make full use of our resources—is perhaps the more urgent and fundamental. This is particularly true in United States, which is of course such a large, rich, and varied nation that international trade must normally be of secondary importance. The failure to reach, much less maintain, full employment in the prewar decade was so conspicuous, and the controversy over the measures to be taken to remedy it so heated, that this primary issue tended to overshadow international economic problems.

While the problem of achieving and maintaining satisfactorily full employment is, I think, going to be common to most of the Western world, for nearly all nations outside the United States it remains intimately bound up with the second question—that of developing international exchange. Most nations cannot achieve satisfactorily full employment without more international trade, unless they gravely reorient their economic life. They cannot proceed intelligently to solve the problems of unemployment and underemployment unless they can forecast to some degree what their export markets will be and on what terms imports will be available. Private investments must depend very largely upon prospects for export industries or the domestic demands for which they provide income. Even such an apparently purely domestic program as rehousing cannot be properly undertaken on a large scale in many countries unless some guess can be made about the future of export industries and import policies and conditions, for housing must be put where people will be working. Consequently to most nations the future of international trade is of vital importance, not only for the direct and obvious gains of the international division of labor, but also because the direction of domestic development and investment is dependent upon it. If the world is all to go back to peaceful work and the problem of unemployment is to be solved, even by vigorous domestic policies, some answer must be found to the economic issues considered in this paper.

It is equally important to realize, on the other hand, that a satisfactory volume of international exchange, and satisfactory solutions to many of the most persistent international economic issues cannot be achieved unless reasonably full employment can be reached, in the major countries at least. So long as unemployment is a serious problem in many countries, and particularly in the great nations who are the large potential importers, international trade and the policies that enable it to flourish are likely to be sacrificed to efforts designed to increase domestic employment without reliance on co-operation from abroad. When total employment and production are at relatively satisfactory levels, nations can afford to act more intelligently from an international point of view.

During the tempestuous twenty years between the wars we all fell far short of achieving that freedom from want which we now recognize as one of the new rights of man. We must do better after this war if our civilization is to survive. We must achieve freedom from want, as Roosevelt said, "everywhere in the world." We shall only do so if we reach some sort of solution to both our fundamental problems; because we can only raise the deplorable standard of living of much of mankind above the "want" level if we make use of our resources both fully and effectively. In doing this we will face some very difficult issues, on which some agreement must be found.

The first and most general of these issues which we must expect to face after the war is the old one which we may sum up in the query: How much economic nationalism? It is, of course, a matter of degree; we need not anticipate having to decide between free trade and autarchy.

In the postwar period this issue seems likely to appear most vividly in connection with the positive programs that will undoubtedly be instituted to reach and maintain a satisfactory level of employment once the immediate postwar boom is over.

It does not take a political expert to forecast that following an Allied victory, many nations will embark upon "new deals." Quite apart from the development of socialism itself, the social temper seems sure to require forthright and vigorous action to provide work and security under all circumstances. Experience preceding, and particularly during, the war has convinced the man in the street—indeed even the man in business—that governments can put men to work and make private business profitable by spending money, and, what is more, that when need arises, the money can be found in undreamt-of quantities. "If we can spend money and go to work for war," the layman asks, "why can we not do the same to keep people alive and make their lives worth living?" The public pressure for long-term programs of large-scale public expenditures seems likely to be practically irresistible, as soon as any significant unemployment develops.

In carrying out these programs of public investment, guaranteed employment, and enlarged consumption, there is danger that nations may be led to restrict or displace imports or fight for export markets. One reason is that investment in industries to produce in competition with imports or with foreign exporters offers an apparent opportunity of using capital "productively." A second reason is that the internal effectiveness of any investment program can be seemingly increased by cutting down the "leakages" into imports and thereby increasing the multiplier. Thirdly, there will be a desire to get away in some degree from a dependence on a few unstable export markets whose fluctuations are even more difficult to compensate by public spending than are those of domestic investment. If some exports are to be less, others must be pushed or imports, too, must be reduced in some measure and replaced by home produced goods.

In addition, of course, most of the old motives for protection will continue in force, though the strategic and military motives, we may reasonably hope, will be far less important than before the war. There will, however, be new as well as old vested interests after this war as there were after the last, ready to demonstrate how much employment they provide—and perhaps how much public expenditure their protection would avoid. Many countries will be left with slender "international margins" and, faced with high levels of demands for imports, may be tempted to protectionism rather than let their exchange rate fall or their small reserves melt away. Finally, there is bound to be a temptation again to look to a surplus of exports over imports as a means of stimulus for domestic employment and incomes, in place of domestic outlets. For many debtor countries, with opportunities to use capital profitably in paying off their debts abroad by this method, this attempt to secure a large export balance will certainly appear a sensible and businesslike policy, if only the export markets can be found.

On the other hand, however, it is obvious that if many countries attempt to restrict imports for any of these reasons, their ultimate purposes are likely to be frustrated by the effects on their export trade of one another's action. Then the advantages of exchange will have been lost without any gain in employment (except perhaps in the greater employment needed to produce the same output uneconomically). It is clearly in the general interest to secure the maximum use of opportunities for international exchange at any given level of general employment, and it is surely in the interest of any particular nation to make more use of exchange if it can do so without sacrificing its level of employment or terms of trade, even though in other circumstances it may be a case of balancing conflicting considerations. Therefore it is desirable to ensure, so far as possible, that the barriers to international exchange should be lowered rather than raised after the war, as well as ensuring a satisfactory and sustained level of employment.

If the postwar decades are to be a period of reconstruction, in which the world is to be re-equipped and new economic or social orders fashioned, it is particularly important that a sensible pattern of international exchange of goods and services should be evolved. Otherwise an enduring structure of industrial and other capital and organization will be built up on the basis of a defeatist attitude to international exchange, an attitude suited to the prewar period when international collaboration was impossible or futile and when the advantages of trade were sacrificed in a frantic search for employment.

Consequently, it seems to me vitally necessary that in the development of postwar programs of reconstruction, increased consumption, and employment, there should be a frank recognition of the need to "share the recovery" between nations and to avoid simply producing or preparing to produce at home what used to be imported. Some international understanding must be reached on allowing the propensity to import full scope in spreading higher incomes from country to country, and perhaps as well some understanding on the industrial sectors in which domestic investment will be directed by official action. It may prove desirable to agree as well that no country will attempt a "free ride" on the recovery of others but will contribute, so far as it can, to the mutual recovery, and at least set about such internal and external adjustments of its economy as would constitute reasonable co-operation in the working out of better international trade.

If by some such arrangements to work in parallel during recovery and reconstruction the nations can achieve a satisfactory level of employment and maintain it for some time, the way should be clear for a real attack on the old barriers to trade inherited from before the war, whose reduction or removal will require some actual transfer of economic resources to make room for cheaper imports and not simply the sharing of expanding markets. Such positive transfers are far more feasible, both economically and politically, in times of prosperity than at other times. They are essential if we are to take real advantage of the opportunities of international specialization and exchange.

One cannot expect it will be easy to achieve international agreement to undertake and share positive recovery and reconstruction programs. It must involve far more than the relatively precise reciprocal concessions of trade and exchange agreements. It will concern facts and principles still not generally understood or accepted even by economists. It will relate to what may be highly controversial domestic policies. Different countries may pursue very different courses in the search of full employment, and some may feel the actions taken by others are likely to fail and that consequently they will not be contributing their share to the dynamic recovery of trade.

Nevertheless, there appears to be a reasonable chance that the political complexions of the Western democracies will be sufficiently alike and the realization of interdependence sufficiently strong, to make possible co-ordinated social and economic programs. The advantages of international trade are great enough to justify the effort that will be needed to achieve them.

In the field of international investment many issues are found to arise after the war. The most important seem likely to concern large-scale lending between governments rather than private investment. Some prewar forms of capital movement will probably continue after the war without giving rise to much argument. For example, direct investment by large corporations in foreign plants or subsidiaries, which is one of the most important modern forms of international investment, particularly for the United States, seems likely to continue with relatively minor adjustments, although it may be expected that some of the special trade barriers which gave rise to investment of this kind will be reduced rather than increased. This form of capital movement, which has been accompanied by expert management and advanced techniques, seems to have been sufficiently useful and successful to warrant our expecting it to continue, and although the most obvious openings have already been filled, other opportunities will undoubtedly open up both in new and old ideas. It is also likely that the provision of medium-term export credits will continue to develop, as it did so notably during the thirties, and will not give rise to much difficulty. If trade should be relatively poor, governments will probably continue to use such credits as a direct means of pushing exports, while if trade is good, we may expect to see more private credit in this field.

On the other hand some forms of capital movement do not seem likely to regain their old position. As we shall note later in discussing exchange matters, the movement of short-term balances and speculative funds between major financial centers, which distinguished the interwar period, will probably be substantially curtailed. It is not of great importance from the point of view of economic development or trade policy. Secondly, the large-scale issue of foreign securities in the major financial markets seems likely to continue its process of decline. This classical form of foreign investment had such a great deal of lurid and unhappy history in the twenties and thirties that both investors and borrowers (as well as underwriters and governments) are apt to continue to regard it with suspicion except in the relatively few cases where the record was good, and there exist close financial and commercial relations between the borrowing and lending nations. Perhaps a reasonably long period of good trade and fairly stable exchange conditions will bring the foreign issue market back to vigorous life, but that is a long way ahead.

The most controversial foreign investment problem will probably be whether or not this continent should lend to Europe for the purpose of reconstruction. I take it for granted that Europe's immediate postwar needs for food and raw materials will or should be met by gifts or by relief loans of a special character. There is some room for questioning, however, whether America will be prepared to continue sending capital to Europe for, say, a decade, as it did after the last war. There is no doubt the need will exist; Europe will be able to rebuild itself far more quickly with outside help, particularly if the destruction as well as the deferred depreciation is very great.

In some respects the risks may be less this time. The victory is likely to be more complete and the preponderant power of Britain, Russia, and America will not be in doubt. It is unlikely that Britain and Russia will let control of Europe slip out of their hands for many years after this bitter experience, even if America should turn its attention elsewhere. The governments established on the Continent will likely be of a socialist character, and more stable than those of the last twenty years. This may not prove at all favorable for prewar capital, but it seems likely to result in greater economic development and more sustained full employment. Such nations are apt to want more imports from abroad than Europe took between the wars, and are likely, I believe, to prove more satisfactory debtors in the long run than more capitalist but less stable regimes. Naturally the borrowing would be done by governments or their agencies. There seems a good chance that many Americans will look with favor and hope upon such a re-established Europe, or at least that western part subject to Anglo-American influence. Under such circumstances, there will be plenty of American export interests ready to urge loans to this new Europe to enable it to use American materials and equipment and eat American foods while it is getting back on its feet. Absurd reparations requirements are unlikely to be present to bedevil the issue this time.

On the other hand, however, several influences will stand in the way of this lending. There will be a far more widespread and acute consciousness of the transfer problem inherent in any service on or repayment of these debts—the same kind of transfer problem that was debated in the twenties and demonstrated in the thirties. Moreover, memories not only of the ill-fated loans of the twenties but of the old war loans themselves are not buried even now. Many Americans are likely to retain some lasting suspicion of Europe's intentions and weakness and there will be fears that somehow loans to Europe may be used to plunge yet another generation into war, whatever watch is kept on her. Finally, European industry will appear as a potential competitor with America in world markets once it is re-equipped. Will we on this continent be ready to finance that re-equipment? And if the loans are not to add to Europe's exporting power, or reduce her need for imports, how can they be justified in the new financial orthodoxy?

It is not in rebuilding Europe, however, that one looks for real hope in the future of international investment. If sustained and large-scale foreign investment is to take place, there must be some great new economy created. Two areas seem to hold some promise as fields for such development: South America and China. Attention in North America has, of course, been concentrated on the former because of its strategic importance under war conditions or conditions of political or economic warfare. Already American capital is helping to reshape Latin-American economies and give them more strength and stability. It is reasonable to expect it will continue after the war, whether or not trade between South America and Europe revives. China, however, appears to present a far greater opportunity for investment on a large scale sustained over several decades. China's immense population and area need roads, railroads, dams, power plants, factories, hospitals, and houses in quantities to challenge even the immense productivity of American industry. The effects that could be obtained in raising the standard of living would be a humanitarian achievement on a scale without parallel in history. Indeed there would be a serious population problem to contend with, simply because of the reduction in the death rate, and the outside world might find its surplus food-producing capacity rapidly disappearing under the force of the demand created by that population.

While there would, of course, be some political and economic risks in such investment, they should not be great in the event of a clear Allied victory. Russia as well as the United States will be interested in China, but she will not be nearly so able to provide real capital on a large scale. The future transfer problem on the servicing and repayment of the debt will be far more distant in the case of China than in the case of Europe, and the challenge of developing China seems far more likely to appeal to the American imagination than the repair of Europe.

This looks to be the opening for that New Imperialism which one hears about these days—a benevolent, liberal, and farsighted, if not actually socialist, imperialism—a TVA imperialism. The new imperialists would have as objectives not a high return on capital but rather a flourishing trade built up on the basis that would be created by the rising standard of living in the capital importing country. More distant objectives would be peace and strategic security for the lending country, achieved not so much through political influence as through the political stability that a prosperous trade and progressive economic and social development would ensure in the borrowing countries.

The major part of the capital involved in such a new international development would appear likely to move through government channels—perhaps by the agency of some sort of intergovernmental corporations. Only a public body would be able to take the farsighted view that would be needed and count as gains the indirect benefits to the lending country as a whole. However, the functioning of this new official imperialism would not seem to preclude a development of considerable private investment at the same time. In particular, it would seem to afford a great opportunity for direct investment by established industrial and commercial concerns to fill in the gaps which governmental investment cannot appropriately fill.

This new imperialism is an attractive idea to those who want to see bold and humane action on an international scale. But one must expect very real opposition to it from many quarters. The potential, private imperialist would seem to be the least of the opposition. More serious will be the criticism of those who would see it as one vast and well-nigh perpetual WPA project, to provide relief to tens of millions of foreigners thousands of miles away. More logical would be the opposition of those who would ask why it is necessary to find an outlet for real investment on another continent when there are many tens of millions at home who are barely above the poverty line. And there would also be those who would fear the time when China's teeming millions, equipped with the latest American machinery, would begin to pour exports into the world's markets in competition with Western industry and labor. To all of those, the best answer would be the assurance of a future in which a satisfactory level of employment could be maintained for Americans and for the Chinese—in which the willingness of any country to export can be welcomed—and in preparation for which it will be good economics as well as good ethics to invest in China or South America.

In addition to the general issues that have been mentioned, there are several important economic issues of a more specialized character which must be noted. One of these has already been the subject of considerable discussion in recent months and a diversity of views among English-speaking economists is evident. The point at issue is whether nations, in their trade policies, should treat other nations alike, without discrimination, or should bargain with them, giving some preferences and even entering into purely bilateral arrangements.

The ten years before the war had seen a great development of discrimination in trade policies—varying from minor tariff preferences to rigorous bilateral payments agreements. Immediately after the war, of course, many of these preferences and practices will be in effect—inherited from before the war and imbedded in old tariff structures and new exchange controls. The most extreme forms of discrimination and exploitation, we may expect, will vanish with the totalitarian regimes which practiced them. But there is room for doubt concerning the milder varieties.

In the first place, there will continue to be political, strategic, and geographic, as well as economic, reasons for nations looking on some other nations as closer or more vital to them than others, and justifying or even requiring embodiment in preferential trade or exchange treatment. This sort of argument may be used to justify some Pan-American grouping, or a British Imperial, or sterling area preference. Furthermore in the future as in the past there may appear to be more hope of reducing trade barriers first within a group (or as limited bilateral concessions) and then progressively enlarging the group, than there would be in attempting to reduce barriers by general agreement or even by the use of the unqualified most-favored-nation clause.

There are more powerful arguments, however. The hard facts of her balance of payments may make it exceedingly difficult for Britain to avoid bargaining and discrimination. For one thing, to put it bluntly, she will have lost most of her invisible means of support. In the past, Britain's enormous excess of imports over exports, which was so important in orienting the trade of the world, was very largely paid for by the receipts she obtained from her overseas investments and from her large merchant marine. The war is making it necessary for her to sell many of her investments and to lose much of her merchant marine. Furthermore, war is making it very difficult for her to retain many of her export markets, which may be lost after the war either to local industry, expanded behind the accidental protection which war affords, or to other exporters. Faced with a serious reduction in her income from abroad, Britain must be prepared by some means or other to import less or export more—or else to live on loans and the liquidation of her remaining investments. It is only to be expected that she will need to follow as vigorous a trade policy as circumstances permit. Nor is this all. Her receipts of dollars and other "hard currencies" seem likely to be particularly reduced as compared with the prewar situation, and no automatic reduction appears likely in her requirements of dollars. Even before the war sterling was none too strong in relation to the dollar. Consequently, it seems probable that Britain, and the sterling area, will face a relative scarcity of dollars after the war, unless some new and radical development occurs to make them available. Under such circumstances it may be that no other course will be open to Britain except to restrict in some way or other the use of dollars to the more essential purposes—which may involve what will appear to be discrimination in trade or exchange policies.

There are apparently some English writers who see an opportunity to make a virtue of this necessity and who emphasize the very useful bargaining power which inheres in a large demand for imports. They note the considerable success which Germany achieved before the war in obtaining export markets and favorable terms of trade by bargaining methods, even though she had almost no reserves and was a debtor rather than a creditor. Britain's own gains from bargaining and mild discrimination before the war were not inconsiderable, while the advantage to her of favorable terms of trade in the thirties is well known. Experience with centralized buying, exchange control, and discriminatory trade policies during the war is showing what can be done when necessity drives. It is natural that many should advocate the use of bargaining and preferences by Britain to help her in meeting the very real trade and exchange difficulties she will face.

On the other hand, spokesmen in the United States, both official and unofficial, are making it quite clear that they hope and expect to see equal treatment in trade policies established as a general rule after the war. This attitude, in opposition to imperial and other preferences and in favor of a wide use of the "most-favored-nation" clause, is of course traditional American policy into which Mr. Hull has instilled a new vigor. There appears—at least to the outsider—to be very little opposition to it within the United States. The motives behind it appear to be long-term ones rather than immediate. Of course the United States, almost alone among nations, need have no fear of a shortage of exchange and can afford to take a long view. Perhaps, too, it can expect to compete with any nation in export markets on equal terms, because of its low mass production costs and advanced techniques. But a more general and important motive appears to exist in a realization of the danger of international friction, ill will, and instability which is created by international bargaining and discrimination. The fact that the State Department is most active in advocating this trade policy suggests this wider motive. Of course, as American spokesmen themselves recognize, one cannot forget that the United States, in putting forward this traditional and liberal policy of no discrimination, does so from behind the ample protection which the Smoot-Hawley tariff still affords against all comers, despite Mr. Hull's fine and persistent efforts.

In the event of an Allied victory, the United States seems certain to get its way in regard to this trade policy. It seems desirable in the general interest of most nations that equal treatment should prevail and that nations can secure the obvious benefits of buying in the cheapest markets and selling in the dearest. Nevertheless, some means will have to be found of solving the dollar problem for the sterling area—and for all the world outside the United States, for that matter. Several possible lines of solution occur to one. In part it may be solved by large American investment in China, which will permit China to use some of these dollars to purchase goods and services from the rest of the world. Perhaps an even larger part of the shortage may be made up by the expansion in United States imports which will occur if the United States can secure a high and stable level of employment and production after the war. It is noteworthy that in the thirties the United States was relatively further from full employment than most other countries and the balance of payments must have reflected this. However, there is no assurance that in fact the marginal propensity to import and the lessened pressure to export will be adequate to bring the dollar balance of payments to a tolerable situation. Of course it would be desirable from the outside point of view to overcome part of this dollar deficiency by a reduction in American tariffs, and while the political difficulties of doing that are recognized, particularly until some degree of prosperity is achieved, the benefits to the American consumer should be realized as well. The most natural way of meeting this relative scarcity of dollars in the outside world would be to permit an appreciation of the dollar in terms of other currencies. The amount of such appreciation that would be required to end the dollar shortage is hard to forecast, and some writers argue that the dollar-sterling position is relatively inelastic to a movement in that rate. Finally, of course, the shortage may be met by stabilization loans or the sustained use of exchange funds. Such operations may be desirable in the early postwar years when the dimensions of the problem are obscure and methods of solving it are being worked out; but I should think it probable that neither the United States nor the other nations concerned would like to envisage a continuing flow of loans simply to meet exchange deficits and to postpone the more fundamental adjustments required in the balance of payments.

Time does not permit me to do more than mention several other issues which deserve attention and which, I trust, the other speakers will discuss. First, in the field of monetary policy there will be the question of whether exchange control is to be retained after the war, and if so, whether it will be used to restrict current account transactions or just capital movements. Before the war, of course, exchange control was regarded as a sign of economic weakness, if not indeed of vice. Because of its usual origins, it was identified with the demoralization of international trade and finance and was associated with totalitarian powers. Nevertheless it worked. Now, in wartime, it has become well-nigh universal and familiar, and most countries are learning to operate it with some smoothness and efficiency. It is only natural that many should be wondering whether all this effective and flexible machinery will be dismantled after the war, or whether some of it will be kept in operation to handle the new, complex, and difficult problems that will be with us during reconstruction, when many overseas countries will be short of exchange reserves and the new future of balances of payments will be uncertain.

Whether or not control will be required in order to restrict or direct trade and other current account transactions will depend upon the answer that is found to the preceding issue concerning trade policy. If discrimination and preferences are to be common and complex, then restriction upon the use of exchange for current account payments will probably be retained and used to carry out these policies effectively by those countries most concerned with them. If, on the other hand, as we are expecting, the equal-treatment trade policy of the United States comes to prevail, then any significant restriction on current account payments by exchange control would appear to be inconsistent and unnecessary. Mere protection can be secured by simpler means.

In regard to control of capital movements, the outlook is more complex. During the thirties and even the twenties movements of liquid balances and speculative capital back and forth between major financial centers created many difficulties and seem now to have served very little real purpose. For those countries which do not need to depend on foreign capital, it is hard to justify all the trouble, expense, and disruption caused by these unbridled comings and goings of "hot money" and its cold-blooded counterparts. When we visualize the very large supplies of liquid balances and marketable gilt-edge securities there will be in major countries after the war, and the natural desire to diversify holdings, it seems apparent that there will be danger of large-scale international movements of this character unless some control is exercised.

Because of this danger and a probable shortage of exchange reserves, some nations with large financial centers—Britain, for example—may well find it desirable to retain exchange control for the purpose of regulating capital movements, even though leaving current account transactions unrestricted. The United States, because of its unique situation, might find it desirable to exert some kind of control over inward movements of foreign capital. On the other hand, there will likely be other countries to whom it will be worth bearing the expense of holding large reserves and running the risks involved in the absence of control in order to attract capital, or to maintain high credit standings built up over many years, or to facilitate a large volume of international trade and transactions.

Apart from control itself, there will be the issue of exchange stability. Before the war the issue of fixed versus flexible exchange rates was a favorite academic question, and the degree of stability to be sought or undertaken in various exchange rates was an important practical issue. In fact, during the decade since 1931 there has been a growing unwillingness to sacrifice internal conditions in order to secure the maintenance of exchange rates, although on the other hand there has been a widespread realization of the danger of competitive or retaliatory action following depreciation.

After the war the difficulties of stabilization seem likely to be greater than before it except insofar as capital movements are restricted. Many countries will be short of gold and exchange reserves, and even if they can borrow or otherwise obtain some, they will probably be reluctant to use them boldly. It will be very difficult to select a rate for stabilization with much confidence that it will prove suitable for a reasonably long period, because conditions will be so different from prewar times, and everything in flux. Nations and their governments will be less willing than ever to sacrifice domestic price levels or interest rates, much less production and employment, in order to maintain exchange rates.

On the other hand, of course, there will be less danger to stability if international trade can be developed on a large scale and if it is solidly based upon fairly well maintained employment in the major countries. On the whole, I think we need not expect either a readiness to undertake definite long-term stabilization nor attempts to depreciate currencies as a form of aggressive trade policy, but there may be some reluctance on the part of those with strong currencies to permit them to appreciate.

It seems obvious that the re-establishment of the gold standard in anything like its old form is not going to be an issue at all after the war. Monetary conditions and monetary policy are now recognized as too important and too close to the heart of fiscal sovereignty to be entrusted to any automatic or even semiautomatic system—even if the latter is ruled by some international authority. This does not mean, however, that gold will not continue to serve a useful monetary function. It will very likely continue to be the most useful and acceptable form in which to hold and transfer foreign exchange reserves, which will always be required. To the former advantages of gold in this respect the war is probably adding another in demonstrating how vulnerable other forms of reserves are in a world where exchange control is common and where international temperatures may quickly drop below the freezing point. Of course, there will be a major problem in the redistribution of the world's gold reserves, which have accumulated so preponderantly in the hands of the United States. That problem will exist, however, whatever form of reserves is used, and is part and parcel of all the problems of international trade and investment. We should note in passing that the continuing use of gold for reserves will serve in part to render more manageable the postwar dollar problem, so long, but only so long, as production remains fairly substantial.

Time does not permit anything but a mention of two other postwar issues that deserve more. The first of these is the problem of agricultural and raw material surpluses, which made themselves so painfully evident during the thirties. The persistent surplus capacity was in part the result of the agricultural revolution and the changes in population trends, and in part the result of the absence of really general prosperity which would have increased demand and offered alternative occupations to producers. The war and the shipping shortage are adding to many of these surpluses, although relieving others temporarily. The distribution of relief supplies after the war, already foreshadowed, will dispose of some of the excess stocks, subject to the limits of shipping possibilities, but the surplus capacity problem will remain.

A real solution to this problem must be found in the higher consumption of agricultural products on the one hand and alternative opportunities for producers on the other. Both will require a far higher level of sustained employment in other occupations than before the war. The increasing consciousness of the need for improved nutrition all over the world offers some real hope. Europe, for example, may be able to turn its own agriculture in large measure of protective foods, leaving markets for staples from overseas, and China's potential demands are enormous. However, a basic solution cannot be achieved immediately and in the meantime the surpluses must be handled. It now appears very likely that international government control schemes, of the ever-normal granary type, will be adopted. Governments are already having to hold stocks and restrict production of many commodities and in many countries. They will undoubtedly be less reluctant than before the war to follow international control schemes, particularly as the United States is taking a lead in working them out.

Such schemes as this will serve a very useful temporary purpose in protecting primary producers against the devastating effects of excess capacity with an inelastic market. The holding of ample stocks appears likely to be a permanent improvement. But there are dangers to be guarded against. These restriction schemes may conceal the real need for a transfer of resources from production or the need to develop a larger consumption. Secondly, the quasi-monopolistic power inherent in them may be abused, just as the quasi-monopsonistic powers of importing nations may be abused in the discriminating trade policies mentioned above.

The final issue to be mentioned, which may in time come to overshadow all the others, is the question of migration in a world where population trends have become widely divergent and where differences in densities of population already are marked. It hardly appears likely that countries of potentially large-scale immigration—like the Americas—will be ready to receive millions of migrants, at least for many years after the war. Perhaps some alternative can be found to migration, for a period at least, by a vigorous development of international trade and investment. This leads us back to the earlier issues raised in this paper.

In concluding, I would like to draw attention to the fact that in relation to almost all these international economic issues, the United States occupies a central position. She will be the dominant naval and air power of the world. She will enjoy a great political prestige, not only from the results of the war, but from the example given and the hope inspired by the spirit of the New Deal before the war. She will be *the* great economic power, not dependent on trade, but using it. She will be much the greatest creditor nation in the world, with nearly all its gold reserves, and the major source of its current saving. She will possess a large proportion of the world's industry and the world's largest merchant marine. Naturally, therefore, we outside shall be looking to her for responsible leadership. I, for one, am confident she will provide it, that isolationism, economic and political, will be over. I think we can expect that the United States will see to it that the "dollar problem" of the outside world is solved, and that she will be prepared to "share the recovery," taking her fair reward in a larger real content of income.

Many of us outside the United States realize the difficulty of the problem facing her in achieving and particularly in maintaining a satisfactorily high level of employment and production, given her high propensity to save and prodigious productivity. We realize, too, that when she shares her recovery by greater imports, her economic problem is a more difficult one. But the fruits of its solution are greater as well.

If the United States is to lead, others must work with her. In particular, I think, responsibility will lie on other fairly advanced countries, not to depend primarily for their economic stimulus on developments abroad, nor to postpone internal adjustments, nor to seek domestic recovery at the cost of imports, but rather to co-operate with the United States in building up international trade and lending on a firm foundation of a high level of employment, consumption, capital creation, and imports.

It is not going to be easy to achieve freedom from want, whoever is to do it, but it can be done. We understand far more clearly than ever before the two basic economic problems—that of using all our resources and that of using them effectively. The nations of the world can solve both these problems after the war if they devote to them the hard work, co-operation, and courage now being devoted to war. But if it is to be our privilege to solve them, in our own way, we must first put our thought and effort into the war itself. Planning for a postwar world will avail us nothing if we do not achieve the victory on which such plans must depend.

Name Index

Abraham, D. 251, 252
Ahvenainen, J. 361
Akerlof, G. 26
Aldcroft, D.H. 243, 264, 315, 335, 421
Alesina, A. 162
Alltmont, R. 406
Almond, G. 266
Andersen, P.N. 414
Andrews, M. 63
Angell, J.M. 527
Arndt, H.W. 242, 264
Arrubla, M. 631
Artus, J.R. 424
Ashton Gwatkin, F. 342, 359, 369
Auge-Laribe, M. 270
Azariadis, C. 28

Bacha, E. 593
Backe, H. 388
Bairoch, P. 363
Balderston, T. 34, 162, 174
Baldwin, R.E. 626
Baldwin, S. 215, 216, 266, 317
Barber, W.J. 37, 41, 169
Basch, A. 381, 392, 409, 414, 415
Bassett, R. 104
Baudhuin, F. 452
Bauer, R. 243
Becker, J. 329
Beenstock, M. 447, 448
Beer, S.H. 267, 354
Bélanger, G. 424
Benham, F. 368, 376, 377, 388, 410, 411
Benjamin, D. 29
Bennett, E.W. 90, 96, 101, 104
Bentham, J. 244
Berger, S. 274
Bernanke, B. 36, 37, 39, 40, 54, 123, 139, 145, 159
Berndt, R. 373
Bernstein, M. 24, 25
Berov, L. 382
Bevin, E. 109, 265, 268
Bhagwati, J. 565
Bingham, R.W. 332
Blank, S. 267
Bloomfield, A. 161

Blum, J.M. 451
Blum, L. 269, 270, 271
Bodin, L. 271
Bohme, H. 251
Bonn, J.M. 320
Bonnell, S. 462
Bonnet, G. 211, 338, 339, 347
Booth, A. 447
Borchardt, K. 28, 36, 179, 372, 421, 427
Bordo, M. 24, 112, 124
Borkin, J. 255
Bouvier, J. 148, 271
Bowden, S.M. 26
Boyce, R.W.D. 166, 336
Bozga, V. 373
Bradbury, Lord 109
Brand, R.H. 278
Brittan, S. 106
Broadberry, S. 24, 25, 30, 40, 46, 180, 343
Broué, P. 271
Brower, D. 271
Brown, B. 243
Brown, E.C. 46, 169, 466
Brown, W.A. 92, 97, 99
Brown, W.B. 369
Bruce, S.M. 215
Brüning, H. 102, 183, 316
Brunner, K. 52, 57, 81, 263, 447
Buiter, W. 452
Bullock, A. 265
Bulmer-Thomas, V. 593, 594, 600, 612, 619, 628
Burnham, W.A. 259
Butlin, M.W. 560

Cagan, P. 28
Cairncross, A. 36, 46, 165, 173, 450, 453, 461, 528
Calvo, G.A. 112
Campa, J.M. 43
Capie, F. 42, 334, 349, 354, 447, 448
Cárdenas, E. 593, 608
Carter, S. 28
Carus-Wilson, E.M. 435
Casey, V. 593
Cassel, G. 322
Cecchetti, S.G. 35

Chamberlain, J. 266, 267
Chamberlain, N. 323, 326, 327, 331, 335, 338, 339, 342, 345, 347, 348, 354
Chang, T.C. 94, 95
Cheng, H.S. 421
Child, F. 406, 407, 427
Choudri, E. 36, 130, 131, 448
Churchill, W.S. 428
Ciocca, P. 148
Clarke, P. 41
Clarke, S.V.O. 315, 350, 452
Clay, H. 89, 93, 95, 102, 103
Clereland, H. 421
Cohen, D. 31
Collier, L. 355
Colton, J. 271
Condliffe, J.B. 92, 421, 450, 476
Connolly, F.G. 161
Cooper, R. 39, 112
Copland, D.B. 497
Corbett, D. 28, 29
Crafts, N.F.R. 39
Craig, G.A. 251
Crouch, C. 247, 264, 267

Dahmen, E. 263
Darity, W.A. Jr 542
Day, E. 343
Deane, P. 551
De Cecco, M. 545
De Long, J.B. 536
de Sola Pool, I. 243
Detieuf, A. 270
Dexter, L.A. 243
Diaper, S. 166
Diaz-Alejandro, C.F. 536, 537, 593, 627, 629
Dimsdale, N.H. 29, 37, 179, 180
Dixit, A. 27, 30
Dominick and Dominick 549
Dorey, N. 271
Döring, D. 174, 373
Dornbusch, R. 32, 112
Drummond, I. 161, 322, 344, 345, 347, 349, 350, 353
Drummond, M. 335
Duisberg, C. 252, 270
Dunn, R.W. 526
Dupeux, G. 270
Dwyer, G.P. 34

Early, E.F. 353
Eaton, J. 524, 531, 533
Ebert, F. 252
Edelstein, M. 526

Edge, W. 205
Edwards, S. 531, 533
Ehrmann, H. 270, 271
Eichengreen, B. 28, 29, 30, 31, 32, 33, 34, 36, 37, 38, 40, 42, 43, 46, 63, 122, 123, 124, 128, 130, 131, 135, 137, 146, 158, 165, 173, 180, 326, 334, 354, 450, 452, 453, 461, 466, 528, 541, 626, 628, 630
Eichholtz, D. 382
Einzig, P. 377, 410, 411
Elliott, W. 358, 359
Ellis, H.S. 96, 372, 378, 383, 410, 411, 412, 413, 458, 626
Emi, K. 586
Erdman, K.D. 421
Eyers, J.S. 369

Falkus, M. 421
Fearon, P. 24, 25, 42
Feder, G. 537
Feinstein, C. 25, 82, 83, 526
Feis, H. 343, 344
Feldman, G. 251, 256
Ferguson, T. 252, 258, 260
Fernandez, D. 122
Feuerlein, W. 547
Field, A. 24, 32
Finegold, K. 260
Fischer, P.T. 278, 536
Fisher, I. 123
Fleisig, H. 34, 322
Fleming, J.M. 112, 454, 628
Fodor, J. 613
Ford, H. 25
Foreman-Peck, J. 184
Forstmeier, F. 373
Fountain, H. 360
Franco, F. 618
Fremling, G.M. 180, 183
Friedman, M. 24, 36, 41, 82, 129, 137, 139, 158, 168, 446
Friedman, P. 407
Fritsch, W. 593

Gardener, L.C. 341
Gaventa, J. 244
Geiss, I. 374
Gerschenkron, A. 243, 249
Gersovitz, M. 524, 531, 533
Gertler, M. 123, 139
Gilpin, R. 267
Glynn, S. 421
Goguel, F. 269
Gordon, R.J. 28

Gourevitch, P.A. 249
Gravil, R. 353
Greene, N. 271
Griffiths, B. 447, 448
Griffiths, M. 122
Guérin, D. 271
Guillebaud, C.W. 372, 406, 409, 410, 414
Gustafson, B. 263

Haberle, R. 253
Haberler, G. 130, 159, 278, 456, 586, 626
Hailsham, Lord 325
Hamada, K. 112
Hamilton, J. 29, 32, 35, 122, 128, 129, 151
Hamilton, R. 253
Hancock, K.J. 264
Hannan, E. 547
Hardach, G. 421, 446
Hardy, C.D. 458
Harris, C.R.S. 543
Harrison, G. 35, 110, 161, 168, 169, 170
Harrod, R. 104
Hatton, T.J. 28, 29, 38, 54, 135, 137
Haubrich, J.G. 39
Hauser, K. 372
Hawtrey, R.G. 109, 319, 348
Hayami, Y. 586, 587
Hayek, F. 175
Heckscher, E.F. 264
Hengel, A. van 164
Hentschel, V. 432
Hexner, E. 366
Heyl, J.D. 258
Hicks, J.R. 52
Hildebrand, K. 329
Hilferding, R. 254, 267
Hillman, H.C. 407
Hirschman, A.O. 273, 353, 406, 412
Hirst, H. 278
Hitler, A. 53, 255, 256, 257, 351, 375, 380, 384, 390, 391, 406, 413, 419, 618
Hodson, H.V. 315, 338
Hoffmann, W.G. 397
Holland, R.F. 39, 369
Holtfrerich, C.-L. 430
Hoover, H. 37, 41, 102, 316, 317, 323, 326, 330, 351
Hopkins, R. 109, 110, 165, 167
Horsewood, N. 29, 37, 179
Howson, H. 421
Howson, S. 447, 453
Hughes Hallett, A.J. 182
Hull, C. 330, 333, 338, 341, 342, 345, 349, 350, 597, 659

Issawi, C. 485

Jackson, J. 37, 171, 346
Jacobsson, P. 89, 161
Jacoby, S. 28
Jäger, J.-J. 399
Jaitner, K. 329
James, H. 36, 39, 40, 159, 161, 165, 314
Jansson, B. 264
Jenks, L. 546
John, A. 39
Johnson, H.G. 448
Jones, G. 279
Jonung, L. 46, 263, 447
Just, R.E. 537
Justo, General 609

Kahn, A. 264
Kaiser, D. 273, 369
Kalecki, M. 271
Kaletsky, A. 528, 543
Katzenstein, P. 242, 267
Kavanagh, D.A. 266
Kemmerer, D.L. 406, 414
Kent, B. 317
Kenwood, A.G. 372, 406, 409
Kerr, C.C. 355
Keynes, J.M. 39, 41, 46, 53, 64, 109, 125, 159, 160, 262, 266, 267, 271, 319, 428, 454, 461
Kilroy, A. 360
Kim, F. 462
Kindersley, R. 526
Kindleberger, C.P. 42, 51, 54, 82, 125, 144, 159, 169, 258, 270, 315, 322, 376, 406, 407, 411, 421, 435, 446, 450, 451, 466
Kitson, M. 42
Klein, B.A. 393
Klug, A. 24, 31
Kobayashi, U. 586
Koblik, S. 262
Kochin, L. 29, 36, 130, 131, 448
Kooker, J.L. 421
Korpi, W. 264
Krugman, P. 112
Kuisel, R. 270
Kunz, D.B. 163, 167
Kurth, J. 243, 249, 255
Kuznets, S. 484
Kydland, F. 124

Lacouture, J. 271
Lafranc, G. 271
Laidler, D. 112

Lambi, I. 243
Lamer, M. 382
Landes, D.S. 242, 249
Lange, P. 242
Laqueur, W. 258
Layton, W. 226, 337
Lebergott, S. 28
Leith-Ross, F. 318, 319, 321, 323, 326, 331, 335, 340, 343, 344, 346
Lewin, L. 264
Lewis, C. 529, 530, 536
Lewis, W.A. 160, 242, 371, 412, 421, 525, 526
Liepman, H. 450
Lindbeck, A. 39, 264
Lindert, P. 29, 124
Lindsay, R. 328, 329, 330, 333, 340
Lipset, S.M. 253
Lloyd George, D. 266, 267
Lockwood, W.W. 567, 586
Lodoño, C. 608
Longstreth, F. 267
Lothian, Lord 321
Loughheed, A.L. 372, 406, 409, 421
Lubbock, C. 109
Luttala, M. 180
Lyttleton, R. 281

MacDonald, C.A. 369
MacDonald, R. 265, 266, 267, 268, 314, 316, 317, 325, 326, 330, 332, 334, 335, 337, 343, 346, 349, 350
MacDougall, G.D.A. 298
Machlup, F. 160
Madden, J.T. 543, 544, 547
Maddison, A. 629
Madgearu, V. 416
Maizels, A. 364, 366, 389
Makin, J. 112
Malthus, T. 639
Marguérat, P. 375, 380, 381, 382, 384, 391, 395
Marjolin, R. 271
Marseille, J. 26
Marston, R. 452
Martin, A. 263
Matthews, R.C.O. 25
May, G. 109
McCulloch, T.K. 342
McDonald, D.C. 537
McKenna, R. 278
Medlicott, W.N. 381
Meltzer, A. 446
Mercier, E. 270

Methorst, H.W. 458
Middleton, R. 46, 160, 466
Miles, M. 112
Mills, T.C. 46
Milward, A.S. 258, 389, 390
Mishkin, F.S. 26
Mitchell, B.R. 551, 560, 561, 631
Mitchell, D.J.B. 61, 73, 83, 84, 458
Moggridge, D.E. 42, 450, 461, 528
Moley, R. 327, 331, 344, 349
Mommsen, H. 373, 389
Momtchiloff, N. 378, 399
Mond, A. 278, 285
Montgomery, A. 264
Moore, B. Jr 249
Moore, J.R. 315
Moret, C. 158
Morgan, J.P. 111, 163
Mosley, O. 265
Mouré, K. 24, 32, 41, 171
Mundell, R. 112, 454, 628
Mussa, M. 112
Myers, M.G. 91, 96

Nadler, M. 543, 544, 547
Nathan, O. 462
Neal, L. 375, 376, 388
Nelson, D.B. 35
Nelson, F.D. 539
Neurath, K. von 337, 352
Newell, A. 37, 52, 53, 63, 64, 69, 71, 73, 83
Nichols, J.P. 338
Nickell, S.J. 29, 37, 63, 180
Norman, M. 100, 101, 107, 108, 109, 110, 168
Nötel, R. 163
Nurkse, R. 447, 448, 465, 541
Nyman, O. 264

O'Brien, P. 485
Ocampo, J.A. 593, 606
O'Connell, A. 593, 613
Odling-Smee, J. 25
Ohkawa, K. 435, 565
Olney, M. 24, 26, 27
Olson, M. 274
Overy, R. 314, 419

Palma, G. 593, 608, 616
Palyi, M. 421
Parkin, M. 112
Patat, J.-P. 180
Pearson, F.A. 11, 448
Peden, G.C. 447

Perrot, M. 450, 460
Petzina, D. 373, 389, 394
Philippe, R. 161
Phillips, F. 319, 335, 344, 347
Pinedo, F. 609
Piore, M. 274
Pittman, K. 343
Platt, D.C.M. 526
Poole, K.E. 393
Portes, R. 533
Prati, A. 162
Prebisch, R. 609, 626

Raff, D. 28
Ránki, G. 400
Rappoport, P. 34
Rathenau, W. 252
Reading, Lord 316
Redmond, J. 30, 427
Reynaud, P. 271
Rhomberg, R.R. 423, 424
Richardson, H.W. 243, 264
Richardson, J.H. 368, 528
Riedel, J. 531, 533
Ritschl, A. 179
Rodd, F. 319
Rodriguez, C.A. 112
Rogowski, R. 251
Romer, C. 26, 34, 46
Rona, F. 89
Roosevelt, F.D. 41, 161, 169, 170, 259, 326, 327, 329, 330, 332, 341, 342, 343, 345, 347, 350, 351, 432, 624
Rooth, T.J.T. 353, 359, 360, 366, 368
Rosett, R.N. 539
Ross, G. 242
Ross, K. 537
Rothschild, M. von 82
Rowland, B.M. 421
Runciman, W. 282, 317, 336, 349, 354

Sabel, C. 274
Sachs, J. 28, 31, 37, 43, 63, 122, 123, 130, 131, 135, 146, 158, 544, 626, 628, 630
Saint Etienne, C. 446
Sakurai, M. 112
Salter, A. 542, 646
Santoni, G.J. 34
Sauvain, H.C. 543, 544, 547
Sauvy, A. 271, 446, 452, 460
Sayers, R.S. 103, 529
Schacht, H. 389, 406, 419
Schattschneider, E.E. 243

Schatz, A.W. 350
Schleicher, K. von 256, 393
Schlesinger, A. 315
Schmidt, C.T. 93
Schmidt, G. 329
Schönfeld, R. 373
Schuker, S.A. 30, 31, 161
Schulze, H. 421
Schumann, W. 382
Schwartz, A.J. 24, 36, 82, 129, 137, 139, 158, 168, 446
Schweitzer, A. 393
Sering, M. 510
Shann, E.O.G. 497
Shibusawa, E. 584
Shinohara, M. 586
Shionoya, Y. 586
Shonfield, A. 242
Simon, J. 320, 325, 328, 333, 335, 340, 349, 355
Simpson, A. 419
Skidelsky, R. 247, 265
Skocpol, T. 260
Smith, A. 244
Snowden, P. 265, 266, 267, 268
Snower, D. 39
Soderpalm, S.A. 264
Solomou, S. 42
Somary, F. 175
Sorbom, D. 264
Stalin, J. 269
Steindl, J. 25
Sternberg, F. 507
Stiefel, D. 163
Stimson, H. 317, 323, 330, 333
Stolper, G. 372, 406
Strakosch, H. 158, 322
Strange, S. 264
Strong, B. 13
Sturzenegger, F. 32
Summers, L. 536
Sundhausen, H. 374
Sutch, R. 28
Svennilson, I. 25, 446, 448
Symons, J. 37, 52, 53, 63, 64, 69, 71, 73

Tabellini, G. 162
Takeuchi, H. 587
Taussig, F. 243
Tavernier, K. 451, 458
Taylor, A.D. 536
Taylor, A.J.P. 384
Taylor, H.C. 536
Teichova, A. 382

Temin, P. 24, 25, 27, 33, 34, 35, 36, 40, 42, 43, 122, 125, 129, 137, 148, 158, 180, 446
Thomas, M. 24, 28, 46
Thorp, R. 560, 561, 593, 608, 609, 627, 631
Tilton, T.A. 263
Tinbergen, J. 536, 551
Tingsten, H. 264
Tobin, J. 464
Toniolo, G. 148, 175
Tonningen, R. van 164
Torgay, O. 377
Touchard, J. 271
Tracey, M. 335
Tullio, G. 180
Turner, H.A. Jr 256

Uhr, C.G. 263
Uriburu, General 608
Urrutia, M. 631
Uzan, M. 30

Vansittart, R. 331, 351
Vernon, R. 249
Volkmann, H.-E. 373
Von Papen, F. 256

Wagenfuehr, H. 278
Waley, D. 323
Warner, C.K. 270
Warren, G.F. 11, 448
Watt, D.A. 315
Wee, H. van der 335, 451, 452, 458

Wehler, H.-U. 251
Weinstein, M. 37
Weir, M. 260
Weisbrod, B. 373, 389
Weiser, L. 406
Wendt, B.-J. 374, 379
Whale, P.B. 98
White, E. 24, 31, 34, 39
Wigmore, B. 43, 169
Wilkie, J. 560, 631
Williams, J.H. 170, 343
Williams, W.A. 243
Williamson, P. 161
Willis, P. 168
Wills, J.J. 357
Wilson, E.A. 629
Wilson, H. 281
Wilson, W. 323
Winch, D. 263, 264, 447
Winfield, C. 355
Winkel, H. 421
Winter, D. 533
Withers, H. 640
Wolf, H. 32, 122
Wolfe, M. 90, 91
Wood, G.E. 46
Worswick, G.D.N. 46
Woytinski, V. 254
Wright, J.F. 46
Wynne, W.H. 91, 96

Yamazawa, I. 586
Youngson, A. 264, 421